Georgia

the Bradt Travel Guide

Tim Burford

edition

www.bradtguides.com

Bradt Travel Guides Ltd, UK
The Globe Pequot Press Inc, USA

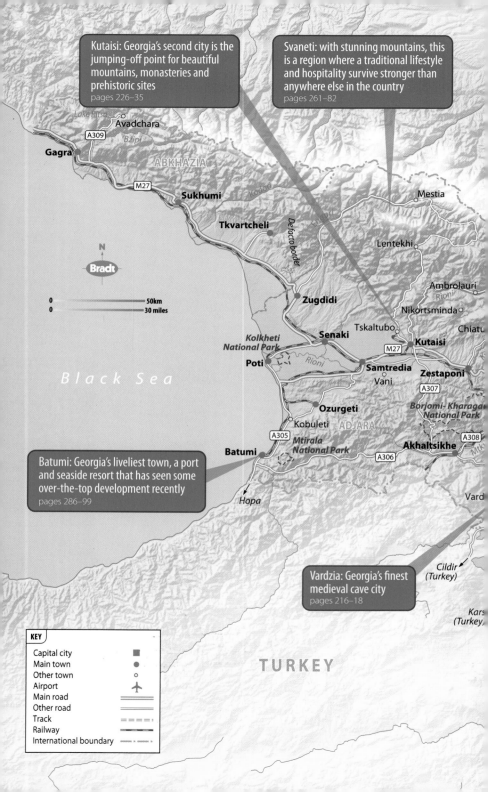

Kutaisi: Georgia's second city is the jumping-off point for beautiful mountains, monasteries and prehistoric sites pages 226–35

Svaneti: with stunning mountains, this is a region where a traditional lifestyle and hospitality survive stronger than anywhere else in the country pages 261–82

Batumi: Georgia's liveliest town, a port and seaside resort that has seen some over-the-top development recently pages 286–99

Vardzia: Georgia's finest medieval cave city pages 216–18

Bradt

N

0   50km
0   30 miles

Black Sea

Lake Mtsa
Avadchara
A309
Bžipi
Gagra
ABKHAZIA
M27
Sukhumi
Tkvartcheli
De facto border
Kodori
Mestia
Lentekhi
Ambrolauri
Rioni
Zugdidi
Nikortsminda
Chiatu
Tskaltubo
Kutaisi
Kolkheti National Park
Senaki
M27
Poti
Rioni
Samtredia
Zestaponi
Vani
A307
Borjomi- Kharaga National Park
Ozurgeti
A308
Kobuleti
ADJARA
Akhaltsikhe
A305
Mtirala National Park
Batumi
A306
Mtk
Hopa
Vard

Vardzia: Georgia's finest medieval cave city pages 216–18

Cildir (Turkey)

Kars (Turkey,

TURKEY

KEY

Capital city	■
Main town	●
Other town	○
Airport	✈
Main road	
Other road	
Track	= = = =
Railway	
International boundary	– · – · –

RUSSIA

Kazbegi: set within stunning mountain scenery, this friendly little town is overlooked by Mount Kazbek and the Gergeti Church
pages 185–92

Uplistsikhe: an evocative cave city close to Stalin's home town, Gori
pages 171–3

Tusheti: the country's remotest and least spoilt national park, only accessible for four months a year
pages 319–26

Kazbek
5033m ▲

Alagir

› Vladikavkaz

Shatili

Roka

Kazbegi

SOUTH
OSSETIA

Pasanauri

Tusheti
National
Park

Tskhinvali

A301

Omalo

Ananauri

Akhmeta

Tbilisi
National
Park

Lagodekhi
National
Park

M27

Uplistsikhe

Telavi

Khashuri Gori

Kaspi

Lagodekhi

orjomi

Trialeti Ridge

Mtskheta

Sagarejo

› Balakan

Bakuriani

Algetis
National
Park

TBILISI

Gurjaani

AZERBAIJAN

A303

Manglisi

Rustavi

A302

Sighnaghi

Akhalkalaki

Khram

Marneuli

M27

Bolnisi

✝

Vashlovani
National
Park

Tashir,
Yerevan ›

Ganja, Baku

Debet

Yerevan

Kur
(Kura)

Iori

Gyumri

ARMENIA

AZERBAIJAN

Mingecevir
Reservoir

Borjomi: a charming spa and base for the country's finest national park and the Bakuriani ski resort
pages 198–207

Tbilisi: Georgia's capital is an intoxicating blend of cultures, both ancient and modern
pages 92–155

Davit-Gareja: cave monasteries dating from the 6th century, scattered in semi-desert on the Azerbaijani border
pages 337–40

Georgia
Don't miss...

Ancient churches
The monastery of Gelati, near Kutaisi, is decorated with fantastic frescoes of saints and Georgian kings
(WC/S) pages 235–7

Svaneti villages
Hidden in the remotest reaches of the High Caucasus and dotted with ancient towers and frescoed churches, the land of the Svans is seen by many as the spiritual heartland of Georgia
(KV/D) pages 261–82

Georgian Military Highway

The Soviet-Georgian Friendship Monument, by the Georgian Military Highway, is a unique viewpoint in the heart of the High Caucasus

(MPi/S) pages 177–95

Tbilisi Old Town

Inhabited at various times by Persians, Tatars, Jews and Armenians, the heart of the Georgian capital is an intriguing array of architectural styles

(BS/S) pages 134–8

Cave cities

Once a working monastery with 3,000 chambers, Vardzia is the site of Georgia's most famous cave complex

(r/S) pages 216–18

Georgia in colour

above   The town of Mtskheta was founded at the confluence of the Mtkvari and Aragvi rivers over 3,000 years ago (Y/S) pages 157–62

right   The Jvari Church, overlooking Mtskheta (OK/S) pages 161–2

below   Shenako is typical of the remote and tiny villages of Tusheti, where you'll virtually always find one or two welcoming guesthouses (MPa/S) pages 323–6 *left* Situated at an altitude of 810–850m, the spa town of Borjomi offers both health-giving waters and a bracing mountain atmosphere (Alv/S) pages 198–201

below left With its cypress trees, fine 18th- and 19th-century buildings and setting high on a ridge overlooking the Alazani Valley, Sighnaghi is reminiscent of a Tuscan hill town (SS) pages 331–5

bottom Davit-Gareja Monastery, near the border with Azerbaijan, is surrounded by an almost lunar landscape of dry steppe (IT/D) pages 337–40

AUTHOR

A guidebook writer and hiking guide for close to three decades, **Tim Burford** has written guides to places as widely spread as Romania, Alaska and Chile, while also leading hiking groups in Britain, Patagonia and above all the Alps. He first went to Georgia in the late 1990s and found it possessed the authentic charm that Romania had in 1991 but soon began to lose. Happily, Georgia's authenticity has been preserved in many ways by a passionate national commitment to its food, drink and customs. These are exactly the things that Tim enjoys discovering when he travels, as much at home as abroad – any excuse to get on a bike and explore.

Brought up in the west of Cornwall, Tim has lived in Cambridge for 20 years, mainly for its cultural opportunities and easy access to Eurostar trains and other travel options; it's also easy to lead a car-free life there. He's heavily involved with the local cycling campaign, but hasn't yet taken a bike to Georgia, alas.

DEDICATION

For Chris and Natalie, to mark 40 years of friendship.

> Spending on feasting and wine is better than hoarding our substance; that which we give makes us richer, that which is hoarded is lost.
>
> Rustaveli

FEEDBACK REQUEST AND UPDATES WEBSITE

At Bradt Travel Guides we're aware that guidebooks start to go out of date on the day they're published – and that you, our readers, are out there in the field doing research of your own. You'll find out before us when a fine new family-run hotel opens or a favourite restaurant changes hands and goes downhill. So why not write and tell us about your experiences? Contact us on ☎ 01753 893444 or e info@bradtguides.com. We will forward emails to the author, who may post updates on the Bradt website at w bradtupdates.com/georgia. Alternatively you can add a review of the book to w bradtguides.com or Amazon.

PUBLISHER'S FOREWORD   *Hilary Bradt*

It's always a pleasure to welcome a new edition of one of Tim Burford's guides, and *Georgia* has been one of his stalwarts. I remember a meeting at the Frankfurt Book Fair many years ago with an Englishman who ran a bookshop called Prospero's Books in, of all places, Tbilisi. He was quite misty-eyed with praise for Tim's guide. This is what I love about publishing guides to unusual destinations. When they hit the spot they dispel a bit of magic in all directions!

Sixth edition published June 2018
First published 1998

Bradt Travel Guides Ltd
IDC House, The Vale, Chalfont St Peter, Bucks SL9 9RZ, England
www.bradtguides.com
Print edition published in the USA by The Globe Pequot Press Inc,
PO Box 480, Guilford, Connecticut 06437-0480

Text copyright © 2018 Tim Burford
Maps copyright © 2018 Bradt Travel Guides Ltd; includes map data © OpenStreetMap contributors.
Tbilisi metro map © Robert Schwandl (UrbanRail.Net), 2018
Photographs copyright © 2018 Individual photographers (see below)
Project Manager: Susannah Lord
Cover research: Pepi Bluck, Perfect Picture

ISBN: 978 1 78477 072 3 (print)
e-ISBN: 978 1 78477 537 7 (e-pub)
e-ISBN: 978 1 78477 438 7 (mobi)

British Library Cataloguing in Publication Data
A catalogue record for this book is available from the British Library

Photographs Alamy Stock Photos: Aldo Castellani (AC/A); Magdalena Paluchowska (MP/A); Dreamstime.com: Actrisavesna (A/D), Anna Bogush (AB/D), Ilia Torlin (IT/D), Joye Ardyn Durham (JAD/D), Karolina Vyskocilova (KV/D), Lukas Blazek (LB/D), Speculator27 (S27/D); Tony Hanmer (TH); Shutterstock.com: Anna Bogush (AB/S), Alexander Ishchenko (AIs/S), Anton_Ivanov (AIv/S), Artur Synenko (AS/S), Baciu (B/S), Boris Stroujko (BS/S), Erni (E/S), Elena-Ms (EM/S), Kavun Halyna (KH/S), Milosz Maslanka (MM/S), Magdalena Paluchowska (MPa/S), Michal Piec (MPi/S), Olesya Kuznetsova (OK/S), roibu (r/S), Roxana Bashyrova (RB/S), Rosliak Oleksandr (RO/S), saiko3p (s3p/S), Sobol Igor (SI/S), tramper79 (t79/S), thomas koch (tk/S), Vahan Abrahamyan (VA/S), Vladimir Zhoga (VZ/S), Wojtek Chmielewski (WC/S), Yurcha (Y/S); SuperStock (SS).
Front cover Tsminda Sameba church, near Kazbegi (MP/A)
Back cover Tbilisi Old Town with ancient sulphur baths and view of Narikala Citadel (AS/S), Man wearing the traditional Svan felt hat (TH)
Title page Turk cap's lily (JAD/D), Architectural detail of the Orbeliani Baths, Tbilisi (AB/S), Adjaran dancers in traditional costume (AB/S)

Maps David McCutcheon FBCart.S and Liezel Bohdanowicz; colour map base by Nick Rowland FRGS; regional base mapping, modified by Bradt, provided by ITMB Publishing Ltd (*www.itmb.com*), 2018

Typeset by Lee Riches, and Ian Spick, Bradt Travel Guides Ltd
Production managed by Jellyfish Print Solutions; printed in the UK
Digital conversion by www.dataworks.co.in

Acknowledgements

Thanks to: Dr Jonathan Aves, Rowan Stewart, Neil Taylor, Ed Manning, Eilidh Kennedy, Arthur Gerfers, Mark Elliott, Koba and Leila, Gela and Cristina, Ana Anganashvili, Vano Vashakmadze, Remaz Rekhiashvili, Mary Ellen Chatwin, Manana Kochladze, Aleko Motsonelidze, David Tarkhinishvili and Jesse Tsinadze in Tbilisi; Tamuna and Nugzar Kvaratskhedia in Kutaisi; Natia Khordiani in Mestia; Alek and Sophiko in Zugdidi; Ramaz Georgadze in Batumi; and above all to Boris and Tsira Arhdabevsky.

Further thanks for their assistance on the second edition to: Peter Nasmyth, Amy Spurling, Hugo Greenhalgh, Eleanor O'Hanlon, Rebecca Weaver and Andrew Barnard, Polly and Susan Amos, Maka Dvalishvili, Besik Lortkipanidze, Lars Nejsig and the Javakhishvili family, Raffi Kojian and Dave Mitchell.

Also Ben and Suki – I'm still waiting to get my Truso map back!

Thanks on the third edition to: Amy Spurling, Boris and Tsira, Laurie Dalton, Till Bruckner, Ed Raupp, Erekle Tavartkiladze, Natia Muladze, Knut Gerber, Ramaz Gokhelashvili, Rati Jabaridze, John Graham, Inga Gotsiridze, Molly Corso, Rob Ainsley and Ian Colvin.

For help with the fourth edition, Laurence Mitchell thanks Nino Ratiani, Giorgi Giorgadze, Eto Jajanidze, Dodo Kevlishvili, Meri Maxatelashvili, Martha Bakhtiari and Bob Thompson in Georgia; Nick Rowlands for comments on the last edition and Tim Burford for copious compiled notes.

Thanks for help on the fifth edition to Tony and Lali Hanmer, Roza and Vitaly Shukvani and Koka Chartolani (and Paata and Rusu) in Svaneti; Ia Tabagari, Giorgi Nebieridze, Mark Richmond, Rauf, Erekle, Eka Tchvritidze and as ever Boris and Tsira Arhdabevsky in Tbilisi; Ana Uturgaidze (Rooms, Kazbegi); Giorgi Giorgadze (Kutaisi); Gulnasi and Sophie (Batumi); Artur Stepanian (Borjomi); Inga Gotsiridze-Furley (Bakuriani); Gaga Mumladze (Borjomi-Kharagauli National Park); Nazy Dakishvili and Gurjeet Batth (Pankisi); Dima Bit-Suleiman (Kisiskhevi); Dato Luashvili (Telavi) and Nato and John Wurdemann and all at Pheasant's Tears (Sighnaghi); and Laura Pidgley and all at Bradt.

Thanks for help with the sixth edition to: Tony and Lali Hanmer, Roza Shukvani and Richard Baerug (Svaneti), Simon Rainauli (Omalo), Svetlana Tushishvili (Telavi), Devi Asmadiredja and Gurjeet Batth (Pankisi), Gia Aliashvili (Gurjaani), John Wurdemann and Nato (Sighnaghi), Ana Svanidze (Fabrika), Giorgi Zangaladze, Giorgi Nebieridze, Irakli Paniashvili, Vazha Natroshvili, Tsira Chelidze and Boris Arhdabevsky (Tbilisi), Tom Allen and Paul Stephens (Trans Caucasian Trail), Gela (Kazbegi), Lia (Gori), Gaga Mumladze (Borjomi-Kharagauli National Park), Sergo and Inga Gotsiridze-Furley (Bakuriani), Inga Tkemaladze (Vardzia), Kote, Giorgi and Kakha (Kutaisi), Sophya Mikeladze and Jack Greenhalgh (Batumi), Wojciech Mania, Martin Barlow and all at Bradt, especially Susannah Lord.

Contents

AUTHOR'S FAVOURITES

Finding genuinely characterful accommodation or that unmissable off-the-beaten-track café can be difficult, so the author has chosen a few of his favourite places throughout the country to point you in the right direction. These 'author's favourites' are marked with a ✳.

MAPS

Keys and symbols City maps (but not regional maps) include alphabetical keys covering the locations of those places to stay, eat or drink that are featured in the book.

Grids and grid references Some maps use grid lines to allow easy location of sites. Map grid references are listed in square brackets after the name of the place or sight of interest in the text, with page number followed by grid number, eg: [84 C3].

LISTINGS Accommodation and restaurants are marked with price codes and listed alphabetically in descending price code order (**$$$$$–$**); in the Tbilisi and Batumi sections they are also listed geographically.

HISTORIC SITES Prices and opening hours are included where they apply. Otherwise assume the site is free and always open.

KEY TO SYMBOLS

—·—·—	International boundary	🖿	Museum/art gallery
········	District/province boundary	🎭	Theatre/cinema
	Roads main/other (town plans)	🏛	Important/historic building
→	One-way street (town plans)	🏰	Castle/fortification
	Pedestrianised road (town plans)	⚲	Statue/monument
‖‖‖‖‖‖‖	Steps (town plans)	$	Bank/ATM
══━══	Railway	✉	Post office
═══════	Main road (regional maps)	⊞	Hospital/clinic
══════	Other road (regional maps)	✚	Pharmacy
═══════	4 x 4/track (regional maps)	†	Church/cathedral
··········	Footpath (regional maps & town plans)	☾	Mosque
✈ ✈	Airport (international/domestic)	✡	Synagogue
M Ⓜ	Metro station/terminus	☆	Nightclub/casino
▭	Railway station	✿	Gardens
⛴	Ferry	⊀	Beach
🚠	Cable car/funicular	▲	Summit (height in metres)
🅿	Car park	●	Other place of interest
🚗	Car hire	✳	Viewpoint
🚲	Bike rental	大	Stadium/sports facility
🚌	Bus station		National park/nature reserve
🄸	Tourist information		Urban park
Ⓔ	Embassy/consulate		Market area

Introduction

Despite recent improvements, many things in Georgia are still run-down, yet it's one of the most heart-warming and exciting of all European destinations. This is above all due to its people, who are some of the most hospitable and generous you could meet anywhere. In addition you'll see fantastic scenery, including Europe's highest mountains, and lovely ancient churches and cave-cities.

This does in part raise the question of whether Georgia is in Europe, Asia, the Middle East, or some other region; travellers can easily spend half their trip debating this issue. If the Caucasus is the dividing line between Europe and Asia, it's unclear which side is European and which is Asian. Armenia and Russia have international phone codes in the European 003 series, yet they are separated by Georgia and Azerbaijan, which have chosen codes in the Asian 009 series. Despite this, since 2007 Georgia has competed in the Eurovision Song Contest (apart from 2009 when they withdrew as a protest against it being held in Moscow). Certainly, the Georgians seem to spend a lot of time squatting on their haunches in an Asian way waiting for the good times to come around, yet civil society (non-governmental organisations, pressure groups, a fair judicial system and so on) is stronger here than in the neighbouring countries.

To illustrate the joys and perils of travel in Georgia, here's an account of a cycle trip in 1995 when the country was still raw and newly independent:

> In a month we managed to cover 1,000km on our bikes; however, we could probably have completed it in half the time but for the Georgians taking Rustaveli to heart and insisting that we share their food with them all the time. There was the man walking by the side of the road who gave us the loaf of bread that he was carrying. There were the policemen who constantly stopped us and, when we expected to have to show our documentation, merely wished to give us a watermelon or figs. Old women would give us apples or walnuts, people driving past in cars would pass out bubble gum while on the move, the list goes on. We were constantly surprised and humbled by the generosity of everyone from the countryside to the cities. We were invited into many people's homes, by cow herders in the mountains, peasants in villages and sophisticates in towns. In every household the inevitable bottle was brought out and the toasting began … needless to say, on some days our cycling was seriously curtailed after such meetings.
>
> Ella Truscott

Twenty years on, Georgia is a little better known to the outside world and foreign visitors are not quite the rarity they once were. Nevertheless, any brave souls attempting to cycle across the country independently can still expect a royal welcome and some serious 'hospitality'. Don't be in too much of a hurry!

Part One

GENERAL INFORMATION

1

Background Information

GEOGRAPHY

With an area of 69,700km² (26,911 square miles), Georgia is slightly smaller than Austria or the Republic of Ireland, and under half the size of the American state of Georgia. More than half this area lies above 900m and almost 40% (2.69 million hectares) is wooded. The country's dominant feature is, of course, the High Caucasus range which forms its northern border. Although its highest peak, Elbruz (in fact Europe's highest peak at 5,642m, or 18,510ft), lies wholly within the Russian Federation, Georgia does have three peaks over 5,000m (Shkhara, 5,068m; Janga, 5,059m; and Mkinvartsveri (Kazbek), 5,033m) and ten more over 4,000m. The Caucasus is, like the Himalayas, a very young and dynamic range; it was formed just 25 million years ago, and linked about 15 million years ago to the Iranian Massif. It stretches for roughly 1,200km and contains over 2,000 glaciers, covering an area of 1,780km². The High Caucasus falls into three parts. The first of these is the Western Caucasus, stretching 440km from the Black Sea to Elbruz, its highest peak being Dombay (4,046m), on the border with the Russian Federation. It's composed of granite, gneiss and crystalline shales, with limestone and sandstone ridges parallel to the north and west, and is very beautiful with canyons and dense vegetation. The 100km west of Elbruz are higher and more alpine, with glaciers. The Central Caucasus covers the 180km from Elbruz, where the range is at its widest (180km), to Kazbek, where it's at its narrowest (60km), and includes all the peaks over 5,000m. Its western half is granite and shale, and its eastern half andesite and diabase, with a last small spot of granite near Kazbek. Elbruz and Kazbek are very ancient volcanoes, while the peaks between, such as Uzhba, Tetnuldi, Shkhara and Dykhtau, are younger upthrust peaks sculpted by glaciers, with gigantic north faces and lots of scree. Finally, the Eastern Caucasus, from Kazbek to the Caspian Sea, is a confused mass of argillaceous slate, with outcrops of diabase, porphyrite and sandstone; its climate is far drier than to the west, with very little glaciation.

The High Caucasus forms the border with the Russian Federation, but nowhere does Georgia directly adjoin Russia itself; the Muslim peoples of the northern Caucasus, who speak at least 30 different languages, live in half a dozen autonomous republics: from west to east Karachai-Cherkesbaijan (or Circassia), Kalbardino-Balkaria, North Ossetia, Ingushetia, Chechnya and Daghestan.

From almost anywhere in the central valleys you'll be able to see the High Caucasus as a long white wall to the north; in many places you'll also be able to see the Lesser Caucasus, to the southwest towards the Turkish border. This is a gentler, more rounded range, rising to 3,301m at Didi-Abuli; the Trialeti Ridge, covered in rich pastures and forests, stretches to the outskirts of the capital, Tbilisi. The two ranges of the Caucasus are linked by the very young Suran (or Likhi) range, which forms the watershed between the Black and Caspian seas and separates eastern and western Georgia, Kartli and Kolkhida.

The country is dominated by one main river, the Mtkvari (Kura in Russian; 1,364km long in total, including 435km in Georgia), which rises in Turkey, enters Georgia near Vardzia, then flows east through Kartli and Tbilisi, and then through Azerbaijan to the Caspian Sea. The main river of western Georgia is the Rioni (327km), which flows from the foothills of Racha through Kutaisi to the Black Sea; others are the Enguri (213km), which flows from Svaneti to the Black Sea, the Iori (320km) and Alazani (351km, the longest wholly within Georgia), which flow through Kakheti and into the Mtkvari, and the headwaters of the Terek (623km in all), which flows north into Russia and eventually into the Caspian Sea.

The main centres of industry and population lie along an east–west axis, from Rustavi through Tbilisi, Gori, Zestaponi, Kutaisi, Samtredia and Senaki to Poti; the only other major cities are two Black Sea ports, Batumi, near the Turkish border, and Sukhumi, in the secessionist republic of Abkhazia.

Georgia has over 2,000 mineral springs producing 130 million litres a day, most of which are wasted. There are over 500 different waters (both hot and cold), of which most contain carbon dioxide, such as those from Borjomi, Sairme and Nabeghlavi; there are also sulphide, nitric and silicon waters (mostly hot), such as those from Tskaltubo, Tbilisi, Nunisi, Tkvartcheli and Makhinjauri, and Gagra, Sukhumi and Aspindza in Abkhazia.

At least 15% of Georgia is limestone, so it's not surprising that there are plenty of fine caves; few of them are set up properly for visitors, but there are great opportunities for exploring. The Gumistavi Cave, near Tskaltubo, is a particularly fine recent discovery, and the Pantiukhin Cave is claimed to be the second deepest in the world at 1,540m (5,050ft). The Tovliana Cave contains snow and ice far underground but has been badly polluted by cavers' rubbish, such as burnt carbide from their lamps. The people of the Tskaltubo area have unwittingly been polluting their own water supply by dumping garbage in caves; some have also been used for agricultural storage and even as hothouses.

GEORGIA'S REGIONS Georgia is much more regional and less centralised than the other Transcaucasian countries, and since independence there has been a marked increase in the power of the regions vis-à-vis the centre. The country includes the two autonomous republics of Abkhazia and Adjara, the formerly autonomous region of South Ossetia (which has seceded), and ten administrative regions (*mkhare*). From east to west these are: Kakheti, Kvemo (Lower) Kartli, Shida (Inner) Kartli (which technically includes South Ossetia), Mtskheta-Mtianeti, Samtskhe-Javakheti, Imereti, Samegrelo, Racha-Lechkhumi and Kvemo Svaneti, Zemo (Upper) Svaneti and Guria.

Kakheti is the easternmost region of Georgia, projecting into Azerbaijan; it's known almost entirely for its vine growing and winemaking. **Kvemo (Lower) Kartli** lies to the south of Tbilisi, across the routes to Armenia; it's largely inhabited by people of Azerbaijani origin who produce much of the food sold in the markets of Tbilisi. Although there are secessionist tendencies and in 1992–95 there was some sabotage of pipelines and railways, both the Georgian and Azerbaijani governments are keen to keep things calm. Further west, around Lake Tsalka, is a population of Greeks raising livestock and growing potatoes.

In general the people of Kvemo Kartli are seen as reformist, wanting to be allowed to make money, while the Kakhetians are conservatives who want to be left alone with their wine.

Shida (Inner) Kartli is the heartland of eastern Georgia; with a population of 343,000 it produces 5–10% of Georgia's industrial output as well as most of its fruit.

It theoretically includes the autonomous region of **South Ossetia** (also known as Samachablo, with a population of about 51,000), which has now seceded.

Mtskheta-Mtianeti, to the north of Tbilisi, straddles the Georgian Military Highway, the main route to Russia; it's an agricultural area with vegetables grown in the lower region and sheep raised in the high mountains. Industry is growing in Mtskheta and Dusheti, and Georgia's main ski resort is at Gudauri.

Samtskhe-Javakheti covers the bleak, empty volcanic tablelands of the southwest of Georgia; 90% of the population is Armenian and in many ways the area is largely autonomous. Few speak Georgian and they are not conscripted into the Georgian army; however, the Russian army base near Akhalkalaki (which closed in 2006) took recruits for the Russian army. Javakheti, near the present border of Armenia and Turkey, was settled by Armenians in the 19th century, after the Russian conquest of the area; here and in **Meskheti**, to the west, there was also a heavily Islamised population of largely Georgian stock, the so-called Meskhetian Turks, who were deported to Central Asia in 1944 and have still not been permitted to return. There's little industry, apart from some low-grade coal, and Swiss and French investment in sugar plants. There are now road crossings to Turkey at Vale and Çıldır, and a 98km extension of the railway from Akhalkalaki to Kars in Turkey (page 63), opened late in 2017, linking Azerbaijan and Turkey, and thus Kazakhstan and China with Europe, moving freight faster than the Trans-Siberian.

Georgia's second city is Kutaisi, capital of **Imereti**; 10–25% of Georgian industrial production is based here, although this share is declining – it's largely dependent on the Chiatura mine (which used to produce a quarter of the Soviet Union's manganese) and the connected ferro-alloys plant at Zestaponi.

Samegrelo (or Mingrelia), in the northwest of Georgia, has historically had a considerable degree of autonomy, partly because the Mingrelian dialect is almost unintelligible to the people of Tbilisi. Politically the area is still strongly associated with Zviadism and opposition to the central government. The regional capital, Zugdidi, is now overloaded with refugees but benefits from illicit trade with Abkhazia. The subtropical climate makes tea and citrus fruits important crops, while traditionally Zugdidi has produced porcelain and Senaki carpets. Exports of tea have crashed since the end of the Soviet Union and many plantations are now being replanted with hazel trees.

To the north of Kutaisi, **Racha-Lechkhumi and Kvemo Svaneti** lie in the foothills of the Caucasus; the only roads here are minor and circuitous because of the hills. Winters are harsh, with much of the population decamping to the city, but nevertheless Racha manages to produce both tea and wine. The chief towns of Racha are Ambrolauri and Oni. Lentekhi, capital of Kvemo Svaneti, is even smaller. Kvemo (Lower) Svaneti was historically part of the feudal system of western Georgia, while **Zemo (Upper) Svaneti** was always self-governing and has developed a far stronger cultural identity. With its stunning Caucasian landscape, its defensive towers, its haunting music and its superb and ancient icons, Zemo Svaneti is the area to which all the more enterprising tourists to Georgia are drawn like moths to the flame.

Guria, a small swampy region on the coast south of Poti, is known for its subtropical crops, stunningly complex polyphonic songs and the humour of its people. People usually come here *en route* to **Adjara**, which dominates Georgia's trade both across the Turkish border and through the port of Batumi. With this trade, subtropical agriculture, beach tourism and some copper and gold mining, Adjara is a prosperous republic.

Finally, the autonomous republic of **Abkhazia**, in the extreme northwest of Georgia, has effectively seceded (pages 30–1) and is less easy for foreign visitors to visit. In the past this was perhaps the most sought-after holiday area of the entire Soviet Union and Russian holidaymakers are starting to return in large numbers, entering by means of the western border near Sochi. It exports citrus fruits, hazelnuts and timber, so there is some tax revenue, and arrangements have been made to share the power produced by the Enguri hydro-electric station between Georgia and Abkhazia; but it'll be a long time before normality returns.

CLIMATE

There's quite a wide range of climates in Georgia, from the warm, humid, subtropical Black Sea Coast, via the colder, wet, alpine climate of the High Caucasus, to the arid steppes of the east.

Temperatures in the mountains range from an average −4.6°C in February to 16.4°C in July and August, with an annual average of 5.7°C. In Svaneti the winter lasts for up to eight months, with an average temperature of −15°C; it gets even colder on the high bare plateaux of Javakheti where temperatures drop to −30°C. On the coast of Adjara, average temperatures range from 5.8°C in January to 23.8°C in August, with an annual average of 14.5°C; on the Abkhaz coast temperatures are slightly lower in winter, noticeably warmer in April and May, but virtually the same in high summer. In eastern Georgia temperatures range from 0.5°C in January to 23°C in August, with an annual average of 11.8°C, and in the south they range from −2.1°C in January to 20.1°C in August, with an average of 9.1°C.

The weather in the Caucasus is more stable than in the Alps. In June there may still be too much snow for high hikes; July and August have the best weather, but even then it can drop to −10°C at 3,000–3,500m. Lower altitudes can often be hot and humid at this time of year, and the inhabitants of Tbilisi and Kutaisi flee to the coast or the mountains.

Precipitation ranges from 2,800mm in Abkhazia and Adjara to 300–600mm in the east (with 462mm in Tbilisi), and about 1,800mm at the main Caucasian passes. There's an average of 1,350–2,520 hours of sunshine per year (3 hours/day in December, over 8 hours from June to August) in Tbilisi.

Climate change is affecting Georgia, with temperatures rising, glaciers shrinking and snowfall decreasing. More extreme weather in the last two decades has resulted

CLIMATE IN TBILISI

Month		Temperature			Humidity %		Rain
	max °C	ave °C	min °C	max/min °F	max	min	mm
January	6	0.9	−2	43/27	79	60	21
February	8	2.6	−1	46/30	75	53	26
March	12	6.6	3	53/35	69	50	32
April	18	12.8	7	65/44	66	49	49
May	24	17.9	13	75/53	61	47	82
June	28	21.8	16	82/60	57	42	54
July	31	25.0	19	88/66	57	40	74
August	31	24.7	19	87/66	60	42	43
September	26	20.3	15	79/58	66	49	40
October	20	14.1	9	68/48	71	53	42
November	13	8.2	4	55/39	78	60	36
December	8	3.3	0	46/31	80	65	23

in flooding, landslides, forest fires and coastal erosion. Rainfall has become far more irregular, with droughts and heavy downpours; in spring 2005 heavy rain, warm temperatures and the consequent sudden snowmelt caused flooding across much of Georgia, with landslides and mudflows in many mountain areas. Summers are drier and hotter (often reaching 35°C), with a wet spring and autumn.

In the last couple of decades, the winter snowline has risen from 1,300–1,500m to 1,800–2,000m, and over the last century glacial volume in the Caucasus has declined by 50%. Georgia's glaciers are currently retreating by between 5m and 25m a year, and it's possible that hardly any glaciers will remain by the end of this century, with reduced water supply affecting both agriculture and hydro-electric generation in the longer term.

NATURAL HISTORY AND CONSERVATION

Despite its small size, Georgia is ecologically very interesting. Located between the forests of northern Eurasia and the tropical deserts of Iraq and Iran, and incorporating Europe's highest mountains and a subtropical coastline, it has Europe's highest level of biodiversity and is a route for many migratory bird species. It is characterised by its complex interaction of west Asian, east European and purely local communities. There's a wide variety of plant communities, with examples of almost all the main habitat types found in Europe and some of those in Asia; many are highly valuable in terms of biodiversity, including subalpine coniferous forests, meadows, wetlands, peat bogs and lakes; coniferous and beech forests; oak woodlands; caves and mountain gorges; unique Colchic forests with evergreen undergrowth; Mediterranean and sub-Mediterranean communities; steppe grasslands; arid light woodlands; and riparian shrub and forest vegetation along rivers such as the Alazani and Mtkvari.

Forest covers 2.7 million hectares (36.7% of Georgia's area), of which only 59,500ha is artificially planted; around 6% of the natural forest is virgin, and 40% has avoided serious human impact.

Overall, Georgia can be split into two main biogeographical regions: firstly the Colchic and Caucasian districts, forest landscapes with plenty of autochthonous animals and plants, and others related to middle and eastern European species; and secondly the uplands of the Lesser Caucasus and the Mtkvari district, with species related in some places to Anatolia and the Middle East, and in others to the arid and semi-arid Turanian region, beyond the Caspian. Between these two main regions are mixed zones, notably the Borjomi Gorge and the Trialeti Ridge, as well as the southern slopes of the High Caucasus in eastern Georgia.

The **Colchic (or Euxine) district** covers most of western Georgia, between the Black Sea, the Meskhetian Mountains, the Surami Ridge and the High Caucasus; the climate is mild and humid, rarely freezing and with a metre or more of precipitation each year, and the characteristic landscape is subtropical forest with well-developed evergreen underwood consisting of many Tertiary relics (such as *Laurocerasus officinalis*, *Ilex aquifolium* and *Rhododendron ponticum*).

The **Caucasus district** lies to the north at 2,000m and higher, with a severe climate and over a metre of precipitation per year. It harbours some of the most diverse and distinctive temperate coniferous and deciduous forests in Eurasia, ranging with altitude from subalpine beechwoods (half of the country's forested area), dark coniferous forests and crook-stem woods to subalpine, alpine and subnival plant communities and, above these, bare nival (ie: dominated by snow) landscapes. Its borders are fluid, with many Colchic elements in the west, and Turanian elements in the east; on the northern slopes there are many eastern European and boreal species, while in the west the very wet southern slopes are dominated by massive weeds.

The plateaux of the **Lesser Caucasus** are largely treeless grassland, either subalpine meadows or mountain steppes, as well as forest and semi-arid steppes. There's a severe continental climate, with annual precipitation between just 400mm and 800mm. The **Mtkvari district** covers much of Kartli and Kakheti, and is largely arid and semi-arid steppe, with xerophytic Turanian (or Armeno-Iranian) species predominating, and forested only along the banks of the Mtkvari. There's a warm continental climate, rarely dropping below –5°C, with under 400mm of precipitation per year.

The 'mixed' zones, at the borders of these main zones, are the most biologically fascinating regions of Georgia. There are three main mixed zones: first, the northern slopes of the **Trialeti Ridge**, from the northwestern side of Tbilisi to the Borjomi Gorge, mostly dry deciduous mountain forests with a temperate climate and 400–800mm of precipitation per year – the fauna and flora are mostly Caucasian, with some Turanian and Colchic elements, and no great diversity; second, the **forests of eastern Georgia**, which are relatively similar to the Trialeti forests, but with more Turanian elements – the climate is subtropical/mild, with 400–600mm of precipitation; and, third, the smallest but most interesting is the **Borjomi Gorge**, which has a well-balanced range of elements from all over Georgia (although Turanian elements are scarce) with a mild temperate climate and 800–1,200mm of precipitation per year. The gorge marks the divide between the humid west and the arid east, and between Mediterranean and Turanian fauna.

Endemic species comprise about 9% of Georgia's flora, a surprisingly high proportion for so small a country, with another 5% endemic to the Caucasus. The highest proportion (for instance 87% of western Georgian scree flora) is in certain mountain areas which were turned into islands when the seas rose around 15 million years ago, in the Miocene epoch; the surrounding areas have since dried out and gone their own way biologically, while the humid subtropical forests of the mountains have survived largely unchanged, and many species there now have their closest relatives in Anatolia and Europe. Indeed, the only relative of the Caucasian parsley frog (*Pelodytes caucasicus*) is *P. punctatus* in France and northern Spain, while the nearest relative of the Caucasian salamander (*Mertensiella caucasica*) and *M. luschani* (in Greece and southwest Turkey) is the gold-striped salamander (*Chioglossa lusitanica*) in Portugal and northwestern Spain.

FLORA Georgia boasts around 4,200 species of **vascular plants** (including 153 trees and 11 lianas), of which 380 are endemic to Georgia and about 600 to the Caucasus; and between 8,400 and 10,000 cryptogamous or spore-bearing plants (including between 7,000 and 21,000 fungi, 2,600 algae and seaweeds, 675 mosses, 738 lichen and 74 ferns). Ten species are extinct, notably the chickpea (*Cicer arietinum*), the Georgian elm (*Ulmus georgica*), the Transcaucasian poplar (*Populus transcaucasica*) and the Eldari pine (*Pinus eldarica*), which now exists only in Azerbaijan. Fifty species are in a critical state, including the royal fern (*Osmunda regalis*), the Mingrelian birch (*Betula megrelica*), the Colchic water chestnut (*Trapa colchica*) and the Caucasian yam (*Dioscorea caucasica*). Around 300 species are now rare, including the Pitsunda pine (*Pinus pithyusa*), the Saguramo camomile (*Anthemis saguramica*) and a type of brassica called *Pseudovesicaria digitata*; about 140 are seriously reduced, including the joint-pine (*Ephedra distachya*), a red-berried undershrub (*Pachyphragma macrophyllum*) and the Mediterranean caper (*Capparis spinosa*). Others of interest include: *Campanula mirabilis*, found only in one gorge in Abkhazia; *Iris iberica*, only in the southeast of Georgia; *Hypericum thethrobicum*, only in Javakheti; *Senecio rhombifolius*, a Caucasian endemic found throughout Georgia; *Solidago turfosa*, in peat bogs; *Epigaea gaultherioides*, in the Colchic forests; *Heracleum sommieri*, in subalpine megaphorbias; *Rhododendron caucasicum*, in alpine habitats; and *Delphinium caucasicum*, in subnival habitats. Around 2,000 vascular species are of economic value (for timber, fruits, dyes, oils, fodder and medicinal properties) and at least 150 fungi are edible.

Lowland Colchic forests are dominated by oak (*Quercus pedunciflora, Q. hartwissiana, Q. imeretina*), chestnut (*Castanea sativa*) and lime (*Tilia* sp), while higher regions are covered by beech (*Fagus orientalis*), fir (*Abies nordmanniana*) and spruce (*Picea orientalis*), with an evergreen understorey. At subalpine levels there are crook-stem and dwarf forests of birch (*Betula litwinowii, B. raddeana, B. medwedewii, B. megrelica*) and oak (*Q. pontica*). Other trees and shrubs found in the Colchic district include hornbeam (*Carpinus caucasica*), pine (*Pinus kochiana, P. pithyusa*), juniper (*Juniperus foetidissima, J. polycarpus*), pistachio (or turpentine; *Pistacia mutica*), Colchic boxwood (*Buxus colchica*), cherry-laurel (*Laurocerasus officinalis*), holly (*Ilex colchica*), bladder-nut (*Staphylea colchica*), Colchic hazel (*Corylus colchica*), rhododendron (*Rhododendron ponticum, R. luteum, R. caucasicum, R. ungernii, R. smirnovi*), rowan (mountain ash; *Sorbus subfusca*), wing-nut (*Pterocarya pterocarpa*), Caucasian wing-nut (*P. fraxinifolia*), small-leaved elm (*Zelkova carpinifolia*) and the extremely rare strawberry tree (*Arbutus andrachne*).

The High Caucasus is also rich in endemics; on the southern slopes at lower to mid altitude there's thick deciduous forest, which on the southwestern slopes is described as 'temperate rainforest' (although it falls far short of Chilean or British Columbian standards). Then between 1,250m and about 2,300m there's mixed deciduous–coniferous forest of birch, dwarf rowan and rhododendron (the lilac-flowered *R. ponticum* below and the bright yellow *R. luteum* at the forest limit), with spectacular flowers in clearings and on the forest edges, such as the yellow Turk's cap lily (*Lilium monadelphum*), purple bellflower (*Campanula latifolia*), columbine (*Aquilegia olympica*), fragrant orchid (*Gymnadenia conopsea*), butterfly orchid (*Platanthera chlorantha*) and marsh orchid (*Dachylorhiza* spp). Around Mestia you'll also find red helleborine (*Cephalanthera rubra*), tall pink campion (*Silene* spp), large yellow loosestrife (*Lysimachia punctata*), henbane (*Hyoscyamus niger, Datura* sp), endemic giant hogweed (*Heracleum sommieri*), hollyhocks (*Alcea* spp), as well as white foxgloves, yellow cinquefoil, and wild strawberries and gooseberries.

Above the treeline (between 1,800m and 2,400m) are subalpine meadows that are very lush to the west: herbaceous plants include masterwort (*Astrantia* sp), maroon lousewort (*Pedicularis* sp), bistort (*Polygonum bistorta*), lilies, columbine, delphinium, ranunculus, bellflowers, orchids, campion, vetch, scabious, pansies and cornflowers. Above these you'll see the white-flowered *Rhododendron caucasicum* and alpine meadows (up to 3,000m), home to perennials, many in rosettes or cushions. These include spring gentians (*Gentiana verna pontica*), Pyrenean gentian (*G. septemfida, G. oschtenica*), purple oxlip (*Primula elatior meyeri, P. algida, P. auriculata* and *P. bayerni*), pink cinquefoil (*Potentilla oweriana*) and yellow cinquefoil (*P. ruprechtii*); sandwort (*Arenaria* sp), chickweed (*Cerastium undulatifolium*), fleabane (*Erigeron* sp) and dwarf forget-me-not (*Myosotis* sp), Snowdon lily (*Lloydia serotina*), rock-jasmine (*Androsace villosa* and *A. albana*), whitlow grass (*Draba bryoides*) and wild pansies (*Viola caucasica, Pulsatilla aurea*), fumitory (*Corydalis conorhiza, C. alpestris*), fritillaries (*Fritillaria latifolia*), the white *Anemone impexe* and yellow *A. speciosa*, prophet flower (*Arnebia pulchra, Trollius ranunculus*), and finally, saxifrages, bellflowers and buttercups.

Many **native plants** have suffered from an increase in trade: in 1994, 515,000 bulbs of the snowdrop (*Galanthus ikeriae*), a species listed in Appendix II of the Convention on Trade in Endangered Species of Wild Fauna and Flora (CITES), were illegally collected in Georgia and subsequently exported by Turkish traders to Western Europe; this trade has now been regulated and apparently kept to a sustainable level. Other species have also been affected by illicit trade, including wild cyclamen (*Cyclamen* spp) and snowflakes (*Leucojum* spp).

FAUNA There are 105–10 species of mammals (the most in any European country), over 350 species of birds (253 nesting), about 52 reptiles and 13 amphibians, around 160 fish and thousands of invertebrates (including 290 molluscs, 150 homoptera and 1,363 lepidoptera). Nearly a quarter of the mammals, reptiles and amphibians are endemic to the Caucasus. Twenty-one species of mammals, 33 birds, and ten reptiles and amphibians are listed as rare, threatened or endangered; these include the goitered or Persian gazelle (*Gazella subgutturossa*), which probably became extinct in Georgia in the 1960s, although it is still found in Azerbaijan. The striped hyena (*Hyaena hyaena*) and Caucasian leopard (*Panthera pardus ciscaucasia*) were thought to have met the same fate, but it now appears that a few remain in the arid steppes of southeastern Georgia. Two species are listed as critically endangered: the Kazbegi birch mouse (*Sicista kazbegica*) and the Mediterranean monk seal (*Monachus monachus*). Large mammals such as red deer, bear, wolf, boar, lynx, golden jackal, ibex, chamois, wild goats and wild sheep (mouflon) are found almost exclusively in the High Caucasus. However, populations of many species have been halved in the last couple of decades, largely due to increased poaching; wildlife has fled from conflicts in the northern Caucasus (notably Chechnya) and from the south in Azerbaijan, then been shot in Georgia (partly by hunters from Russia).

Mammals There are four species of wild goat: the west Caucasian tur (*Capra caucasica*), the east Caucasian tur or Daghestanian goat (*C. cylindricornis*), bezoar or pasang (*C. aegragus*) and chamois (*Rupicapra rupicapra*), and all are suffering from being hunted. The bezoar has been in decline since the 19th century, and there's now a maximum of 100 on the northeastern slopes of the High Caucasus. The Daghestanian goat, endemic to the eastern Caucasus, is endangered, with its population falling from about 5,000 in 1985 to a current estimate of around 1,000; the west Caucasian tur, endemic to the western Caucasus, is listed as vulnerable, but its population has also been halved from around 5,000 in 1985, with perhaps 1,000 in Svaneti. In the eastern Caucasus, the chamois is endangered, its population having fallen from around 6,000 in 1985 to perhaps 2,000 today.

A bounty system for hunting predators operated until 1993, and poaching has continued since then; the population of the Eurasian or common wolf (*Canis lupus lupus*) in particular has fallen sharply. The red deer (*Cervus elaphus maral*) is also endangered by hunting; in eastern Georgia numbers fell from 2,500 in 1985 to 880 in 1994, and there were an estimated total of 500 in the whole of Georgia in 2014; however the population in Lagodekhi has recently doubled, possibly owing to the fall in the wolf population. Likewise, lynx (*Felis lynx orientalis*) numbers have fallen from over 500 in 1990 to just 100 today. The brown bear (*Ursus arctos syriacus*) is vulnerable, its numbers having fallen from over 3,000 in the 1980s to fewer than 500. In fact the main hazard for hikers in the mountains is the nahgaaz or Caucasian sheepdog, used to guard sheep; this supposedly gentle giant (in medieval times visiting ambassadors would nervously ask for the lion next to the throne to be removed) is seen as a national treasure, and competitive shows (often won in the past by Aslan Abashidze! – page 283) are very popular. Bear gall, as well as skins and horns, are smuggled into Turkey. Tougher legislation is under consideration and bounties are no longer paid for killing animals that attack flocks, while reintroduction programmes are under way for wolves and other large mammals.

Mid-sized mammals in the mountains include the badger (*Meles meles*), pine marten (*Martes martes*), stone marten (*M. foina*), marbled polecat (*Vormela peregusna*), wildcat (*Felis silvestris*), fox (*Vulpes vulpes*), hare (*Lepus europaeus*) and weasel (*Mustela nivalis*), which here fills the niche of the marmot, scavenging in campsites. Other endangered species include the jungle cat (*Felis chaus*) whose range stretches from here to Indochina, the European otter (*Lutra lutra*), the Caucasian mink (*Mustella lutreola caucasica*) and the golden jackal (*Canis aureus*). The Persian squirrel (*Sciurus anomalus*) is suffering from an invasion by the European squirrel (*S. vulgaris*).

Twelve species of small mammal are endangered or vulnerable, largely due to overgrazing or agricultural expansion; these include the red-backed vole (*Clethrionomys glareolus ponticus*), the Transcaucasian golden hamster (*Mesocricetus brandti*), the pygmy or grey hamster (*Cricetulus migratorius*), the shrew (*Sorex volnuchini*), the birch mice (*Sicista caucasica, S. kluchkorica, S. kazbegica*) and the Prometheus mole vole (*Prometheomys shaposhnikowi*), most of which have been split up into isolated groups. Many of these are endemic to the Caucasus: the Transcaucasian golden hamster; the black-chested hamster (*Mesocricetus raddei*); shrews (*Sorex volnuchini, S. raddei, S. caucasica*) and the water shrew (*Neomys schelkownikowi*); birch mice (*Sicista caucasica, S. kluchorica, S. kazbegica, S. armenica*); the Prometheus vole; Caucasian moles (*Talpa caucasica, Terricola daghestanicus, Terricola nasarovi*); the yellow-breasted mouse (*Apodemus fulvipectus*), as well as the Black Sea field mouse (*Apodemus ponticus*); and hybrids with the house mouse (*Mus musculus*).

Cetaceans There's been little research on the cetaceans of the Black Sea, but the harbour porpoise (*Phoecoena phoecoena*), bottlenose dolphin (*Tursiops truncatus*) and common dolphin (*Delphinus delphis*) are all present.

Reptiles There are around 52 species of reptiles in Georgia (the total keeps changing as lizards are reclassified), 25% of which are endemic to the Caucasus. The dominant lizard species is *Lacerta praticola*, while *L. rudis, L. derjugini, L. parvula, L. unisexualis, L. clarcorum, L. valentini and L. mixta* may or may not be separate species. Much the same applies to the *Vipera* (*Pelias*) *kaznakovi* complex. Threatened species include Schneider's skink (*Eumeces schneideri*), the lidless skink (*Ablepharus pannonicus*), the leopard snake (*Elaphe situla*) – perhaps the most beautiful in Europe – and the Transcaucasian ratsnake (*E. hohenackeri*), the dwarf snake (*Eirenis collaris*), the boigine snake (*Malpolon monspesulanus*), the racerunner (*Eremias arguta*), the turtle (*Clemmys* (*Mauremis*) *caspica caspica*), the snake-eyed lizard (*Ophisops elegans*), the commonest lizard in the Anatolian steppes, the javelin sand boa (*Eryx jaculus*), the garter snake (*Natrix megalocephala*), the Caucasian viper (*Vipera kaznakovi*), the Transcaucasian long-nosed or sand viper (*V. ammodytes transcaucasiana*), the Levantine viper or giurza (*V. lebetina obtusa*; up to 1.8m in length) and Dinnik's viper (*V. dinnicki*).

The population dynamics of the Caucasian salamander and rock lizards are particularly fascinating to scientists, with lots of more or less distinct species living together, with some hybridising and some not. Some of the lizards also live in all-female colonies, reproducing by parthenogenesis (asexually). There's the possibility of lots of interesting micro-evolutionary research to be done here, but the potential is almost unknown to foreign scientists.

Amphibians Georgia's amphibians consist of four species of Caudata: the Caucasian salamander (*Mertensiella caucasica*), the banded newt (*Triturus vittatus ophryticus*), the smooth newt (*T. vulgaris lantzi*) and the southern crested newt (*T. cristatus karelini*), and nine species of Anura – the frogs and toads *Pelobates syriacus syriacus*, *Pelodytes caucasicus*, *Bufo viridis viridis*, *B. verrucosissimus*, *Hyla arborea shelkownikowi*, *H. savignyi*, *Rana macrocnemis*, *R. camerani* and *R. ridibunda*. A quarter of these are endemic to the Caucasus (*Mertensiella caucasica*, *Pelodytes caucasicus*, *Bufo verrucosissimus*, and hybrids of *Rana macrocnemis* and *Hyla arborea*). The Caucasian salamander is, in fact, found only in the Lesser Caucasus of Georgia and Turkey, not the High Caucasus. *Pelobates syriacus*, *Mertensiella caucasica* and probably *Hyla savignyi* are threatened, and *Pelodytes caucasicus*, *Bufo verrucosissimus* and *Rana macrocnemis* are in decline.

Fish A quarter of Georgia's fish species are endemic: the ship sturgeon (*Accipenser nudiventris*) is probably extinct in Georgia, while *A. guldenstadti* and *A. sturio* are endangered. Eastern European fish have been introduced into the lakes of the Javakheti Plateau, virtually wiping out local fish species; the Crucian carp (*Carassius carassius*) is also harming newt populations.

Birds Georgia acts as a 'funnel' for birds migrating from their breeding grounds in Siberia and northern Europe to their winter homes, so it's hardly surprising that very few are endemic to the Caucasus, and even these are subspecies rather than distinct species. Twenty species are endangered: the lammergeyer or bearded vulture (*Gypaetus barbatus*), the black or cinereous vulture (*Aegypius monachus*), the griffon vulture (*Gyps fulvus*), the Egyptian vulture (*Neophron percnopterus*), the peregrine (*Falco peregrinus*), the lanner falcon (*F. biarmicus*), the short-toed eagle (*Circaetus gallicus*), the marsh harrier (*Circus aeruginosus*), the Imperial eagle (*Aquila heliaca*) and lesser-spotted eagle (*A. pomarina*) (the Georgian populations of both are under 85 pairs), the golden eagle (*A. chrysaetos*), the booted eagle (*Hieraaetus pennatus*), the Caucasian snowcock (*Tetraogallus caucasicus*), the black francolin (*Francolinus francolinus*), the grey partridge (*Perdix perdix*), the black stork (*Ciconia nigra*), the spoonbill (*Platalea leucordia*), the crane (*Grus grus*), the demoiselle crane (*Anthropoides virgo*) and the glossy ibis (*Plegadis falcinellus*), as well, probably, as some woodpeckers and passerines. Certainly the Syrian woodpecker (*Dendrocopus syriacus*) is vulnerable, as, amazingly, is the pheasant (*Phasianus colchicus*); having taken over the world it is suffering in its land of origin from loss of forest and increased hunting.

Many raptors migrate along the flyway down the Black Sea Coast; lammergeyer live year-round in the High Caucasus, but the population has dropped from 40 pairs to 20 pairs in the last 50 years. Others nest in the mountains but can often be seen hunting in the semi-desert of Davit-Gareja; other mountain species include the Caspian snowcock (*Tetraogallus caspius*) – from the Eastern Caucasus to Iran, the Caucasian snowcock (*T. caucasicus*) – more to the west, and the Caucasian black grouse (*Tetrao (Lyrurus) mlokosiewiczi*) – typically Caucasian, and probably a relict species. There's an isolated population of the alpine finch or great rosefinch (*Carpodacus rubicilla*), which otherwise lives in Central Asia; the scarlet grosbeak (*C. erythrinus*) breeds from Sweden to Japan and passes through to winter between Iran and China. An endemic subspecies of the rock partridge (*Alectoris graeca*) (which is kept as a domestic fowl in Armenia) can be seen near the snowline.

Other species found in the High Caucasus include Kruper's nuthatch (*Sitta kruperii*), the white-winged or Guldenstat's redstart (*Phoenicurus erythrogaster*), Radde's accentor (*Prunella ocularis*), the red-fronted serin (*Serinus pusillus*), the grey-necked bunting (*Emberizia buchanani*) and rock bunting (*E. cia*), the alpine accentor (*Prunella collaris*), the redwing (*Turdus iliacus*) – only in winter – and a subspecies of jay (*Garrulus glandarius krynicki*).

In the deserts you may find the trumpeter bullfinch (*Rhodopechys sanguinea*), the rufous bush robin or tugai nightingale (*Cercotrichas galactotes*), the chukar (*Alectoris chukar*) and, in winter, great bustard (*Otis tarda*) and little bustard (*O. tetrax*).

Perhaps the most important bird habitats are the wetlands of the Black Sea Coast and the Javakheti Plateau, where you may see migratory birds such as white spoonbills (*Platalea leucorodia*), red-breasted geese (*Rufibrenta ruficollis*), red-necked grebe (*Podiceps grisigena*), white pelican (*Pelecanus onocrotalus*), Dalmatian pelican (*P. crispus*), squacco heron (*Ardeola ralloides*), great white egret (*Ardea alba*), little egret (*Egretta garzetta*), white stork (*Ciconia ciconia*), black stork (*C. nigra*), glossy ibis (*Plegadis falcinellus*), ruddy shelduck (*Tadorna ferruginea*), ferruginous duck (*Aythya nyroca*) and other ducks, herons, geese and cormorants.

CONSERVATION Royal **hunting reserves** known as *korugi* (similar to Britain's New Forest) are first mentioned in the *Law Book of Vakhtang VI* (1709). Georgia's first nature reserve in the modern sense was created in 1912 to protect the wolves of the Lagodekhi Gorge; by the end of the Soviet era there were 15 reserves, totalling 168,800ha (1,680km^2, or 2.4% of the country's area), in addition to forests and other protected zones, now covering a total of 4.4% of the country. The WWF (now the World Wide Fund for Nature) set up an office in 1989, and started to create a Western-style system of Protected Areas, with a hierarchy from Protected Landscapes through Nature Reserves to National Parks; in March 1996 parliament declared the law on Protected Areas, creating the first modern National Park, at Borjomi. This replaces the Soviet *zakaznik* system of totally closed reserves with a flexible system allowing sustainable use of many areas. The Kolkheti, Tusheti and Vashlovani national parks were established between 1998 and 2003. The Department of Protected Areas was created in 2004 within the Ministry of Natural Resources and became the independent Agency of Protected Areas (w apa.gov.ge/en) in 2008, since when the Mtirala, Javakheti, Machakhela, Algeti, Saguramo and Kazbegi national parks have been created. A National Park of Glaciers based on the Pshav-Khevsureti Protected Area is planned. There are now ten national parks spanning over a total area of 276,723ha.

Georgia also signed the International Convention on Biodiversity in 1994 and the CITES agreement in 1996. Land privatisation began in 1992; by mid-1995, 38% of arable land (around 20% of all agricultural land) had been privatised, and in 1999 a land-registration programme made farmers the official owners of their land. Since 1996 hunters have required permits, but this has generally been ignored. In 2005, an Environmental Protection Inspectorate (or the ecological police) was set up, but initially had no budget except what was provided by international donors.

The WWF also set up an environmental education programme, which involves teaching the teachers, making television programmes, and opening ecocentres for school groups.

There's an **active 'green' movement** in Georgia, which grew out of a 1989 campaign against a planned dam in Svaneti; the Georgian Greens are now affiliated with Friends of the Earth, and Zurab Zhvania, prime minister from 2003 to 2005, was first elected as a member of the Green Party. Since 1991 they have been campaigning against the truly dreadful pollution of the Black Sea and for a sustainable forestry industry; the government imposed a tax of US$46 per square metre of timber, but the International Monetary Fund (IMF) forced its withdrawal. Nuclear issues have a high profile, even though the research reactor in Mtskheta was closed in 1990, and plans for a second nuclear power station in Armenia were abandoned in 1996 after big protests. In 1997, 11 servicemen on the Red Army's former Lilo base near Tbilisi developed skin burns, which after three months (and no help from the Russians) were diagnosed as radiation burns; eventually nine radiation sources were found, including stores of depleted uranium bullets and capsules from Geiger counters. Around 300 radiation sources were found at the former nuclear missile base of Vaziani, 30km east of Tbilisi. Russia was unable or unwilling to provide any information, which led to large demonstrations at the Russian embassy in 1998. In addition, strontium fall-out from Chernobyl in Ukraine caused illness in western Georgia. The oil pipelines across Georgia have undergone surprisingly strict and detailed Environmental Impact Assessments, but there's scepticism about the standards in Azerbaijan and the Central Asian states.

Georgia inherited many **environmental problems**, largely due to Soviet industrialisation, with pollution by oil, heavy metals and fertilisers, disrupted water-catchment areas, and erosion due to uncontrolled logging and overgrazing. The numbers of sheep in the mountains are still 2.5 times optimum levels, and 30% of pastures are affected by erosion, silt from which covers spawning beds. Forests and wetlands continue to be converted to farmland, causing serious ecological damage.

What foreigners notice at once, however, is the amount of **litter** strewn around, especially along main roads; Georgians don't even notice it, but littering from cars became illegal in 2015. A very few recycling bins appeared in 2017, and a national tourism strategy drawn up in 2018 has the litter problem as a top priority. Foreigners also notice a lot of stray dogs, but those with ear tags have been sterilised and vaccinated against rabies, and they all seem fairly well fed and happy.

HISTORY

It can be said that the history of Georgia goes back to the dawn of time. Noah's great-grandson Thargamos settled in the land of Japhet, somewhere between the Ararat and Caucasus mountains; the Georgians claim descent from him via his great-grandson Karthlos (while the Armenians claim descent from his brother Haik), and therefore still call themselves Karthians, or Kartvelebi, and their country Sakartvelo. Remains of protohumans (*Homo erectus georgicus*) about 1.75 million years old and human remains about 200,000 years old have been found (at Dmanisi), as well as Palaeolithic artefacts. The Middle Bronze Age Kurgan and Trialeti cultures developed here, known as the Early Transcaucasian Culture (ETC) when they spread into present-day Turkey, Iran and Syria in the third millennium BC; this was seemingly a peaceful expansion, spreading wine culture rather than conquering. By the 2nd millennium BC, tribes were on the verge of statehood, and Medea and her father King Aetes probably did live between the 14th and 13th centuries BC on the Black Sea coast. The tribal union of Diauehi was recorded in the 12th century BC, and the state of Colchis (Kolkhida or Egrisi) certainly existed here by the 9th century BC, when tribute was demanded by Assyria, with Greek trading ports by the 6th century BC. The oldest (and somewhat lurid) account of Georgia is by Xenophon, who retreated from Persia at the end of the 5th century BC. In the east of the country the state of Kartli (known to the Greeks as Iveria) was created by one of Alexander the

Great's generals, overthrown in 335BC by King Parnavaz I. In the 1st century BC it was an ally of Rome, ruled for a time by Mithridates IV Eupator, King of Pontus, who turned against Rome and also seized Colchis. He was finally beaten in the Third Mithridatic War (66–65BC) by Pompey, who incorporated Colchis into the Roman Empire, though few traces remain (although Roman remains, including *qvevri*, have been found in Zalissa (now Dzalisi), 20km northwest of Mtskheta, and in Gonio, south of Batumi). Iveria remained a Roman satellite state until AD298, when Rome signed a treaty with Persia, recognising the Persian-born Mirian III as king of Iveria; he founded the Chosroid dynasty which ruled for two centuries. In AD337 Mirian, following his wife Nana, was converted to Christianity by Nino, a slave from Cappadocia. Thus Georgia became the world's third Christian state, preceded only by Armenia (AD301) and Ethiopia (AD330). In the 4th and 5th centuries Colchis (now known as Lazika) also came under

THE MYTH OF JASON AND THE *ARGO*

In Greek mythology, Jason was the son of Aeson, King of Iolcus, near Volos in Thessaly. After his uncle Pelias seized the throne Jason was reared by the centaur Chiron on Mount Pelion (the concept of the centaur has its origin on the steppes to the north of the Caucasus, where men were first seen riding horses). When Jason grew up, Pelias ordered him to bring him the legendary Golden Fleece from Colchis, expecting never to see him again. Jason built a ship called the *Argo*, and assembled a crew of 50, including such heroes as Hercules, Orpheus, Theseus, Castor and Pollux. After overcoming storms, monsters and seductive women, they at last reached Colchis, where the king, Aetes (son of Helios and brother of Circe and Phaethon), agreed to give Jason the fleece if he succeeded in further trials such as yoking two fire-breathing bulls to a plough and sowing the dragon's teeth of Cadmus (which sprouted as armed men). He won the love of Medea, daughter of Aetes and a sorceress who gave her name to the science of medicine; she secretly helped him win the fleece and escape from Colchis. They returned to Iolcus, supposedly sailing up the Danube and carrying the *Argo* overland to the Adriatic. Pelias was killed but his son drove Jason and Medea from the city; they took the fleece to Orchemenus in Boetia, and settled in Corinth, living there for many years. Jason abandoned Medea when he fell in love with King Creon's daughter Glauce; Medea took revenge by making a magic robe that burnt to death both father and daughter. For breaking his vow to Medea, Jason was condemned to be a wanderer until, as an old man, he at last returned to Corinth and was killed when the prow of the *Argo* fell over and crushed him. The Jason myth dates from around 1400BC but the definitive compilation came only in the 4th century BC with the *Argonautica* of Apollonius of Rhodes, who worked out their actual route; it was a great success and Apollonius became director of the great Library of Alexandria, one of the Seven Wonders of the Ancient World.

The first voyage myth, it is in part a metaphor for the expansion of Greek trade, the fleece and Medea's gifts of magic oil and stone being exchanged for technology, represented by harnessing bulls and ploughing. The legend of the fleece itself arose from the use of sheep fleeces to trap particles of gold from mountain streams in the countries around the Black Sea, as witnessed by the writers Patrick Leigh Fermor in Romania and Tim Severin in Georgia.

Persian influence. By the end of the 5th century the Chosroid king of Kartli, Vakhtang Gorgasali (AD442–502), ruled a feudal state which included Abkhazia, Ossetia and much of Armenia; he moved the capital of Kartli from Mtskheta to Tbilisi, and secured autocephalous (self-governing) status for the Church, which became established in the 6th century thanks to the 13 Assyrian Fathers (page 44).

However, from the mid 6th century the Persians took control again, followed by the Byzantine Empire, and then the Arabs who had conquered Georgia by the mid 7th century, leaving its kings in power as long as they acknowledged the supremacy of the caliphs: their dominance lasted until the 9th century. The Armenian family of the Bagratids (who claimed descent from David and Bathsheba via Bagrat or St Pancras) had moved to the Georgian borderlands by the late 8th century; Ashot Bagration became chamberlain to the Byzantine emperor and soon de facto ruler of Kartli and, in AD866, Adarnase IV took the title of king; their dynasty ruled until the Russians took over in the 19th century.

MEDIEVAL GEORGIA Bagrat III became King of Kartli in AD975, and by 1008 had united east and west Georgia for the first time (excluding Tbilisi); in 1068 the Seljuk Turks under Alp Arslan came out of Central Asia, creating havoc and finally defeating the Byzantine Empire at Manzikert in 1071. However, the kings were allowed to keep their thrones, although Georgia remained a backwater until it was again united under King Davit IV Agmashenebelis (David the Builder). Born in 1073, he took over from his father Giorgi II in 1089, annexed Kakheti in 1105 and, in 1121, drove the Seljuks out of Tbilisi, making it his capital the next year. He made Georgia the most powerful state in the Near East, and economic strength led to a cultural Golden Age in the 12th century. Davit died in 1125, and was succeeded by his son Demetre I (1125–56) and then Giorgi III (1156–84).

Georgia's favourite monarch remains Davit's great-granddaughter Queen Tamar (Tamar Mepe in Georgian – this is sometimes mis-translated as King Tamara, as *mepe* simply means monarch), who was born in 1154 and who ruled jointly with her father Giorgi III after crushing a revolt in 1178, and then alone from 1184 to 1213. In 1185 she married Prince Giorgi Bogoliubskoi of Suzdal, a vicious, drunken adventurer (a typical Russian in the eyes of many Georgians) who was soon divorced and expelled for sexual (perhaps homosexual) misconduct; after the fiasco of this political union she married the far more suitable David Soslan, an Ossetian prince, who led her armies and fathered Giorgi IV Lash and his sister and successor Queen Rusudan (said to have been 'fearless only in her lusts'). Tamar extended Georgian rule from the Black Sea to the Caspian, defeated the Turks at the battles of Shamkhori (1195) and Basiani (1202), and after the sack of Constantinople by the Fourth Crusade in 1204 she set up a new Byzantine Empire in Trebizond (now Trabzon) under her kinsman Alexius Comnenus, who had been brought up in Georgia. The Golden Age was brought to an abrupt end in 1220 by Chinghiz (Genghis) Khan and his Mongol hordes, followed by the Black Death from 1366, and by Temur Lang (Tamerlane) who invaded six times between 1386 and 1403. The last king of a united Georgia was Alexander I (1412–43); on his death the country was divided between his three sons, with the eldest taking Kartli (with his capital in Tbilisi), the second Imereti (based in Kutaisi) and the third Kakheti (based in Telavi). As the centralised state fell apart, other noble families took control of smaller areas, such as the Dadianis in Mingrelia, the Gurielis in Guria, and the Gelovanis in Svaneti. After the fall of Constantinople in 1453, Persia and the Ottoman Empire vied for control of the area in a protracted and destructive struggle – Georgia was split between them, although the kings were left on their thrones as long as they did what they were told. Shah Abbas (ruler of Persia from 1587 to 1629) established his rule over Kakheti and Kartli, punishing an uprising in 1615–16 by killing 60,000–70,000 and deporting 100,000.

RUSSIAN RULE The 18th century saw the rise of a third power in the region: Russia, which claimed to protect the Orthodox from Islamic oppression, and specifically Daghestanian raids. It began the process of conquering the northern Caucasus in 1722 under Peter the Great, who died three years later. As the Persian empire declined the Ottomans invaded, and the enlightened Vakhtang VI of Kartli fled into exile in Russia in 1723; fortunately he had constructed irrigation channels and other public works (and written the history of Georgia) before he left. In 1744 the Persians installed Erekle (or Heraclius) II as King of Kakheti, and his father Teimuraz II (who had ruled Kakheti since 1733) as King of Kartli; Erekle also ruled Kartli from his father's death in 1762 and struggled heroically to resist Persian dominance (fighting more than 200 battles). Although he did finally have to call for Russian help, Frederick the Great of Prussia saw him as an invincible equal due to his youthful exploits with Nadir Shah on his campaign in India, sacking the Mughal capital Delhi in 1739. In 1768 the first Russo–Turkish war began, and in 1769 the Russian general Todleben crossed the Caucasus, taking Tbilisi and Kutaisi, but was recalled before he could capture Poti; in the Treaty of Kutchuk-Kainardji of 1774, the Turks gave up their claims to western Georgia, and agreed not to help the Muslim tribes of the Caucasus against Russia, though in fact they continued to do so.

In 1783 Persia's new shah, Ali Murad, tried to reimpose his sovereignty, and Erekle II was forced to ask for Russian aid; the Treaty of Protection was signed in Gurgievsk on 24 July 1783, and Count Paul Potyomkin (cousin of the Russian empress Catherine the Great's lover, Grigori Potyomkin) reached Tbilisi later that year, becoming the first viceroy of the Caucasus in 1785. Also in 1785 the Chechens of the north Caucasus rose in a revolt that lasted until 1791; to deal with this Russian troops were withdrawn from Tbilisi in 1787, and in 1795 the city was razed by Shah Aga Mohammed Khan of Persia, who killed 50,000 and took 20,000 slaves. Catherine refused to help, even though there had been plenty of warning (much like Stalin refusing to help the Warsaw uprising), but the Russians then attacked Persia, thus seizing Azerbaijan. However, Catherine died the next year and her successor, Paul I, withdrew to the River Terek. Erekle II died in 1798 followed in December 1800 by his successor, George XII, and in March 1801 Paul was assassinated; his successor, Alexander I, at once violated the Treaty of Gurgievsk and abolished the monarchy of eastern Georgia (Kartli and Kakheti), annexing it as the province of Tiflis. In 1802, he installed a viceroy, Prince Paul Tsitsianov (Georgian born and Russian educated), who deported the remnants of the royal family to Russia and in 1804 occupied Imereti.

Russia was at war with Persia from 1804 to 1813, and with Turkey from 1807 to 1812, and in 1812 Napoleon invaded Russia; amidst all this confusion Russia was still able to crush revolts in Kakheti (1802 and 1812–13) and Imereti (1819–20), the last Georgian king, Solomon II, fleeing in 1810. Tsitsianov was killed in Azerbaijan in 1806, but by 1813 Persia had been forced to give up its claims to Georgia and Daghestan. In 1825 Nicholas I became tsar and in 1827 appointed as Viceroy Prince Alexander Paskevich, who captured Yerevan and Tabriz. In 1828 Russia made peace with Persia (retaining eastern Armenia) then began another war with Turkey; Paskevich captured Kars, Akhaltsikhe, Erzurum and Poti. The Treaty of Adrianople

Josef Vissarionovich Djugashvili probably had more influence on people's lives than anyone else in the 20th century, bringing between 45 million and 66 million of them to a premature end. Nazism killed around 25 million and Chinese communism about 65 million. Yet he did have charm and charisma, and 45 years after his death one Russian in six calls him their greatest leader (which admittedly is not saying much).

He was a Georgian, born in the Russian quarter of Gori. Although his birthdate was officially given, from around 1922, as 21 December 1879 (9 December by the Old Style calendar), it seems he was born a year earlier and may have changed it once he had absolute power in order to have a nationwide celebration of his 50th birthday. His mother did laundry, and his father was an alcoholic cobbler. He was born with a webbed left foot, was pockmarked by smallpox from the age of six, and acquired a crooked left arm when he was run over by a cart; it seems likely that these deformities in some way fuelled his ruthless ambition, together with his mother's obsessive desire for him to succeed as a priest and beatings from his father which made him hate authority.

He was a star pupil at the church school in Gori, and won a scholarship to study at the seminary in Tbilisi in 1894. In 1895 and 1896 seven of his poems were published in *Iveria* (edited by Ilia Chavchavadze), but he was soon involved in revolutionary politics. He was expelled from the seminary in 1899, and worked as an accountant and record-keeper at the Tbilisi Meteorological and Geophysical Observatory until March 1901.

After the violent demonstration of May Day 1901, he was expelled from Mesame Dasi (the Social Democrats) and went underground in Batumi and Baku. He was arrested in 1902 after strikes in the Rothschild oil plants and sent to Siberia, escaping in 1904 and returning to Batumi and then Tbilisi. At this time he first met Nadezhda Alliluyeva, then aged three, whom he was to marry 16 years later, and who was to shoot herself in 1932. In 1903 the Social Democrats split into two groups: the Bolsheviks and Mensheviks. Koba, as he then called himself, supported the more radical Bolsheviks and their leader, Lenin, and took a new *nom de guerre*, Stalin, suggesting 'Man of Steel' in Russian. From this time on, his loyalty was to Russia and to international communism, rather than to Georgia; although he had no oratorical skills or charisma, he had plenty of energy, organisational talent and a retentive memory. He roamed the Caucasus, fomenting strikes and spreading the message of socialism, as well as staging robberies to raise funds, together with Simon Ter-Petrossian (known as Kamo), who was also from Gori, although Armenian.

Between 1902 and 1913, Stalin was frequently arrested and sent to Siberia, but he always escaped. In 1912 he founded the party newspaper *Pravda* ('Truth') and Lenin rewarded Stalin's loyalty by appointing him to the Bolshevik Central Committee; he began to gain influence in the party, but was arrested again in 1913 and this time had to stay in Siberia until the March revolution of 1917.

IN POWER In the Bolshevik government Stalin served as commissar of nationalities (fomenting trouble in Baku), and in 1920 as commissar of the army heading for

(now Edirne) in 1829 restored Erzurum and Kars to Turkey (prompting many Armenians to flee), but Guria was reunited with Georgia. In 1856, having lost the Crimean War, Russia again turned its attention to the Caucasus; Prince Alexander

Berlin, being blamed by Trotsky for its defeat in the Battle of Warsaw. In 1922 he became general secretary of the party's Central Committee, and on Lenin's death in 1924 used all the levers of power to crush his rivals as he manoeuvred into a position of absolute power, despite Lenin having specifically instructed the party to beware of him.

Initially he advocated moderate economic policies and an end to world revolution, which aroused the opposition of the leftists led by Trotsky, Kamenev and Zinoviev; by 1928 he had driven them from any position of power, and then adopted leftist policies such as rapid industrialisation and agricultural collectivisation, arousing the opposition of the rightists. By the end of 1929, Stalin was the undisputed master of the Soviet Union, and communism died in any meaningful sense.

Having seized the land of the *kulaks* (bourgeois peasantry) in 1928, Stalin was able to fund industrialisation by exporting their grain stocks, and continued collectivisation despite dogged resistance from the peasants and a famine in 1932 which may have cost more than ten million lives. Sergei Kirov, the Leningrad party secretary, protested, and was murdered in 1934; Stalin used this as a pretext for his first purge, arresting virtually all his senior colleagues and staging the Moscow show trials between 1936 and 1938. Only 41 of the 139 deputies elected to the Central Committee in 1934 survived, and millions more died as he purged the party, the professions and intellectuals throughout the Soviet Union. By 1938 there was no doubt that this was a dictatorship.

By concluding a non-aggression pact with Nazi Germany in 1939 (including a secret clause agreeing to a joint attack on Poland), Stalin bought time for further industrialisation and rearmament before the Nazi attack in June 1941. The Soviet people made immense sacrifices in what they know as the Great Patriotic War, but its huge reserves of manpower (expended extravagantly by Stalin) and industrial power, coupled with ferocious winter weather and the contributions of the Allies, finally brought victory. Stalin (now a *generalissimo*) was far more of a hands-on commander than any of the other Allied leaders, while also out-manoeuvring them diplomatically.

There was no relaxation after the war; the imposition of communist rule on eastern and much of central Europe led to further waves of repression and the outbreak of the Cold War with his former allies. In 1953 his health failed, but he claimed to have discovered a plot by his doctors to kill him; a massive new purge seemed imminent, but he died on 5 March 1953. In 1956 his successor Nikita Khrushchev denounced his crimes and in 1961 his body was removed from the Red Square mausoleum. Under Brezhnev criticism of Stalin was muted, but again in 1987 Gorbachev told a party congress that his crimes were 'enormous and unforgivable'. The huge death toll of the purges and collectivisation was finally revealed, and with the opening of the Soviet and KGB archives more and more is becoming known.

Nevertheless he is widely seen, particularly in Georgia, as a 'strong man', the sort of leader who might pull the country out of the morass, and his crimes are widely overlooked as a price worth paying.

Baryatinski (a veteran of the never-ending campaigns against the Muslim tribes of the northern Caucasus) became viceroy and in 1857 occupied Mingrelia and Svaneti; by 1859 he had been able to defeat the Chechen leader Shamyl, who had

Lavrenti Pavlovich Beria, born in 1899 near Sukhumi to Megrelian parents, was involved in undercover revolutionary activities in Baku and elsewhere before the revolution, and it's likely that he was an agent for the British as well. He only joined the Bolshevik Party in 1917; in 1921 he became head of the Cheka (secret police) in Transcaucasia, where he implemented Stalin's purges so effectively that in 1938 he became head of the NKVD, the secret police of the whole Soviet Union. In 1940 he ordered the massacre of at least 22,000 Polish officers and intellectuals at Katyn; during World War II he also organised the partisan campaign behind the German lines, the mass deportation of various ethnic groups and the Soviet Union's atomic bomb project. He became a politburo member and deputy chairman of the Council of Ministers in 1946; suspected of involvement in Stalin's death and of planning to take power himself, he was arrested in June 1953 and executed on 23 December 1953. He probably didn't kill Stalin but may have given him warfarin which brought on other complications, and he certainly delayed calling for doctors after Stalin's stroke – there's no doubt that he loathed Stalin by then.

Although he has a terrible reputation in the West, he was by no means the worst of the purgers – he reached the top only after the 1936–38 terror, and he began to empty the Gulag camps then and after Stalin's death. He was surprisingly pragmatic and might well have been a better leader than the more idealistic Khrushchev, initiating a more thorough process of de-Stalinisation. He was briefly part of a ruling 'troika' with Malenkov and Molotov, but overconfidence and his lack of a party base led to his downfall. Although Armando Ianucci's 2017 film *The Death of Stalin* showed him being shot on the day of Stalin's funeral, he and his sidekicks were in fact given a trial of sorts six months after their arrest and then executed the same day. It's also now clear that he was an appalling sexual predator and rapist.

led a very effective guerrilla revolt since 1837. In 1864 the Circassians of the north Caucasus were crushed (and 600,000 fled to Turkey), and the next year Abkhazia was also incorporated into the Russian Empire. Another Russo–Turkish war followed in 1877–78, with Russia capturing Kars and Adjara (both reoccupied by Turkey in 1918).

Under Russian rule economic development proceeded apace, but the Georgian populace did not benefit greatly. By the late 19th century, 58% of Georgia's area was owned by Russians and by the government, and the merchant class was overwhelmingly Armenian. Ilia Chavchavadze (1837–1907) and Akaki Tsereteli (1840–1915) led the group of intellectuals known as 'the men of the '60s', or *Tergdaleulebi*, who began to infuse a sense of national consciousness in the Georgian people; in the 1890s another wave of Russian-educated men returned to their homeland, including Noe Zhordania (1868–1953). Political unrest grew in Georgia as elsewhere in the Russian Empire, with the various strands of Marxist thought as influential as elsewhere. On 28 October 1905, 60 people were killed when Cossacks broke up a Social Democrat meeting in Tbilisi, and in 1907 Ilia Chavchavadze was killed; this was long blamed on tsarist agents, but the feeling now is that in fact the Bolsheviks wished to remove his persuasive voice for moderation.

After the Russian revolutions of 1917 Georgia briefly regained independence, but found itself the pawn of larger countries competing for access to the Caspian oil fields. In April 1918, Transcaucasia (Georgia, Armenia and Azerbaijan) declared itself an independent federal state, but on 26 May 1918 Georgia broke away, having been persuaded by Germany that it would provide protection against the Bolshevik threat from north of the Caucasus. German troops helped to drive the Turks, supposedly their allies, out of Batumi; a week after the defeat of Germany and Turkey at the end of 1918, 15,000 British troops landed in Batumi to occupy Transcaucasia (stopping fighting between Georgians and Armenians in the Akhalkalaki area after Turkey's withdrawal). Britain and its chief commissioner, Oliver Wardrop, wanted to maintain Georgia as a buffer against Bolshevism, but the Social Democrat (Menshevik) government led by Zhordania from June 1918 refused to form an alliance with Denikin's White Russians, the last tsarists. Zhordania's government introduced universal suffrage, health insurance and some nationalisation and land redistribution; but this wasn't enough for the Bolsheviks in Russia who imposed a blockade, leading to food shortages. In May 1920, a Bolshevik coup attempt in Tbilisi and a revolt in South Ossetia failed; in January 1920 the Allies granted de facto recognition to all three Transcaucasian republics, and a year later Britain and France granted full *de jure* recognition. Zhordania felt protected by the League of Nations, but Prime Minister David Lloyd George was more interested in a deal with Moscow; the British troops left early in 1920, and on 16 February 1921 the Red Army invaded, occupying Tbilisi nine days later.

The takeover was engineered by the Soviet ambassador Sergei Kirov and Sergo Ordjonikidze (a Georgian Bolshevik, who in 1937 'committed suicide at Stalin's urgent suggestion, being granted in return a state funeral', as Fitzroy Maclean, then a diplomat in Moscow, put it) on Stalin's instructions and against Lenin's wishes; in Moscow it was denied that it was happening and Lenin was very unhappy with the brutality used. A Russo–Turkish treaty restored large areas of historically Georgian territory to Turkey (where they remain today), while Georgia retained Akhalkalaki, Akhaltsikhe and Batumi. Georgia became a Soviet socialist republic, but in December 1922 was absorbed into the Transcaucasian Soviet Federative Socialist Republic; this was dissolved in 1936 (with the adoption of the USSR's second constitution), and Georgia became a Union Republic. The Soviets closed around 1,500 churches and monasteries, leading to a revolt in 1921–22; in August 1924 there was another uprising and General Mogilevski was killed when his Georgian pilot deliberately crashed. This was brutally suppressed by Stalin and Ordjonikidze and 7,000–10,000 were killed, followed by widespread emigration. There were further purges in 1936–37 and 1953. Nevertheless, communism brought some social and material advances and the Georgians fought bravely in World War II (although some fought in the SS against the Soviet Union). Stalin died in 1953, and in 1956 Khrushchev's speech denouncing his crimes led to anti-Russian (and pro-Stalin) riots which were crushed on 9 March by tanks, with more than 100 being killed in Tbilisi.

THE END OF THE SOVIET UNION In 1972 Eduard Shevardnadze, then the republic's interior minister, was promoted to First Secretary of the Georgian Communist Party, and followed the Brezhnevite line of the time, although he took action against corruption. In 1985, Mikhail Gorbachev became leader of the Soviet Union and chose Shevardnadze as his foreign minister. Although there had already been some surreptitious glasnost pre-Gorbachev, from 1985 political agitation escalated (with 80% of Georgian men avoiding their military service). In February 1989 the Abkhazian campaign for secession (begun in the 1970s) was renewed, followed by counter-demonstrations in Tbilisi and then hunger strikes against Russian involvement. On

9 April 1989 (a date now commemorated by street names in many towns), tanks were sent on to the streets of Tbilisi and Russian troops attacked the demonstrators (using sharpened entrenching tools and gas), killing 21 of them (mostly young women), who at once became martyrs. Jumber Patiashvili, First Secretary of the Georgian Communist Party, resigned and Shevardnadze flew in from Moscow to calm things down. As the Soviet Union began to fall apart, the Georgian Supreme Soviet declared Georgian law superior over USSR law in November 1989, and then declared Georgia 'an annexed and occupied country' in February 1990; in March the Communist Party's monopoly on power was abolished.

In August, the statue of Lenin in Lenin Square (now Freedom Square) was removed (supposedly to permit 'repairs' to the square), and multi-party elections were held in October and November 1990. These were won by a coalition of nationalist parties led by Zviad Gamsakhurdia, a university lecturer and translator of French and English poetry. The son of the writer Konstantin Gamsakhurdia (most of Georgia's Gamsakhurdia Streets are named after him, not Zviad), he had co-founded Georgia's Helsinki monitoring group in 1976, was jailed for five years but controversially was released after two after recanting on television. (Merab Kostava, who co-founded the Helsinki group and did not recant, stayed in prison from 1977 to 1987 and died in October 1989 when his car supposedly hit a cow.)

Georgia was the first Soviet republic to elect a non-communist government, Gamsakhurdia becoming chair of the new Supreme Soviet. He was a naïf and charismatic nationalist, working on the assumption that the Georgians had long been a persecuted minority in their own country, and set out to rectify this injustice (proposing, for instance, to limit the franchise to Georgian speakers); this led to the worst outbreak of messianic nationalism in any of the former Soviet republics. Opposition groups refused to recognise the legitimacy of a legislature and government elected under the Soviet system and organised demonstrations and hunger strikes, which Gamsakhurdia met with repression. He had no understanding of democracy, believing that winning an election gave him absolute power and the right to treat all criticism as an attack on the nation; it was soon clear that he was succumbing to clinical paranoia. He also nearly bankrupted Georgia by isolation both from Russia and the Commonwealth of Independent States (CIS), and from the West. The referendum on the future of the Soviet Union in March 1991 was boycotted, except in South Ossetia, Abkhazia and Red Army barracks, which all turned out, unsurprisingly, to be strongly pro-Union. On 31 March, the Georgian government held its own referendum in which 93% (of a 95% turnout) voted for independence; on the anniversary of the 9 April 1989 killings the Soviet declared independence and in May Gamsakhurdia was elected president with 86% of the vote. Things went very wrong after the August 1991 Soviet coup attempt – Gamsakhurdia at first failed to condemn it, then declared a state of emergency in Tbilisi, clamped down on the media and arrested opposition leaders Jaba Ioseliani and Georgi Chanturia. Demonstrations gathered momentum, turning in December to fighting. Gamsakhurdia was besieged in the parliament building by paramilitaries who released Ioseliani and Chanturia and also about 8,000 common criminals whom they equipped with Kalashnikovs.

Between 113 and 200 people were killed in street fighting, which wrecked a few buildings near the parliament and Freedom Square; in January 1992 Gamsakhurdia fled to Armenia and Chechnya. A military council had little choice but to invite Eduard Shevardnadze to take charge again. He returned in March and was designated chair of the State Council, which replaced the Military Council; Ioseliani was deputy chair and Tengiz Kitovani (once a sculptor, then leader of the National Guard) was minister of defence.

THE SHEVARDNADZE PRESIDENCY In October 1992, elections (boycotted in South Ossetia, Mingrelia and parts of Abkhazia) were held for the State Council (formerly the Supreme Soviet). No party won more than 29 seats out of 235, and it was the National Guard and Mkhedrioni paramilitaries who were now running the country as one massive protection racket, controlling petrol and cigarette distribution and setting up roadblocks to 'tax' motorists; for most of 1992–93 the interior minister

EDUARD SHEVARDNADZE

The youngest of five children, Eduard Shevardnadze was born in Mamati, Guria, in 1928. His parents wanted him to become a doctor but he chose politics, joining the Communist Party at 20 and working his way up to be Georgia's Minister of Internal Affairs, ie: head of the secret police. In 1972, aged just 44, he was appointed Secretary-General of the Georgian Party, with a mission to cut corruption. At his first politburo meeting, it's said that he asked those present to raise their hands if they agreed that corruption should be eliminated; naturally they all agreed, and he asked them to keep their hands up while he went round the table; all those with foreign watches were sacked. In fact, he failed to make much impact in this area, but his reforming policies presaged perestroika, and when Gorbachev became Soviet leader in 1985 he appointed Shevardnadze foreign minister. He is still especially popular in Germany where he is seen as having brought about the fall of the Berlin Wall and German reunification more or less single-handedly. In 1989 he resigned in protest at Gorbachev's repressive attempts to slow the break-up of the Soviet Union, although he did serve again as foreign minister during the Soviet Union's final days, before returning to Georgia.

As chair of parliament from 1992 he had no formal powers but rapidly built up a semi-presidential apparatus while parliament was too fractured to play a real role; in 1995 he became president. Although his own party, the Citizens' Union of Georgia (CUG), dominated parliament, Shevardnadze ruled outside formal political structures, preferring an informal network of contacts and cronies, which is very much part of Georgian culture and a breeding-ground for corruption.

The CUG comprised both progressive 'greens' and reactionary 'reds', and its political identity was unclear; some reformers, such as Zurab Zhvania, established themselves in positions of power, but without being allowed to rival Shevardnadze. This helped him effectively to blackmail the electorate, saying 'it's me or it's chaos'. Shevardnadze was re-elected president in 2000; in September 2001 he announced that he was relinquishing the chair of the CUG, and began to plan a slow transition to post-Shevardnadze politics. He followed a classic 'divide and rule' strategy, giving hope to both the 'young reformers' led by Zhvania and the conservatives led by Targamadze. Eventually the country tired of his fence-sitting and swept him from power; however, he stayed in his palace until his death in 2014 and often appeared on television to give his opinions.

Although most people accepted that Shevardnadze was clean of corruption himself, he was seriously tainted by the activities of his nephews, particularly Nugzar Shevardnadze who dominated the cigarette and kerosene trades; he may not have directly used access to the president, but he certainly assumed that his name made him untouchable.

Background Information **HISTORY**

1

(in charge of the police) was Temuraz Khachishvili, a convicted criminal put in place by the Mkhedrioni. Economic policy was chaotic, with a disastrously loose credit policy and pyramid investment scandals.

Throughout 1992 unrest continued in the west, stronghold of the Zviadists (supporters of Gamsakhurdia); in June they seized Tbilisi's TV Tower, recaptured only with the loss of 40 lives. In August, Kitovani precipitated fighting in Abkhazia by his recklessness when the interior minister was kidnapped; he was finally forced to resign in May 1993. In August the Council of Ministers resigned after parliament rejected the 1993 budget, and Shevardnadze also resigned when parliament refused to let him declare a state of emergency; crowds blockaded the government building and parliament rejected his resignation. A state of emergency was declared in September, but already the country seemed ungovernable; in October Abkhazia was lost (page 30), and Zviadist rebels captured Poti and Samtredia, and began advancing east. The only way out, as in the 18th century, was to call for Russian help; Georgia finally agreed to join the Commonwealth of Independent States, Russian troops arrived in late October and within weeks defeated the Zviadists. Gamsakhurdia himself was cornered by government troops in January 1994 and committed suicide; he was buried (eventually) in Chechnya and moved to the Pantheon in Tbilisi in 2007. Russia was given permission to maintain four bases in Georgia (Vaziani near Tbilisi, Akhalkalaki, Batumi and Gudauta in Abkhazia) for 25 years, although they in fact closed in 2006.

The winter of 1993–94 saw the start of large-scale operations against organised crime and paramilitary groups, first the National Guard and Zviadist groups, and then in May 1995 the Mkhedrioni were finally disarmed. By the summer of 1994 basic law and order had been re-established, but there then followed a wave of political assassinations, the most prominent victim being Giorgi Chanturia in December 1994. Some land and housing were sold in 1993, but economic reform really began with price liberalisation in 1994, with gas prices increasing five times, electricity ten times and bread up to 280 times. A new constitution was approved by parliament in August 1995, virtually as drafted by Shevardnadze; it established a presidential republic with a minister of state instead of a prime minister, acting as adviser to a president directly elected for a maximum of two five-year terms.

The militia leaders were unhappy at being marginalised, and on 29 August a car bomb exploded in the courtyard of parliament – the closest of the many attempts on Shevardnadze's life since 1992. However, Shevardnadze, the 'silver fox', managed to play the gangsters off against one another until all were in jail, gradually bringing reformers into government.

A new currency, the lari, was successfully introduced and elections were held under the new constitution in November 1995. The results were something of a surprise, with only three parties over the 5% barrier for party-list seats: over 60% of the electorate voted for parties which polled under 5%, and the Citizens' Union of Georgia (CUG or SMK), set up by Shevardnadze as a personal vehicle, won almost half these seats with a quarter of the vote. With further seats filled by a first-past-the-post system, the CUG won a total of 107 seats, followed by the National Democratic Party with 34 seats and the Union for Georgian Revival (led by the Adjaran strongman Aslan Abashidze) with 31 seats. Shevardnadze won the presidential election with 75% of the votes. Parliament elected the moderniser Zurab Zhvania to be its chair or speaker; trained as a biologist, he was leader of the Greens before joining the CUG. Real structural economic reforms began at last, with an IMF stabilisation programme, a Partnership and Co-operation Agreement with the European Union, and similar deals with neighbouring countries. The reformers were nominally in charge, but the overlap continued of law enforcement and criminal gangs.

In October 1999 inadequately clean parliamentary elections were held: the CUG won 42% of the vote and 132 seats (56% of the total). In April 2000, the presidential election (again less than fully free and fair) was won by Shevardnadze with 80% of the vote (Stalin's grandson Evgeni Djugashvili was refused registration when it was decided that he was not a Georgian citizen). In January 1999, Georgia was admitted into the Council of Europe, and in June 2000 into the World Trade Organization (in both cases well ahead of Armenia and Azerbaijan).

THE STRUGGLE FOR THE SUCCESSION In August 2001, justice minister Mikheil Saakashvili proposed confiscating luxury houses built by ministers and senior officials, unless they could prove they were built with legitimate funds (many were worth US$200,000 or more, though even cabinet ministers earned only US$200 a month), but Shevardnadze refused to overturn the principle of the presumption of innocence. Saakashvili specifically accused three ministers of corruption and resigned on 19 September, two days after Shevardnadze had announced that he planned to relinquish the leadership of the CUG and wouldn't seek a third term as president in 2005. The showdown between the CUG's 'young reformers' – led by Saakashvili, Zhvania and Nino Burjanadze, head of the parliament's foreign relations committee – and the Soviet-era old guard, led by interior minister Kakha Targamadze, became increasingly bitter as it turned into a battle for the succession to Shevardnadze. Shevardnadze's perpetual balancing act worked when he was popular, but was less effective once he sank to just 6% in the polls. Suffering from diabetes, he was seen as ageing, tired and confused. The CUG halved in size, from 98 to 50 deputies, with at least two new factions forming; the opposition likewise realigned itself, with Aslan Abashidze's Union for Georgian Revival the dominant force.

Shevardnadze parroted his commitment to rooting out corruption but achieved little. Zhvania forced a showdown with Targamadze leading to their both resigning on 1 November, and Shevardnadze, with his support now almost non-existent, had no choice but to dismiss the whole government. He was still unable to have a proper clean-out and the 'power' ministries and security apparatus remained entangled with organised crime.

Shevardnadze created a new alliance, For A New Georgia, out of his faction in the CUG plus the National Democratic Party, the Socialists and the Greens, as well as unions and business groups. Zhvania, now clearly opposed to Shevardnadze, left the CUG in early 2002 and formed his own party, the United Democrats; likewise, the more confrontational Saakashvili (elected Mayor of Tbilisi in November 2002) created the National Movement, allied with the Republicans and Conservatives. Shevardnadze claimed victory in parliamentary elections in November 2003, leading to demonstrations by up to 15,000 people calling for his resignation after exit polls and independent observers showed that he had in fact lost. Saakashvili and his associates insisted on peaceful protest, backed up by a sharp statement from the US ambassador complaining that many people had been 'denied their constitutional right to vote' – presumably not what Shevardnadze expected. After almost three weeks, official results gave Shevardnadze's For a New Georgia 21.3% of the vote, Revival 18.8%, and Saakashvili's National Movement 18%. Busloads of protestors came to Tbilisi to prevent the new parliament from meeting, and the head of the Security Council admitted fraud and called for new elections (but not Shevardnadze's resignation); Aslan Abashidze sent his supporters to Tbilisi for pro-Shevardnadze counter-demonstrations. When the parliament met, protesters stormed in as

Shevardnadze was in the middle of a speech declaring a state of emergency; he was rushed away by bodyguards and Nino Burjanadze, now speaker of parliament, declared herself temporary president. The next day, 23 November 2003 (St George's Day), Shevardnadze resigned, having been abandoned by the army and the police. Due to the roses carried by the protesters, this became known as the Rose Revolution.

THE SAAKASHVILI ERA Zhvania became prime minister and in January 2004 Saakashvili, the only opposition candidate, won a presidential election with 88% of the vote. In parliamentary elections in March, the National Movement-Democrats (uniting Saakashvili's, Zhvania's and Burjanadze's supporters and the Republicans) took 67% of the vote and 135 of the 150 party-list seats; the Rightist Opposition alliance was the only opposition grouping over the threshold, with 7.6% and 15 seats.

Saakashvili soon fell out with the Republicans, then with Aslan Abashidze, who cut three bridges linking Adjara to the rest of Georgia in May 2004; Saakashvili gave him ten days to disarm and return to constitutional rule, sending the army on manoeuvres just across the border, while activists were smuggled in to lead protests and seduce Abashidze's guard away from him. Fortunately he was also persuaded to go peacefully to Russia, and Adjara returned to being a normal part of Georgia.

In February 2005 Zhvania was found dead, supposedly of carbon monoxide poisoning, although many people assumed he'd been murdered. He was replaced by finance minister Zurab Noghaideli, although he had less power than the interior and defence ministers. In May 2005, US President George W Bush visited Tbilisi and was greeted with great enthusiasm (although an Abashidze supporter did throw a grenade at him, which failed to explode).

The Rose Revolution was great PR, with corruption tackled vigorously and the entire police force replaced. Tariffs were cut from 16 bands (up to 30%) to just three: 0, 5 and 12%, and a flat 20% income tax was introduced, with collection rates rising sharply.

In January 2006, banker Sandro Girgvliani was murdered after an argument in the Sharden Bar, apparently on the orders of interior minister Vano Merabishvili's wife; four men were jailed but there were widespread accusations of a cover-up and calls for Merabishvili to resign. In March a prison riot, that the government claimed was part of a nationwide plot by the 'criminals-in-law' (the top dogs who controlled Georgia's prisons as well as much criminal activity outside), was put down with seven deaths; opposition demands for an investigation were voted down. Merabishvili remained in office, and was still Georgia's most powerful figure after Saakashvili, having widened the Interior Ministry's responsibilities; he was jailed after Saakashvili's departure for abuse of office and bribing voters.

Saakashvili began to lose much of his earlier popularity, owing to the Zhvania and Girgvliani affairs and to his constant publicity-chasing – on the ski slopes, opening the new Rustavi prison several times, and similarly the tunnel to Batumi (first at one end, then the other…). More substantially, he managed relations with Russia very badly, causing massive damage to Georgia's economy and compounding this by triggering a war with its powerful neighbour in August 2008.

THE RUSSIAN CRISES Externally, despite efforts to move towards the West and specifically NATO and EU membership, Georgian politics is dominated by its poor relations with Russia, which has always sought to dominate the surrounding countries. After the outbreak of the latest Chechen war in 1999 Russia tried even harder to manipulate Georgia, wanting the country to allow Russian troops in to seal the border with Chechnya; this was refused (although Russian jets and helicopters did drop bombs on the Georgian side of the border), so from 2000

Russia required visas for Georgians (up to a million of whom work there), though not for Abkhazians or Armenians. Russia accused Georgia of harbouring Chechen terrorists (and even al-Qaeda guerrillas) in the Pankisi Valley in Kakheti, an enclave populated by Kists or Islamic Chechens. In 2001, various foreigners were kidnapped and held in Pankisi; this was linked to just about every possible political faction, but was simple criminality and in time they were freed. British banker Peter Shaw was kidnapped and held with a chain around his neck in a tiny cellar in Pankisi from June until November 2002. Less happily, the brother of the AC Milan footballer and Georgian captain Kakha Kaladze was kidnapped and murdered in 2001.

In mid-2002 Georgia (backed up by the USA) twice accused Russia of bombing Pankisi, but Russia accused Georgia of staging it. In August, 1,000 Georgian Interior Ministry troops, trained by US Army Special Forces, went into Pankisi and arrested a few criminals, failing to find any al-Qaeda training camps. Even so, in September Russia accused the Georgian government of being 'fellow travellers' of international terrorism and threatened economic sanctions and even a Russian 'anti-terrorist' operation across the border.

After the Rose Revolution, Russia was determined to block Georgian entry to NATO by keeping the Abkhaz and South Ossetian conflicts active; Saakashvili retaliated by blocking Russian entry to the World Trade Organization. In January 2006, Russia doubled the price of gas supplied to Georgia and later that month, during a particularly cold spell, an explosion (presumably sabotage) cut the gas pipeline from Russia to Georgia, leaving most of the population without heat or power for a week (gas supplies had also been briefly cut off in the winter of 2000 due to 'Georgia's lack of co-operation on Chechnya'). In March Georgian wine was banned by Russia, supposedly due to impurities, soon followed by Georgian mineral water and fruit. In fact, the ban hurt Russian retailers and consumers as much as it did Georgia; the quantity of Georgian wine sold in Russia was always far greater than that actually produced, and any health risks were entirely due to the fake wine produced in Russia, a country in which 35,000 people a year die due to bad booze. Saakashvili reacted by blithely saying 'What doesn't kill you makes you stronger', and sought alternative markets for Georgian wine in Asia, but he was widely blamed for provoking the crisis.

As Russia became sure of its stranglehold over European gas supplies, it became increasingly willing to offend the West and to take a harder line with Western-minded neighbours. In July 2006, Russia's only border crossing with Georgia was suddenly shut 'for repairs', and in November, Gazprom announced that the price of Georgia's gas would double again in January; a few days later it suggested it could leave the price unchanged if Georgia sold it the pipeline instead, a proposal greeted by the sound of Georgian jaws hitting the ground at the sheer brazenness of the blackmail attempt. In the end Georgia agreed to pay the higher price, but can now buy most of its gas from Azerbaijan.

In September 2007, former defence minister Erekle Okruashvili accused Saakashvili of corruption and was himself arrested two days later on corruption charges. For once, the opposition formed a united front and organised a mass protest; after demonstrators had blocked Rustaveli Avenue for four days they were brutally driven away by police water cannon, sparking international outrage, and a state of emergency was declared. The next day Saakashvili gambled by calling early elections for January 2008; he won 53% of the vote, sparking claims of vote-rigging. Almost at once Badri Patarkatsishvili, who had won 7% of the vote for president after his Imedi television station had been closed down in the state of emergency, was charged with plotting a coup; he died in England in February from what appeared to be a heart attack. Further mass demonstrations took place against Saakashvili in 2009, following the August 2008 conflict with Russia (page 33).

At the end of 2009, controversial amendments were introduced to election laws, clearly intended to favour Saakashvili's United National Movement Party (UNM) in the May 2010 local elections, and the capital's roads and historic quarters were renovated at breakneck pace, with the Peace Bridge also being constructed. A media campaign attacked former ambassador to the UN Erekle Alasania, leader of the Free Democrats and a strong candidate to be mayor of Tbilisi and probably for the presidency, too, before long. The UNM won the local elections, but international observers registered 'deficiencies' in the process.

In May 2011 the opposition again organised mass protests, which were cleared by riot police; four people were killed, two by the cars of the protest leaders as they fled. The reclusive billionaire Bidzina Ivanishvili (see box, page 35) announced plans to form a party with the specific aim of removing Saakashvili from

MIKHEIL SAAKASHVILI

The idealistic young man who drove Shevardnadze from power was born in Tbilisi in 1967; his father was a well-known doctor and his mother a historian at Tbilisi State University. He studied international law in Kiev, Strasbourg and Columbia Law School in New York, acquiring fluent English, French, Ukrainian and Russian along the way, as well as a Dutch wife, Sandra Saakashvili-Roelofs, with whom he has two sons.

In 1995 he was persuaded by his old friend Zurab Zhvania, who had been commissioned by Shevardnadze to recruit talented young Georgians, to return to Georgia and enter politics. Together with Republican Party leader David Usupashvili and Conservative Party founder Koba Davitashvili, they were leading members of the Georgian Young Lawyers Association, which became a pro-reform pressure group.

Saakashvili and Zhvania both entered parliament in 1995 for Shevardnadze's CUG and were soon noticed. Saakasahvili was successful as chair of the parliament's judiciary committee and in January 2000 became vice-president of the Parliamentary Assembly of the Council of Europe. In October 2000 he became justice minister and implemented major reforms, but was unable to root out top-level corruption, despite producing documents at a cabinet meeting that showed some colleagues had built huge houses with illicitly gained cash.

He was finally ground down by the 'power' ministries (notably Kakha Targmadze's Interior Ministry), or else decided he had to provoke a showdown, and resigned in September 2001, founding his own party, the National Movement, in the social-democratic mould.

In 2002, with the backing of the Labour Party, he became Mayor of Tbilisi, and built a strong power base by delivering local services and fixing roofs and drains. As a crusader against corruption and poverty, he built a populist bandwagon that clearly won more votes than Shevardnadze's For a New Georgia in November 2003's elections, and harnessed the general indignation to bring up to 100,000 people on to the streets in non-violent protests for two weeks, until Shevardnadze was forced to resign. Saakashvili had to wait until the elections of January 2004 to become Europe's youngest president. He was forgiving of his predecessor, saying: 'History will judge him kindly.'

He immediately replaced the country's flag with a new one, and set out vigorously to tackle corruption. These efforts and a new tax code had considerable office, and at last the opposition began to pull together, forming the Georgian Dream coalition.

In September 2012 a video was released of systematic abuses (including sexual assault with a broom by senior officials) at Gldani Prison in Tbilisi and the prison and interior ministers resigned. In the parliamentary elections of October 2012 both sides claimed victory, with Georgian Dream leading in the party lists and Saakashvili in the constituency seats; but Saakashvili admitted defeat before too long and promised to lead a peaceful opposition (while remaining as president). It was a polarising campaign but, in the end, a fair vote. It was above all the government's repressive use of the judicial system for political ends that lost it the election, since when the conviction rate and the fear of persecution have fallen.

To show its democratic, pro-Western credentials, Georgia has deployed peace-keeping troops in Afghanistan since 2004 (and remains the largest contributor of troops there after the USA), in Iraq since 2008 and in the Central African Republic since 2014.

effect in increasing government revenues and thus expenditures too; Georgia was named the world's leader in economic reform and one of the best to do business in, well ahead of its neighbours.

Saakashvili's fiercely pro-USA and pro-NATO stance earned him friends across the Atlantic but created enemies elsewhere, most notably in Russia. Despite – or, perhaps, because of – his economic and political reforms he was increasingly criticised for authoritarianism. Critics pointed to Georgia's worsening human rights record and he was accused of election rigging, as well as smearing opponents and crushing protest rallies. Saakashvili's populism often tipped into demagoguery and authoritarianism, for instance in a 2004 media law and the favouritism shown to some television stations (notably Rustavi-2) and pressure on others. As it turned out, the slavish TV support for him was undermined by opposition use of social media. He'll also be remembered for his taste in brash contemporary architecture (see box, page 47) as part of his project to modernise Georgia in a hurry. It is hard to feel too sorry for him though; as is so often the case, initial reforming zeal led to a conviction that no-one else could do the job and thus an urge to keep power by any means, and a belief that he could take on Russia led to the disastrous war of 2008 (page 33).

Bizarrely, after leaving the presidency, and the country, in November 2013, he became an advisor to the Ukrainian government due to his experience in dealing with Vladimir Putin. Clearly, they should have listened to his advice and done the opposite. From 2014, various Georgians became ministers in the Ukrainian government and in May 2015 Saakashvili's bizarre trajectory continued with his appointment as governor of the Odessa region and giving up his Georgian citizenship; he then fell out with the president, accusing him of being captured by corrupt oligarchs. He resigned his post in November 2016 and was stripped of his citizenship when he was abroad in July 2017 (when it seemed that he might be a viable rival for the presidency); he literally forced his way back into the country (accompanied by crowds of supporters and TV cameras) and was arrested, after a rooftop stand-off, in December. He was released on bail then deported to Poland; in February 2018 he moved to his wife's home country, the Netherlands, but Georgia is still seeking to extradite him to stand trial for abuse of office.

ABKHAZIA Under Georgia's 1921 constitution Abkhazia was virtually autonomous; Stalin made Abkhazia an autonomous republic in 1930, but he also encouraged large numbers of Georgians to immigrate and by 1989 the population of 450,000 was 46% Georgian, 18% Abkhaz, 14% Armenian, 14% Russian and 3% Greek. Perestroika encouraged the growth of secessionism and in 1989 demands for teaching at the University of Sukhumi to be in Georgian rather than Abkhazian led to fighting and 14 deaths. In August 1990 the Abkhaz Supreme Soviet voted for independence as a Union Republic within the Soviet Union, but was persuaded to reverse this; in the referendum of March 1991 virtually the whole non-Georgian population of Abkhazia voted in vain to stay in the Soviet Union, seeing it as less of a threat than being part of an independent and nationalist Georgia.

Although the 1921 constitution was restored in 1992, the Abkhaz were convinced that Tbilisi was bent on denying them autonomy and saw no choice but independence; therefore a Republic of Abkhazia was declared in July 1992 (though without the required two-thirds majority). The next month Shevardnadze's defence minister, Kitovani, sent the National Guard into Abkhazia, ostensibly to protect transport links with Russia, and full-scale conflict broke out. The Abkhaz leader, Vladislav Ardzinba (a historian in Moscow until 1987), retreated to the Russian army base at Gudauta; with help from Russia and Muslim paramilitaries from the northern Caucasus he had regained control of northern Abkhazia by October. By spring of 1993 the front line seemed stable along the River Gumista, north of Sukhumi, although the city was largely destroyed by Russian bombing. Shevardnadze flew to Moscow to urge Yeltsin to bring his generals under control, but he found that Russia was determined to dominate the former Soviet Republics. By July there was a ceasefire and UN observers arrived in August; however, the Abkhazians launched a surprise attack in September and soon 'liberated' Abkhazia (Shevardnadze went to Sukhumi vowing to defend it himself, but had to flee ignominiously by air). Around 8,000 people were killed between August 1992 and October 1993.

Between 200,000 and 350,000 Georgians and others fled, about 400 dying in the mountains on the border with Svaneti. In July 1994, 3,000 CIS (mainly Russian) peacekeepers moved in, and in August the first 5,000 refugees returned.

Gali, the ethnically Megrelian (Georgian) border district of Abkhazia, was virtually unscathed in 1993–94 and became a demilitarised zone; but in 1998 Georgian paramilitaries killed up to 20 Abkhaz militiamen before being driven out of Gali, with between 60 and 200 deaths, and at least 30,000 refugees took to the roads again. Over 2,000 buildings were burnt down by the Abkhaz in the buffer zone patrolled by the Russian peacekeepers (which even Russian officials later admitted was too close to turning a blind eye to ethnic cleansing). Many Georgian refugees began crossing by day to work the fields in Gali, returning to sleep in Zugdidi, and in 1999 they began to return to their homes. Between 40,000 and 60,000 refugees have returned to Gali, some commuting daily across the ceasefire line and others migrating seasonally following agricultural cycles.

The two sides continued to talk, with Abkhazia insisting on equal confederal status with Georgia, and Georgia insisting on an asymmetric arrangement with more power for Tbilisi. As discussed in the box on pages 80–1, Russia was clearly fomenting instability in Georgia to keep it out of NATO and boost its own Caspian–Black Sea pipeline. It is claimed that the Russian airfield at Vaziani (just east of Tbilisi) was the base for the 1995 attempt to assassinate Shevardnadze, and Moscow has failed to extradite Igor Giorgadze and Guram Absandze, both accused of involvement in the plot; Giorgadze appeared regularly on television but Russia's police responded to an Interpol warrant by denying it knew where he was, until he was granted asylum in 2006. In 1999, Russia opened its border with Abkhazia (although it had been very porous for a long while).

In October 1999, Abkhaz presidential elections produced a 99% vote for Ardzinba, the only candidate, and a referendum on independence was approved by 97%; a week later the Abkhaz parliament formally declared independence, and the new Abkhaz premier Anri Jergenia spoke of applying to join the Russian Federation, though this was still a step too far for Putin. In 2001, Russia failed to withdraw (as agreed in 1999) from Gudauta, the base for the CIS peacekeepers and also for dodgy Russian arms shipments worldwide.

The upper part of the Kodori Gorge, adjoining Svaneti, still in Georgian hands, became a flashpoint; in 1999 first Georgian government officials and then UN observers were kidnapped there. In 2001 Georgian guerrillas, reportedly aided by Chechen fighters, launched raids there resulting in at least 30 deaths, and a few days later a UN helicopter was shot down near the Kodori Gorge, killing nine – it seems likely that Russian missiles from Gudauta, and possibly Russian personnel, were involved. In 2006, Georgian special police were sent to the gorge to arrest the renegade governor turned warlord, Emzar Kvitsiani, and disperse his paramilitary Hunter battalion, and the Abkhazian government-in-exile was moved from Tbilisi to the Kodori (renamed Upper Abkhazia).

Saakashvili pledged to reunite Abkhazia and South Ossetia with the rest of Georgia by 2008, but despite signs that a military solution might be attempted this did not happen. Russia lifted its sanctions on Abkhazia and granted citizenship to most residents, while Saakashvili continued to call for Russian peacekeepers to be replaced by an international force. It might seem odd to the independent observer that the separation of Kosovo from Serbia, used by Russia as a precedent for separating Abkhazia and South Ossetia from Georgia, has not been taken up by Russia as a template for its own Chechnya region. The lifting of sanctions against South Ossetia and Abkhazia in March 2008 was seen as the first step towards recognition of their independent status by Russia. This raised concerns within the EU which had recognised Georgia's territorial integrity since the break-up of the Soviet Union. In April 2008, a Georgian drone was shot down over Abkhazian territory; the Georgian government asserted that it possessed video footage showing that a Russian MiG-29 had been involved, an accusation denied by Russia and Abkhazia. This event would turn out to be a forerunner of the short but brutal Russian–Georgian war that unfolded in the summer of that year (page 33).

Sergei Bagapsh died of lung cancer in May 2011, 18 months after being re-elected for a second presidential term; he was succeeded by his vice-president Aleksandr Ankvab, defeating Bagapsh's perennial rival Raul Khajimba, leader of the Forum of National Unity of Abkhazia. Russian-backed protests led to Ankvab fleeing to the Russian base in Gudauta in May 2014; elections in August were won, by just 559 votes, by Khajimba, who whipped up feeling against the Megrelian (Georgian) population of Gali, blaming them for his three previous defeats. In October 2014, a draft treaty with Russia (clearly a quid pro quo for Russian support against Ankvab) triggered a storm of protest; in Tbilisi it was seen as a step towards Abkhazia's incorporation into the Russian Federation and in Abkhazia it was seen as curtailing the powers of the army (a pillar of national identity) and leading to the abolition of Russian–Abkhaz border controls. Surprisingly, Russia took into account virtually all the Abkhaz objections and also offered to invest US$260 million by the end of 2017; the treaty was signed in November.

To Moscow's annoyance (and Georgia's), however, Abkhazia is becoming closer to Turkey, exporting coal, hazelnuts and mandarins (worth up to US$50 million per annum); perhaps half of Abkhaz GDP comes from Russian pensions and aid (sometimes it seems that the main economic activity is building and extending Russian army bases), and it's mainly Russians who support the tourism industry, which was worth US$100 million per annum until it fell 60% in 2017 owing to worries about crime and (delicious irony) an increasing preference for Russians to visit Georgia instead.

South Ossetia The Ossetians are ethnically totally distinct from all their neighbours and, as the majority population in South Ossetia (an autonomous region since 1922), felt entitled to protection from an independent and nationalist Georgia. Demands in 1989 for unification with North Ossetia, within the Russian Federation, were rejected heavy-handedly by Georgia, but in 1990 South Ossetia declared independence within the Soviet Union, confirmed by a referendum. In December the Georgian Supreme Soviet abolished the autonomous region and declared a state of emergency there.

The Shevardnadze government released the chair of the South Ossetian Supreme Soviet from prison, blaming Gamsakhurdia's runaway nationalism for all the preceding problems. However, another referendum called for integration with the Russian Federation and in 1992 Georgian troops attacked the capital, Tskhinvali; 400 Georgians and over 1,000 Ossetians were killed before a ceasefire was brokered in June. Monitors from the Organisation for Security and Co-operation in Europe (OSCE) and Russian peacekeeping troops managed to maintain this until 2008, and many refugees returned home. However, many South Ossetians were unable to forgive the brutality of the Georgian military. Lyudvig Chibirov was elected president in 1996 and South Ossetia seemed to have effectively seceded (with its budget entirely financed by Moscow) until North Ossetia rejected the idea of unification. In 1999, relations worsened after Chibirov's party lost elections (held illegally, according to Georgia) to Russian-oriented communists, who won more than 80% of the seats, and the Georgian government cut the electricity supply to just 30 minutes per day. In 2001 Chibirov himself lost a presidential election (also unrecognised by Georgia), to the more radical Eduard Kokoiti, a 37-year-old Moscow-based businessman, and in March 2002 the South Ossetian parliament asked the Russian Duma to recognise its independence. Saakashvili's rapid success in bringing Adjara back into the fold led him to try for the same result in South Ossetia, leading to rapid militarisation there. Saakashvili claimed Russia was using the illegal gun trade in Tskhinvali, a market claimed to be worth US$20 million a year, to undermine Georgia's economy, and in August 2004 sent in Interior Ministry troops to close it down, resulting in several dozen deaths. In 2005 he offered an autonomous parliament and government but this was dismissed by Kokoiti. In July 2006 Oleg Albarov, secretary of South Ossetia's National Security Council, was killed by a bomb, allegedly for being willing to talk to Georgia – but the attack was blamed by South Ossetia on Georgia. Five days later a bomb exploded in front of the home of a South Ossetian MP; he was unharmed, but two teenagers were killed and four passers-by were wounded. In September missiles were fired at two Georgian helicopters, one carrying Georgia's defence minister, and one Georgian and three South Ossetian policemen were killed in a clash outside Tskhinvali. Kokoiti, running against token opponents, was re-elected president in November 2006, and another referendum called for independence – Georgian passport-holders were not allowed to vote and only South Ossetia and Russia took the results seriously. Georgia set up a parallel administration in a Georgian-majority village outside Tskhinvali.

The tensions between Georgia and Russia over the question of South Ossetian and Abkhazian sovereignty came to a head in the summer of 2008, both sides insisting that it was the other that had initiated the conflict. Georgia, accused of shelling South Ossetian villages, killing six civilians, claimed that it had merely responded to South Ossetian attacks on Georgian-controlled villages; Russia claimed it was 'unable to control the Ossetian militias'. In fact there had been a Russian military build-up from 2006, also in Abkhazia from April 2008. Stupidly responding to provocation, Saakashvili launched a brutal military attack against Tskhinvali on the night of 7–8 August. Russian forces counter-attacked in South Ossetia and bombed targets deep within Georgian territory, and then Russian marines landed on the Black Sea Coast. A third front was opened on 10 August when Russian and Abkhaz forces moved towards the Kodori Gorge, but the Georgian forces retreated at once to Svaneti. The Georgian army held off the invasion for a couple of days, as Russian forces shot down several of their own planes; a Russian general was wounded by shrapnel, and tank commanders resorted to using mobile phones and shop-bought GPS (ie: US satellites) instead of the faulty equipment they had been issued with (it was a totally transformed Russian army which got involved in Ukraine). However, overwhelming force eventually told and after five days Russian troops had occupied the Georgian cities of Poti, Senaki, Gori and Zugdidi, stopping outside Tbilisi only due to US pressure. An American plane was kept at Tbilisi airport, preventing Russian bombing, and likewise a ship of the US 6th Fleet brought humanitarian aid to Batumi; visits by the Lithuanian and Polish presidents also deterred the Russians. This was also the first cyber war, with attacks on Georgian government servers. A ceasefire brokered by the French-led EU was agreed on 12 August although skirmishing continued for a while. Russia withdrew its forces to buffer zones around South Ossetia and Abkhazia by 8 October and has kept troops in South Ossetia.

The war may have been short but it was costly: more than 400 Georgians died, thousands were injured; Tskhinvali was left in ruins, many ethnic Georgian villages were razed to the ground, and an estimated 20,000 ethnic Georgians and 24,000 Ossetians were displaced. About 17,500 have been housed in new settlements around Gori and elsewhere. Late in August, militias were still looting Georgian villages in South Ossetia while Russian troops looked on. Despite Georgia's refusal to recognise its existence as a bona fide political entity, South Ossetia remains, de facto, an independent territory that is recognised, along with Abkhazia, by just four nations – Russia, Nicaragua, Venezuela and Nauru.

The war finally ended the Georgian belief in quick fixes to solve the Abkhazia and South Ossetia disputes; they now realise that they'll have to entice the secessionists back with prosperity and stability in the longer term. Likewise, Georgians have lost any expectations of speedy integration into the West and particularly NATO. Meanwhile, the conflict convinced Putin that he could seize Crimea without Western interference. However, Russian troops have several times moved the South Ossetian border fence south, to within 500m of Georgia's east–west highway – and over a 1.6km section of BP's Baku–Supsa pipeline – leading to international outrage but predictably little action (while Russia claims that it's NATO's exercises in Georgia that are a threat to regional stability).

In December 2011, former South Ossetian Education Minister Alla Dzhioyeva won, according to unofficial results, the election for de facto leader as the population rejected the corrupt and authoritarian Kokoiti regime, defeating the Kremlin's nominee Anatoly Tibilov; the Supreme Court of South Ossetia annulled the election, accepting Tibilov's absurd charges that Dzhioyeva had bribed voters, and barred her from new elections in March 2012. A raid on her headquarters by around 200 masked security personnel left her in hospital, and Tibilov was elected to succeed Kokoiti. He appointed Dzhioyeva deputy premier and David Sanakoyev (defeated in the presidential runoff) foreign minister, and opened criminal investigations into how most of the 27.3 billion roubles allocated for reconstruction by the Kremlin in 2008–11 had simply vanished.

Following Abkhazia's 'friendship, cooperation and mutual help' treaty with Russia, South Ossetia was happy to accept a treaty with even less autonomy; Tibilov said that he simply wanted to join the Russian Federation. With a population of just 20,000, few natural resources apart from timber, and virtually all its food imported from Russia at inflated prices, there may be little choice. In April 2017 a referendum changed the territory's name to South Ossetia-Alania (moving away from the Georgian-derived name Ossetia), and Tibilov lost the presidential election to Anatoliy Bibilov, a former Russian special forces officer.

AFTER SAAKASHVILI Bidzina Ivanishvili created an alliance to defeat Saakashvili and to make him prime minister for no more than two years, and used his immense wealth to achieve that. He appointed a government of calm pragmatic types, many with experience of life and business in the West. A number of members of the Saakashvili regime disappeared, although some have been jailed and had their ill-gotten gains confiscated; Georgian Dream's determination to extradite others to face justice has been widely seen abroad as an unfair witch-hunt, and in December 2012 Saakashvili, still president, threatened to dismiss the government.

In October 2013 Giorgi Margvelashvili, a little-known academic who became the Georgian Dream government's Minister of Education and Science, was elected president. In November, Ivanishvili stepped down as prime minister after just over a year, installing his long-standing associate Erekle Garibashvili as his successor. Saakashvili left Georgia soon after stepping down as president in November 2013 (moving to the USA and then Ukraine; see box, page 29) and has refused to return; he has since been charged with abuse of office in connection with assaults on opposition politician Valeri Gelashvili and Sandro Girgvliani (page 26), and the November 2007 protests, and also for spending almost GEL400,000 on cosmetic treatments. He still leads the main faction of the UNM and appears on Rustavi-2, attacking the government for letting Russia annex Abkhazia and for ignoring a 'crime wave'.

An EU Association Agreement and DCFTA (Deep and Comprehensive Free Trade Area) came into effect in July 2016 (with visa-free travel to the Schengen area in 2017).

People complain of a sense of stagnation, but it's largely due to the contrast with Saakashvili's hyper-activity and to growing disunity within the ruling coalition; in fact the government is busy with infrastructure projects. Its main external achievement has been to keep a balance between Russia and the West (only implementing one of the 15 sanctions imposed on Russia after its annexation of Crimea, for instance). Parliamentary elections in the autumn of 2016 and local elections a year later were both won by Georgian Dream, comfortably outspending the opposition parties. The new mayor of Tbilisi is the former national soccer captain Kakha Kaladze, who was heavily involved in the campaign against Saakashvili and then became energy minister, where he impressed by working hard to understand the brief.

One controversy has been over electoral changes to move towards fully proportional representation in parliament: since 2011 there have been 77 deputies representing single-mandate constituencies (varying between 6,000 and 150,000 voters) and 73 elected proportionally on a party-list system, and there was pressure to switch to a proportional system of regional constituencies. Georgian Dream tried to maintain a system that benefitted the ruling party, but this was blocked by the president; finally in September 2017 the new constitution was approved, with fully proportional representation after 2018 and an end to direct presidential elections. From 2024 there will be a parliamentary system of government, with the president chosen (for a maximum of two five-year terms) by an electoral college of MPs and others. The government was also streamlined slightly, with 14 ministries instead of 18.

BIDZINA IVANISHVILI

Currently worth just under US$5 billion (one-eighth of Georgia's GDP), according to *Forbes* magazine, Bidzina Ivanishvili made his fortune by importing computers to Russia in the 1980s, then co-founding a bank and branching out into metals, mining and real estate. He left Russia when Putin came to power in 2002, living in France before retiring to his native village of Chorvila (near Sachkhere), which was transformed by his donations into an oasis of prosperity; he also subsidised struggling artists and actors, renovated theatres and secretly paid for the construction of the grandiose Sameba Church in Tbilisi and the Narikala cable car. In addition to his home in Chorvila and a huge seaside retreat, he built his sci-fi glass 'business centre' on a ridge overlooking Tbilisi, hung with replicas of his collection of contemporary art (the originals are in a vault in London). His latest hobby is apparently buying the oldest and tallest trees in the country, uprooting them and transporting them to his Black Sea residence south of Ureki (where he is also supposed to have collections of zebras, lemurs and penguins).

Having attempted to build a new society from behind the scenes, he finally decided to directly enter politics with the explicit purpose of ousting President Saakashvili. Having announced in December 2011 that he was creating a new party and opposition coalition and intended to become prime minister himself, for a very limited period, he didn't appear in public for another ten days, leading to speculation about his reclusiveness and possible messiah complex. His aims were to eradicate corruption, create an independent judiciary and the conditions for restoring Georgia's jurisdiction over Abkhazia and South Ossetia, boost foreign investment and to improve relations with Russia, the USA and the EU. He refused to foment street protests, insisting on coming to power only through the ballot box, although the fact remains that his wealth was the key. In fact, he functions perfectly well in public, but doesn't hedge his words like a true politician and is suspicious of colleagues, preferring power to be shared among small parties rather than held by one big one. It seems that the mayor of Tbilisi, Davit Narmania, fell out of favour, as apparently did his successor, Kakha Kaladze, before he'd even taken office.

Having seen a new president elected in 2013, he left office as promised and continues to work for a civil society, boosting NGOs to continue Georgia's transformation into a 'typically European' society and country. Having attacked the Saakashvili administration for its lack of transparency, he has, however, created something even more opaque, an elected government that he continues to direct from behind the scenes.

Ivanishvili's albino son Bera is Georgia's most famous rapper; born in Paris, he lives in Hollywood.

Also in 2015 government attempts to take control (via a proxy owner) of Rustavi-2, Georgia's biggest and arguably most popular TV station, which usually backed the opposition, led to protests and to conflict between President Margvelashvili and Prime Minister Garibashvili; wiretap recordings were leaked of Saakashvili and a Rustavi-2 executive discussing barricades and protests, but the takeover attempt was stopped only by a ruling of the European Court of Human Rights. The main casualty was Garibashvili, who resigned at the end of 2015 (or was pushed) and was replaced by Foreign Minister Giorgi Kvirikashvili, who had been chief executive of Ivanishvili's Cartu Bank.

ECONOMY

During the Soviet period, Georgia's industry was, of course, state-owned and directed from Moscow; it was a major supplier of electric locomotives and jet fighters to the Soviet Union, and the city of Rustavi was founded in 1948 to supply metallurgical products. Although there was more private production in agriculture, it was also excessively oriented to the production of tea, citrus fruit, grapes and wine for the rest of the Soviet Union, leaving Georgia dependent on imported grain and meat. Nevertheless Georgia had a higher standard of living than most other republics. Naturally there has been major restructuring since independence, and coupled with an energy crisis and the collapse of the Russian market this meant that much of Georgia's industry simply closed down, with production virtually halving in 1992.

In 1993 Georgia withdrew from the rouble zone, introducing a temporary coupon currency, and then in 1995 its own currency, the lari. By the end of 1993 a combination of pyramid savings frauds, the Abkhazia war (which cost 50 million roubles a day) and a disastrous policy of printing money had caused hyperinflation. Consumer prices rose by 15,606% in 1994: savings were wiped out, industry shut down, half the economy went underground and the tax base fell from 40% of GDP to under 10% – the lowest in the former Soviet Union. This led to Georgia applying to the IMF for help, and committing itself to the required reforms. From September 1994 prices were freed, and privatisation began in 1995, with the electrical supply industry split up and sold off in 1998, and land, water supply, ports and telecommunications following.

The economy turned around in 1995; in 1996 and 1997, Georgia had the fastest-growing economy in the Newly Independent States, with GDP growth over 11% for 1996 and 1997 (admittedly from a very low base), but 1998 was a bad year, with a poor harvest, and an appallingly low rate of tax collection; the lari had to be devalued in the wake of the Russian economic collapse. GDP grew by 3% in 1998 and 1999, and by just 1.9% in 2000 (to US$4.8 billion), after a drought hit agriculture again. Nevertheless manufacturing output rose by 10%, and mining by 75%, and services grew steadily as a share of the economy. Average incomes crept above the subsistence level, but in fact expenditure was 36% above reported income on average, indicating that people were rather better off than they let on. In 2002, GDP grew by 5.4%; tax collection improved slightly, with some high-profile raids to spread the message, and in 1998 excise stamps, printed by the German company that is also printing the euro notes, were introduced on alcohol and tobacco, to reduce evasion. As a result of the shortfall in tax revenues, IMF loans were delayed and public spending was cut across the board, except for social spending.

The retirement age was raised by five years, to 65 for men and 60 for women; a State Social Allowance was introduced in 1998, intended mainly as a top-up for lone pensioners, of GEL9 a month, in addition to the basic GEL15. This is still a big issue as the allowance has not kept up with inflation (it's just 18% of the average salary) and it's normal to see old women begging in the cities (it's better in the villages, where food is available).

After the Rose Revolution the Saakashvili government produced some remarkable economic achievements, with more privatisation and an anti-corruption drive yielding big increases in tax revenue. The civil service was cut and the tax code simplified, persuading international lenders to restructure Georgia's debt and provide more aid. This allowed the government to pay, and increase, pensions, to refurbish infrastructure, and to strengthen the military. By 2007 many big construction projects (notably pipelines, worth US$195 million, the new terminal at Tbilisi Airport, worth US$65 million; the Khulevi oil terminal, worth US$45 million, and hotels in Adjara, worth US$100 million) were also complete.

The economy almost doubled in size in the first five years of the century, from GEL6.7 billion in 2001 to GEL11.5 billion (US$6.4 billion–US$1,424 per capita) in 2005. Russian sanctions from 2006 and the South Ossetia war in 2008 severely affected Georgia's economy, with GDP falling by 3.9% in 2009, and foreign investment falling from US$525 million in the second quarter of 2008 to a mere US$150 million in the third.

Georgia struggled with high inflation in the 2004–08 period and agreed with the IMF to cut the fiscal deficit from 4% of GDP to 2%, which kept inflation to around 9% at the start of 2007. By 2012 it was estimated at 3.3% and in January 2015 it stood at 1.4%.

Unemployment (and underemployment) remains a perennial problem; in 2014 it was estimated that 14% of the labour force was unemployed, varying between 26% in Tbilisi and 4.1% in Samtskhe-Javakheti, Guria and Mtskheta-Mtianeti – this is because anyone owning half a hectare of farming land, even if it is not used, is classified as employed even if receiving state benefits, while many of Tbilisi's unemployed are actually working in the shadow economy (now 22% of the economy, down from 53% in 2003). The proportion of people below the poverty line fell from 32% in 2004 to 21% in 2016, but Georgia has more poor working people than anywhere in the world – only 18.8% of those employed earn GEL900/month or more, and four in five of those employed earn less than the average salary (GEL940/month, about US$379); 71% (and rising) are in debt. The Georgian currency came under pressure following the 2008 war but financial stability was maintained thanks mainly to international aid (Georgia is one of the highest recipients of US aid). In 2014 there was a 25% drop in remittances from Georgians working in Russia (to US$116 million) due to the collapse of the Russian economy and the fall of the rouble, so that the lari's value also fell by 9% against the US dollar. Remittances from Georgians working abroad account for 9% of the country's GDP (up from just 2% in 2002); Russia remains the largest source, but in 2014 30% came from EU countries (mainly Greece and Italy).

Real GDP grew by an average of 9.6% per annum in 2003–07 and by 5.6% per annum in 2010–14 but fell to just 2.8% in 2015 and 3.4% in 2016 (US$14.378 billion, US$3,853 per capita), before picking up to just over 5% in 2017, with the same forecast for 2018.

Up until 2008 Russia had been Georgia's main trading partner, but trade with Turkey grew steadily throughout the first decade of the 21st century and by 2009 formed the largest share of Georgia's trade, accounting for almost 20% of its exports and 18% of its imports. The Deep & Comprehensive Free Trade Agreement with the EU means that over a quarter of trade is now with EU members, and Georgia hopes for similar benefits from its Free Trade Agreement with China, the first in the

GOD GAVE GEORGIA TO THE GEORGIANS – BUT CAN THEY HOLD ON TO IT?

Rowan Stewart

A lot of rhetoric flows about the beauty and hospitality of this fertile land. The tourist potential of Georgia is immense and it appeals to foreign investors, especially the tourism sector. However, business control and the majority of profits will remain firmly with the foreign investor, leaving minimal financial benefit for Georgia and, more particularly, the local community.

Tourism is a powerful and unpredictable beast, as other parts of the world can testify; its capacity to ravage communities and environments, distort local economies and prostitute cultures is frightening. Handled carefully, it can bring considerable benefits to local people as well as providing a friendlier, more authentic experience to visitors. The skills and training gained in the trade are easily transferable. If organised properly, local ownership of tourism facilities can provide much-needed income. Furthermore, it improves the chance of local cultures being presented to visitors in an accurate and respectful way. By placing control with local people, villagers are to some extent protected from outsider 'fat-cats' and from a dehumanising tourist invasion which reduces villages to zoos, and cultures to roadside spectacles. Throughout the world a new kind of tourism is coming to life which rejects multi-national ownership and control. With so many large elegant houses standing empty, so many skilled, well-educated people unemployed and its excellence at hospitality, Georgia is ideally placed to choose this new kind of tourism.

Today the elegantly carved balconies of Tbilisi gaze disdainfully down on Guinness bars and McDonald's. Will this small pristine land succumb to a new invasion of foreign investors bent only on exploitation?

region. Georgia's foreign trade increased to US$9.56 billion in the first 11 months of 2017 (up 12.9% year-on-year), with exports up 27% to US$2.43 billion and imports up 8.8% to US$7.12 billion. Surprisingly, Georgia's third most important export, after copper ores and concentrates, and hazelnuts, is cars (and minibuses) – imported, fettled up and sent onwards at a profit. Next come ferroalloys, wine, crude oil and mineral waters. In 2013, Russia lifted its ban on Georgian wine and now takes 63% of Georgia's wine exports; however, Georgia has worked hard to find new markets and now sells wine to 46 countries. Wine exports grew 33% by volume and 36% in value on 2014, with brandy exports doing almost as well.

Foreign direct investment collapsed due to the 2008 war, from US$1,750 million in 2007 to US$658 million in 2009, then recovered to US$1,763 million in 2014 and has since dropped to an estimated US$1,347 million in 2017. The major source of investment in 2015 was Azerbaijan, and 44% of the total went into transport and telecomms, 14% into the financial sector, 10% into construction, 7% each into energy and manufacturing, 4.5% into hotels and restaurants and just 2% into agriculture. Saakashvili's reforms have made Georgia very attractive to investors, with almost no corruption – Georgia was 44th in Transparency International's 2016 world rankings, above Italy and Brazil, and 16th in the World Bank's 2017 report on the ease of doing business. However, the poorly educated workforce is seen as the key barrier to future growth, along with transport infrastructure and hazardous waste management.

Since the Russian embargo on Georgian **wine**, the country's winemakers have worked hard to open up new markets (and to make better, less sweet, wines for them). The recent Free Trade Agreement with China (now the world's biggest consumer of red wine) will make a huge difference, but wine exports to China were already up 158% in 2015. In the first nine months of 2017 total wine exports were 52.7 million bottles (up 63% year-on-year) worth US$116 million (up 55%), along with 11.3 million bottles of brandy, up 89%.

In the future, one of the best sources of foreign exchange will be **tourism**; in the Soviet era four million tourists a year (and 47% of all foreign visitors to the Soviet Union) came to Georgia, almost all to the Abkhazian coast. The loss of Abkhazia, coupled with the occupation of Georgia's hotels by refugees from Abkhazia and the general economic crisis, almost wiped out the tourist industry. Tourism soon began to grow again, from a very low base (just 1,500 in 1997), but the 2008 South Ossetia war with Russia was another considerable setback as many countries like the UK and USA issued travel advisories against travel to Georgia. The top end of the business is over-regulated, but there's also a huge number of rooms available informally. In 2011 there were 2.8 million tourist arrivals which rose to 6 million by 2016 (1.6 million of them from Turkey) and at least 7 million in 2017 (accounting for 7% of GDP and 7% of employment and generating over US$2 billion in foreign exchange).There are plenty of visitors from Armenia, Russia, Poland and Ukraine, with the numbers from Israel, Germany and the UK also increasing fast, but the big growth in the last couple of years has been from Iran, Azerbaijan and the Gulf states, while the numbers from Turkey are dropping as a result of delays at the Sarpi border crossing. The statistics are a bit unbalanced as they include a remarkable number not staying overnight and a growing number of transit visitors – in August 2017, for instance, 1,080,449 foreigners arrived (27.4% more than in August 2016), of whom 573,368 were defined as tourists, 274,878 in transit and 232,203 day visitors. About 40% of the transit visitors are Russians continuing to Armenia or Turkey, who may or may not be travelling as tourists.

In 2015 the government worked with the World Bank to develop a strategy to attract high-value tourists, aiming for US$6.6 billion in revenue by 2025; the growth in tourist numbers has been so hectic that it may make sense to concentrate on fewer, higher-yielding visitors, but that risks depriving people running small guesthouses and other village businesses of the benefits of tourism.

AGRICULTURE Agriculture suffered as much as the rest of the economy, with production in 1995 half that of 1990; but it offers promise for the future, with Georgian products now allowed into the EU and ideal conditions for new crops such as almonds. Although its share of GDP has fallen from 38% in 1995 to just 9% in 2016, it still employs almost half the workforce. This was the only Soviet Republic where farmers were able to keep some of their land, and privatisation of collectivised land began in 1992. Only 13.2% of agricultural land (although over half the better-quality land) had been privatised by 1998. In 2013 a law allowed the creation of agricultural co-operatives, but unfortunately people confuse them with collective farms.

PEOPLE

With 15 major ethnic groups (and up to 80 in Tbilisi), Georgia is the least homogeneous of the Transcaucasian states. The population has fallen steeply, due to emigration and ageing, since the 1989 Soviet census, when it was 5.5 million; now it is probably about 3.7 million. Many Georgians live and work abroad (mainly in Russia) and Russians, Armenians, Jews and Greeks have left the country; it's hoped that the situation is now stable. It is estimated that almost 84% of the population is Georgian, 6.5% Azeri, 5.7% Armenian, 2% Ossetian, 1.5% Russian and other groups, including 95,000 Kurds, 52,000 Ukrainians, 12,000 Jews, 8,600 Belarussians, 6,000 Assyrians and 4,000 Tatars. Germans, invited to come as colonists in the 1780s by Potyomkin, first viceroy of Caucasus, were deported to Central Asia in 1941 but then left for Germany. As of 2010 there are about 260,000 Internally Displaced Persons or refugees, mainly from Abkhazia. Life expectancy is 74 on average (70 for men and 78 for women), and the population is ageing, 16.4% now being over 65 years old. The birth rate is one of the highest in Europe (and rising), while the abortion rate is falling. The population density is 78 per square kilometre overall, and up to 300 per square kilometre in the fertile plains; 56% of the population is urban (one-third of them in Tbilisi).

Overall, the Georgians are marked by what the historian W E D Allen called 'aesthetic irresponsibility'; or as the writer Laurens van der Post put it, they and the Irish both 'realise the positive creative uses of irresponsibility'. They are impulsive and passionate people for whom hospitality and having a good time are the highest aims. Unlike the more serious Armenians, who have suffered from genocidal attacks more than once, the Georgians have managed to dance their way through history and come out laughing. The Georgians grew out of a blend of Neolithic and Bronze Age cultures, and the present-day nation is still a mix of very different types: the Megrels or Mingrelians in the west who are quick, smart, boastful and can't be stopped from feeding guests; the naïve and funny Svans; the extremely hospitable and talkative Imeretians; the slow and careful Rachvels; the political and humorous Gurians; the calm wine-loving Kakhetians; not to mention the Karts, Khevsurians, Pshavians, Mokhevians and Meskhians. As for the Adjarians, they are said to have all the above qualities; they are ethnically and linguistically Georgian but about 30% are Muslim in religion.

Some groups share ethnicity and religion with the majority population but are linguistically distinct: these include the million or so Megrels, the Svans, and the Laz, most of whom (around 200,000) live across the border in the Hopa region of Turkey. Related to the Megrels, the Laz are very extrovert and humorous, and tend to have reddish hair; the Laz and Megrelian languages are basically the same but with different alphabets.

MINORITY COMMUNITIES The **Armenians** form the largest ethnic minority in Georgia and are found all over the country; however, the vast majority live either in Tbilisi (200,000) and in the Javakheti region (Javakhk in Armenian, around Akhalkalaki and Ninotsminda), where they form a majority of the population. Their ancestors settled here as refugees from western Anatolia during the 19th-century Russo–Turkish wars, and also just before and after World War I. It's a bleak area with poor infrastructure, and there is some discontent with the bad conditions here. Tbilisi, on the other hand, has always been a major centre of Armenian culture and continues to produce many leading figures in Armenian life. Their lingua franca has always been Russian, and few in the rural areas speak Georgian. The Armenian government is not particularly interested in changing its borders, but it takes an interest in the wellbeing of the Armenian population in Georgia.

Russians are scattered thinly across Georgia, apart from small groups of religious dissidents such as Molokans and Doukhobors, mainly in the centre and south. Some arrived in the 19th century, but the bulk came during the Soviet period, settling mainly in urban and industrial areas such as Tbilisi and Rustavi as well as in Abkhazia. These later arrivals tend not to speak Georgian and many have emigrated in recent decades, mainly to Russia but also to Canada and elsewhere. This has drained away many of Georgia's skilled workers and technicians. However, Georgians see Russian men as drunks and the women as sexually easy ('sleep with Russians, marry a Georgian' is the Georgian male's credo).

The **Azeri** population occupied the southeastern corner of the country, around Marneuli, Bolnisi and Gardabani, in the early 17th century when it was de-populated by the Persian wars. This is an underdeveloped area and life is tougher than these hard-working farmers deserve, although they are relatively well off. They are mostly Shia Muslims, although not fervently so. Between 1926 and 1989, when the national population doubled, their population quadrupled. Not all are ethnically Azeri in the purest sense, but it's generally accepted that all the Turkophone Muslims in Georgia can be included in this category, and the government of Azerbaijan does take a certain degree of responsibility for them.

Until recently the majority of the 165,000 **Ossetians** in Georgia lived outside the then autonomous region – mainly in Tbilisi and Rustavi, and also in some rural areas. An Indo-European people, speaking an Iranian language, they are unrelated to the other peoples of the Caucasus. They are held to be the descendants of the Alans, one of the many nomadic peoples who came out of Asia and settled in the north Caucasus. During the last two centuries they have increasingly moved into the highlands on the south of the Caucasus, living peacefully for the most part (and inter-marrying) with the Georgians. Now many have moved to South Ossetia, and there's a tendency towards learning Russian rather than Georgian, especially now that cultural ties have been strengthened with the north Caucasus. Most are Orthodox Christians, although some of the later arrivals are Sunni Muslim, and paganism still plays a strong part in their religious lives.

The **Abkhaz** are considered to be one of the aboriginal peoples of the Caucasus, entitling them to an autonomous republic under Stalin's scheme for ethnic relations (while the South Ossetians, having arrived relatively recently, were entitled only to an autonomous region). Even before secession, they almost all lived in Abkhazia, but they formed just 18% of the republic's population; since secession they have formed a much higher proportion of its population, due to Georgians and other groups like Armenians and Russians leaving. Closely related to the Adigh peoples of the northern Caucasus, they have preserved their traditional culture and their highly prized oral literary heritage. The population is made up of both Christians and Sunni Muslims, although many Muslims emigrated to Turkey after the Russian conquest in the 19th century.

Greeks live in the Tsalka and Tetri-Tskaro areas of Lower Kartli (the so-called Anatolian Greeks, or Rums), and on the Black Sea Coast (the Pontian Greeks). Although it's tempting to assume that the latter have been there ever since the classical Greeks established trading ports, in fact they arrived from 1829, fleeing persecution in Turkey. Although most are Orthodox Christians, some have converted to Islam. There's a steady flow back to Greece, although some speak Pontian Ancient Greek rather than the modern language, and most of those in Lower Kartli (a poor isolated community) speak Turkish; many have also moved to Tbilisi.

Most of the **Kurds** in Georgia are Yezidi (Mithraist pagans), descended from refugees from Ottoman persecution. They live mainly in Tbilisi and Rustavi, but although fairly well integrated socially, they preserve their distinct ethnic identity, language and cultural traditions. There was also a small rural (Muslim and Turkish-speaking) population living in southern Georgia, which was deported to Central Asia in 1944.

It's a proud boast in Georgia, and largely true, that **Jews** have lived there for 2,600 years without suffering persecution (ironically, yet another way for Georgians to show their superiority to the Russians). It may have helped that they have the same appetite for wine as the Georgians. The population numbered about 80,000 in the 1970s but is now reduced to around 13,000, divided between Ashkenazim (European or Russian Jews) and Georgian Jews (Georgian-speaking, and considered as Sephardim due to their religious ritual); over half live in Tbilisi, with many of the rest in the west of the country. As a rule they feel very attached to Georgia, and although most have now emigrated to Israel and, to a lesser extent, the USA, they maintain close links with Georgia and preserve Georgian cultural traditions.

Georgia and Turkey are the only two countries that are home to all three families of **gypsies** – the Rom, Dom and Bosha– with just 4,400 or so in Georgia.

Finally, a group that currently is scarcely represented in Georgia are the so-called **Meskhetian Turks**. Under the Ottomans, Javakheti was heavily Islamicised from 1624, producing a population of mixed Georgian and Turkish ethnicity; in November 1944 all 70,000–120,000 of these people were deported to Central Asia, for supposedly pro-Turkish (and thus possibly pro-Axis) sentiments – even though most of their menfolk were serving in the Red Army. Unlike most other deported groups they were not allowed to return after the Stalinist era, and struggled to establish themselves in their new homes. After the break-up of the Soviet Union, and mob violence against them in Uzbekistan in 1989 (officially ascribed to a dispute over the price of strawberries), they began demanding to return home, moving to the northern Caucasus and Azerbaijan. Now they number around 300,000, of whom 100,000 live in camps in northern Azerbaijan. Georgia is reluctant to take them back, due to its lack of resources, but in 1996 agreed to a plan for 5,000 to return, subject to their learning the Georgian language and other conditions. Nothing happened, and in 1998 a demonstration in their support in Tbilisi met with a heavy-handed response; due to international pressure an initial 5,000 should soon return. The government is still procrastinating, as it is already struggling to cope with the displaced people from Abkhazia and South Ossetia, but some have now been moved from Russia to the USA.

LANGUAGE

While the Turks and Azeris speak Turkic languages, and the Armenians, Ossetians and Russians speak Indo-European languages, **Georgian** is the most important of the Caucasian group of languages. This is divided into three families: the South Caucasian or Kartvelian – comprising Georgian (Kartuli), Megrelian, Laz and Svan (the closest to proto-Georgian), spoken by 3.5 million people in all – and the relatively similar northeastern and northwestern Caucasian families, spoken by about a million people each. These comprise about 40 languages in an area the size of France, although Strabo recorded that in the 1st century BC the Romans needed no fewer than 70 interpreters in the Dioscurias (Sukhumi) area alone. Just in Daghestan there are 14 ethnic groups and 29 languages, and it's no surprise that the name Caucasus derives from the Arabic for 'mountain of languages'.

Efforts have been made to place the Caucasian languages in a 'super-group' with the Indo-European, Turkic, Semitic, Finno-Ugric and even Chinese languages, but no links have been proved. Nor has it been possible to prove links with Basque, although some scholars speak of an Ibero-Caspian group.

The Caucasian languages are all grammatically complex; the northwestern languages have verbs with a huge variety of inflections, while the northeastern ones have simple verbs, but complex nouns, with up to eight grammatical classes (such as male, female, animal and mass noun), and up to 46 cases. The southern languages, eg: Georgian, have both a large case system for the noun and complex verbs. Likewise, they all have complex sound systems. The northwestern languages have only two distinct vowels, but highly complex consonant systems. The northeastern languages have fewer consonants, but large numbers of vowels. The southern languages are simpler but still have enormous clusters of consonants, 'back-of-the-throat death-rattles' that utterly baffle foreigners. Georgians love to test foreigners with tongue-twisters such as '*Baqaqi tskalshi kikinebs*' (the frog is croaking in the water), and a similar one about the duck (*ikhwi*) going quack (*khaadha*) in the water. Just to make things even harder, there are no capital letters.

Naturally, **Russian** is still used as the lingua franca of the area; virtually everyone over 30 in Georgia is bilingual, and few have any hang-ups about using the colonisers' language. However, Russian is being replaced by English as the second language in schools. **Turkish** may be useful in Batumi and also Kutaisi.

The Georgian alphabet has five vowels and 28 consonants, and looks like nothing else on earth, except the Armenian alphabet. An alphabet may have existed in the 3rd century BC but was supplanted by Greek and Aramaic; the present alphabet may have begun to evolve with the arrival of Christianity, and was certainly in use by AD450; after the 10th century the present Mkhedruli ('Cavalry') script, smaller and easier to read, was adopted. There are a variety of forms of many letters, but at least there's no upper or lower case. The Abkhaz language uses an extended Cyrillic (Russian) alphabet.

See pages 347–9, for vocabulary and other practical information.

RELIGION

Tradition holds that **Christianity** was introduced to Georgia in the 1st century by the apostle Andrew the First-Called, who travelled around the Black Sea before becoming the first Patriarch of Constantinople, and also by the apostles Simon and Matthew. However, it didn't become the sole official religion until AD380, while Georgia was converted in AD337, making it the world's third Christian nation. St Nino, a slave from Cappadocia, cured a child by placing her hair shirt on him and praying; Queen Nana heard of this and Nino cured her by prayer of some

THE LEGEND OF SAINT GEORGE

St George, the patron saint of Georgia and England, was a senior Roman army officer who was martyred in Palestine in about AD303; like St Nino, he was from Cappadocia and Georgians claim they were cousins. The legend that he saved a Libyan princess by killing a dragon arose in the 12th century, possibly from the myth of Perseus slaying a sea monster near the site of George's martyrdom. He had nothing to do with England but, also in the 12th century, Crusaders picked up the habit of praying for his help in battle and in 1347 England's Order of the Garter was founded in his name. Nor does he have anything to do with the name 'Georgia', which comes from *gurj*, the ancient Arabic and Persian name for the country, perhaps derived from *gorg* or wolf, a pagan idol. George is also patron of Portugal, Aragon, Catalonia, Ethiopia and Lithuania, and of horsemen, landowners, herdsmen and travellers.

In addition to the normal St George's Day on 6 May, St Nino also instituted a festival on the date of his martyrdom on 23 November, both of which are celebrated in Georgia.

unknown malady, and converted her to Christianity. King Mirian followed his wife in converting when Nino was able to cause a thunderbolt to destroy the pagan idols, followed by an eclipse of the sun which she didn't lift until he agreed to convert. However, Christianity was not firmly established until the 6th century, when the Assyrian Fathers came from Antioch; it's uncertain whether they were Georgians or Chalcedonians, but it's clear they could speak the language before they arrived. They founded several monasteries in Kartli and Kakheti, such as Shio-mghvime, Zedazeni, Samtavisi, Alaverdi, Nekresi and Davit-Gareja, and spread the Gospel throughout the country. Between AD790 and 861 more monasteries were founded by St Gregory of Khantza. In the 10th century classical texts such as Zeno's *On Nature* and works by Porphyrius were preserved in Georgian monasteries, and the texts of Buddhism were first translated by St Euthymius in the Georgian monastery on Mount Athos, in Greece. Bachkovo, the second most important monastery in Bulgaria, was founded in 1083 by the Georgian Grigorii Bakuriani, who renounced the governorship of Smolyan and Edirne to be a monk, and his brother Abasius.

For centuries the **Orthodox Church** was split by theological disputes and heresies: first, Arianism, which denied the full deity of Jesus claiming that he was created by God, and 'there was a time when he was not'; and then from the 4th century Monophysitism, the doctrine that Jesus had only one nature, rather than two, divine and human. Finally, in the 5th century, Nestorianism argued against the Virgin Mary being called 'mother of God', claiming she was mother of Christ only in his human aspect. Monophysitism was popular in the monasteries of Davit-Gareja and it survives as official doctrine of the Armenian Church; however, the Georgian Apostolic Autocephalous Church has followed the official Orthodox line. It was granted autocephaly or self-governing status in AD466; this was abolished in 1811, when authority was transferred to the Moscow patriarchate and seminaries were closed, cutting short a revival that had begun at the end of Persian domination.

Likewise, in 1917 there was a brief revival before the Bolsheviks repressed religion from 1921; by 1943 Stalin felt he'd broken its back and recognised autocephaly. In the post-Stalinist period there was a limited revival in the Church's fortunes, and from 1988 some churches were reopened. However, it never played the sort of role in the nationalist movement that the Roman Catholic Church did in Poland and Lithuania, partly due to its conservative hierarchical nature and its addiction to being allied with authority, and partly due to the Catholicos, Ilia II, having been selected in 1977 by the KGB. Then just 44, Ilia was an energetic reformer, but after the end of the Soviet Union the Georgian church became nationalist and isolationist; politicians chose to give the church money in return for its support and turned a blind eye to its blocking of reforms, whipping people up into frenzies about music festivals, drugs and gays.

While the Orthodox Church may seem utterly conservative, many monks are even more fundamentalist and regard the Catholicos and priests as dangerously liberal. In particular, the decision to join the World Council of Churches was seen as virtually heretical (Orthodox doctrine being that there are no other legitimate churches), and Ilia was forced to reverse this in 1997. Nevertheless, the next year he celebrated the 20th anniversary of the election of Pope John Paul II, who then visited Georgia in 1999; things were different when Pope Francis visited in 2016, when the Orthodox faithful were told to boycott his mass. In February 2017 a senior archpriest was arrested at Tbilisi airport with cyanide in his luggage; he was planning to fly to Germany, where Ilia was in hospital, and to assassinate the patriarch's personal secretary. This scandal finally blew the lid off the paranoid closed world of the church establishment and may lead to more openness and modernisation. The True Orthodox sect, which also exists in Russia and Greece, is also active here, and has links with extreme nationalist groups. Fundamentalist groups such as Jvari (the Cross) and the Society of Saint David the Builder have been accused of orchestrating attacks on Baptists, Pentecostalists and Jehovah's Witnesses; but Saakashvili tackled harassment of those following non-traditional faiths, for instance by sending police to break into a church and arrest a priest blamed for attacks on Jehovah's Witnesses. The 14,000-odd **Jehovah's Witnesses** have seen widespread discrimination, due mainly to their pacifism, but are now highly visible on the streets handing out leaflets. The tiny **Roman Catholic** congregation is due largely to Turkish oppression of Orthodox believers in the 17th century, mainly in Meskheti.

As described on pages 41–2, there are various **Muslim** communities (mostly Shia) and a very long-established **Jewish** presence (pages 41–2), with synagogues in Tbilisi, Kutaisi and Batumi. Most of the Kurds are **Yezid** or openly **pagan** rather than Muslim, but in fact pagan influences can be found throughout Georgia, and above all in the remoter mountain areas. Decorative motifs are often derived from nature worship, and fertility rites and offerings can be found in many places, notably trees with pieces of cloth tied to the branches, as at a Cornish holy well. This is especially so in Svaneti – see pages 261–6 for more details

There are also many premature deaths in Svaneti, mainly due to traffic accidents, although inter-family feuds are not as prevalent as they once were – see box, page 264 for the elaborate funeral rites there. Georgian **cemeteries** are usually fenced plots on the edge of fields, rather than next to a village church; in the west of the country the graves can be very elaborate, often roofed and with benches, and sometimes a family plot will be more like a *dacha* or summer house. Easter in particular is a time for feasting at the graveside. **Weddings** are also big events in Georgia, traditionally lasting for two or three days, with brain-damaging quantities of alcohol consumed. On summer and autumn Saturdays (the Tbilisoba weekend seems particularly popular in Tbilisi) you'll see many convoys of over-excited people rushing to and from churches, hooting and yelling and driving even worse than usual. Women in particular should dress respectfully to enter churches, and cover their heads; in Tbilisi there is less need for this.

CULTURE

ARCHITECTURE Lovers of architecture will already be aware of Georgia's churches. On a compact ground plan they combine simple and efficient forms with attractive proportions and perfect harmony with their setting. The oldest, dating from the 4th to 6th centuries, are basilicas derived from the law courts of Rome and Byzantium, a tradition transmitted via Syria and Asia Minor. These are relatively long, straight buildings with a semi-circular apse at the east end for the altar and priest. In Georgia they take two forms: first, triple-aisled with a common ceiling and no transepts, and then from the late 6th century a uniquely Georgian form known as the triple-naved basilica, which has longitudinal walls and doors rather than arches, and again no transepts. Bolnisi Sioni is the only survivor of the first type, with later and less pure forms at Anchiskhati and Urbnisi.

Domed churches derive from the form of eastern Georgian homes since the 3rd or 4th millennium BC; from the 6th century AD these developed into cruciform churches, with a central cupola at the centre of a cross. In a cruciform church the central area becomes the liturgical focus of the church, under a dome that symbolises the sphere of heaven. Again there are two types: first, with a semi-

1

circular apse at the east end and the other ends square (such as Samtsevrisi); and, second, the tetraconch form, with apses on all four arms of the cross. This developed fast around the turn of the 7th century, when the Jvari Church at Mtskheta, with smaller chambers filling the spaces between the arms, became the prototype for many others such as Ateni Sioni, Dzveli-Shuamta, Martvili and Dranda. This architectural flowering was stopped by the Arab invasion in the second half of the 7th century, although hybrid forms did appear in the 8th and 9th centuries, with a fusion of central domed church and triple-church basilica, such as at Kvelatsminda (Gurjaani) and Vachnadziani. The Georgian Renaissance brought a new climax in the 11th and 12th centuries, with much bigger churches such as Svetitskhoveli (Mtskheta), Bagrati (Kutaisi) and Alaverdi. In these churches, too, the interior seems unexpectedly large, since the compact proportions of the ground plan keep the volumes tightly packed. Almost every new Georgian church looks like this, including in places where the 'standard' cross-and-dome form never really existed, such as Svaneti.

RELIGIOUS ART Many of the churches are decorated with **frescoes**, which are also largely based on Byzantine traditions. Until the mid-9th century the church discouraged the painting of human images, and in the Great Iconoclasm of AD726–843 all religious art other than images of the cross and symbolic birds and plants was destroyed. However, Byzantine art then entered a Golden Age, named after the ruling Macedonian dynasty, in which the development of the cruciform church was matched by the flowering of fresco and mosaic art. This was now organised thematically with Christ Pantocrater (Lord of All) in the central dome, the Virgin in the apse over the altar, and the Life of Christ and the saints painted elsewhere.

In the Greek tradition the figures portrayed in religious art were strongly modelled but unemotional, with a calm dignity and stern grandeur. However, Georgia was also marked by the much freer and more humanistic tradition of Antioch and Alexandria, in which figures were portrayed more naturalistically and with concern for their emotional impact. There are few ancient mosaics in Georgia, but fresco art reached its peak between the 11th century and the first half of the 13th. The best are those preserved in the churches of Ateni Sioni, Kintsvisi, Timotesubani and Ubisi; and in the cave monasteries of Bertubani and Udabno (at Davit-Gareja) and Vardzia, as well as in Svaneti. Others worth looking at are in the churches of Nekresi, Zemo Krikhi and Gelati.

Icons Icons (religious images) were also produced, of three types: silver, painted on wood, and combined (silver and painting), the silver surface of the icon being generally covered with gilt. The images, of Christ, the Virgin and saints, followed the same stylistic patterns as the frescoes. The standard of metalwork in Georgia is amazing (pages 149–51).

The sack of Constantinople by the Fourth Crusade was closely followed in Georgia by the Mongol invasions, bringing an end to the high period of Georgian religious art. However, in the secular sphere (illuminated manuscripts, for instance), Persian influence later led to much fine work in Georgia.

Painting and sculpture Perhaps it's unfortunate that Georgia's best-known **paintings** are those of Pirosmani, as his charming naïf works have nearly hidden from foreign view the country's many other fine artists. Many of these worked in Paris in the 1920s and 1930s and were well known at the time. Perhaps the best known was **Elene Akhvlediani** (1901–75), who was born in Telavi. Her mother was

As president, Mikheil Saakashvili saw architecture as a key part of his campaign to modernise Georgia at speed; he commissioned foreign architects to produce iconic (and amazingly expensive) statements such as the new parliament in Kutaisi and his own presidential palace. In Tbilisi he also built the Peace Bridge, various buildings for the Justice and Interior ministries and the Bank of Georgia, as well as the new airport; he also fostered a capitalist free-for-all that allowed glitzy new towers to be shoehorned into very unsuitable areas of historic urban fabric. But it's worth noting that he spread the work evenly across the whole country, with almost every good-sized town getting a Public Service Hall (every one striking and totally different to all the others) and a new police station (more uniform in style, with a green glass façade to indicate the new transparency), while a remote town like Mestia also received a new airport (and a striking bridge leading to it) and a commercial centre. Border posts were also given special attention.

Most of his modern projects have been interesting and not entirely tasteless, but his treatment of existing buildings and urban settings was less successful. The 'old quarters' of towns like Sighnaghi and Gori and the Rabati (fortress) area of Akhaltsikhe have been over-restored and turned into tacky settings for kitschy restaurants and tourist hotels; the old town of Tbilisi has quite simply been devastated, either left to collapse or dismantled and rebuilt using a concrete structure with nothing authentic about it. He also insisted, against the forceful advice of UNESCO and many experts, on rebuilding, but essentially ruining, the Bagrat Cathedral in Kutaisi. Why the great moderniser felt the need to get into bed with the reactionary church is unclear, but he was in good company, as Bidzina Ivanishvili paid for the construction of the new Sameba Cathedral in Tbilisi.

Saakashvili said in an interview that 'If I hadn't been a politician, I should have been an architect' – perhaps wanting to be remembered as Misha the Builder, echoing the great king Davit Agmashenebelis. Well, at least Georgia was spared that. It's worth noting that Ivanishvili has his own vanity projects, both public and private. And it's worth remembering that far more damage is being done by the monks returning to ancient churches and making them fit for use again, as they have little interest in architecture or heritage conservation.

Background Information CULTURE

1

a princess but her father was poor; however, they managed to send her to Tbilisi's Second Gymnasium in 1911 and then to the Tbilisi Art Academy. She spent two years in Italy, and three in Paris, where she exhibited in the Salon des Indépendents, before returning to Georgia in 1927, where she worked for Koté Marjanishvili as a stage designer. After a long and varied career, she was declared a People's Artist of Georgia in 1960, and awarded the Rustaveli Prize in 1971. She had a wide range of styles, none especially challenging, and was the most romantic of the Georgian painters, with a great interest in traditional rural life. She also produced designs for films, and many illustrations for books, by Longfellow and Mark Twain among others, and for some children's stories.

David Kakabadze was born to a peasant family near Kutaisi in 1889, studied science in St Petersburg until 1918, but was then able to change to an artistic career, going to study in Paris in 1920 before living in Tbilisi from 1927 until his death in 1952. **Lado Gudiashvili** was born in Tbilisi in 1896 and lived in Paris from 1920 to 1925 and then in Tbilisi until his death in 1980. He toed the party line during the Stalinist period (although for some reason his characters often have no ears), but also produced bitterly ironic graphics for private consumption, and played an important role in post-Stalin liberalisation. **Niko Pirosmani** (once known as Piroshmanvili) was born in 1862 and moved to Tbilisi when he was orphaned; he worked as a self-taught sign painter, earning drinks with his quirky portraits. He was 'discovered' in 1912 by three artists down from Moscow on their holidays, but despite increased earnings his lifestyle did not change. In 1918, he was found unconscious in a basement and taken as an unknown beggar to hospital, where he died. Only 200 of a possible 2,000 of his paintings survive. The contemporary art scene is surprisingly lively; one of my favourites is Gogi Lazarashvili (b1946), and younger artists include Giorgi Kochiashvili, Thea Djordjadze (based in Berlin), Levan Songulashvili and Eteri Chkadua (both based in New York); there's also graffiti artist Bacha Khoperia, aka Dr Love or the Georgian Banksy.

There's also a strong tradition in Georgia of public art, most notably monumental **sculpture** and mosaics that somehow managed to avoid being totally derailed by communist dogma (there are a few surviving Stalin busts across the country). Iacob Nikoladze (1876–1951) was a student of Rodin and father of Georgian sculpture. The best-known sculptor is Elgudja Amashukeli (1928–2002), whose *Mother Georgia* (1958–63), *King Vakhtang Gorgasali* (1967) and *Pirosmani* (1975) in Tbilisi, and *King David the Builder* (1995) in Kutaisi, are all characterised by stylised monumentalism and muscularity. His contemporary Merab Merabishvili was responsible for the statues of Griboedev (1961) west of Saarbrücken Platz in Tbilisi, and of Erekle II in Telavi. A possible successor is Merab Berdzenishvili who created the statues of the poets Galaction Tabidze and David Guramishvili (1966) near Chavchavadze Avenue 21, of Paliashvili (1973) outside the Opera House, and of King David the Builder (1997) outside the Hotel Iveria, all in Tbilisi. Radish Tordia, Iden Tabidze and Apolon Kharebava created many of the mosaics at Tbilisi's metro stations and other public places. In Moscow the 'monstrous creations' of **Zurab Tsereteli** (b1934) are impossible to avoid (thanks to his schoolboy friendship with Mayor Luzhkov) – freakish iron reanimations of Russian folk tales and other high kitsch. A recent project was a 100m-high statue of Columbus to be donated to the United States to commemorate the 'discovery' of the Americas in 1492. Columbus, Ohio, rejected it, followed by New York, Boston, Cleveland, Fort Lauderdale and Miami; finally, it was erected in 2016 in Puerto Rico, where Columbus had landed in 1493. The city of Moscow also agreed to buy a 94m version of the statue, calling it 'Peter the Great' (as founder of the Russian navy); Dervla Murphy described it as 'monumental kitsch … a grotesque agglomeration of ships and sails and rigging seeming to rise out of the river, dwarfing every building in sight' and many Muscovites talked of blowing it up. Now loaded with money and honours, he lives in Moscow; although he has a house with a very strange and wonderful garden in the hills outside Tbilisi (just visible to the left of the Manglisi road soon after the Vake cemetery), there was very little of his work to be seen in the city, except for the psychedelic mosaic façade of the former Soviet Propaganda Centre (1977), another on the Ortachala bus station (1973), and the statue of St George and the Dragon now installed in Freedom Square, until he created his own museum, MOMA-Tbilisi (page 140).

THEATRE A uniquely Georgian style of theatre, stylised but emotionally powerful, has developed and is rightly seen as one of its national treasures. Under great directors like Robert Sturua (who runs the Rustaveli Theatre in Tbilisi), this style is turned loose on foreign classics as much as on Georgian texts. Shakespeare is a particular favourite, with very successful world tours of plays such as *Richard III*, which oddly is seen as his greatest work. ('It's magnificent, but it's not Shakespeare,' was the comment of the Royal Shakespeare Company's director Adrian Noble.) It's remarkable how many Shakespearean references Georgian journalists use.

GIFT, the Georgian International Festival of the Theatre, was founded in 1997 with a bravura publicity campaign and made a great impact, with many highly renowned international artists and companies appearing for next to nothing; the 1998 festival was smaller, due to funding problems. The festival, in or around October or November each year and based at Tbilisi's Marjanishvili Theatre, is well worth seeing, although there were accusations of political interference by the Saakashvili government when pro-opposition directors were sacked.

BALLET The Georgian National Ballet is usually abroad nowadays, thanks to a worldwide reputation for athleticism and spectacle, including sabre dances and knife-throwing. The State Ballet, now run by Nina Ananiashvili, ex-prima ballerina of the Bolshoi and the American Ballet Theatre (described by the *Daily Telegraph* as one of the 12 greatest ballerinas of all time), is undergoing a remarkable revival; the ballets of George Balanchine (page 235) are of course very important to them.

FILM Georgia had a highly successful cinema industry, based at the Gruzhia film studios in Tbilisi's Digomi suburb. Sandro Akhmetil worked with the Rustaveli Theatre from 1928 to 1935 before directing films to such effect that he now has a metro station named after him. Koté Marjanishvili also worked at the Rustaveli, and the main square on the left bank of the Mtkvari is named after him. Both men were shot in Stalin's reign of terror.

Sergei Paradjanov was born to an Armenian family in Tbilisi and lived in Kyiv until his death in 1990, so, although he filmed quintessentially Georgian subjects as in *The Surami Fortress*, he's not generally thought of as a Georgian director. Misha Chaiureli, Stalin's favourite director and a personal friend, made historical and propaganda films, and his daughter Sophiko Chiaureli starred in Paradjanov's masterpiece *The Colour of Pomegranates*. The successful biopic *Pirosmani* was directed by Eldar Shengelaia, son of the director Nikoloz Shengelaia and the actress Nato Vachnadze, after whom the *Nato*, the Georgian equivalent of the Oscar, is named. One of the most successful Georgian films is *Repentance* (*Monanieba*; 1986, directed by Tenghiz Abuladze), about a dictator who was a thinly veiled composite of Stalin and Beria; it won six prizes. Temur Babluani's *The Sun of the Sleepless* (1991) won a Silver Bear at the Berlin Film Festival. The director Nana Jorjadze, meanwhile, earned an Oscar nomination for *Chef in Love* (with the French comic star Pierre Richard) in 1996 and was elected a member of the Academy of Motion Picture Arts and Sciences. Another success has been *13 Tzameti*, written and directed by Gela Babluani, which won two awards at the 62nd Venice Film Festival and the World Cinema Jury prize at the 2006 Sundance Film Festival. Fine directors such as Jorjadze, Otar Iosseliani, Mikheil Kobakhidze, Dino Tsintsadze and Erekle Kvirikadze are doing well abroad (especially in France), as well as actors such as Dato Bakhtadze, Nutsa Kukhianidze and Merab Ninidze. The mountainous Georgian landscape itself has also become a star: *The Loneliest Planet*, a German–US produced thriller directed by Julia Loktev and starring Mexico's Gael Garcia Bernal and Israeli actress Hani Furstenburg was shot entirely in Georgia in 2010. Both *Corn Island* and *Tangerines* (a Georgian-Estonian co-production) were nominated as Best Foreign Language Film in 2015's Academy Awards.

The Hollywood film *5 Days Of August*, directed by Renny Harlin of *Die Hard 2* fame and starring Andy Garcia as Mikheil Saakashvili, was shot in Tbilisi in 2009 and released in 2011, telling the story of the 2008 South Ossetian conflict from a pro-Georgian perspective. Saakashvili allowed use of his residence and office for filming, and the Georgian army provided military uniforms, tanks and helicopters. In contrast, the Russian internet film *War 08.08.08: The Art of Betrayal* (w war080808.com) portrays, in documentary form, how the same conflict is seen by the Russians. In 2017 Nana Ekvtimishvili and Simon Groß's *My Happy Family*, the story of a woman deciding to leave her husband and live alone, in defiance of patriarchal norms, and Rezo Gigineishvili's *Hostages*, about the failed 1983 attempt by a group of young Georgians to defect from the USSR by hijacking an Aeroflot flight from Tbilisi, both did well at the Berlin International Film Festival and were bought by Netflix and HBO Europe respectively. Mariam Khatchvani's *Dede*, also about a woman living in an even more traditional setting (Ushguli in 1992), is notable for being in the Svan language and has also been successful. Tamta Gabrichidze's documentary *Sovdagari* (The Trader) won a jury prize at the 2017 Sundance Festival.

LITERATURE The classic work of Georgian literature is *The Knight in the Panther's Skin*, by Shota Rustaveli, who was Queen Tamar's treasurer; the writer Fitzroy Maclean described it as 'a fine allegorical poem of great breadth of vision, harmoniously fusing the currents of Neoplatonist philosophy and eastern romance.' It foreshadows the literature of courtly (platonic) love of the European Renaissance, but was only translated into English after World War I by Marjory Wardrop, whose brother Oliver was then Britain's chief commissioner of Transcaucasia. In the 19th century there was a fine crop of romantic poets, led by Alexander Chavchavadze (1786–1846), a friend of the Russians Pushkin and Griboedov (who married his daughter); others included Nikoloz Baratashvili (1817–45) and Akaki Tsereteli (1840–1915), who is not to be confused with the radical journalist Georgi Tsereteli (1842–1900). Galaction Tabidze (1892–1959) is the most popular of Georgia's 20th-century poets, whose suicide is still bitterly regretted. His less famous cousin Titsian Tabidze (b1895) was shot in the purge of 1937 (he was a close friend of Boris Pasternak, who translated his work into English, and whose genuine love of Georgia probably helped save him in the purges; many of his translations of Georgian poetry were done in Tabidze's flat on Griboedov kucha in Tbilisi). Currently Russia's hottest novelist (though living abroad since 2014) is Grigori Chkartishvili, a prolific author (under the un-Georgian pseudonym Boris Akunin) of excellent historical mysteries. You'll find detailed information at w rustaveli.tripod.com/lithistory.html.

MUSIC Georgia has a wonderful and highly distinctive tradition of **polyphonic singing**, which developed several hundred years before it appeared in western Europe. Instrumental music and music for dancing are also quite common, but as later developments from the vocal tradition. Folk songs span many genres, with women singing traditional lullaby and healing songs, while men, often accompanied by large quantities of wine, sing war and feasting songs; some festival songs may have been sung by men and women together.

Igor Stravinsky said that Georgian polyphony was 'more important than all the discoveries of new music'. This was recognised when it was named part of humanity's intangible cultural heritage by UNESCO in 2001 and the Research Center for Traditional Polyphony of Georgia was founded at Tbilisi State Conservatoire. Its website (w polyphony.ge) is a great source of information on Georgian song.

Georgians sing in a tuning all their own, which baffled the 19th-century musicologists who first tried to transcribe Georgian folk songs and church chants into Western notation. Georgian **folk music** is modal and often breaks out of simple 'major' or 'minor' classifications, being characterised more by the dissonance and resolution of close harmony. This produces a rich sonorous flow of sound stabbed from time to time by startling disharmonies, often repeated, before returning to the smooth flow. Parallel firsts, fifths and octaves, long 'banned' in the West, still predominate in Georgia; minor and major thirds are both considered dissonant, hence the frequent use of non-resolving fourths and sevenths.

Polyphony and harmony are both supposed to have existed in Georgia when both Orient and Occident were still monodic. It's easy to see the roots of polyphony in Georgian **choral song**, in which a single melody was supported by an organ-point or plain chant, to keep the lead singer in pitch; in Georgia the plain chant is usually sung by the middle part. This very strong drone may have evolved for the church acoustic. The 11th-century scholar Ioanne Petrisi explained the nature of the Trinity in terms of the harmonic and melodic functions of the three voices – the *mzehekri mazkhr* or top voice (in fact a mid tenor), *zhir*, a middle voice or low tenor, and *bam* or bass. The various genres of folk song include *mushuri* (working songs), *supruli* (table songs, including toasts), *satrpialo* (love songs) and *sagmiro* (epic songs – a long solo from the oral tradition or from a 19th-century writer such as Chavchavadze). Songs are mostly in the form of a strophic rondo, with or without a refrain, with syllabic setting as a rule. Rhythmically, there's often a swift alternation of 3/4 and 6/8 in the same phrase, accounting for the 'bouncy' nature of Georgian secular song.

The most complex polyphony is to be found in the western regions, above all in Guria, where the composer Honegger was defeated trying to notate a seven-part song; every voice is given a special degree of freedom, with even the bass improvising freely and taking solos. *Naduri* songs (from *nadi*, voluntary co-operative labour for harvesting or house-building) are unique to Guria, with two choruses of four voices alternating; the top voice (*gamkivani* or *krimanchuli*) simply indulges in yodel-like wordless cries, the tenor or *damtskebi* carries the poetic text, the third voice or *shemkmobari* carries the organ-point, and the bass or *bani* sings a wordless melodic counterpoint to the tenor. The Mingrelians also excel in weaving voices, with 'composed' *ritenuti* and *accelerandi*. Mingrelia is the only place where you may find mixed choruses of men and women. Wordless (glossolalic) phrases (like 'hey-nonny-no' in an English madrigal) are especially common in the west of Georgia.

Svaneti, high in the Caucasus, has kept alive a primeval and ethereal style of three-part singing, with pentatonic harmonies (unlike the rest of Georgia). This is often accompanied by the *changi*, the Svan harp, which looks as if it's come straight off a Greek vase, or the lute-like *chianuri* (which can only be played by men). Svaneti is also rich in round-dances called *perkhuli*, which gradually accelerate to end in fantastic male dance solos, and in female mourning songs. The funeral traditions here and in Racha combine pre-Christian wailing traditions with Christian singing, mainly by women though sometimes by men, but not together.

In eastern Georgian songs the bass often sings a long steady wordless drone, over which the heroic tenors sing ornamented tunes with words in close harmony; church chants show similarities to the region's secular music, although all parts sing words. Some of the richest, most sonorous and wine-soaked songs predictably come from Kakheti, while further south you find the long, lyrical *orovel*, a rare example of a solo song originally sung while ploughing or riding an oxcart. These are closely related in name and sound to the *horhovel* songs of Armenia.

Church music, which shows a direct line of descent from Byzantium, is slower and softer than secular music with harmonies and melodic patterns more interwoven, and a static rhythm. Hymns are sung with great intensity and voices overlapping to give continuous moving harmonies, as if the singers are not breathing. The unique Orthodox chant tradition of medieval Georgia survives in the form of manuscripts from the 10th century onwards and from handwritten transcriptions from the early 20th century into Western musical notation. Chant developed as Byzantine texts were translated in Palestine and Mount Athos in the 9th and 10th centuries by Georgian monk scholars such as Giorgi Mtatsmindeli and Grigol Khandzteli.

Three-part homophonic chant is believed to have begun during this period, as academies were founded to propagate church traditions such as chanting, centred on Gelati monastery near Kutaisi. Students spent up to seven years learning their craft from *sruligalobeli* (master chanters) before being initiated as chanters themselves.

The *neumas* (musical notation) was gradually lost from the 17th century, and only deciphered in the mid 20th century, although local styles were passed down verbally, while medieval neumatic notation is still undeciphered. A hymn to the Virgin by King Demetre I (1125–56), 'You are the Vine' (*Shen Khar Venakhi*), has also been sung at weddings for a century or more. The mixture of a strong secular singing tradition and the professional school of church chant yielded a genre of 'folk-sacred' songs such as *chona*, fertility songs performed just before Easter, and *alilo*, carols sung around the village on Christmas Eve (5 January). Though group singing is the dominant traditional form of music, **instruments** abound in Georgia, the oldest yet found being a 3,000-year-old bone shawm (*salamuri*) from near Mtskheta. The *doli*, a round skin-covered drum, beat out 5/4 rhythms to accompany ancient Georgians into battle (as attested by Xenophon, writing about the Mossynoeci tribe). There are two traditional bagpipes, the *chiboni* from Adjara and the *gudatsviri* from Racha. Singing is often accompanied in western Georgia by the lute-like *chonguri* (with four strings) or in eastern Georgia by the panduri (with three strings, and frets). Introduced instruments include the clarinet-like *duduki* and the oboe-like *zurna*, both from Armenia.

Since the 19th century Western harmonies have combined with Georgian three-part singing to form a popular genre known as **'urban music'**, which can now be heard in every car and bar of Georgia. It has catchy tunes and sentimental lyrics, sung in simple harmony and sometimes accompanied by guitar or piano. The most famous example is 'Suliko', a song of homesickness by the poet Akaki Tsereteli, which as everyone will remind you was Stalin's favourite.

In the communist period, the Rustavi Choir was the best known of Georgia's professional ensembles, and produced some fine recordings, now on CD, which serve as a good introduction to Georgian song. Similarly the Tsinandali Choir produced an enjoyable collection, *Table Songs of Georgia*, in fact all from Kakheti. French companies such as Ocora have produced some good compilations of field recordings, including a fine collection from Svaneti. However, in post-communist Georgia it's the Anchiskhati Choir and a group called Mtiebi ('Morning Star') who emerged first as the leaders in rediscovering and preserving the most authentic examples of Georgian song. The Anchiskhati Choir's five CDs are available from Marika Lapauri-Burk, Max-Brauer-Allee 68, 22765 Hamburg, Germany (\ +49 40 389 2222; w *lile.de*). Their first CD, *Anchiskhati Choir – Sacred Music from the Medieval Ages – Georgian Polyphonic Singing*, is a great introduction. Others to look out for include Zedashe (w *zedashe.bandcamp.com*, *zedashe.com*), Basiani (w *basiani.ge*), Elesa and the women's choir Mzetamze; Georgian choirs have also appeared in the West, such as the London Georgian Singers, the Canadian groups

Kavkasia and Darbazi, and in the USA Iveria (w *iveria.org*), which has released a CD, *Songs from the Republic of Georgia*.

In addition, *99 Georgian Songs: A Work Book for Singers* by Mtiebi's founder, the late Edisher Garakanidze, is published by the Centre for Performance Research at the University of Wales, 6 Science Park, Aberystwyth SY23 3AH (w *thecpr.org. uk/99-georgian-songs-black-mountain-press*). Songbooks are available online from Village Harmony in Vermont (w *northernharmony.pair.com/store/*), who also organise an annual singing camp in Sighnaghi ($1,700 for 14 days). John Graham (☎ +1 609 906 3665 (US); m +995 599 365372 (Georgia); e *jagraham@wesleyan. edu*; w *johngrahamtours.com*) also runs music courses in Sighnaghi and tours of medieval monasteries and Svaneti (as well as Tao-Klarjeti, now in Turkey), focusing

KATIE MELUA

Katie (originally Ketevan) Melua has put Georgia on the map for a whole generation of Westerners. However, as a folk-jazz-bluesy singer-songwriter inspired by Eva Cassidy, Ella Fitzgerald, Freddie Mercury, Nick Drake, Joni Mitchell and Bob Dylan, she seems an unlikely candidate for chart success, even with her classically Georgian good looks and her lack of ego.

Born in Kutaisi in 1984, she came to Britain in 1992 when her surgeon father took a job in Belfast, moving to Surrey in 1997. As a student at the BRIT School for Performing Arts, she was discovered by producer Mike Batt; fortunately Melua was unaware of his earlier career as creator of *The Wombles*. Melua's career was kickstarted when Terry Wogan ignored the BBC playlist to play her songs instead.

Her first album, *Call Off the Search*, was released in 2003, with songs by Melua, Batt, John Mayall and Randy Newman; it sold 1.7 million copies in the UK, making her the country's best-selling female artist two years running, and three million abroad. Her debut single, 'The Closest Thing to Crazy', written by Batt, was a top-ten hit in the UK. Her follow-up album *Piece by Piece*, released in 2005, was darker but just as successful.

In 2005 she became a British citizen, partly so as to be able to travel without needing visas almost everywhere, but she retains Georgian citizenship. She's never been seen as a turncoat in Georgia – probably because few over the age of 20 recognise the name, and those who do think of her as 'half-Georgian' – and returned in 2005 to record with a traditional male-voice choir. She gave her first concert there in November 2005 and says she'd like to do an album of Georgian folk songs. A year later she performed the world's deepest gig on a Norwegian oil rig, a record 303m underwater. Her 2010 album *The House*, produced by William Orbit, showed a move towards electronica, but 2012's *Secret Symphony* was a horribly misjudged orchestral album. Having completed her six-album contract with Mike Batt, she recorded the leftfield seasonal concept album *In Winter*, with the Gori Women's Choir.

Melua's sense of humour came to the fore after a tongue-in-cheek media debate about the scientific accuracy of some lyrics in her song 'Nine Million Bicycles'. She duly produced a spoof 'corrected' version which went: 'We are 13.7 billion light-years from the edge of the observable universe. That's a good estimate with well-defined error bars and with the available information, I predict that I will always be with you.'

For more information, see w katiemelua.com.

on wine, food, culture and above all ecclesiastic chant, with three leaders who sing in the churches – unforgettable. If you read German, see also *Musik aus Georgien* by Thomas Houssermann (Erka Verlag, 1993). Ts'utisopeli (w *tsutisopeli.com*) is an ethnomusicological project documenting, recording and sharing folk music in eastern Georgian villages and has more than 400 songs on its website. The **Georgian Harmony Association** (*c/o Michael Bloom, 5 Alder Lodge, 292 Bury St West, London N9 9LL;* ✆ *020 8360 9991;* e *info@georgianharmony.org.uk;* w *georgianharmony.org. uk*) puts on workshops in the UK and singing holidays in Georgia; you could also join the Maspindzeli choir in London (w *maspindzeli.org.uk*).

In the field of **classical music**, the great bass Paata Burchuladze (b1955) is Georgia's main claim to fame; he's very much in the Western operatic tradition rather than the Russian, and remains in great demand worldwide. Less well known are conductors Jansugh Kakhidze and Evgeni Mikeladze, pianists Eliso Virsaladze, Khatia Buniatishvili, Elizabeth Leonskaja, Nino Gvetadze and Mariam Batsashvili, mezzo-sopranos Anita Rachvelishvili and Nino Surguladze, and violinists Lisa Batiashvili and Marina Iashvili. There's also jazz piano prodigy Beka Gochiashvili. The Tbilisi opera house is named after the composer Zakaria Paliashvili (1871– 1933), who established classical music in Georgia with his operas *Abessalom and Eteri* (1918, a monumental tragedy), the lyric-dramatic *Daisi* (1923, prefiguring Khachaturian but with a 'Georgian' tone in its peasant crowd scenes) and the heroic-patriotic *Latavra* (1927). Mikhail Ippolitov-Ivanov (1859–1935), a student of Rimsky-Korsakov, was conductor of the Tbilisi Symphony Orchestra for a decade, and his *Caucasian Sketches* (1895) is based on Georgian folk tunes. It may be interesting to know that Stravinsky based *Les Noces* on Georgian harmonic and melodic patterns. The leading Georgian composer of the 20th century was Gia Kancheli (b1935), whose violent early symphonies have given way to increasingly subdued, wistful later works.

Armenia, by contrast, is known for lively instrumental music (derived from the Islamic world) with drums and the *duduk*, like a reedy clarinet (usually played in pairs, with the second instrument providing a drone). The other traditional style is that of the *ashugs* or troubadours, who were poets and storytellers as well as musicians. The most famous was Sayat Nova (1712–95) who was based in Tbilisi, at the court of Erekle II.

Georgia has suddenly become highy visible in the world of **fashion** – Demna Gvasalia, creative director of Balenciaga and Vetements, was born in Sukhumi, and others such as Irakli Rusadze of Situationist, George Keburia, Sesili [Cecily] Kemularia, Sofia Tchkonia, George Shaghashvili and Diana Kvariani are all creating waves.

SPORT The most popular sport in Georgia remains **soccer**, but the national team has little impact internationally, fighting hard to achieve draws with Wales and Ireland in qualifiers for the 2018 World Cup. The biggest games in Tbilisi recently have been the 2015 UEFA Super Cup final, a nine-goal thriller between Barcelona and Sevilla, and the 2017 UEFA Under-19 championships. On the other hand, Georgia's **rugby** team is world-class, qualifying for the 2003, 2007, 2011, 2015, and 2019 world cups (not totally surprising, as almost the whole team plays professionally in France, plus a few at Bristol, Worcester and London Irish); now ranked 12th in the world, they're consistently winning the Rugby Europe Championship (the second tier of European competition, sometimes referred to as the Six Nations B) and pushing to join the Six Nations proper. Their forwards can take on the best in the world, but the backs are not quite there yet, with a lack of creativity in attack.

In **tennis**, Nikoloz Basilashvili, who plays mainly on the ATP Challenger Tour, is at 59 in the world rankings. Georgia's finest players were Aleksandre Metreveli, who lost to Jan Kodeš in the Wimbledon men's singles final in 1973, and Leila Meskhi, who reached the quarter-finals of the US Open in 1990 and was ranked 12th on the women's tour in 1991.

The government is keen to promote **hiking**, not only to boost tourism; in addition to the volunteer-led Trans Caucasian Trail (see box, page 275), the Georgian National Tourism Administration is working on a 600km network of trails across the country, to link national parks and other protected areas within five years. National standards for marking the first mountain tracks were created in 2016, essentially following the European norms.

The Saakashvili government was particularly keen to develop **skiing**, which has proved to be particularly popular with Poles, Ukrainians and others from Eastern Europe. The main resorts are Gudauri (pages 180–3) and Bakuriani (pages 207–9); and several resorts in Svaneti, as well as Goderji and Bakhmaro, are growing fast.

2

Practical Information

WHEN TO VISIT

Georgia may not suffer from many power cuts these days, but winter is still not the smartest time to visit, unless you are just interested in Tbilisi and the ski resorts. High summer can be too hot and humid, but spring and autumn are ideal times to visit; in particular the golden autumn colours can be spectacular, and the wine harvest makes this a great time to visit Kakheti; however, beach resorts such as Kobuleti close by the end of September.

HIGHLIGHTS

Given the difficulties and unpredictabilities of travel in Georgia, some visitors confine themselves to Tbilisi, with brief excursions to places such as Mtskheta and Davit-Gareja. However, the rewards for venturing outside the capital are great for those prepared to make the effort. To the east, Kakheti is ideally placed for an outing of two to four days, sampling wines and churches, and to the north the Georgian Military Highway leads into the heart of the High Caucasus. The country's main axis is the highway from Tbilisi to Kutaisi and on to Poti or Batumi, or to Zugdidi and Abkhazia; this begins by following the Mtkvari and then crosses into the Rioni Basin in the west of the country. Batumi is one of the most pleasant and laid-back cities in Georgia, although the Black Sea's beaches are not really worth visiting. From Zugdidi it's also possible to head north into the heart of the Caucasus, to the region of Svaneti, where unique architecture and semi-pagan customs are preserved.

SUGGESTED ITINERARIES

Almost all itineraries start in the capital, Tbilisi, although it's also common to arrive at Kutaisi or Batumi airports or overland from Turkey. From Tbilisi, it's easy to head east for a couple of days to Kakheti to enjoy a bit of wine tourism and visit the ancient monasteries of Davit-Gareja. Otherwise you'll head west on the country's main highway past Mtskheta, either swinging north to Gudauri and Stepantsminda (Kazbegi) in the High Caucasus, or continuing to Gori and Kutaisi and then the coast at either Poti or Batumi. There are other options to turn north into the High Caucasus, notably from Kutaisi to Racha and from Zugdidi to Svaneti; equally, from Khashuri, between Gori and Kutaisi, you can head south to Borjomi in the Lesser Caucasus, continuing to the cave city of Vardzia and either looping east to Tbilisi or (in summer) west to Batumi. The itineraries suggested below are feasible by rental car, bus or *marshrutka* (minibus).

ONE WEEK From Tbilisi head west to Mtskheta and Gori, detour south to Borjomi and Vardzia, then return to the main highway to visit Kutaisi, finishing in Batumi.

TWO WEEKS From Tbilisi head west to Mtskheta and then north to Stepantsminda in the heart of the High Caucasus; then follow the one-week itinerary west to the Black Sea and return to Tbilisi. Leave time to finish with some restorative wine tourism in Kakheti, east of the capital.

THREE WEEKS This option gives plenty of time to explore the mountains; follow the one-week option west to Kutaisi for an optional side-trip north to Racha, then go via Zugdidi to Mestia and Ushguli in Svaneti. If you don't get enough hiking there you can also divert to Stepantsminda on the way back to Tbilisi, before finishing in Kakheti, east of the capital – in addition to wine, there's also the Tusheti National Park, perhaps Georgia's most remote wilderness (road access only from June to mid-October).

TOURIST INFORMATION

There is a very useful website for advance planning (w *georgia.travel*) and a number of helpful **tourist information centres** throughout the country that can provide maps, brochures, itinerary suggestions and practical help. The best of these is in Tbilisi at Freedom Square, but there are others at Batumi, Kutaisi, Borjomi, Akhaltsikhe, Gori, Sighnaghi and Telavi (see individual towns for other locations). The **Department of Tourism and Resorts** (*Chanturia 12, 0108 Tbilisi*; \ +995 32 436996; e *georgia@tourism.gov.ge, marketing@tourism.gov.ge*; w *georgia.travel*) can be contacted to answer specific questions; they also have a 24-hour English-language helpline (\ *0800 800909*).

Using the internet for research you will find that searches for 'Georgia' inevitably produce vast amounts of material on the US state – try 'Tbilisi' or 'Caucasus' instead. See page 354 for useful websites.

MAPS If venturing anywhere outside Tbilisi, you should pick up the 1:500,000 map of Georgia published by GeoLand in Tbilisi (page 131) or the 1:610,000 map published by International Travel Maps and Books (w *itmb.ca*), both available in major stores such as **Stanfords** (*12 Long Acre, London WC2E 9LP*; \ *020 7836 1321*; w *stanfords.co.uk*). A 1:800,000 German map called *Georgien – Reisekarte* is produced by ERKA-Verlag (w *erka-verlag.de*), also based in Tbilisi. Several 1:1,000,000 maps of the entire Caucasus are also available through Bartholomew's at Stanfords and other shops. Tourist offices in Georgia also give away a reasonable 1:950,000 map of Georgia for free in addition to quite detailed provincial maps (1:200,000 to 1:350,000).

TOUR OPERATORS AND TRAVEL AGENTS

UK

Birdfinders Westbank, Cheselbourne, Dorset DT2 7NW; \ 01258 839066; m 07768 691997; w birdfinders.co.uk. 1-week birding tours for £1,495 plus flights.

Cox & Kings 30 Millbank, London SW1P 4EE; \ 020 3773 6246, 020 7853 5014; w coxandkings. co.uk. Offers private tours of Georgia from £2,070 for 7 nights to £2,595 for 10 nights, & a 10-night group tour combined with Armenia (£2,245).

Exodus Grange Mills, Weir Rd, London SW12 0NE; \ 020 3733 2877; w exodus.co.uk. This company operates a 14-day 'Highlights of Georgia & Armenia' cultural tour (*from £1,949*).

Explore Nelson Hse, 55 Victoria Rd, Farnborough, Hants GU14 7PA; \ 0843 561 1721, 01252 883626; w explore.co.uk. They offer 'Hiking in the Caucasus' (*8 days from £1,155*), 'Discover Georgia' (*9 days from £1,335*), 'Land of the Golden Fleece' (*16 days* *in Georgia & Armenia from £1,989, or £2,699 with Azerbaijan extension).*

Naturetrek Mingledown Barn, Wolf's Lane, Chawton, Hants GU34 3HJ; ☎01962 733051; w naturetrek.co.uk. An 8-day birding trip from £2,295/£1,995 inc/exc flights.

Regent Holidays Colston Tower, Colston St, Bristol BS1 4XE; ☎020 3588 2971; w regent-holidays.co.uk; see ad, inside front cover. Regent is the leading British operator, offering tailor-made tours to suit any budget or interest & can book accommodation, transport, guides or other services. Long w/ends cost from £715 in Tbilisi; their 8-day 'Cultural Landscapes of Georgia' tour costs from £2,100pp, with add-ons available to Svaneti (*4 days from £560*) & Armenia. They also offer the only tours to Abkhazia, at £3,150 for 12 days. All prices inc flights.

Ride World Wide Staddon Farm, North Tawton, Devon EX20 2BX; ☎01837 82544; w rideworldwide.co.uk. Offers 8-/10-day horseback trips for £1,530/£1,795, exploring the little-touristed area south & southwest of Tbilisi including the 12th-century monasteries of Gudarekhi & Pitareti.

Scott's Tours 141 Whitfield St, London W1T 5EW; ☎020 7383 5353; w scottstours.co.uk. This small company, originally specialising in tours to Russia, can organise tailor-made tours of Georgia.

Silk Road Tours 8 Oak Cottages; Green Lane, London W7 2PE; ☎020 8728 2478; w silkroadtours.co.uk. Specialists in the Caucasus, Middle East & Central Asia, offering a 9-day private trip of Georgia (*£1,375*), as well as combos with other countries.

The Slow Cyclist Foxbury, Upton Estate, Banbury, Oxon OX15 6HT; ☎020 7060 4487; w theslowcyclist. co.uk. A new 7-night 'Vineyards, Wildflowers & Mountains of Georgia' cycling & hiking trip in Kakheti & Tusheti, for £1,795 pp exc flights.

Steppes Travel 51 Castle St, Cirencester, Wilts GL7 1QD; ☎01258 787507; w steppestravel.co.uk. Tailor-made or group trips to Georgia, as well as Armenia & Azerbaijan; a 7-day 'Highlights of Georgia' trip costs £1,610, an 8-day 'Food & Wine' tour £2,700, & a 13-day walking tour including Svaneti, Kazbegi & Kakheti from £2,995.

Travel Local w travellocal.com. A UK-based website where you can book direct with selected local travel companies, allowing you to communicate with an expert ground operator without having to go through a 3rd-party

travel operator or agent. Offers trips such as a long w/end walking break to Svaneti (*4 nights from £530 pp, or 7 nights from £1,150*), 'Classic Georgia' (*6 days, £640*), 'Georgia's Foodie Highlights' (*7 days, £760*) or 'Highlights of Georgia' (*10 days, £960*). Your booking with the local company has full financial protection, but note that travel to the destination is not included. Member of ABTA, ASTA.

Travel the Unknown Riverbank Hse, 1 Putney Bridge Approach, London SW6 3BQ; ☎020 7183 6371; tf 1800 604 6024 (N America); w traveltheunknown.com; see ad, 2nd colour section. A 12-day Georgia Explorer trip (*£1,875*), including Borjomi-Kharagauli National Park & Martvili Canyon, as well as tours combining Georgia with Azerbaijan & Armenia.

Undiscovered Destinations PO Box 746, North Tyneside NE29 1EG; ☎0191 296 2674, tf 1800 614 2967 (N America), 1300 956 415 (Australia); w undiscovered-destinations.com. The 11-day Peaks & Valleys of the Caucasus trip (with GeorgiCa; page 59) goes to both Tusheti & Svaneti.

Wild Frontiers Adventure Travel 78 Glentham Rd, London SW13 9JJ; ☎020 8741 7390; w wildfrontiers.co.uk. A range of adventurous trips such as the 'Wild Walk in Svaneti' (*10 days from £1,545*), or 'Land of Myths & Mountains' (*9 days from £1,425*), visiting Kazbegi, Juta & Roshka. It also combines Georgia with Azerbaijan & Armenia, a 15-day trip costing £2,850, as well as horse treks (*9 days from £1,645*) & custom trips; all exc flights.

USA
From the USA there are more expensive trips on offer.

Ker & Downey 6703 Highway Bd, Katy, TX 77494; ☎+1 281 371 2500; tf +1 800 423 4236; w kerdowney.com. Luxury 'handcrafted holidays' from US$700–850/day, plus a 2-week tour of Georgia, Armenia & Azerbaijan.

MIR Corporation 85 South Washington St, Suite 210, Seattle, WA 98104; tf +1 800 424 7289; ☎206 624 7289; w mircorp.com. MIR offers a variety of packages: among others, a 12-day 'Taste of Georgia' tour from US$5,095 & a 15-day 'South Caucasus' tour from US$7,395; plus private trips. All exc flights.

Wilderness Travel 1102 9th St, Berkeley, CA 94710; tf +1 800 368 2794; w wildernesstravel.

com. This top-end company offers 11-day trips for about US$4,195, including strenuous hiking in Tusheti.

WORLDWIDE

ERKA Reisen Postfach 4240, Robert Stolz Str 21, 76626 Bruchsal, Germany; ☎ +49 7257 930390; w erkareisen.de. This German company offers tours for Germans, naturally, including climbing, riding & farm stays.

Sundowners Overland Level 1, 51 Queen St, Melbourne VIC 3000, Australia; ☎ 3 9672 5300, 1300 559860, NZ 0800 770156, UK & Europe 020 8877 7660, rest of world +61 3 9672 5386; w sundownersoverland.com. Group tours of Georgia & Armenia (*from £1,545 for 11 nights*) & independent journeys (*from £2,875 for 12 days*).

Village Ways Khali Estate, PO Ayarpani, Almora 263601, Uttarakhand, India; ☎ 01223 750049 (UK), 05335 20774 (France), 992 088 2409 or 986 900 5642 (India); w villageways.com. Working with local communities, the 'Grass Routes – Mountains & Vineyards of Georgia' tour visits Kakheti & Tusheti for 9 days.

GEORGIA

Adventure Club Jomardi Robakidze 7, 0159 Tbilisi; m 570 100244, 599 141160; w adventure. ge. Adventure tours, especially rafting.

Argotour Paliashvili 28/8, Tbilisi; ☎ 32 229 2779; w argotour.ge. This company's branches are open 7 days a week (⏲ 09.30–19.00 Mon–Sat, 10.00–18.00 Sun). Historical, skiing, rafting & spa tours, plus w/end breaks in Tbilisi.

Badagoni Tours Digomi 1/11/64, Tbilisi; ☎ 32 251 6701; m 593 937751; e zazamakharadze@ yahoo.com, zazamakharadze@gmail.com; w badagonitour.com. Specialising in wine tours but offering a range of other excursions.

Batumi Birding Melashvili 5, 6010 Batumi; ☎ 422 241777, 558 217706; w batumibirding. com. New company based on the Batumi Raptor Count (page 301) but expanding to cover Georgia & neighbouring countries.

Caucasus Travel Peritsvaleba 22, Avlabari, 0103 Tbilisi; ☎ 32 298 7400; e online@caucasustravel. com; w caucasustravel.com. Set up in 1991 by some of Georgia's leading climbers as Caucasian Travel, it was renamed when it was found that this could give offence; now it's the leading agency dealing with incoming tourists & has associated

companies offering car hire, business consultancy & adventure tours. Service is superb & they're totally reliable regarding what is possible or safe; their website is an excellent reference tool. Their city tour costs US$50–95 depending on numbers; day trips to Davit-Gareja cost US$70–160.

Concord Travel Barnov 82, 0179 Tbilisi; ☎ 32 222 5151; w concordtravel.ge. Concord has a wide variety of tours on offer, including wine, adventure & archaeological.

Exotour Galaktion Tabidze 9, 0105 Tbilisi; ☎ 32 291 3191; w exotour.ge. A company providing a good range of services – food & wine, hiking, horseriding & off-road jeep tours.

Explore Georgia Shevchenko 5, 0108 Tbilisi; ☎ 32 292 1911; w exploregeorgia.com. A full range of hiking, climbing, horseriding, mountain-biking & caving trips.

Georgian Adventures (GATA) Barnov 42, 0171 Tbilisi; m 599 535589; e georgianadventures@ gmail.com; ⓕ georgianadventures. Trips to Lagodekhi & Khevsureti & 14 w/end tours for expats; also rafting.

Georgian Discovery Tours Chavchavadze Av 80, 0162 Tbilisi; ☎ 32 229 4953; w gdt.ge. This Georgian–Swiss company offers tailor-made tours.

GeorgiCa Travel Erekle II St 5, 0105 Tbilisi; ☎ 32 225 2199; w georgicatravel.ge; see ad, page 55. This company offers cultural tours, trekking, horseriding, cycling & climbing. They can book accommodation & car hire, & offer trips with other Caucasian & Silk Road countries.

Geotour Rustaveli Av 18, 0114 Tbilisi; ☎ 32 245 0110; m 599 156840; w geotour.ge. A wide range of culture, adventure & wine tours, plus hiking, riding, rafting & skiing. Also offer tours to Armenia & Azerbaijan.

Kaukasus Reisen Tumanianis 15, Tbilisi; ☎ +49 170 337 7228; m 599 570554; e kaukasus@gmail. com, w kaukasus-reisen.de. Adventure tours (German- & English-speaking), including a 14-day introductory tour for €1,380 (land-only); trekking & riding in Tusheti from €1,340 for 11 days; or a 12-day trek in Khevsureti or Svaneti for €1,280.

Living Roots Baratashvili 18, 4200 Sighnaghi; w travellivingroots.com. Excellent company specialising in finding the most authentic off-the-beaten-track cultural experiences, with emphasis on wine & music.

Omnestour Abesadze 4, 0105 Tbilisi; ☎ 32 293 3400; e info@omnestour.ge; w omnestour.

ge. Efficient, friendly company offering historic, adventure & cultural tours.

Real Georgia Tours 101 Freedom Square, Tbilisi ; m 555 561671, 596 122777; w realgeorgiatours.com

Sunny Travel Bakhtrioni 7, Tbilisi; ⟍32 242 1618; e geo_sunnytravel@yahoo.com. Adventure & cultural tours, including horseriding & day tours of Tbilisi & Davit-Gareja.

Tbilisi Tourist Centre Akhvlediani 5, 0108 Tbilisi; ⟍32 298 5075; e ttc@wanex.net; w ttc. ge. General & cultural tours mainly for Germans, as well as cycling & hiking in the Borjomi-Kharagauli National Park.

Ugo Travel Pavle Aslanidi 14, Tbilisi; ⟍32 243 6058; m 597 293841; w ugogeorgia.com. Liithuanian-owned company offering professional tours, including all sorts of outdoor activities.

Visit Georgia Ingorovka 4A, Tbilisi; ⟍32 292 2246; w visitgeorgia.ge. Large, well-established company offering a wide range of tours; prices vary with the standard of hotels. As well as individual & group tours they offer wildlife, hiking & archaeology.

Wild Georgia Tsinamdzgvrishvili Av 17, 0102 Tbilisi; m 599 941320; e eka@wildgeorgia.ge, inanycase23@yahoo.com; ⧉. Hiking & horseriding in Tusheti & from a vineyard in Kakheti, with excellent local guides.

Independent guides
These are just a few of the English-speaking guides available in Tbilisi for private tours.

Expert Guides Georgia Sumbatashvili-Iuzhini 36A, 0180 Tbilisi; m 598 527211; w expertguides. ge; ⧉ expertguidesgeorgia

George Varsimashvili 'George's secret places tour' m 599 148485; ⧉ George Zardiashvili m 599 988815; e dailytoursingeorgia@yahoo.com; w privatedailytoursingeorgia.weebly.com

Ilia Sebiskveradze m 551 477171; e iliasebiskveradze87@gmail.com; ⧉ ilosebiskveradze

Shota Elisashvili m 577 495884; e shotael@ yahoo.co.uk

Tariel Tabashidze ⟍32 264 8928; m 899 648928; e tariel_tabashidze@yahoo.com

RED TAPE

Citizens of the European Union, USA, Canada, Australia, New Zealand, Japan, Israel and many other countries do not require visas for visits to Georgia of up to a year. Otherwise you'll need to buy a single-entry visa at an embassy or consulate, or online at w **evisa.gov.ge** (*queries to* e *contact@evisa.gov.ge;* ⟍ *322 945050*). Visas are no longer issued at rail or sea entry points. Citizens of 94 countries can now stay for up to 360 days, after which you just need to leave the country and re-enter to stay another 360 days, and you're even allowed to work in Georgia.

For further information, contact the Ministry of Foreign Affairs (*Chitadze 4, 0118 Tbilisi;* ⟍ *322 94 5000, 240 1010;* e *inform@mfa.gov.ge;* w *mfa.gov.ge;* ⊕ *10.00–14.00 Mon–Fri*). It's better not to overstay – there's a penalty of GEL190 (*US$75*) for up to six months beyond your visa's expiry or GEL360 beyond that, and you may not be allowed back for three months.

It's easy enough to cross from Georgia to Abkhazia but you cannot travel from Russia to Georgia via Abkhazia; however, it's not possible to visit South Ossetia or Tskhinvali for the time being. British and US embassies advise against visiting both Abkhazia and South Ossetia.

There was a great deal of petty corruption and grafting at Georgia's borders in the past, with officials demanding a few dollars from travellers, but this has been cleaned up since the Rose Revolution. The problem now seems to be racism, with too many cases of people of colour being refused entry, even with a visa.

EMBASSIES The main embassies are based in Tbilisi and there are a number of consulates in Batumi.

Tbilisi

E Armenia [105 E2] Tetelashvili 4, 1 block west of Marjanishvili Sq; ☏295 1723, 295 0977; **e** armemb@caucasus.net; **w** georgia.mfa.am/en; ⏲ 09.00–18.00 Mon–Fri, visas 10.00-13.00

E Azerbaijan [95 G6] Gorgasali 4; ☏224 2220; **e** tbilisi@mission.mfa.gov.az

E Canada [104 D5] (consulate) Rustaveli 34, 3rd fl; ☏32 218 2072; **e** ccogeorgia@gmail.com

E China [104 B4] Barnov 52; ☏225 2670; **e** zhangling@access.sanet.ge; **w** ge. chineseembassy.org

E European Union [105 H5] Chkheidze 38; ☏294 3763, 294 3769; **e** delegation-georgia@ eeas.europa.eu; **w** eeas.europa.eu/delegations/ georgia_en

E France [95 F7] Krtsanisi 49; ☏272 1490; **e** ambafrance@access.sanet.ge; **w** ambafrance-ge.org

E Germany [94 D2] Due to earthquake damage, the embassy is semi-permanently on the 4th floor of the Sheraton Metechi Palace Hotel, Telavi 20; ☏244 7300; **e** info@tifl.diplo.de; **w** tiflis.diplo. de; ⏲ 08.30–17.30 Mon–Thu, 08.30–14.30 Fri. Consular/visa section is at Davit Aghmashenebelis 166; ☏243 5399; ⏲ 09.00–13.00 Mon–Fri

E Iran [94 A3] Chavchavadze Av 80; ☏291 3657–60; **e** embassy@iran.ge

E Israel [95 E3] Davit Agmashenebelis 154; ☏255 6500; **e** press@tbilisi.mfa.gov.il; **w** tbilisi. mfa.gov.il

E Italy [105 E7] Chitadze 3A; ☏299 6418; **e** embassy.tbilisi@esteri.it; **w** ambtbilisi.esteri.it

E Russian Federation [94 A3] c/o embassy of Switzerland, Chavchavadze Av 51; ☏291 2406, 291 2645; **e** russianembassy@caucasus.net; **w** georgia.mid.ru

E Turkey [94 B6] Chavchavadze Av 35; ☏225 2072; **e** tiflisbe@dsl.ge; **w** tbilisi.emb.mfa.gov.tr

E Ukraine [94 A3] Chavchavadze Av 76; ☏231 1161; consul ☏231 1454; **e** emb_ge@mfa.gov.ua; **w** georgia.mfa.gov.ua

E UK [95 F7] Krtsanisi 51; ☏227 4747; **e** british. embassy.tbilisi@fco.gov.uk; **w** ukingeorgia.fco. gov.uk; ⏲ 09.00–17.00 Mon–Fri except Georgian & British holidays

E United Nations [94 D7] Eristavi 9 (on the UN Circle); ☏25 1126; **e** uno.tbilisi@unic.org; **w** ungeorgia.ge

E USA [94 C1] Balanchini 11, Didi Dighomi; ☏227 7000 (embassy), 227 7724 (consular section); **e** support-georgia@ustraveldocs.com, consulate-tbilisi@state.gov; **w** usembassy.ge; ⏲ consulate 08.30–17.30 Mon–Fri

Batumi

E Armenia [289 E2] Gorgiladze 5/5; ☏422 273812; **e** armgenconsulatebatumi@mfa.am; **w** batumi.mfa.am/en; ⏲ 10.00–13.00, 15.00–17.00 Mon–Thu

E Azerbaijan [288 D4] Parnavaz Mepe 62; ☏422 276700; **e** batumi@mission.mfa.gov.az; **w** batumi.mfa.gov.az; ⏲ 09.00–18.00 Mon–Fri

E Iran [288 D5] Parnavaz Mepe 83; ☏422 228601-3; **e** cg.iri.batumi@gmail.com; **w** batumi. mfa.ir; ⏲ 09.30–13.30 Mon–Fri

E Turkey [288 C2] Mehmet Abashidze 8; ☏422 274789/90; **e** consulate.batumi@mfa.gov.tr; ⏲ Mon–Fri 09.30–13.00 & 14.00–18.00

E Ukraine [288 C6] Melikishvili 71; ☏422 231600; **e** gc_gep@mfa.gov.ua; ⏲ 09.00–13.00, 14.00–18.00 Mon–Fri

GETTING THERE AND AWAY

BY AIR Direct flights from London were introduced in 2017, both from Gatwick with Georgian Airways to Tbilisi (*Wed: dep 22.00, arr 06.00; from £100/dir inc checked bag & meal*) and from Luton with Wizzair to Kutaisi (*Thu & Sun: dep 18.00, arr 03.15; from £20; in Jan hand luggage only*).

You can also go via Istanbul – **Turkish Airlines** (*THY*; **w** *turkishairlines.com*) give the most options: from Britain there are eight flights a day from London (both Heathrow and Gatwick), two from Manchester and one each from Birmingham and Edinburgh, the latter connecting with a midnight flight from Istanbul (Ataturk) that reaches Tbilisi at 04.30 (there's also a 14.00 flight that arrives at 17.00); they also fly from Ataturk to Batumi. Turkish budget carriers also provide good connections via Istanbul: **Pegasus** (**w** *flypgs.com*) has daily flights from London

Stansted via Istanbul Sabiha Gökçen (SAW) which depart Stansted at 12.30 and arrive Tbilisi at 02.40, and return at 05.30 to arrive at noon. This is relatively cheap, from around £200 return, but as well as highly inconvenient arrival and departure times at Tbilisi it requires lengthy stopovers in each direction at Istanbul's modern but uninteresting – and expensive – second airport. Pegasus also fly from SAW to Batumi and Kutaisi. **Atlas Global** (w *atlasglb.com*) fly from London Stansted daily at 13.30 via Istanbul's main Ataturk airport, arriving in Tbilisi at 03.15, with comparable fares but with full service.

THY is a Star Alliance member, offering worldwide connections. Others are **Lufthansa** (w *lufthansa.com*), which has daily flights at 21.00 from Munich, arriving at 04.00 (with connections from Heathrow and elsewhere); and **LOT** (w *lot.com*), which has five flights a week from Warsaw, arriving at 05.00 (with a connection from Heathrow at 18.15).

The only Oneworld members flying to Tbilisi are **Qatar Airways** (w *qatarairways. com*) and the Siberian airline S7 (w *s7.ru*); and the only Skyteam members are China Southern Airlines (w *global.csair.com*) and **Aeroflot** (w *aeroflot.ru*), which has reasonable (but not cheap) connections through Moscow (Sheremetyevo), leaving London Gatwick at 10.40 and reaching Tbilisi at 02.00. **Ukraine International Airlines** (w *flyuia.com*) have flights from Kiev daily at 19.25, arriving in Tbilisi at 00.10. The return flight is at the very inconvenient time of 06.45. However, there are decent connections to/from London Gatwick, Amsterdam, Berlin, Brussels, Munich, Paris and Zurich in both directions; they also fly four times a week from Kiev at 11.30 (too early for connections from western Europe), arriving at 16.15. It's also worth considering **Air Baltic** (w *airbaltic.com*), with flights via Riga up to three nights a week, leaving at 23.30 and arriving in Tbilisi at 04.00. All these airlines use modern Airbus and Boeing planes, and fares are broadly competitive, starting from around €200 return in winter.

Other low-cost airlines fly into the new Kutaisi Airport (linked by modern minibuses with Kutaisi, Tbilisi and Batumi), notably **Wizzair** (w *wizzair.com*) from London Luton, Barcelona, Berlin, Bucharest, Budapest, Dortmund, Milan, Paris (Beauvais), Prague, Rome, Warsaw and Vilnius.

From North America you'll usually have most options with Turkish Airlines, with return fares starting from around US$600 including taxes from New York (JFK). They also fly from Chicago (*US$800*), San Francisco (*US$900*), Toronto (*CDN$1,200*) and Vancouver (*CDN$1,00*). Ukraine International Airlines fly from New York via Kiev four times a week (with code-shared connections from Los Angeles and San Francisco), costing from US$600 return.

From Asia and Africa it's easiest to fly via the Gulf, with low-cost airlines such as **Air Arabia** (w *airarabia.com*) and **Fly Dubai** (w *flydubai.com*) serving cities such as Mumbai, Delhi, Nairobi and Dar Es Salaam. Qatar Airways serves these and further-flung destinations such as Johannesburg, Auckland, Hong Kong, Tokyo and Perth via Doha. The Omani low-cost carrier Salam Air Muscat (w *salamair. com*) plans to fly to Tbilisi from June 2018. Turkish Airlines is also a possibility, with flights from Singapore via Istanbul from US$680; China Southern fly three times a week from Beijing via Urumqi, from £400 each way.

The main Georgian operator is ,**Georgian Airways** (w *georgian-airways.com, airzena.com*), still sometimes referred to as Airzena. In 1991, the Georgian division of Aeroflot became Orbi Georgian Airlines; it flew ancient Soviet planes and maintained them so badly that US embassy staff were not permitted to use the airline. In 1999, the charter line Airzena bought the bankrupt Georgian Airways, as it now is, and Air Georgia, and the state now holds just 20% of the company. In

2000 it leased two Boeing 737s, which fly to Amsterdam, London Gatwick, Paris, Vienna (code-sharing with Austrian Airlines) and Tel Aviv.

BY RAIL International railway services from Moscow originally ran via Baku (Azerbaijan) to Tbilisi (3,214km, taking three days) until the opening in 1942 of a line along the Black Sea Coast. This became the main route (2,509km, taking 41 hours), but is now closed owing to the secession of Abkhazia. There have been various attempts at building a direct route through and under the Caucasus, but all were abandoned and it seems unlikely to be tried again. (Writer Fitzroy Maclean records how it used to be announced in Tbilisi that 'the train to the Soviet Union will leave from platform such-and-such...')

However, at the end of 2017 the new (and much delayed) BTK (Baku-Tbilisi-Kars) railway opened, linking Azerbaijan and Turkey via a new line from near Akhalkalaki to Kars (29km in Georgia and 76km in Turkey), with trains switching from the Russian broad gauge to the Turkish standard gauge at Akhalkalaki. Although three ten-carriage sets of passenger carriages (with first- and second-class sleepers and a dining car) have been delivered from Switzerland, there seems to be no great rush to start passenger services. This despite the line costing over a billion dollars (largely paid by Azerbaijan's state oil fund) and potentially carrying a million passengers a year as well as five million (and ultimately 17 million) tonnes of freight. More usefully, there are overnight trains from Baku and Yerevan to Tbilisi; both are run in the Russian style (although the carriages have been modernised), with *kupé* (KP) four-berth second-class compartments and *spalny vagon* (SV) two-berth first-class compartments; the Yerevan train also has *platskartny* third-class open couchettes. Travelling towards Tbilisi, you will be woken twice for lengthy passport checks; coming from Tbilisi you can get this out of the way earlier and get a decent night's sleep.

The train from **Baku (Azerbaijan) to Tbilisi** is liable to serious delays, with perhaps a couple of hours at the Georgian border post and the same at the Azeri border. Leaving Baku every night at 21.50, it takes around 14 hours for 550km, and fares start at about US$14. You can book online via w ticket.ady.az (unreliable, but now in English), but only for the train from Baku. Select the Baki–Tiflis train and either an 'SV' (first class) or 'KP' (second class) carriage or 'PL' (seated), then enter name and passport details before paying. Collect the ticket at the station at least an hour before departure – go to counter 22 with your passport and a printout of the booking confirmation email. From Tbilisi, you'll have to buy your ticket at the station (cash only); the train leaves at 19.30 daily and reaches Baku at 09.15. From Baku there's a weekly train to Moscow, taking 52 hours.

The train from **Yerevan (Armenia) to Tbilisi** takes about 10½ hours to cover 374km, but allow a bit more time for delays. From late September to mid-June it leaves Yerevan for Tbilisi at 21.30 on even dates, returning at 20.20 on odd dates. In summer it runs nightly and is extended to Batumi – it leaves Yerevan at 15.30 and arrives in Tbilisi at midnight and Batumi at 07.10; returning, it leaves Batumi at 15.35 and Tbilisi at 22.15, reaching Yerevan at 07.30. Women travelling alone have found it a frightening experience. One-way fares are between US$21 and US$45, depending on class; the best class, SV, can be a very civilised way to travel, if you're in no rush. There's even free Wi-Fi nowadays!

BY BUS
From Turkey Coming from Turkey, you're most likely to travel by bus (the rail link from Kars to Tbilisi via Akhalkalaki opened at the end of 2017 but still has a

2

limited passenger service). There are two main routes, along the Black Sea coast to Batumi, and by the Vale border crossing to Tbilisi; a less useful third crossing has opened at Çıldır in Javakheti.

There are many buses from Istanbul, Ankara and Turkey's Mediteranean coast direct to Batumi and Tbilisi, with drop-offs (and pick-ups heading towards Turkey) at roadside kiosks in Kobuleti, Samtredia, Kutaisi, Khashuri and Gori. You could also head for Trabzon (there are several buses an hour from Istanbul, taking 15–18 hours for the 1,110km journey and costing US$28–35; no-frills airlines are not usually much more expensive); from here buses run east to Hopa every half-hour, taking 3 hours to cover the 165km (*US$10*). From Trabzon Airport, just to the right outside the terminal, Havaş (w *havas.net*) operates frequent shuttle buses directly to Hopa, from where you can take a taxi to the border. There are a couple of decent hotels, and various fleapits, in Hopa, which is also served by one or two buses a day from Erzurum, which is 5 hours to the south and can be reached by the Doğu Ekspresi sleeper train, which leaves Ankara at 18.00 daily (with a high-speed connection from Istanbul at 13.30) and arrives at 14.00. The border crossing at Sarpi, another 20km to the northeast, is effectively a huge bazaar, and there's plenty of transport on both sides of the border northeast of Hopa. It costs US$2 in a minibus, US$4 by shared taxi or US$15 by private taxi from Hopa to Sarpi, and GEL0.80 (*US$0.50*) by minibus or GEL10 by taxi onwards to Batumi; remember to put your watch forward 2 hours. There are direct buses from Trabzon's Otogar to Batumi (and on to Tbilisi), as well as minibuses leaving from just outside from mid-morning onwards.

The **Vale route** is used by through buses from Istanbul and Ankara to Tbilisi (and on to Baku), costing US$25 from Ankara and US$40 from Istanbul (a 30hr marathon); these can be picked up at Ardahan, north of Kars. To reach the Vale crossing independently, take a train or bus to Kars, then (from the international bus station) a minibus to Posof (*4hrs*), and a taxi or minibus to the border (*30mins*) and finally a taxi to Akhaltsikhe (*30mins*). These are very comfortable air-conditioned, Turkish-built and Turkish-operated vehicles:

🚌 **Doğu Karadenizi Express** Dikmen Caddesi 29/37, Istanbul; ☎ +90 464 612 4253, 0850 840 0853; w dogukaradenizekspres.com.tr

🚌 **Jon Tur** Tbilisi: ☎ 322 722607; m 598 459210, 595 508189, 551 501411; e jontour2@gmail.com. Daily to Trabzon & Istanbul.

🚌 **Luks Karadeniz** Istanbul: ☎ +90 212 658 3453, 658 3353, call centre ☎ 444 0053; Tbilisi: ☎ 322 75 4179; m 599 552885, 555 442481; Kutaisi: ☎ 431 263170; m 555 577980, 555 578010; Batumi: m 593 931527, 577 780608, 593 951850; w lukskaradeniz.com. Daily at 10.30 to Istanbul & 18.00 Trabzon & Ankara.

🚌 **Mahmut Turizm** Emniyet Otoparkı No 5/C, Aksaray, Istanbul; ☎ +90 212 633 0220, 212 632 9979, 212 588 6555; Tbilisi: ☎ 32 275 2639; m 599 172263. Daily at 08.00 to Trabzon & Istanbul, also to Baku & Tehran.

🚌 **Mavi Karadeniz** Rize: ☎ +90 464 212 0905; Tbilisi: m 568 417070; e info@mavikaradenizliler.com

🚌 **Metro Turizm** tf 444 3455; m 577 788105; Istanbul: ☎ +90 212 658 3232; e info@metroturizm.com.tr; Trabzon: ☎ +90 462 325 7286, +90 462 325 7737; w metroturizm.com.tr. Perhaps the most comfortable buses; twice daily from Istanbul, Ankara & Trabzon to Tbilisi.

🚌 **Ulusoy** (Istanbul: at the Otogar, office 128; ☎ +90 212 658 3000/1; Inönü Caddesi 59, Taksim; tf +90 212 444 1888; Ankara: at the Otogar; ☎ +90 242 331 1310; Trabzon: ☎ +90 462 325 2201, 321 1281, 212 692 1777; e musteri@ulusoy.com.tr; w ulusoy.com.tr

🚌 **Vardar Turizm** Istanbul: ☎ +90 212 529 5451/7/9, 212 658 3350; w vardarturizm.com.tr

From Greece
Buses from Greece to Tbilisi (*US$80 from Thessaloniki/US$100 from Athens*) are run by the companies listed below. In Tbilisi, contact Almazidi

Tour, Athens Express, Borjomi Tour, Gomareti Tour (🔌 *275 2005;* m *593 645707;* e *gomareti17@mail.ru*), Irina Tour, Kakheti Tour, Nike Express (🔌 *275 3547, 230 5466;* m *597 554554*), Nugzari Tour (🔌 *275 3622*), Oktava Travel (🔌 *275 3471*) or Panagiotis Travel (🔌 *275 3315*), all at the Ortachala bus station, from where each operates a weekly bus.

🚌 **Elas Travel** Athens: 🔌 210 028 6268;
Thessaloniki: 🔌 231 522 5194
🚌 **Kakheti Tur** Athens: 🔌 210 522 4410;
Thessaloniki: 🔌 231 055 1145
🚌 **Manglisi Turi** Thessaloniki): 🔌 231 050 0702

🚌 **Nugzari Tours** Athens 🔌 210 523 3205;
Thessaloniki: 🔌 231 023 9080; Tbilisi: 🔌 322 275
3622
🚌 **Oktavi Travel** Thessaloniki: 🔌 231 023 3964,
231 056 6445; Tbilisi: 🔌 322 275 3471

From Armenia
There are also minibuses and shared taxis between Yerevan (Armenia) and Tbilisi, as well as a train (page 63). Marshrutkas leave Yerevan's Central Bus Station on Admiral Isahakov Avenue every 50 minutes and take 5–7 hours, costing US$20. You can also wait until a shared taxi is full; this will take 5–6 hours and cost about US$35, as long as all four seats are taken. There are also buses from Yerevan's railway station that leave whenever they're full.

A few buses run from Vanadzor and Gyumri (in Armenia) to Tbilisi. There's also a daily marshrutka from Yerevan to Akhalkalaki taking 8 hours (*US$7*), continuing three times a week in summer to Batumi and taking 15 hours (*US$25*). Take your own food and drink.

From Azerbaijan
From Baku to Tbilisi there's less traffic so you're less likely to find a taxi; the train is slower and more erratic than the Yerevan service. There are a few buses (*US$15*), mostly overnight: these leave the Autovoksal (near the 20 Januari metro station) between 20.00 and 22.00, taking 8 hours plus an hour or two at the border. In Tbilisi, contact Next Trans (m *599 670367, 597 785595*). See box, page 340 for the more scenic route via Lagodekhi and Shekhi.

From the Russian Federation
Finally there are also buses, marshrutkas and shared taxis via Kazbegi between Tbilisi (Didube and Ortachala) and Mineralni Vodi in the Russian Federation, some of them continuing all the way to Moscow (*US$60*).

🚌 **Mimino Trans** Tbilisi: m 599 685005;
Krasnodar: m + 7995 210 5050; Rostov:
m + 7918 513 4455; e miminotrans.kr@mail.ru

BY SEA Another option is to arrive by ship; with the completion of new docks, train–ferry services were introduced in 1999 from Varna (Bulgaria) and Chornomorsk (formerly Ilyichevsk, Ukraine) via Constanţa (Romania) to Batumi and Poti, also carrying cars, trucks and passengers. The route is served by the *Greifswald*, a large and comfortable ferry; built in Germany in 1988, it carries trucks and railway wagons and has a restaurant, non-smoking lounge, playroom and conference room, as well as a swimming pool and sauna. There's a weekly circuit, leaving Chornomorsk on Thursday morning and Constanţa on Thursday night and returning from Georgia on Sunday, so that it takes around 60 hours from Chornomorsk to Batumi via Constanţa but only 40 hours for the direct return. Tickets can be booked through **Ukrferry-Tour** (*Sabanskyy Lane 4A, Odessa 65014;* 🔌 *+380 482 347663/344059;* e *ukf@ukrferry.com;* w *ukrferry.com*). In Georgia book through **UBG-Agency**, which has offices in Tbilisi (*Kazbegi Av 12A;* ↘*322 223987;* e *agency@uga.ge*), Batumi (*Kutaisi 34;* ↘ *422 274119;* e *ugagencybatumi@gmail. com*) and Poti (*Gegidze 20/1;* ↘*493 221998;* m *599 915696;* e *ugagencypoti@gmail. com*). Fares start from US$110 per person in a four-berth cabin, including three meals; a car costs US$300.

Ferries (usually 'Kometa' hydrofoils, taking 6 hours) run from Sochi (in Russia, just beyond the border with Abkhazia) to Batumi: contact **Batumi Express** (*Batumi:* m *593 333966; Sochi:* ↘*+7 918 409 1296*).

Finally, if you need to send goods or equipment to Georgia, your best bet is either the Belgian company **Nomad Express** (*Belcrownlaan 23, 2100 Deurne;* ↘*+32 3 360 5500;* w *gosselingroup.eu; Georgia: Mirian Mephe 36, Didi Dighomi, Tbilisi;* ↘ *32 259 6600-3;* e *georgia@gosselingroup.eu;* w *gosselinmobility.eu*), or **Georgian Express** (*Davit Agmashenebelis 46, 0102 Tbilisi;* ↘ *32 294 0770;* e *tbilisi@georgia-express.com, georgiaexpress1@yahoo.com;* w *georgia-express.com*).

HEALTH   *with Dr Felicity Nicholson*

Reform and privatisation of Georgia's corrupt and run-down health service began in 1995; a state medical insurance company and 12 health funds were funded by a payroll tax of 3% on employers and 1% on employees. After the Rose Revolution any social safety net was abolished, so that those who could not afford insurance were sometimes forced to sell their homes; now there is state-backed insurance for all. In addition the abolition of the prescription system turned out to be a liberalisation too far, and it has been re-introduced. The health service is improving as the economy grows, and the share of GDP spent on health has risen from under 1% to just over 10%. Although British citizens are covered by a reciprocal agreement and need only proof of UK residence (ie: UK passport) for free treatment, they will still have to pay cash for drugs and many other services; as a rule US health insurance is not valid in Georgia without paying a substantial premium. Treatment is expensive (US$600 for a hernia operation). Embassies have lists of good English-speaking doctors in Tbilisi.

Pharmacies (*aptiaki* in Georgian) are plentiful and easy to find, and many are, in theory, open 24 hours. The Aversi, GPC and PSP chains have modern shops in many towns and all over Tbilisi – these show their names in Latin script, while others will at least have an *Apotheka* sign. You should expect generic drugs, but if you bring in an empty packet of whatever medicine you're looking for or name the main ingredient, the pharmacists will usually find a generic for you.

BEFORE YOU GO   You are advised to be up to date with vaccinations against tetanus, diphtheria and polio, now available as an all-in-one ten-year vaccine (Revaxis). You should also be covered for hepatitis A and very occasionally typhoid for longer trips and more rural travel. Other vaccines that may be advised include a course of hepatitis B and rabies vaccine. Hepatitis B vaccination is essential if you will be working in a medical capacity and is usually recommended when working with children. Having the pre-exposure rabies jab is particularly important as there's a shortage of the rabies immunoglobulin used for treatment following bites, scratches or even licks from any warm-blooded mammal. The courses for rabies and hepatitis B comprise three injections over a minimum of 21 days (for hepatitis B you need to be 16 or over for this super-accelerated course), so you should go to see your GP or travel clinic specialist well in advance of your trip. Tuberculosis (TB) is common in Georgia with ≥40 cases per 100,000 population (Travel Health Pro,

2018). The disease is spread through close contact with infected sputum or through eating unpasteurised dairy products. Vaccination may be considered for those under 16 who are living or working with the local population for three months or more. Tuberculin-negative individuals under 35 years of age should be considered for vaccinating if they are at risk through their occupation. The vaccine becomes less effective with age, so vaccinating people over the age of 35 is considered only if they are at very high risk of disease.

TRAVEL CLINICS AND HEALTH INFORMATION A full list of current travel clinic websites worldwide is available on w istm.org. For other journey preparation information, consult w travelhealthpro.org.uk (UK) or w wwwnc.cdc.gov/travel (USA). Information about various medications may be found on w netdoctor. co.uk/travel. All advice found online should be used in conjunction with expert advice received prior to or during travel. See page 129 for pharmacies in Tbilisi.

HEALTH HAZARDS
Tick-borne encephalitis Human cases of tick-borne encephalitis (TBE) in Georgia are unknown, but there is some evidence of possible risk. Vaccination with TBE vaccine is not recommended, but all attempts to avoid tick bites should be employed. Ticks are most active between early spring and late summer and are prevalent in parks, meadows and forested areas. Avoiding unpasteurised dairy products is also recommended. See also box, page 68.

Malaria There is a very low risk of malaria in Georgia from June to October in the rural southeastern part of the country beyond Sighnaghi and Davit-Gareja. Taking malaria prophylaxis is not routinely recommended for most travellers. A small subset of travellers who have significant underlying health problems may be advised to take malaria tablets. There is no malaria in the rest of the country. Malaria is transmitted by mosquitoes that emerge from dusk until dawn. It is sensible to use insect repellents that contain DEET (around 50%) or Icaradin (20%), wear trousers and long-sleeved tops, and ensure that your accommodation is as mosquito-proof as possible when travelling in these remote areas.

HIV/AIDS HIV does not seem to have been a big problem here so far (unlike in Russia); by the end of 2017 there had officially been 7,266 cases (of whom 1,201 had died), but the number of reported cases is rising every year. Transmission is slightly more likely to be through sexual contact than through infected syringes. Occasionally immigrants or long-term expats may be asked for proof that they are free from HIV infection. Check whether you need this when applying for visas or work permits.

Rabies Rabies risk exists in Georgia, especially in rural areas. Rabies is carried by any mammal and is passed on to humans through a bite, scratch or even a lick on intact skin. You must always assume any animal is rabid, and seek medical help as soon as possible. Meanwhile scrub the wound with soap under a running tap or while pouring water from a jug for about 15 minutes. Find a reasonably clear-looking source of water (but at this stage the quality of the water is not important), then clean with an antiseptic. This helps stop the rabies virus entering the body and will guard against wound infections, including tetanus.

Pre-exposure vaccinations are advised for everyone, but are particularly important if you intend to have contact with animals and/or are likely to be more than 24 hours

Ticks should ideally be removed complete, and as soon as possible, to reduce the chance of infection. You can use special tick tweezers, which can be bought in good travel shops, or failing this with your finger nails, grasping the tick as close to your body as possible, and pulling it away steadily and firmly at right angles to your skin without jerking or twisting. If possible, douse the wound with alcohol (any spirit will do) or iodine. Irritants (eg: Olbas oil) or lit cigarettes are to be discouraged since they can cause the tick to regurgitate and therefore increase the risk of disease. If you are travelling with small children, remember to check their heads, and particularly behind the ears, for ticks. Spreading redness around the bite and/or fever and/or aching joints after a tick bite imply that you have an infection that requires antibiotic treatment. In this case seek medical advice.

away from medical help. Ideally three doses should be taken over a minimum of 21 days. Contrary to popular belief, these vaccinations are relatively painless.

If you are bitten, scratched or licked by any mammal, then post-exposure prophylaxis should be given as soon as possible, though it is never too late to seek help, as the incubation period for rabies can be very long. Those who have not been immunised will need a full course of injections and a blood product called rabies immunoglobulin (RIG). This product is expensive (at least US$800 and possibly more) and may be hard to come by. However, if you have had the pre-exposure course then you need only two doses of vaccine which makes it very much easier to manage – another reason why pre-exposure vaccination should be encouraged. Even having one dose of rabies vaccine can be helpful if time is short.

Tell the doctor if you have had the pre-exposure vaccine, as this should change the treatment you receive. And remember that, if you do contract rabies, mortality is 100%, and death from rabies is probably one of the worst ways to go.

Altitude Most people will not have major problems with altitude below 2,500m unless they have underlying health problems, but parts of Georgia are above 2,500m and so time is needed to acclimatise to the lower levels of oxygen. A general rule of thumb is once you are over 3,000m, do not sleep more than 300m higher than the day before. You can climb higher during the day as long as you come down again to sleep. A rest day every two to three days also helps. If acclimatisation is inadequate then High Altitude Illness (HAI) can develop. There is an excellent booklet that can be downloaded free of charge from w medex.org.uk which explains what happens to your body at altitude, the symptoms of altitude illness and what to do to avoid it.

Dentistry Some dental treatment should be provided free under the UK's reciprocal agreement, but be sure to find a good English-speaking dentist.

Drinking water It is always advisable to drink bottled water and to clean your teeth with bottled water to minimise the risks of an upset stomach. Meat and other foodstuffs are usually safe as long as they have been properly cooked. Care should be taken over milk and other milk products if there is doubt as to whether it has been pasteurised (see risk of TB, pages 66–7, and possibly tick-borne encephalitis, page 67). About a third of the former Soviet Union's spas are in Georgia, and it's easy to find mineral waters such as Borjomi, Bakhmaro, Likani, Sno and Nakhalakhevi.

Smoking More likely health hazards include passive smoking and car crashes. Georgia has among the highest levels of tobacco use in the world, with most men (except monks) seeming to smoke most of the time, as well as 28% of pregnant women and 35% of breast-feeding women. Around nine billion cigarettes are consumed every year in Georgia, 2,200 per capita, against a world average of 1,600 per capita, and the 11,000 smoking-related deaths per year account for about 10% of mortality. Men now live a surprisingly long time but are generally in poor health. The excise on tobacco is relatively high at GEL0.90 per pack (three times Russia's) so 60–70% of the market is contraband; but tax is even higher in Turkey, so cigarettes are also smuggled there from Georgia. When the Ministry of Health tried a poster campaign in Tbilisi, all the billboard sites were bought up at once by Philip Morris, manufacturers of Marlboro cigarettes.

In 2005 smoking was banned in public places (including the metro, theatres and parliament); from May 2018 smoking (including e-cigarettes) will be banned in all enclosed spaces except homes, prisons and casinos, and from 2020 in sports stadiums. However it will for some reason still be allowed in taxis.

Drugs Until recently Georgia's anti-narcotic laws were very strict – anyone caught with cannabis twice in 12 months faced up to 14 years in prison; more than 300,000 people have been forced to take urine tests over the past seven years, triggering widespread protests. However, in November 2017 the constitutional court effectively decriminalised possession of the drug, over-ruling opposition from the governing party and the Orthodox Church, and you can now carry enough for personal use.

Other dangers There's apparently been a rise in thyroid gland illnesses in western Georgia, which may be linked to strontium from Chernobyl.

SAFETY

Georgia is a very safe country, still with too few tourists for them to be targeted by thieves. **Abkhazia**, which has effectively seceded, is more problematic, and with no diplomatic representation you are very much on your own there if you get into trouble. The bordering area around Zugdidi is also considered to be risky. **South Ossetia** is closed to tourists, and crime levels are higher than elsewhere here too, partly due to the wide availability of guns; the same used to apply to Svaneti, where unwary tourists were almost routinely robbed until a few years ago, but this is now as safe as anywhere else in the country. Tusheti, Pankisi and Khevsureti are also safe – they were closed to tourists due to the Chechen war but there's no problem now. In **Tbilisi**, you should take the same commonsense precautions as in any other big city.

There's little public drunkenness in Georgia, and there are usually plenty of people on the streets, even late at night; there is some pickpocketing, particularly in the metro, but few other problems. The days of Kalashnikov-toting Mkhedrioni (political gangsters) running the whole country as one big protection racket are long gone!

The **police force** used to be incompetent and corrupt, but after the Rose Revolution it was reformed and properly paid at last, and its popularity rose from 2% to 75% in polls. In particular, the new 'patrol police' (who deal with traffic and who should salute you when they pull your car over) have a good reputation – but the 'balaclava police' (part of the Security Ministry), who staged dramatic raids on tax dodgers and the like, often with television cameras in attendance, were seen as out of control under Saakashvili. In fact, there now seem to be too many patrol police, not doing much apart from driving around in new cars with red and blue lights flashing pointlessly and loudspeakers telling stopped drivers to move on, but doing nothing about seat belts, mobile phones, red-light jumping, speeding or dangerous driving in general (see below).

The US embassy has useful, if over-cautious, **advice online** (w *travel.state.gov/ content/passports/english/country/georgia.html*). Since 2012, there's now only one **emergency phone number** (✆ *112*).

ACCIDENTS Accidental death rates are surprisingly low in Georgia, less than half the rates in Russia and the Baltic States. This is undoubtedly linked to the low rates of vodka consumption. The Russian response to economic collapse in 2014 was to cut vodka prices, as in previous crises. Even in 2012, 30% of all deaths in Russia were alcohol-related deaths, four times the rate in Georgia.

DRIVING AND ROAD SAFETY Given the undisciplined and excessively macho approach to driving, the constant use of mobile/cell phones, and the refusal to wear seat belts properly (many Georgian drivers sit on the lap-strap), it's not surprising that the death toll is high on Georgia's roads. Often drivers on both sides of the road will attempt to overtake at the same time, making a two-lane road into a three-lane one, with inevitable consequences. They also drive on the horn, not the brake, as it's always the other guy who is wrong or incompetent. Pedestrians are at risk too, as drivers assume they'll get out of the way – bad luck if your sight or hearing isn't too good. There are lots of three-legged dogs, as a warning to you. The level of tolerance for dangerous driving is ridiculous, and the death toll is rising – from 514 in 2013 to 581 in 2016. Roughly half the deaths are linked to alcohol, but **drink-driving** is finally being taken seriously by the police, and smart cameras are being introduced in major cities to tackle speeding, red-light jumping and other traffic offences.

Speeding is also a major factor, and there's a US$100 fine for those unlucky enough to be caught out – but in 2014 the fee for non-payment of traffic fines was cut from US$186 to US$56; if this isn't paid a driver now loses his/her licence for just six months, rather than for two years (as before), or can pay US$186 to get the licence back. In mountain regions such as Svaneti very few people take driving tests at all.

Only 10% of Georgia's 1.2 million cars are under ten years old, and 44% are over twenty years old; in addition to pumping out noxious fumes, these are of course less than totally safe; mandatory technical inspection of vehicles was abolished in 2004; a new Road Safety Law should have restored it from 2013, but this was delayed until January 2018. Every day 170 cars enter Georgia on average, 77% of them over ten years old – the import duty on cars up to four years old has now been cut in an effort to bring down the average age of the country's vehicles. In addition there are now much higher duties on right-hand-drive cars (imported second hand from Britain, Ireland and Japan), of which there are far too many on the roads, given the Georgian driver's imperative need to overtake all the time.

WOMEN IN GEORGIA

Sexism in Georgia is as bad as anywhere in the world, but as a rule foreign women see only the positive, chivalrous side of the Georgian male's world-view. In smaller towns and villages you may notice some stares and comments, but much less so than in neighbouring countries. There are some notable female politicians, notably Justice Minister Tea Tsulukiani, and three former foreign ministers, Tamar Beruchashvili, Salome Zourabichvili and Maia Panjikidze, and 39% of Georgia's judges are women.

Nevertheless, the proportion of women in parliament has fallen considerably from 30% in Soviet times, hitting a low of 5% in 2008 before recovering to 12% in 2016. In 2016 just 1.6% of local councillors were women, and not a single mayor. According to UN research, one in 11 married women in Georgia has been subjected to domestic violence; but the real number could be much higher as victims rarely speak out. Three-quarters of Georgian women believe domestic violence is a private matter and should remain within the family, and police refuse to get involved.

In 2016 videos were leaked on YouTube showing married female politicians (government and opposition) apparently having sex with men who were not their husbands, accompanied by threats against four others to release further videos unless they resigned. One of these was an unmarried TV journalist who declared on air: 'I am Inga Grigolia, a woman, daughter, mother, and friend. I have a wonderful boyfriend, I have sex, and I plan to continue to live the way I live.' There was a lot of public support for the victims, and increasing awareness of the huge difference in sexual standards between men and women. There were five arrests, but it's clear that not all the videos made illegally by Saakashvili's secret police were destroyed as promised after Georgian Dream came to power.

Men may actually have a bit of a raw deal (it's not fair that when they dress in black they're said to look like gangsters while women in black are said to look like Medea) – but they've foolishly kept the bad jobs for themselves (manual labour, driving trucks and so on), as well as the mind-rotting ones like sitting around smoking in hotel lobbies, supposedly supervising or providing security, so it's no surprise that women are getting ahead, especially in public service.

LGBT TRAVELLERS

Despite the fact that discrimination against LGBT people is illegal, homosexuality is still viewed as a major deviation from Orthodox Christian values in Georgia – the Church itself is very anti-gay and priests have led violent protests against gay pride marches. In a 2017 survey, Georgia was rated as the world's third-most homophobic country, with 93% of Georgians saying they would object to having a gay neighbour. In October 2017 there were protests against Guram Kashia, captain of Georgia's soccer team (who plays for Vitesse Arnhem), wearing an LGBTQ armband as part of a Dutch Football Union pro-diversity campaign – but the same month the first openly gay candidate stood for Tbilisi's city council (although she wasn't elected).

INFORMATION FOR TRAVELLERS WITH A DISABILITY

The UK's **gov.uk** website (w *gov.uk/guidance/foreign-travel-for-disabled-people*) provides general advice and practical information for travellers with disabilities preparing for overseas travel. **Accessible Journeys** (w *disabilitytravel.com*) is a comprehensive US site written by wheelchair users who have been researching wheelchair-accessible travel full-time since 1985. There are many tips and useful contacts (including lists of travel agents on request) for slow walkers, wheelchair travellers and their families, plus informative articles, including pieces on disabled travelling worldwide. The company also organises group tours. Global Access News (w *globalaccessnews.com/index.htm*) provides general travel information, reviews and tips for travelling with a disability. The **Society for Accessible Travel and Hospitality** (w *sath.org*) also provides some general information.

As you might expect, attitudes are changing faster in the capital than elsewhere – thanks to dating apps such as Grindr and Tinder, and inclusive nightclubs such as Bassiani, gay people there can now be much more open and confident in their identity. Recent changes in legislation are due more to pro-Western alignment rather than any real buy-in by politicians. Nevertheless, there are a small number of pro-gay bars in Tbilisi, such as Success [104 C4] (*Vashlovani 3;* ↘ *32 299 8230*), Café Gallery [104 D5] (*Griboedov 34;* ↘ *32 299 5747*), Salve [112 C2] (*Leselidze 25;* m *591 692727*) and Divan [112 B3] (*Tabidze 3/5;* m *599 018884;* f *divantbilisi*). It is also normal for two men or women to share a room with each other.

WHAT TO TAKE

Given the risk of power cuts, although they're not so common these days, it's sensible to bring a torch (flashlight) or candles. In addition, it's wise to have some toilet paper and your own soap or shower gel, and pens can be hard to find; a sheet sleeping bag may be a comfort in some hostels. You should also consider bringing presents for people you stay with (page 89).

MONEY

The unit of **currency** is the lari (GEL), which is divided into 100 tetri. The lari derives its name from the Latin *libra* or scales, while tetri simply means 'white'.

Banking hours are from 09.30 to 17.30 Monday to Friday. The main banks will change travellers' cheques, although they are choosy and erratic in the brands they accept; Thomas Cook and American Express are the most widely accepted. You should also bring some cash US dollars or euros (carried in a money belt or some other secure place). Sterling can only be changed in a few places in Tbilisi and Batumi (and only at poor rates). Russian, Armenian, Azeri and Turkish cash can be exchanged in a few places in Tbilisi and Batumi and near the border crossings, but other currencies are of little use. It's far easier to exchange cash than travellers' cheques, with exchange counters all over the place, especially around markets and bus stations.

ATMs can now be found in all cities and most towns (not necessarily at the actual bank offices); they are safe and reliable and the obvious way to fund your travels. You don't have to take your card back before receiving your cash, so don't forget it; in some machines you actually have to press 'Cancel' for it to be returned. Don't confuse ATMs with the Pay Boxes found in the streets everywhere for paying bills and topping up mobile phones and metro cards. Visa and MasterCard are accepted by the more expensive hotels, restaurants and supermarkets.

Western Union (w *westernunion.com*) and MoneyGram (w *moneygram.com*) have lots of agents in Georgia, all prominently signed, so it's easy but expensive to have money sent to you from abroad.

TYPICAL PRICES

1-litre bottle of water	£0.50	Meal: cheap	£2–4
Bottle of wine	£4	Meal: mid-range	£15+
Fuel		Museum entry	£3–6
petrol	£0.60/litre	Public transport	
diesel	£0.60–0.70/litre	city bus	£0.20
Loaf of bread	£0.25	city taxi	£2

BUDGETING

Costs are generally low. In restaurants, cafés and taxis, it's normal to tip by rounding up the total rather than by adding a percentage. It's usual to haggle in markets, where you can get up to 30% off (not for food).

GETTING AROUND

The main mode of public transport is the marshrutka, or minibus. Shared taxis are also available (faster and more expensive, but not vastly more dangerous than a marshrutka, as a rule), usually waiting outside bus stations, for instance at Telavi. Hitching is also possible, sometimes with a small payment expected, but rapes have been reported.

BY BUS Marshrutkas used to leave only when full (to bursting) but most routes now have a regular hourly service; there are more frequent departures between major towns, and at least one or two a day to most villages. These use fairly substantial bus stations in cities, while smaller places may just have a yard by the railway station or in the centre of town. Departure bays will show the destinations in Georgian, but if you look at the rear of this sign you may find the same information in Cyrillic or even Latin script. Comfortable modern buses (some overnight) run from Tbilisi to Kutaisi, Batumi and Zugdidi. The last bus from a town to a nearby village often leaves at about 17.00 or earlier, and the last service inbound to town may well be even earlier. Fares are generally about GEL1 per 20km, eg: GEL8 from Tbilisi to Lagodekhi, GEL18 from Tbilisi to Batumi or GEL10 from Kutaisi to Batumi.

Any bus or marshrutka with spare space (which doesn't necessarily mean a seat) will stop for anyone who flags it down; this can be tricky as it's hard to read the destination boards (only rarely in Cyrillic or Latin script as well as Georgian) until the last moment. Therefore (once you've learnt to read 'Tbilisi') heading towards the capital is an easier business than heading away from it! In most cases you'll pay as you get off at the front of the bus, so you should remember the name of the place where you boarded. If you have a ticket you may be expected to hand it in as you get off.

CITY TRANSPORT City transport is also mainly by bus and marshrutka, although there's a metro in Tbilisi. City buses take a long time at each stop; drivers won't open the rear doors (for boarding) until everyone has got off (and paid) at the front, but even so some people always wait to slip off at the rear, or to board at the front. Nevertheless, the buses will get you to your destination in the end, and they are very cheap. There are also plenty of semi-official taxis, without meters.

BY CAR Driving can take a bit of getting used to, given the poor state of minor roads and the excessive urgency of the other drivers. The cost of a car with driver is not high, so this may be the easiest solution; in Tbilisi it's easy to hire a taxi (including 4x4 vehicles) at the Didube bus station. You'll pay about US$40 a day for a car with driver in Tbilisi, and US$60 a day outside Tbilisi (plus fuel, and food and accommodation for the driver). The only major international car-hire chains represented in Tbilisi are Avis, Budget, Europcar, Hertz and Sixt (page 102), with cars costing from US$50/day, plus insurance waivers, etc. A licence from almost any of the developed Western countries is valid in Georgia. Speed limits range from 50km/hour in cities to 110km/hour on highways, although these are universally ignored.

Contrary to general belief, Georgians are not totally lunatic drivers. They have some concern for life and limb, and perhaps more for their vehicles, skirting very carefully around speed-ramps and pot-holes and taking bends at fairly reasonable speed. Problems arise with laws and signals, which are widely ignored, and in relation to other cars (page 70). Fuel costs around GEL2/litre for normal, GEL2.20/litre for super and GEL2–2.20/litre for diesel; lead-free fuel is widely available now. Fuel pumps are not usually self-service; Georgians use loyalty cards but still pay cash, usually taking only about GEL20's worth of fuel at a time.

Distances are not great: by road it's about 85km from Tbilisi to Gori, 128km to Khashuri, 230km to Kutaisi and 384km to Batumi (349km by rail). A new highway is opening in sections from east to west, with a temporary gap through the mountains between Khashuri and Zestaponi – the Imereti Bypass section has reduced journey times by up to an hour, but means that one can no longer assume that all marshrutkas will go via Kutaisi.

BY RAIL There has been a remarkable revival of Georgia's railways, making it the safest and most pleasant option for tourists travelling to the west of the country. The tracks were previously neglected and pounded by heavy trains transporting oil from Baku, but now the pipelines are open and new passenger trains have been introduced, in addition to the long-distance overnight trains – although there are still enough oil trains to cause delays. The main line from Tbilisi to Samtredia is almost all double-track, and all Georgia's railways are electrified, though at one time power cuts were causing US$30,000 of damage a month to delicate traction equipment, and causing oil trains to take an average of 35 hours from Baku to Batumi instead of the scheduled 21 hours. Now, new day trains link Tbilisi with Batumi (*5hrs*), Poti (*4hrs 50mins*), Ozurgeti (*8hrs 10mins*) and Zugdidi (*5hrs 25mins*).

Modern double-deck electric trains were ordered from Swiss company Stadler for Moscow's airport express, but owing to a fall in the rouble they couldn't afford them all, so the Georgia and Azerbaijan railways made an offer that Stadler couldn't refuse; now four of them are in Georgia, operating two daily non-stop services each way between Tbilisi and Batumi. Unfortunately there's a very poor service to Kutaisi, the country's second city, which is bypassed by the main line; you can use Rioni station, just south, as a sort of parkway station. In 2018, supposedly, a new station is due to open at Kutaisi Airport, with all mainline trains diverting to call there; this will also help passengers trying to reach Kutaisi from the west. The overnight train from Tbilisi to Zugdidi is one that is particularly worth considering: for the same price as being crammed in a minibus for a day (*currently GEL18*), you can enjoy a comfortable berth with clean sheets and good service, although the day train is also a good option.

The ticket offices are computerised, so you can go to any window, but allow time for your passport details to be typed in. The Georgian Railways website (**w** *railway. ge*) is adequate for checking schedules (in English – 'Online tickets' then 'Schedule'), but to buy tickets online it's better to use **w** tkt.ge/en/Railway or **w** biletebi.ge/startup.aspx?id=90, where you can register with Facebook and use foreign credit cards. There's no need to print your e-ticket: you can simply show the reference number and your passport to board the train. The day trains have second- (perfectly adequate) and first-class seating, while there are three classes of accommodation on the night trains: *platzkart* is a hard seat, *coupé* is a four-bed compartment, and *spalny vagon* (SV or *esveh*) is a two-bed compartment.

BY AIR Domestic flights to Batumi, Mestia, and Ambrolauri are operated by Service Air and booked through Vanilla Sky (page 266). They use the Natakhtari airfield just north of Mskheta, off the Georgian Military Highway.

Having toured throughout North America, Asia, Europe and Australia, I am convinced that there is no place on the planet as well suited for bicycle touring as Georgia. Georgians are the world's most hospitable people and there is no better way to be embraced by that hospitality than to arrive on a bicycle. Unlike any other method of travel, if you arrive as a 'velotourist' you will immediately command both curiosity and respect, and you will be welcomed with consistently open arms. We literally had multiple people grabbing us, pulling in different directions, begging us to stay with them – not for financial gain, but out of a genuine spirit of hospitality. It is awesome and will deeply influence the way you deal with guests for the rest of your life. In addition, Georgian food is amazing, a joyous celebration of life itself.

Georgia has a unique history that makes it a fascinating place to travel. This history is alive at every corner, discussed at every table, a veritable feast for the mind as much as food is for the belly, hospitality for the soul and scenery for the eyes. Now is an excellent time to travel before it is forever changed by the inevitable throngs of Western tourists.

Nevertheless, Georgia is not for the faint of heart. Though the human spirit is thriving, the infrastructure is not and the roads are often bad while there's far too much fast traffic. Bring all of your own gear, tools and spare parts.

ADDRESSES Many street names were changed after independence, as communist figures such as Lenin went of fashion; new signs have replaced worn and faded old ones, but these may only be in Georgian whereas the old ones were also in Cyrillic script. Some towns have signs with Latin script too, but elsewhere this may indicate there's a guesthouse or embassy on the street. In any case many people, especially taxi drivers, are more likely to recognise the old names than the current official ones. There are also grammatical differences between Georgian and Russian even where the names have survived unchanged. Likewise, streets named after people often have an 's' tacked on the end in Georgian. It's worth noting that street names are often shown not at the street corners but on house numbers, and many city buildings are very long, so that you may be told to go to, for example, No 20, third entrance (or even third building); you may also be given a floor to go to (the ground floor counts as the first) as well as an apartment or office number. Six-digit Soviet postcodes beginning with 38 have been replaced with four-digit ones.

Out of town, places are located with reference to the kilometre signs along most roads; these count from both ends of the road (eg: km2/154), so that the total on the two sides always adds up to the total distance (eg: 156km). Remember that 'street' is *kucha*, 'avenue' is *gamziri* and 'square' is *moedani*.

ACCOMMODATION

For a long time, finding somewhere to sleep was difficult outside Tbilisi; many of the older Soviet-period hotels were used to accommodate Georgian refugees from Abkhazia. Thankfully, there are now many new, better hotels, especially in Tbilisi. In any case this problem gave Georgia the chance to start again on a small-scale sustainable basis, with family homes opening as simple homestays. With a bit of improvement, above all in the bathroom area, many have become decent guesthouses. Many are well up to European standards, while those in remoter areas such as Svaneti and Tusheti are more basic, although this is compensated for by the ambience. Increasingly they're not bothering with websites, and using Facebook, booking.com, hostelworld.com and airBnB instead.

There are plenty of guesthouses in Tbilisi, but these evolved as upmarket abodes for businesspeople and official visitors. Some really are luxurious, and some might appear amazingly pricey for a country in which the standard of living is still low. Until recently there were few affordable alternatives, but in the last decade plenty of hostels and mid-range hotels have emerged to fill the gap. In hotels a single room often has a double bed, and you may just be able to pay a bit more for a second breakfast; but a double room often has twin single beds.

Details of local guesthouses can usually be obtained from tourist information centres. Otherwise two organisations are trying to coordinate and list rural homestays: **Elkana** has three offices (*Gazapkhuli 16, 0177 Tbilisi;* \ *32 536 486/7;* e *ruraltourism@elkana.org.ge,* w *ruraltourism.ge; Shalva Akhaltsikheli 9, Akhaltsikhe;* \ *790 506776;* e *farezi@elkana.org.ge, rop@elkana.org.ge; Guria* \ *790 536487;* e *guria@elkana.org.ge*); and the **Georgian Tourism Association** has an office in Tbilisi (*Melikishvili 18/II, 0179;* \ *32 220 195;* m *577 734686;* w *tourism-association.ge/guesthouses*). See also w *davisvenot.ge.* Houses in beach/spa villages often have signs offering *komnati* or *sdaetsya* ('rooms' in Russian). If in doubt, you can simply ask a taxi driver or policeman if he knows anyone who has a room free; in villages you'll never be allowed to go without a bed. Georgian hospitality is renowned, and you'll usually find liberal amounts of alcohol included in the cost of a homestay, as well as food. Although hotel beds can be absurdly soft, in homes they're usually firm enough, and washing facilities, which are quite clean in hotels, tend to be even more so in homes. Most hotels include value-added tax of 20% in their rates, but it's worth checking; smaller ones and guesthouses don't pay it.

EATING AND DRINKING

Georgian cuisine is far closer to that of Turkey and Iran than that of Russia, with plenty of garlic, walnuts, cumin and coriander; huge feasts are traditional, though not as huge as in the Brezhnev years, when food was absurdly cheap. Meat is central, but a Georgian meal is served with many dishes (many cold), including vegetable ones, on the table at once and everyone helping themselves to whatever they want (so the concept of pairing specific wines and foods doesn't work here). Menus are rarely displayed outside restaurants, especially in English, and dishes come as and when – don't expect a flight of orders to arrive simultaneously. It's best to pace yourself, as it's likely to be a long evening with plenty of wine. In Tbilisi there are fast-food joints selling *shwarma* (kebabs), burgers, hot dogs and a poor approximation to pizza. Cafés everywhere sell *khachapuri* (pages 78–9) and other traditional snacks. Street traders sell *marozhni* (ice cream) and *semichki*, the sunflower seeds which are chewed and spat out everywhere, and probably use more energy than they provide. Those who would like to try their hand at reproducing some of the dishes they enjoyed in Georgia will find a wealth of inspiring and knowledgeable food and wine bloggers discovering Georgia.

MEAT AND FISH Traditional meat dishes include *kharcho* (a spicy soup of mutton or beef with garlic, rice and vegetables, also with walnuts in Mingrelia); *jigari* (a stew of liver, heart, kidney, onion and parsley); *ostri* (a stew of beef, tomato and onion); *chakapuli* (a stew of lamb, scallions and greens in their own juices with tarragon and plum sauce); *chakhokhbili* (a drier but equally tasty stew, originally of pheasant, but now usually chicken, with herbs, diced tomatoes, red pepper, garlic and onion); *kupati* (kidney stuffed with minced meat and spices); *ojakhuri* (pork, potatoes, onion and garlic, often swimming in fat); *chanakhi* (lamb with tomatoes, greens, garlic and green peppers); and *abkhazuri* (an Abkhazian meat purée with onion, garlic, pomegranate, herbs and spices).

Chicken is also used, in the form of: *satsivi*, pieces of chicken (or turkey) in a sauce of walnut, cornflower, garlic and saffron (a traditional New Year dish); *tabaka*, pressed fried chicken; *chikhirtma*, chicken soup with egg; and *shkmeruli*, roast chicken in garlic sauce. *Mtsvadi*, pork or mutton skewered and grilled on a vinewood fire (also known as *shashlik*), is very popular for outdoor feasts; *kebab* means meat patties grilled on a barbecue, while *shwarma* (döner kebab) is standard fast-food fare. *Basturma* (ie: pastrami, as used in New York delis) is air-dried pressed mutton. *Tolma* is the same as Turkish dolma, cabbage leaves stuffed with minced beef, rice, spices and herbs. *Chanakhi, shkmeruli, lobiani* and *ojakhuri* are usually cooked and presented in a clay pot (*ketsi*), as are mushrooms. Fish, usually with dill, is also popular, notably sturgeon and trout, such as *kefalia*, small fried trout from the mountains of Adjara. A true Georgian speciality, *khinkhali* are envelopes of dough (like little money bags) stuffed with minced meat, historically associated with mountain regions such as Mtiuleti, Pshavi and Khevsureti. The standard version contains mixed pork and beef in broth with carraway, coriander and parsley; in Mtiuleti it's without herbs, in Tusheti (where pork is forbidden) they're made of beef or lamb. They can also be stuffed with melty *sulguni* cheese or with potatoes, mushrooms or spinach. They're served everywhere, including cheap khinkali houses that are often open 24 hours; hold onto the knot (*kudi*) and bite a hole to suck the broth out cleanly (not necessary with meat-free versions, which may not even have a knot).

VEGETABLES AND HERBS Vegetable dishes include several with aubergine (eggplant, *badrijiani*), for instance fried and rolled with walnuts and garlic paste (*badrijiani nigvzit*) or with hazelnut paste, or as *ajapsandali*, stewed like a

RESTAURANT PRICE CODES

Prices are based on the cost of a main course per person.

$$$$	GEL30+	US$13+
$$$	GEL15–30	US$6.70–13
$$	GEL8–15	US$3.50–6.70
$	under GEL8	under US$3.50

ratatouille with tomato and peppers. Bean dishes include *lobio* (kidney beans stewed with coriander in a clay pot), *karabakh loby* (green beans in sour cream and tomato sauce) and *mtsvane lobio niguzit* (a bean salad in a walnut dressing). *Pkhali* is a generic term for walnut and vegetable pâtés, often rolled in balls and topped with pomegranate seeds, such as aubergine or minced spinach with walnuts, spices, garlic; similarly, shredded beetroot tops are served with red peppers and pomegranate seeds, and red beans with walnuts, garlic, celery and coriander. Beetroot is also served with walnuts, or mashed with garlic. Salads include *tarkhun* (long green leaves with an aroma of aniseed, eaten with kebabs), raw cabbage salad, and the ubiquitous Georgian salad of tomato and cucumber with onion and parsley, and often with walnut. Fermented, pickled or marinated vegetables are important, especially *jonjoli* (Caucasian bladdernut flowers, often foraged), served cold with raw onion, coriander and sunflower oil.

Fresh herbs are very important, and you'll see huge bundles of parsley, basil and dill in every market, as well as marigold flowers and *qviteli* or Imeretian saffron. Bunches of coriander (*kinza*) are used for sprinkling water over produce in markets, to keep it fresh, and it is eaten raw (for long life), as well as used in cooking. Food is spicier in western Georgia, and better for **vegetarians**, with more use of maize and nuts. Saying (*me*) *khortss ar v-ch'am* means *I don't eat meat*. In many restaurants you can ask for fasting food, for the periods (about a third of the year in the Orthodox tradition, not just Lent) when meat, fish, and oil are forbidden.

There's a range of **pastes and sauces** eaten with shashlik and other dishes; the best known is *tkemali*, a sour plum sauce with *ombalo* or pennyroyal (it can be green, made from unripe plums in spring, or red, made with ripe plums at the end of summer). Others are *adjika* (a hot red pepper and coriander paste from the west of Georgia, which also comes in dry and green varieties), and *bazha* (a sauce of crushed walnuts with either pomegranate juice or red wine vinegar and a combination of spices, garlic and saffron known as *tkhmali-suneli*). *Masharaphi* is a pomegranate dressing. On the table you may find a small pot of *svanuri marili* (Svan salt), a blend of salt, garlic, fenugreek, coriander and red chilli pepper, perhaps with black pepper, caraway, saffron or dill.

CHEESE AND BREAD
Georgian cuisine is quite heavy, dominated by meat, cheese and bread, but balanced by vegetable side dishes; oddly, though, milk itself is not drunk much. There are various cheeses, divided into *brindza*, the bog-standard salty factory cheese found in shops everywhere, and far more interesting local and largely homemade cheeses. The most popular is *imeruli qveli* (Imeretian cheese), a salted cow's-milk cheese, like a firmer feta that crumbles easily when cool and melts smoothly when hot. *Sulguni* is a mozzarella-like cheese associated with Mingrelia (where it should be made from buffalo milk) and Svaneti, and *sulguni shebolili* is a smoked version; *nadughi* ('second boiling') is a low-fat ricotta-like whey cheese that can be served with mint wrapped in sulguni. *Chechili* or *tenili* is also mozzarella-like, produced in dense strings that are usually braided and rolled into a figure of eight. *Gudiskweli* is a very salty cheese made of sheep's milk in Tusheti in a bag (*guda*) of sheepskin (with the wool inside). *Matsoni* is an unpasteurised yoghurt (known in Mingrelia as *kebzhalia*), and *kefir* is the equivalent of the Central Asian buttermilk known as *kumiss*.

Khachapuri, literally cheese-bread, is the national snack and is served with every meal. It takes many forms: in homes and restaurants it's usually a cheese-filled bread, while on stalls nationwide (though especially associated with Tbilisi) it's *pelovani*, a folded cheese-filled pastry. Cooks will tell you that there are four varieties: the basic *imeruli* (ie: Imerian), bread stuffed with cottage cheese (*khacho*) that looks something like *pizza bianca*; *megruli* (ie: Mingrelian), similar but with sulguni on top too (the Christmas version has a boiled egg inside and is hung to smoke in a chimney for two days); *achma*, made of thin layers of filo-like pastry (boiled then baked) interleaved with goat's cheese and folded into a square, much like pelovani; and the legendary heart-attack on a plate, *adjaruli* (ie: Adjaran), boat-like with a lightly fried egg on top swimming in molten butter. You may also find *pkhovani*, with cheese and spinach. In Kazbegi and Ossetia they make *khabajini*, a spinach and potato khachapuri, and in Svaneti khachapuri is stuffed with greens and perhaps ground millet and hemp seeds; *kubdari* is the Svan national dish, bread stuffed with meat (or trout). *Chebureki* are pies (like the Ukrainian and Russian *pirozhi*) of unleavened dough and filled with spiced mutton; *lobiani* is a Racha speciality, bread stuffed with kidney bean paste, herbs, and possibly bits of bacon, and *kartushki* are greasy potato rolls found in bus stations.

Other breads (*puri*) are also excellent; various types are produced by slapping dough on the sides of a *tone* or clay oven set in the floor, like an oversized tandoor (now often with electric elements rather than wood fuel). These include the standard *deda-puri* (mother's bread), the spear-shaped *shoti*, and the flat, unleavened Armenian bread known as *lavash*.

In Kakheti you'll find thin flattened loaves, a bit like unleavened baguettes. In the west of the country maize is used rather than wheat, both for *mchadi*, a heavy but delicious crusty pan-fried cornbread (often served with *lobio*), and for *ghomi*, a form of polenta served with sulguni cheese.

DESSERTS AND FRUIT Desserts (only for special occasions) such as *halva* and *baklava* show influence from the south; walnuts are also used in many ways, such as in cakes, crushed and wrapped in a flour and honey paste, and best of all as *nigozis muraba*, picked green, marinated in slaked lime and water, and boiled in the shell with sugar, until you can easily bite through the shell and the nut is the texture of marron glacé. Also quintessentially Georgian is *churchkhela*, made by threading walnuts or hazelnuts, almonds and raisins on a string, covering them in flour, dipping them repeatedly in simmering grape juice and hanging out to dry; made at the grape harvest each year, they look like brown candles. The definitive version comes from Kakheti, where it's made with wheat flour and walnuts (*k'ak'ali*); in Imereti they use maize flour and hazelnuts (*tkhili*). Traditionally for warriors, nowadays it's great fuel for hikers. Also produced during the grape harvest, *pelamushi* is condensed grape juice and cornflour, served like a porridge, while *tklapi* is similar but rolled out and dried in the sun.

Fruit is also excellent, and all sorts of health benefits are now being discovered; in addition to the citrus fruits grown by the Black Sea, there are various relatives of the persimmon (*Diospyros lotus* and *D. kaki*), such as the *karalioke* (Russian for 'royal fruit'), similar to the Israeli sharon fruit, which can be eaten hard, with no need to peel; and the *khulma*, which looks similar but must be soft when eaten. November is the season for these, producing the striking effect of trees with no leaves but large numbers of golden fruit. The pomegranate (*Punica granatum*) grows wild between the Caucasus and the Middle East and bears many-seeded red fruit up to 13cm in diameter. In addition to being eaten fresh, its seeds and dark red juice are used in cooking. It's associated with the goddess of love, fertility, spring, youth and eternity, and does in fact contain lots of antioxidants while the seeds are high in potassium, vitamin C and polyphenols, which protect the heart. The medlar

The programme known as Traceca (Transport Corridor Europe–Caucasus–Asia) was set up in 1993 by Georgia, Azerbaijan, Armenia and five Central Asian states, and has since been joined by Ukraine, Mongolia and Moldova. It's a sort of re-creation of the Silk Route, with substantial funding from the European Union, which mainly went into refurbishing railways and ports and introducing new train-ferries across the Caspian and Black seas. For cotton exports from Central Asia, a route via Georgia and across the Black Sea is around 2,000km shorter than one through Russia to the Baltic ports, although Russian Railways are still faster. Similarly, in 1995 the major companies involved in the extraction of oil from the Caspian and beyond announced that their 'early oil' would be moved through improved pipelines through both Georgia and Russia (which both opened in 2001), while continuing to debate the route to be taken by the larger modern pipeline needed for bulk flows. The refurbished Soviet pipeline from Baku to Supsa (34% owned by BP) was soon carrying 150,000 barrels/day (three million tonnes/year). For the longer term, the best route was also through Georgia, to Ceyhan on Turkey's Mediterranean coast (to remove tankers from the Bosphorus, which is 700m wide at its narrowest, with nine sharp bends, and faced a possible five-fold increase in tanker traffic); however, Russia did all it could to promote its route to Novorossiysk, even though this passes through Daghestan and close to Chechnya. This promotion may have included fomenting instability in neighbouring countries, perhaps even abetting an assassination attempt on Shevardnadze. Iran also offered a route to the sea, but this was vetoed by the USA. The Ceyhan route was the longest, at 1,700km, and the most expensive. However, Turkey managed to halve its estimate of the construction cost, claiming that it had been using German labour costs and hadn't realised that Turkish wage rates could be used. In 2001, BP (which has a 30% share) finally committed itself to the US$3 billion BTC (Baku–Tbilisi–Ceyhan) Project, after three years' hesitation; this was perhaps linked to BP's shift from being a British company to being an American one.

Opened in 2005, the BTC pipeline can carry 1.2 million barrels/day, but is currently only carrying half that amount. It was followed the next year by the parallel South Caucasus Pipeline to take Azeri gas from the Shah-Deniz field to Erzurum via Tbilisi, breaking the Russian monopoly of supplies to Georgia. BP's Shah-Deniz-2 project will expand the SCP (worth US$2 billion of investment to Georgia), tripling its capacity by 2018.

In parallel with Traceca, from 1996 Georgia, Ukraine, Azerbaijan and Moldova began to form a bloc of nations seeking to escape Russia's overpowering influence; Uzbekistan also joined, and the GUAM charter was adopted in 2001, followed by a free-trade pact (without Uzbekistan) the next year. It received new impetus from the US-led anti-terrorism campaign after 11 September 2001; oil was already crucial to Bush's foreign policy (indeed the 'multiple pipelines' policy dates from the Clinton

(*Mespilus germanica*) is a small tree up to 6m in height, with brown acidic fruit, like apples, up to 5cm in diameter. The fruit remains hard until frost, after which it is picked and kept in a cool dry room until soft, when it is eaten raw or in preserves. Figs and soft fruits are used for conserves, served with tea after dinner.

WINE There's been wine in Georgia almost as long as there have been Georgians: at least 6,000 years, or 8,000 vintages as Georgians prefer to put it. Stone wine presses years), but secure supplies have become even more important, and so Azerbaijan and the countries through which pipelines could run are seeing more American support. For a while the USA embraced Russia as an ally in the war against terrorism, adopting a see-no-evil policy to human rights abuses in Chechnya and to the bullying of Georgia; but Putin's adventures in Georgia and Ukraine have ended that. In 2011 Russia opened Nord Stream, the world's longest undersea pipeline (covering 1,222km under the Baltic from Russia to Germany), bypassing Poland and Ukraine, but an expansion project (Nord Stream II) has been blocked by the EU (although Germany still wants to buy more Russian gas). The US$45 billion Southern Gas Corridor project will allow gas from Azerbaijan to cover nearly 20% of western European demand from 2019, using the upgraded South Caucasus Pipeline through Georgia, the new 2,000km Trans-Anatolian Pipeline (TANAP) through Turkey, and finally the new Trans-Adriatic Pipeline (TAP) from Albania to Italy. There's also talk of a Trans-Caspian Gas Pipeline to feed in gas from Turkmenistan and possibly Kazakhstan. In 2014, Putin abandoned the South Stream project for a gas pipeline under the Black Sea from Russia to Bulgaria, due to EU opposition, but immediately replaced it with the Turkish Stream project, which will feed gas to Greece and the rest of the European Union from 2019, avoiding Ukraine and Georgia and undermining non-Russian sources of gas. Almost 90% of Georgia's gas consumption is now supplied by Azerbaijan in lieu of pipeline transit fees , and most of the rest is supplied by Russia's Gazprom, also as transit fees for gas supplied to Armenia. Georgia is the route for most of Armenia's trade, as Armenia's borders with Turkey and Azerbaijan are closed. Most of this also takes the main railway line to Batumi; Armenia is particularly keen to see a resolution of the Abkhaz conflict and the reopening of its rail route to Russia. Armenia is also in favour of an Iran–Armenia pipeline project, to secure Armenia's fuel supply and possibly carry gas from Iran to Europe.

There's an increasing emphasis on links with China, which is working hard on a plan to create an 'Iron Silk Road' to Europe, including the Trans-Caspian international transport route (TCITR) via Kazakhstan, Azerbaijan, Georgia and train-ferries to Ukraine. This is an alternative both to Russia's Trans-Siberian railway and to shipping via the Suez Canal. In December 2017 it was announced that former British prime minister David Cameron would head the One Belt, One Road initiative, the largest infrastructure project in history, affecting two-thirds of the world's population; the UK is to invest £750 million, dwarfed by the £150 billion/year that China will pay. In Georgia, the Chinese are investing in the port of Poti, as well as building new railway tunnels through the central mountains.

Russian policy is currently directed more against Ukraine than Georgia, and to creating as much of a grip on EU gas supplies as it can, but controlling the southern Caucasus corridor has long been vital in the Russian geopolitical outlook, before and doubtless after Putin.

and clay containers have been found dating from the 3rd millennium BC, and vine leaves and stems have been found in Bronze Age tombs. It seems that our word 'wine' derived from the Georgian *ghvino*. Wine is absolutely central to the Georgian lifestyle and to their self-image, and everyone (especially men) drinks large quantities and will want you to do the same. In theory Georgians drink red wines in winter, and whites in summer, but in practice it can be hard to tell the difference, as even 'red' (literally 'black' or *shavi*) wines may in fact be straw-coloured. There are lots of amber

The set-piece Georgian feast is known as the *supra*, meaning literally 'tablecloth', from the Arabic *sufratun*; it's a marathon of food and drink in which men will drink up to four litres of wine over 3–5 hours. In theory they're not allowed to leave the room, but in practice some sort of an excuse can usually be found.

The key feature of the supra is the ceremony of toasting, led by a *tamada* or toastmaster (assisted by a *merikipe*, who fills the glasses and stokes the conversation but stays sober; both, of course, are always male). It's almost sacramental, with the first dozen or so toasts (of 20 or more) following a prescribed order. The first will be proposed by the master of the house to the tamada (unless he's playing this role himself), then the tamada will propose toasts to the person being celebrated, if any (for example, for a homecoming or a birthday), to his family or the host family, to the elderly (if any are present), to siblings, to the ancestors, to the dead, to children (ie: the future), to the parentland, to women and mothers, to the winemaker, and to 'our son' (any local hero, which could include Stalin or Tamar). For the toast to the dead, wine is poured on to bread, or on to the ground, and men may stand; for the toast to women those slaving in the kitchen will emerge to join in for a few minutes. After this, things become more flexible, with toasts to specific people, present or not, and guests may ask for permission to propose a toast themselves (a sure way for a foreigner to win approval). In regions such as Svaneti the pattern differs slightly, with, for instance, a toast to St George. Between the toasts there may well be singing.

Each *sadghegrdzelo* or toast is in fact a speech of ten to 15 minutes, during which it's not permitted to touch your wine (although water or soft drinks are always available); when it's done the tamada will drain his glass, or ideally a horn, and turn it upside-down, everyone says '*gaumarjos*' (victory), and you will have to drain your glass in one swallow too. Never have I drunk so much and tasted so little as at a Georgian supra; it's largely irrelevant whether Georgian wine fits contemporary Western tastes when so little of it makes contact with the taste buds. When it gets too much for you, ask permission to propose a toast, toast the host family, and leave.

Most meals are, of course, informal family affairs, but wine will be produced for a guest, and one-line toasts will be proclaimed: 'To Britain!', 'To Georgia!', 'To Thatcher!', 'To Stalin!' being a hardly atypical exchange. As at a supra, you should not drink wine outside toasts, and you must then, at least initially, drain your glass in one. Wine is never drunk without toasting, while beer is never drunk with toasting (except for a toast to 'the police and the president'), except in remote places like Khevsureti where they have to drink beer instead of wine and make awful *chacha* from bread.

or orange wines, made with white varietals but with the skins, seeds and stalks left in contact for up to six months, producing something with tannin that's more like a red and is great with food. Most families make their own, ideally in *qvevri*, large sealed clay vessels set into the floor of a room known as the *marani*. In every ancient site you visit, such as Vardzia or Uplistsikhe, there'll be a marani or three.

There are at least 525 varieties of grape in Georgia, and more or less every village produces its own wine, effectively semi-organically. In addition to traditional home/

village winemaking, a modern 'European' industry was established from the 1870s, earning respect at the 1900 Exposition Universelle in Paris; but in the Soviet period the focus was entirely on producing cheap alcohol for Russians, notably the dreaded semi-sweet red which is now slowly vanishing. Only five varieties were permitted, designated by numbers (Tsinandali was No.1, generic Saperavi No.5), followed by three years of prohibition under Gorbachev. After independence companies such as Georgian Wines and Spirits, Teliani Valley, Tbilvino and Telavi Wine Cellar introduced modern techniques at the upper end of the market, with temperature-controlled stainless-steel tanks replacing concrete, leading to some very good wines suited to foreign tastes and the world market. What is happening now is more interesting, as many winemakers are rediscovering the ancient qvevri method of natural wine-making – although the few remaining manufacturers of these huge clay pots can barely keep up with demand. Even the large modern wineries are mostly now making some qvevri wine on the side. In 2013, qvevri wine-making was added to UNESCO's list of the world's intangible heritage. The largest qvevri are three or four 'tonnes' (3,000 or 4,000 litres), treated with beeswax for hygiene while still allowing the clay to breathe, so that the wine is at the temperature of the earth that holds it and is imbued with the essence of its terroir. There are no additives; only the natural yeasts on the grape skins are used, with the skins, stalks and pips gathering in the narrow foot of the jar, for the duration of the winter or longer. The grapes are first trod by foot in a wooden trough or *satsnakheli* before being poured into a qvevri, stalks, pips, skins and all; this juice is stirred four times a day for about ten days then left for 20–40 days, after which the skins, seeds and stalks (collectively known as *chacha*) may be removed before the wine is sealed up for malolactic fermentation over the winter (five to six months); it may then be aged for perhaps a year, still in a qvevri.

The trend now is not just to use qvevri but to make entirely natural wines, without any additives (not even yeast) except perhaps for a tiny dose of sulphur dioxide; in 2011 there were five or six winemakers bottling and selling natural wines and in 2017 about 80, and a legion of mainly American wine bloggers are enthusing about the wines and even getting small vineyards and making their own. This goes hand in hand with a quest to rediscover ancient grape varieties – of Georgia's 525 indigenous varieties about 45 are in commercial production, but the leading natural wine restaurants in Sighnaghi and Tbilisi already have examples of 75.

Kakheti, the region least affected by the Black Sea climate, produces around 70% of Georgia's wine, its classic grapes being Saperavi (for red wine), which has deep colour, rich plummy flavours and crisp natural acidity, and Rkatsiteli (mainly for whites), acidic with spicy and floral notes and a very dry aftertaste. Saperavi in particular is exciting for winemakers because it's a bit quirky, having red skins and red juice (rather than the more usual white juice – whence its name meaning dye or colour); it's clearly very ancient given the large number of clones or mutations across the country (such as Saperavi Budeshuri and Atenis) and it's now being planted in Australia and elsewhere. It's similar to Syrah (Shiraz) but lighter-bodied, though full of inkiness and tannins. Other well-known Kakheti varieties include Tsolikouri, Kisi and Mtsvane, but there are many more, with some villages having their own varieties.

Rkatsiteli goes with most foods, likewise Tsolikouri from western Georgia; and modern wines made with Mtsvane, Khikhivi, Kisi or Tsitska go well with salads and fish. Qvevri wines are high in tannins, so should not be drunk without food; in particular they go well with heavier fatty meals including most meats and mature cheeses. This also applies to Saperavis – some are particularly good when young,

2

Oliver Moss

On 22 July 2006, I set off from the familiarity of London's Hyde Park along with 200 other drivers and cars, on the road trip of all road trips: the Mongol Rally. The purpose of the rally is to make your own way from London to Mongolia's capital Ulaanbaatar to raise money for various charities, in a car with an engine size below 1,000cc (eg: Nissan Micras, Fiat Pandas, Ladas, Minis, Ford Escorts) which would normally be deemed wholly unsuitable for such a journey. The route you take is largely up to you.

After reaching Prague on the second night, the teams started to head off in different directions according to their planned route. Some headed north through Scandinavia, St Petersburg, across the Urals and down into Mongolia; others headed across Poland to Moscow and through Kazakhstan; others through Ukraine and Central Asia; and others down through the Balkans, across Turkey, the Caspian and Central Asia. I, with my team of four Fiat Pandas, decided to take the last of the described routes. We spent a total of three days in Georgia, which under normal circumstances would barely seem sufficient. But the innate sense of hospitality and friendliness for which Georgians are well known, and the fact that we crossed the entire country from the western border with Turkey to the eastern border with Azerbaijan, meant we left this compact and stunning country with huge reluctance and a longing to return in the future.

On our first day, after a long wait at the border, we sat down to a late lunch in a beachside café overlooking the Black Sea. Having heard of the banquets that are the average Georgian meals, and the local wines of which they are so proud, we had to ask the staff to halve the dozen or so courses they were trying to lavish on us. The food was superb and very filling, with enormous amounts of cheese and meats and wine: it seemed rude to turn them down when they attached such devotion and pride to their meals.

going well with almost any food. In the centre of Georgia, Kartli is known for the Chinuri and Goruli Mtsvane grapes (for dry white wines with a bit of spritz, especially from the Ateni valley), as well as other Georgian and indeed French varieties. Kvanchkara, a semi-sweet red wine from just two villages in Racha, goes well with cakes, fruit and desserts and is famed as Stalin's favourite (supposedly he sent his secret police to secure the best supply) and is still somewhat overpriced; the dry Alexandrouli and Mujuretlui wines go well with typical Racha dishes such as smoked ham, rabbit, goose kharcho or lobio. Nearby in Lechkumi, Ojaleshi is the main indigenous varietal. In Imereti they make lighter, more flowery wines using the Aladasturi, Dzvelshavi, Otskhanuri Sapere and Odzhaleshi grapes for red wines and Tsitska, Tsolikouri and Krakhuna for whites; here some vines are still allowed to grow high on trees and the grapes are collected in a pointed basket known as a *gideli* which is lowered down on a rope. This doesn't affect the taste, but does give rise to a specific genre of worksongs. In the high, bleak south of the country they grow Meskhuri Mtsvane (Meskhetian Green) and Meskhuri Shavi (Black); at the far end of the country, in Guria and Adjara, the most common grape is the late-ripening Chkhaveri, while in Adjara they also grow Satsuravi, in Guria Aladasturi and Tsolikouri, and in Mingrelia Chvitiluri.

Sparkling wine ('Georgian champagne' or *champanska*) is produced in factories nationwide rather than in homes; it's inexpensive and ranges from more or less dry to ultra-sweet in taste.

The first night we spent in the port city of Batumi, an interesting place rather than beautiful, with colourful markets set against crumbling grey Soviet apartment blocks, and dilapidated buses pushing their way through the thronging streets. The next day we embarked on a memorable journey to Tbilisi, crossing mountain passes where medieval castles overlooked long-abandoned Soviet factories, driving through stunning, green, wooded valleys with crystal-clear rivers winding and roaring their way down from the Caucasus mountains, and passing through villages where pony and trap and horse and plough were still in widespread use.

When we got to Tbilisi, we were taken out on a city tour by a contact of mine, proud to show off his city and culture. Unlike the other major cities, Tbilisi is a beautiful old city, the jewel of the Caucasus, with grand buildings, windy cobbled streets, and ancient castles nestled in a deep valley. We went out for another traditional Georgian feast complete with toasts every few minutes, before heading to our hotel.

The main concern before entering Georgia was the reports of potential violence surrounding the disputed breakaway republics within the country. However, we never felt unsafe – in fact, we were made to feel so welcome that the image we had before we arrived was quickly forgotten, and we forged a new one of a beautiful, welcoming and fascinating country.

Unfortunately not all of our cars made it to Mongolia, as was perhaps expected. The first burst into flames on a particularly dodgy Azeri road, the second finally gave up the ghost in northern Kazakhstan, but the final two limped over the line some five weeks after setting off from London: battered, dusty and falling to pieces, but covered in hundreds of good luck messages from people along the way who had helped us to complete such an incredible journey.

For more information, visit w theadventurists.com/mongol-rally.

OTHER DRINKS The national **beer** was Kazbegi, a nice tangy German-style brew which has been produced in Tbilisi since 1881; it's not so widely seen now, but it's still a Tbilisi custom to go down to the riverside brewery on a hot afternoon with plastic bottles and buy it straight from the tap. Many village shops now also sell draught beer in the same way, for just GEL3/litre. Argo, a premium beer, was created by the Kazbegi company in the 1990s, and in 2017 was relaunched under new owners. You'll also find other *chekhuri* (Czech-style) beers such as Mtieli, from the Natakhtari brewery (founded in 2005) and Zedazeni (founded in 2012). They all seem to make various kinds of lemonade as well, notably *tarkhuna* (tarragon lemonade), as well as raspberry, barberry and even saperavi flavours. Russian beers such as Baltika are also available, as well as German Krombacher and Paulaner and Czech Staropramen at high prices. Microbreweries are just beginning to appear in Tbilisi but there's not much of a scene yet.

Vodka is drunk in Georgia, but far less than in Russia and the other Slav countries; the national spirit is *chacha*, a firewater (between 48° and 75°) made at home, as a rule from the leftover grape skins and pips, although in Svaneti and Khevsureti, where grapes don't grow, they use bread instead! It's intriguing to wonder whether there's any linguistic connection with *chicha*, the fermented maize drink of the Andes. Although the Georgians love to drink, there's very little public drunkenness and few of the alcohol-related problems that are found north of the Caucasus.

2

Soft drinks are easily available, both the ubiquitous Coca-Cola and Fanta, and local fruit juices, which are slightly cheaper as well as rather healthier. Borjomi mineral water is also sold almost everywhere; the milder Borjomi Light was introduced in 2001. Nabeghlavi, Bakhmaro and Sairme are other excellent mineral waters. Lagidze Water is a soda water flavoured with fruit syrups that's famous in Georgia yet not widely available.

Real coffee (*kava*) is available in many cafés, as well as Turkish coffee in some places, and you'll usually be able to find tea (*chai*) – it's generally from Sri Lanka, as while Georgia produces tea, it's mostly green tea for the Russian samovar market.

SHOPPING

Larger shops open from 09.00 to 20.00 Monday to Saturday; kiosks and house-front 'markets' are usually open from 08.00 at the latest until in some cases midnight or later, and are usually open on Sundays too. Only foreign-owned shops and restaurants (and 24-hour places) actually post their opening hours.

In Tbilisi there are quite a few 'antique salons', in which you can buy items such as ceramics, wood- and metalwork, and carpets. An export permit (and attached photo) is needed from the Ministry of Culture (*Rustaveli Av 37, 3rd floor, room 16, Tbilisi;* ✎ *32 299 0285*) to export carpets and some other items. You may find it simpler to take wine to your loved ones, or, if you really want to perplex them, sticks of churchkhela (strings of nuts coated in grape syrup that look like knobbly candles), but be aware that wine will have to be put in your checked-in luggage if you are flying – a risky business.

Among the more interesting items are the male national dress, the *chokha*, a sort of frock coat with a row of pockets across the chest to hold cartridges, and the *akhalukhi or* silk inner coat. More exotic perhaps is the *nabadi* or *burka*, the shaggy sheepskin cape worn by mountain shepherds. A dagger or *khandzali* is always worn by men with the national dress: it should have an elaborately decorated side, for weddings,

PUBLIC HOLIDAYS AND FESTIVALS	
1 January	New Year's Day
7 January	Christmas (Orthodox Church)
19 January	Epiphany (Orthodox Church)
3 March	Mother's Day
8 March	International Women's Day
9 April	Remembrance Day
April/May	Easter Sunday and Easter Monday (Orthodox Church): 28 and 29 April 2019, 19 and 20 April 2020, 2 and 3 May 2021
26 May	Independence Day
28 August	Assumption of the Virgin (Mariamoba) (Orthodox Church)
14 October	Sveti-tskhovloba (Mtskhetoba) – Mtskheta town festival
23 November	St George's Day (Giorgoba), now also celebrated as the anniversary of the Rose Revolution, and of Aslan Abashidze's departure from Adjara a year later

and a plain one, for funerals. A winehorn or *khantsi* is another possible present, or a *Svanuri kudi*, the round felt Svan hat. See page 133 for suitable shops in Tbilisi.

MEDIA AND COMMUNICATIONS

MEDIA Several English-language **newspapers**, largely business-oriented, are published in Tbilisi, and subscriptions are available for most: *The Messenger* (*GEL3*) and the *Georgian Times* (*GEL2*) appear Monday to Friday; *Caucasian Business Week* (*free*) appears on Mondays; *Georgian Journal* (*GEL2*) appears on Thursdays; and *Georgia Today* (*free*) appears on Fridays. All have websites that are updated most days, and w agenda.ge is a web-only news source. The amount of world news you'll find in them is minimal, but they're a useful window onto Georgian life, politics and business. The papers can be picked up free in major hotels. Friday's *Messenger* is good for culture and what's on.

Nationwide, the dominant **television** broadcaster is Sakartvelos Sazogadoebrivi Mauts'q'ebeli or the Georgian Public Broadcaster; its Channel 1 reaches 85% of the population and Channel 2 reaches 55%. Having been a state system, and hardly neutral, it is now making the transition to being a genuinely public broadcaster (which seems to consist largely of pumping out Turkish serials). Other channels are Adjara, Imedi, Maestro, Mze and Rustavi-2, and satellite and cable TV is available in almost every hotel and elsewhere. The independent Rustavi-2 television station earned a good reputation towards the end of the Shevardnadze era, especially for its hard-hitting investigative programme *Sixty Minutes*, but then became tediously pro-government under Saakashvili; it still peddles his scare stories about crime waves and the Russian threat.

TELEPHONE The telephone system has traditionally been so decrepit that most people ignore it, using mobile phones instead. However, there has now been investment in modern equipment, with Siemens, Alcatel and Daewoo installing new exchanges and a fibre-optic line under the Black Sea from Varna (Bulgaria) to Poti, now extended across Georgia to Azerbaijan, *en route* to Shanghai. In Tbilisi in particular there are now good connections for broadband internet. The number of lines has risen to more than 830,000 (around 20 lines per 100 people in urban areas, around four per 100 in rural areas), but some villages still don't have phone lines. Note that there's Wi-Fi in all hotels and guesthouses, and also at Public Service Halls.

Mobile phones work on a GSM system using Siemens-Motorola kit that is compatible with Western systems. Probably the supplier with the best coverage is MagtiCom, a joint venture with American company Telcell which was run by Shevardnadze's son-in-law, Georgi Jokhtaberidze. After the Rose Revolution he was

USEFUL NUMBERS

The emergency service should have an English-speaking operator, but otherwise you'll need to speak Georgian or Russian.

Police, fire or ambulance	112
Long-distance operator	07
Taxi	008
Directory enquiries for Tbilisi	09, elsewhere 05

arrested at the airport and only freed after paying US$15 million to the state treasury, allowing it to pay salaries and pensions on time at last. The main alternatives are Geocell and Beeline; together they cover 98% of Georgia's populated area and have three million users.

Bring your own phone, and buy a SIM card for GEL10 at most, including GEL5 credit, from a corner shop. In truly remote areas such as Khevsureti there's no mobile (or fixed) phone coverage, but some satellite phones are available, at GEL9/minute. Public coin or card phones have disappeared.

Georgia's **country code** is 995, and the code for Tbilisi is 32, so from most countries you'll dial 0099532, followed by the seven-digit number. All other places have six-digit numbers; other codes are 422 for Batumi, 431 for Kutaisi, 493 for Poti and 350 for Telavi. Within the same town, just dial the number; otherwise dial 0 then the code and number. Mobile numbers begin with 5 and two digits, then a six-digit number; you'll need to prefix this with +995 (rather than 00995).

POST AND COURIERS The state postal service had virtually disappeared, but has now re-invented itself as **Georgian Post** (╲ *32 224 0909; w gpost.ge*); post offices are few and far between, but at least there is now a vaguely reliable service. Whether sending to or from Georgia, you should stick to postcards if possible. Airmail to western Europe costs GEL5 (*US$2.50*) and takes about ten days; it's possible to buy pre-stamped envelopes for internal mail for GEL2 at cigarette kiosks. Blue-and-white letter boxes can be found on main streets, but it's best to find stamps before leaving Tbilisi (page 130). Incidentally, the first Georgian stamp was the 'Tbilisi Unica' of 1857, which was the first in the Russian Empire; now it survives nowhere in the former Soviet Union, and only in two collections in the world. It's featured on a GEL0.80 stamp, against a photo of 19th-century Tbilisi. Letters to UK cost GEL5, domestic postage is GEL2.

The courier companies DHL, TNT, UPS and FedEx all have offices in Tbilisi (pages 129–30) and they offer the most reliable international mail service; however expats in Georgia seem more likely to use USA2Georgia (*Beliashvili 1;* ╲ *32 242 1818, 32 219 2080;* ⊕ *09.00–21.00 Mon–Fri, 11.00–18.00 Sat; w usa2georgia.com*); US Shop (*Kandelaki 17, Tbilisi;* ╲ *32 221 2128,* m *597 925511; w usshop.ge*); or Inex (*Tsereteli 57, Didube, Tbilisi;* ╲ *32 249 2625/6;* ⊕ *08.00–23.00 daily; w inex.ge*).

OTHER PRACTICALITIES

TIME Georgia is 4 hours ahead of GMT. Georgians are not early risers, but can be lively well into the night.

PUBLIC TOILETS Public toilets are few and far between, although petrol stations are increasingly likely to have them. Where you do find one, pictograms are now more common than the Cyrillic symbols, M for men and Ж for women.

ELECTRICITY Electrical power is supplied in theory at 220v 50hz, using European-standard two-pin plugs; however, it's subject to surges, and in winter there may be power cuts.

BUSINESS

Georgians are known as wheeling-dealing businessmen, and Russians in particular also associate them with organised crime – unfairly, as most of the gangsters in

Moscow are in fact Chechens and indeed Russians. Laws and accountancy norms are being brought into line with EU standards; but to do business here you will have to come to terms with a culture of clannish loyalties.

Economic data can be obtained from the Economist Intelligence Unit (w *eiu. com*). In Tbilisi, the International Chamber of Commerce is at Kakabadze 29 (☎ *32 298 8176;* w *icc.ge*). AmCham, the American Chamber of Commerce in Georgia, is at Asatiani 36A, Tbilisi (☎ *32 222 6907;* w *amcham.ge*); they have an online database of businesses in Georgia, and publish the useful and interesting *Investor.ge* every two months (available free online).

For **casual work**, about your only option is teaching English – try International House Tbilisi, Centre for Language Studies (*26 May Sq 2, Tbilisi;* ☎ *32 294 0515;* w *ihtbilisi.ge*); the Byron School (*Griboedov 2, Tbilisi;* ☎ *32 298 3478;* w *byronschool. ge*); and the English Language Centre (*Barnov 51A, Tbilisi;* ☎ *32 222 2326;* e *the-elc@internet.ge;* w *the-elc.com.ge*).

CULTURAL ETIQUETTE

Georgians, though poor, are fantastically hospitable people; this is in some cases a form of subconscious domination or possession rather than pure generosity, but you still have to deal with the question of how to pay them back. Payment with money will never be accepted and may be seen as offensive, but presents for children are usually welcome (postcards or picture books about your home country, coloured pencils, toys, chocolate, etc). American cigarettes will usually be accepted by men, but the hardest problem is to find suitable gifts for the women who work so hard for so little in the way of thanks; in the remoter villages even make-up is inappropriate, but headscarves, napkins and tablecloths are much appreciated.

CULTURAL DOS AND DON'TS Perhaps the most important rule is to learn to accept a drink even when it's the last thing you want. Restaurant bills are never split; they're always paid by one person, almost always a man. Adult Georgians don't wear shorts except for sport. In churches shorts and low-cut dresses are unacceptable, and this is true in general in the remoter mountain areas. Women cover their heads in church (though not always in Tbilisi) – perhaps pack a scarf to cover your shoulders, although often they are provided. Queues are surprisingly orderly.

TRAVELLING POSITIVELY

The best way to find out what's going on in the Georgian NGO scene is by reading the excellent newsletters published (on paper and online) by the Caucasus Environmental NGO Network (CENN). Details for this and other organisations are listed here.

Caucasus Environmental NGO Network (CENN) Betlemi 27, 0105 Tbilisi; ☎ 32 275 1903–4; w cenn.org

Iare Pekhit Abashidze 24A, 0179 Tbilisi; ☎ 32 223 5309; w iarepekhit.org. A small new group working for a better deal for pedestrians, more green spaces, etc in Tbilisi.

Let's Do It! – Georgia m 555 755977; e sally. bokhua@gmail.com; w caynex.ge/ka/lets-do-it. A youth group working to persuade society of the importance of a clean & green environment & organising World Cleanup Day in September.

The Noah's Ark Centre for the Recovery of Endangered Species (NACRES) Abashidze 12A, 0179 Tbilisi; ☎ 32 223 3706; w nacres.org

Sabuko Society for Nature Conservation (Birdlife Georgia) Nutsubidze 72, 1st floor, flat 71, Tbilisi; m 577 960559; w sabuko.org

Teach & Learn with Georgia Gmir Kursantta 1, 0167 Tbilisi; ☎ 32 220 0220; m 558 177574; w tlg.gov.ge. TLG recruits native English, French & German speakers to co-teach for at least a year alongside local teachers in schools; the Georgian government provides return flights, accommodation, medical insurance, a vacation & US$300/month.

World Vision Georgia Davit Agmashenebelis 61, 0102 Tbilisi; ☎ 32 215 7515; e ana_chkhaidze@wvi.org; w wvi.org/georgia. Working mainly with children of poor families.

WWF-Georgia Aleksidze 11, 0193 Tbilisi; ☎ 32 223 7500; e atsintsadze@wwfcaucasus.org; w panda.org/caucasus

UPDATES WEBSITE

You can post your comments and recommendations, and read feedback and updates from other readers online at w bradtupdates.com/georgia.

Part Two

THE GUIDE

3

Tbilisi თბილისი

Telephone code: 32 (followed by a 2 and six digits)

Tbilisi lies at about 380m altitude, on the same latitude as Rome, Barcelona, Boston and Chicago. It stretches for 20km along the River Mtkvari (the Kura in Russian), with mountains on three sides: Mtatsminda to the southwest, Mount Tabori and the Solalaki Ridge to the southeast, and the low undulating Makhat Ridge to the northeast, beyond which is the so-called Tbilisi Sea, now a reservoir, and then the Samgori steppe.

The average temperature in Tbilisi is 13.2°C (24.4°C in July and 0.9°C in January), and average annual precipitation is 505mm (the wettest months are May with 75mm and April with 61mm). A damp spring is followed by a summer which can be oppressively hot and stuffy, then a fine autumn with lower humidity; the first snow appears on the mountains in mid-October, but winter in the city tends to be damp and misty with minimal snowfall, but higher pollution levels. This is a seismically active zone: seismologists reckon that the strongest earthquake likely to occur here will be 4.5 on the moment magnitude scale, and this was tested in 2002 when a quake of magnitude 4.3 (Richter 4.8) struck. Six people died (two from heart attacks) and over 2,000 buildings were damaged in the old city, but none actually collapsed.

Perhaps the most evocative accounts of Tbilisi come from the 1930s, because of the contrast it offered to the rest of the USSR: Boris Pasternak called it 'a city as if not of this world', and Arthur Koestler said:

> I loved Tbilisi more than any other town in the Soviet Union, perhaps because it was still so untouched by the drabness and monotony of Soviet life. The town has an irresistible charm of its own, neither European nor Asiatic, but a happy blend of the two.

Fitzroy Maclean, who came here a dozen times or more, called it 'one of my favourite towns anywhere'. Of his first visit he wrote:

> Immediately the town took my fancy. It had a graceful quality, a southern charm, an air of leisure, which I had so far found nowhere else in the Soviet Union. In the old city the houses, crazy structures with jutting verandas, hang like swallows' nests from the side of a hill. Beneath them a mountain stream tumbles its rushing waters and more houses cluster on the far side.

Tbilisi is far busier now than it was then, but its mix of ancient churches next to hip restaurants and of old ladies in black shuffling home from the market beside young people with ripped jeans and the latest phones give the city a very specific allure.

HISTORY

The city's name derives from *tbili*, meaning warm, referring to the 30 hot springs on the northeastern slopes of Mount Tabori – which produce three million litres of water a day, at between 24°C and 46.5°C – and in the 12th century supplied 65 bathhouses. Tiflis is the Persian name, also used by Russians and Armenians; the locals (or Tbilisebi) just say *kalaki* or 'the town'.

Legend has it that King Vakhtang Gorgasali ('Wolf-Lion'; AD446–502) went hunting from his capital in Mtskheta, and his sparrowhawk wounded a deer or pheasant, which was miraculously cured (or alternatively cooked) by a hot spring. Vakhtang decided to move his capital to this health-giving spot (the water is even said to restore eunuchs), though it was his son King Dachi who completed the walls of the new city and moved the capital here. In fact there's evidence of habitation since at least 3000BC , and it's not surprising given the combination of defensible hills with the hot springs. The city suffered 40 invasions between AD627 and 1795, by Persians, Byzantines, Arabs, Khazars and Seljuk Turks (many of them several times); in 1121 King Davit IV (the Builder) recaptured the city and rebuilt it (allowing the Muslims to stay), building his palace across the river in the Isani ('fortified place') district. The next year Tbilisi became capital of the most powerful state in the Near East, and then centre of Georgia's cultural flowering under monarchs such as Tamar. Then the invasions recommenced, with the Mongols in the 13th century, Temur Leng in the 14th and the Ottomans in the 15th. Georgia was divided into weak principalities, and from 1632 Tbilisi was governed by imposed Shahs (including Khusran-Mirza, an illegitimate member of the Bagratid family who had converted to Islam and who ruled for 26 years as King Rostom I). In 1744, they were driven out by King Teimuraz II and his son Erekle II, and in 1762, Tbilisi became capital of eastern Georgia. In 1795 the Shah of Persia, Aga Mohammed Khan, utterly destroyed Tbilisi (almost nothing survived; the churches you see now were rebuilt afterwards) and drove out the entire population.

After this disaster Erekle appealed for protection to the tsar and Georgia entered the Russian Empire. Tiflis (as the Russians know it) recovered but was soon largely inhabited by Armenians and Russians, with Georgians mainly in the Avlabari quarter, across the river beyond the Metekhi Church, which had been the Armenian quarter in Tamar's time, and is again now. The Russians developed the Garetubani area (the present centre, around Freedom Square and Rustaveli Avenue) only in the 1850s, when merchants' villas (characterised by so-called 'Italian' courtyards lined with glassed-in 'shushabandi' balconies) began to creep up the foothills of Sololaki and Mtatsminda. Across the river, towards the railway station, the Chugureti district was settled by Poles and Germans, invited to settle in the Russian Empire in 1817. During this period it was the capital of the entire Transcaucasus, and many great figures came here. In 1829 Pushkin passed through on his way to Erzurum, in 1851–54 the young Tolstoy wrote his first significant stories here, and Gorki also wrote and published his first story here in 1892; he called Tbilisi his second home. The city was also visited by Tsar Nikolai I in 1837.

There are some fine Art Nouveau buildings (known as Moderne here), notably the National Library. Huge changes came in 1933–41, under Stalin's henchman Beria, when the Mtkvari embankments were built and Tbilisi became much longer, stretching along the river. The Circus, Dinamo Stadium and Rustaveli Cinema were built, and the first high-rise apartment blocks appeared; from 1951 the so-called 'attractive new housing developments' of Digomi, Varketili, Avchali and Gldani were built. Varketili is an extremely deprived area which has developed a particularly good community organisation to tackle its problems; if you should happen to go there, note block No 303, the Leaning Tower of Tbilisi, which has a cant of 1m. A few buildings in the Freedom Square/Rustaveli area were destroyed in the civil war of 1991–92, but most gaps have been filled by new

Tbilisi International Christian Fellowship

Ethno Tsiskvili, Ludis Moedani, Phaetoni, Kakhelebi (Digomi), Jan Homer Tennis Complex, Baptist church, Astra Park Entertainment Centre, US Embassy, Mtskheta

Bank of Georgia HQ

Didube Metro, bus station

DIDUBE

Allwine

Zhvania Square

Kandelaki

Central Republican Hospital

City Sport

MediClub

Cheese Corner, Salewa, post office, FINCA Bank, Mogzauri, Innova Medical Center

Khvanchkara

Vazha-Pshavelas

Sameditsino Instituti

bikes.ge

Bagrationi Bridge

Khidi

Tsereteli

Delisi

Tolibashi

Kazbegi

Alitalia

Mitskevich

Pekini

Georgia Technical University

Mtkvarze

Mushtoid Park

Si

Assyrian-Chaldean Catholic Church

K Gamsakhurdia Sukhumi State Drama Theatre

Magellan Sport

SABURTALO

Book House

IMSS

Kakha Bakuradze Movement Theatre

Mikheil Tumanishvili

University (main block)

Arena 2 Sports Centre

Saburtalos

Bakhtrioni

Georgian Wine Culture Centre

Shumi

Politekhnikuri

Adjara

Abashidze

Arena Pool

Old Hippodrome

International House

26 May Square

Sports Palace

King David Residences

Cartu

see inset below

Mziuri Park

Queen Tamar Bridge

Neptune Pool

Victory Square

Ilia Chavchavadze Av

Vake Pool

LOT

Paliashvili

VERE

Russian Federation

Iran

Vake Park

Abashidze

VAKE

Vake Cemetery

Ukraine

Mtskheta

Manglisi

Museum of Georgian Ethnography

Turtle Lake

N

Bradt

0 — 1km

0 — 1mile

Vake

David Tatishvili Medical Center

Mziuri Park

Liberty

Turkey

Tbilisi State University Medical Diagnostic Centre

ILIA CHAVCHAVADZE AV

Backstage 76

Air Baltic

Fromagerie

Air Arabia

English Book in Georgia

PAM Club

PALIASHVILI

Aegean Airlines

Kindzmarauli Marani

bikes.ge

Cito Medical Centre

PALIASHVILI

Azerbaijan Airlines

Parnassus

Levon Travel

Cheese House

Senate Club

Gemorcheuli

ABASHIDZE

Poka Nunnery's

UN

Alcorium

Fly Dubai

American Medical Centers

Lufthansa

UN Circle

MTSKHETA

BusinessTravelCom

Berika International/ Czech Airlines

Cable car

Atlas Global

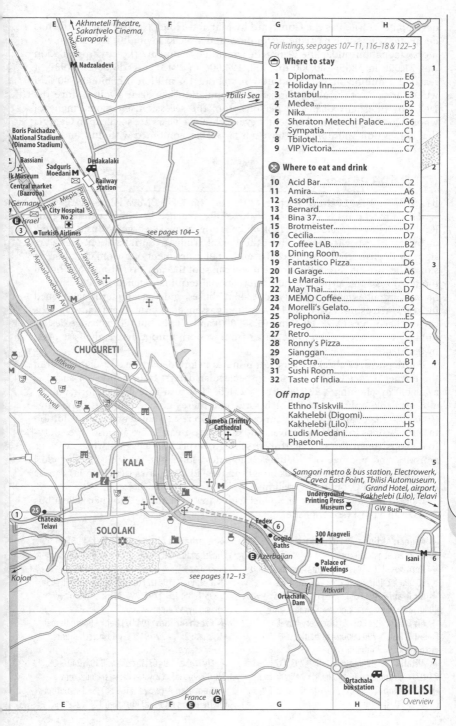

For listings, see pages 107–11, 116–18 & 122–3

⌂ **Where to stay**

1	Diplomat	E6
2	Holiday Inn	D2
3	Istanbul	E3
4	Medea	B2
5	Nika	B2
6	Sheraton Metechi Palace	G6
7	Sympatia	C1
8	Tbilotel	C1
9	VIP Victoria	C7

✖ **Where to eat and drink**

10	Acid Bar	C2
11	Amira	A6
12	Assorti	A6
13	Bernard	C7
14	Bina 37	C1
15	Brotmeister	D7
16	Cecilia	D7
17	Coffee LAB	B2
18	Dining Room	C7
19	Fantastico Pizza	D6
20	Il Garage	A6
21	Le Marais	C7
22	May Thai	D7
23	MEMO Coffee	B6
24	Morelli's Gelato	C2
25	Poliphonia	E5
26	Prego	D7
27	Retro	C2
28	Ronny's Pizza	C1
29	Sianggan	C1
30	Spectra	B1
31	Sushi Room	C7
32	Taste of India	C1

Off map

	Ethno Tsiskvili	C1
	Kakhelebi (Digomi)	C1
	Kakhelebi (Lilo)	H5
	Ludis Moedani	C1
	Phaetoni	C1

see pages 104–5

see pages 112–13

Samgori metro & bus station, Electrowerk,
Cavea East Point, Tbilisi Automuseum,
Grand Hotel, airport,
Kakhelebi (Lilo), Telavi

TBILISI
Overview

Tbilisi HISTORY

3

developments, such as the Courtyard by Marriott Hotel. Nearby, the old town is decaying, with some pastiche restoration under Saakashvili, but less action and more stagnation under the Georgian Dream government. The city's population was 71,000 in 1865, 120,000 in 1900, 194,000 in 1913, and 519,000 in 1939; it reached a million in 1977, and now has about 1.4 million inhabitants, 40% of whom are not ethnically Georgian. Its population has been swollen since the 1990s by internally displaced persons from the secessionist regions, many of whom have no stable employment; nevertheless used cars are so cheap in Georgia that congestion and pollution have got far worse, combined with dust and sand from a construction boom.

GETTING THERE AND AWAY

BY AIR Tbilisi's **Lochini Airport** [95 H5] (*formerly Novo-Alexeyevka; TBS;* **w** *tbilisiairport.com*) is 18km east of the centre, reached by bus or taxi along the Kakheti Highway (a short stretch of which is now named George W Bush Avenue), or by train (just twice a day) from the Voksal, Tbilisi's central station. There are signs in English from the city centre and a tall monument of a woman holding a sun at the turn-off. From the air, see if you can spot the *kurgans* (Bronze Age burial mounds) near the airport. A new international terminal opened in 2007, able to handle aircraft as large as A330 and A340 Airbuses, and a second terminal opened in 2017, increasing capacity to four million passengers a year. There's now an Avis car-rental counter (❬ *92 3594;* m *595 587000*) and ATMs, but the exchange desk is unlikely to be open when most planes from western Europe arrive; they are open by 05.30, however.

For **departures** check-in is 60–90 minutes before departure and flights within the former Soviet Union can suffer spectacular delays. Information (of sorts) is available by phoning ❬ 231 0421 or ❬ 231 0341. Up-to-date flight information is also available online at **w** tbilisiairport.com. There's a coffee shop at departures (⊕ *08.00–23.00*) and a 24-hour Turkish-Georgian restaurant at arrivals in addition to 'British' pubs in both the arrivals and departure areas. There are also three duty-free shops (open for all departures) selling overpriced Georgian wines, various whiskies and a range of perfumes, cigarettes, sunglasses and electrical goods. Remember that duty-free goods bought in non-EU countries (ie: Georgia) can be taken into the EU, but there are limits.

It's also possible to arrive at Kutaisi with a low-cost airline and then take a bus transfer to Tbilisi (see opposite).

✈ **Aegean Airlines** [94 B7] Paliashvili 66; ❬ 290 7090; **w** en.aegeanair.com

✈ **Aeroflot** [105 F4] Davit Agmashenebelis 10D; ❬ 290 0900; **e** info@avio.ge; **w** aeroflot.ru

✈ **Air Arabia** [94 C6] Chavchavadze Av 15; ❬ 240 0040; **e** airarabia@gasa.ge; **w** airarabia.com

✈ **Air Baltic** [94 B6] c/o Discovery Travel, Paliashvili 61; ❬ 290 0900; **e** airbalticgsa@ discovery.ge; **w** airbaltic.com

✈ **Alitalia** [94 B2] Kazbegi 14B; ❬ 293 7373, 293 73803; **e** customercare@alitalia.it; **w** alitalia.com

✈ **Atlas Global** [94 C7] Arakishvili 8; ❬ 225 0330; **w** atlasjet.com

✈ **Azerbaijan Airlines (AZAL)** [94 D6] Chavchavadze 28; ❬ 225 888; **e** tbilisi@azal.az; **w** azal.az

✈ **Belavia** [104 D2] Davit Agmashenebelis 95a; ❬ 295 1685, 291 1791, 295 3815; **e** georgia@ belavia.by; **w** en.belavia.by

✈ **Czech Airlines** [94 D7] Berika International, Mtskheta 2; ❬ 2 22 7941; **e** info@czechairlines. ge; **w** csa.cz

✈ **Fly Dubai** [94 C7] Taktakishvili 10 ❬ 240 0808, 240 0909; **e** info@voyager.ge; **w** flydubai.com

✈ **Georgian Airways** [105 E6] (Still sometimes referred to as Air Zena) Rustaveli 12; ❬ 248

5511, 248 5577; e info@georgian-airways.com;
w georgian-airways.com
✈ **LOT** [94 A3] Chavchavadze Av 43 (Victory Sq);
↘255 4455; e lot@lottravel.ge; w lot.com
✈ **Lufthansa** [94 C7] Abashidze 24; ↘247 3990,
291 2080; e viatravel@viatravel.ge, lufthansa.
tbilisi@dlh.de; w lufthansa.com
✈ **Pegasus** [112 B2] Courtyard by Marriott Hotel
(Freedom Sq); ↘240 0040; w flypgs.com

✈ **Qatar Airways** [105 F6] Pirimze Plaza
Bldg, Vekua 3; ↘243 9608/09, 248 6000;
w qatarairways.com/ge
✈ **Turkish Airlines (THY)** [95 E3] Davit
Agmashenebelis 147; ↘295 9022, 294 0703;
e tbsmarketing@thy.com; w turkishairlines.com
✈ **Ukraine International Airlines** [105 E5]
Marie Brosse 2; ↘243 8614; e georgia@flyuia.
com; w flyuia.com
✈ **Wizzair** [104 A3] Chavchavadze Av 2; m 595
641525, 599 526007; e info@aviabiletebi24.ge

Airport transfer Bus route 37 (a blue MAN bus) runs from the airport along the Kakheti Highway to Samgori (for metro and bus stations), Avlabari, the Baratashvili Bridge, Freedom Square, Rustaveli, Kostavas and Tamar avenues, giving a handy tour of the central area, and after half an hour reaching Station Square, where they leave from the stops in front of the railway station. The bus runs 24 hours a day (every 15–20 minutes, or every 30–40 minutes overnight) and costs just GEL0.50 (*US$0.30*) – you'll need a MetroMoney card or coins. **Taxis** cost GEL25 (*US$15*) by day, or GEL30 (*US$17*) at night, usually after 20.00 (confirm the price before departure); transfers can also be organised through hotels and hostels, for GEL25–30. A **railway** branch to the airport's armadillo-like station opened in 2008, but trains currently leave only at 07.50 and 16.55 from the city's central station, taking around 35 minutes and returning 45 minutes later; pay the fare of GEL0.50 on board. Heading east to Kakheti, it's less than 2km to the highway, if you want to flag down a **marshrutka**, but it's easier to arrange a transfer with your hotel, which can include a detour via Davit-Gareja.

From Kutaisi Airport, used by low-cost flights, **Georgian Bus** (m *555 397387*; w *georgianbus.com*) runs connecting minibuses direct to Pushkin Square, taking 4 hours; return tickets can be bought online or across the road at Bar Warszawa (⊕ *10.00–04.00*).

BY RAIL In 2010, the massive Soviet railway station [95 E2] (pages 148–9) was converted into a modern shopping complex with a supermarket and jewellery shops on the ground floor, and clothing retailers on the first and second floors. The ticket hall is on the third floor on a bridge over the tracks – from the metro station go up the external ramp road to the second floor (at platform level), then go up on the escalator. There are English-language timetables; a monitor next to the ticket counters (⊕ *until 23.00*) shows the availability of tickets and berths on night trains, in Georgian and English. For rail information, call ↘313 on the phones provided, or see w railway.ge, which gives a brief outline of services. On the next floor up there's a food court with a variety of fast-food stands, all reasonably priced, plus a play area. Left-luggage is at the west end of platform 1(⊕ *06.00–22.00 daily*). Trains leave for Borjomi at 06.30 and 16.15, for Batumi at 08.00, 17.30 and midnight, for Poti at 08.30 and 17.50, for Zugdidi at 09.00, 18.15 and 21.45, and for Ozurgeti at 09.00 and 21.45, although precise times may change. For those arriving late at night there's a hotel up on the sixth floor.

BY BUS International buses from Azerbaijan, Armenia, Turkey and Greece arrive at **Ortachala** [95 H7], southeast of the centre, in theory the main bus station, with exchange desks but no ATM, and some cheap hotels. Ortachala also handles some services to Kakheti, and the Metro Class buses (↘ *275 0595*; m *577 159415*;

w *geometro.ge; GEL20–25*) leave for Batumi at noon, 15.00, 20.00, midnight and 01.00, with Wi-Fi, air conditioning and reserved seats. The main terminal is in fact at **Didube** [94 D1] (✆ *234 4924*), to the northwest, but it is a disgraceful mess; emerging from the metro station through a crush of stalls, traders and bus touts, you'll find in front of you a yard full of minibuses and shared taxis. Marshrutkas for Mtskheta (and taxis to Davit-Gareja) wait about 50m ahead and to the right, and beyond them the hourly marshrutkas to Kazbegi (sometimes with signs in Latin or Cyrillic scripts). Otherwise turn left from the metro subway and ask for your destination (such as Kaspi, Gori, Borjomi, Zestaponi, Kutaisi, Akhaltsikhe and elsewhere). Alternatively, go a couple of hundred metres to the right – first you'll come to the Autovoksal Okriba, fairly new but just used as parking for buses, with what should be ticket offices rented out as shops; and then the old terminal, where you'll find vile toilets and left-luggage and exchange facilities. Marshrutkas leave hourly to Batumi (⊕ *09.00–17.00*), as do the really quite decent coaches to Kutaisi; there are also frequent marshrutkas to destinations such as Marneuli, Akhaltsikhe, Sacchere, Kutaisi, Poti, Zugdidi and Batumi. Metro coaches to Zugdidi (m *599 201506;* w *geometro.ge; GEL15*) leave from here at noon, 19.00 and 01.00, as well as buses and shared taxis to Russia (for those who have visas).

Buses for destinations in the **west** of the country, and **north** to Kazbegi, leave Didube until mid afternoon; later on you're best off going to the Dedakalaki (Capital) bus station on the rear (or north) side of the main railway station [95 E2] (✆ *218 0567*). At the front of the station you can find marshrutkas and shared taxis to relatively close destinations such as Rustavi, Marneuli and Kaspi. This is much more orderly and pleasant than Didube. A couple of ticket kiosks serve timetabled buses for Chiatura, Kutaisi, Senaki, Samtredia, Poti, Zugdidi and Ozurgeti, as well as marshrutkas that leave when full, with the last departures at about 19.00. Buses to Batumi leave at 10.00, 13.00, 16.00 and midnight, and marshrutkas leave roughly every 2½ hours from 09.00 to 19.00, and at midnight; there are also hourly marshrutkas to Batumi from the Sports Palace.

Marshrutkas **eastwards** to Kakheti leave from Ortachala (in front of the terminal), and from the Samgori metro station [95 H5]. Arriving at Samgori by metro from the centre, go to the left-hand end of the platform, turn right and go up to find local buses to Sagarejo, for instance; marshrutkas leave from a yard a short distance west, known as the Naftlugi bus station. Shared taxis and some marshrutkas also leave from just behind (north of) the Isani metro station [95 H6] (*Atskhuri 47*), where services from Samgori also pick up passengers, although they may already be full at this point. From Ortachala, marshrutkas leave from 08.00 to 18.00 every 40 minutes for Telavi (*GEL7*), every 20 minutes for Kvareli (*GEL8*), hourly to Dedopolis-Tskaro (*GEL7*), to Akhmeta (*GEL8*) at 10.00, 14.00, 17.00 and 19.00, to Gremi (*GEL8*) at noon, 15.00 and 16.00 and to Duisi (*GEL10*) at 07.30. From Samgori they leave from 09.30 to 16.45 every 45 minutes to Telavi (*GEL7*), every 20 minutes to Sagarejo (*GEL3*) and six times daily from 09.00 to Sighnaghi (*GEL6*); also at the far end for towns south of Tbilisi such as Marneuli, Bolnisi and Dmanisi. From Isani marshrutkas leave for Gurjaani every 20 minutes (*08.30–19.00; GEL6*), to Tsnori every 40 minutes (*GEL6*) and to Lagodekhi (*GEL7*) 15 times between 08.00 and 18.15.

The occasional bus to Tsiteli Khidi (the Krasni Most or Red Bridge, the main border crossing to **Azerbaijan**) also leaves from Samgori and from opposite the Isani metro station; they connect with minibuses on the far side of the border. Marshrutkas for Manglisi leave from Station Square at 11.00 and hourly from 13.00 to 18.00 and from Victory Square (Gamarjvebis Moedani). Marshrutkas to

Marneuli and Bolnisi leave from the Ortachala roundabout. Buses to Rustavi leave from Didube and the Dinamo Stadium.

Heading towards **Armenia**, there are buses from Ortachala to Yerevan (*GEL30*) every 50 minutes from 07.30 to 15.00, to Stepanavan at 08.00, to Artiki at 08.45, to Vanadzor at 09.20, to Gyumri at 10.30 and to Spitak at 15.00, plus to Yerevan from the rear of the railway station at 11.00 and 17.00. However, the easiest way to get to Yerevan is with the comfortable cars waiting opposite Avlabari metro station (*09.00, 11.00, 13.00; GEL35 pp for a full car*). For Baku (Azerbaijan), there's a departure from Ortachala at 14.00 daily plus at 16.00 on Mondays (*GEL30*).

Buses to **Turkey and Greece** (a very long haul) leave from Ortachala; see pages 64–5 for details of operators (it's best to buy tickets a day ahead). Buses leave Ortachala for Trabzon at 17.00 and 20.00 (*around 12hrs; US$30*), for Ankara at 10.30, 18.00, 18.30 and 19.00 (*around 26hrs; US$50*), for Istanbul at 08.00, 10.00, 10.30, 11.00 and noon (*34hrs; US$59*), and for Antalya (*31hrs; US$80*) and Izmir (*29hrs; US$70*) at 10.00. For Thessaloniki (*36hrs; US$80*) and Athens (*42hrs; US$100*) there are departures on Monday at 14.00, Tuesday at 13.00, Wednesday, Thursday and Friday at 10.00, and Sunday at 09.00.

Heading north to **Russia**, there are shared taxis from Didube to Mineralni Vodi, and daily buses from Ortachala at 11.00 to Mineralni Vodi and at 14.00 to Vladikavkaz (*GEL60*), Pyatigorsk (*GEL80*), continuing on Monday, Tuesday, Thursday, Friday and Sunday to Rostov-on-Don (*GEL140*). There's a through-bus from Ortachala to Moscow (*GEL200*) on Thursdays at noon. Finally, there's a bus at noon daily from Ortachala to **Tehran** (℡ *275 3442*; m *599 220614*; *US$50*).

TRAVEL AGENCIES The leading Georgian ticket agencies are **BusinessTravelCom**, offering air and hotel reservations, car and bus rental and other travel services; they're at Mtskheta 17 [94 C7] (℡ *299 9662*; m *592 075353*; ⏰ *10.00–17.30 Mon–Fri, 10.00–14.00 Sat*). **Georgian Avia Service Agency** [112 B2] (*GASA; Courtyard by Marriott Hotel, Freedom Sq 4; Tbilisi Airport; & East Point Mall; all* ℡ *240 0040*; e *contact@ gasa.ge;* w *gasa.ge*), **Levon Travel** [94 D6] (*Chavchavadze Av 20;* ℡*225 0010;* e *sales@ levontravel.ge;* w *levontravel.ge*) *and the slightly less slick* **Berika International** [94 D7] (*Mtskheta 2;* ℡*222 0941;* e *berika@berika.ge;* w *berika.ge*) are travel agencies that deal more with residents than visitors, but can book flights with all major airlines. **Promethea Voyages** [105 E6] (*formerly CGTT Voyages; Besiki 4;* ℡ *222 1425/6;* e *contact@promethea-voyages.com;* w *promethea-voyages.com*) is a French-owned company operating across the former Soviet Union.

See pages 59–60 for tour operators.

GETTING AROUND

Tbilisi has a two-line metro system, as well as buses and swarms of private marshrutka minibuses. Public transport runs from 06.00 to midnight. Since 2010, all metro, bus and cable car users must use a MetroMoney card, sold at metro and cable car stations. The minimum initial payment is GEL5 (GEL2.50 for the card deposit plus GEL2.50 credit) and these can be topped up as necessary at stations or pay machines. This can be refunded if you return the card within a month of purchase. Each journey (up to 90 minutes in duration, with free transfers between lines or to buses) subtracts GEL0.50 from the total value of credit on the card. You can still use coins on marshrutkas, but you need a MetroMoney card for **cable cars** (from Rikhe Park to Narikala and from Vake Park to Turtle Lake). The funicular up to Mtatsminda uses its own system.

METRO [map, opposite] The metro (w *ttc.com.ge*) opened in 1966 and extends for 27km, with 22 stations. There are two lines, mostly deep underground, meeting at Station Square (Sadguris Moedani), and trains run roughly every 4 minutes. Baggage is not generally permitted on the metro, but foreigners with rucksacks are allowed.

The principal line runs largely parallel to the Mtkvari from north to southeast, from Akhmeteli to Didube, Station Square, Marjanishvili, Rustaveli Square, Freedom (or Liberty) Square, Avlabari, Isani, Samgori and Varketili; the other line runs westwards from Station Square through the Saburtalo district mostly along Vazha-Pshavelas Avenue to Universiteti. The system seems to have been built on the cheap, with stations unusually far apart and platforms only five carriage-lengths long (and three- and four-carriage trains); however, the trains and four central stations were refurbished in 2006, and announcements and signs are now in English as well as Georgian.

BY TAXI There are thousands of taxis on the road in Tbilisi at any time, all unregulated, though a few do have meters. You shouldn't pay more than GEL6 (*US$3*) around town or GEL10–15 (*US$3.50–5*) to go to Turtle Lake or the Tbilisi Sea (fares double late at night). Two dependable taxi companies that may be pre-booked are **Gig Taxi** (✆*278 7878*) and **NBO Taxi** (✆*242 0111*). **Taxi.Ge** (✆*274 7474; w *taxi.ge*) is also good but slightly pricier at GEL0.60/km.

BY MARSHRUTKA AND BUS Marshrutkas (yellow Ford Transits) are a phenomenon that barely existed under the Soviet Union: the franchise for each line is owned by someone (often a member of parliament, for some reason) whom minibus owners/drivers pay for the right to work. They run from dawn to 23.00 (later in summer). Fares are GEL0.80, compared with GEL0.50 for buses (touch a MetroMoney card or pay with coins, and take a ticket at the bottom of the machine). In 2006 a fleet of 500 relatively new, yellow Dutch **buses** were introduced and marshrutkas were summarily banned from the main axis of Rustaveli, Kostavas and Chavchavadze avenues. The marshrutkas (which should have been reorganised to be feeders to the metro and the new buses) simply moved to the inadequate parallel streets, with no information available about where they could be found or their destination other than the basic route information board (in Georgian) displayed in their front window. They're now back on the main avenues, but stop only at designated stops (they'll stop anywhere on other streets). Modern blue MAN buses powered by compressed natural gas are now being introduced.

Buses run every 10 minutes or so. They're slower and cheaper than marshrutkas, but have more space and in general provide a more relaxing experience; you can feed coins into the payment machine as you board, or use a MetroMoney card.

Bus stops have dot-matrix screens giving live updates on the next departures (principal services only; in Georgian and English alternately), or you could try phoning ✆ 272 3433 for information, or texting the stop's ID number to m 93344; stops also have QR codes. There's an online bus journey planner at w transiten. ttc.com.ge/#, and the app w tm.ge/routes/site.php?lang=2 gives marshrutka routes; the Moovit app gives real-time information. Bus route 87 is a handy loop, from Baratashvili Street via Freedom Square, Rustaveli Avenue, Kostavas, Pekini and Vazha-Pshavelas Avenue to Delisi metro, then around by the university to Chavchavadze Avenue and back along Rustaveli to Baratashvili Street.

Ortachala **bus terminal** [95 H7] is served by buses 44, 71 and 80 from Baratashvili Street and by a dozen marshrutka routes; some of these terminate at the roundabout just to the west. The Didube bus station [94 D1] is best reached by

metro, but many bus routes pass it, notably 15 and 27 from Station Square, 20 from Orbeliani Square, 33 from Baratashvili, 46 from Avlabari (via Rustaveli) and 51 from Vake. The Samgori bus station [95 H5] is also best reached by metro, but buses 25 and 39 come here from Baratashvili, as well as the 101 from Ortachala.

Electric **trolleybuses** and **trams** ceased running at the end of 2006 as one of the early reforms following the Rose Revolution. However, as the buses that replaced them are polluting and barely able to cover their costs, there's talk of laying down new tram lines. There are also two **sightseeing bus** companies, Bus Hopper (m *595 170502*; w *hoponhopoff.ge/en*; *GEL40 for 24hrs*) and City Sightseeing [113 G1] (*Rkinis Rigi 11*; 243 8088, 243 8808; m *514 217722*; w *https://cstbilisi.com*; *GEL20 for 24hrs*). City Sightseeing uses an open-top double-decker, and also offers a boat tour below the Metekhi Cliffs for an extra GEL12. Boat tours are also provided by Borani, at the north end of the Metekhi Bridge [113 F3] (m *596 135858*; w *borani.ge*). Both buses go out to Mskheta too, costing an extra GEL10 with Bus Hopper or GEL16 with City Sightseeing; this is the cheapest and easiest way to get up to the Jvari Church.

There are also some brilliant specialist tours, notably the Tbilisi Soviet Concrete Walking Tours ('*In concrete we trust*'; e *brutaltours@gmail.com*; w *brutaltours. com*; €*25–40/day*), Taste Georgia (m *599 039106*; w *tastegeorgia.co*; *US$85/day*), and the Culinary Backstreets food tours (w *culinarybackstreets.com/culinary-walks/tbilisi/*; *US$85/day*). Good free walking tours of Tbilisi are put on by Tbilisi Hack (m *599 922937*; e *tbilisifreewalkingtour@gmail.com, tbilisihack@gmail. com*; w *tbilisifreewalkingtour.com*), starting daily at noon in front of the Old City Hall [112 C2] on Freedom Square, as well as the more offbeat Fabrikahood Tour, leaving from the Fabrika hostel [105 F2] (*Ninoshvili 8*) at noon on Wednesdays and Saturdays.

CAR HIRE As well as the international chains, there are local companies offering jeeps, saloon cars and minivans, with or without drivers, for US$95–110 (US$25 more to include a driver). Be sure to check what your insurance covers; Georgian companies may tell you that third-party cover is neither needed nor available. You can also use w gotrip.ge to enter a destination and see a list of drivers and cars, languages spoken, and prices. There are 24-hour petrol stations at the airport junction, Ortachala, and on the Mtskheta Highway, and there are plenty of others on the river embankments.

International companies

🚗 **Avis** [112 B2] Freedom Sq 4; 292 3594; m 599 190391; e reservations@avis.ge; w avis. ge; at the airport [95 H5]: 292 3594; m 595 587000

🚗 **Budget** [104 D4] Rustaveli Av 37 (Rose Revolution Sq); 223 4112; w budget.com.ge

🚗 **Europcar** [113 H2] Samghebro 6; 275 4471; m 551 348844; w europcar-georgia.com

🚗 **Hertz** (Inc Dollar & Thrifty) [113 G1] Leselidze 53; 272 3530; m 597 994453; w hertz. com.ge; at the Radisson Blu Hotel [104 D4], Rose Revolution Sq; 230 7890; m 574 551133

🚗 **Sixt** [113 G1] Leselidze 44; 243 9911; w sixt.com.ge

Local companies

🚗 **Cars4Rent** [112 C3] Dadiani 24A; 230 6095; e info@world4you.travel; w cars4rent.ge

🚗 **Geo Rent Car** [112 C3] Lermontov 9; 293 0099; m 595 930099; e georentcar.ge@gmail. com; w georentcar.ge

🚗 **GSS Car Rental** [112 C2] Dadiani 10 & [105 F6] Purtseladze 14; m 571 446644; w gsservices.ge

🚗 **Jeep Rent Ltd** [104 B4] Tatishvili 19; 210 6310; m 551 106310; w jeeprent.ge

🚗 **Naniko Rentacar** [113 G1] Leselidze 49 & [104 A3] Barnov 82; 214 7675; m 574 288855; w naniko.ge

🚗 **RACE (Rent a Car Enterprises)** [112 D2] Leselidze 22; m 514 577555, 514 896896; w race. com.ge

🚗 **Royal Geo Rentacar** [112 D2] Leselidze 22; m 591 191923; w geocarrent.ge

🚗 **Star Rentacar** [112 D2] Leselidze 27; m 570 700330; w carrentalgeorgia.ge

CYCLE HIRE There's very little cycling in Tbilisi, owing to the polluted congested roads and very poor standards of driving and car parking.

🚲 **Bikes.ge** [94 B6] Abashidze 51 (Vake); ✆225 0828, m 551 263737; & [94 C2] Iosebidze 61 (Saburtalo); ✆237 1884; m 551 263737; w bikes. ge; ⏰ 10.00–20.00 daily

🚲 **Mogzauri** [94 A2] Vazha-Pshavelas 91; ✆231 9101, m 568 659985, 599 504113; w mogzaurirent.ge; ⏰ 10.00–19.00 daily

TOURIST INFORMATION

Tbilisi has an efficient **tourist information centre** [112 B2] (✆ *32 215 8697;* m *595 997752;* e *tictbilisi@gmail.com;* w *gnta.ge;* ⏰ *10.00–21.00 daily*) opposite City Hall on Pushkin Square. The helpful English-speaking staff has free maps and booklets to give away, and can advise on transport and help book accommodation in the city and beyond.

WHERE TO STAY

After the Abkhazian War, the Soviet-era block-hotels in Tbilisi and across Georgia were taken over by refugees and for a while there was almost nowhere to stay. Soon a crop of small, pricey guesthouses sprouted up for businessmen; these often have no sign on the street (both for security and for tax evasion), and should be booked in advance. In the last decade a new generation of backpacker-oriented homestays and hostels has appeared, mostly in the Old Town and the Marjanishvili district, and there are also plenty of new small hotels, as well as a couple of Marriotts for the business market. Now that the refugees have been relocated from the Soviet-era hotels, these have been rebuilt as modern facilities: the Radisson and Holiday Inn towers are now open, but plans for Novotel, Intercontinental and Park Hyatt hotels seem to be on hold. It might seem as though Tbilisi now has a huge over-provision of hotels, but very few have more than a dozen rooms.

Most **hotels** cater for Georgian tastes with huge (cold) rooms and echoing apartments; a few, such as the Kartli, have smaller, snugger European-style rooms. All but the very cheapest have their own generator; few have lifts. Remember that you'll have to pay an extra 18% tax in many cases.

Most of the **hostels** listed offer freeWi-Fi, tea, coffee and cooking facilities. Most can be booked online through sites like w hostelworld.com, w hostelplanet.com or w hostels.com. There are many other hostels in Tbilisi (mainly Sololaki), many of which are lucky to last one season.

For **budget** travellers looking for something slightly better than a hostel bed, the best bet is probably a private room in a city homestay. For longer stays you might want to rent an apartment (*see* w *besttbilisiapartments.com or* w *rental.ge/apartments. htm*); there's also the Citadines apart-hotel behind Freedom Square 4 [112 B2] (✆*254 7030;* e *tbilisi@citadines.com;* w *citadines.com*). And of course, AirBnB (w *airbnb. com*) is a great source of apartments, rooms and bed-and-breakfast options.

HOSTELS & HOMESTAYS

🏠 **Formula 1 Guest House** [104 D6] (7 rooms) Kote Meskhi 13a; ✆m 574 456789;

e ghformula1@gmail.com; w formula1georgia. com. A little hard to find, up a steep hill in the Mtatsminda district a 10min walk west of Rustaveli;

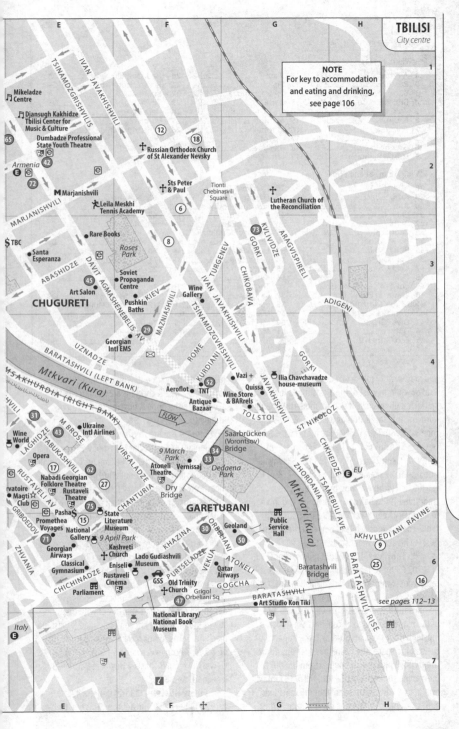

NOTE
For key to accommodation
and eating and drinking,
see page 106

Mikeladze Centre

Djansugh Kakhidze Tbilisi Center for Music & Culture

Dumbadze Professional State Youth Theatre

Armenia

Russian Orthodox Church of St Alexander Nevsky

Sts Peter & Paul

Tionti Chebinasvili Square

Lutheran Church of the Reconciliation

Marjanishvili

Leila Meskhi Tennis Academy

Rare Books

Roses Park

TBC

Santa Esperanza

Soviet Propaganda Centre

Art Salon

CHUGURETI

Pushkin Baths

Wine Gallery

Georgian Intl EMS

Mtkvari (Kura)

BARATASHVILI (LEFT BANK)

Aeroflot

TNT

Antique Bazaar

Wine Store & BARrels

Vazi

Quissa

Ilia Chavchavadze house-museum

Ukraine Intl Airlines

Wine World

Opera

9 March Park

Saarbrücken (Voronfsov) Bridge

Nabadi Georgian Folklore Theatre

Rustaveli Theatre

Atoneli Theatre

Vernissaj

Dedaena Park

Dry Bridge

GARETUBANI

Promethea Voyages

Pasha

State Literature Museum

Public Service Hall

Geoland

EU

Georgian Airways

National Gallery

9 April Park

Kashveti Church

Lado Gudiashvili Museum

Classical Gymnasium

Eniseli

Rustaveli Cinema

Parliament

GSS

Old Trinity Church

Qatar Airways

Grigol Orbeliani Sq

Baratashvili Bridge

BARATASHVILI

Art Studio Kon Tiki

see pages 112–13

Italy

National Library/ National Book Museum

⊖ **Where to stay**

1	A & M....................D5	10	Iliani.........................B2	20	Radisson Blu Iveria..............D4
2	Beaumonde................D5	11	Ilja's..........................B4	21	Rooms Hotel Tbilisi...........C4
3	Betsy's......................C5	12	Irina Japaridze..........F2	22	Stamba...........................C4
4	British House............B4	13	Kartli.........................B4	23	TiflisLux.........................D5
5	Classic......................B4	14	Lia's Guesthouse........D5	24	Vere Palace....................B2
6	Fabrika.....................F2	15	Marriott Tbilisi..........E6	25	Vinotel..........................H6
7	Formula 1	16	Mirobelle...................H6	26	Waltzing Matilda Hostel.....D5
	Guest House..........D6	17	Opera.........................E5	27	Why Not? Hostel...............E5
8	Green Stairs...............F3	18	Prestige......................F2		
9	Hostel Baratashvili.....H6	19	Primavera...................B3		

✖ **Where to eat and drink**

28	Alubali..............................C4	46	Factory 27.......................B4	64	Nali..............................D4
29	Amber Bar..........................F4	47	Flashback.........................F6	65	Nasimi............................E2
30	Atoneli 21..........................F6	48	Funicular Lounge...........C7	66	O, Moda, Moda............A4
31	Baan Thai...........................E5	49	Green Terrace................A3	67	Old London....................C4
32	Barbarestan.......................D1	50	Hello Coffee...................G6	68	Picasso...........................C3
33	Bauhaus............................F5	51	House of Khinkhali.....D4	69	Rainer's Pizzeria &
34	Book Corner Café.............F5	52	House on Madatovi..... F4		Biergarten.................. B4
35	Buffalo Bill.......................C4	53	Hurma Café....................B3	70	Rhea's Squirrels............D7
36	Café Goethe......................C4	54	Iveria Café......................D4	71	Sake Sushi Bar.............E6
37	Café Literaturuli...............B3	55	Keti's Bistro....................C4	72	Second Cup....................E2
38	Café Red............................D3	56	Keto & Kote.....................C4	73	Shavi Lomi...................G3
39	Caliban's Coffeehouse......D5		The Kitchen..........(see 21)	74	Shemoikhede
40	Canudos Ethnic Bar...........D4	57	La Fondue.......................B3		Genatsvale..................D3
41	Csaba's Jazz-Rock Café.....C3	58	Luca Polare.....................D1	75	Sophia Melnikova's
42	Deniz.................................E2	59	Maharajah.......................C3		Fabulous Douqan..... E5
43	Dive Bar............................E5	60	Marco Polo.....................D5	76	Strada..............................D3
44	Dublin...............................C4	61	McDonald's.....................C4	77	Wheels.............................C3
45	Eco Garden....................... E3	62	Minimalist......................E5	78	Zala.................................B4
	Fabrika........................(see 6)	63	Mukha Café.....................C3		

you may want to take a taxi up at night. Steps also lead down from west of the Mtatsminda funicular station on Chonkadze. It's clean, modern & friendly, with en-suite sgls & dbls as well as 4- & 5-bed rooms, all with TV & Wi-Fi. Price inc b/fast. **$$$**

✳ ⌂ **SKAdaVELI** [112 C1] (4 rooms, 1 en suite) Vertskhli 27; m 595 417333; e Skadaveli@ gmail.com; w ska.ge. Rooms (with Wi-Fi & AC) & a kitchen (with washing machine) along a traditional Tbilisi balcony in the lower Old Town. Irekli is very helpful & rooms are spacious with tables, desk lamps & lots of power sockets (& no TVs), so ideal for longer stays. **$$$**

✳ ⌂ **Fabrika** [105 F2] (98 rooms) Ninoshvili 8; ☎ 202 0399; w fabrikatbilisi.com. A former silk factory just 5mins from Marjanishvili metro station has seen a spectacular re-invention & now houses perhaps the best hostel in the Caucasus (& one of the biggest), as well as cool bars & eateries, a hipster barber shop, art studios & the Impact Hub co-working space. The hostel has spacious dorms (*from US$7*) plus private rooms (from US$40) & mezzanine suites (from US$100), all with fantastic firm beds & towels; there are laundry machines in the basement with a free dryer & irons. B/fast

(*US$7*) is simply superb, with omelettes made to order, & pizza & cocktails are available in the evenings in the huge & buzzing ground-floor lounge (page 119). **$–$$**

⌂ **Hostel Baratashvili** [105 H6] (11 rooms) Akhvlediani Khevi (Ravine) 3; m 559 776267; e booking@beacon.ge; w beacon.ge/baratashvili. In a good solid red-brick building, in a central but pleasantly residential district, this new hostel has mixed dorm & private rooms, all with AC, Wi-Fi & balconies looking out over a nice little public garden to the river & Public Service Hall; there's also a terrace & secure parking. **$–$$**

⌂ **TiflisLux** [104 D5] Griboedov 30; m 577 988143; w tiflislux.ge; **f**. Up an alley off Griboedov, this self-described boutique hostel & guesthouse has dorms & private rooms in a delightful Art Nouveau apartment with tiled stoves (not in use), 2 kitchens, a lounge & washing machine. Some rooms have en-suite bathrooms, AC & TVs. Balconies & a large terrace give great views. The regular TiflisLux Hostel at Barnov 23 is less good. **$–$$**

⌂ **Envoy Hostel** [113 H2] Betlemi 42; ☎ 292 0111; w envoyhostel.com. This big, well-established hostel is not the cheapest in town, but a good b/fast is included; there's a kitchen & common room, & a rooftop terrace with great city views (& beers from the friendly reception staff). They also run a tour company, with a sister hostel in Yerevan (Armenia). $

Green Stairs [105 F3] (4 rooms) Tsinamdzgvrishvili 53; 294 1552; m 593 331236; e vazha@lycos.com; w greenstairs.info. Another small hostel 5mins from Marjanishvili metro, though in a very untouristy area, this one has private rooms rather than dormitories. It's simple but comfortable & quiet (well away from the street); owner Vazha is very helpful. $

Irina Japaridze [105 F2] (12 rooms) Ninoshvili 19; m 599 111669; e irina5062@ gmail.com; guesthouse.irina. This is the 1st street on the left after the Russian church (taking Marjanishvili north from the metro). It's clean & spacious, with a dozen rooms (dorms & doubles), 4 bathrooms & 2 kitchens, TVs & great views over the city, plus free internet access & a washing machine (*GEL5 for a full load*). It's very popular with Israelis & even hosts celebrations of major Jewish holidays. $

Pushkin 10 Hostel [112 C2] Pushkin 10; m 577 651156; w pushkin10.ge. In a 3rd-floor apt right on Freedom Square, this very friendly hostel is like a home from home, with its cosy lounge, kitchen, & a pile of pancakes for b/fast. $

Tina's House [112 B2] (2 rooms) Sulkhan-Saba 5; m 593 139122; e t_gotsiridze@hotmail. com; w tbilisihomestay.com. Just off Freedom Sq, at the rear of the Marriott Courtyard Hotel. Tina works at the National Museum & Zviad is a taxi driver, so excellent & affordable tours can be arranged as well as airport pickups. Dbl rooms with shared bathroom, kitchen, washing machine & a filling b/fast (extra charge). $

Waltzing Matilda Hostel [104 D5] (8 rooms) Chavchavadze 11; 298 8343; m 593 997957, 597 730642; . A popular & very lively hostel near the Opera, not Australian- but Russian--owned, this has 2 large dorms & 6 smaller rooms, plus common room, kitchen & roof terrace. $

Why Not? Hostel [105 E5] Grishashvili 30; m 599 007030; e whynot.tbilisi@gmail.com; w whynothostels.com. With Polish, American & Georgian staff, this is one of the funkier & more cosmopolitan hostels in Tbilisi; sheets & towels inc. common room – & an excellent b/fast. It's

just moved to the sulphur baths area (where there aren't many other hostels). $

HOTELS
The hotels below are listed broadly from east to west, on the left/north bank & then the right bank. To book from abroad, prefix phone numbers with +99532.

Avlabari
Handy for the airport.

Sheraton Metechi Palace Hotel [95 G6] (220 rooms) Telavi 20; 277 2020, tf 0800 960501 (UK); e smpht@sheraton.com; w sheraton.com/ tbilisi. The city's premier hotel for many years, this has packed a lot of living into its short life - opened in 1989, in 1994 it was taken over by Kalashnikov-toting Mkhedrioni, supposedly there to guard the place; instead there were lurid stories of shootings in the bar & drug dealing in the corridors. The US embassy banned its officials from going there (although the EC office was there); famously, a sign on the door read 'Handguns allowed, semi-automatics to be left at reception'. In 1997 the Marco Polo group sold the building at a loss to Sheraton, & now it's like any other international business hotel, with its 7-storey atrium & glass lifts, & is home to various embassies & airline offices; nevertheless it's been overtaken by the Marriott & Radisson downtown. $$$$$

Old Tbilisi [113 H4] (24 rooms) Ketevan Tsamebuli 27; 277 3840–3; w hoteloldtbilisi.ge. On the cliffs above the Mtkvari River on the main road to the airport, this is a very nouveau hotel that is not particularly aimed at Westerners. Rates inc b/fast & internet access. $$$

Kopala [113 G3] (20 rooms) Chekhov 8–10; 277 5520; w kopala.ge. In a fantastic setting above the Metekhi Church (not to be confused with the newer Kopala on Rikhe Park), views are best enjoyed from the roof-top terrace rather than the restaurant, which serves small portions of average food. The rooms are nice, with AC, satellite TV, minibar, internet access, safe & hairdryer; there's a gym, sauna & business centre. $$$–$$$$, apts $$$$$

Dzveli (Old) Metekhi [113 G4] (15 rooms) Metekhi Rise 3; 299 0536; 293 4571; e dzmetekhi@hotmail.com; w oldmetekhi. tripod.com. A historic building set on the cliffs of the Mtkvari River, 10 of the rooms have balconies with a view of the city. All have AC, minibar, safe & satellite TV; there's also a good restaurant, which offers a 10% discount for hotel guests. Inc b/fast & tax. **$$$–$$$$**

🏠 **Georgian House** [113 G2] (12 rooms) Vakhtang VI 38; 📞 279 1919, 279 1920; w georgianhousetbilisi.com. Conveniently situated just uphill from Avlabari metro, close to Sameba Cathedral, this good-value small hotel has decent en-suite rooms with Wi-Fi, satellite TV, AC & minibar, as well as a pleasant terrace & brick cellar-bar. Inc tax & b/fast. **$$$**

🏠 **GTM** [113 F4] (32 rooms) Metekhi Rise 4; 📞 227 3348/9, m 599 990422; e hotel-gtmkapan@mail.ru; w gtm.ge. A modern, business-style hotel in a prime location, with views over the river & Old Town; rooms are good & clean with cable TV & free laptop internet access. There's a restaurant, conference hall, swimming pool, sauna, gym & billiards. Rates inc b/fast. **$$$**

🏠 **Mirobelle** [105 H6] (14 rooms) Samreklo 14; 📞 277 4977; m 557 754141; e mirobelle@live.com; 📘 mirobelle.hotel. Just a couple of hundred metres from the Sameba Cathedral, this is fairly new & squeaky clean but a bit over-priced, with friendly English-speaking staff & a good b/fast. **$$$**

Chugureti

🏠 **Vinotel** [105 H6] (13 rooms) Akhvlediani Rise 4; 📞 255 5888, m 596 555885; w vinotel.ge. Excellent new boutique hotel by the river (opposite the Public Service Hall), with a good restaurant & excellent wine cellar (with plenty of local natural wines); the antique furnishings are a bit over the top but every detail is perfectly placed. **$$$$$**

🏠 **Prestige** [105 F2] (25 rooms, 5 suites) Marjanishvili 51; 📞 294 0505, 294 2974; e hotelprestige_ge@yahoo.com; w hotelprestige.ge. Fairly handy for the railway station, this small hotel has AC rooms with satellite TV & minibar, plus a restaurant-bar & parking. **$$$**, suites **$$$$**

🏠 **Istanbul** [95 E3] (16 rooms) Davit Agmashenebelis 148; 📞 291 1182–3; w hotelistanbul.ge. In a former military school on the Turkish section of Davit Agmashenebelis, this has a cramped staircase & lift, but decent rooms with TV, minibar, free laptop connection & good bathrooms. English is spoken & there is a restaurant & bar. B/fast inc. **$$$$**

Old Town

🏠 **Mercure Tbilisi Old Town** [113 G4] (102 rooms) Gorgasali 9; 📞 200 6060; e H9417-RE@accor.com; w mercure.com/gb/hotel-9417-mercure-tbilisi-old-town/index.shtml. Opened in 2015 & not yet quite up to the standard of Mercure hotels elsewhere, this is still a comfortable 4-star place in a part of town that doesn't have many top-end hotels. B/fast is excellent, & there's a gym, spa & 2 saunas. **$$$$$**

🏠 **Ambasadori** [112 D1] (39 rooms, 3 suites) Shavteli 13; 📞 243 9494; w ambassadori.com. Close to Baratashvili Bridge, this is the grandest of Tbilisi's locally owned hotels, with business centre, casino, spa, Italian restaurant & a lift to the roof-top swimming pool. All rooms have AC, & the more expensive suites inc b/fast in the 4th-floor terrace café (🕐 until 02.00). **$$$$–$$$$$**

🏠 **Zaira** [112 D3] (7 rooms) Leselidze 31; 📞 298 9734; w hotel-zaira.tbilisi-hotels.com/en. In another courtyard off the old town's main drag, this hotel is accustomed to international business visitors; some English is spoken. Rates inc b/fast & tax; rooms have a balcony & microwave & there's free internet access. **$$$**

🏠 **GT** [112 D3] (21 rooms) Leselidze 28; 📞 247 8166; m 599 478160, 593 269920; e georgia-tbilisi@list.ru; w gthotel.ge. In a quiet courtyard just off the Old Town's main drag, this is a squeaky-clean & remarkably good hotel, with efficient reception staff, rooms with huge balconies & a roof terrace with great views. **$$$$**

🏠 **Villa Mtiebi** [112 D1] (8 rooms, 1 suite) Chakhrukhadze 10 (at the end of Ietim Gurji St); 📞 292 0340/1; e tbilisi@hotelmtiebi.ge; w hotelmtiebi.ge. In a discreet & beautifully restored 19th-century building, with a lovely b/fast hall/winter garden, rooms all have AC, satellite TV, CD player, minibar, laptop access, free umbrella, hairdryer & orthopaedic mattress plus a large bathroom. There's also free internet access, gym, sauna & small swimming pool. Rates inc b/fast but exc tax. **$$$$**

🏠 **Sharden** [112 D4] Khanzteli 32; 📞 292 2027, 292 1980; w hotelsharden.com. Just above the Norashen church, this is recommended mainly for its location (& great online deals) – it's a fairly functional place with variable service. There's a simple b/fast & a nice cellar-bar, but no restaurant. Some rooms are small, others quite spacious; the lift only goes to the 2nd floor. **$$$$**

🏠 **Boutique Hotel No12** [112 D3] (12 rooms) Beridze (formerly Khodasheni) 12; 📞 255 2212; m 599 125520; w no12hotel.com. A beautifully contrived patio, above the basement b/fast room, leads in to this charmingly decorated little place, with smallish rooms in Andalusian style with stained-glass lampshades & tiles; the upstairs rooms are quieter. The b/fast is excellent. **$$$$$**

🏠 **Kalasi** [112 D2] (42 rooms) Leselidze 25; 📞 243 9600/1; w hotelkalasi.ge. A modern glass-fronted block (but with antique furniture in the foyer) on the old town's main drag (rooms at the front can be noisy); rooms are a bit small but clean, with good AC, Wi-Fi, buffet b/fast & laundry service. **$$$$**

🏠 **Ata** [112 C2] (5 rooms) Leselidze 17; 📞 298 7715; e hotelata@gmail.com; w myhotels. ge/hotelata. A modern block on a side road off Leselidze, the adequate large rooms have small TVs, metal doors & electric water-boilers; Nana speaks fair English. Inc b/fast. **$$$**

🏠 **Ibis Styles** [112 B3] (120 rooms) Tabidze 4; 📞 200 2424; e HA413@accor.com; w ibis.com/gb/ hotel-A413-ibis-styles-tbilisi-center-/index.shtml. On a pedestrianised street just off Freedom Square, this brand new place is a genuine 3-star hotel, in a city where everything else claims to be a 4-star; there's a rooftop café but no business centre, gym or parking, so it's better for leisure than business travel. 2 rooms are adapted for guests with reduced mobility. The Ibis Stadium should open in 2018 near the Dimano Stadium, a modern tower behind a Neoclassical façade. **$$$$$**

🏠 **Courtyard by Marriott** [112 B2] (118 rooms) Tavisuplebis Moedani (Freedom Sq) 4; 📞 277 9100; e courtyard.tbilisi@marriotthotels. com; w courtyardtbilisi.com. Opened in 2002, this 4-star sidekick to the Marriott proper offers all necessary amenities at a slightly more affordable price. All rooms have 2 phone lines & dataport, voicemail, cable/satellite TV, AC, safe, hairdryer & iron. There's a health club, swimming pool & sauna, & a bar & brasserie, notable for its Sun brunch (🕐 noon–16.00). Price inc b/fast & tax. **$$$$$**

🏠 **Iota** [112 B3] Lermontov 10; 📞 240 3010; w iotahotels.com. A brand new contemporary design hotel, the only one in this area, this has comfortable rooms with excellent bathrooms; punctilious English-speaking staff in the hotel but less so in the rooftop Ghumeli café & Iota Garden restaurant – the food in general seems unexciting & there's a shocking $20 charge for b/fast. **$$$$$**

New Town

🏠 **Marriott Tbilisi** [105 E6] (110 rooms, 17 suites) Rustaveli 13; 📞 277 9200; tf 0800 221222 (UK), 1 888 236 2427 (USA); w marriott.com/ tbsmc. Built in 1915 as the Majestic & reopened in 2002, this is Tbilisi's grandest hotel. Innovations include Tbilisi's first wine bar, the Patio open-air summer restaurant & ice machines on each floor (1 of which is smoke-free). **$$$$**

🏠 **Opera** [105 E5] (15 rooms) Vaso Abashidze 4; 📞 299 6799; m 551 982624, 599 155554; e info@hotelopera.ge, hotels.tbilisi.com@gmail. com; w hotelopera.ge; 📘. Just off Rustaveli, next to the opera house, this has always been a favourite with its friendly English-speaking staff; it's in a prime location & not too noisy. They've just added an extra storey; 4 rooms are 'luxe' with balcony & bath. **$$$$**

🏠 **Radisson Blu Iveria** [104 D4] (249 rooms & suites) Rose Revolution Sq (Vardebis Revolutsis moedani) 1; 📞 240 2200; e tbilisi.info@ radissonblu.com; w radissonblu.com/hotel-tbilisi. Once the run-down Hotel Iveria, which housed internal refugees for many years, has been transformed into a stylish, glass-fronted tower, Tbilisi's leading business hotel. The wide range of rooms & suites include 62 that connect with each other & 10 with facilities for guests with disabilities. There's free Wi-Fi throughout, a spa, health club & indoor pool, & also smart Italian & Asian-fusion restaurants, the Surface Bar (at ground level) & the Oxygen Bar (the highest bar in the city, on the 18th floor). **$$$$$**

🏠 **David** [112 A3] (11 rooms, 2 suites) Iashvili 16; 📞 293 5006; m 574 646600; e hoteldavid5@ gmail.com; w davidhotel.ge. Opened in 2001, rooms are a little Soviet-style, but in other respects the style is oriental. Rooms have satellite TV, fridge & internet access for laptops, & the bathrooms have tubs. The corridors are spacious & airy, & there's a pleasant little tea house. **$$$$**

🏠 **Diplomat** [95 E6] (9 rooms, 1 suite) Bolo Agmarti 4; 📞 292 2088; e hoteldiplomat@gol.ge; w diplomat.ltd.ge. A very comfortable modern hotel up at the top of Sololaki, the Diplomat's rooms are AC with satellite TV & minibar. There's a business centre with internet access & a sauna, gym & pool are available. It's on the Kojori Highway just above the terminal of marshrutkas 41 & 137. Prices inc parking & laundry. **$$$$–$$$$$**

Vere

🏠 **Beaumonde** [104 D5] (19 rooms) A Chavchavadze St 11; 📞298 6003; w hotelbeaumonde.com. This is a comfortable, friendly place with an atrium sitting area (with fireplace), free beer & wine, both European & Russian billiards tables, & big fish in a tank in the dining area. $$$$

🏠 **Lia's Guesthouse** [104 D5] (8 rooms) Arsena 35; 📞292 0858; m 577 499449, 577 287279; e arsena35@yahoo.com; 📘 liasguethouse. A classy guesthouse where rooms have ornate antique-style furniture (& TV). Prices inc excellent b/fast; dinner is also available if required. $$$$

🏠 **A & M** [104 D5] (Manana Skhirtladze's guesthouse) (6 rooms) Zubalashvili 51; 📞293 6397; m 599 656397; e anano@inbox.ru; w anano.ge. Manana claims to have been the first to open a guesthouse in Tbilisi (6 months before Betsy) although she has now moved a block downhill to this building, with en-suite rooms, as well as meeting rooms, bar, gym & pool, & a roof terrace with a good view. There's free Wi-Fi with a scanner & printer. Book ahead; rates inc meals & laundry. $$$$–$$$$$

🏠 **Stamba** [104 C4] (160 rooms) Kostava 14; 📞32 202 1199; w stambahotel.com. The even more luxurious sister of Rooms Hotel, in a former publishing house next door, with a stunning jungle atrium & a rooftop swimming pool. $$$$$

🏠 **Rooms Hotel Tbilisi** [104 C4] (125 rooms) Kostavas 14; 📞202 0099; w roomshotels.com. The former Pravda printing plant on the corner of Chovelidze St has been transformed by the people who created Rooms Hotel Kazbegi (page 186) into Tbilisi's coolest hotel – behind a façade of reclaimed wood & black metal there's a huge self-portrait of Eteri Chkadua riding backwards on a zebra, & a library-style lounge with more contemporary Georgian art & hand-painted red-&-orange floor tiles, & a discreet reception area off to the left. The city's movers & shakers are drawn to the dimly lit lounge, the deck overlooking the street, & the courtyard bar created in an alley at the rear. The bedrooms with AC feature dark wood, leather & retro light fittings, though bathrooms can be a bit small; & there's a free gym. $$$$$

🏠 **Betsy's Hotel** [104 C5] (45 rooms & 12 suites) Makashvili 32/34; 📞293 1404; w betsyshotel.com. Founded in 1993, for many years Betsy's Guesthouse was a Tbilisi institution & Betsy herself Georgia's best-known expat; now she has retired but the name lives on. It was used more by NGO workers than by business visitors or tourists, & the Friday Happy Hour is still popular with expats. Having expanded into adjacent blocks, it's now too big to be a boutique hotel, let alone a guesthouse. Most rooms have balconies & views across the city; some are executive suites with free fibre-optic broadband. There's a lift, spa, sauna & a small pool (oddly sited between the hotel & the road), plus a restaurant (closed at lunchtime) & a branch of Caliban Coffee. $$$$$

🏠 **British House** [104 B4] (8 rooms) Chovelidze (formely Belinski) 32; 📞298 8783, 292 3998; e hotelbritishhouse@gmail.com; w british-house.ge. Just a short walk up from Rustaveli Av, this smart hotel (originally British-owned) is popular with both tourists & expat business visitors alike. $$$$

🏠 **Ilja's Hotel** [104 B4] (4 rooms) Bakradze 16: m 593 118099; e iljastemberg@gmail.com; w iljashotel.com; 📘 iljashotel. Close to the metro & the best restaurants of Vera, this attractive new Swedish-owned place offers only b/fast & snacks (including wine!), but discounts are available for longer stays (the entrance is around the corner on Machavariani). $$$

🏠 **Kartli** [104 B4] (5 rooms) Barnov 32; 📞299 5429; m 598 801999; w hotel-kartli.com. German-owned, this is one of the more switched-on places in town with an excellent restaurant, a German-style pizzeria & beer garden. Tours are available (w erkareisen.com) plus airport transfers. $$$

🏠 **Classic** [104 B4] (7 rooms) Gurgulia 18; 📞225 1280; e info@classic.ge; w myhotels.ge/hotelclassic. Down an alley formerly known as 2nd Barnov Lane at Barnov 43, the Classic has AC, free Wi-Fi & a friendly, family atmosphere; English is spoken. $$$

🏠 **Primavera** [104 B3] (29 rooms) Kuchishvili 8; 📞225 1146/7; w primavera.ge. An American–Georgian joint venture, this is a fine, modern building on a less fine street close to the Philharmonic. Rooms have AC but not all are smoke-free. There's a free swimming pool, gym & jacuzzi on the 5th floor & a Georgian-Italian restaurant, & there's a lift with steep afterthought wheelchair ramp. $$$$

🏠 **Vere Palace Hotel** [104 B2] (42 rooms, 9 suites, 2 apts) Kuchishvili 22/24; 📞225 3340–2;

w verepalace.com.ge . This luxurious hotel has seen the Pope, the Patriarch of the USA & Canada, & rock group Uriah Heep among its clientele. Beyond the lobby with its antique chairs, there's a business centre & Wi-Fi, restaurant & bar plus roof-top swimming pool, fitness centre & sauna. $$$$–$$$$$

🏠 **Iliani** [104 B2] (24 rooms) Anjaparidze 1 (at Nikoladze); \223 4086, 233 5711; e hotel@iliani. com; w iliani.com. This modern block, just off Kostavas, has simple rooms with AC, balcony, cable TV & minibar. There's free Wi-Fi; the friendly staff speak English, but the lift & corridors are cramped. There's a pleasant garden & an extension including conference facilities & a roof-top terrace. $$$$

Vake

🏠 **VIP Victoria** [94 C6] (12 rooms, 3 suites) Arakishvili 1 Lane 3; \229 1877, 225 1247; e victoria@global-erty.net; w myhotels.ge/vip-victoria; 🅵. A modern, tastefully decorated hotel, handy for the upmarket restaurants on Abashidze, that caters mostly for a business clientele. En-suite rooms with balconies, cable TV, AC & free internet. Good b/fast inc. $$$–$$$$

Saburtalo

🏠 **Holiday Inn** [94 D2] (270 rooms) 26 May Sq 1; \230 0099; w hi-tbilisi.com. Far more upmarket than you might expect, this glass-fronted tower was full of refugees just a few years ago; now it has a spa & swimming pool, & rooms featuring rain showers & work stations. Half the

rooms are non-smoking; only 3 cater for visitors with disabilities. The metro station is across the (busy) road. Wi-Fi inc, b/fast extra. $$$$$

🏠 **Tbilotel** [94 C1] (47 rooms) Daraselia 8, nr Zhvania Sq; \238 7804–6, m 551 212509; w tbilotel.ge. A well-run place with good English spoken at reception, AC, satellite TV, Wi-Fi & lift (without steps!). Rates inc b/fast. $$$$

🏠 **Sympatia** [94 C1] (14 rooms, 12 suites) Daraselia 4, nr Zhvania Sq; \237 0590, 299 5588 w elitetravel.ge/en/hotels/tbilisi/hotel-sympatia. A big, modern business hotel, with a lift (but lots of steps to reach it), conference halls, billiards, gym, sauna, jacuzzi, & a roof terrace with indoor & outdoor pools. All rooms have AC, Wi-Fi, satellite TV & minibar, & the price inc b/fast & tax. $$$

🏠 **Nika** [94 B2] (6 rooms) Mitskevich 38; \238 2931; m 599 382931; e nikaguesthouse@yahoo. com. Reached by bus 47 from Station Sq, this friendly guesthouse is popular with Peace Corps Volunteers visiting Tbilisi. Rooms are small but have TVs, some English & German are spoken, & there's a nice garden with safe car parking. Rates inc b/fast. $$–$$$

🏠 **Medea** [94 B2] (6 rooms) Mitskevich 40; \237 0125; e hotelmedea@posta.ge; w hotelmedea.co.nr. A pleasant suburban house with a friendly, spacious feel, perhaps not the most slickly managed of places. Rooms have dbl beds (as well as the more usual twin sgls), balcony, satellite TV & bath; laundry & car service are available, & a minimum of English is understood. Price inc b/fast, tax & internet access. $$$–$$$$

✖ WHERE TO EAT AND DRINK

The **Old Town** is better served by cafés and bars than places for a proper sit-down meal; nevertheless, there are a few decent choices to be found along pedestrianised Sharden and Erekle II near Sioni Cathedral, and there's a row of cellar restaurants along Dadiani that dish up delicious Georgian staples like khinkhali at low prices. **Vere**, above Rustaveli and Rose Revolution Squares, is home to many of the city's best restaurants. Kiacheli and Akhvlediani (also known as Perovskaya) streets, west of Rose Revolution Square, are lined with pubs, most of which offer live bands plus food of some type, although it tends to be a featureless blend of Georgian and international styles.

Not surprisingly, there is a good range of places to eat and drink in the affluent (but rather dull) residential quarter of Vake. Many of the smarter places serving Mediterranean and European food (often at western European prices) are lined up along Abashidze Street west of the UN Circle; there's not much Georgian food available here, however. In **Chugureti** on the left bank, the area around Marjanishvili metro station has a number of simple restaurants and fast-food places (many halal),

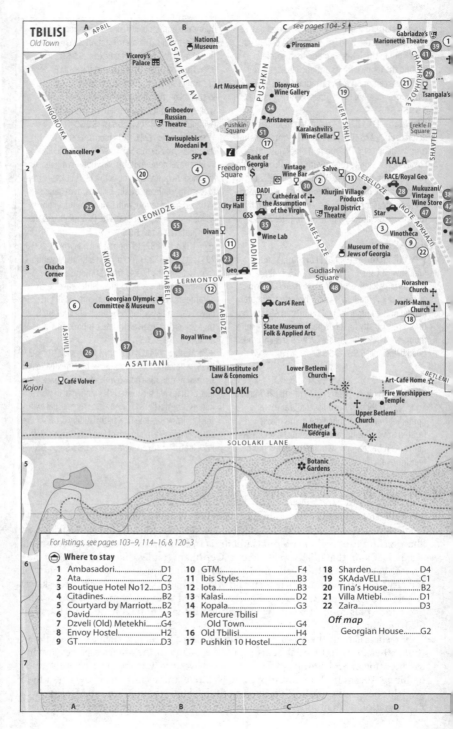

TBILISI
Old Town

A 9 APRIL

National Museum

Viceroy's Palace

see pages 104–5

Gabriadze's Marionette Theatre

Pirosmani

Art Museum

Dionysus Wine Gallery

Griboedov Russian Theatre

Aristaeus

Karalashvili's Wine Cellar

Tsangala's

Erekle II Square

Chancellery

Pushkin Square

Tavisuplebis Moedani

SPX

Freedom Square

Bank of Georgia

Vintage Wine Bar

Salve

KALA

RACE/Royal Geo

Mukuzani/ Vintage Wine Store

Khurjini Village Products

City Hall

Cathedral of the Assumption of the Virgin

Royal District Theatre

Star

Vinotheca

Divan

Wine Lab

Museum of the Jews of Georgia

Geo

Gudiashvili Square

Norashen Church

Jvaris-Mama Church

Georgian Olympic Committee & Museum

Cars4 Rent

Chacha Corner

State Museum of Folk & Applied Arts

Royal Wine

Café Volver

ASATIANI

Tbilisi Institute of Law & Economics

Lower Betlemi Church

Art-Café Home

SOLOLAKI

Fire Worshippers' Temple

Upper Betlemi Church

Mother of Georgia

Kojori

SOLOLAKI LANE

Botanic Gardens

For listings, see pages 103–9, 114–16, & 120–3

Where to stay

1 Ambasadori............D1
2 Ata.........................C2
3 Boutique Hotel No12......D3
4 Citadines................B2
5 Courtyard by Marriott....B2
6 David......................A3
7 Dzveli (Old) Metekhi....G4
8 Envoy Hostel.............H2
9 GT...........................D3
10 GTM.........................F4
11 Ibis Styles...............B3
12 Iota.........................B3
13 Kalasi.......................D2
14 Kopala.......................G3
15 Mercure Tbilisi
    Old Town..................G4
16 Old Tbilisi..................H4
17 Pushkin 10 Hostel........C2
18 Sharden.....................D4
19 SKAdaVELI..................C1
20 Tina's House...............B2
21 Villa Mtiebi.................D1
22 Zaira.........................D3

Off map
    Georgian House........G2

112

Inset

Anchiskhati Church
☆ Kalakuri

Presidential Palace

Egoist/☆
Tbilisi Voice
Vinomania Wine Gallery
Vernissage
Naniko
Old Cellar (Dzveli Marani)
Great Synagogue
Wine House
Armenian Church of St George †
Georgian House

Safe
Sixt
City Sightseeing
Hertz
Medicinal herbs
Gorgasali Square
Maidan 91
Château Mukhrani
Europcar
Khareba
State Museum of Georgian Folk Songs & Instruments

0 ——— 50m
0 ——— 50 yds

Shangri La ☆

Mtkvari (Kura)

Peace Bridge

Pirosmani

aucasian Carpets allery

Sioni Cathedral †

Carvasla (Museum of the History of Tbilisi)

Schuchmann

Gorgasali Square

Arts Centre

Rikhe Park

Europe Square

Borani boat tours

Diwine

Metekhi Bridge

Metekhi Church

Armenian Chuch †

SKY Bar ☆
Sachino Palace

Aviabari Sq
Basis $ $ Tera

Avlabari

Tbilisi State Armenian Dramatic Theatre

KETEVAN TSAMEBULI

Airport

METEKHI RISE

FLOW

GORGASALI

Alco Room
Firma Narikala
Bathhouses

Narikala Citadel

Jumah mosque

Mtkvari (Kura)

Ortachala

Akhundov Museum of Azerbaijani Culture

0 ——— 200m
0 ——— 200 yds

Tbilisi WHERE TO EAT AND DRINK

3

✕ Where to eat and drink

23	9 Mta.....................B3	34	Culinarium-Khasheria.....F5		Pastorali..............(see 38)
24	Alani Restaurant & Brewery.............F4	35	Eno...........................C3	48	PurPur......................C3
25	Azarpesha................A2	36	Entrée.....................G1	49	Racha.......................C3
	Begemot Coffee & Books............(see 55)	37	Ezo............................A4	50	Samikitno................H2
26	Black Dog.................A4	38	G.vino.....................D2	51	Shemoikhede Genatsvale............C2
27	Café Kala..................D3	39	Gabriadze's Café.......D1	52	Tiflis Maidani............H1
28	Café Le Toît..............D2	40	Ghvino Underground.....B3	53	Tredici.......................E3
29	Café Leila..................D1	41	The Hangar Bar........D1		Veliaminovi.........(see 35)
30	Café Linville...............C2	42	KGB..........................D2	54	Warszawa................C1
31	Café Littera................B4	43	Kiwi Vegan Café........B3	55	Woland's Speakeasy..............B3
32	Chardin 12................G1	44	Le Cabernet...............B3		
33	Creator Bar................B3	45	Machakhela...............H2		
		46	Maspindzelo..............G4		
		47	Moulin Electrique..........D2		

particularly along Davit Agmashenebelis where there is a concentration of small, good-value Turkish cafeterias, although most do not serve alcohol.

When Georgia's first branch of **McDonald's** opened in 1999, next to the Rustaveli metro station [104 C4], it was the only expat-friendly place for a quick coffee and a snack (there are now others on Marjanishvili Square [105 E2] and at Kostavas 71 (*26 May Sq*) [94 D2] and Tsereteli 34 [94 D1]); they're smoke-free, have Wi-Fi and good toilets – but now café chains such as Entrée (page 120) fill that rôle better. The area around Marjanishvili Square must also have the greatest concentration of take-away khachapuri places (and halal restaurants) in the entire city – a cheap way to fill up at breakfast or lunch.

Most bars simply serve their locals and don't bother with any sign beyond that supplied by Estrella Damm, Guinness or Paulaner; others make more of an effort and can really be quite stylish and even pricey (these are more likely to have signs promoting their Czech beers). Many bars serve food and may be listed under Restaurants.

On the **Left Bank** there are various bars and cafés, none of any great distinction. There's more excitement in the **lower Old Town**, where Sharden (with Rkinis Rigi and Bambis Rigi) is now very commercial and very crowded, with cafés and bars all offering very un-Georgian hookahs. Nearby, as mentioned previously, the pedestrianised Erekle II is lined with pleasant cafés. The **upper Old Town** starts with the pretentious nouveau lounge-bars and restaurants on the pedestrianised lower block of Galaction Tabidze, above which more interesting venues are slightly more scattered. You won't find any pubs in **Vake**, but there are some classy café-patisseries and also roadside coffee stands.

Until recently it was almost impossible to find a café open before 10.00, but now there are American-style coffeeshops opening from 08.00. The nearest to a chain is **Coffeesta** (*Rustaveli 52 (Academy of Science building)* [104 D4]; *Chavchavadze Av 8* [94 D6]; *Leselidze 40* [113 G1]; *East Point Mall* [95 H5]; w *coffeesta.com*; ⊕ *08.00–23.00 daily*), which is mostly smoke-free and has good Wi-Fi; they also do lunch snacks and in summer iced coffees and frappés. Others include **Hello Coffee** [105 G6] (*Mtkvari 2*) and **Second Cup** (*Davit Agmashenebelis 106 (Marjanishvili Sq)* [105 E2] *& 26 May Sq 1* [104 C3]). In addition, bookshop-cafés (page 123) seem to be a Tbilisi thing.

Unless otherwise stated, restaurants are usually open from around noon until 23.00 or midnight. More basic cafés tend to close earlier, while fancier, trendier places stay open until the early hours.

RESTAURANTS

The restaurants are listed from east to west, first on the right bank then on the left bank.

The Right Bank
Old Town

✘ **Maspindzelo** [113 G4] Gorgasali 7; ☏230 3030; w mgroup.ge/en/maspindzelo; ⊕ 24hrs daily. A lively khinkali restaurant that's reminiscent of a German bierkeller, with an entertaining violinist wandering about. Good Georgian food, but poor service. $$

✘ **Culinarium-Khasheria** [113 F5] Abano 27; ☏272 1157; e geoculinarium@gmail.com;

f khasheria; ⊕ 11.00–02.00 Mon–Fri, 07.00–02.00 Sat, 07.00–midnight Sun. A new venture by Tekuna Gachechiladze of Café Littera & the Culinarium cookery school, inspired by the traditional 'khashi bars', all-night joints serving tripe soup to boozers – the modern version seats most of its guests at long shared tables, rapidly dishing up exciting updates on traditional recipes such as the tripe soup with Japanese kombu & ginger, a khinkali soup with shitake mushrooms, pkhali vegetable purées with tahini, & offal sausage on chestnut polenta. $$$

✘ **Samikitno** [113 H2] Maidan Sq; m 577 710788; w vdcapital.ge/en-samikitno; ⊕ 24hrs.

These budget restaurants, serving classic Georgian dishes (but especially various types of khachapuri), are a smaller version of the Taglaura restaurants (see below); there's a great upstairs terrace here. Others (some combined with a Machakhela outlet) are at Rustaveli Av 24 [105 E5] (*at Lagidze*), Davit Agmashenebelis 106 [105 E2], Pushkin 5 (*on Freedom Sq*) [112 B2], Atskuri 45 (*Isani*) [95 H7], Kostavas 25 [104 C3], Kazbegi 26 [94 A2] and Mosashvili 11 [94 A6]. $

✗ **Machakhela** [113 H2] Leselidze 26; ☎ 210 2119; w vdcapital.ge/en-machakhela; ⏰ 24hrs daily. A chain of what look like fast-food joints but they have wood-fired ovens & actually take their time producing excellent khachapuri & acharuli 'boats' with aubergine stew, spinach & cream or meat sauces; there's also Wi-Fi. Other branches are at Arakishvili 5 (*Vake*) [94 C6], Tsereteli 77, Marjanishvili 16 [105 E2], Kazbegi (*at Tamarashvili*) [94 A2], Kostavas 77 [94 D2], Vazha-Pshavelas 4 [94 C2], Khizanishvili 31, Javakheti 16 & at Tsereteli metro station [94 D2]. The same company owns the more upmarket Taglaura restaurants, of which 3 (*Vakhushti Bridge on the right bank of the Mtkvari;* m 555 207700; *Gulia 1, Ortachala;* m 555 247700; *Beliashvili St, Digomi;* m 555 237700; $) are combined with a Machakhela outlet & 1, on the Okrokana Rd (m 577 417700; $) is a standalone – this one has a lovely wooded garden with views across the hills to the Botanical Gardens.

✗ **Tiflis Maidani** [113 H1] Rkinis Rigi 6 (on the embankment); ☎ 275 1188, m 599 250625; e tiflismeidani@gmail.com; ⏰ noon–01.00 daily. A deceptively rustic cellar, Maidani serves expensive Georgian food, with live Georgian music & dancing from 20.00 Tue–Sat. $$–$$$

✗ **Chardin 12** [113 G1] Sharden 12; m 577 480460; 🅵; ⏰ 11.00–01.00 daily. French-style café with live jazz; it's popular for drinks & a chat, but the food has recently got a lot better. The best of a bad bunch in this touristy area. $$$

✗ **Gabriadze's Café** [112 D1] (aka Ar Daidardo or the Sans Souci) Shavteli 13; ☎ 298 6594; m 577 556594; w gabriadze.com; ⏰ 11.00–02.00 daily. Attached to the famous puppet theatre whose founder, Rezo Gabriadze, designed the whole interior, from tables and chairs to the handmade curtains, as well as paintings & sculptures, this deservedly popular place serves traditional Georgian food but with unusually subtle flavours, notably

chicken dishes such as shkmeruli, roasted in a clay pan with a garlic sauce (& a similar dish with blackberry sauce), or cutlets of ground chicken fried with coriander, garlic & spices & served on a bed of ghomi (polenta) & bazhe (walnut sauce); there's also a legendary apple cake with vanilla ice cream. $$$

✗ **Café Leila** [112 D1] Shavteli 18; m 555 949420; ⏰ noon–02.00 daily. Right in the touristic heart of the old town, this charming café has a menu that's mostly vegetarian (some fish) & mostly Georgian (some felafel, hummus & the like). It's not especially cheap, & it may be hard to find space. $$

Sololaki

✗ **PurPur** [112 C3] Abo Tibilebi 1; ☎ 247 7776; m 574 441212; w purpur.ge; ⏰ noon–02.00 daily. There's a great atmosphere here, upstairs in one of the few buildings on Gudiashvili Sq that isn't crumbling; the food doesn't always match the friendly service & retro/shabby-chic setting, with its mismatched fabrics & lamps. There's live jazz piano from 21.00 daily. $$

✗ **Eno** [112 C3] Dadiani 8; ☎ 293 3932; ⏰ 13.00–01.00 Tue–Sun. The owners of Ezo have recently opened this excellent grill & wine-bar nearby, with a simple open kitchen. The food is fresh & simple, basically grilled meat & veg & wonderful salads (such as a mushroom & walnut mix). The wines are all natural, many of them from small artisanal producers. $$

✗ **Veliaminovi** [112 C3] Dadiani 8; m 551 906920. Very popular, often filled with locals. $–$$

✗ **Racha** [112 C3] Lermontov 12 (at Dadiani); m 577 460532; ⏰ 11.00–22.00 daily. Food & wine from Racha, of course, in this popular cellar dive; no English spoken. $$

✗ **Le Cabernet** [112 B3] Machabeli 4; m 577 404428; 🅵 le.cabernet; ⏰ noon–23.30 daily. A fine French restaurant that specialises in steaks; the fixed lunch is good value. $$$$

✗ **Café Littera** [112 B4] Machabeli 13; m 595 031112, 598 507272; ⏰ 11.00–23.00 daily. Georgia's first celebrity chef Tekuna Gachechiladze has created a delightful restaurant in the back garden of the Writers' House of Georgia. Opened in 2015, it stirred up instant controversy, as she uses mussels instead of meat in her chakapuli (a stew with sour plums, tarragon & wine), & lighter, healthier almonds instead of walnuts, &

other near-blasphemous changes to Georgian cuisine. In fact the beautifully presented food tastes wonderful. Gachechiladze also runs the Culinarium cookery school (▪ *culinarium.ge*) & the Culinarium-Khasheria restaurant (page 114). **$$$–$$$$**

❋ ✗ **Ezo** [112 A4] Kikodze 16; ☎ 299 9876; ▪ EZO.Restaurant; ⊕ 13.00–01.00 Tue–Sun. Another courtyard restaurant (Ezo means 'Yard') at the corner with Asatiani; they give a creative twist to Georgian cooking, largely using organic ingredients from the owners' own farm. Veal with herbs is always popular, as well as jonjoli (bladdernut flowers) with walnut sauce, & there are daily specials. On Sun there's a small farmers' market as well. **$$$**

✗ **Azarpesha** [112 A2] Ingorovka 2; ☎ 298 2346; m 579 704080; w azarpesha.com; ⊕ 11.00–23.00 daily. 2 blocks uphill from Freedom Sq, Tbilisi's 1st wine restaurant is the place to experience any of 100 Georgian natural wines in conjunction with fine Georgian-fusion food, offered as soups & small plates such as bruschetta, moutabal (aubergine spread) & leek mimosa (*GEL7–12*), large plates such as lamb saddle ragù, pork loin, pkhlovani & other vegetarian dishes (*GEL12–20*) & divine desserts such as lavender crème brûlée (*GEL8–10*). The décor is delightfully unpretentious, with traditional tablecloths & vases of flowers, & ancient drinking horns on the walls. **$$$**

❋ ✗ **Poliphonia** [95 E5] Amaghleba 23; m 557 637143, 599 393538; e magdapoliphonia@gmail.com; w poliphoniatbilisi.com; ▪ poliphoniatbilisi. The owners of Azarpesha opened this at the end of 2016 as a simpler organic restaurant that would be accessible to younger people, & it was soon 1 of Tbilisi's most popular eating spots. The cosy brick cellar is decorated in a mix of Art Nouveau & Oriental styles, with old carpets & chandeliers; seasonal Georgian-fusion food such as pork with honey & sour cornelian cherries, oyster mushrooms or roast pumpkin with pomegranate sauce is matched with a short but carefully chosen list of natural wines from small family wineries. **$$$**

On & near Rustaveli Avenue

✗ **Shemoikhede Genatsvale (Step In, Darling)** [112 C2] Pushkin 5; ☎ 299 7887; ▪ shemoikhedeams; ⊕ 09.00–23.00 daily. A

branch of this popular & affordable Georgian chain, known for excellent khinkali; service can be patchy but the price is right. The central branches – also at Maidan Sq [113 H2], Kakabadze 2 & Marjanishvili 5 (page 119) – seem all to be in cosy cellars, but those out at Kazbegi 16A & Oniashvili 2 (*on Zhvania Sq*) are modern buildings. **$–$$**

✗ **Sake Sushi Bar** [105 E6] Besiki 4; ☎ 251 9966. Tbilisi's first genuine sushi bar, just off Rustaveli, has Japanese dishes adapted to Georgian tastes. Also offers business lunch packages. **$$$**

✗ **Baan Thai** [105 E5] Tabukashvili 35; ☎ 229 9780; ▪ BaanThaiCuisineTbilisi; ⊕ 11.30–23.30 daily. 1 of Tbilisi's best Thai (& Cambodian) restaurants; staff speak English & also do deliveries, & it's non-smoking! Also does deliveries & take-aways. **$$**

✗ **Marco Polo** [104 D5] Rustaveli Av 44; ☎ 293 5383; m 555 459010; ⊕ 09.00–01.00 daily. Georgian & European food in a tastefully furnished (but smokey) city bar. **$$$**

✗ **House of Khinkhali** [104 D4] Rustaveli 37, at the south entrance to the Rose Revolution Sq pedestrian underpass; m 593 142253; ⊕ 24hrs. This Tbilisi institution is the place for a huge meal of dumplings (including vegetarian options) at low cost – nothing at all flashy, but they're used to foreigners. Some people prefer Khinkali Centre (m *555 991399*), at the same address but facing the Academy of Science, with a less basic décor & a wider choice of khinkali; at the Rustaveli Sq end of the same building, Khinkhlis Sakhli (Khinkali Hse) is less good. **$**

Close to Rose Revolution Square

✗ **Alubali** [1043 C4] Akhvlediani 6; m 599 362749; ⊕ noon–midnight. New in 2017 (& entered from Ekaladze, next to the Old London pub), this charming 'secret garden' restaurant specialises in Megrelian food & mainly 'orange' wines; the garden is covered in winter. **$$**

✗ **Csaba's Jazz-Rock Café** [104 C3] Vashlovani 3; ☎ 292 3122; ⊕ noon–04.00 daily. On a side street off Akhvlediani, this café offers Hungarian food, as well as music (*20.30–22.30*). **$$$**

✗ **Picasso** [104 C3] Miminoshvili 4; ☎ 298 9086; ⊕ 11.00–midnight daily. Chinese restaurant with Wi-Fi, between Kostavas & Akhvlediani by the Super Babylon department store. **$$**

✗ **Maharajah** [104 C3] Akhvlediani 24; ☎ 299 9799; ▪ maharajahbar; ⊕ 11.30–23.30 daily.

A curry house serving fairly authentic dishes. Live music & belly dancing at w/ends. $$$

Vere

✗ Keto & Kote [104 C4] Zandukeli Dead End 3; ☎ 293 0200; ⏰ 11.00–01.00 daily. The most exciting new restaurant in this vibrant area – it's up above the Rustaveli metro station (go down the alley, turn right at the end & go through to the garden). You can eat in the old-style interior or the garden with great city views; the food is Megrelian-influenced, with excellent megruli khachapuri, mchadi, elarji & phkali, as well as great desserts. The service can be haphazard. $$$

✗ Café Goethe [104 C4] Zandukeli 16; m 574 880331; ⏰ 11.00–19.30 Mon–Fri. Run by Rainer Kaufmann of the Hotel Kartli, this serves good, cheap food in the lovely garden of the German cultural centre. $$

✗ The Kitchen [104 C4] Kostavas 14; ☎ 240 0099; w roomshotels.com/the-kitchen. At the über-stylish Rooms Hostel, the restaurant is pioneering a local form of New American cuisine with seasonal local ingredients. Also owned by Rooms (*Chovelidze 7;* ☎ *202 0299;* e *lolita@ roomshotels.com*) is Lolita, a café & bistro with an open kitchen & a wood-fired oven producing a range of lighter dishes & snacks. $$$

✗ Keti's Bistro [104 C4] Chovelidze 3; ☎ 202 0303; . Opposite Rooms Hotel at the bottom of Vere, this is a cosy new place with an open kitchen & a pleasant courtyard serving a blend of Georgian & French provincial cuisine, using fresh ingredients from local farmers (Georgian truffles are a feature, & the steak is excellent). The menu is fairly limited, as is the wine list, & portions seem small for the price. $$$

✗ Zala [104 B4] Chovelidze 24 at Zandukeli; m 599 710808; ⏰ noon–midnight daily. A small loft-style (non-smoking) space serving excellent Georgian food with a modern presentation – there's a mixed sharing plate of appetisers, lots of meat-free choices (especially an avocado-citrus salad with walnuts & blue cheese) but also a great pork belly & burger. $$

✗ La Fondue [104 B3] Tatishvili 7; m 557 409554; ⏰ 11.00–23.00 Mon–Fri, 18.00–23.00 Sat–Sun. This new French-run place specialises in fondue & raclette, as you might guess, but also serves Breton galettes & crêpes, & a great chocolate gateau! Just behind the

Philharmonic, tables & an open kitchen are in a loft above the entry lounge. $$

✗ Rainer's Pizzeria & Biergarten [104 B4] Barnov 39; ☎ 298 5439; w hotel-kartli.com; ⏰ noon–23.00. Just up the hill from the Philharmonic at the Hotel Kartli, Rainer's serves a mix of German, Italian & New Georgian cuisine & also delivers pizza. $$

✗ O, Moda, Moda [104 A4] Barnov 64; ☎ 243 0041; omodamoda; ⏰ 11.00–01.00 daily. A bizarre but very successful blend of a vintage clothing shop & a café-bar-restaurant – the only sign on what looks like a normal 19th-century house is some small Georgian text on the door, but there's a tasty brunch menu until 13.00 (with great coffees & an excellent omelette Benedict) & then snacks & salads rather than main meals, indoors or in the garden. Drinks range from traditional tarragon lemonade & syrupy Lagidze sodas to mulled wine & cocktails. $$

✗ Green Terrace [104 A3] Kekeldize 11; ☎ 224 0203; GreenTerraceTbilisi; ⏰ noon–midnight daily. Below the Barnov viaduct, this stylish, wood-faced building covered in greenery, houses a café (with great cakes) downstairs & a spacious restaurant upstairs serving international cuisine such as goulash, pizza & pasta. $$–$$$

✗ Prego [94 D7] Barnov 84; ☎ 225 2258; m 593 229749; w prego.ge; ⏰ 10.30–01.00 daily. An affordable Italian restaurant that serves particularly good pizza at this branch; there are others at Marjanishvili 2 [104 D3] & Erekle II 15 [112 D2] (*both* ☎ *255 6688*), where the daily specials are the best bet (& not to be confused with eg: Prego Reale (*Vazha-Pshavelas 2A at Pekini;* ☎ *237 3610*), although this is decent enough). $$

Vake

✗ Fantastico Pizza [94 D6] Napareuli 3A; ☎ 272 8908; ⏰ 11.00–02.00 daily. A great, cheap Italian place (for pizza, pasta & desserts) on a side street near the university & UN Circle. It's smokey, but they do take-away. Also at Kazbegi 14 [94 B2] (☎ *272 8908;* ⏰ *10.00–02.00 daily*). $–$$

✗ May Thai [94 D7] Mtskheta 1; ☎ 223 2372; RestaurantMayThai; ⏰ 11.00–22.30 daily. This Thai place is probably more use as a take-away (*from GEL6*) than as a restaurant. $$

✗ Cecilia [94 D7] Abashidze 10; ☎ 230 9559; e ceciliakafe@gmail.com; ⏰ 11.00–23.00 daily. Excellent Italian food, thanks to importing authentic ingredients (though at a cost) – they serve pizza, pasta, soup, cakes & ice cream, plus fine coffee & good service. $$$

✕ Sushi Room   [94 C7] Abashidze 12; ✆224 2599; m 597 010733; ⏰ 10.00–01.00 daily. Pricey but reliable sushi. $$$

✕ Dining Room   [94 C7] Paliashvili 38; ✆225 0900; ⏰ noon–midnight daily. A classy & well-established restaurant with a French- & Italian-inspired menu that may include chestnut soup, escargots, steak & tasty dolci. $$$$

✕ Le Marais   [94 C7] Abashidze 32; ✆290 3993; m 599 153904; w lemarais.info-tbilisi.com; ⑤ ; ⏰ 11.30–late. Authentic upmarket French restaurant, with stylish décor & a Michelin-starred chef serving classics including seafood & foie gras. $$$

✕ Amira   [94 A6] Mosashvili 24; ✆290 7701; m 599 179699; w amira.tbb.ge; ⏰ 11.30–midnight daily. An excellent & fairly upmarket Lebanese restaurant; plenty of veggie options including the meze. $$$

❋ **✕ Il Garage**   [94 A6] Mosashvili 26; ✆222 7588; ⏰ noon–22.00 Mon–Sat. The most authentic Italian restaurant in Tbilisi; it's moved from the original garage but is still intimate & relaxed. A free portion of bruschetta is followed by huge portions of pasta or pizza – & don't miss the homemade limoncello! $$

Saburtalo & Digomi

There's a cluster of riverside restaurants in Digomi, to the north of Saburtalo, which are popular with both locals & tourists.

✕ Phaetoni   [94 C1] Beliashvili 105, Digomi; m 577 660020; ⏰ 10.00–02.00 daily. Phaetoni is well known for its nightly live folk-singing & dancing, & for good traditional Georgian food. $$$

✕ Ethno Tsiskvili   [94 C1] Beliashvili 99, Digomi; ✆200 5555; w tsiskvili.ge; ⏰ 10.00–02.00 daily. Near to Phaetoni, this is a restaurant-museum incorporating a restored water mill & Ludis Moedani (Beer Square), a pubby red-brick restaurant (⏰ 10.00–midnight daily). $$$

✕ Kakhelebi   [94 C1] Beliashvili 41, Digomi; ✆218 4222; e sales@kakhelebi.ge; ⑤ kakhelebi. ge. Also in Digomi is 'The Kakhetians', serving food from the east of Georgia – but you're best off going to the original branch, actually on the Kakheti Highway out east beyond the airport [95 H5]

(*Saknavtobi 2, Kakheti Hwy, Lilo Settlement;* ✆*294 3300;* m *599 481505;* ⏰ *09.00–21.00 daily*) – this is one of the city's best & most authentic regional restaurants, with excellent service. $$$

✕ Retro   [94 C2] Gamrekeli 2; ✆237 7351; m 571 511722; ⏰ 10.00–01.00 daily. Just off Bakhtrioni near the Holiday Inn, this serves the best Adjaran khachapuri in Tbilisi – the flagship dish is known as *acharuli tsomgamodlili*, with a lighter crispier dough, & without the egg whites. $

✕ Sianggan   [94 C1] Pekini 41 (Zhvania Sq); ✆23 7 9688; ⏰ 11.30–23.00 daily. A flashy Chinese place in the Las Vegas casino; serves Hong Kong specialities & Beijing smoked duck. $$–$$$

✕ Ronny's Pizza   [94 C1] Vazha-Pshavelas 3 (*at Pekini*); ✆247 2472; w ronnyspizza.com; ⏰ 11.00–23.00 Mon–Sat, 13.00–23.00 Sun. Founded by a pair of American artists, a tiny pizza place with just 3 tables that serves authentic American-style pizza with thick crusts & real mozzarella. There are other branches at Paliashvili 43 [94 B6] (*Vake*) & in Digomi (*Gldani 3 micro 5A*). $$

✕ Bina 37   [94 C1] Mgaloblishvili 5A, 2nd entrance, 8th floor, apt 37; m 599 280000; ⑤ ; ⏰ 13.00–23.00 daily. On the top floor of an apartment building in Vedzisi, at the far northern end of Saburtalo, this is something else – a restaurant in a duplex flat which actually contains a marani with 43 qvevri, where they make remarkably good wine from grapes trucked in from Kakheti. The food is top-end classic Georgian cuisine, & the whole experience is delightful. $$$

✕ Taste of India   [94 C1] Kandelaki 23; m 577 587333; ⑤ ; ⏰ 11.00–midnight daily. Formerly Little India, this is perhaps the most authentic & most expensive North Indian restaurant in Tbilisi; there's German beer, Wi-Fi, a non-smoking area, & deliveries are available. $$$

Left Bank
Chugureti

✕ Shavi Lomi   [105 G3] Kvlividze 28; ✆296 0956; e shavilomi@gmail.com; ⏰ noon–midnight daily. Formerly right at the top of Sololaki, this renowned restaurant, which more or less created modern Georgian cooking, recently moved to the semi-wasteland beyond Fabrika. In a fairly grand domestic interior, enjoy mchadi cornbread, pkhali walnut & vegetable patés, pickled vegetables & stews. $$$$

✕ House on Madatovi [105 F4] Davit Agmashenebelis 25; m 555 859292; ⊕ 11.00– 23.00 daily. An excellent & affordable Georgian restaurant on the recently pedestrianised southern end of Davit Aghmashenebelis. Excellent food, from the shoti bread via fantastic salads to veal & mtsvadi with pomegranate seeds; the décor is charming too. $$

✕ Fabrika [105 F2] Ninoshvili 8; ✆202 0399; w fabrikatbilisi.com. In addition to Tbilisi's best hostel (page 106), this former silk factory houses a huge lounge filled with sofas & hammocks, throbbing chillout music & cool English-speaking staff in black T-shirts & jeans, serving beers & cocktails, pizza & pasta. In the courtyard are various funky bars & cafés, including DiveX (with live bands & local craft beers), Pipes Burger Joint (the best in town) & a branch of Moulin Electrique (page 120). $$

✕ Deniz [105 E2] Davit Agmashenebelis 107; m 593 982783; ⊕ 08.00–midnight daily. 1 of several dependable (but smokey) Turkish cafeterias along this stretch, with no menu but helpful waitresses & excellent food. Beer is available in the upstairs section. $–$$

✕ Nasimi [105 E2] Davit Aghmashenebelis 116; ✆294 6694; f nasimirestaurant; ⊕ 08.00– midnight daily. In a yard set back from the road, this cafeteria-style halal restaurant (no alcohol) serves a good lahmacun ('Turkish pizza', a circle of dough topped with minced meat, onions, tomatoes & other vegetables, parsley & spices, & baked). Also at Kostavas 76 [104 C3]. $

✕ Barbarestan [104 D1] Davit Agmashenebelis 132; ✆294 3779; m 577 415835; ⊕ 10.00– midnight daily. This cute family-owned restaurant bases its menu on the 1874 cookbook of Duchess Barbare Eristavi Jorjadze, using produce from small-scale farmers as far as possible, including ham from Racha, honey from Svaneti & cheese from the nuns of Poka (page 221). The restaurant is a former butcher's shop (complete with meat hooks), which is also reminiscent of 19th-century Tbilisi. $$$

✕ Strada [104 D3] Marjanishvili 5; m 595 992288; w stradacafe.ge; ⊕ 10.00–02.00 daily. A favourite of middle class Tbilisians & expats, this sleek modern café-restaurant has an attractive courtyard & serves a range of eggs, waffles & pancakes for brunch (until 13.00, or 14.00 at w/ ends), then American-European & Korean-Asian menus, including deep-pan pizza, plus live music

in the evenings. Also at Euli 7 (just off Vazha-Pshavelas in Saburtalo; m 595 992277) & soon at Mosashvili 11 in Vake. $$$

✕ Shemoikhede Genatsvale (Step In, Darling) [104 D3] Marjanishvili 5 (on the ramp left down to the embankment); ✆291 0005; f Shemoikhede; ⊕ 11.00–23.00 daily. This chain specialising in khinkhali has other branches (page 116) but this bierkeller-style place is probably the best of the bunch. $–$$

CAFÉS & BARS
Left Bank
⊑ Eco Garden [105 E3] Davit Agmashenebelis 68; ✆274 3274; m 599 121892; e ecogarden919@ gmail.com; f Ecogarden; ⊕ 11.00–midnight daily. In the attractive garden of the Folklore State Centre of Georgia, with an interesting gallery, it serves decent Georgian & European food (with lots of vegetarian options, & an English menu); live music includes a folk group playing 'Tbilisi city music' on Fri from 21.00. $$

⊑ Café Red [104 D3] Marjanishvili 8; ✆220 1211; w redcafe.ge; ⊕ 08.00–23.000 daily. An elegant café with Art Nouveau features & a terrace attached to the Marjanishvili Theatre; offering Western-style b/fasts followed by fast meals such as salads, soups, pizza & pasta. Also at Leonidze 2 [112 B2] (Freedom Sq) & Vazha-Pshavelas 71. $

⊑ Luca Polare Finest Ice Cream & More [104 D1] Davit Agmashenebelis 125; ✆238 0802; w lucapolare.com; ⊕ 08.00–02.00 daily. Probably Tbilisi's best, certainly its priciest, ice creams. The 'more' includes salads, cakes, juices & coffees, including iced soya-milk frappés & the like, plus Wi-Fi. Also at Leselidze 34 [112 D3], Eristavi 12 (UN Circle) [94 D7], Pekini 7A [94 C2] & the East Point Mall [95 H5]. $

♀ Amber Bar [105 F4] Davit Agmashenebelis 49; m 514 490049; f AmberbarTbilisi; ⊕ noon– 01.00. In the newly pedestrianised Neu Tiflis zone, this open brickwalled space has become 1 of Tbilisi's coolest hangouts – it's a wine bar that aims to let guests enjoy wine in the European manner, without the compulsory Georgian-style toasting & swigging. The mostly natural wines come from 70-odd producers, while the chef (a former wrestling champ, apparently) produces mainly appetisers such as cheese sticks in a walnut crust, a bean dip, bruschetta with pear, walnut & blue cheese, & Imeretian kupati (sausages). $$

3

Old Town

G.vino [112 D2] Erekle II 6; ✆293 2121; m 598 932121; ⏰ 13.00–01.00 daily. Far more authentic than the other places along this very touristy street, this showcases Georgian wines & serves good food too, including plates of Georgian tapas, to a backing of mellow jazz. $$$

Pastorali [112 D2] Erekle II 6; m 592 311919; ⏰ 09.00–02.00 daily. 1 of the best places to eat on this busy traffic-free street lined with good terraces for watching the world go by. They do good standard Georgian fare, including khachapuri & salads with walnuts. $$$

Café Le Toît [112 D2] Leselidze 22; m 559 497497; ⏰ noon–01.00 daily. This lovely café looks like your granny's front room with its retro chintzy wallpaper & furniture; there's a small bar, an enterprising kitchen, Wi-Fi & nice roof-top views. There's quiet-ish music in the day & often live piano or guitar from 19.00. $$

Café Linville [112 C2] Abesadze 2; ✆293 3651; m 5932221; Linville.Cafe; ⏰ noon–02.00 daily. Arty café-restaurant just off Leselidze with a vintage-apartment style ambiance & comfy sofas & random umbrellas (plus a fish tank in an old TV); there's good jazz & a varied menu including excellent crêpes. $$

Tredici [113 E3] Sioni 13/40; m 599 074422; e clavestbilisi@gmail.com. In an attractive historic building (don't miss the ceiling frescoes) opposite the Carvasla, this non-smoking café has a show kitchen, where they'll show you how Georgian dishes are prepared, & seating on the traffic-free street outside. There's good music & free Wi-Fi, but as ever here service can be poor. $$

Entrée [113 G1] Leselidze 47; m 599 887016; w entree.ge; ⏰ 08.00–22.00 daily. This Franco-Georgian bakery-café offers delicious baked goods like croissants & quiches, saltimbocca sandwiches, Italian ice cream, a variety of b/fasts (*until 11.00*) & excellent coffee. No smoking; there's Wi-Fi & WCs, signs are in English as well as Georgian. Also at Amaghleba 12 [95 E6], Taktakishvili 3 [94 C7], Ateni 1 [94 D6], Gagarin 25 [94 C1], Mtskheta 7 [94 D7], Nutsubidze 82 [94 A1], Zandukeli 19 [104 B4], Kazbegi Av 36 [94 A2], Chavchavadze Av 78 [94 A4], Davit Agmashenebelis 86 (*Marjanishvili Sq*) [105 E2], Abashidze 35 [94 C7] & 76 [94 A6], Petriashvili 19 (*at Barnov*) [104 A3] & Pekini 7 [94 C2] & 24 (*at Mitskevich*) [94 C2]. $

Café Kala [112 D3] Erekle II 8; m 599 799737; w kala.ge; ⏰ 10.00–02.00 daily. A trendy bar with Western prices & beers, & a wide menu including kebabs & Uzbek pilaf; jazzy music live nightly 21.00–23.30. $$$

The Hangar Bar [112 D1] Shavteli 20; ✆293 1080, 291 1080; w thehangar.biz; ⏰ noon–late Mon–Sat, from 10.00 Sun. One of the main expat drinking holes, this Irish-American pub has free Wi-Fi & major sporting events screened live. It incorporates the Old Love café, once renowned for its oriental sweetmeats & startling décor, with plaster lion heads in the jaws of which a cigarette can conveniently be perched. $$$

Alani Restaurant & Brewery [113 F4] Gorgasali 1; ✆272 1628; ⏰ 09.00–midnight daily. On the embankment between the baths & Maidan Sq, this is the place for great Ossetian khinkali & khachapuri (with cheese & potatoes) & for their own beer (good but not always kept well). There's also a smokey, noisy cellar restaurant. Service is poor & there's a risk of overcharging. $$

Gabriadze's Café [112 D1] (aka Ar Daidardo, ie: the Sans Souci) Shavteli 13; ✆298 6594; w gabriadze.com; ⏰ 11.00–02.00 daily. A great place for a drink, although it has only foreign beers, as well as wine & lots of teas; there's Wi-Fi, & one of Georgia's best pianists plays here from 22.00 nightly. $$

KGB [112 D2] Erekle II 10; ✆298 5013; m 599 674488; w kala.ge; ⏰ 10.00–02.00 daily. With the slogan 'We're still watching you' above the door, the emphasis here is on ironic Soviet kitsch, with dishes such as Lenin's Favourite & Proletarian Pizza. $$

Moulin Electrique [112 D2] Leselidze 28; m 551 722323; ⏰ 10.30–01.00 Mon–Fri, 11.30–02.00 Sat–Sun. A very hip place in a courtyard, with outdoor seating or a smokey interior; it's most popular for snacks & drinks, especially craft beers (from the local Shavi Lomi brewery), Illy coffee & iced tea, but the food is also good, with several vegetarian options. $$

Warszawa [112 C1] Pushkin 19; m 574 805564; barwarszawatbilisi; ⏰ noon–04.00 daily. Tbilisi's first shots bar (basically vodka, of course) – drinks at GEL2–5, knock 'em back & be on your way. But, in fact, there's a cellar bar too with long shared tables where you can order wine, or bring beer & food (soup, sausages, herrings) down some tricky steps. $$

Sololaki

Kiwi Vegan Café [112 B3] Machabeli 6; m 514 000175; kiwi.vegan.cafe; noon–23.00 daily. This achieved fame of sorts in May 2016 when it was attacked by Georgian nationalists wielding sausages & protesting against its support for LGBTQ activists. In truth it is more of a meeting place for supporters of right-on causes than a gourmet destination, but they do serve cheap & tasty snacks. $$

Rhea's Squirrels Gallery-Café [104 D7] Chonkadze 29; m 595 505522; 11.00–23.00 Tue–Sun. Supporting & employing people with mental disablilites, this is Tbilisi's first 'social café', well placed opposite the funicular's lower terminal (& wheelchair-accessible, of course). A plain, quiet space of white-painted concrete (smoke-free & with Wi-Fi), it serves b/fast (including matsoni & honey from Samtskhe-Javakheti), lunch (combos for GEL12–14; 13.00–15.00), quiches, khachapuri & salads. $

Ghvino Underground [112 B3] Tabidze 15; 230 9610; m 599 506427, 599 393538; w vinounderground.ge; noon–23.00 daily. Just above the pedestrianised section of Tabidze (next to Tea Underground) 'Wine Underground' is an attractive cellar owned by a group of Georgian natural winemakers & stocks a good range of their wines (to drink in or take away, with plenty of tasting advice). The menu (after 17.30) offers some anarchic combinations of raw & fermented vegetables, dried meats & some hardcore artisanal cheeses. $$$

Funicular Lounge [104 C7] w funicular. ge; 18.00–02.00 daily. The upper terminal of the Mtastminda funicular houses several good restaurants including the cafeteria-style Puri Guliani (13.00–midnight daily), serving a great range of snacks such as khachapuri, the top-end Funicular Restaurant (18.00–midnight daily), & a lounge-bar above – when the Soviet building was renovated in 2014, this was given a sophisticated modern look with Italian furniture & fixtures, while the 1960s fresco 'Tribute to Pirosmani' by Koka Ignatov was beautifully restored. Its terrace is the best place in town for sundowner cocktails. $$$

Black Dog [112 A4] Asatiani 33; m 555 586688; blackdogbartbilisi; 14.00–02.00 (Sun until midnight). Opened at the end of 2016, this soon became established as the city's first proper neighbourhood pub, & a smoke-free & pet-friendly one to boot. There's not much real ale or craft beer yet in Georgia, but whatever does appear you'll find here. They serve various bitters & pale ales, a porter, lager & even a Belgian witbier (all on gas rather than handpumps), & a Georgian-American version of pub-grub, such as burritos with Georgian pickles, chicken fingers & pepper poppers stuffed with sulguni, & burgers (*vegetarian GEL10, cheeseburger GEL11*). $$

Woland's Speakeasy [112 B3] Machabeli 2; m 596 309494; ; 19.00–01.00 daily. At the rear of a bookshop-café stairs lead down to a red-brick basement where you'll find craft beers & fancy cocktails (*GEL20*), plus a pub quiz (*Tue 20.00*) & live blues or country music (*Sun 21.00*). It's smoke-free except for a cigar lounge. $$

9 Mta [112 B3] Tabidze 10; m 599 459994; Beer9Mta; noon–02.00 daily. Opened early in 2018, this will at last bring craft beer into the Tbilisi mainstream, with 24 beers on tap, including 3 of their own; also snacks & light meals. $

Creator Bar [112 B3] Machabeli 10; m 593 088959; creatorbar.tbilisi; 18.00–02.00 Mon–Fri, 13.00–04.00 Sat & Sun. At the corner of Lermontov, this grungy cellar hosts live rock bands on Thu, blues Fri & Sat & jazz on Sun. $

On & near Rustaveli

Caliban's Coffeehouse [104 D5] Rustaveli 34; 292 3592; 09.30–20.00 daily. Coffee shop attached to Prospero's Books, very popular as a meeting place for expats. The coffee & tea are pricey but good; also at Betsy's Hotel (page 110). $$

Minimalist [105 E5] Tabukashvili 21 m 599 093444; w fotografia.ge; Tue–Thu noon–20.00, Fri–Mon 10.00–20.00. At Fotografia, Tbilisi's only art photography gallery. Minimalist offers rare African coffees served using the latest technology, as well as craft beer in bottles. $

Sophia Melnikova's Fabulous Douqan [105 E5] Stamba Dead End 22; m 592 681166; ; noon–02.00 daily. Just down the hill from Rustaveli, left on Tabukidze & all the way to the rear of the Literary Museum (the sign on the gate is only visible when it is closed), this bohemian café offers good home cooking (excellent khinkali) & chilled vibes to an arty, alternative crowd, indoors or in the courtyard. $

Atoneli 21 [105 F6] Atoneli 21; m 593 111056; ; 18.00–02.00 daily. A grungy cellar-bar, one of the cheaper places to drink in the city centre. $

♀Bauhaus [105 F5] Dedaena Park; m 599 377622; ⓕ bauhauscafetbilisi; ⊕ 13.00–01.00 Mon–Thu & Sun (to 02.00 Fri/Sat). A wild arty café by the Dry Bridge, with snacks available as well as drinks; there are live & DJ gigs. $

♀Dive Bar [105 E5] Rear of Laghidze 12 (at Mari Brosse); m 597 067473; ⓕ DiveTbilisi; ⊕ 18.00–01.00 Mon–Thu & Sun (until 03.00 Fri–Sat). With a slightly older crowd of friendly expats & Georgians who've travelled, this bar has an underground feel, with its concrete floor & seating on wooden crates; no food but cheap beer (including Georgian craft brews) & cocktails & occasional live music. $

♀Flashback [105 F6] Vachnadze 5; m 599 586835; ⓕ flashback19; ⊕ 17.00–02.00 daily. Affordable beer, chacha & imported spirits, with a pretty boho young crowd, snacks available including Mexican spicey potatoes. $

Along Akhvlediani & Kiacheli

☕Mukha Café [104 C3] Akhvlediani 15; ☏292 0053; m 577 737440; ⓕ Mukhatsakatukha; ⊕ 11.00–01.00 daily. Essentially a café-deli in the daytime, selling b/fast, tartini & sourdough sandwiches & 'pizza' of lavash bread topped with olive paste, cheese & veggies, this offers more leisurely dining in the evenings, with French-oriented dishes based on local products, & jazz. $

♀Buffalo Bill [104 C4] Akhvlediani 16; ☏293 6052; m 599 370022; ⊕ 11.00–02.30 daily. A Wild West-themed bar with rock & country music (live from 20.30 nightly) plus Wi-Fi. $$

♀Dublin [104 C4] Akhvlediani 8 (cnr Ekaladze); ☏298 4467; ⊕ 11.00–03.00 daily. Another Irish pub with live music nightly; odd, then, that its menu is more Georgian than you'd expect (but includes Mexican dishes). $$

♀Nali [104 D4] At the angle of Kiacheli 4/1; ☏243 0420; w nali.ge; ⊕ noon–03.00 daily. Near Rose Revolution Sq, this pub has a 'happy hour' from 16.00 to 19.00 & live music at 21.00 daily. There's a good range of affordable food. In the same building is the Althaus tea house, serving 80 types of tea & a terrace (⊕ noon–midnight daily). $$

♀Old London [104 C4] Akhvlediani 6; m 593 259116; ⓕ oldlondon.ge; ⊕ 16.00–03.00 daily. Wood-panelled 'English' pub theme with live bands. $$

♀Wheels [104 C3] Akhvlediani 16; ☏298 8733; m 599 900800; w tbilisipub.tripod.com; ⊕ 13.00–01.00 daily. Tbilisi's first Irish pub, this has a wood-panelled bar & a homely dining area. $$

♀Canudos Ethnic Bar [104 D4] Samaia Sq (at the top of Javakishvili); m 598 262670; ⊕ 15.00–03.00 daily (until midnight Sun). Linked to a backpackers' hostel, this is a party place for alternative young travellers & their local equivalents, with a bright, wood-floored interior plastered with travel-related items & a garden with fountain. There's cheap beer & snacks including a huge Italian sandwich. $

Vere

☕Iveria Café [104 D4] Rose Revolution Sq; m 570 501445; ⊕ 08.30–midnight daily. A stylish Corten steel-&-glass box with great views across the river, this rather upmarket café serves a range of breakfasts (GEL5/16/26), excellent salads & sandwiches; it's one of the few places in the city where you can have soya milk in your coffee. $$

☕Brotmeister [94 D7] Eristavi 16 (on UN Place); m 577 631200; w brotmeister.ge; ⊕ 08.00–22.00 daily. Since 2015 this Austrian bakery chain has served a great range of breads, muffins & pastries, with excellent coffee. After b/fast-time they also serve excellent soups, salads & pancakes. Also at Taktakishvili 7/9 [94 C6], Abashidze 69 [94 A6], Pekini 14 [94 C2] & Dolidze 38 [95 E3]. $

☕Factory 27 [104 B4] Zandukeli 27; m 595 255552, 593 937161; ⊕ 11.00–01.00 daily. A pleasantly post-industrial café, serving excellent light meals with plenty of vegetarian choices; there's a small courtyard below street level, enlivened by graffiti art, where you can sit wrapped in a blanket on summer evenings. $

☕Hurma Café [104 B3] Melikishvili 21; m 591 100097; ⓕ hurmacafeshop; ⊕ 09.00–23.00 daily. Stylish new café with efficient English-speaking staff that does a particularly good brunch (until noon). $

Vake

☕Assorti [94 A6] Abashidze 81; ☏243 3444, m 579 165151; e info@assorti.ge; ⊕ 09.00–23.00 daily. A pricey but classy bakery, producing its own bread, khachapuri, pastries & cakes, as well as salads & tarts. Also at Mosashvili 1 [94 B6] (near Chavchavadze Av 64; m 579 165252), Mtskheta

8 [94 D7] (m *579 162244*), Nikoladze 5 [104 B2] (m *579 165353*), Nutsubidze 86A [94 A1] (m *579 161188*) & Pekini 22 [94 C2] (m *579 168282*). **$$**

⌨ **MEMO Coffee** [94 B6] Abashidze 49; m 598 257999; w memocoffee.ge; ⊕ 10.00–22.00 daily. A place for hardcore coffee fans, serving everything from matcha latte to affogato, as well as tiramisu & sandwiches. **$**

♀ **Bernard** [94 C6] Abashidze 29; m 568 560088; ⊕ 24hrs. A decent enough place for Czech (& German) beer & khinkali – it's cheap, but service can be pretty slow. Also at Shartava 40 [94 C1] & Tabidze 3 [112 B3]. **$$**

Saburtalo

♀ **Acid Bar** [94 C2] Kazbegi 3A; m 599 101238; ⊕ noon–02.00 daily. Among the coolest bars in town, with creative décor including bench sofas & booths; Georgian & international food & drink available. Also at Chavchavadze Av 16 [94 D6] & Leonidze 9 [112 B3]. **$$**

⌨ **Coffee LAB** [94 B2] Kazbegi 27; ☎322 505405; 🅵 coffeelabgeorgia; ⊕ 09.00–23.00 daily. An artisan coffee shop that also sells coffee beans, coffee machines, oh & sandwiches too. **$**

⌨ **Morelli's Gelato** [94 C2] Sulkhan Tsintsadze 8; ☎222 3242; w morellisgelato.com; ⊕ 11.00–23.00 daily. Totally authentic gelato, plus coffee & snacks. **$**

⌨ **Spectra** [94 B1] Vakeli 25; m 597 791310; ⊕ 10.00–midnight daily. In the further reaches

of Saburtalo near the Medical University there are various Middle Eastern cafés catering to foreign students – this one offers grilled chicken, sub sandwiches, pizza & koshary (Egypt's national dish, a vegetarian mix of lentils, noodles & rice topped with a spicy tomato & chickpea sauce), as well as a kind of shepherd's pie. **$**

BOOKSHOP-CAFÉS

⌨ **Begemot Coffee & Books** [112 B3] Machabeli 2; ☎299 1227; m 596 309494; w begemot.ge; ⊕ 09.00–21.00 daily. This café serves great coffees & sandwiches & has plenty of books for sale, as well as a book-swap section; there's also a sliding bookcase at the rear leading down to Woland's Speakeasy (page 121) in the basement. **$**

⌨ **Book Corner Café** [105 F5] Tarkhnishvili Lane 13B; ☎223 2430; m 577 468388; w bookcorner.ge; ⊕ 11.00–03.00 daily. Similar to the Literary Cafés but with better food (soup, flatbreads, vareniki cheese dumplings & cake). There's a new branch below the Dry Bridge (in Dedaena Park, where booksellers have riverside display/storage chests like in Paris) which has a hipper but less literary feel to it. **$**

⌨ **Café Literaturuli (Literary Cafés)** [104 B3] Tarkhnishvili 2; ☎222 5133; ⊕ 10.00–01.00 daily. Also branches at Pekini 31 [94 C2] (*at Kazbegi*; ☎*237 8902*); & Abashidze 22 [94 C7] (☎*222 0276*); all incorporate interesting bookshops & hold book launches & talks. **$**

ENTERTAINMENT AND NIGHTLIFE

Cafés and bars often stay open until 02.00, but after that Tbilisi doesn't have a wild nightlife (with one exception), with just a couple of clubs open to 06.00. As well as the places listed, some of the bars and cafés on Akhvlediani and Erekle II also have live music. From July to September some close to move their operations to the Black Sea coast. There's also a concentration of commercial DJ and karaoke clubs in the Rkinis Rigi area (near the Maidan and Metekhi Bridge).

The Georgian **film** industry is having a bit of a revival at the moment, and the numbers going to the cinema are rising, with the odd new cinema opening, too. Most films are in Georgian and Russian but some English-language films are shown undubbed at the Amirani and Cavea cinemas – information at w kinoafisha.ge (which also covers the Rustaveli Cinema). **Theatres** close at the end of June for the summer (*for information, see w info-tbilisi.com/events/ theatres; book via w biletebi.ge or w tkt.ge*).

NIGHTCLUBS

☆ **Art-Café Home** [112 D4] Betlemi 13; m 599 708079, 577 940117; ⊕ 17.00–02.00 daily.

With 3 floors including a rooftop bar, cool décor & staff, this is a good place to warm up for a night out.

☆ **Backstage 76** [94 A6] Vake Park (near the Abashidze St gate); m 599 242001; w 76backstage.wixsite.com/backstage76; ⏰ 17.00 until late Tue–Sun. A tapas bar that stages some experimental music & jazz, as well as video shows & DJ sets.

☆ **Bassiani** [95 E2] Tsereteli Av 2; m 557 204047; w bassiani.com. A nightclub that quite simply rivals the best in Berlin & London, & a cultural phenomenom that's made a stand for openness & tolerance in a society that has ostracised the gay community & drug-users in particular. It attracts the leading European techno & house DJs, & up to 1,200 ravers, to this vast, dark, smokey space (flash photography strictly forbidden) created out of a huge swimming pool beneath the Dinamo Stadium. No regular hours or prices – check the website, & register there to buy tickets at half the cost at the door. At the same site is **Spacehall** (m 595 310001; w spacehall. com; ⓕ spacehall bassiani.com/spacehall), a multifunctional space for concerts, conferences & workshops.

☆ **Café Gallery** [104 D5] Griboedov 34; ☎299 5747, 292 0053; w cafe-gallery.ge; ⓕ cafegallery. ge. A quiet café by day (serving good pizza), with art exhibitions & a garden, after midnight at w/ends this becomes a wild disco that's very popular with gays & LGBTQ-friendly crowd.

☆ **Egoist** [113 G1] Bambis Rigi 8; m 598 329361; ⏰ 22.00–05.00. Part of the Unique complex (known for overcharging & poor service), this is a decent enough club for this very commercial area, with 2 DJs playing a variety of pop, R&B, house & progressive music. Entry is free (but subject to the door staff's whims) & it's possible to book a table with a minimum spend of GEL150 on food or drink.

☆ **Elektrowerk** [95 H5] Salosi I Turn 2; m 577 782497, 596 963636; ⓕ elektrowerkvenue. An exciting new venue in a former electric motor factory out in the Samgori backstreets – international & local bands play here, as well as other performances.

☆ **Heaven** [104 A3] Petriashvili 1; m 599 169414; ⏰ Thu–Sat 20.00–03.00. In a former wine factory, you climb a spiral staircase to reach a small bar & then a high-ceilinged room where DJs play house & techno at w/ends.

☆ **Kalakua** [113 E1] Shavteli 13; ☎299 6683; m 571 223333; w kalakuri.info-tbilisi.com;

⏰ 22.00–late Thu–Sat, 20.00–late Sun. Popular with the gilded youth of Tbilisi; European & Japanese food, DJs & karaoke; popular bands live on Sats.

☆ **Khidi** [94 D2] Bagrationi Bridge, Right Embankment; w khidi.ge. Opened in 2016, 'the Bridge' can welcome up to 1,000 revellers over its 3 floors – yes, inside the bridge.

☆ **Magti Club** [105 E5] Rustaveli 22; m 595 182222; ⓕ ClubMagti; ⏰ 19.00–06.00 Tue–Sun; GEL25 inc cocktail. Cellar club with live jazz, blues, soul & even 'ethno-folklore' & experimental music.

☆ **Mtkvarze** [94 D2] Agladze 2; m 599 193344; w mtkvarze.com; ⏰ 23.00–08.00 Fri & Sat. In a former fish restaurant by the river in Didube, with chandeliers still in place, there are 2 rooms with what was the best sound system in town until Bassiani opened. Local DJs play techno & house music at w/ends.

☆ **PAM Club** [94 A6] Paliashvili 60; ☎250 0125; ⓕ clubpam; ⏰ 17.00–02.00. This is the place if you want to get away from techno – there's a mix of jazz, rock, alt-rock & experimental music here, plus food & drink, including some excellent Belgian beers.

☆ **Safe** [113 H1] Rkinis Rigi 11; m 595 5620050, 557 700044; ⏰ lounge 15.00–late, club 22.30–07.00 daily. Behind the big bank vault door there's a good bar, lights & sound system but not much space for dancing.

☆ **Senate Club** [94 A6] Mishveladze 5; ☎599 223344; w senateclub.ge; ⓕ SenateClub; ⏰ lounge noon–05.00 daily, club 23.00–06.00 Thu–Sat. On the edge of Vake Park, this mock-Roman farrago is popular with the residents of this affluent area.

☆ **SKY Bar** [113 G3] Metekhi 22; m 592 323232; ⏰ 19.00–late Thu–Sun. In Avlabari, this has theme nights, live bands & DJs playing 80s & 90s hits. No under-21s admitted.

☆ **Tbilisi Voice** [113 G1] Bambis Rigi 8; m 597 211211; ⏰ 16.00–06.00 daily. Karaoke & hookah.

☆ **Underwheel Club** [104 B7] Mtatsminda; m 591 492323; ⓕ Club.Underwheel. A wonderful setting, under the Ferris wheel high above the city.

CASINOS

☆ **Adjara** [94 D2] 26 May Sq 1; ☎233 5519; w casinoadjara.com. Attached to the modern Holiday Inn, for blackjack, poker & roulette.

☆ **Iveria** [104 D4] Rose Revolution Sq 1; 📞 240 2245; w casinoiveria.com. A glass box attached to the Radisson, this is the classiest of Tbilisi's casinos.
☆ **Shangri La** [113 E2] Mtkvari right embankment, by the Peace Bridge; 📞 220 0701; w shangrila.ge. A garish blaze of neon by the river, this is the city's most modern casino.

THEATRES

🎭 **Abashidze Music & Drama State Theatre** [94 D2] Davit Agmashenebelis 182; 📞 234 8090, 234 7959; w musictheatre.ge
🎭 **Akhmeteli Theatre** [95 F1] Vekua 8; 📞 262 5437, 262 5973
🎭 **Atoneli Theatre** [105 F5] Atoneli 31; 📞 293 3238
🎭 **Dumbadze Professional State Youth Theatre** [105 E2] Davit Agmashenebelis 99/1; 📞 295 3927, 295 7874; e childrentheatre@gmail.com; w mozardi.ge
🎭 **Gabriadze's Marionette Theatre** [112 D1] Shavteli 13; 📞 298 6590; w gabriadze.com. Puppet theatre for adults with 4 shows in repertory: *The Battle of Stalingrad*, *The Autumn of My Spring*, *Ramona* & the new *Marshal de Fantie's Diamond*.
🎭 **Griboedov Russian Theatre** [112 B2] Rustaveli 2; 📞 293 5811, 293 1106; w galleria.ge/en/griboedov-theatre. Swallowed up in the new Galleria shopping centre, this has staged Russian-language drama since 1845, including the classics.
🎭 **K Gamsakhurdia Sukhumi State Drama Theatre** [94 B2] Vazha-Pshavelas 16; 📞 237 1650; w teatrisokhumi.ge
🎭 **Kakha Bakuradze Movement Theatre** [94 D2] Davit Agmashenebelis 182 (Mushtaid Park); m 599 015567
🎭 **Marjanishvilis State Academic Theatre** [104 D3] Marjanishvili 8; 📞 295 5966; w marjanishvili.com; ⊕ box office 11.00–19.00 Tue–Sun. This is also home to performances & rehearsals of Fingers Theatre (📞 *295 3582*) – dancing fingers that perform Georgian dance, the cancan & a version of *Hamlet*, all in great costumes. The Marjanishvili's New Stage is at Marjanishvili 5.
🎭 **Mikheil Tumanishvili Film Actors' Theatre** [94 D2] Davit Agmashenebelis 164; 📞 234 2899; m 599 501816; e info@tumanishvilitheatre.ge; w tumanishvilitheatre.ge. Home to GIFT, the Georgian International Festival of Theatre in honour of Mikheil Tumanishvili (w giftfestival.ge).

🎭 **Nabadi Georgian Folklore Theatre** [105 E5] Rustaveli 19; 📞 32 298 9991; m 599 961077. A stylised tourist show of music & dance is staged here.
🎭 **The Royal District Theatre (Samepor Ubenese Teatri)** [112 C2] Abesadze 10; 📞 299 6171; e rd_theatre@caucasus.net. This theatre was built as a caravanserai in 1898, became a cultural centre under Beria, & was abandoned in 1987. In 1992 Isa Grigoshvili, leading lady of the Rustaveli Theatre for 30 years, was sacked for going on a tour of Germany without permission, although she claimed it was because of her Zviadist politics; she her husband & son decided to set up an independent company in the Royal District Theatre & were ready to reopen in 1995, when a Jewish group claimed it as a former synagogue. A furious legal battle erupted & all the city's unemployed actors joined an 'act-in', 24hrs a day for 10 days, until they won the right to open as a theatre. It now stages some of the city's liveliest drama.
🎭 **Shalikashvili Pantomime Theatre** [104 D4] Rustaveli 37; 📞 299 6314, 298 2506; m 595 500203. Now led by Amiran Shalikashvili Junior, son of the founder, this is one of the world's great mime ensembles.
🎭 **Shota Rustaveli State Theatre** [105 E5] Rustaveli 17; 📞 272 6868; w rustavelitheatre.ge. Recently refurbished, with 2 modern theatres seating 300 & 800 people, plus a studio theatre.
🎭 **Tbilisi State Armenian Dramatic Theatre** [113 H3] Avlabari Sq, Ketevan Tsamebuli 8; 📞 274 7764; 📘
🎭 **Theatre Veriko** [104 B2] Anjaparidze 16; 📞 222 1338
🎭 **Zakaria Paliashvili State Opera House** [105 E5] Rustaveli 25; 📞 214 3203, 204 4554; w opera.ge, ballet.ge. Reopened in 2016 after a very thorough refurbishment (Bidzina Ivanishvili apparently paid US$38m for the latest sound & lighting kit). In addition to the main auditorium there are also the Red, Blue & Mirror Halls for vocal & chamber concerts & exhibitions.

CINEMAS

🎬 **Amirani Cinema Plaza** [104 B3] Kostavas 36; 📞 299 9955; e amirani@amirani.ge; w amirani.org. Under the Philharmonic, this is the main venue for art films (mostly dubbed into Russian) & home of the Tbilisi International Film Festival in Dec (w tbilisifilmfestival.ge).

Astra Park Entertainment Centre [94 C1] Chachava 8; ☎237 3737; m 595 884490; f AstraPark. Well north of the centre in Digomi, this promises 7D cinema.

Cavea East Point [95 H5] Tvalchrelidze 2; & Cavea Tbilisi Mall, Mtskheta Hwy km16; both ☎200 7007; w cavea.ge

Kashe (or Cache) Cinema Club [104 C3] Kiacheli 9; ☎299 0551; m 599 440818; e kiacheli9@gmail.com

Rustaveli [105 F6] Rustaveli 5; ☎255 5000, 293 2253; w rustaveli.com.ge. The only traditional movie house left in the centre.

Sakartvelo [95 E1] Guramishvili 2/9; ☎269 6647/51

MUSIC Classical music is performed at the **Philharmonic**, now officially known as **Tbilisi Concert Hall** [104 B3] (*Melikishvili 1;* ☎*299 0599; w tbilisiconcerthall. com; box office at rear,* ⊕ *11.00–14.00, 15.00–19.00 daily*), and at the **Djansugh Kakhidze Tbilisi Center for Music & Culture** [105 E1] (*Davit Agmashenebelis 123;* ☎*296 2207; w kakhidzemusiccenter.com*). The Tbilisi Symphony Orchestra was founded in 1993 by Djansugh Kakhikdze (1935–2002), splitting away from the Georgian State Symphony Orchestra, and is now conducted by his son Vakhtang. The Georgian Philharmonic Orchestra, directed by Nikoloz Rachveli, plays at the **Mikeladze Centre** [105 E1] (*Davit Agmashenebelis 127;* ☎ *291 5505; w georgianphilharmonic.ge/en/mcenter*). Other venues are the **summer theatre** also at Davit Agmashenebelis 123 (page 148), the **opera house** (Zakaria Paliashvili State Opera House) and the **Rustaveli Theatre** (Shota Rustaveli State Theatre) (pages 125 and 140), and the **Conservatoire's concert halls** at Griboedov 8 [104 D5] (☎*299 9144, 293 4624; e grandhall@conservatoire.edu.ge; w conservatoire.edu.ge; box office* ⊕ *11.00–14.00, 15.00–17.00 daily (until 19.00 before performances)*).

The city at last has a venue for larger pop/rock concerts in the **Old Hippodrome** (*Tamarashvili 13; m 595 090832;* f *hippodromepark*), which is also intended to be a hub for film shoots, fashion shows, conferences and other creative events.

FESTIVALS The city's festival, **Tbilisoba**, is held on a weekend in October, with food, music, dancing and other events in the Rikhe Park and elsewhere; it's actually a Soviet creation and is seen as rather downmarket, with its emphasis on pop music, beer and shashlik. Autumn is also the time for music, with the **Autumn Tbilisi Music Festival** (w *kakhidzemusiccenter.com*) from mid-September to mid-October, followed by the **Tbilisi Jazz Festival** (w *tbilisijazz.com*) in October or early November and the **Tbilisi Wind Festival** (w *tbilisiwindfestival.com*) in November. The **Art Gene Folk Festival** (w *artgeni.ge*) is held in July at the Museum of Ethnography. The month-long **TIFT** theatre festival (w *tbilisiinternational.com*) takes place in October and November, at roughly the same time as GIFT, the Georgian International Festival of Arts in Honour of Mikheil Tumanishvili (w *giftfestival.ge*). There's an excellent **film festival** (w *tbilisifilmfestival.ge*) in December, while the **Ciné-Doc documentary festival** (w *cinedoc-tbilisi.com*) now takes place in May.

More alternative youth-oriented festivals include **SOU** (Stream of Unconsciousness; w *soufestival.com*), an annual festival of contemporary music and visual arts, which starred Björk in October 2017; **Tbilisi Open Air** (w *tbilisiopenair. ge;* f) and **Ezo** – a festival of love, peace and freedom (and music, arts, yoga and table tennis), organised by a vegetarian community called Mzesumzira (*Sunflower;* f *festivalezo*) held on summer Saturdays at Mtsatsminda Park. Also on the food and drink front, there's the **New Wine Festival** in mid-May at Mtatsminda Park (and the city's natural wine restaurants put on the Zero Compromise wine-tasting event the day before).

In 2018 there will also be a series of special events to celebrate the centenary of Georgia's declaration of independence from Russia.

ACTIVITIES

BATHS Although Tbilisi has been famous for its sulphurous hot waters since Vakhtang Gorgasali moved his capital here in the 5th century, most of the city's baths date from the 19th century. They have always been central to community life, being used for checking that prospective sons/daughters-in-law have no physical defects, and for gay cruising. Bathing in the single-sex public section costs just a few lari – it's a colourful and friendly experience, but there's not much point if you can't follow the chatter. To enjoy the full experience, you and a few friends should take a private room, for GEL50–80/hour (you may want a couple of hours to really relax) – in fact you'll have two rooms, one for (un)dressing and resting (with shower and toilet), the other with a large tub with hot sulphur water flowing through it and a marble massage table. Most baths also offer larger 'luxe' rooms, for GEL90–120/hour. You can pay GEL10–20 extra for a massage; after about 20 minutes a masseur of the same sex as you (traditionally Azeri, and communicating only with gestures – and wearing only shorts) will enter first to exfoliate (with a scrubbing glove) and then brutally massage you. Ordering tea is the traditional way to wrap up the experience, but beer is also available. There'll be a price list at the entrance – towels will be included in the higher-priced packages, otherwise you can pay for them, as well as soap, shampoo, snacks and tea, and maybe even a hair dryer.

The best-looking ones are the **Orbeliani** or **Chreli ('Motley') Baths** [113 F5] at the top of Abanos kucha, with their blue-tiled façade and minaret-style towers – built in the second half of the 17th century, the façade was remodelled in the 19th century. They're very popular (it's best to book), but reasonably priced, with both public baths (⏰ *06.30–22.00 daily*) and private rooms (⏰ *08.00–midnight daily*); prices range from GEL40/hour (for one or two persons) to GEL100 for up to six, with two pools (hot and cold), or GEL250 for up to nine with VIP service. The older baths in the brick domes just below, including the **Sulphur Baths** and the **Royal Baths** (signed in English), are simple but welcoming. The Sulphur Baths (⏰ *24hrs daily*) have rooms at GEL30–50, and the Royal Baths (⏰ *08.00–midnight daily*) have a wider range (*GEL40–80*), for between two and ten people, some with a sauna or a bath the size of a small swimming pool, and a public bath for women only. Nearby, at the foot of Grishashvili, an alley marked '24/24 King Erekle's Bath' leads to the **Erekle Baths** (⏰ *24hrs daily*), perhaps the cheapest in town (*starting at GEL30 for a room for four, plus GEL20 for a scrub and massage*), and fairly decrepit inside.

Just beyond in Aliyev Park (*at Gorgasali 3, beneath the Tiflis Veranda Hotel*) are the **Public Baths no. 5** (*public bath* ⏰ *07.00–21.00, private* ⏰ *24hrs daily*), the city's oldest. The entry has some attractive tiles and mosaics, but the interior is drab and draughty in places. The separate male and female public baths cost from just GEL3/hour; private rooms cost GEL50–100/hour, and a scrub and massage cost GEL10 (public) or GEL20 (private). Behind the same hotel, the **Bakhmaro Baths** (*Grishashvili 5*; ⏰ *07.30–01.00 daily*) are quieter, with just ten rooms (*seven at GEL20–50, two at GEL60 and a VIP room, for up to 20 persons, at GEL100*). It's worth turning right off Grishashvili towards the Bohema restaurant to find the **Queen's Baths** (⏰ *07.00–00.30 daily; massages 09.00–23.00*); built in Moorish style, these have attractive stained glass but smaller rooms than most; it's also much less touristy than the baths at the bottom of the hill.

On the left bank are the **Gogilo Baths** [95 G6], across the road from the Sheraton Metechi Palace Hotel, which has a health club with pool and sauna, available to non-residents for a daily charge. There's another sauna on Ghvinis Aghmarti, between Avlabari Square and the Metekhi Church. The **Pushkin Baths** [105 F3] (*Kiev 4, off Davit Agmashenebelis*), known for being very cheap and gay-friendly, were refurbished at the end of 2017 so may have been cleaned up in various ways.

SPORTS The main spectator sport (other than watching other people work) is **soccer**: Lokomotiv (w *fcloco.ge*) play at the 27,000-seat Mikheil Meskhi Stadium, Vake Park [94 A3], while Dinamo Tbilisi (w *fcdinamo.ge*) and the national team play at the 55,000-seat Boris Paichadze National Stadium [95 E2] (page 148); this was refurbished in 2006, just before the World Cup finalists France and Italy visited.

The Paichadze and Meskhi stadiums are also used by the Lelos, the national **rugby** team (page 54); a new 30,000-capacity stadium is planned in Didi Digomi. The country's leading clubs (both semi-professional) are Tbilisi Caucasians and Lelo Saracens (formerly Lelo Tbilisi), who both play at the Avchala Stadium, in Gldani on the way to Mtskheta, which only has 3,000 seats.

The most quintessentially Georgian sports are **wrestling**, **weight-lifting** and **power-lifting**, with major tournaments held in the Sports Palace on 26 May Square [94 D2] (w *sportspalace.ge*).

The city's main **tennis** clubs are the Jan Homer Tennis Complex [94 C1] (*Ljubljana 18, Digomi;* 254 0077) and the Leila Meskhi Tennis Academy [105 E2] (*Marjanishvili 29, Chugureti;* 295 3800; w *leilameskhitennisacademy.ge*); courts (*about GEL20/hr*) are also available at the Mziuri Tennis Courts in Vake Park [94 A3] (m 593 28848) and City Sport in Saburtalo [94 B2] (*M Asatiani 7A;* 239 1981; m 577 790200, 599 947294; e *tbilisi.citysport@gmail.com*).

Climbing and bouldering have become very popular – the Tbilisi Chess Palace and Alpine Club in Vere Park [104 C3] (*Kostavas 37A, a fine piece of Soviet Modernism from 1973*) has a small gym with bouldering walls, and there are some higher but basic walls at the Vake Park gym. The Arena 2 sports centre in Saburtalo [94 A2] (*University St 6;* 239 1707) has better facilities and a very helpful owner who can provide gear if needed.

The Tbilisi **marathon** (w *tbilisimarathon.ge*) takes place in October.

SWIMMING The city's main **swimming** pool is the outdoor Vake Pool [94 A3] (*Chavchavadze Avenue 49B*), which has natural warm water and is popular with expats before work, all year round; there's also a covered pool and fitness club here (225 2575; 07.00–23.00 Mon–Fri, 09.00–22.00 Sat & 09.00–21.00 Sun; GEL90/day, GEL300/month valid 07.00–18.00 Mon–Fri, or GEL440/month unrestricted). Almost next door is the Neptune Pool [94 A3] (*Chavchavadze Av 49A;* 225 0486; w *neptune.ge*; 07.00–23.00 Mon–Fri, 07.00–22.00 Sat & Sun; GEL50/day, 10-day pass GEL200, GEL400/month), with a 25m pool with retractable roof, as well as a fitness club with saunas and gym. In Saburtalo, the Arena Pool [94 A2] (*University St 2;* 239 0289; arenasportcomplex; 07.00–23.00 Mon–Fri, 07.00–21.00 Sat, 09.00–19.00 Sun; GEL30/day, GEL165/month) has an indoor pool, sun terrace, cafeteria, gym and saunas.

You can also take the kids to Europark, out towards Didube [95 E1] (*Ninua 3;* m 597 923388; w *europark.ge*; 10.00–20.00 daily; GEL30 Mon–Fri, GEL40 Sat–Sun), which has four pools with slides, wave machines and artificial rivers. There's also swimming at the Tbilisi Sea (page 149), where the Tbilisi Sea Club (247 6060; w *tbilisiseaclub.ge*; 09.00–19.00; GEL15/day) has two large pools and a small children's pool with a slide. The iconic Laguna Vera pools at Kostavas Lane 34, known for their 1970s Soviet architecture and mosaic, closed in 2013 and are under threat of demolition, alas.

OTHER PRACTICALITIES

There are plenty of **ATMs** around town; some machines dispense US dollars, as well as Georgian lari. There are **exchange offices** (*many* ⊕ *24 hrs*) all over the city, especially on Rustaveli and Chavchavadze avenues, as well as on Tamar Mepis below the Voksal, opposite the Samgori and Isani metro stations and at the airport, where you can exchange cash – euros, dollars, roubles and sometimes British pounds and Swiss Francs – for Georgian lari.

All hotels and hostels have **Wi-Fi**, as do many cafés. There's also the city's Tbilisi Loves You free public Wi-Fi service, which seems to work in metro stations but rarely connects elsewhere. Alternatively, Tbilisi has some cybercafés: there are a couple of good places close to Marjanishvili metro station [105 E2], in the alley between Marjanishvili 28 and 30, and at Davit Agmashenebelis 81, 108 and 109. Across the river, there are places down an alley at Rustaveli 18 [105 E5], Leselidze 6 [112 C2] and Chavchavadze Avenue 22 [94 D6].

There are several free **English-language newspapers**, largely business-oriented, that you can pick up in the better hotels – the best established is *Georgia Today* (**w** *georgiatoday.ge; issued every Fri*), along with *Georgian Journal* (**w** *georgianjournal. ge; issued every Thu*) and *Caucasian Business Week* (**w** *cbw.ge; issued every Mon*). An online-only equivalent is Agenda.ge (**w** *agenda.ge*), which is updated daily. There's also *Investor.ge*, a glossy mag from the American Chamber of Commerce in Georgia which can also be picked up in major hotels every two months.

There are plenty of *aptekas* (**pharmacies**), most now part of the Aversi, GPC and PSP chains, and many open 24 hours (with a night window). Medicinal herbs are sold at Leselidze 53 [113 G1]. The Stomatological (Dental) Clinic of Tbilisi State Medical University is at Davit Agmashenebelis 126 [104 D2] (❧ *295 3282*); there are lots of private **dental clinics** in Vake and Saburtalo (especially on Mitskevich, it seems).

BANKS

$ Bank of Georgia [112 C2] Pushkin 3; ❧244 4444; **e** customerservice@bog.ge; **w** bankofgeorgia.ge. On the north side of Freedom Sq, with a beautiful hall (dating from 1902).

$ Basis Bank [113 G3] Ketevan Tsamebuli Av 1; ❧292 1921/2; **w** basisbank.ge

$ Cartu Bank [94 A3] Chavchavadze 39A; ❧292 5592; **w** cartubank.ge. Formerly AbsoluteBank; owned by Bidzina Ivanishvili.

$ FINCA Bank [94 A2] Vazha-Pshavelas 71; ❧220 7410/1; **w** finca.ge

$ Liberty Bank [94 A6] Chavchavadze 74; ❧255 5500; **w** libertybank.ge. Formerly the People's Bank of Georgia.

$ Pasha Bank [105 E6] Rustaveli 15; ❧226 5000; **w** pashabank.ge

$ TBC Bank [104 D3] Marjanishvili 7; ❧227 2727; **w** tbcbank.ge; also [112 D2] Leselidze 22; ❧227 2727. Founded in 1992, now the largest bank in Georgia, & the 2nd largest in the Caucasus.

$ Tera Bank [113 G3] Ketevan Tsamebuli 3; ❧255 0000; **w** terabank.ge

COURIERS

Federal Express [95 G6] Ketevan Tsamebuli 39; ❧274 8240, 274 8940; **e** fedexge@post.ge; **w** fedex.com/ge; ⊕ 10.00–19.00 Mon–Fri

Georgian International EMS [105 F4] Davit Agmashenebelis 44; ❧32 235 4094; **e** info@gpost. ge; **w** ems.post; ⊕ 09.00–19.00 daily. Also at Chavchavadze Av 21 [94 D6] (❧ *222 7403*).

TNT Express Worldwide [105 F4] Davit Agmashenebelis 25/5; ❧291 0220; **e** tamuna. khelaia@tnt.com; **w** tnt.ge; ⊕ 10.00–18.00 Mon–Fri

✝ **Armenian Church of St George** [113 H2] Samghebro 5, Gorgasali Sq; ⊕ 09.00 daily

✝ **Assyrian-Chaldean Catholic Church of Simon the Tanner** [94 A2] 34/38 Marika Baratashvili Dead End; ⊕ noon Sun

✝ **Baptist church** [94 C1] Vefkhistkaosani 60, Didi Digomi; ⊕ 11.00 Sun (English)

✝ **Church of SS Peter & Paul** [105 F2] Ivan Javakhishvili 55; ⊕ 09.00 Mon–Sat (Georgian); 10.00 (English), 11.30 (Georgian), 17.00 (Latin) & 18.00 (Polish – summer only) Sun

✝ **Georgian Orthodox Sioni Cathedral** [113 E3] ⊕ 09.00 Sun. Magnificent singing.

☪ **Jumah Mosque** [113 F5] Botanikuri 32; ⊕ 13.00 Fri

✝ **Lutheran Church of the Reconciliation** [105 G2] Terenti Graneli 15; ⊕ 11.00 Sun

✝ **Roman Catholic Cathedral of the Assumption of the Virgin** [112 C2] Abesadze 4, in the Old Town; ⊕ 10.00 daily, noon & 18.00 Sun, 17.30 winter/18.00 summer Mon–Fri (Georgian)

✝ **Russian Orthodox Church of St Alexander Nevsky** [105 F2] Ivan Javakhishvili 69; ⊕ 09.00 daily

✡ **Synagogue** [113 G1] Leselidze 47; ⊕ 09.00 daily

✝ **Tbilisi International Christian Fellowship** [94 A1] Bessarion Jgenti 11, Nutsubidze; ⊕ 16.00 Sun (interdenominational, English)

United Parcel Service [113 H3] (Meridian Express) Ketevan Tsamebuli 15–17; ☏ 218 0144; e info@mexge.com, w ups.com/ge; ⊕ 10.00–18.00 Mon–Fri

INTERNET SERVICE PROVIDERS
The main providers for home use are:

Caucasus Online Tsinamdzgvrishvili 160; ☏ 200 0022; w co.ge/en
Geonet Vazha-Pshavelas 41; ☏ 247 0000; e info@geonet.ge; w geonet.ge.

MEDICAL SERVICES
✚ **American Medical Centers** [94 C7] Arakishvili 11; ☏ 250 0020; w amcenters.com/tbilisi
✚ **Central Republican Hospital** [94 B1] Vazha-Pshavelas 29; ☏ 239 5714
✚ **Cito Medical Centre** [94 C7] Paliashvili 40; ☏ 229 0671, 225 1948; w cito.ge. A Swiss–Georgian joint venture.
✚ **City Hospital No. 2** [95 E3] Constitution St 2; ☏ 295 4423

✚ **David Tatishvili Medical Center** [94 B6] Tengiz Abuladze 20; ☏ 291 3119, 91 3242; e usdc@gol.ge
✚ **IMSS** [94 C2] Bakhtrioni 10A; ☏ 292 0928; m 599 266669, 599 100311; w imss.ge
✚ **Innova Medical Center** [94 A2] Euli 7A; ☏ 223 3232; w innovamedical.ge
✚ **MediClub** [94 B1] Tashkent 22A; ☏ 225 1991; m 599 581991; w mcg.ge
✚ **Tbilisi State University Medical Diagnostic Centre** [94 D6] Chavchavadze Av 5; ☏ 222 4428, 223 0492; emergency doctor m 599 581991

POST OFFICES
Post offices can be found at Chavchavadze Av 21 [94 C6], Vazha-Pshavelas 69 [94 A2], Gorgasali 4 [95 E2], Tamar Mepe 9 [95 E2], Station Sq 4 [95 E2] & Pekini 39 [94 C1], with the same opening hours as the 'main' post office below.

✉ **Main post office** [105 F4] Davit Agmashenebelis 44; ⊕ 09.00–17.00 Mon–Fri, 10.00–14.00 Sat. Technically the main post office & where you should check for *poste restante*.

SHOPPING

Most Tbilisebi buy **food** at markets and corner shops, but there are some modern supermarkets, many open 24 hours, the best of which are listed on page 132. The excellent Populi and Ioli neighbourhood supermarkets have all been converted to 24-hour Spar outlets. There are also a couple of shops selling artisan Georgian cheeses (including three in the block of Marjanishvili northeast of the metro station). There are lots of **wine** shops along Leselidze (*mostly* ⊕ *10.00–22.00*), and a number of other good options elsewhere (pages 132–3), in addition to a selection of good wine bars that sell some interesting bottles. Various wineries also have their own outlets – these close at about 19.00.

For **books**, try the numerous stalls along Rustaveli Avenue, especially under the Academy of Science arcade. Those will all be in Georgian and Russian, but the shops listed below do stock some books in English. There are also various bookshop-cafés (page 123).

For detailed Georgian **maps**, the best place to look is Geoland [105 G6] (*Telegrapis chichi 3, facing the Public Service Hall on the right bank;* \ *292 2553;* e *info@geoland. ge;* f *geoland-garmin;* ⊕ *10.00–19.00 Mon–Fri*). It produces excellent 1:200,000 travel maps (*GEL10; or GEL50 for all 6 covering the whole country*), twelve 1:50,000 hiking maps, a road map of the country and a Tbilisi map (*all GEL10 each*). They will also print off (in about 20 minutes) old Soviet military maps (with place names in Latin script, and a modern UTM grid) and other maps from the 1970s and 1980s. They also stock Garmin GPS gear and Camping Gaz canisters.

Carpets are, of course, a speciality throughout the Middle East. Common in the Islamic countries, they are made in Georgia too, especially in Kakheti. The best places to buy carpets (including Georgian ones) are across the Caspian in the bazaars of Bokhara, Ashgabat and other cities. In Tbilisi, as well as the places listed below, you can buy carpets at Leselidze 10, 27 and 42 (at Sioni), & under the Dry Bridge [105 F5]. There's also the excellent reWoven project in Marneuli (page 341), working to keep the Azeri carpet-making tradition alive.

Shops selling Georgian wine and carpets tend to have a sign in English.

BOOKS

Biblusi Books [104 A2] w biblusi.ge/info/ map. Branches at Rustaveli 40, Kostava 47, Chavchavadze Av 10, Davit Agmashenebelis 121, Tsereteli 49, Iosebidze 49, Khizanishvili 50, Kavtaradze 1, Zhvania Sq, the railway station foyer, major shopping centres & half a dozen sites across the city.

Book House [94 C2] Bakhtrioni 11

English Book in Georgia [94 D6] Chavchavadze Av 14; w englishbookgeorgia.com. A wide range of mainly educational books, available online for delivery or collection from their shop.

International House [94 C2] 26 May Sq 2; w ihtbilisi.ge/en/bookshop. Well stocked with classics, modern literature & language-learning books.

Parnassus [94 D6] Chavchavadze Av 22; w parnasi.ge

Prospero's Books [104 D5] In the courtyard at Rustaveli 34 (Caliban's Coffeehouse); \ 292 3592; m 577 917991; w prosperosbookshop.com; ⊕ 09.30–21.00 daily. This is the best place for English-language guides & novels, as well as news magazines & maps; they also buy & sell 2nd-hand

books. Also at Betsy's Hotel (page 110) & Vazha-Pshavelas 1 (in the National Archive Centre).

Rare Books [105 E3] Davit Aghmashenebelis 77; ⊕ 10.00–19.00. English books available 2nd-hand, though most are fairly old.

Santa Esperanza [105 E3] St Petersburg 12, off Davit Agmashenebelis; w santaesperanza.ge

CARPETS

Caucasian Carpets Gallery [112 D3] Erekle II 8; m 577 405311; e gallerycarpets@yahoo.com; w carpetsintbilisi.com; ⊕ 10.00–20.00 daily. The best option for authentic carpets & kilims from the Caucasus & Central Asia.

Firma Narikala [113 F5] Abanos 1

Maidan 91 [113 H1] On the south side of Gorgasali Sq, Samghebro 5; \ 272 3546

FOOD & DRINK
Artisan shops

Aristaeus [112 C1] Pushkin 19; ⊕ 10.00–21.30 daily. Cheese & more.

Chacha Corner [112 A3] Lortkipanidze 11 (*formerly Lermontov 25*); m 591 197757; ⊕ 10.00-23.00 daily.

A wide range of chachas, from rare grapes, as well as the standard Rkatsiteli & Saperavi, & gin from Racha, grain alcohol from Svaneti, honey vodka from Guria, & various brandies.

Cheese Corner [94 A2] Nutsubidze 163; w cheesecorner.ge; ⏰ 10.00–21.00 daily. Also at Berdzenishvili 6 [94 B6] & Sharden 3/5 [113 G1].

Cheese House [94 D6] Paliashvili 7; ▪ cheesehouse; ⏰ 10.00-20.00 daily. Also at & Kazbegi 20A [94 B2].

Fromagerie [94 B6] Chavchavadze Av 50; m 591 555546, 599 703927; ▪ Fromagerie.Ge; ⏰ 10.00–21.00 daily

Gemorcheuli [94 B7] Abashidze 31; ⏰ 09.00–22.00 daily. Organic groceries & dairy products, etc. Also at Kipshidze 9B [94 B3] & Vazha-Pshavelas 5/4 [94 C2].

Khurjini Village Products [112 D2] Katalikosi 15; ⏰ 10.00–23.00. Just off Leselidze, this sells a fantastic range of natural products from all over Georgia – spices, honey, teas, sweets, wines & chachas.

Poka Nunnery's [94 D7] Paliashvili 30. Cheese & jam from the nunnery by Lake Paravani (page 221).

Hypermarkets

Carrefour ⏰ 09.30–22.00 daily. The French giant has huge stores in the Tbilisi Mall (*on the edge of town at km13 of the Mtskheta Hwy*) & the East Point Mall (*on the Kakheti Hwy*), & smaller Carrefour Market shops at the rear of the railway station (*Tsotne Dadiani 7*) & on the lower level of the Georgian Trade Center (GTC), home to the former central market (*Orbeliani Sq*), now with fashion & jewellery boutiques on the upper level.

Goodwill ⏰ 10.00–22.00 daily. Georgia's 1st hypermarket (with some interesting German foods), it's now owned by Carrefour. Branches at Parnavaz Mepe 1 , Didi Dighomi, by the highway northwest to Mtskheta, & in the Pixel Business Centre (*Chavchavadze Av 34*).

Supermarkets

Smart w smart.ge. Mainly found at petrol stations, but also has 24hr branches in the old post office at Rustaveli 31 [105 E5], at Chavchavadze Av 37 [94 B6] & on the Kakheti & Mtskheta highways.

Zemeli [104 D4] Rustaveli 37, opposite McDonald's.

Wine bars

Café Volver Organic Wine & Food [112 A4] Asatiani 56

Château Mukhrani [113 H2] Samghebro 6, Maidan Sq

DADI [112 C2] Dadiani 4

Ghvino Underground [112 B3] Tabidze 15. See also page 121.

Karalashvili's Wine Cellar [112 C2] Vertsikle 19

Old Cellar (Dzveli Marani) [113 G1] Leselidze 51

Schuchmann [113 E3] Sioni 8. With a molecular version of Georgian cuisine, eg: salad with sulguni sorbet, or desserts with nitrogen.

Tsangala's Wine Shop & Bar [112 D1] Shavteli 12

Wine shops
Along Leselidze (Kote Apkhazi)

Mukuzani at Gocha's Winery [112 D2] Leselidze 27/15 at Katalikosi

Vinomania Wine Gallery [113 F1] Leselidze 45; ⏰ until 02.00

Vinotheca [112 D3] Leselidze 31

Vintage Wine Bar [112 C2] Leselidze 11. Shop & wine bar with bottles up to GEL250.

Vintage Wine Store [112 D2] Leselidze 27

Wine House [113 G1] Leselidze 55

Elsewhere in Tbilisi

Alco Room [113 F4] Abanos 13

Alcorium [94 D7] Eristavi 9 (*UN Place*)

Allwine [104 A2] Kandelaki 7 (*Zhvania Sq*) & Chavchavadze Av 10

Dionysus Wine Gallery [112 C1] Pushkin 25

Diwine [113 F3] Metekhi Rise 2

Georgian Wine Culture Centre [94 C2] Bakhtrioni 11A

Royal Wine [112 B4] Tabidze 23

Wine Gallery [105 F3] Tsinamdzgvrishvilis 39

Wine Store & BARrels [105 G4] Davit Agmashenebelis 15

Wine World [105 E5] Laghidze 2

WineLab [112 C3] Dadiani 10

Winery outlets

Château Mukhrani [113 H2] Samghebro 6, Maidan Sq

Château Telavi [95 E5] Amaghleba 21

Eniseli [105 F6] Jorjadze 3/5 (*at Gudiashvili 11*)

Khvanchkara [94 A2] Vazha-Pshavelas 41

Kindzmarauli Marani [94 B6] Chavchavadze Av 56

Shumi [94 C2] Sulkhan Tsintsadze 18
Tibaani [104 A3] Janashia 18/11
Tolibashi [94 A2] Kazbegi 35A
Tsinandali [104 D4] Radisson Blu Hotel (page 109), Rose Revolution Sq
Vazi + [105 G4] Tsinamdzgvrishvili 4
Winery Khareba [104 D5] Rustaveli 50 & [113 H1] Gorgasali 1 (*off Maidan Sq*)

SOUVENIRS

For **souvenirs** such as daggers, drinking horns & national costume (page 86), look in the shop in the Opera underpass [105 E5] & the pavement in front of the Academy of Science [104 D4], or the souvenir shops on Leselidze. There's a small shop at Vertskhli 26 [112 D2], just off Leselidze, selling Georgian costumes. Artworks & handicrafts can also be bought at:

Alexander Gotsi [104 C3] Kiacheli 12; ⓕ gotsialexanderi. Superb handmade leatherwork.
Antique Bazaar [105 F4] Uznadze 9. A huge shop on the embankment near the Saarbrücken Bridge.
Art Salon [105 E5] Griboedov 11 & [105 E3] Davit Agmashenebelis 68
Art Studio Kon Tiki [105 G6] Chakhrukhadze 28
Caucasus Nature Jewels [113 E3] In the Tbilisi History Museum, Sioni 8; ⏰ closed Mon. Supports local artists & craftspeople & also national parks. Also in the Radisson Blu Hotel (page 109).
Pirosmani [112 C1] Pushkin 25 & [113 E2] Erekle II 8. Handmade jewellery & other souvenirs.
Quissa [105 G4] Javakhishvili 12
Vernissage [113 G1] Leselidze 49

SPORTS GEAR

There are shops selling Chinese sports gear around the Dinamo Stadium [95 E2], & also Adidas outlets at Rustaveli 1 [112 B1] & Marjanishvili 17 [105 E2] & the Competitive World of Sport [94 C2] (*Vazha-Pshavelas 12*).

Magellan Sport Shop [112 B2] Mitskevich 68; ✆ 237 1919; ⓕ TheNorthFaceMagelani. This North Face outlet stocks a range of specialist gear for skiing, snowboarding, fishing & other outdoor pursuits.
Mogzauri [112 A2] Vazha-Pshavelas 91; ✆ 231 9101; m 568 659985; w mogzaurirent.ge; ⏰ 10.00–19.00 daily. This British-Georgian shop sells & rents mountain bikes, skis, snowboards, sleeping bags, tents & other gear. Also at Gudauri (pages 180–3).
Salewa [94 A2] Nutsubidze 193; m 599 547500. Outlet for excellent Italian mountain gear.
SPX (Sport Point Extreme) [112 B2] Rustaveli Av 2/4; ✆ 322 970167. In the new Galleria Tbilisi, this sells good-quality imported sports gear.

MARKETS Tbilisi's **central market** (Bazroba) [95 E2] is by the station, a bustling place, where you'll find better quality (at higher prices) upstairs; between here and the Dinamo Stadium is an even more chaotic open-air market known as the **Deserters' Bazaar**, after soldiers who fled the Czarist army in the early 19th century and sold their guns and equipment there; nowadays it's the main source of food for many of Tbilisi's families and restaurants, and gives a wonderful insight into Georgia's rich food culture. The Station Square area is also the place for all sorts of services such as mobile phone repairs – but beware pickpockets in this area. There's an open-air flower market, between Baratashvili and 9 April Park, but the old food market here has closed and there is now a branch of Carrefour on the ground floor and fashion outlets upstairs. The **Lilos bazroba** is a huge flea market 20km east beyond the airport on the Kakheti Highway, where you can find anything you need; don't forget to bargain. This is really the wholesale market for the whole country, with direct buses from cities such as Kutaisi, and several marshrutka lines terminate here, as well as bus 41 from Samgori metro.

Artists sell their work at weekends at the **Vernissaj** [105 F5], the open-air market in the park by the Dry Bridge; above, by the road between the bridges, there is a thriving street market where Soviet-era memorabilia, military uniforms, second-hand books, magazines, coins, banknotes, records and cameras are all sold alongside household items and all manner of bric-a-brac. The lingua franca here is predominantly Russian and this is the place to come if you are in search of a Stalin bust or communist lapel badge. There are also people carrying labels advertising houses and flats for sale. Around the corner is a car bonnet market that mostly deals in tools and spare parts.

A DAY'S TOUR OF TBILISI

This provides an outline of a tour of Tbilisi which should take about a day, although if you visit all the museums as you go around it'll take far longer; it can also be speeded up by taking minibuses along the main streets, and by omitting its western extremities.

THE OLD TOWN The Old Town of Tbilisi (the Kala) lies higgledy-piggledy on the crowded slopes between the river and the citadel of Narikala. Here, in an area inhabited, at various times, by Persians, Tatars, Jews and Armenians, you can visit a mosque, a synagogue, and Armenian and Georgian churches, all still in use, and a Roman Catholic church, built in 1804 and reconsecrated by the Pope in 1999.

Freedom Square to the Metekhi Bridge The best starting point for a day walk is **Freedom Square** [112 B2] (Tavisuplebis Moedani), one of the busiest stations on the metro (which calls it Liberty Square). Laid out by the Russians between the 1820s and 1870s, it was originally known as Yerevan Square, then Theatre Square and was then Lenin Square until 1990; the statue of Lenin in its centre was replaced by a grassy roundabout, on the site of the city's first opera house, built in 1846 (the south wall was unearthed 30 years ago when the Rustaveli Avenue/Pushkin Street pedestrian underpass was built). A very tall column, the **Monument of Freedom and Victory**, with a kitschy gilded statue of St George and the Dragon by the sculptor Zurab Tsereteli atop it, now has pride of place in the centre of the square. The square is dominated by the **City Hall** [112 C2], built as a police station in the 1820s and remodelled in 1882–86 by the German architect Peter Stern, with a third storey and clock tower added in 1910–12; this is an attractive building with stripes of sandy green and white and mauresque stucco. The west side of the square was gutted in the civil war, but modern buildings such as the Courtyard by Marriott Hotel have now filled the gap. To the northwest is Pushkin Square, really an extension of Freedom Square where the chaotic oriental bazaars were cleared away by Beria; now, old men play backgammon here beneath the trees and a bust of Pushkin. There's also a **tourist information office** here with plenty of free booklets, maps and helpful English-speaking staff, as well as the grave of Kamo, a Bolshevik activist who was killed by a car in 1922, in what was almost certainly a murder organised by Stalin. The **Art Museum** [112 C1] (pages 150–2) faces Pushkin Square, in a Neoclassical building which was built in 1827–34 as a hotel, then served as a seminary until 1908, and became an art gallery in 1933. Noe Zhordania, the prime minister of independent Georgia from 1918 to 1921, studied here, as did Stalin.

To the left of City Hall (across Dadiani Street), Leselidze Street leads down into the Old Town – it's officially been renamed Kote Apkhazi Street (as Konstantin Leselidze was a Soviet general), but even those who've noticed are mostly ignoring the change. A 19th-century Russian construction, this was roughly the dividing line between the Upper and Lower parts of the Old Town and is now lined with souvenir shops and snack bars.

However, the Old Town's historic main street is Shavteli, running parallel to the river through a pleasantly shabby area; US$1.3 million has been spent to pedestrianise it and to add features like life-size statues sitting on benches. To reach it, continue down Pushkin (on the east side, opposite the Art Museum), on a walkway over the 12th–13th-century ruins of the Dighomi Gate, unearthed only in 2012. The blocks on the west side of Pushkin date from the 1950s and 1960s, while on the east side many houses were built into the **city wall** in the 19th century and now host touristy restaurants, as well as a wedding registry. The west end of Shavteli is marked by the Misrule statue (seemingly children playing) that used to indicate the Children's Art Gallery and Dolls Museum; turning right you'll pass the rather contrived surrealist tower of the **marionette theatre** [112 D1]; turning right again at the junction just beyond and then left, you'll come to the house-museum (rarely open) where the poet Nikoloz Baratashvili lived from 1841 to 1845.

Continuing on Shavteli, immediately on the left at No 7 is the **Anchiskhati Church** [112 D1], the oldest and one of the most loved in Tbilisi, with the best choir, singing on Saturdays (☉ *16.00–19.00*) and Sundays (☉ *09.00–noon*). Founded by Vakhtang's son in the early 6th century, it's a three-nave basilica with two pairs of bare brick columns and stone walls flanking its narrow three-bay aisles. It has been rebuilt several times, most notably in 1675; the present frescoes (with wording in Old Church Slavonic script) probably date from the 18th century. Its name means 'the icon from Ancha', after a wonderful 6th-century icon in a golden frame (now in the National Museum), which was moved here in 1664 from Ancha, in Turkish-occupied territory. The gate-tower, with a residence above the gate, was built in 1675 and is most unusual with its Islamic-influenced brickwork.

Shavteli continues past an attractive park and an old people's home and chapel, before leading into **Erekle II Square** [112 D2], the historic centre of old Tbilisi, with a cast-iron fountain from France, once the site of open-air courts and punishment. On the north side of the square is the balconied palace of Giorgi XII (well restored but now semi-permanently closed); semi-underground towards the embankment are the remains of the 17th-century baths of King Rustum and Vakhtang VI's press (1709). To the east is the former governor's palace (built in 1802 and now a police building).

Passing through an ugly unfinished area (where Bidzina Ivanishvili is planning a five-star hotel and cable car terminal) at the rear of the Shangri-La casino, a path leads left to the **Peace Bridge** [113 E2], an arresting if somewhat over-sized footbridge, opened in 2010, which stretches across the Mtkvari River to Rikhe Park (page 146). With its interactive LED lighting, the bridge is supposed to symbolise Georgia's transition from the past to a better future, but owing to its unfortunate resemblance to a giant sanitary towel is referred to by some wags as 'Always Ultra'. Remaining on the right bank, you'll enter **Erekle II Street**, now pedestrianised, busy with trendy art galleries and bars and lots of tables and chairs on the street; it's very nice at weekends, especially Sundays, the only time you see expats strolling in jeans instead of driving in 4x4s.

Forking left at the end of Erekle II on to Sionis Street (instead of joining Leselidze), you'll come to the **Sioni Cathedral** [113 E3], seat of the Catholicos of Georgia, who lives in the villa immediately to the west. The original Church of the Assumption was built between AD575 and AD639, but little of that is left; the present church is a typical domed Georgian church built of tuff stone from Bolnisi in the 12th century, but it's nothing special architecturally. However, it is the centre of religious life in the city, partly due to the presence of St Nino's Cross, which she made by binding two vine branches together with her own hair (hence the drooping arms of the Georgian cross); a replica is displayed to the left of the iconostasis, but it's hard to see much as even this is in an ornate early 14th-century reliquary which also contains a piece of Doubting Thomas's skull. The frescoes and iconostasis (1850–60) are by the Russian Grigori Gagarin. The row of taps in the courtyard date from the 18th century, when the church was turned into a mosque by Shah Abbas. Across the road is the handsome bell-tower or *kolokolnaya*, the first example of Russian neoclassicism in Georgia but now in very poor repair; it was built in 1812 at the wish of the Russian viceroy prince Paul Tsitsiani, who had died in 1806 and been buried in the cathedral. This is also where the playwright Griboedov married Alexander Chavchavadze's daughter Nina. To the north of the cathedral (towards the river) is the original bell tower, built in the 13th century and 1425, and restored in 1939. On the west/right side of Sioni (on either side of the kolokolnaya) are two caravanserais or trading centres for visiting merchants (at numbers 36 and 40), supposedly being restored, and then on the left at No 8 is the Tbileli caravanserai or **Carvasla** [113 E3], built in 1650, rebuilt in the 1820s and again in 1912 with an Art Nouveau façade, which now houses the Museum of the History of Tbilisi (page 152). The interior has a high atrium and three galleries overlooking a fountain, which was once a drinking pool for pack animals. Immediately beyond, on the left, Bambis Rigi (Cotton Row) curves right to continue as Rkinis Rigi to the Metekhi Bridge; parallel to the right is Sharden Street (named after the French traveller Jean-Baptiste Chardin, who visited Tbilisi several times between 1666 and 1672). This area is packed with very tacky hookah bars, restaurants and art galleries; in particular Bambis Rigi, a wonderful unified piece of Art Nouveau architecture (1905), has been ruined by tasteless clutter.

Maidan and Abanotubani At the end of Sharden (at the west end of the Metekhi Bridge), steps lead up to **Gorgasali Square** [113 H1], popularly known as the Maidan. In medieval times this was the site of the city's bazaar, and it is still surrounded by Silversmiths' Street, Blacksmiths' Street and so on, marking where various trades were once concentrated. There were two bridges across the Mtkvari here, and a mosque, until 1951 when Beria replaced them with the present Metekhi Bridge; but when the river is low the foundations are still visible to the west. Just to the left of the south side of the square is the **Armenian Church of Surb Gevorg (St George)** [113 H2], founded by the Armenian merchant Umek in 1251, although what you see now is largely 18th century and fairly standard in form, apart from the choir gallery. The grave of the great Armenian poet and musician Sayat-Nova, beheaded in 1795, is outside the door. Continuing eastwards on Samghebro, the first turning to the right leads up to the **Narikala Citadel** [113 E5] (page 145); you'll emerge on Botanikuri, which leads steeply up the hill to the right through the old Azeri quarter to (as you might expect) the **Botanic Gardens** [112 C5] (pages 154–5), passing the **Jumah mosque** [113 F5], the only one left in the city (with Sunni and Shia now worshipping together), at No 32. Built in 1895, it's red brick with a relatively discreet minaret, opposite a memorial to the Turkish artist Ibrahim Isfahanli (1897–1967). You're free to enter but should, of course, remove your shoes. Just east of the Maidan, the courtyard of the Monastery of the Forty Martyrs of Sebaste was excavated in 2015, and there's now a walkway from which you can see the remains of a 2nd–3rd-century bathhouse and of a later wine cellar, walls and palace; there's also an Archaeological-Ethnographic Museum displaying some 12th–14th-century ceramics. Immediately beyond is Abanos kucha, named after the **bathhouses** [113 F5] found here (pages 127–8). At the end of the road just to the right you'll see the most striking bathhouse, the late 17th-century Chreli ('Motley') Baths (famously visited by Pushkin in 1829), with a façade of bright-blue tiles and two short minarets, recalling the design of a mosque. The other old bathhouses are underground, their presence betrayed only by rows of brick domes which you can walk over. The oldest surviving is the Erekle, on the corner of Abanos and Akhundov; opposite this is the early 17th-century Simbatov baths, while the 18th-century Bebutov baths are on Akhundov. In 1817 Sir Robert Ker Porter, court painter to Alexander I, was able to bribe his way into the women's baths and was shocked to find that 'they seemed to have as little modest covering on their minds as on their bodies'. The area immediately around the bathhouses and mosque has long been at the centre of the city's **Azeri quarter**: the small park in front of the bathhouses bears the name and bronze bust of Heydar Aliyev, the former president of Azerbaijan. In 2011–12 this area was nicely repaved and pedestrianised, with the Tsavkisistksali riverbed opened up, creating a pleasant promenade up the Leghvtakhevi gorge to a waterfall below the Botanic Gardens.

South of Gorgasali Square Returning to the Maidan, there are two churches at this end of Leselidze, the first of which is the Georgian **Jvaris-Mama Church** [112 D3], built in the 16th century and modified in 1825; it's small and tall, with newly painted interior walls. The other, larger, church is the Armenian **Norashen Church** [112 D3], built in 1793 and now closed for repairs. The **Great Synagogue** [113 G1] (1903) at Leselidze 47 has a blue and gold lower hall (without a women's gallery) for daily services (at 09.00) and a brighter upper hall with gallery and large chandeliers for Sabbath and festivals. There's also a ritual bath and kosher butcher, bakery and the David restaurant. In the courtyard of Leselidze 28, there's also the Bet Rachel or Ashkenazi synagogue, reopened in 2009.

For the best sense of how Tbilisi's Old Town used to be, you should explore the back alleys of **Kala**, on either side of Leselidze. Many of the buildings here fell into poor repair in the latter part of the 20th century, due to neglect and earthquakes, and the area was placed on the list of the world's most endangered monuments and sites. There's been extensive restoration work in the last few years, but under Saakashvili this too often involved demolition and rebuilding with a pastiche version of the original façade and balconies. It's still possible to get a feel for how life was in this densely populated area, with its narrow winding streets and multi-storey houses with *musharabi* balconies and stained-glass windows overlooking courtyards. Historically, Kala fell into two parts – Zemo Ubani (the Upper District) centred on Batonis Moedani (King's Square, now Erekle II Square) and the largely Armenian Kvemo Ubani (the Lower District) around Tsikhis Moedani (Fortress Square, now Vakhtang Gorgasali Square) up to Narikala.

The Betlemi area, on the slope below the Narikala Fortress, has been inhabited since the 5th century but the oldest houses now extant date from the 17th century, and most are 19th century, with far older churches hidden in between. From Leselidze, take Asatianis kucha (formerly Bebutov) up to the left of the Jvaris-Mama and Norashen churches; there are good Moderne (Art Nouveau) buildings at Asatiani 38, 44, 50 and 66. You'll pass the tiny Tumanian Square on the left and soon emerge into Puris (Bread) Square, which is not much bigger. From the corner of Asatiani and Betlemi you can climb steps to the **Ateshga**, or **Fire Worshippers' Temple** [112 D4], a rock-cut altar built by the Persians between the 5th and 7th centuries, and converted to a mosque in the 17th century. From here (or taking Betlemi Rise from Asatiani), an alley leads on to the **Upper and Lower Betlemi (Bethlehem) churches** [112 C/D4] (founded in the 7th century but both now largely 18th century, and both painted inside in the last few years). There's a bell tower to the east of the upper church, and there is a fine view from its charming garden over the roofs and wooden balconies of the Kala and across the river to the Presidential Palace and Sameba Cathedral. Just behind the church you'll find steps leading up to the *Mother of Georgia* statue [112 C5]. More steps lead down to the lower church and back to Asatiani; at No 28 is the striking former Girls' College (looking down Dadiani, which leads to Freedom Square), now the Tbilisi Institute of Law and Economics [112 C4]. Immediately north of Asatiani on Machabeli are two of the earliest and most exuberant examples of Art Nouveau in Tbilisi: No 13 was built in 1905 for the cognac magnate Davit Sarajashvili who left it to the Writers' Union; and No 11, Beria's residence in the 1930s, now houses the **Georgian Olympic Committee and museum** [112 B3] (⏲ *10.00–17.00 Mon–Fri; free*), which has lots of interesting electronic displays (and wrestling videos) but only in Georgian, alas.

It's three blocks further downhill to Gudiashvili Square [112 C3], currently the Ground Zero of dereliction and neglect – bizarrely, the city has created a tranquil haven in the centre of the square, while the buildings around it are collapsing. The most notorious is No 2, the **Lermontov House** (one of the city's finest balconied houses, built in the 1830s), where the writer stayed in 1837. Continuing from the square downhill and at once turning left, you can go back down Anton Katolikos to Leselidze, through a nicely restored area with the new Museum of the Jews of Georgia (page 154).

Garetubani and the Dry Bridge
If you go down Pushkin from Freedom Square to Baratashvili Street (leading to the **Baratashvili Bridge** [105 G6], rebuilt in 1966 as the Stalin Bridge, with a lower urine-stinking pedestrian level) and turn left, you'll pass the city's former central market, the former US embassy (in the splendid 1860s Orbeliani Palace) at the foot of 9 April Park, and the **Dry Bridge** [105 F5] or Mshrale Khidi (1851); this crosses a former channel of the Mtkvari (now a busy highway) to **Dedaena Park** [105 F5] (formerly Madatov Island), where artists display and sell their works *en plein air*, and the wonderful Vernissaj street market is devoted to Soviet-era bric-a-brac on the road above. Returning towards Baratashvili Bridge, the modern **Public Service Hall** [105 G6] (also known as the House of Justice) appears to have been air-dropped in, with its parachutes (more often compared to mushrooms) still on the roof. It's actually bustling and very useful, with fast, corruption-free service (w *my.gov.ge*).

THE NEW TOWN
Rustaveli Avenue Rustaveli Avenue (Rustavelis Gamziri in Georgian) leads off to the northwest from Freedom Square. Laid out in 1810, almost 1.5km long and lined with plane trees, it's a fine, stately avenue that's spoilt by the amount of traffic roaring up and down it these days. There are pedestrian underpasses, but not many and not at the metro stations. On the north/right side at No 3 is the **National Museum** [112 B1] (pages 149–50), built in 1910–29, which houses the national collections of archaeology, history, natural history and ethnography, based on the collections of the Caucasian Museum, founded in 1852. A treasury houses a superb collection of pre-Christian gold; jewellery and icons from the Christian era are in the treasury of the Art Museum. Just beyond the museum is the **Rustaveli Cinema** [105 F6], built in 1939 by Nikolai Severov (who also designed the National Museum), with idealised statues of Soviet youth on the façade. Behind them is the **National Library** [105 F6], housed in three imposing former banks (all built 1907–15) along Gudiashvili Street; the easternmost block is a fascinating neo-Romanesque creation with lovely murals on its ceiling (including an external arcade). In November 2017 the **National Book Museum** (*Gudiashvili 5;* w *nplg.gov.ge;* ⏲ *10.00–18.00 Mon–Fri*) opened here, displaying rare books, including a Georgian–Italian dictionary published in 1629, a Book of Psalms, the first book printed in Georgia, in 1709, various editions of *The Knight in the Panther's Skin*, in Georgian and translated,

and Ilia Chavchavadze's library with some private belongings. Below the library is the **Old Trinity Church** [105 F6] (built in 1790, with more recent frescoes and a Baroque iconostasis), busy with weddings at weekends.

Immediately on the left at the start of Rustaveli is the modern Galleria Mall (opened at the end of 2017), incorporating the Freedom Square metro station and the **Griboedov Russian Theatre** [112 B2] behind it; originally a *caravanserai*, there's been a theatre here since 1845. At its far end, steps lead up to the Chancellery, then Rustaveli rises to the Young People's Palace, built in 1807 as the Russian **Viceroy's Palace** [112 B1], with an arcade in front added in 1865–68. Stalin installed his mother here at one time and it then served as the Pioneers' Palace, housing the Soviet youth organisation and a Museum of Children's Toys. It's still used for youth activities, and is the best place to find classes and displays of Georgian folk dance and the like.

Beyond this is easily the most dominating building on Rustaveli, the **Parliament Building** [105 E6]. This was built as a U-shaped block in 1938 (on the site of the Alexander Nevsky Church, built in the 19th century for the Russian army); a very solid portico of tuff was built by German prisoners of war and the building opened in 1953. It was on the steps before the Parliament that the massacre of 9 April 1989 took place, and you'll still see memorials to the dead here. This was also the focus of the 1991–92 civil war, with Gamsakhurdia and his supporters holed up inside; the side wings were gutted, but the portico resisted the National Guard's shellfire, giving rise to comments on the superiority of German building to Soviet efforts. It stands opposite the site of the Artists' House and the lovely Hotel Intourist (built in the 1870s), both sadly destroyed in the civil war; in 2017 a hideous new building was completed in their place, which is to become the national art gallery.

Immediately beyond the Parliament (by an underpass beneath the avenue) is the **Classical Gymnasium** [105 E6] or High School No 1, founded in 1802 as the first European-style high school in Transcaucasia; it educated many of the leading figures of recent Georgian history, including Kostavas, Gamsakhurdia, Sigua and Kitovani. It's a good example of Russian neoclassicism, with statues of Ilia Chavchavadze and Akaki Tsereteli (1958) in front. Next, at Rustaveli 12 the 1950s Ministry of Transport and Communications bears a plaque commemorating those killed by Soviet security forces on 9 March 1956.

At No 9 on the north side is the **Kashveti Church of St George** [105 E6], built in 1904–10 by the German Leopold Bielfeld, on the site of a 6th-century church demolished as unsafe at the end of the 19th century. It was based on the 11th-century church of Samtavisi, and the altar apse was decorated in 1946 by Lado Gudiashvili (who lived just behind the church and for his pains was expelled from the Communist Party and lost his job at the Academy of Art). There's a separate church in the crypt, used for Russian-language services. Henry Mowatt, a Scottish engineer who worked on the Surami rail tunnel and married a Georgian, is buried here.

The attractive 9 April (formerly Alexandrov) Park is behind the church (with decent public toilets), and next to it, at Rustaveli 11, is the **National Gallery** [105 E6] (page 152) in a fine Neoclassical building known as the Khram Slavi (Temple of Glory), built in 1885–88 by Alexander Saltzmann, with a modern rear extension added in 2011. Beyond this, at No 15 (opposite the Ministry of Transport and Communications) is the Hotel Tbilisi, built in 1915 as the Hotel Majestic and gutted in the civil war. It reopened in 2002 as the luxurious Marriott Hotel (page 109). Behind it at Chanturia (formerly Georgiashvili) 8 is the **State Literature Museum** [105 E5] (✆ 299 8667; w *literaturemuseum.ge*; ⊕ *10.00–18.00 Tue–Sat*), a nice 19th-century building facing the park – the literature displays are closed, but it houses temporary art shows, both upstairs from the uphill door and just inside the lower doors.

Beyond the hotel, at No 17, is the splendid French Neoclassical façade of the famous **Rustaveli Theatre** [105 E5], built in 1899–1901 and refurbished in 1920–21 for the new Rustaveli Theatre Company and again in 2002–05. It boasts marble staircases, classical statues, and frescoes by Lado Gudiashvili, Moise Toidze and David Kakabadze in the Kimerioni (Chimera) café. Rustaveli 19 was built as the Palace Hotel in 1910 and is now part of the theatre.

On the south side of the avenue, behind Rustaveli 24 at Griboedov 8, stands the **Conservatoire** [104 D5] (music college), built in 1904; there's a museum (*in room 301, up one flight and at the end of the corridor to the right;* ⊕ *noon–17.00 Mon–Fri; free*) with Rachmaninov's piano and lots of vintage photos and drawings of opera sets. On the ground floor at the east end of the building are the recently refurbished Grand Hall and a lovely chamber recital hall where Horowitz played. The poet Titsian Tabidze lived at Griboedov 18 from 1921 to 1937, where his friend Boris Pasternak allegedly did many of his translations of Georgian poetry. The imposing Supreme Court stands on the next street uphill, Brothers Zubelashvili. You can continue along Griboedov to Rose Revolution Square, passing the **Academy of Arts** [104 D5] at No 22 – a very fine building erected in 1858, with rather splendid murals in the hall and mosaics above the staircase; it's currently closed for major refurbishment.

If you continue from the theatre along the north side of Rustaveli, you'll come to the **Zakaria Paliashvili State Opera House** [105 E5] at No 25. Founded in 1851 and burnt down in 1874, it was replaced with the present Moorish building in 1880–96; it saw the start of Shalyapin's career before it too burnt down again in 1973. It was rebuilt in 1977, and reopened in 2016 after a six-year, £28 million, refurbishment, paid for by Bidzina Ivanishvili; there are various displays in the foyers, including memorabilia of Zacharia Paliashvili's operas. Outside is a statue of Paliashvili (by Merab Berdzenishvili, 1973); this is next to his grave and that of Vano Saradzishvili, the first great Georgian singer. Beyond another underpass, No 27 (built in 1909 as a military school, then the national archives) now houses the **Museum of Modern Art–Tbilisi** [105 E5] (w *momatbilisi.ge;* ⊕ *11.00–18.00 Wed–Mon, noon–19.00 in summer;* GEL5) created by the ubiquitous Zurab Tsereteli (page 48). There are temporary displays by other artists on the ground floor, with Tsereteli's powerful paintings and sculptures in the large upstairs space; a mezzanine displays lots of photos of him schmoozing with the famous and powerful.On the same side of Rustaveli, at No 29, is an imposing colonnaded building built in 1938 as the **Marx-Engels-Lenin Institute (IMELI)** [104 D5], which housed the obligatory Lenin Museum, with a copy of his Kremlin study; there are four blank cartouches high on the façade where the heads of Marx, Engels, Lenin and Stalin were removed in 1991. It was the seat of the State Council when Shevardnadze returned to take power, then the constitutional court, before it was sold to developers who removed the roof, expecting the building to collapse and allow them to raze it and replace it. It failed to oblige, and public outcry finally forced them to restore it, while building an ugly tower (now the Biltmore hotel) at the rear that blights the whole city. Beyond this is a brutalist block built in the late 1970s, housing the main post and telephone offices, the PostBank and a Smart supermarket. Opposite at Rustaveli 42 was the first major Soviet public building in Tbilisi, constructed in 1926–28; it's also brutalist plain concrete but with a few Neoclassical details, and very modern for the period, perhaps influenced by Czech functionalism.

Here, the modern plaza of Rose Revolution Square opens up to the right while Rustaveli kinks to the left past the **Academy of Sciences** [104 D4], a large, pompous building (built in 1953–58) in which 7,000 research staff once laboured. In its courtyard is a flattened, circular building housing the terminal of the cable car to Mtatsminda, built in 1958 with British cables and closed in the early 1990s after collapsing. The avenue ends at the small **Rustaveli Square** [104 C4], on the site of the former Moscow Gates, where a statue of the poet (by Koté Merabishvili, 1937) now stands by the Rustaveli metro station, next to Tbilisi's first McDonald's. Above this is **Vere**, an attractive district that is popular with younger expats and professionals.

Rose Revolution Square to the Philharmonic
Rose Revolution Square [104 D4] (then Republic Square) was laid out in 1981, above a road underpass and a shopping complex (now closed and very dark, except for an interesting new contemporary art gallery); in 1991 it was the rallying point for the opposition to Gamsakhurdia. It's now been pleasantly landscaped, with metal planters and wooden benches, and offers fine views across the city to the High Caucasus (to the northwest). To the north is the high-rise glass tower of the Radisson Blu Iveria, the product of a total renovation of a very run-down Soviet-period hotel built in 1967 that was inhabited, for many years, by the internally displaced and refugees from Abkhazia. At the west end of the square, most traffic swings left to Rustaveli Square; ahead are two minor streets, Kiacheli (to the right) and Akhvlediani (still better known as Perovskaya), lined with some of the city's liveliest pubs. Confusingly, the Elena Akhvlediani house-museum [104 C4], one of the most enjoyable in the city, is at Kiacheli 12. Traffic from Rustaveli Square passes under the Rose Revolution Square plaza and drops down Vere Hill to the Marjanishvili Bridge, leading to the left/north bank of the Mtkvari.

The city's main traffic axis continues west as Kostavas kucha (the former Lenin Street), and soon splits in front of the striking circular building of the Tbilisi Concert Hall, still generally known as the **Philharmonic** [104 B3], built in 1969–71, largely of glass; a bronze sculpture, *The Muse* (1971, by Merab Berdzenishvili), stands in front of it. To the right/north of the square in front of the Philharmonic is the **Vere (formerly Kirov) Park** [104 C3]; to the right in the park (ie: at the end of Kiacheli) you'll find a flight of steps that descend to the petrol station on the embankment road, passing the **Lurdzhi Monastery** [104 C3], and the very Russian **Church of St John the Theologian** [104 C3] (1901) next to it. The Lurdzhi Church is smaller, and can be identified by the faded blue roof that gives it its name. Built in 1155 and rebuilt in the 16th and 17th centuries, it's high with virtually no nave, and an unusual round cupola added in 1873; it's richly decorated and a modern belfry has been added. In communist times it housed a museum of medicine, while the Russian church was quite clearly left untouched; now the tables are turned and it's the Russian church that externally looks abandoned. This is entered from the far side and is painted in eggshell blue and white, with a gold iconostasis that just manages not to be too over the top. From here you can go up to the Vere district (page 141), or continue to the newer parts of the city.

Around 26 May Square
Forking right in front of the Philharmonic (behind which is Phikris Gora or Dream Hill, an enclave of nice hotels), Kostavas soon drops down to the ugly roundabout and flyovers of **Heroes' Square** [104 B1] (Gmirta Moedani), in a ravine filled in in the 1930s; there's a modern white obelisk in the centre, an Eternal Flame with guards at the heroes' memorial, and lots of graffiti art in the underpasses. To its left is the **zoo** [104 A1] (page 155) and the Mziuri (Sunshine) children's park, and to the right is the **circus** [104 B1], built in 1940, and (by the massive new King David Residences, which I call the Salt & Pepperpot Towers) the

bridge across the Mtkvari to Tamar Mepis Gamziri (Queen Tamar Avenue) and the railway station [95 E2]. Carrying on straight ahead, Kostavas climbs again past some very decent Stalinist/Neoclassical buildings to **26 May Square** [94 D2], laid out from 1940, with the domed Sports Palace (1961; with a statue of a buff naked athlete in front) and the Technical University metro station to its right and the high-rise Holiday Inn ahead (this was the Hotel Adjara, cleared of refugees in 2005, totally rebuilt and re-opened in 2010). The main road continues to the left of the hotel as Pekini Avenue, passing through the affluent but unlovely Saburtalo district and becoming the main road towards Mtskheta. There are some fine examples of 1970s Soviet tower blocks in Saburtalo and, beyond it, the Nutsubidze Plateau, including 14th-floor connecting walkways. Above Nutsubidze, **Lisi Lake** is a new private development where you can swim, go out in a boat or rent bikes to cycle around the lake; there are cafés and a nearby horseriding centre – but the most striking feature (visible from across the city) is the flying saucer of the Emergency Control Centre, which handles the city's 112 calls.

To the right of the hotel, Kostavas leads to the main building of **Georgia Technical University** [94 D2], a fine white-and-ochre Neoclassical pile, behind which the Saakashvili Presidential Library, in his trademark architectural style, overlooks the Bagrationi Bridge, crossing to Didube on the left bank. Continuing towards Mtskheta, the headquarters of **the Bank of Georgia** at Gagarin 29A [94 C1] (built in 1975 as the Ministry of Highways Construction) is one of the most iconic examples of Soviet modernism, a huge grid of interlocking cantilevered blocks like a pile of Jenga sticks above the Mtkvari. There are entrances both on Gagarin and on the embankment road, 33m below, but it's not actually easy to visit, as the only easy way to see it as a whole is to drive in and park beneath it.

Vake The Vake (Plain) district is the city's most affluent area, with many of its best restaurants and patisseries on streets such as Abashidze, parallel to the left of Chavchavadze Avenue. The district was built by Beria on top of the mass graves of the victims of his purges; the Bolsheviks had already executed many of the Georgian aristocracy here in 1923, and a public toilet was built on the site, now replaced by a memorial. Vake was once home to the communist bourgeoisie, and now, because it still has the city's best phone/internet and power supplies, is home to most of the city's expatriates and NGOs.

Forking left in front of the Philharmonic, Melikishvili kucha (widened in 1948) leads past the massive Soviet-era ex-Hotel Sakartvelo and the Tbilisi No.1 wine cellars to the **Tbilisi State University** [104 A2], the country's leading academic institution, housed in a fine domed building built in 1900–16, as well as some rather less attractive blocks behind this and a large modern complex on the western edge of the city, beyond Saburtalo. There's always a crowd of students blocking the pavement here, a great social coming and going which is the nearest thing to a *passeggiata* that Tbilisi offers. The main road continues west as Ilia Chavchavadze Avenue, lined with upmarket shops and coffee bars. To the right at No 21, marked with a jokey statue, there's an entrance to the **Mziuri Park** [94 C6] (pleasant but with an unfinished feel, and surrounded by tatty high-rises), and nearby the statues of the poets Galaction Tabidze and David Guramishvili (1966, by the omnipresent Merab Berdzenishvili).

Further out on Chavchavadze are the three bulbous towers of the Alliance Highline project, including Tbilisi's tallest residential tower and a Wyndham's Hotel (due to open in 2020), and the twisted Axis Towers, including a Pullman Hotel (opening in 2018). After 3.8km (with frequent buses) Chavchavadze finally reaches

Victory Square (Gamarjvebis Moedani), overlooking **Vake Park** [94 A3] to the left/ south. Laid out in 1946, this is a spacious and well-tended area of 226ha, where the grave of the Unknown Soldier lies at the foot of a flight of steps up to the statue of Victory, erected in 1976. A tiny cable car (⊕ *08.00–22.00; GEL1*) rises over the park to Kus Tba (Turtle Lake) [94 B4], where there are cafés; there's an asphalt loop around the lake, and some fairly informal paths (and mountain bike trails) lead back down (or indeed up), or you can hike up beyond the lake and across to Mtatsminda (see below) in a couple of hours. There's a small charge for swimming, which is good if you can avoid being run down by a pedalo (*GEL20/hr*) or row boat (*GEL8/hr*). The lake can also be reached by a 3km road, from just beyond the park, halfway along which is the open-air **Museum of Georgian Ethnography** [94 A4] (page 152), which has an Asian-fusion restaurant with a great view. There's also the Squirrels' Park, opened in 2006, with free children's games and wooden picnic huts. Just beyond the park, at the western end of Chavchavadze Avenue, is the **Vake Cemetery** [94 A3], with its tall cypresses, grand tombstones and ivy-clad mausoleums, which featured as a setting for the 2013 film *Repentance*. The main road climbs through pine forest to the so-called 'mountain resort quarter' of Tskneti (now swamped by tasteless dachas built with illegal money after 'accidentally' burning down an area of forest) and to Manglisi and Akhalkalaki.

OTHER AREAS It is of course possible to extend this brief tour of Tbilisi in various directions if you have the time and stamina.

Mtatsminda

If you turn right/south from Kostavas up Tamriko Tshovelidze (still better known as Belinskis), you can turn left on to Gogebashvili and at its end right onto Makashvili, which runs along the slopes of Mtatsminda. With wide views over the city, Chonkadze then Kakabadze pass the Russian church of St Michael of Tver (1910) and a few houses before reaching the crossroads just below the **Mamadaviti (Father David) Monastery** [104 C7], up a few tight cobbled hairpin bends. It's named after St David, one of the Assyrian Fathers, who lived here in a cave in the 6th century before moving on to Davit-Gareja (pages 337–40). The present church was built in 1859–79, in plain brick on an artificial terrace. However, what's of interest here is the **Pantheon** [104 C7] or graveyard, a repository of the remains of the leading figures of Georgian culture. These include the poets Nikoloz Baratishvili, Galaction Tabidze, Akaki Tsereteli and Georgi Leonidze, painter Lado Gudiashvili, dissident Merab Kostava and educationalists, critics and philosophers such as Iacob Gogebashvili, Niko Nikoladze and Vazha-Pshavelas, as well as Stalin's mother. Grottoes in the cliff face house the Russian playwright Griboedov and his widow Nina, daughter of Alexander Chavchavadze, and the secular saint Ilia Chavchavadze (no relation).

A little further along Chonkadze is the mosque-like lower terminal of the Mtatsminda **funicular** [104 C7] (⊕ *09.00–04.00 daily; GEL2 each way, midnight–04.00 GEL3; you need to buy a stored-credit card per group for this & the amusement park rides*) which was built in 1903–05 by Belgian engineers, an odd contribution from so flat a country, and rebuilt in 2012; it climbs for 5 minutes at 55° (with a path winding up and criss-crossing it) to reach its upper terminal, at an altitude of 727m on the edge of Mtatsminda, the Holy Mountain, so called because of St David's Cave. Above the terminal is the vast restaurant complex (❨ *298 0000*; w *funicular.ge*; *page 121*) built by Beria (an 80m-high statue of Stalin was planned on top).

There are other restaurants in the spacious but rather lame **amusement park** [104 B7] (w *park.ge*; ⊕ *summer 11.00–04.00 daily, 11.30–21.00 Sat–Sun, from 11.00* *winter*) behind the terminal, with attractions such as a rollercoaster, water ride, climbing wall, trampolines and ice rink that all have to be paid for (*GEL1–2*) with the stored-credit card. The main attractions are, in fact, the stunning views (as far as Kazbek, weather permitting, best seen from the Ferris wheel) and the fact that in summer the temperature is up to 5°C cooler than the city, so that it's lively until 04.00. Behind it is the massive TV Tower, like a 210m oil rig visible from all over the city; this had lurid flashing lights put up for Christmas in 2005, and they have not been turned off since. The Pantheon and Funicular Restaurant (and the Kartlis-Deda statue, Parliament, Presidential Palace, Chancery, Peace Bridge and Sameba, Sioni and Mtskheta churches) are also lit at night.

Buses 90 and 124 come up here from the city; there's an ATM and ticket office at the bus terminal. Otherwise, it's a pleasant 20-minute walk through pine woods to reach the Kojori road. If you happen to be coming up by car, it's a very sharp right turn into the park at a no-entry sign, virtually opposite a yard with a wire sculpture of an elephant with a mahout on its back.

East to Ortachala From Gorgasali Square [113 E4], the main road to the east along the Mtkvari embankment is Gorgasalis kucha, built in 1851 as Vorontsov ulitsa. About 100m beyond the bathhouses it passes the kneeling statue of the painter Pirosmani (1975, by Elgudja Amashukeli), the Tbilisi Balneologic Health Resort (founded in 1938 by Shevardnadze's father, and apparently run now by Saakashvili's father!) and at No 17 the **Akhundov Museum of Azerbaijan Culture** [113 H5] (✆272 1571; ☉ *11.00–18.00 Tue–Sun; free*). This is part of a recently renovated complex with wine bar, the Monsieur Jordan café (☉ *10.00–22.00 daily*) and art gallery, in the house where Mirza Fatali Akhundzade (creator of Azeri drama; 1812–78) lived from 1834. Not far beyond is the huge Azerbaijan embassy and then the '300 Aragveli' monument, a 23m-high stela raised in 1961 on the spot where, in 1795, King Erekle II was rescued from Aga Mohammed Khan by 300 men from the Aragvi Valley (on the Georgian Military Highway), who were all killed in the process. This was also the scene of one of the closer assassination attempts on Shevardnadze. Note that the 300 Aragveli metro station is actually on the far side of the river.

Continuing eastwards, you'll pass the equestrian statue (1982) of Pyotr Bagration, who distinguished himself in the campaign against Napoleon in 1812. To the left is the Ortachala Dam, and on the cliff top beyond this is the former **Palace of Weddings** [95 G6]. Built by the communists in 1984 to attract couples away from church weddings, it's very modernist, but with a classical statue (of a naked male) in front of the blatantly phallic carillion tower. The palace was bought in 2002 and used as a private mansion by the reclusive oligarch Badri Patarkatsishvili until his death in 2008 (he's buried in the garden); it's now used for weddings and banquets again. It can be reached by going straight across the road from the 300 Aragveli metro station, but you can no longer get inside.

To the east, the road now follows the course of the channel that used to make a small island, past the Finance and Justice ministries, the Public Prosecutor's Office and the city's main prison. The **Krtsanisi Palace**, built by Beria and home to the president until Shevardnadze neglected to move out, is hidden away just to the south. In fact, Saakashvili refused to move in, preferring to build the new Avlabari Residence. This area is becoming the new embassy quarter, with the British, Germans and Swiss moving here. The highway continues past the Ortachala bus station, built in 1973 to replace the cramped former terminal by the Marjanishvili Bridge; however, most bus services use the chaotic yard at Didube, and Ortachala's echoing hall is used mainly by international services, to Azerbaijan, Armenia and

Turkey. On the façade you can see *The Wheel*, a mosaic by Zurab Tsereteli; to the rear there's another fine mosaic (1979) on a fire station.

Beyond Ortachala the main road continues along the river and then splits, to Rustavi and Baku to the left, and Marneuli and Yerevan to the right.

Narikala Perhaps the best way to reach the *Mother of Georgia* statue and the Sololaki Ridge is by the cable car [113 F3] (⏰ *10.00–midnight; GEL2.50 with MetroMoney card only*) from Rikhe Park to Narikala, opened in 2012; this gives great views, especially from the one car with a glass floor, although the journey takes under 2 minutes. Otherwise your options are the steps and pathway up from the Upper Betlemi Church; Orbiri Street, climbing steeply from near the Armenian church to the Narikala Citadel; or Sololaki Lane, a road, lined with lime and cypress trees, that turns off the Kojori Highway and passes beneath the eyesore of Ivanishvili's business centre with its flying saucer helipad. It takes 5 minutes to reach the ruins of some medieval fortifications and a view to the right over the Botanic Gardens (there's a turnstile and a rough path down), as well as a new zip-line (page 154); and the 20m-high aluminium statue of *Kartlis-Deda* or *Mother of Georgia*, visible from all over the city. There's a great view down to the Old Town, marred by huge amounts of litter; there are lots of charms tied on a tree behind the statue. This was made in 1958–63 by Elgudja Amashukeli; sword in one hand and bowl in the other, it shows Georgia as hospitable but ready to defend herself. Also nearby are the ruins of the ancient Shakhtakhi Fort (from 'Sahis Tahti' or Throne of the Shah), which was used as an observatory in the 7th–9th centuries.

Heading east along the ridge, you'll pass the cable car terminal then fork left onto a rough path around to the gate of the **Narikala Citadel** [113 F5]. This was built in about AD360 by the Persians (who called it Shuris-tsihke), expanded by King David the Builder and restored by Mustafa Pasha's Turks in the second half of the 16th century, before being ruined by an earthquake in 1827. It's always open and entry is free, although there's a minimal charge for parking. Locals often come up here for picnics and to enjoy the evening views of the city. Near the car park is the 12th-century **Church of St Nicholas**, rebuilt in 1997, with a painted interior and a simple, modern, stone iconostasis. The fort walls are either over-restored or untouched (and being destroyed by people climbing on them); you can walk along the battlements, although there are some very steep steps. At the citadel's south end, you'll see the square Istanbul Tower, which was a prison under Turkish rule.

Left bank of the Mtkvari The left or north bank of the Mtkvari is, with the exception of the Metekhi Church and the area immediately behind it, relatively recently developed; although it contains little of touristic interest, there is much of practical use here. Its heart is the area to the south of the railway station, along Davit Agmashenebelis Gamziri (David the Builder Avenue), laid out by German colonists in the 19th century.

Metekhi Church On a crag over the Mtkvari, facing the Maidan, is the Metekhi Church [113 F4]; the view of this church, with the equestrian statue of Vakhtang Gorgasali (1967) overlooking the city he founded, is one of the most widespread images of Tbilisi.

The earliest churches on this site were built in the 5th and 8th centuries, but the present Church of the Virgin was built in 1278–89 by King Demetre II the Self-Sacrificer (so called because he answered a summons by the Mongols to near-certain death rather than cause an invasion). The ground plan is actually quite complex, with a cross filled out to a square, and lateral apses projecting at the eastern end. Four free-standing pillars support a central dome (rebuilt in 1748). The external stonework is very worn, and the interior is bare.

The present churchyard was long occupied by a castle which was ruined by Shah Aga Mohammed Khan in 1795 and rebuilt in 1819 as a prison, which housed Beria's offices and less willing guests such as Kalinin, Gorki and Kamo, the last of whom escaped down the cliff on half a dozen sheets tied together. This was demolished in 1937 when the present bridge and the Mtkvari embankment road were built. The church was used as a youth theatre until it was finally restored for worship in 1988. Below, by the bridge, are two chapels, including a tiny one dedicated to St Abo Tbileli (a 7th-century Arab convert, killed here by Muslims), built by hand in the 1990s.

Upstream, beyond the Europe Square roundabout (where a piece of the Berlin Wall was installed in 2017) and the mouth of the tunnel under the Avlabari Cliffs, is **Rikhe Park** [113 F2], once a resting place for camel caravans from Persia. This was a scruffy area but has recently been beautified with dancing fountains and quirky sculptures, as well as the Narikala cable car terminal and the Peace Bridge (page 135), and beyond them, the giant 'tubes' of Saakashvili's performing arts centre, still standing closed. It's now attractive and busy (even though there's no shade), and is the main site of the Tbilisoba Festival on a weekend of October (page 126), when stages are set up for performers and the whole area is hidden by the smoke from shashlik stalls (also up on Rose Revolution Square). To the right, Baratashvili Hill descends to the bridge of the same name from Avlabari Square; to the north, looking down on the bridge, is Saakashvili's new presidential palace with its striking egg-shaped glass cupola, like a mini-Bundestag. There has been much speculation as to how much this building cost, although Saakashvili himself claims it was a mere GEL13 million; it may be used to house a new Technological University. This part of Avlabari is prone to earthquakes and was rather run-down, but is now seeing some regeneration on the back of the palace and the Sameba Cathedral, with quite a few small new hotels opening. You can get here from the north side of the Echmiadzin Church along Meskhishvili and to the left.

Just west, Akhvlediani Hill (formerly Uritskis Hill) leads down to the river beyond the Baratashvili Bridge and a nice little park with a statue of the poet Nikoloz Baratashvili, by Boris Tsibadze (1975).

Avlabari The highway from Kakheti passes the airport and enters Tbilisi alongside the railway before turning to dive under it; traffic turns right on to Ketevan Tsamebulis Gamziri, just east of the Sheraton Metechi Palace Hotel, and then reaches Avlabari Square and metro station [113 G2], the heart of Tbilisi's Armenian quarter. From the Metekhi church you can get here by climbing up Ghvinis Aghmarti (Wine Hill), a steepish street below the walls of the Sachino Palace, mostly made of rows of riverbed stones alternating with double rows of brick. Alternatively, head up Metekhi Rise, lined on the right with the fine merchants' homes (now hotels and restaurants) whose triple-decker balconies you may already have admired from across the river, and turn left onto Metekhi Street.

At the west end of Avlabari Square is the Echmiadzin Church, named after the Armenian equivalent of Canterbury; built in 1804, it was cracking apart due to vibration from the metro trains passing underneath, but has recently been repaired. Across the main road a flight of steps and an alleyway lead to the Chapel of the Transfiguration, set on the battlements of the **Sachino Palace** [113 F3]; although the Avlabari cliffs have long been fortified, all that remains is this chapel and a round pavilion both built in 1776 for Queen Darejdan, wife of Erekle II. They're set in an attractive garden, from which there are views stretching from the bathhouses to Tbilisi State University. The chapel has a simple, vaulted nave and sanctuary with a very low dome at the west end under a belfry with external bell ropes. There are some early 20th-century frescoes, and plenty of whitewashed areas.

To the left, Meskhishvili leads towards the massive new **Sameba (Trinity) Cathedral** [95 G5] on Mount Elia, begun in 1995 and finished in 2004. Regarded as an eyesore by many people, it is equally venerated by many others, who cross themselves whenever they glimpse it on the far side of the city. It was built on the Armenian Khojavank cemetery, which was treated with a scandalous lack of respect. It's the largest religious building in the Southern Caucasus, with an interior area of 2,380m^2. It's certainly way out of scale for a Georgian church, even though it's in an exaggerated traditional Georgian style; a long esplanade with fountains leads past a belfry to the cathedral with a sort of triple-decked west end. The apses are very high but the windows only reach two-fifths of the way up; the dome is supported by eight freestanding pillars. The interior is now full of icons, priests and people; there are five additional chapels in the crypt.

Chugureti To the west is the Chugureti district, largely settled by Germans and Poles from around 1820; one block inland at Chkheidze 38, the EU embassy is a surprisingly beautiful three-storey building (built in 1888) quite out of keeping with this tatty red-brick district. The main road swings away from the river, soon passing the **Ilia Chavchavadze house-museum** [105 G4] (*Javakhishvili 7; closed for long-term refurbishment*) and continues to the railway station and out towards the northwestern suburbs.

However, soon after a relatively uninteresting early 19th-century church on the embankment, Tolstoy kucha leads off to the left to Saarbrücken Moedani, at the north end of the **Saarbrücken Bridge** [105 F5] (formerly Vorontsov, then Marx), and on as Davit Agmashenebelis Avenue. This was built as Mikhailovskaya in the 1830s, and was then known as Plekhanov under communism. Despite appearances, it's not a one-way street – a few marshrutkas do go the 'wrong' way, so be careful; this southern end near the Dry Bridge has in any case recently been closed altogether, creating a short pedestrianised stretch known as **Neu Tiflis**. Historic buildings have been refurbished and are now occupied by bars, restaurants and stylish shops – it's far nicer than the Charden area across the river. Continuing up the avenue, the first buildings of real interest are No 60, the **University Hospital**, a neo-Gothic pile built in the 1860s, and opposite it at No 61 the former House of Political Education or **Soviet Propaganda Centre** [105 F3], a brutalist block built in 1977 with, on its façade, a lurid high-relief mosaic (42m by 12m) by Zurab Tsereteli, celebrating the 60th anniversary of the Bolshevik Revolution; it's now the Mosaic Business Centre.

A little further along Agmashenebelis you'll come to Marjanishvili Square, laid out in 1948–56, with a metro station in its northern corner facing the city's second McDonald's; Yevgenii Primakov, Russian prime minister in 1998–99, grew up nearby on what was then Leningrad Street. A block towards the river at Marjanishvili 7, the striking **TBC Bank HQ** [105 E3] was built in 1912 as the Economic Society of Caucasian Officers, and shows temporary exhibits in a gallery upstairs (⊕ *13.00–17.00 Mon–Fri; free*); opposite is the Marjanishvili Theatre, built in 1907 with fine Moderne ironwork and recently refurbished.

Marjanishvili kucha (formerly Kirochnaya) leads north from Marjanishvili Bridge and Square and, after two blocks, crosses Ivan Javakhishvili (formerly Kalinin); on the corner to the left (at No 69) is the city's main **Russian Orthodox** church [105 F2] (1864), and just to the right at No 55 is the **Roman Catholic church** [105 F2], a low-key Neoclassical building (1870–77), both now in great condition, thanks to foreign funds. A block to the east on Chitaia is Chikobava (formerly Sovietskaya) Square; on its far side, beyond the statue of Gorki on Terenti Graneli, is the modern **Lutheran Church of the Reconciliation** [105 G2], built in 1997. The Germans' first church was where Marjanishvili Square now is, but this was replaced in 1897 with a larger church (by Leopold Bielfeld, who also designed the Kashveti Church on Rustaveli Avenue), and then demolished in the 1940s when the square was laid out.

Continuing westwards from Marjanishvili Square on Davit Agmashenebelis, there are some grander Art Nouveau buildings, such as No 108 (with stucco pilasters) and No 101 (with caryatids supporting a balcony; built by Bielefeld in 1897 as a hotel), and a nice park behind. This stretch of the avenue became a cultural zone under communism; at No 136 is the Akhvlediani Children's Art Gallery and No 123 houses the Composers' Union and the **Djansugh Kakhidze Tbilisi Center for Music & Culture** [105 E1], with a garden in which the State Symphony Orchestra gives summer concerts. Just beyond it at No 127 is the **Mikeladze Centre** (home to the Georgian Philharmonic Orchestra) [105 E1], a fine Neoclassical pile built as the Cultural Centre of the Railwaymen of Georgia in 1950 and set back from the road in front of a park. Here, too, is the Tumanishvili Movie Actors' Theatre and documentary film studios, in a pseudo-medieval castle and tower built in 1930. Just behind the splendid former Apollo Theatre (1909) at No 135 is the Art Palace (a mansion built in 1895 by Peter Stern), housing the **Museum of Theatre & Film** [104 D1] (⊕ *11.00–17.00 Tue–Sun; GEL2*) at Kargareteli 6; temporary exhibits are inside the main entrance, then you'll come back outside, turn right and go upstairs to six period rooms furnished with film costumes, lots of portraits of actors and singers, and paintings by Gudiashvili, Pirosmani and Kakabadze. At Davit Agmashenebelis 150 (right at the back) is the Observatory in which Stalin worked in 1899–1901, just before the junction with Tamar Mepis, leading from the railway station to the river.

Didube Beyond Tamar Mepis, Davit Agmashenebelis soon reaches the **Silk Museum** [94 D2] (page 153) on the right, overshadowed by the Boris Paichadze National Stadium, better known simply as the **Dinamo Stadium** [95 E2], beyond a statue of Paichadze (1915–90; perhaps Georgia's greatest footballer) shooting for goal. This was built in 1937 on the site of a fort and then rebuilt in 1976 to accommodate 70,000 fans. Between the museum and the river is the well-kept **Mushtaid Park** [94 D2], with dodgems, a Ferris wheel and a miniature railway with a preserved narrow-gauge steam locomotive.

It is here that you enter the Didube district, also settled by Germans in the 19th century. The main road is Tseretelis Gamziri, a block to the right/northeast, which passes first the Orthodox **Church of the Nativity of the Virgin** (1883) where there's another pantheon of lower-league celebrities such as football players (and poet Terenti Graneli), and then the **Baptist church**, before reaching the huge modernist **Exhibition Centre**, which now houses furniture showrooms and the like. It's quite a bit further to the Didube bus station, which is best reached by metro.

Rather than heading into the wilds of Didube, it's probably preferable to turn either left to the Tamar Mepis Bridge and Heroes' Square, or right to Station Square, where you can catch the metro. The huge brutalist **railway station** [95 E2] (also page 97), built in 1969–88, was one of the last works of Soviet modernism in Tbilisi, resembling an airport terminal more than a station. It was renovated and essentially turned into a shopping centre in 2010. It is also a terminal for many of the city's marshrutkas and buses, and the **main market** [95 E2] is immediately to the southwest, so the whole area is always heaving with people. Behind the station roads lead up past the Gypsy palaces of Lotkin to the **Tbilisi Sea** (Tbilis Tskalsatsavi), the natural Lake Djairan enlarged in 1951 to form a reservoir (fed by the Iori River); there are restaurants and beach resorts here, but the water is not really clean enough for swimming. However, it is good for windsurfing, though you have to bring your own board. At its southern end (at the top of the Varketili district), the massive Tbilisi Sea Plaza is being developed by China's Hualing group to be the most important trading centre in the Caucasus; the Hotels & Preference Hualing Tbilisi luxury hotel (w *hotelspreference.ge*) opened in 2015, with a massive recreation centre and gym, gardens with an artificial lake, and of course a Chinese restaurant. About 3km north is the **Gino Paradise Aquapark** (⊙ *215 8585;* m *599 880989;* w *ginoparadise.ge;* ⊕ *noon–23.00 daily; from GEL39 for 3hrs*), opened in 2013, with a 25m pool, wave pool, waterfall, 'wild river' and six slides up to 30m high, as well as a spa. At the northern end of the lake, the huge **Chronicles of Georgia** monument (1985) is yet another grandiose project by Zurab Tsereteli, like Stonehenge colliding with an Egyptian temple.

WHAT TO SEE AND DO

MUSEUMS
National Museum [112 B1] (*Rustaveli 3;* ⟍ *299 8022;* w *museum.ge;* ⊕ *10.00– 18.00 exc Mon & holidays; GEL7*) Reopened after refurbishment in 2011, the National Museum now has a nice modern foyer with a tiny coffee stand and two shops (selling books, postcards and Geoland maps), and a display of the earliest hominid relics found outside Africa, including the skull of an old man who survived for years after losing his teeth, suggesting care for the elderly and hence compassion and social structure. The first stone tools at Dmanisi, over two million years old, were found in 1984, followed by bones from at least five 1.77 million-year-old hominids and from sabre-toothed cats, short-necked giraffe, giant ostrich, giant cheetah, elephant, rhinos, horses and deer.

The museum's star attraction, however, is the amazing treasury of largely **pre-Christian gold and silver**. Whereas the Greeks preferred filigree decorations and the Persians encrustation, the Georgians chose granulation (*tsvara*), with tiny lumps creating texture; they also set their jewellery with semi-precious stones, such as cornelian (found all over Georgia). Going around to the left, the display falls into three parts, the Trialeti or Great Barrows Culture (3rd–2nd millennium BC), 'Colchis rich in gold' (8th–3rd centuries BC) and Kartli-Iveria (3rd century BC to 4th century AD). Gold-mining in fact began in the 4th millennium BC; in the 3rd millennium the Barrow Culture of the Trialeti Plateau produced tiny pins (plain or with semi-precious stones and granulation), then diadems, pendants and vessels. A tiny golden lion with an intricately worked mane, dating from 2600–2300BC, is one of the most remarkable pieces in the whole collection; slightly later pieces include a king's sceptre, a silver cup with a frieze of religious ritual and hunting, and a gold bowl from about 1800BC encrusted with precious stones. A millennium then passed without gold- or silverwork until the Colchian culture developed in the west – finds from Vani, produced in the 5th century BC, include a superb diadem and very finely granulated necklaces, including one with 31 tiny turtles (symbolising longevity) hanging from it, others with swastikas, and an enamelled pendant, the oldest in Georgia. There are also hooped earrings, gold bracelets with cornelian beads, signet rings, and coins imitating Greek and Roman originals. Also from the

3

5th century BC, there's jewellery from Iveria, including silver bowls, earrings, gold buckles and sheep's-head rings, a lovely pair of gold pendants showing horses with a type of harness only used in Georgia, and a necklace of frogs (symbolising fertility). You'll also see an imported pectoral with cloisonnée inlay from Achaemenid Egypt.

From the mid 4th century BC Colchian goldsmithery changed, with new styles of bracelets and signet rings, and wreath-like headdresses replacing diadems. Rich burials from the 4th and 3rd centuries BC have been found in eastern Georgia, yielding discoid plaques from horse harnesses, torques and silver *phialai* (dishes) from Iran.

The display then leaps forward to the 2nd century AD, and a tiny part of the Hellenistic-style treasure buried with the royal family and ruling elite of Kartli in the Armaziskhevi cemetery in Mtskheta, such as the sheath of Aspavruk the Pitiakh's dagger, his gold and cornelian signet, and an intaglio buckle. There's also fine Roman silverware and a cameo, Roman and Sassanian silver *phialai*, glass pitchers, agate vessels and cloisonné inlays. Finally, by the early 3rd century, granulation was giving way to encrustation, and gold served mainly as a support for precious stones: from the late 3rd to early 4th century AD there's a writing set found in the Svetiskhoveli churchyard in Mtskheta, consisting of a silver box, gold plaque and a gold inkpot case. On your way out, you can see a silent video on the technique of cloisonné enamel, developed in Vani from the 2nd century BC.

A **numismatic exhibition** opened in 2016, displaying more than 3,000 coins from the first millennium BC (huge bronze discs and cowry shells from the Indian Ocean) up to 1834, including Colchian tetri, copies of coins issued by Alexander the Great and the Emperor Octavius, Georgian-Sassanian drachms, Jafarid dirhams and silver coins produced in Georgia for the first Bagratids, David the Builder, Giorgi IV Lash and Queen Rusudan.

Upstairs there are temporary shows plus the **Oriental Collections**, with a small first room showing Egyptian pieces then a larger galleried room with 18th–20th-century Iranian paintings and steel ewers with gold overlay, and finally a room devoted to East Asia, with 19th-century bronzes and gouache on silk from Tibet, a 14th-century celadon bowl, 18th to 19th-century porcelain, jade, ivory and gouaches on rice paper from China, and 18th-century Satsuma porcelain, netsuke, and Samurai armour and swords from Japan, as well as an Utamaro print. Finally, there's a leap to the **Museum of Soviet Occupation**, covering the period from 1921 to 1991, with images, documents and items depicting the brutal Soviet rule that led to 80,000 Georgians being shot, 800,000 deported and another 400,000 killed in the Great Patriotic War, with examples of prominent musicians, artists and poets lost in Stalin's terror, along with Nagan revolvers used to kill them. Finally there's coverage of the rather ineffectual dissident movement led by Zviad Gamsakhurdia and Merab Kostava. In the centre, a long carpet leads to a Stalin-era desk from where you might learn your fate; around the upper gallery original documents are displayed, including the Certificate of Merit awarded to Stalin's henchman Kamo in 1928. The atmosphere is powerful but the displays should be much better – English labels are patchy and videos are without sound.

Art Museum [112 C1] (*Gudiashvili 1;* \ *299 9909;* ☉ *10.00–18.00 exc Mon; GEL3, plus GEL45 (up to 10 people) for the required guided tour (1hr); catalogues are available in English, French & German for GEL20*) The Art Museum houses the Treasury of gold- and silverware and cloisonné enamel from the Christian era, which is if anything even more amazing than the collection in the National Museum. There's little else here now other than temporary shows, as the building is being prepared for major restoration. Naturally most of the exhibits are icons, in fine golden frames – three-dimensional sculptures of the saints were forbidden by the Orthodox Church, but relief was permitted. Many are of St George, who is often shown lancing the Roman emperor Diocletian rather than a dragon or devil, as a symbol of the triumph of Christianity over paganism; St George is also shown being tortured. Encaustic enamels, in which the colours were mixed with wax, were (from the 6th century) another speciality, reaching a peak in the 10th to 12th centuries; the technique of firing them so that the colours were melted, but not the gold frame, was lost in the 15th century.

After passing full-size copies of frescoes from Betania, Svaneti and Davit-Gareja, you'll start in a small room with a selection of jewellery (and decorations from horse bridles) from 5th-century BC Colchis, similar to the treasures from Vani in the National Museum's treasury and with an equally superb range of techniques such as granulation, filigree and inlaying.

The long second room starts with some Byzantine- and Assyrian-influenced crosses and Hellenistic heads, then highlights include the Zarzma icon of the Transfiguration (AD886) and a 9th-century encaustic enamel of the Virgin Agitria (Showing the Way) with Child. There's also a 10th-century cloisonné Virgin and icons from Racha and Svaneti, then the superb chalice from Bedia (in Abkhazia), made in AD999 from a single piece of gold with a relief of Christ, the Virgin and Apostles. Then there's the famous 11th-century tondo from Gelati, a circular silver plaque with a high relief of St Mammes on a lion (it wouldn't eat him so he was martyred by soldiers). There are more incredibly fine cloisonné enamels (with a lapis colour that's typical of Georgia), notably 13th-century ones of St George from western Georgia.

Queen Tamar's pectoral cross has almost mystic significance for many Georgians, as a tangible link with one of their greatest rulers; it was made at the end of the 12th century, of gold set with emeralds, rubies and pearls, and has a 13th-century starotech or case. The triptych Icon of the Saviour from Ancha was enamelled in the 6th century and brought to the Anchiskhati Church in Tbilisi in the 17th century; its frame was made for Tamar in the second half of the 12th century, with a grape motif that never repeats itself. The wings of the frame were added in the 14th century, well after the Georgian Renaissance but still proof of good craftsmanship, while the cherubim on top are from the 19th century.

The Khakhuli triptych has a similarly tangled history: the head of Christ is a 6th-century encaustic wax painting, to which the Virgin (the largest piece of cloisonné enamel in the world) was added in the 10th century. These, with 115 cloisonné enamel medallions mostly dating from 1125–55, were set in a gold frame (with gilded silver wings) in the first half of the 12th century, after it was brought to Gelati from Khakhuli, now in Turkey. The Russian governor of Imeretia, Levashev, tore out much of the gold and jewels in 1859; only the Virgin's face and hands have been recovered. The Martvili Icon of the Virgin, dating from the first half of the 12th century, is of gold with small enamels of the Evangelists in the corners and in the middle of the right side a medallion of St Peter from the 9th century, the oldest known Byzantine enamel.

The third room shows how Georgian metalwork lost its way somewhat after the Mongol invasions of the 13th century, when the secrets of enamelling were lost; good pieces were produced again from the 15th century and, from the 16th century, icons from eastern Georgia show Persian influence, with floral motifs rather than vines. The 15th-century cross of Gori-Jvari is 2m tall and bears 16 silver plaques, with reliefs of St George. The Atskuri triptych is unusual in depicting the birth of the Virgin; the faces are sadder than in the Golden Age, hinting at hard times in 16th-century Georgia.

By the 18th century, emphasis was on secular jewellery; in the fourth room there's a display of the jewels of Katarina Dadiani, daughter of Alexander Chavchavadze, and possessions of other notable families. Finally, there's a small room of embroidered clerical robes.

In addition, an exhibition of the Masterpieces of the Museum of Fine Arts Collection was due to close in December 2017, as part of the project to transfer the art collection to the new building at Rustaveli 7 and also to the adjacent building on Gudiashvili – but these things tend to be delayed, possibly by a year or more. Wherever you find it, it should include paintings by Bernardo Daddi, Lucas Cranach the Elder (*The Procuress*, which was stolen in 1994 and returned by the thieves ten years later), Guido Reni, Jan Steen, Jacob van Ruisdael, Rodin, Picasso and Kandinsky, as well as the Georgians Pirosmani, Gudiashvili and Kakabadze, and medieval icons and other artefacts.

National Gallery [105 E6] (*Rustaveli 11;* ✆ *215 7300;* ☉ *10.00–18.00 exc Mon & holidays; GEL7*) With a modern extension added in 2011, this now houses the Georgian art collection that was held in the former seminary on Pushkin Square. Entering at the rear, there are temporary exhibitions on the ground floor (as well as a shop), then you'll go upstairs to the original Temple of Glory (page 139), starting in the central hall housing half a dozen sculptures by Iacob Nikoladze, with photos of other works by him across Tbilisi. On one side is a large room devoted to Kakabadze (including half a dozen 'Imeretian Landcsapes', a very avant-garde still life and some Kandinsky-like abstracts) and Gudiashvili, and on the other side another devoted to Pirosmani.

Museum of the History of Tbilisi (or Carvasla) [113 E3] (*Sionis 8;* ✆ *298 2281;* ☉ *10.00–17.00 except Mon; GEL5*) Around the atrium of the Carvasla caravanserai (a wonderful space with cast-iron pillars), the museum displays a range of interesting models, costumes, musical instruments, an Underwood typewriter with Georgian keys, paintings, interesting historic photographs and replica shops and restaurants. The upper floor (presumably once displaying the history of communist Tbilisi) now houses temporary exhibits, offices and empty rooms, while on the lower level there are craft shops and a wine bar.

Museum of Georgian Ethnography [94 A4] (*also known as the Open-Air Ethnographic Museum; Berdzenishvili (Turtle Lake Rd) 25;* ✆ *270 9045/6;* ☉ *10.00–18.00 exc Mon, closes 17.00 in winter; GEL3*) This open-air museum displays about 70 buildings from all over Georgia, in vernacular local style and traditionally furnished. If you take the cable car up to Turtle Lake it's about a 15-minute walk down the road to the museum. The lower houses, nearer the entrance, are furnished and open, while those further up can usually be safely viewed from a distance. You'll see *darbazi*-type and flat-roofed houses from the east of Georgia, gable-roofed wooden houses from the west, and three roofing types: thatch in western Georgia, red channel tiles, and shingles. Going around to the left (clockwise), you'll come first to a big, open-plan house from Abacha in Mingrelia, with a sleeping platform; then a farmstead, also from Mingrelia, with attractive, wooden panelling around a *bukhari* or chimney. An 18th-century house from Imereti is built of logs on a stone base, also open-plan with a central chimney; above is a house from Lanchkhuti (in Guria), which has an ingenious babywalker on the veranda, and a smithy which is still in use.

The shorter route back passes another Imeretian house, with the traditional Georgian marani or wine store; the alternative is to climb up the hill, near large and impressive houses from Adjara and a Svan defensive tower (a copy of the 28m tower of Etseri) on the ridge above Turtle Lake. Returning down the hill you'll pass a house from Teliani (near Kaspi) just before the ruined 6th-century Sionis Church from Tianeti and a row of tombs (one, with an inscription in Old Georgian, under glass); beyond this a stone building half-set into the hillside is from Giorgitsminda in Kakheti. Finally, hidden away right at the bottom is a 2m phallic stone from Abkhazia. As you go around you'll see odds and ends such as old muskets, wooden claws to protect the fingers while scything, and cots with a pipe leading to a gourd for urine below. At weekends and in summer costumed staff will be cooking or baking bread.

Lado Gudiashvili Museum [105 F6] (*Gudiashvili 11, just below the Kashveti Church;* \ *293 2305;* w *ladogudiashvili.ge;* ⊕ *11.00–18.30 Tue–Sun; GEL5*) The fantastical painter's home has been rebuilt as a modern gallery, with a display of his work, mainly from private collections and changing every year, plus temporary shows. See also the dandyish statue of Gudiashvili in nearby 9 April Park.

Elena Akhvlediani Museum [104 C4] (*Kiacheli 12, 1 flight up & on the right, with posters on the door;* \ *299 7412;* ⊕ *10.00–18.00, closed Mon; GEL3*) The best of Tbilisi's house-museums is the home of Elena Akhvlediani (1901–75), where you'll find a room with a huge wooden column in the middle, modelled on peasant architecture, as well as small wooden galleries and hanging rugs. Akhvlediani's paintings are hung up to five high on the walls, and you'll also see examples of her theatre and film designs and book illustrations, as well as photos and mementoes. Although not the most challenging of artists she did have a very wide range of styles, and is loved for her warm depictions of daily life.

State Museum of Folk and Applied Arts [112 C4] (*Dadiani 28;* \ *299 9722, 299 6152;* ⊕ *10.00–18.00 Tue & Thu–Sun, 10.00–21.00 Wed; GEL3*) Founded in 1913 as the Museum of the Caucasian Kustar (craftsmen) Committee to encourage crafts in the Russian Empire, this displays carpets and *kilims* (most made in the 1930s), costumes, silver and ceramics upstairs (ask for English-language information); downstairs are historic photos and temporary shows.

State Museum of Georgian Folk Songs and Instruments [113 H2] (*Samghebro 6;* \ *245 7721;* ⊕ *11.00–18.00 Tue–Sun; GEL3*) Just off Maidan Square, this small museum is good for children, who can touch and even play instruments such as a *calliope*. The first room has displays of traditional Georgian wind, string and percussion instruments, the second has Asian instruments, used by Armenian, Azeri, Jewish, Assyrian and Yezidi musicians, and the third has 19th-century European classical and mechanical instruments, such as an orchestrion, accordion, mandolin and banjo, and musical boxes.

Silk Museum [94 D2] (*Tsabadze 6;* \ *234 0963/7;* w *silkmuseum.ge;* ⊕ *11.00–18.00 Tue–Sun; GEL3*) In the shadow of the Dinamo Stadium, this is one of the oldest museums in Georgia, built in 1892 to help develop the silk industry and still using the original display cabinets. A helpful guide will explain the silkworm's life cycle and show machines for chopping leaves to feed them, plus a butterfly-sexing carousel, 4,000-odd cocoons from across China and elsewhere, natural dyes and finally the textiles and embroideries that are the final product.

Museum of the Jews of Georgia [112 C3] (*Katalikosi 3;* ☎*298 5992;* ⓕ *jewishgeo;* ⊕ *11.00–17.00 daily; GEL3*) Tbilisi's Domed Synagogue, dating from the 1880s, was converted into a museum in 1940. Closed from 1951 to 1992 and again from 2014 to 2016, it is now fully renovated, displaying a range of mainly 19th- and 20th-century artefacts of the Jewish community, established here since at least 585BC (after Nebuchadnezzar's conquest of Jerusalem and the Babylonian exile). Georgia's Jewish population peaked at about 100,000 in the 1970s and now numbers perhaps 4,000. There are also some attractive portraits by Misha (Mordekhai) Janoshvili (1929–88); captions are in Georgian and English, and there's no need for men to cover their heads.

Underground Printing Press Museum [95 H3] (*Kaspi 7;* ☎ *274 6821*) Not far north of the 300 Aragveli metro station, an anonymous-looking house hides a secret chamber, 17 metres underground via a well shaft, where from 1903 to 1906 a now very rusty press produced thousands of Bolshevik leaflets (in Georgian, Russian and Armenian). There's no proof that Stalin was ever here, but the people who run it are true believers who still think that he was a good guy and that he ran the press himself.

Tbilisi Automuseum [95 H5] (*Police Turn;* m *599 545628;* w *automuseum.ge*) It's not easy to find (a couple of miles east of the centre towards Kakheti, south of the East Point Mall), but car enthusiasts will find it very worthwhile, with its 25 Soviet cars and seven motorbikes.

OTHER PLACES OF INTEREST
Botanic Gardens [112 C5] (☎ *272 3406/9;* w *nbgg.ge;* ⊕ *09.00–18.00 daily; GEL2*) These gardens are one of Tbilisi's least-known treasures, a beautiful place to wander for an afternoon, with both cultivated beds and greenhouses and wilder, quieter areas higher up the slopes. The main entry is at the top of Botanikuri, above Gorgasali Square, and it can also be reached by paths from the second hairpin of the Kojori Highway, at the junction to the Sololaki Ridge, or near the Kartlis-Deda statue; if you enter this way guards will send you down to the main gate to pay. Since June 2017, it's also been possible (at a cost of GEL30) to take a zip-line into the gardens from the top of the Narikala cable car (near the Kartlis-Deda statue).

The gardens were established as a royal pleasure ground in 1636 on the right bank of the Tsavkistiskhevi (Fig Ravine), with a natural waterfall, and became a municipal garden in 1801, growing vines, vegetables and fruit. In 1845 it was taken over and expanded by the Russian Viceroy Mikhail Vorontsov (who also founded the lovely gardens in Yalta), using the steep valley, and a Muslim cemetery. In the 1890s it became an academic body, publishing its proceedings and a seed exchange list from 1895, and the *Bulletin of the Tbilisi Botanic Garden* from 1905; from 1897 it was organised into bio-regional sections (such as pine grove, saline soils and Turkestan). In the Soviet period it expanded on to the right bank of the stream and became more practical in outlook, as well as opening sections in Kutaisi and Zugdidi. Taken over by the city in 2000, it was desperately short of money and in a terrible state until being rescued by oligarch Bidzina Ivanishvili; unfortunately he has now been given land within the gardens in exchange for less suitable land outside, in order to build his US$500 million Panorama development, including cable cars from Freedom Square and Erekle II Square.

In its 128 hilly hectares (of which 85ha are cultivated) there are 4,500 species, including 2,300 species and forms of trees and shrubs, and over 900 species of tropical and subtropical plants in greenhouses ⊕ *Tue–Thu afternoons*). Local people see the gardens mainly as a venue for picnics and wedding photos; an EcoCentre, funded by the Worldwide Fund for Nature, is being set up here, as a key part of an environmental education programme.

There's a fine specimen of Pitsunda pine (*Pinus pithyusa*) inside the entrance, from where a gravel path leads up the valley to bridges below the waterfall; the main building and greenhouses are across the valley to the left, with a winding asphalt road continuing up the valley, not very interesting at first with fields and scrubby shrubs, as well as some succulents and thorny shrubs, and some hidden gardens stumbled across at random. Things improve near the head of the valley where you'll enter conifers (with bamboo) and then untended scrub of birch or alder, ending at a locked gate. It's possible to loop back to the left, below the cliffs, or to the right down a cypress alley (on a gravel path).

Zoo [104 A1] (*Kostava 64, at the Heroes' Sq roundabout;* ☎ *233 2901;* w *zoo.ge;* ⊕ *May–Sep 09.00–21.00 daily, Oct–Apr 10.00–18.00 daily; GEL2*) Tbilisi's zoo was criticised in the past for its small, concrete-floored cages, but since 2006 it has moved the animals to more suitable housing and opened a veterinary centre. It had a few camels, lions, tigers, hippos, zebras, gibbons, baboons, bears, hyenas and peacocks, and also a kids' funfair, which needs to be moved away from the animals. The elephants were moved to more natural surroundings in 2008. Proposals for a New York-style 'central park' to link the Saburtalo and Vake districts mean that the zoo may be moved to a new location at the Tbilisi Sea; this became more urgent after a flash flood virtually destroyed the zoo in June 2015, drowning three keepers, and 16 others outside the zoo. Some animals escaped and a lion and a tiger were shot by police, after the tiger had killed a man – in all, more than half the zoo's 600-odd animals drowned or were killed by the authorities. Twenty penguins had been moved here from a zoo in Torquay less than a year before, and only eight survived – one was last seen in the river approaching the border with Azerbaijan. Georgia's Patriarch blamed the flooding on the communists, who in 1927 melted down church bells and crosses to raise the money to build the zoo.

GEORGIA ONLINE

For additional online content, articles, photos and more on Georgia, why not visit w bradtguides.com/georgia?

4

Shida (Inner) Kartli
შიდა ქართლი

Heading west from Tbilisi, you pass through the heartland of Georgia, beginning with Mtskheta, the country's spiritual capital. Most tourist agencies in Tbilisi run day trips to Mtskheta and Gori, with your car or theirs, and Tbilisi bus tours also come out here (page 102).

MTSKHETA მცხეთა *Telephone code 32 (followed by a 2 and six digits; same as Tbilisi)*

Named after Mtskhetos, son of Kartlos, and overlooked by Mount Kartli, supposedly still home to the soul of Kartlos, Mtskheta (pronounced 'Skayta') is at the heart of Georgia's spiritual identity. Inhabited for 5,000 years, the site at the confluence of the Mtkvari and Aragvi rivers was the centre of the pagan cult of Armazi (the local version of the Zoroastrian fire god Ormazd of Persia), adopted in the 4th century BC by King Parnavaz I of Kartli, who established his capital 2km southwest of present-day Mtskheta. It was known to the ancient Greeks as Armosica and to Pliny as Armasicum, and is now Armazistsikhe (Armazi Castle). There are traces of older Hittite and even Sumerian cults; the surrounding hilltops all housed pagan shrines which have now been replaced by churches. From the 4th century BC until the 5th century AD this was the capital of Iveria (present-day Kartli), the scene of the royal family's conversion to Christianity, and continued as seat of the Georgian Church until the 12th century. The town's churches are included on UNESCO's World Heritage List. The main cathedral, though no longer seat of the Catholicos, is far more impressive than Tbilisi's Sioni Cathedral, and effortlessly dominates the town (now little more than a village), especially as seen from the main highway across the river. There's another couple of fine ancient churches in Mtskheta, and the Jvari Church, high on a crag across the Aragvi, is one of the most architecturally important in Georgia, setting the pattern for virtually all those built in the following centuries.

The Jvari, Svetiskhoveli and Samtavro churches have been on UNESCO's World Heritage List since 1994, but in 2009 they were put on the list of World Heritage in Danger due to damage to stonework and frescoes and by uncontrolled construction of ugly buildings in the buffer zone; the government clamped down on this and in 2016 UNESCO took the site off the danger list, but saying 'there are still challenges in improving the site management mechanism and the coordination between the different management stakeholders'.

GETTING THERE AND AWAY At the Didube **bus** terminal in Tbilisi (page 98) there's always a marshrutka loading for the 25–30-minute trip to Mtskheta; buy tickets (*GEL1*) at the cash desk before boarding. Marshrutkas also leave roughly every 30 minutes for Gori and more frequently for Kutaisi, passing below the Jvari Church. A taxi should cost GEL25.

Buses cross the Didube Bridge heading for the equestrian statue of King David the Builder (and a spectacular statue of St Nino above) where they join the main highway to Western Georgia. If you come directly from the city centre along Pekini you'll first pass the most striking piece of modern architecture in Tbilisi, the Ministry of Highways Construction (now the headquarters of the Bank of Georgia; page 142), the modernist effect now spoilt by the new (traditional-style) church in front. The highway (two hectic four-lane carriageways here) passes through the usual outskirts clutter of restaurants, petrol stations and big-box shops, with on the eastbound side the Tbilisi Prosecutors Office, a stark black frame (supposedly representing the uncompromising nature of the legal system) with overhanging glass blocks suspended in the air, reminiscent of the Highways Ministry. After the US embassy (an ugly, big, white building away to the right, opened in 1992) and the Tbilisi Mall, the highway leaves the city limits at km16 and swings left along the right/south bank of the Mtkvari (passing the Zahesi hydro-electric station, built in 1927 and now very small and old-fashioned). After just 2km, the Jvari Church is signed (in Latin script) to the right, but it's still 7km away and you shouldn't get off the bus here. It's just 1km more to the turning to Mtskheta, which takes off to the right and goes under the main highway just before it crosses the Mtkvari. Coming by road from the west you should get off here, immediately after the bridge, and go 200m west to a bus stop; marshrutkas from Tbilisi are often full, but there will eventually be a bus, or a taxi may be waiting. Alternatively, you may be set down just east of the Aragvi bridge by some steps, at the top of which marshrutkas run along the local road into town.

It's a deceptively long way into town from here, following the river past the town, then after 4km crossing a bridge (with what seems to be a statue of a skateboarding eagle at its south end; the foundations of Pompey's Bridge, dating from 65BC, are visible when the water is low) and doubling back. Cross the bridge and swing right to continue on Kostava for 1km to the post office at the start of the one-way system. You'll glimpse the cathedral on your right and then the Armazi cinema (with a colourful fresco depicting Georgian history) hidden by trees on your left; it's built over the remains of the Old Town gates, visible beneath. Immediately afterwards, you'll arrive at a plaza with the Samtavro Church to the left, where you should stop.

The main highway to the west passes below the Jvari Church, high on its rock, crosses the Aragvi at km25.5, and meets the local road from Mtskheta. It's another couple of kilometres to the flyover at the start of the Georgian Military Highway, just after the km27 marker.

Returning to Tbilisi, marshrutkas pass Samtavro and the cinema and pick up along Davit Agmashenebelis, the next road up the hill.

The railway station lies just southwest of the bridge, and a couple of **trains** a day still call here, leaving Tbilisi at 09.00 and 21.45, arriving 25 minutes later, and continuing on to Gori and stops along the route to Ozurgeti.

Running east from the cathedral, Arsukidze is the town's main commercial street, lined with souvenir shops and guesthouses; it ends by the confluence of the Aragvi and Mtkvari rivers, at the tiny 7th-century Antioch church of the nunnery of St Stephen, with its peaceful garden (not many visitors get this far). **Boat rides** start here, operated by Mtskheta Cruise (m *593 373044;* e *mtskheta.cruise@gmail. com;* f *mtskheta.tour*) at Arsukidze 12, where there's also a café in a very pleasant garden; trips last 30 minutes, with an audio guide in 16 languages, and wine and cheese tasting is available.

WHERE TO STAY The tourist information centre can organise accommodation in one of the guesthouses (*all* **$$–$$$**), and there may be signs for rooms in houses close to the cathedral; otherwise there are just a few hotels.

Hotels

Gino Wellness Davit Agmashenebelis 37; `32 222 5115; w ginohotel.com. A fine modern hotel with comfortable rooms & a spa & outdoor pool, but service is often poor. **$$$$**

Hotel Mtskheta Palace (8 rooms, 3 suites) Davit Agmashenebelis 7,500m west from the north end of the bridge; `32 291 0202, 251 3131, 251 2777; m 593 078585, 599 111246; e mtskhetapalace@gmail.com; w mtskhetapalace.ge. For a long time the only upmarket hotel in Mtskheta, though it now seems dated. It has a covered pool & sauna, & 3 dbl rooms with AC, TV & a good bathroom with toiletries & hairdryer, 5 larger ones & 3 suites with massage shower, like a vertical jacuzzi. All inc b/fast. **$$$–$$$$**

Bagineti Kostava 39; m 592 007500, 593 631786. At the northwestern corner of the cathedral wall, this small, new place is pretty amateur but has decent rooms with TV, AC & Wi-Fi. **$$$**

Old Capital Erekle II 7; m 593 631786. Just to the right from the cathedral gate, this comfortable, new hotel has TV & AC in all rooms; it also offers a luggage storage service. **$$**

Guesthouses

Ekaladze Gia (2 rooms) Arsukidze 85; `32 251 2582; m 598 449255

Guesthouse Jishkariani Ilia (6 rooms) Arsukidze 67; m 551 707172

Guesthouse Mtskheta-Kapanadze Arsukidze 63; m 595 380898, 574 789777

Kapanadze Nazi (3 rooms) Kostava 22, opposite the cathedral gate; `32 251 2865; m 551 512865

Khizanishvili Zaqro Arsukidze 93; `32 251 2402; m 593 360609, 599 113822

Machitadze Nana (4 rooms) Gamsakhurdia 14; `32 251 2413, m 599 353104. On the much quieter road from the cathedral towards the station.

Merebashvili Gulnara Arsukidze 15; m 593 174492

Mtskheta Sanapiro Sanapiro 6; m 597 182244. New & squeaky clean in 2014; by the river south of the cathedral, they offer boat rides & have a café.

Tamarindi (7 rooms) Arsukidze 23; `51 2764; m 579 037772. Also offers jeep tours.

✕ WHERE TO EAT AND DRINK

✕ Armazis Tskaro Armazi, 3km west from Mtskheta station; m 599 696992; ⏲ 11.00–23.00 daily. A fascinating restaurant with covered dining terraces on both sides of a stream connected by lots of footbridges; ideal for large family groups. Large portions of classic Georgian dishes such as khinkali. **$$**

✕ Café Tatin Mamulashvili 20; m 593 571217; ☒; ⏲ 10.00–23.00 daily. Delightful French-style café-restaurant with a great view from the terrace, serving very affordable handmade pizza, khinkali, soups, salads & desserts. **$$**

✕ Check-In Garden Restaurant Gamsakhurdia 17; m 558 907709, 577 907705; ⏲ noon–22.00 daily. There's good food & wine in this period house & its lovely riverside garden. **$$**

✕ Georgian Chamber of Wine Davit Aghmashenebelis 69; `32 224 0030, m 595 017799; w ktwchamber.ge; ⏲ 11.00–23.00 daily. Opposite the Samtavro nunnery, Kakhetian Traditional Winemaking has a wine cellar & restaurant aimed at tour groups; however the rooftop terrace is a lovely spot for a sunset drink looking over the historic centre. **$$**

✕ Old Taverna (Dzveli Taverna) At the top of Arsukidze; ⏲ 10.00–22.00 daily. A perfectly decent but not particularly fast place to try the usual Georgian dishes (note that the beet soup is actually beef). **$$**

✕ Opizari Mamulashvili 2; ⏲ 11.00–23.00 daily. Modern & fairly upmarket restaurant at the road junction on the way to Samtavro. **$$**

✕ Salobio Restaurant About 4km towards Tbilisi by the riverside & the highway bridge; ⏲ 09.00–23.00 daily. This has always been a favourite outing for the people of Tbilisi, offering a wide range of traditional dishes such as lobio (beans in a clay pot, for which Mtskheta is famed), chadi, pirozhki, khinkali, shashlik & khachapuri. The nearby Metropol & Serafin restaurants are similar. **$$**

✗ **Café Guga** Mamulashvili 6; ✆ 10.00–23.00 daily. The best food in town, with indoor seating & private wicker summer huts. **$**

OTHER PRACTICALITIES There's an **ATM** at United Georgia Bank (*Davit Agmashenebelis 37*); you'll find others opposite the Samtavro nunnery and more on Arsukidze. There is a **tourist information centre** (*Arsukidze 3;* ✆ 32 251 2128; e *ticmtskheta@gmail.com;* ✆ *10.00–18.00 daily*) with English-speaking staff, plus toilets and a couple of souvenir shops in the pompous wedding hall opposite the cathedral.

WHAT TO SEE AND DO The **Mtskhetoba Festival**, usually attended by the president and Catholicos, as well as over 100,000 others, is held on 14 October (and the previous evening); there's also a **Festival of Performing Arts** in early June.

Sveti Tskhoveli (✆ *08.00–22.00 daily*) The Sveti Tskhoveli Cathedral of the Twelve Apostles rises on the site of the palace of the kings of Iveria, to which part of Christ's crucifixion robe was brought soon after his death by Elias, whose sister Sidonia died of joy clutching it so tightly that it had to be buried here with her. The cedar which grew out of her grave in the early 4th century was felled to build St Nino's first church here, and one column supposedly hovered in the air until Nino brought it down by prayer; in addition, miraculous sap is said to have flowed from it at her behest.

The church derives its name of Sveti Tskhoveli or 'Life-giving Column of Light' from this; it could also be said that the name is pagan in origin. The first church here was built of wood in the 4th century AD; this was replaced by a three-nave basilica by AD575, and the present church was built for Patriarch Melchisidek in 1010–29, incorporating the tiny 6th-century building. It was damaged by an earthquake in 1283 and again by Tamerlane at the end of the 14th century before being restored in 1412–31 (by Aleksandre the Great) and 1656; in 1837 the narthexes to the south and north were removed. Built just a few decades before the great Norman cathedrals of England, you may find some similarities in style, notably the round arches.

Perfectly proportioned, with its great pepper-pot dome of green tuff rising high above the village and the river, it sits in a large square of walls added by Erekle II in the second half of the 18th century. The main entrance (to the west) was added in the 11th century and above it you'll see two carved bulls' heads, which are pagan fertility symbols. The exterior of the church is well decorated, with carvings of red stone set in limestone, but not excessively so; note particularly the beautifully carved vines on the western façade, and a hand holding a bevel-square over the central arch of the northern façade. This illustrates the story of the builder Arsukidze's hand being chopped off by his jealous teacher (though there are various versions of this story).

The church has a three-bay nave that seems huge by Georgian standards; incorporated into the second bay to the right is a 15th-century copy of the church of the Holy Sepulchre in Jerusalem. In the next bay is a high-sided 17th-century pavilion built over the tomb of Sidonia, and to the left/east of this is the patriarch's stone throne, also 17th century. Immediately ahead you'll find the royal tombs, of which three (all of grey marble) can be identified: the last two kings, Erekle II (1720–98) and Georgi XII (1746–1800), lie on either side of the altar steps, and Vakhtang Gorgasali, founder of Tbilisi, is the second back from Erekle.

The most notable frescoes are in the centre of the south wall of the south transept, although much is missing; what's left of this 17th-century Apocalypse is a wheel of the zodiac radiating out of a central Christ figure, with the Apostles to the right and a sea with monsters to the left. Intriguingly, the writer Daniel Farson states that there were undeniably two flying-saucers painted at eye level on the altar fresco of Christ, and another over the arch; others felt they were just floating faces shining down. In any case they had been whitewashed over by 1991.

There is excellent singing here on Saturday and Sunday mornings; knees, shoulders and women's hair should be covered at all times – take a shawl from a basket in the porch.

Samtavro (⊕ *09.00–19.00 daily*) Just 5 minutes north, beyond the plaza with the Armazi cinema, the Samtavro nunnery (the archbishop's residence from the 5th century, taken over by nuns in the 19th century) stands on the site of Georgia's first church, with a tiny chapel in the grounds marking the spot where Nino lived in a log hut; built in the 4th century, this was rebuilt in the 9th as a cross-domed church and painted in the 18th and 19th centuries, although the frescoes are poor and black with smoke. The main Church of the Transfiguration was built by the Catholikos Melkisedek and King George I in the first half of the 11th century (the dome was restored after damage by a 13th-century earthquake); the most notable feature is the richly carved tombs of King Mirian and Queen Nana, the 4th-century founders of the Chosroid dynasty, incongruously set under a 19th-century Italianate marble and mosaic canopy in the church's southwest corner, just left of the entrance. Otherwise the church is big and spacious, with bare walls, a 14th-century iconostasis and some very battered 16th–17th-century frescoes in the dome and above the altar. Externally, there are good decorative carvings on the north and east walls and the dome; the bell-tower (obviously shaken by earthquakes) dates from the 15th century.

The grave of the monk known since 2012 as the Holy Father St Gabriel, Confessor and Fool for Christ (1929–95) is in the churchyard and has become a popular pilgrimage goal, rather overshadowing the 6th-century St Abibos, buried beneath the altar of the Church of Transfiguration. There's a shop and one-room museum (⊕ *10.00–19.00 daily*), with some ancient photos of the nuns.

Jvari The Jvari (Cross) Church (⊕ *08.00–19.00 daily; free*) stands on a spur of the Saguramo Hills, 150m above Mtskheta, and now seems to grow out of the rock. It's one of the finest examples of old Georgian architecture, a marvellously simple but sophisticated edifice, in advance of most European ecclesiastical architecture of the period. Built between AD586 and 604 by Patriarch Stephanoz I, it was the first 'apse-buttressed' cruciform church, in which the gaps between the arms of the cross are filled by small chapels, producing a virtually perfect square ground plan; this allows a wonderfully lofty and spacious interior in which four pillars support an octagonal drum and a round dome covering the entire central space. It stands on the spot where Nino first set up her cross overlooking the pagan shrines of Mtskheta; the ruins of a late 6th-century church survive just north of the present church, with the remains of a defensive tower to the northeast. It was also the first Georgian church where reliefs played a significant role on the façades – there's an exceptionally fine bas-relief of a pair of winged angels bearing a cross above the south door, and other carvings on the east end. Closed in 1911, it was reconsecrated in 1988, and still appears partly ruined, the main columns seemingly hewn out of raw rock. Inside there's the huge plinth of St Nino's Cross in the centre, and a low wooden iconostasis.

Getting there and away Mtskheta and the Jvari Church are quite close as the crow flies, but they're separated by the Aragvi River. If you don't have a car the easiest option is the hourly shuttle (*from 11.00 daily; GEL5, minimum 4 people*) from the tourist office; otherwise you can take a **taxi** from Mtskheta to Jvari (*GEL20, inc waiting time*), but you could also take a **marshrutka** from Tbilisi along the main highway (for instance, to or from Gori or Kutaisi) and ask to be set down at the roadside immediately below the church, at about km21/531, from where you can hike up in about 15–20 minutes. By car, you'll turn right/east on the Tbilisi bypass (the E60, signposted to Telavi) then take a very sharp turn left; the road is a 6km long, looping route around the Lake of Tears, supposedly filled by weeping pilgrims, and ending at a large car park, with a tiny drinks stall and a toilet below it.

Walking back to Mtskheta Once you've seen the church, it's possible to descend, either by the road, or directly down the northern hillside, by a clear 4x4 track that turns left off the tarmac road just off the top. Once on the flat, follow the track across the meadow to an underpass a little way south of the Aragvi restaurant on the far side of the highway; it'll take 30–45 minutes. A path leads down beyond the restaurant to a footbridge (where locals swim); once across the river, turn right along the road and then cut through to the left to the road past the derelict campsite, or continue for 5 minutes along the road to the open-air theatre below the 14th-century castle of Bebristsikhe. This rises beside the road between the historic village and the modern town of typical communist blocks, set tactfully (for once) 1–2km to the north; from the castle it takes 10 minutes to walk to the left/south to the Samtavro Church.

For those who wish to do the walk to the church in reverse, from the centre to Jvari, head north past the Samtavro Church and turn right around the north side of the derelict Univermag shop. Then, go right following the tarmac road past the former campsite in Teatroni Park, and right again at the junction to find the footbridge on your left.

AROUND MTSKHETA

To the northeast of Mtskheta, beyond the main highway and the Jvari Church, is the Saguramo Nature Reserve, which became the **Tbilisi National Park** in 2007; it's mainly of recreational importance and not very species-rich, although there are wolves and bears, and a wildlife rescue centre.

At km24 on the main highway a road turns to the right/north to Saguramo (4km), where there are some luxurious holiday homes and a modern winery; you can visit the **house-museum of Ilia Chavchavadze**, the reformer who became a secular saint after his murder nearby at Tsitsamouri in 1907 by agents either of the Tsarist regime or of the Bolsheviks (pages 20 and 328). From Tskhvarichamia, 15km east of Saguramo, the Tbilisi–Tianeti road switchbacks steeply to the Sabaduri Pass (1,445m) through forest and meadows dotted with campsites and barbecue grills, the most popular part of the national park.

A rough road from Saguramo leads about 7km south to the **monastery of Zedazeni** (also known as Aktimo), set on a hilltop at 1,390m in the heart of the reserve. It was founded by Ioane Zedazneli (St John of Zedazeni), one of the Assyrian fathers, who lived here in a cave from AD501 to 531, attracting many fellow hermits; the Church of St John the Baptist was built over his tomb, just south of the cave, in the 7th–8th centuries and has a 7th-century fresco of St George and the Dragon. Ioane's disciple founded Kvemo (Lower) Zedazeni at the foot of the mountain, and a three-nave basilica (with an unusual rectangular sanctuary) was built in the AD860s and 870s; now reopened, it's sending out monks to repopulate other disused monasteries.

In the hills 12km west of Mtskheta, the **monastery of Shio-mghvime** is built in a limestone canyon in a spectacularly picturesque manner, though the buildings look more like a farm than a monastery; it was founded in the 6th century by the Assyrian monk Shio Mgvimeli, another of the 13 Assyrian Fathers, who voluntarily spent his last 20 years in a cave. A simple cruciform church was built over his grave in 560–80, as well as the Monastery of the Virgin, built on a nearby hilltop by Davit Agmashenebelis in 1103–23 (and restored in 1678), a 12th-century refectory, and a 7km aqueduct at the end of the same century.

The road to Shio-mghvime is signed from the Samtavro nunnery; there are no buses, but taxis wait near the nunnery. This passes the Gvtismshobeli and Mgalobliant-Kari churches (both just to the north of the road and both 17th century), then the Tsminda Demetre and Kaloubiani churches (both to the south and both 12th century). The first three are within 2km of Mtskheta and make a pleasant walk.

THE ROADS WEST FROM MTSKHETA

From its junction with the Georgian Military Highway, the main highway west to Kutaisi and western Georgia runs to the north of the hills along the north side of the Mtkvari; it's a fast (110km/h) road through fairly empty, featureless countryside, except for the spectacular 16th-century **castle of Ksani** visible to the south as the road crosses the river of the same name at km40.5. A few kilometres east of Ksani (south from km32) is the village of **Chardakhi**, where you can visit Iago's Winery (m *593 352426, 599 551045*; e *chardakhi@gmail.com;* f *iagowinery*), one of the best places outside Kakheti to discovery natural qvevri wines. Iago began the conversion to organic agriculture in 1998 and started to use qvevris in 2005; he now produces just 5,000 bottles a year, from local Chinuri grapes, one type with and one without skin contact, and they're always sold out by May. He keeps just enough to serve in the excellent restaurant run by his wife Marina (also a winemaker). The wine is superb, with a soft, fine texture that's partly due to heavy vine-pruning to produce lower yields.

A different wine experience is available at **Château Mukhrani** (m *595 991315/16;* e *1878@mukhrani.com;* w *chateaumukhrani.com*), owned by the Mukhranbatoni family since 1512. The francophile Prince Ivane Mukhranbatoni brought French architects to build the château in 1873–85 and established a modern French-style winery in 1875, winning many international prizes. This was re-established in 2007 with the most modern set-up for making wine and for handling tourists. Guided visits are available daily from 10.00 to 18.00, and the Samepo Marani 1878 restaurant is open from 10.00 (*until 18.00 Mon–Thu & until 22.00 Fri–Sun; advanced reservations required; $$$$*).

ARMAZI An alternative, if you want to meander along visiting ruined castles and ancient churches in villages that see almost no visitors despite being just a few hours from Tbilisi, is to follow the south bank of the Mtkvari. This was the historic road to Gori but is now used mainly by local traffic, with lots of vicious speed ramps; but it's still the obvious route for cyclists. Leaving Mtskheta, the main road to Tbilisi crosses the Mtkvari and turns to the left; to the right/west a minor road passes the railway station and continues towards Armazi, Akhalkalaki and, after 57km, Gori. About 1km west of the station a road turns left across the railway towards the Armazi Monastery, 3km south; for a pleasant hike up to it, continue another 1km west to the 'Archaeologists' House', where the site of Parnavaz's capital (page 157) is being excavated. Marked by a sign reading 'Armaztsikhe-Bagineti', this was constructed in three phases between the 3rd century BC and the 6th century AD, and there are still remains of a temple, royal tomb, palace, baths and wine cellar. On the hillside across the river is the Kaloubiani Chapel, off the road to Shio-mghvime, but sadly there's no way across the river here. Virtually opposite the archaeologists' gate you can take a tiny path diagonally up over the railway embankment to the km0.3 marker. A path, and for a while a water pipe, run along the true right side of a dry ravine into low forest of oaks and hornbeams, with lots of birds in residence and the odd squirrel. The path continues on either side of the stream bed; after about 15 minutes it turns right at some shacks and climbs steeply uphill for a couple of minutes before dropping back to the stream bed. You'll see Armazi Church on the far bank; fork left at a junction to reach it after about 30 minutes in all. It's a simple brick structure dating from the 12th century, now reclaimed and being refurbished by monks. If you cross the stream and fork left, following the stream and then climbing up to your right, you'll come in about 20 minutes to a saddle below the ruined tower of Armazistsikhe (Armazi Castle), spectacularly set amid cliffs of dramatic strata, with views to the chapels on the hilltops around Shio-mghvime. It's possible to climb down on the far side of the saddle and loop back to the stream, but I wouldn't recommend doing it alone.

AKHALKALAKI AND AROUND At the west end of Armazi village (all modern concrete blocks) a comical eagle sculpture points the way left under the railway; the road, fairly well served by marshrutkas, soon heads south away from the wooded river valley into dry sandy hills, and at km36 reaches **Akhalkalaki** (New Town – one of many), where you could visit the Art Villa Garikula (m *597 744040;* w *garikula.com*), 1km south of the road junction on the east side of the Tedzami river. A once grand house, owned by the Academy of Arts, it has been let to a private foundation (originally an art-squat) which now hosts artists' residencies (with facilities for serigraphy, lithography and bookbinding) and puts on events on summer Saturday evenings, and the annual Fest i Nova or Festival in Honour of the Brothers Zdanevich (the foundation's chairman is the grandson of Kiril Zdanevich, who with his better-known brother Ilia (1894–1975) discovered Pirosmani and was active in avant-garde movements such as Futurism and Dada). You can visit the sculpture garden, and new studios and galleries are under construction, as well as a café just inside the gate (they also make genuine *méthode champenoise* sparkling wine and fruit chacha). The house itself (built in 1885) is slowly being restored, but basic accommodation is available, with more planned; in the 19th century it was much visited by artists and writers, but then became an orphanage under Soviet rule. Paint marks show the way to the villa from the Gorelovka marshrutka stop: these run every couple of hours from Tbilisi via the main highway and Kaspi (*GEL3*). There's also a ruined 18th-century square fort in the centre of the village, with two old churches.

By the graveyard at the south end of Akhalkalaki is a simple 10th-century basilica church, with traces of frescoes on its west wall; from here (near where most of the Tbilisi marshrutkas turn around) it's just 2km south and steeply uphill to **Ertatsminda** (20km from Kaspi), a settlement of stone houses which has something of the feel of a real mountain village. The church, built in the 13th and 14th centuries, is known for a priest who was martyred after leading invaders the wrong way to save the village. The exterior is lovely, with carved crosses on all four façades and a blind Romanesque-style arcade above the aisle roof line; the cruciform interior is high and bare, with bits of fresco in the transepts, and a bishop's throne.

From here, a 4x4 track leads southwest for 23km (giving great views back to the Caucasus) to the tiny hamlet of **Rkoni**, where there's a footbridge (and ford) across the Tedzami by the parking area – it's a 2km walk to Rkoni monastery (with a 7th–8th-century church, altered in the 11th century), a medieval bridge and an 18th-century fort, low on the ridge just to the south. It's possible to continue (on foot or mountain bike) through the Algetis National Park, across the Trialeti Ridge, to Manglisi. A three-day hiking route follows the Tedzami Valley to Mgebriani and then takes an ancient trail south across the Trialeti Ridge by the Kldecari (Rocky Gate) Pass, 15km beyond Rkoni monastery, and the Sabolia Gorge to Choliani, north of Lake Tsalka (page 346), which is on the main road from Akhalkalaki (the other, more important one) to Tbilisi. An easier hike follows yellow-stripe hiking signs to the left at the south end of Rkoni, to Ikvi (1.75km) and Gostibe (12km), at the end of a rough track from Akhalkalaki. The 11th-century **Ikvi church** is famed for its superb external stone carvings and for its 12th–13th-century frescoes, being restored after serious rain damage in 2011.

Akhalkalaki is a long thin village with a topless defensive tower near its northern end at km38/71; just beyond this a road turns left to Gori (22km, passing the Uplistsikhe cave-city), while straight on to the north it's 15km to Kaspi; marshrutkas run this way between Kaspi and Gori. It's just a couple of kilometres north on the Kaspi road to the village of **Metekhi**, where the 13th-century Metekhis Sioni Church has a unique tapering pepper-pot dome design. Otherwise it's a simple cruciform shape within a square plan, with carved crosses on all four façades.

KASPI AND SAMTAVISI Kaspi is a small town with a huge cement plant on the railway 48km west of Tbilisi; however, there's nothing to see and no services for travellers beyond an ATM by the station. The only trains are to Tbilisi at 05.30 and back at 21.30. It's 9km south of the Tbilisi-Kutaisi highway at Igoeti (km55/497), where there's usually a taxi waiting. About 200m east up the Tbilisi-bound ramp there's a small 9th-century basilica of brick on stone foundations; about 600m west (still within Igoeti) is the junction to the superbly decorated **church of Samtavisi**, definitely a worthwhile stop for anyone taking the road between Tbilisi and Kutaisi. Without a car this is more easily done eastbound, as any marshrutka will stop and take you on to Mtskheta and Tbilisi, while westbound you'll have to struggle with reading destination boards.

Continuing northwest on the old road, the Samtavisi road continues straight ahead where the old highway swings left (formerly known as the Curve of Death), with the modern highway on a viaduct above – in 2007, when this was being built, a pagan temple (dating from the 7th century BC) was found here on **Grakliani Hill**, where an open-air museum is planned. The church is soon visible, but is bigger than it seems; in fact, it's about 1.5km away (and 11km from Kaspi). Stick to the main road through the village, then turn right where a bridge comes into view ahead, to reach a gate on the north side of the church complex. To the left as you enter are the remains of the bishop's palace; the bell-tower under which you enter dates from the 17th century, but the church itself (the burial place of St Isidore of Samtavisi) is a unified structure dating from 1030–68. Outside, the north, west and south sides are relatively simply decorated, although the north side has what seems to be a fake clock; the east end is richer (perhaps the best stone-carving in Georgia), with the two deep recesses that are typical of Georgian architecture marking the shape of the altar apse within and the lateral apses on either side. They draw the eye upwards to the incised cross and the dome above, stressing the verticality of the building. Inside, the church is high and bare, with the central dome set on four free-standing pillars that are not quite parallel. There are some battered fragments of 17th-century frescoes in the altar apse, and in the cupola (you'll notice that the figure of Christ is always the right way up for the priest, not the congregation), and tombstones dating from the 11th century. If you want to spend more time in the area, there's a fine-looking **fort** which is easily reached by a track northeast from the next village to the north, Pantiani.

GORI ადიი გორი *Telephone code 370*

The dual-carriageway from Tbilisi to Kutaisi runs several kilometres to the north of Gori, a fairly unattractive city known above all as the birthplace of Georgia's most infamous son, Stalin. Even if you choose to boycott the Stalin Museum, Gori is nevertheless the base for visiting the cave-city of Uplistsikhe and several fine historic churches, notably Ateni Sioni.

There have been fortifications on the hill dominating Gori since the first half of the 1st millennium BC; the Roman general Pompey besieged it in 65BC, but there was no real civilian settlement here until 1123 when King David the Builder established a city, partly settled by Armenian refugees. In 1892, when Stalin was 13, Gorky described Gori as: 'quite small, no bigger than a fair-sized village.... The whole place has a picturesque wildness all its own. The sultry sky over the town, the noisy, turbulent waters of the Kura, mountains in the near distance with their 'City of Caves' and further away the Caucasus range, with its sprinkling of snow that never melts.' The population at this time was 9,000 at most, but is now 54,000, with a relatively high proportion of Roman Catholics.

Gori is not a particularly attractive town, having been devastated by an earthquake in 1920 and rebuilt by the communists, and these days seems to have a somewhat schizophrenic attitude towards its historical connection with Stalin. Until 2010, a 17m-tall statue of Stalin stood in the central square, the only survivor of thousands of similar edifices that once graced every city square throughout the Soviet Empire. Although the others were removed elsewhere in the Soviet Union in the years following Khrushchev's denunciation, the Gori statue remained, defended by the town's citizens on the premise that however dreadful the despot's crimes against the Soviet people may have been, he was still, in Georgia at least, a hero of sorts in the 'local boy makes good' mould. Attempts to remove the statue were thwarted by proud locals and it was not until 24 June 2010 that cranes were brought in to remove it. The operation took place at night without debate or warning – clearly the act of a young government in a hurry to demonstrate its pro-West credentials. President Saakashvili had plans to erect a monument to the victims of the 2008 Russia–Georgia war in its place, although for the time being Stalin Square is devoid of any statuary (although it still bears the dictator's name). The statue may have gone but Stalin's shadow will remain for long years to come, it would seem.

Gori was quite badly damaged during the conflict with Russia in August 2008; although several military targets were attacked by Russian planes, bombs also fell in the town centre, causing considerable damage to residential buildings and an estimated 60 civilian deaths. Many residents fled the city as Russian forces and South Ossetian militia moved in following the aerial attack – troops that are accused of carrying out widespread looting and arson before their eventual withdrawal on 22 August. Scars from this episode can still be seen in the town, as can the human fallout of the conflict in the shape of large estates of prefab refugee housing across the Gori district.

GETTING THERE AND AWAY There are seven **trains** a day from Tbilisi (*GEL1*), three of them leaving the capital between 08.00 and 09.00; they take just under an hour, except for the two all-stops services to Borjomi, which take 1 hour 45 minutes. The town centre lies on the left/east bank of the River Liakvi at its confluence with the Mtkvari, and its railway station is on the far, south side of the Mtkvari; it's been well modernised, including remarkably good toilets at the west end of the platform. From here take marshrutka route 2, or climb the steps at the west end of the platform to reach the bridges over the tracks and the river, and carry on northwards along Stalin Prospekt for 15 minutes to reach Stalin Square.

From the north side of the square, Chavchavadze Street leads past the theatre and a circular Public Service Hall to the **bus** station about 500m west, south of the market; some buses leave from a second terminal across the bridge to the west. There are also **marshrutkas** every 15 minutes from Didube, taking around an hour (*GEL5*). Marshrutkas for Tbilisi wait by a ticket kiosk outside the main terminal, with shared taxis for Tbilisi outside the Public Service Hall. For other destinations you should buy tickets inside the terminal.

Heading west – to Kutaisi, say – from Gori is a trickier prospect as most transport passes the town on the main highway without diverting into the town itself. Apart from taking a train – they pass through westbound at around 09.00, 09.30, 10.00, 19.00 and 23.00 (in addition to the very slow trains to Borjomi at about 08.00 and 18.00) – the best bet is to take a local marshrutka to the junction of Khashuri, or a taxi or marshrutka up to the highway.

Roughly midway between Samtavisi and Gori on the new highway the fence along the border of South Ossetia is barely half a kilometre to the north, having been illegally pushed south since the 2008 war; you'll also see large settlements built for IDPs from South Ossetia along the highway. The junction to Gori is at km80/472 (about 60km west of Mtskheta), and it's 4km more to the centre; from the west turn off at km468.5/83.5 if you have your own wheels, or (in either direction) continue to the Tskhinvali junction at km83/475, where taxis (*GEL6*) wait.

WHERE TO STAY Map, page 169

Guesthouses are generally better than hotels here – ask at the tourist office. All charge GEL25 per person plus GEL5 for breakfast (**$$**).

Hotels

Hotel Gori (10 rooms) 3km from town on the highway to Tbilisi; m 590 776669, 599 131205. You'll see this hotel, the best place to stay in Gori, on the left as the bus from Tbilisi begins to turn off into Gori; you can loop under the dual-carriageway to reach it. It's a very nice 4-star place, about the standard of a European Best Western & much more affordable. The staff speak enough English, & there's a good restaurant, with Georgian dishes from about GEL6 (or GEL30 for caviar). **$$$$**

Hotel Georgia Stalin Av 26; 370 707576; m 599 396163; e sastumrosaqartvelo@mail.ru; w hotelgeorgia.blogspot.com. Centrally located on the north side of the old Hotel Intourist (now closed), this has friendly staff & good soundproofing, but still has a very Soviet feel to it. **$$$**

Hotel Victoria (16 rooms) Tamar Mepis 76; 827 07 5586; m 877 402372. Rooms are huge & have TV, shower & fridge. It's adequate for a stopover, with Soviet-era notions of style & service. Rates inc b/fast & tax. **$$$**

Royal House (6 rooms) Samepo 45; m 599 909129; HotelRoyalHouse. This new place just south of the centre has quickly established itself as the best hotel in town, with spacious rooms & friendly service (inc coffee & cake on arrival, if you time it right). **$$$**

Guesthouses

Levani (3 rooms) Davit Agmashenebelis 29; 370 273147; m 599 138514; e kapanadze. tamar@gmail.com; w guesthouselevani.blogspot. co.uk **$$$**

Savane Christopher Kastel 28; m 599 206060. A bit hidden away on the west side of the fortress (there's no sign outside), this is a very friendly guesthouse with comfortable wood-panelled rooms. **$$**

Hostel Kalifornia Rustaveli 79; m 593 300802, 551 300802; e okalifornia@mail.ru. Opposite the new cathedral, this guesthouse now calls itself a hostel, with a 10-bed dorm as well as 2 private rooms, a kitchen (with free tea & coffee) & a washing machine. **$**

✳ **Nitsa** (4 rooms) Kutaisi 58; ✆ 370 277567; m 599 142488; e liazauta@gmail.com; **f** Guesthousenitsa. This wonderfully hospitable place has a common/dining room, kitchen, & 4 rooms with shared bathroom & WC; it's a friendly, arty family, & Lia speaks English. **$**

Nukri (3 rooms) Marabdeli 24; m 577 432143; e nukritalakhadze@gmail.com. Just south of the station, this friendly place is run by a retired army officer, who insists on sharing his own wine & chacha; with 3 rooms & a shared bathroom, it has a rather retro interior in perfect condition. Excellent b/fast. **$**

✖ WHERE TO EAT AND DRINK *Map, opposite*

As well as those listed, there are a few bars on Stalin Avenue near the war memorial (such as **Sport Café** at No 11 and **Bar Shardin** at No 17). There are also supermarkets to the rear of the tourist office and south of the centre on Stalin Avenue. Outside town, the **Hotel Gori** (page 167) has an excellent restaurant, and the **Venezia** (m *595 507870, 599 726902*) and **Nacharmagevi** (m *577 257711*), 5km north on the Tskhinvali road (1km beyond the highway junction) are spacious, rural places that specialise in family parties.

✖ **Chinebuli** Shartava 2 (at Kutaisi); ✆ 370 225040; m 551 375444; ⊕ 09.00–23.00 daily. Facing the tourist office in a seemingly nameless modern stone building with brick features, this is one of the best places in town for solid Georgian food. **$$**

✖ **Hunter Restaurant** Stalin Av 6 (south of Stalin Sq); ⊕ 10.00–midnight daily. Decorated with dead animals rather than serving game; it actually offers the usual khachapuri, khinkali & kebabs, but with slow service. **$$**

✖ **Berikoni** Tsereteli 1; m 598 431062; ⊕ 09.30–23.30 daily. The best of the limited choice in the old town; nice views from the upstairs hall. **$**

✖ **Café Nikala** Chavchavadze 36; m 595 454444; **f** nikalagori; ⊕ 09.00–22.00 daily. Just east of Stalin Av opposite the university, this is a nice, modern restaurant & bar, next to the Al Forno fast food joint. **$**

✖ **Café-Bar Champs Elysées** Stalin Av 13; m 557 777558; ⊕ 10.00–midnight daily. A fancy café (aka Shanzelize) opposite the City Hall that serves good pancakes & salads & has Wi-Fi. **$**

✖ **Cake House** Stalin Av 22. Despite its name, this also serves beer & Turkish coffee; free Wi-Fi. Not to be confused with Café 22 in front, which serves coffee, hot-dogs & kebabs. **$**

✖ **El Depo** Stalin Av 19; ⊕ 24hrs. A lively 24hr pub that's good for beer & khinkali. **$**

✖ **L'Avenue** Stalin Av 24; m 598 353949, 598 382325; **f** Lavenue; ⊕ 11.00–midnight daily. A decent new café-bar for b/fast & later meals (Georgian & European food) plus coffee & cocktails. **$**

✖ **Rain Home** Chavchavadze 22; m 599 500909; ⊕ 09.00–midnight daily. A decent new bar-restaurant that's appeared in the park just west of the Eristavi Theatre. **$**

OTHER PRACTICALITIES There's a helpful **tourist information centre** north of the Stalin Museum (*Kutaisi 23A;* ✆ *27 0776;* e *ticgori@gmail.com;* ⊕ *10.00–18.00 daily, until 19.00 in summer*). There are plenty of **ATMs**, including at the Bank of Georgia and TBC on Stalin Square, Bank Republic at the post office and ProCredit west of the centre (*Chavchavadze 10*). The **post office** is at Stalin Ave 15 (⊕ *09.00–17.00 Mon–Fri, 09.00–14.00 Sat*). Peace Corps Volunteers who visit the town for training also rave about the **swimming pool** behind the sports school southwest of Stalin Square.

GORI

Hotel Gori,
Venezia,
Nacharmagevi,
Tskhinvali, Tbilisi

Gori History &
Ethnography
Museum

Stalin
Museum

Stalin
Park

KUTAISI

26 MAY

GOGEBASHVILI

Goris-Tsikhe
Castle

Cathedral of
the Virgin Mary

STALIN AVENUE

STALIN AVENUE

SAAKADZE

5

Market

GURAMISHVILI

CASTEL

Bus
station

Museum of
Martial Glory

14

SAMEBA

CHKHEIDZE

KOSTAVA

DAVIT AGMASHENEBELIS

Public Service
Hall

KARTLI

7

OLD TOWN

9

2

$

New
cathedral

1

CHAVCHAVADZE

8

16

TSAMEBULI

GELDIASHVILI

11

17

Stalin
Square

12

CHAVCHAVADZE

10

City Hall

GURAMISHVILI

AMILAKHVARI

6

RUSTAVELI

AMILAKHVARI

Swimming
pool

18

ROBAKIDZE

BAGRATIONI

EVDOSHVILI

ROMELASHVILEBI

STALIN AVENUE

SHAPTOSHVILI

15

4

TAMAR MEPIS

3

TAMAR MEPIS

ROMELASHVILEBI

Mtkvari

GORIJVARI

Mtkvari

N

Bradt

0   200m
0   200yds

Nukri (200m),
Uplistsikhe,
Ateni Sioni

Railway
station

Shida (Inner) Kartli GORI

4

For listings, see pages 167–8

🛏 **Where to stay**

1	Hostel Kalifornia	5	Nitsa	**Off map**
2	Hotel Georgia	6	Royal House	Hotel Gori
3	Hotel Victoria	7	Savane	Nukri
4	Levani			

❌ **Where to eat and drink**

8	Bar Shardin	14	El Depo	**Off map**
9	Berikoni	15	Hunter	Hotel Gori
10	Café Nikala	16	L'Avenue	Nacharmagevi
11	Cake House	17	Rain Home	Venezia
12	Café-Bar Champs Elysées	18	Sport Café	
13	Chinebuli			

WHAT TO SEE AND DO

The Stalin Museum (*Stalin Av 32;* ☎ *370 225398;* e *stalinmuseum@yahoo.com;* w *stalinmuseum.ge;* ⊕ *10.00–18.00 daily exc holidays; GEL15 inc guide, railway carriage GEL5 extra*) To the north of Stalin Square, the large plaza of Stalin Avenue, lined with imposing buildings, has replaced the jumble of slummy shacks in which Josef Djugashvili grew up; the two-room house, then Sobornaya (or Cathedral

169

Street) 10, in which he was born in 1879, remains beneath a glass-roofed Doric temple (thought by some to be more like a metro station) erected by Beria in 1939. An empty plinth stands in front of this ready for the erection of the statue removed from Stalin Square in 2010; it's currently face-down in a garden near Gori, and will probably not return. There is a smaller statue to the rear of his birthplace (with a replica on the landing of the museum staircase) and two busts at the top of the stairs, so it's hard to see that the cult of personality is dead yet.

Immediately behind Stalin's birthplace is the massive Italianate museum to his memory that was defiantly built in 1957, the year after Khrushchev's denunciation of Stalin and his crimes. This was officially closed in 1989, but school groups continued to be shown around; the pretence of closure has long ended and it's open to all again.

To the people of Gori there's little purely political significance to the museum: Stalin is simply the only important thing ever to come out of Gori, and is revered as the 'strong man' rather than for his views or deeds. There's no doubt that the locals are far too quick to overlook his immense crimes, but you would in any case be foolish to expect any mention of the Ukrainian famine or the Terror in a museum like this, and if you ask you'll be told they're waiting for proof, much like George W Bush on climate change.

Most texts are in Georgian and Russian only, with some English photo captions, but you'll have a guide whose English may or may not be up to the task of explaining things; most take a suitably Soviet attitude to their work, but one or two are friendly and open. The displays are upstairs (without a lift); the first room deals with Stalin's youth and revolutionary career, up to Lenin's death – it's remarkable what a good-looking youth he was (in a romantic revolutionary style), and how literary, writing quite passable poetry, working in secret presses and then being the first editor of *Pravda*. In the second room, bringing events up to World War II, he gradually becomes more Stalin-like, with the bristling moustache and bushy eyebrows and hair (which prevented his hats from fitting for many years). Kalinin and Gorky remain prominent, but Trotsky can only be seen in one small photo, and there's no mention of Lenin's testament warning the Communist Party against Stalin ('a coarse, brutish bully acting on behalf of a great power'). It was once thought that Stalin might have been a double agent for the tsarist secret police in the pre-revolutionary period, but it's less clear which foreign power Lenin might have been thinking of – quite possibly Britain, which was vilified for its occupation of Transcaucasia.

The third room covers the Great Patriotic War – even if we can't forgive Stalin's crimes, we should give him credit for saving us in the war. The museum culminates with a sort of symbolic lying in state by a bronze death-mask of Stalin, followed by an anticlimactic room of gifts to Stalin. Off the grand staircase is a room with a mock-up of his Kremlin office, the pen he used at Potsdam, his 1919 cavalry sword and the piano from his dacha. Finally, in 2010 the museum responded grudgingly to pressure to cover Stalin's crimes by converting a basement room into a mock NKVD office and cell with limited coverage of the Terror and gulags. The place is still basically a distasteful shrine, with no real attempt to tell the truth, that Stalin killed anywhere between 20 million and 60 million people. Naturally you can buy Stalin postcards, mugs, key-rings and fridge magnets here. Beside the museum it's also worth glancing at Stalin's massive private rail carriage, on six axles to carry the weight of its armour-plating. There is an additional charge if you want to go inside.

Gori History and Ethnography Museum (*Kirion II 12;* ⊕ *09.30–17.30 Tue–Sun; GEL3*) Hidden behind Stalin Avenue 29, this has a remarkable collection of relics from the early Bronze Age Kura-Araxes culture, much of it from a burial mound

about 7km away, and then the early Kurgan period, from the mid 3rd millennium BC. More recent artefacts include bronze bulls from the 8th or 7th centuries BC, Greek and Parthian coins and Roman luxury goods. From the top of the stairs, where there's a copy of a drawing of Gori Castle made for the Pope in the 17th century, you should go around to the left and then right to the ethnographic display of mainly 20th-century clothes, weapons, musical instruments and jewellery. Various carved and inscribed stones can be seen outside even when the museum is closed.

Elsewhere in Gori Just southwest of the History and Ethnography Museum is the Neoclassical **Cathedral of the Virgin Mary** (built as a Catholic church in 1810), and rising beyond it is the **Goris-Tsikhe Castle** (⊕ *always; free*), colourfully lit up at night. This is best reached from the east side: just south of the cathedral, turn right at a stone cross to follow a paved pathway that curves up to the castle gate. Just to the right of here, beneath the fortified walls, is an interesting sculpture of giant warrior figures (moved from Tbilisi in 2009). Another path leads up from the road by the market to the entrance on the south side of the castle. The best view of the castle from below is from the west, where the walls form a series of defensive enclosures tumbling down the hillside. Although the fortifications (mostly from the 7th and 13th centuries) have been rather over-restored, the castle offers good views of the Mtkvari Valley, the solid snowy wall of the Caucasus beyond South Ossetia to the north, and, on a high spur across the river to the southwest, the 6th-century **Church of Gori-Jvari**. This was rebuilt in the 12th century and the 1980s; taxis charge GEL20, although it's a delightful walk of around 3 hours there and back. To reach it, head south along Stalin Avenue, cross the river and railway then follow the Ateni road that winds up the hillside and eventually becomes a dirt trail leading to the church. The Gorijvari spa resort is just west of the church (m *599 449213;* e *kurortigorijvari@gmail. com;* ⊕ *Jun–Sep*). In town there's also a **Museum of Martial Glory** (*Stalin Av 19;* ⊕ *10.00–17.00 Tue–Sun; GEL3*) by a ceramic relief memorial to the dead of 1941–44 and an eternal flame. The museum contains a lot of dull photos with Georgian and Russian captions, the odd mortar and a statue of Stalin. There's minimal coverage of the 2008 war (a few bombs in the foyer, uniforms and photocopied medal citations), but the intention is to create a Museum of Russian Aggression. Behind the museum, east of the castle, is the so-called 'old town', essentially comprised of the heavily renovated 19th-century brick buildings lining Tsereteli.

AROUND GORI

UPLISTSIKHE (⊕ *10.00–18.00 Tue–Sun*) About 10km east of Gori along the Mtkvari Valley, visible from trains along the main line, is the unmissable cave-city of Uplistsikhe (meaning the castle of the mythical Uplos, son of Mtskhetos). The Silk Road ran along the hills to the north (hence the positions of Gori, Kaspi and Mtskheta, all on the north side of the Mtkvari), and excavations in the area have shown evidence of settlement from the second half of the 4th millennium BC onwards. Uplistsikhe was a religious centre by 1000BC (its temples dedicated mainly to the sun goddess) and a trading centre by at least the 5th century BC. It was also a major centre, with a population of perhaps 20,000, in the Hellenistic and Roman periods. Later it became more isolated and was inhabited by monks until it was destroyed in the 13th century by Chinghiz's son Khulagu. Over the centuries the site has suffered greatly from the elements, although channels were built to carry off storm water and prevent flash floods (drinking water was brought 5–6km from a spring just 44m above, through a beautifully engineered system of ceramic pipes and a tunnel). Most of the caves have been at least partly eroded away, so that it takes a considerable feat of the imagination to really understand what the city was like.

The tour of the ruins is only for the able (and requires gripping footwear), starting with steps, then scrambling up rocks and following an ancient pathway past grain pits to the remains of a theatre built in the 2nd or 3rd century AD, complete with orchestra pit; the auditorium side has now all collapsed into the river and been washed away, and the stage roof is held up by concrete pillars. There's even a bread oven in the middle of the stage. The 'Blackberry Hall', so called because of the bramble roots dangling from cracks in the ceiling, may have been a pagan temple. The largest hall in the city is known as Tamar's Hall, although Queen Tamar never lived here; its front wall has gone, but it's otherwise intact. The marani (wine-storage room) next to it, one of three in the city, dates from after her time. There's an underground prison, 8.5m deep, just below Tamar's Hall, and to the south is what must have been a pharmacy, with eight layers of storage spaces (about 15cm cubes), where traces of herbs and wrapping parchments have been found. To the north of Tamar's Hall is another hall, now roofless, which was once a church – there's very little left except for the stumps of four columns, and a basin for the blood of sacrificed animals. Further up there's a very obvious conventional church, a three-nave basilica built of red brick in the 9th–10th centuries, which survived the Mongol onslaught, although all 5,000 resident monks were killed. The church's frescoes were all whitewashed in the 19th century. At the highest points of the site you'll see scraps of medieval defensive walls.

On the way back down you'll pass the market, with its stone stalls, and finish by going down through a 41m tunnel (designed to be used by water carriers, as well as for emergency exits) to emerge on the track beside the river. This leads to a village immediately to the west, whose inhabitants were removed in 1968 (though at least one house is clearly in use again). You might be tempted to set out to walk back to Gori along the north bank of the river, but you should be aware of the deep gullies blocking the way.

A World Bank cultural heritage project paid for an interpretation centre (often locked; ask to see the video with English subtitles, a useful preparation for visiting), walking itinerary and better guides. The cave complex has been on the tentative list of potential UNESCO World Heritage Sites since 2007. At present there are reasonably well-informed guides, whose services cost GEL20 on top of the ticket price of GEL3; some speak English although most have only Georgian and Russian. There are plenty of people flogging postcards, but no real interpretative materials. In addition, cracks are developing in many of the caves, which may soon crumble away; some are supported by concrete pillars, and metal roofs protect some excavated sites, but there's no fencing or limitation on where you can explore.

Getting there and away A return **taxi** from Gori to Uplistsikhe costs GEL30–40 including a reasonable amount of waiting time, or GEL10–15 one-way. Alternatively, a local **bus** (*GEL3; with a sign in Latin script*) leaves the bus station in Gori at 30 minutes past the hour, passing the railway station (by an odd one-way system), forking left in the first village, Khidistavi, and then turning left at an English sign to Uplistsikhe. After a bridge across the railway the bus heads to the right through the village of Velebi and follows the river for 1.5km to Kvakhvreli; get off after 25 minutes where the bus turns right (away from the river) and head left over the bridge, from where it's a 15-minute walk to the site. To take the bus back to Gori, you should walk back another block to a junction by a bend in the river. There's a new café and restaurant by the road and a souvenir shop and toilets by the ticket office. The road runs below cliffs of weathered yellow sandstone which act as a heat trap, with bushes in bloom and bees and butterflies even in winter, as well as rare lizards and two species of hamster; there are eagles in the hills to the north. The best time to visit is late afternoon or early evening, when the setting sun brings a special warmth to the rocks; in summer it can be very hot in the middle of the day.

ATENI SIONI From the road junction at the west end of Khidistavi, an asphalt road, also served by regular local buses from Gori (*GEL0.70*), leads south to Ateni following the left/west bank of the Tana stream. The village of Patara (or Little) Ateni stretches from km2.5, with metal frames training Atenuri vines out over the road from almost every house. At km6.5 the tiny Ateni Church hides to the left of the road; built of green tuff in the 7th century, with a dome added in the 9th or 10th century, it's just 5m by 6m in area and very sparsely decorated.

It's another 1.5km to the Church of Ateni (or Atenis) Sioni: this is one of the loveliest churches in Georgia, due, above all, to its setting at a bend of the narrow Tana Gorge, which is especially stunning in winter. Terraced fields by the river give a Central Asian feel, while just to the south there's a great view down the valley to Mount Kazbeg. The writer Fitzroy Maclean said of it that it made:

> [...] as great an impression on me as any [church] in Georgia; [...] architecturally Ateni Sioni impresses by its simplicity, but what struck me most of all was its magnificent position and the feeling it gave me of age, serenity and strength.

It was built by a certain Todos in the first half of the 7th century in the new style initiated at Jvari (Mtskheta) at the end of the 6th century; its decoration is finer than at Jvari, and it's in a better state of preservation. The lower parts are in red sandstone, with yellow-green tuff above. The ground plan is a tetraconch cross, its arms ending internally in four half-circles, with corner rooms rather than aisles and transepts. The spacious interior effectively has eight columns, supporting four squinches and a relatively low dome. There's just a low minimalist iconostasis. The interior was entirely painted in the late 11th century; the image of the Archangel Gabriel in the apse, painted in 1080, is a highpoint in Georgian art, as is the *Dream of Joseph* in the south transept. Externally, the façade is a copy of Jvari in local stone, restored in the 16th century; note also the two carved stags (pagan symbols) in the tympanum of the north door, and a hunter in a Sassanid headdress and a herd of stags on the west façade.

Taxis charge about GEL30 return from Gori, including waiting time (or GEL50 combined with Uplistsikhe); but it's well worth taking a marshrutka (hourly from Gori) all the way to the end of the road, in the heart of the rugged Trialeti range, and then back to Ateni Sioni; then you can walk down to the village to catch a bus back down the valley.

A booklet and map entitled *Walking Tracks in Ateni Valley* (free from tourist offices) was published by the National Tourism Administration in 2013 and is key to a project to develop green tourism in the area. The Tana (or Ateni) Valley, rising from 600m to 2,200m in the Trialeti range, offers opportunities for rock-climbing (and even ice-climbing, on a waterfall near Biisi), birdwatching, horseriding and mountain biking. The booklet describes ten hikes, of which three are easy; one of these (5km total) starts from a bridge near the south end of Ateni village and climbs gently southeast to the lower Danachvisi Church, just below the 9th-century Vere Fortress. Two harder routes continue from here: one (12km) swinging right/south to the upper church of St George on a 1,643m hilltop (a wonderful viewpoint), the other (11km) looping left to the Ghvtimshobeli Church and returning down the next valley to the north to

Chechelantubani. There are longer routes starting further along the valley, and multi-day hikes (not in the booklet) to Borjomi, Manglisi or Tsalka.

Quite a few good guesthouses have appeared in Khidistavi, such as Gogi Dvabishvili's Wine Cellar (*Tsereteli 8;* m *599 737563;* **f** *KhidistaviWine;* **$$**), and in Ateni, such as Grand Ateni (*Stalin Av 15 6th Lane, No 6, Gardateni;* m *598 194206;* **$**) and Vacheishvili's Guesthouse (*Didi Ateni;* m *577 270032;* **$**), just beyond Ateni Sioni church, where a former government minister makes natural Chinuri, Atenuri and Tavkveri wines and has a restaurant and guesthouse.

SOUTH OSSETIA Gori would also be the base for visits to **Tskhinvali**, capital of Samachablo or South Ossetia, if the political situation were normal. However, travel to the breakaway region is not possible at the moment. From a tourism perspective, there's little to see in Tskhinvali anyway, which was a drab place of typically communist concrete blocks even before the 2008 conflict reduced much of it to ruins. However, there are a few things worth seeing around Tskhinvali. In the Georgian village of **Nikozi** (south of the de facto border, but too close for comfort) there's a 5th-century cruciform cathedral, rebuilt in the 14th century, and the ruins of an episcopal palace built in the 9th and 10th centuries. There's also fine walking in the hills to the north of the South Ossetian capital, which have largely escaped the erosion of the Kazbegi area, although at the present time this is unreachable. Roads continue northwards to Oni in Racha, and towards the Roka Tunnel into North Ossetia, although both are closed to foreigners.

WEST OF GORI

Continuing westwards from the Gori junction, the highway immediately climbs to the low Gori Pass, with a tunnel at km87 and very striking Saakashvili-style service stations for uphill traffic on either side, as well as wind turbines to the north. Soon after you'll pass another village church that is well worth a brief halt: from the **Urbnisi** intersection, at km93.5, follow the asphalt road south through the village until you see the church to your left. Passing through a stone gateway topped by an octagonal brick bell-tower, you'll enter a churchyard in which a surprising number of large qvevri wine jars are lying around. The church is a relatively long three-nave basilica, built in the 6th century and rebuilt in the 10th and 17th centuries; the lower part is of stone, with the upper part of thin Roman-style bricks, supported by two brick arch-buttresses on either side, an unusual sight in Georgia. There are also a few inscribed stones on the exterior and a high relief cross on the east end. This is also the junction (or, from the west, leave the highway at km456) for **Ruisi Church**, visible just north of the highway, a typically Georgian cross-and-cupola church built in the 7th–9th centuries and rebuilt in the 11th century. King George II was crowned here in 1072, and an ecclesiastic council was called by King David the Builder in Ruisi and Urbnisi in 1103–04. The belltower was added in the 17th century; there's now a nunnery here.

SOUTH OF KARELI There's a group of interesting and attractive churches south of the Mtkvari between Gori and Khashuri, at Samtsevrisi, Tsromi and Kintsvisi. From km101 (km451 from the west) a road leads a couple of kilometres south to Kareli, a small town on the railway on the south side of the Mtkvari. Minibuses and taxis shuttle the 2km to the bridge and level crossing just beyond, and then left to the rail and bus stations (there's just one train a day). Marshrutkas run hourly to Gori until 16.00 (some continuing to Tbilisi), six times a day to Khashuri (the last at 14.40), and at noon, 15.00 and 18.00 to Zguderi, to the south beyond Kintsvisi.

From the T-junction 100m south of the level crossing, this road heads right/ southwest to the modern town centre and left at a roundabout. At km2 a minor road leads right for 2km to **Samtsevrisi**, at the far end of which two old churches (visible from the Tbilisi–Kutaisi highway and railway to the north) stand on hillocks on either side of the road. The first, in a cemetery to the left/south, is a tiny dome church built in the first half of the 7th century, with a small bit of 16th-century stonework to the southwest; it's a 'free-cross' church, with a horseshoe apse in a cross plan, and is simply a perfect example of its type. The other, about 1.5km from the junction, is a small, simple basilica beside the well-preserved ruins of a 16th-century castle, with a circular underground chamber which could have been a dungeon or water cistern. The road continues parallel to the Mtkvari for another 8km to Akalsopeli (reached by a couple of marshrutkas a day), and perhaps 5km more to **Tsromi**. The Church of the Redeemer here, built in AD626–34, is the oldest of its kind in Georgia, with four free-standing columns to support the cupola; its roof has mostly been ruined by earthquakes, but it's important as the model for many churches in Georgia and far beyond. It can also be reached across a footbridge from Gomi, on the main road from Tbilisi to Khashuri and Kutaisi, and from the west from km124 on the highway via Khtsisi (8km in all).

Continuing south from the junction at km2 (before Samtsevrisi), you'll see a couple of very odd towers on the hillside to the east, and after 6km more you enter the village of **Kintsvisi**, where a sign by a bridge marks a road to the left leading to the Kintsvisi Monastery in 3.5km. With the help of a few short cuts, it takes about 40 minutes to walk up, climbing from fields to oak and beech forest to the lower edge of the conifer belt. The monastery has reopened, with lots of restoration work under way, and you'll first pass the priest's modern house before curving right up to the church at the end of the road.

Built in 1207–13, of brick despite standing on limestone hills, the Church of St Nicholas has a single-bay nave and aisles, with a large porch to the west and others to the north and south. The three apses at the east end are the same length, the central one being distinguished only by being slightly wider and by its solid stone iconostasis. The church's frescoes are absolutely magnificent, if damaged by mould (now being treated), in particular the 13th-century Resurrection (a copy of which you can see in Tbilisi's Art Museum) on the north side (including a stunning image of the Archangel Gabriel), and a Virgin and Child in the apse, as well as portraits of royalty (including one of the four surviving portaits of Queen Tamar painted during her lifetime) and the 14th-century encyclopaedist Zasa Panaskerteli-Tsitsishvili; the painting of the cross inside the dome is typically Georgian. There's also the small stone Church of St George, probably also built in the 13th century, to the west of the main church, and the eastern half of the 10th-century Church of the Virgin poised on the edge of the hill to the west, with a fantastic Virgin and Child, in Sutherland-esque swirling robes, rather exposed to the elements but still in good condition. A fourth church has recently been built over the grave of the abbot who died in 2006; the monks here are not an austere lot and have a castellated mansion about 500m beyond the churches.

It's a long way on a very rough road, but theoretically it would be possible to head west from just north of Kintsvisi through Zguderi and on to the churches of Tkemlovani and Timotesubani (pages 206–7); perhaps a route best suited to the hardier type of mountain bikers.

KHASHURI AND SURAMI

Continuing westwards, the main road passes through an unattractive district of light industry and then, from km116, a stretch of road with several Turkish truck stops before the new highway ends at Agarebi at km118 (it'll continue to the northwest, bypassing Khashuri and Surami). Founded in 1872 as the rail junction of Mikhailovo, **Khashuri** (km126–131; pronounced 'Hashuri') boasts glass and textile factories, but its chief significance is as the junction of routes west to Kutaisi and southwest to Borjomi, Akhaltsikhe and the Turkish border. The road passes to the south of the centre, and at km129/423 (45km from Gori, 113km from Tbilisi, 32km from Borjomi) reaches the road junction (at a roundabout with a big cross on a fountain), as well as a 24-hour fuel station and ATM. Trains take just under 2 hours from Tbilisi; the station has been nicely renovated, and there's an ATM opposite. Turning right/west from the station you'll pass a shashlik joint and bar (with the tower of an 18th-century fort visible to the left) to reach the main square, and just south of it the **Hotel Iveria** (*Davit Agmashenebelis 2;* \ *368 246458,* m *557 268558;* f *IveriaHotel;* **$$**). Marshrutka 1 runs from the railway station to the roundabout, about 10 minutes' walk west, and on to Surami. Marshrutkas to Kutaisi and Batumi halt just west of the roundabout, and those to Borjomi wait about 100m down the road to Borjomi and Akhaltsikhe. There are also taxis here, and ticket offices for buses to Turkey. The town has no other services or features of interest.

The main road to Kutaisi and the west soon climbs through pine forest to the Rikoti Pass and into Imereti, while a 4km loop runs through the climatic resort of **Surami**, which is a better bet than Khashuri for food, drink and accommodation; they're linked by frequent local marshrutkas. The poet Terenti Graneli was detained in the TB/mental hospital here in 1930–34. First, as the main road climbs up on to the hillside to the north of the town, it passes a dramatic small castle (⊕ *always; free*), which served as residence of the dukes of Kartli from the 11th century and held off the Shah's armies in 1743–45, to the south of the road at km133. This can be easily reached by a lane past a small brick church, built in the 18th and 19th centuries, with two barrel domes – not the more recent church just west of the road on a rock in the pine forest. Rough steps lead up into the castle, where a few stones remain of the palace and one-nave church. The film *The Surami Fortress*, by the great Tbilisi-born Armenian director Sergei Paradjanov, tells the legend of a young man built into the castle's walls to preserve them. Just north of the castle, on the dirt roads between the town and the bypass is a surprisingly modern synagogue – this was known as a centre of Jewish population, but there's little other sign of it now. In the centre of town is a large mineral spring, producing a mildly metallic water that's surprisingly drinkable.

The best place to stay is the **Hotel Batumi Palace** (*Rustaveli 186;* m *599 262848;* **$$**), on the main road through Surami; there's also the **Hotel Kidobani** (*26 May St 49;* m *555 169810;* f *kidobanihotel;* **$$**), near the former station, plus a good anonymous guesthouse just east on Rustaveli at the turning to the former station, and a few others along the main highway such as the **Grizli** (m *558 565751;* **$**).

There are scores of wicker stalls baking and selling excellent sweet bread along the main highway (and after the tunnel there are lots of beehives and stalls selling honey to go with the bread). After being reunited with the road through the town to the left, the main road soon reaches the **Rikoti Pass** where, at km141 there's a choice of a tunnel, 1.75km long, or the more scenic old road over the 997m pass, 4km of tight, hairpin bends signposted as the Rikoti Tunnel Bypass. Trains use a far longer tunnel to the south, leading to Kutaisi via Marelisi and Kharagauli, and there's also a back road from the town of Surami over the Surami Pass (949m) and on beside the railway.

5

The Georgian Military Highway

საქართველოს სამხედრო ხა

The Georgian Military Highway has existed as a route since before the 1st century BC, but had only evolved into a bridle track by the time the Russians finally converted it, through the Herculean efforts of 800 soldiers, into a carriage road in 1783. In 1829 Pushkin followed this route, as did many other great Russian writers, such as Lermontov, Gorky, Tolstoy and Mayakovsky, all inspired in various ways by the experience. Chekhov wrote in a letter, 'I have survived the Georgian Military Highway. It isn't a highway, but poetry.' In 1846, Shamyl attempted to close the highway in his rebellion against Russia, and it was his failure which persuaded the other tribes of the northern Caucasus not to join him, though his rebellion continued until 1864. The route finally lost much of its importance with the opening of the railway via the Caspian coast in 1883. Just over 100 years later the Roki Tunnel opened between South and North Ossetia, although given the instability of these regions it never became a major through route and now only links the two Ossetias.

The Georgian Military Highway still serves as a link to the province of Khevi (The Valley), around Kazbegi, which lies on the northern slope of the Caucasus, and offers the easiest access from Tbilisi to the high mountains. Unfortunately the hillsides are heavily eroded in this area, due largely to overgrazing but also to tourism. It suffers greatly from snow and ice and the pass is frequently closed in winter.

NORTH OF MTSKHETA

The highway starts with a flyover junction just after km27 on the highway from Tbilisi to Kutaisi, immediately to the northwest of Mtskheta. From here it's 58km to Pasanauri, 124km to Kazbegi, and 168km (just over 100 miles) to Vladikavkaz in Russia.

The road runs along the right/west bank of the Aragvi, in a wide valley between sandy foothills; it's lined at first with large wedding-style restaurants and conference-type hotels, of which the best is the Kapiloni at km5/134 (*Misaktsieli; 15 rooms;* m *595 771177, 596 755777;* **$$$**), with conference facilities and a swimming pool. Just before km3/136 a side road leads 5km west to **Tsilkani**, where there's a church built as a basilica in the 5th and 6th centuries and remodelled as a dome church in medieval times. Founded by one of the Assyrian Fathers in the 4th century, this was one of the first churches in Georgia, and was famous for its icon of the Virgin painted by St Luke on a board from Christ's cradle. This road continues to Mukhrani, where wine is produced on what was the Bagration family estate (more usually visited from the Tbilisi–Kutaisi highway; page 163).

THE GEORGIAN MILITARY HIGHWAY & KHEVSURETI

N

Bradt

0   **20km**
0   **15 miles**

Vladikavkaz

Fiagdo

Sunza

A301

R U S S I A N   F E D E R A T I O N

Ingushetia

Chechnya

Terek

Argun

Zemo Larsi

Daryal Fortress
Gveleti
Tsdo
Kazbek 5033m
Gergeti
Kazbegi Nature Reserve
Stepantsminda
Resi
Gergeti Trinity Church
Sioni
Truso Gorge
A301
Sno
Khobi
Almasiani
Ivaris Pass 2379m
Gudauri
Khade
Mleta Kvesheti
Naghvarevi

Arkhoti
Shatili
Anatori
Akhieli
Juta Pass 3287m
Khevsureti
Mutso
Khonischala
Arkhotis Pass 2935m
Ardoti
Khone
Juta
Roshka Pass 3056m
Mt Chaukhi 3842m
Roshka
Datvis-Jvaris Pass 2676m
Khakhabo
Andaki
Abudelari Lakes
Biso
Gudani
Khakhmati
Atsunta Pass 3431m
Gudamakari Pass 2347m
Korsha
Hegho, Omalo (page 321)
Barisakho
Pshavi

Pshavis Aragvi

Black Aragvi

White Aragvi

Mt Didi Borbalo 3294m

South Ossetia

Pasanauri

Iori

Georgian Military Highway

Largvisi

Ksani

Pankisi Gorge

Alazani

Zhinvali Dam
Ananauri

A301

Dusheti
Zhinvali
Tianeti
Alaverdi

Bodorna
Kvetera
Sioni Reservoir
Akhmeta

Lake Bazaleti
Sioni

Kutaisi
De facto border
Samtavisi
Gori, Khashuri
Igoeti
Tsilkani
Bochorma
Telavi

Natakhtari Airfield
Saguramo
Tbilisi National Park
Metekhi
Kaspi
Mukhrani
Chardakhi
Iori
Gombori Pass 1650m
Akhalkalaki
Ksani
Shiom-ghvime
Mtkvari
Mtskheta
Gombori Pass 1650m
Ertatsminda
Zedazeni
St Anthony
Otaraani
Telavi
Armazi
Jvari
Martkopi

Digomi
Ujarma
Gurjaani, Sighnaghi
Khashmi
Ninotsminda

Algetis National Park
TBILISI
Tbilisi Sea
M27
Sagarejo
Manglisi

Betania
A302

Birtvisi
Orbeti
A303
Kojori
Rustavi
Rustavi
Tsalka

At km15.5/123.5 another road leads 8km west to **Lake Bazaleti**, formed according to legend by the tears of the Georgians at the death of Tamar's child; it's too full of weeds for swimming, but fishing is popular. The Bazaleti Lake Hotel complex (🕻 *32 275 5366;* w *bazaletilake.ge;* **$$$$**) has boats and bikes as well as a swimming pool and three-room apartments for four to five persons in four-star 'cottages', plus one- and two-room hotel suites; all prices include three meals a day. To the north of the lake is **Bodorna Monastery**, where the medieval domed Church of St Mary (rebuilt in the 18th century) has a row of hooks outside for hanging sacrificed sheep, and caves in oddly shaped yellow cliffs were used as refuges from the Tatars. Further north (10km from the lake) is **Dusheti**, which was the capital of the Aragvi princes in the 17th century and received a municipal charter late in the 18th century; now it's just a small village with some Art Nouveau buildings. From here it's 5km back to the Georgian Military Highway, at km19.

At km26/113 a minor road turns right to Tianeti (page 318) in Kakheti; after 2km a more minor road (now being paved) turns off to the left to follow the Pshavis Aragvi Valley to Khevsureti (pages 192–5). The Georgian Military Highway rises above the right bank to pass a monument to the 300 Aragveli (page 144) at km27 with a viewpoint to the **Zhinvali Dam** at km28; this has flooded the area of the confluence of the Aragvi and the Pshavis Aragvi, where the forested mountainsides begin to press in on either side. Companies from Tbilisi are now organising rafting trips on the Pshavis Aragvi.

ANANAURI The highway climbs along the hillside to km34/105 (where there's a café with good views), then descends past the crenellated Restaurant Ananauri (m *577 968896, 577 455022;* e *ananuri.rest@hotmail.com*) at km35/104, before dropping to cross a modern viaduct and reach the amazing churches of Ananauri just before km37 (ie: after km102 from the north; 45 minutes from Tbilisi). These stand within a crenellated wall at the head of the reservoir; the village, which stood below, has largely been destroyed and relocated to the north. Amazingly, it was seriously proposed to build the dam higher and flood the churches too, but a popular protest movement of a kind that was almost unheard of in Soviet times managed to defeat this plan.

The entrance on the south side of the wall leads you to the **lower church**, the larger and more recent of the two crammed together here. Dedicated to the Dormition of the Mother of God, it was built in 1689 and is big and bare inside, with two pillars supporting the barrel dome, and frescoes of saints and the Last Judgement on the south wall. The interior was damaged by fire in the 18th century, and many fine frescoes were lost. However, its carved external decorations are superb, above all on the south wall where a huge cross stands on the backs of two dragons, flanked by two vines (being eaten by deer) above two odd moustachioed angels and two lions; there's another angel up at the top left corner. The pagan elements in the design clearly show Persian influence. There are also stones with carved rams' heads, an older pagan motif, now piled up inside the gateway.

Immediately above this church is a 12th-century **watchtower**; the west wall of the church pressed up against this carries wonderful carvings, presumably for the eye of God alone. Above that is the smaller **Hvtaeba** or **Saviour's Church**, built in the 1650s. Although externally of stone, the interior is of brick and it too is bare, with the remaining frescoes largely ruined by graffiti, mainly Russian. It has a two-bay nave and aisles, with a barrel dome above the crossing, lit by deep-set lancet windows. At the top of the slope, set into the ring wall, is the solid Sheupovari (Intrepid) **tower**, which has five chambers, one above the other, all made safe with concrete and connected by wooden ladders. It's well worth climbing to the top for views of the church domes and the surrounding hills, and you can also walk most of the way around the battlements. At the lower end of the complex is a small 17th-century **bell-turret**, nowadays looking out over the lake as well as a ruined Armenian church. Down some steps by the bell-turret is a hiding place where soldiers could lurk before rushing out to attack intruders.

Ananauri was in the wars many times, most famously in 1717 when Prince Bardsig, the Eristav of Aragvi, seized the wife of Prince Chanche, Eristav of Ksani. Chanche allied himself with the Lesghians of the northern Caucasus, and captured Ananauri; he reclaimed his wife successfully, but the Muslim Lesghians burnt the churches and destroyed many of the frescoes.

In the village, just north, you'll find the Restaurant Mtiuleti (m 595 165124) and a couple of decent new guesthouses.

PASANAURI The road continues between thickly wooded hillsides that reminded Fitzroy Maclean of Perthshire. At km53 you'll see the first of the remaining watchtowers, which once stood at every curve in the valley, providing a relay chain of signal stations for times of danger. The only town between Mtskheta and Kazbegi is Pasanauri, which consists of just two streets, Rustaveli (northbound) and Kostava (southbound) between km59 and km60.

This is a climatic resort at 1,014m, where the White (Tetri) Aragvi, the main river, is joined by the Black (Shavi) Aragvi from the northeast; the water of the Black Aragvi is often noticeably darker, with the two flowing side by side before merging. There's little to do here other than rest and walk to the **Chabarukh Gorge** (where there's a waterfall) and the **Gudamakari Gorge** (following the track to Makari, northeast from the south end of town), and to the **Church of St George of Lomisi**, at 3,000m on a ridge to the west; this is the centre of a pagan cult, where boys are taken at the age of 11 or 12 for initiation, a ceremony apparently described by the anthropologist Margaret Mead.

Where to stay, eat and drink The Hotel Aragvi (*Rustaveli 77;* \ 92 0529; m 899 233220; $$) is very run-down, but there are various unpretentious family-run hotel-restaurants along the road just north, which provide decent and friendly accommodation. The Pasanauri area is famed for its khinkhali, so don't miss them. There are some truckstop restaurants just north of town, but it's worth pushing on to the rather surprising Hof Bräu München Gudauri (m 595 353113) at km 63/76, which really does serve fine Bavarian wheat beers with its khinkali; there's a footbridge to the left bank nearby if you want to walk it off afterwards.

Guesthouse Korugi (7 rooms) km62; m 599 540139, 579 540139; e korugi@pasanauri. ge; w pasanauri.ge. A large modern chalet which also offers rafting & mountain biking. $$

Hotel Kvesheti (14 rooms) km75; m 599 543288, 599 114377; w hotelkvesheti.com. A decent & fairly new place in spacious grounds; can arrange trekking, horseriding & rafting. Rates are HB. $$

GUDAURI Continuing northwards in the Mtiuleti district, the valley is still relatively wide. Small villages offer the occasional café (and the Hotel-Restaurant Aragvi at km72/67), while footbridges give access to walks up side-valleys to the east. Near km66 you'll see a watchtower high to the left; at km73 you'll see one to the right and another pair ahead, and near km74 there's a tower to the left. The road passes through the villages of **Naghvarevi** at km75–76 (followed by stalls selling conical sheepskin hats) and **Kvesheti**, with a chapel and a stumpy tower to the right; then there's another tower to the west, and after the bridge to Zemo (Upper) Mleta (1,556m; km79/60) there's a spring and roadside stalls selling drinks, woolly socks and sheepskin hats. The road then climbs 640m up the Mleti cliff, with the help of six hairpin bends from km82/57 to km87/52 (there's talk of building a long tunnel from here to Kazbegi beneath Gudauri). As you climb, Gudauri and the High Caucasus finally come into sight; first the Red Mountains, and then the Seven Brothers, both massive ranges of red volcanic rock. Near the top (just after a roadside shrine at a hairpin) is a viewing platform with metal rails giving great views as you lean out over the abyss.

At the top are the scattered Ossetian villages of Qumlistsikhe and then Gudauri which, at 2,000m, is the highest settlement on the Georgian Military Highway, and one of Georgia's two main ski resorts. Two hours or less from Tbilisi at km89/50, it's an unplanned mess: the centre is marked by a petrol station, supermarket and police post, with a road west to a new church and scattered chalets and hotels. Hairpin bends lead up to some modern hotels by the turning to New Gudauri, a big new apartment development (with restaurants and casino) 900m east at the mid-station of the chairlift and the base of the gondola, before leaving Gudauri at km 93/46.

Where to stay Prices for hotels are high, but most do include meals (normally breakfast and dinner in ski season). Alternatively, there are a few cheaper hostels.

Hotels

Hotel Carpe Diem (53 rooms) 32 251 0770; w carpediem.ge. 130m from the main road down the New Gudauri road near the top of the resort, this is a comfortable place with brightly coloured rooms & a decent restaurant; it's now being extended. $$$$$

Hotel Club 2100 (38 rooms) m 571 210000; w club-2100.com. New in 2013, this big, modern hotel above the centre of the resort (at 2,100m, of course, & km90.5) is non-smoking throughout & has a sauna/jacuzzi (⏰ 24hrs). You can also book through AlpinTravel (📞 +41 81 720 2121; w alpintravel.ch) who operate heli-skiing packages. $$$$$

Hotel Truso (14 rooms) 32 214 6900; m 599 276644; w hoteltruso.com. A simple, older place right in the centre, several hundred metres from the lifts. Restaurant, Wi-Fi, satellite TV & sauna. $$$$$

Marco Polo (123 rooms) 32 220 2900; m 599 111900; w marcopolo.ge/en. Turning right/east at the Wissol petrol station/Smart supermarket, there's a short, unsigned road to this 4-star establishment, built by an Austrian entrepreneur in 1988. It struggled in the absence of direct flights from western Europe, but it may now have a brighter future. Renovated in 2011, it offers all the comforts required of a hotel of this class, inc an indoor swimming pool & tennis

courts, gym, sauna & jacuzzi. Although primarily established for skiing (with the chairlift starting immediately behind the hotel), it's also an ideal base for walking & mountain-biking in summer. $$$$$

ApartHotel New Gudauri m 577 242012; e booking@newgudauri.ge. The centrepiece of the New Gudauri development, with luxury ski-in ski-out apartments (with kitchen) & upmarket Georgian/European restaurant. $$$$

Gudauri Hut (33 rooms) m 595 939911; e gudaurihut@gmail.com; w gudaurihut.com. Just above the police station in the centre, this is a biggish place with en-suite rooms with TV & there's a sauna in the basement. $$$$

Hotel Good Aura (16 rooms) m 571 503011; w hotelgoodaura.com. A modern place to the left behind the police station, there's a restaurant, sauna, climbing wall & transfers to the lifts. $$$$

Hotel Ozone (20 rooms) Qumlistsikhe km88; m 599 550983, 595 355112; e gakozon@ yandex.ru. Down at 1,850m, they provide a free shuttle to the chairlift, 500m away. There's a sauna & a bar in a separate building. $$$$

Hotel Soncho (19 rooms) m 595 968500 3; w gudauri.info/accommodation/hotels. At km92, just before the police post (with an English sign), an asphalt road turns right/east, leading in a couple of hundred metres to this biggish chalet-style building with a cosy lounge & en-suite twin rooms. Meals are about GEL10 each. **$$$$**

🏠 **Skihouse-Panorama** (10 rooms) Qumlistsikhe km88/51; m 599 330003; e hotelpanoramagudauri@hotmail.com; w skihouse-panorama.com. Run by a paraglider pilot, this hotel is right at the bottom of the resort (with a shuttle to the lifts); all rooms have satellite TV. It also has a minibus, a small pool & sauna. Rooms are FB, & are a little cheaper in Apr. **$$$$**

🏠 **Hotel Shamo** (16 rooms) m 599 500142; w allgudauri.ge. Further from the lifts in Qumlistsikhe, this family-run place has a lounge & bar, & offers good meals. Rates are HB. **$$$–$$$$**

Hostels

🏠 **Gagieti Hostel** (10 rooms) m 592 033600; e ninobuchukuri@gmail.com; w gagieti.ge. Immediately below the police station on the main road, this very welcoming place has a good

restaurant next door serving healthy food, organic where possible. Ski rental available. **$$$$**

🏠 **Gudauri Dacha** (5 rooms) m 597 032396, 599 096615; e gudauridacha@gmail.com; 🟦. This snowboarders' place has a couple of rooms with en-suite bathrooms while others have shared facilities; filling Georgian b/fasts & dinners. **$$$**

🏠 **Snow House** (10 rooms) m 599 170104, 599 153577; e snowhouse.gudauri@gmail.com; w snowhouse.ge. Above the centre near the mid-station of the lifts, this hostel also houses a ski-school & equipment rental, & for just US$5/ day extra you can avail yourself of an instructor's services. **$$$**

🏠 **Happy Yeti Hostel** (6 rooms) Qumlistsikhe; m 571 268800; e booking.gudauri@gmail.com; w happyyetihostel.com. Run by a Polish/Ukrainian crew, this comfortable, modern place has shared dorms each with their own bathroom, a pub & washing machine; 2 hearty meals inc. **$$–$$$**

✕ **Where to eat and drink** There are good restaurants at the **Hotel Truso**, **Gagieti Hostel** and the **Gudauri Hut**, all in the centre, just above the 24-hour Smart supermarket, which also has a café, and up at the Carpe Diem and New Gudauri. On the mountain, there are various places to eat near the lift stations, such as the renowned **Khade (or Khizhina) Hut** at 2,650m, which serves Georgian and Uzbek cuisine, as well as cocktails.

What to see and do In winter the place is heaving with skiers and snowboarders, of course, many of them from Poland and Ukraine. The Sukhia ski race, effectively the Georgian championship, is held here in odd years (in even years it's in Bakuriani). There are two main ways up the mountain: first, the 1,010m Pirveli chairlift runs from the main resort (behind the Marco Polo hotel at 1,990m) to the mid-station, from where you can take the 2,310m Soliko lift to Khade (2,650m; see above), and then the Kudebe lift to Mt Kudebe (3,006m); alternatively take either the Gudaura (aka Good Aura) ten-seat gondola from New Gudauri or the new Shino chairlft from near the Hotel Cross Pass on the Military Highway, then the Snow Park and Sadzele lifts up to Sadzele West (3,279m, below the 3,307m peak of Mt Sadzele), from where skiers have a vertical drop of almost 1km. There are 57km of pistes, the longest at 5km, with plenty of snow from late December until the end of April. Most of the runs are in the area below Khade and the Snow Park, where mountain bike trails were added in 2015. **Night skiing** is available, as well as **heli-skiing** (from 4,200m), with Heliksir (*Pekini 28, Tbilisi;* ✆ *32 224 3503;* m *595 350900;* w *heliski.travel*). Gear can be rented through hotels and hostels, at the bases of the lifts and from Mogzauri (m *568 659985, 592 778856;* w *mogzaurirent. ge*). Instruction is available through hotels and hostels or from Kankavebi (m *599 153577*), Mtis Skola (m *599 929113*) or Skiniki (m *599 364647*).

A ski pass for the 2017/18 season was GEL40/day or GEL232/week (GEL190 for 5 days in a week); the chairlifts run from 10.00 to 16.00 (to 17.00 in April) and on Saturdays from 19.30 to 22.00, and in summer from 11.00 to 16.00 (*GEL7, day GEL15*).

In summer you could stop for mountain biking (with a couple of lifts working) or the odd day's **hiking**, but not more. It's possible, on foot or horseback, to cover the distance between the Khade Hut and the Khade Gorge (1,600m) in about 3 hours. The Khade Gorge still has more than 50 defensive towers in seven villages. A 12km dirt road leads down to Kvesheti on the highway below the Mleti cliff. **Paragliding** is possible all year with experienced pilots, from GEL200 – contact Fly Gudauri (m *568 114453*; w *flygudauri.com*), the Georgian Paragliding Federation (m *598 403606*; ▓), Wild Guru (m *595 162255*; w *wildguru.com*) or Mykhaylo Aleksyeyenko (▓ *myxacc*).

INTO THE TERGI VALLEY From Gudauri, the road climbs slightly to an avalanche gallery then dips briefly into the Devil's Valley, which as the poet Lermontov explains is really a mistranslation of Frontier Valley; above to the right is the original Russian road, which makes a pleasant short hike. From a car park at km96 an asphalt path leads to the left to a large viewing platform looking over the 'Stone Chaos' of the Gudaur Abyss 500m below and the 'zebra-striped' summit of Gud-Gura opposite. If the view is too much for you, there's a 70m-long Soviet mural on the inside of the platform, known as the Soviet-Georgian Friendship Monument, created in 1983 to celebrate the 200th anniversary of the Treaty of Gurgievsk; some of the colour has gone but the outlines are clear.

From here it's not far up to the **Jvaris Ughelt** or Cross Pass, better known in Russian as the Krestovy Pereval (2,395m), at km98.5 (127km from Tbilisi); often closed between November and May, it's the highest point of the route and there are many fine descriptions, notably by Lermontov and Dumas, of the struggle to cross the pass in foul weather. There's a small marker at the pass on the present road, but visible to the east immediately north of the pass is the cross erected by Yermolov in 1824, replacing the so-called Tamar's Cross, in fact erected by King David the Builder. This stands on the old road, rather higher than the present one, and is visible from the Devil's Valley at the top of a steep rise.

Descending the Bidara Valley into the watershed of the Tergi (Terek in Russian) River, you'll pass five avalanche galleries, which traffic uses only in winter; you could hike the old road, across the valley to the left. The alpine meadows are interrupted (high on the slopes to the left and between the bottom two galleries) by rocks stained red by the sweet mineral waters that are common here; the bearded vultures seem to dye their 'beards' red by drinking the iron-rich water.

Almasiani (1,960m), the first part of the village of **Khobi**, lies to the left of the road at a police post (km106.5/32.5), by some caravan-cafés. This is the start of a superb hike (marked by yellow signs from the junction) to the west up the **Truso Gorge** (nicely described by Tony Anderson as 'a geological fantasy on the duel between water and rock'), which follows a dirt track alongside the Tergi for 3km to the village of Nogkau. Beyond here there was until recently only a 4x4 track through the very tight gorge to the historically Ossetian hamlets of Ketrisi, Abano and Resi in the lovely wide upper valley. Now, a new road goes over the ridge to the south from Nogkau, but it is also possible to hike through the gorge for about 3km from Kvemo Okrokana to a collapsed bridge. Otherwise a taxi (page 186) will take you most of the way to Ketrisi, beyond which you can walk past a monastery, the hamlet of Abano (ie: Bath) and a tiny nunnery (with just three nuns, tucked alongside a defensive tower) and then the border post at Zakagori, which is as far as you can go (although the guards should let you go up to a ruined fortress on the hill to the right). This is wonderfully spectacular scenery, with the steep slopes of this glacial valley on the southwestern flank of Mount Kazbek rising high above the defensive towers of the villages; there are many more mineral springs at the foot of the cliffs to the south side. The valley is an excellent spot to see bearded vultures and brightly coloured alpine specialities like wallcreepers. There's good camping here too, unlike the Sno Valley where you allegedly need to keep a fire alight all night to keep wolves away. The upper valley is inhabited in summer by Ossetians, and the borders of South and North Ossetia meet at the top of the valley; do not go beyond the Georgian border post (which makes a pleasant day hike) unless you have a permit from the Ministry of Internal Affairs. With camping gear it's also possible to follow the Esikomi valley south from Ketrisi to the barren Keli volcanic plateau and the glacial Kelitsadi lake, with great views north to Mount Kazbek.

At about km107 the Military Highway crosses two bridges and passes the second part of Khobi (1,932m); you'll have your first view of the immense Mount Kazbek ahead (just as on the beer labels), before the road passes through the Baidari Gorge (named after Toti Baidarashvili, an Ossetian mountaineer posted here in the 18th century by King Erekle to rescue travellers from snow). The only villages are away to the west, perched on the cliff on the left bank of the Tergi, and reached by a loop road from a new bridge just before km113.

The next village by the road (148km from Tbilisi) is **Sioni**, where you'll see the church and watchtower on a crag overlooking the road (at km116/23) more or less opposite the turning to a bridge to the villages across the river; to reach them you need to continue to a junction after a green caravan. From here, head right/east for 700m to a T-junction, then follow the road back southwards for 1km, all on asphalt except for the final zigzags up to the church. This is a three-naved basilica built in the late 9th and early 10th centuries; externally it is quite rectangular, although internally there is an apse behind the altar, as well as a five-arched stone iconostasis. The watchtower, beyond an abandoned modern building, is a late medieval construction; at ground level there's no door (a ladder having been used for access), but tasteless Russian graffiti instead.

SNO AND JUTA The northern end of Sioni is **Arsha**, where there's a 9th–10th-century fortress, a fine restaurant (page 187), a couple of guesthouses and the Hotel Tergi (*km119*; m *555 237000, 599 321313*; e *levan_pitskhelauri@yahoo.com*; **$$**), which is simple, friendly and very cheap. Just to the north (before km120/19), a road leads east through Achkhoti, just off the highway, and to the villages of Sno and Juta, another highly recommended hiking route (you can start from the north side of the bridge at km122). **Sno**, where the asphalt ends, is about 4km along the wide glaciated valley, beyond a bizarre sculpture park that has the heads of local writers strewn around the hillside like glacial boulders, as well as pagan stone altars that women are not permitted to approach; nevertheless, it's the birthplace of Ilia, the Catholicos of the Georgian Church. There's a ruined fortress (built in the 16th or 17th century) within a circular wall by the bridge in the centre of the village, a couple of guesthouses and not a lot else.

From Akhaltsikhe (2km beyond Sno), it's possible to hike south through the Artkhmo gorge to the abandoned villages of Miguda and Artkhmo, with some striking waterfalls. It's about 16km further to the end of the side road at **Juta**, the highest village in the area at 2,200m and one of the highest in Europe (pages 279 and 325). It is home to 20 Khevsur extended families (just three in winter), mostly named Arabuli on account of having traded with 'Arab' caravans, living in solid houses with verandas; transfers from Kazbegi can be arranged with Mountain Freaks (page 186). Otherwise it's a 4-hour hike, or GEL40–50 by taxi (*45mins*). Immediately southeast of Juta is the seven-peaked Mount Chaukhi (3,842m), *right*　Traditional clay *qvevri* vessels are key to the huge revival in natural wines in Georgia (MPa/S) pages 80–4

below　At Tbilisi's Dry Bridge flea market you can buy carpets, Stalin busts, houses and flats, bad art and anything else you want (MPa/S) pages 133–4

bottom　*Churchkhela*, made of nuts on a string dipped several times into grape juice, are the symbol of the autumn grape harvest (MM/S) page 79 above left **Making *khachapuri*** (SS) pages 78–9

above right **Chess players in Sukhumi, Abkhazia** (SS) pages 259–60

below left **Carding wool in Svaneti** (TH)

below right **Harvesting Rkatsiteli grapes** (SS) page 83

above left   Man wearing the traditional Svan felt hat (TH) page 266

above right   Adjaran dancing, from the southwest of Georgia, is even more athletic and exhibitionist than elsewhere in the country (tk/S)

right   Musicians playing the *duduki*, a clarinet-like pipe from Armenia, at Davit-Gareja Monastery (AC/A) page 52

below   Men singing and playing the panduri (VZ/S) page 52 *above*   The Bagrat Cathedral, controversially refurbished and re-roofed, overshadows the city of Kutaisi (t79/S) page 234

left   Tbilisi's Orbeliani Baths are covered in intricately patterned tiles (S27/D) page 127

below   Surami Fortress, the former residence of the Dukes of Kartli, has given rise to a legend that a young man was built into its walls to preserve them (AB/D) page 176

above   The stunning Koruldi Lakes are the goal of one of the most popular hikes in Svaneti (s3p/S) pages 274–6

left   The High Caucasus offers a range of beautiful and exciting hikes for all levels of ability (RO/S)

below   Borjomi-Kharagauli National Park is a protected wilderness area that is home to a vast variety of habitats (B/S) pages 201–6

above   Traditional life continues all year round in
          Ushguli, one of Europe's highest villages (TH)
          pages 279–82

right   At 2,000m, Gudauri is Georgia's main ski resort
          (A/D) pages 182–3

below   Tusheti National Park is one of the remotest and
          most beautiful parts of Georgia, being accessible
          by road for only a few months of the year (SS)
          pages 319–26

above left   Bearded vulture or lammergeyer (*Gypaetus barbatus*) (E/S) page 12
top right   White-winged redstart (*Phoenicurus erythrogaster*) (LB/D) page 13
above right   Caucasian snowcock (*Tetraogallus caucasicus*) (EM/S) page 12

the north face of which offers 800m-high cliffs for climbers (best in September/October). There are a few basic **homestays ($$)** in the village; ask for Soso Arabuli (m *595 515149*), Iago Arabuli (m *599 533239, 593 422951*) or Maia Chincharauli (m *593 203716*). In summer, you can also stay in a hut or big solid tents at Zeta Camp (m *577 501057*; e *zetacamp@yahoo.com*; w *zeta.ge*; **$$**), which offers organic meals and hot showers, in a stunning setting a 10-minute hike up the Chaukhistskali valley southeast from Juta at 2,300m. You can also push on for another 10 minutes to the Fifth Season guesthouse (m *555 011515*; e *arabuli.gela@gmail.com*; f *fifth. season.juta*; **$$**), a traditional stone house newly built by hand that's a popular hangout for artists escaping Tbilisi in summer (in fact some just come for the day).

A well-marked track leads on for 5km to a climbers' campsite at 2,250m on a plateau below the Chaukhi Massif, where there's lots of good, accessible climbing (it's also possible to camp right below the massif at 2,600m). This is also the most direct hiking route (from July on) to Pshavi (page 193), taking just 10 hours to Roshka (page 194) via the Chaukhi or Roshka Pass (3,056m). It's a steady 4-hour climb to the pass, then there's a very steep loose descent (much worse in the other direction, especially as Roshka is almost 400m lower than Juta), so this route is not passable for horses. In any case it's more interesting to cross the Juta Pass (3,287m) north to the headwaters of the River Assa and Akhieli (just four houses and an abandoned tall tower); it's part of the three-hamlet community of Arkhoti, a beautiful valley (with gorges, waterfalls and perfect peace) that's very isolated, with fairly easy access to Ingushetia to the north but only two hard passes into Georgia to the south. From Juta it's 21km or a day's hike each way to Arkhoti, or 52km (four days) as a loop via the two passes. It's a 10-hour hike across the Arkhotis Pass (2,935m) south to Roshka. It's also possible to hike south along a pony track from between Sno and Juta over the 2,347m Gudamakari Pass (page 180) to the Black Aragvi Valley and Pasanauri.

STEPANTSMINDA (KAZBEGI)
სტეფანწმინდა (ყაზბეგი) *Telephone code 245*

Another 4.5km brings you to Stepantsminda (Kazbegi), at 1,797m and km124/15 (153km from Tbilisi); this is the only town in Khevi province (or Mokhavia) and the only place with anything resembling shops and accommodation. However, with a population of just 2,000 and relatively little through traffic to Russia, commercial opportunities are inevitably limited, although it's worth looking for the local woollens, such as socks and hats.

It's a small, sleepy place, dominated by free-range highland cattle and pigs. Known in the 19th century as Stepan-Tsminda (St Stephen), the town was then named after Alexander Kazbegi (or Qazbegi; 1848–93), a local noble who became a much-loved pastoral poet, living as a shepherd for seven years; it has now reverted to Stepantsminda, but Kazbegi remains the more widely used name. The square, dominated by a monument to Kazbegi, is lined with 4x4 taxis and marshrutkas, as well as a couple of cafés and hotels.

GETTING THERE AND AWAY **Marshrutkas** leave from the Didube terminal in Tbilisi every hour until 19.00, as well as shared taxis from the same place; services back from Stepantsminda leave hourly from the square. Others run from Tbilisi as far as Pasanauri, and one goes as far as Gudauri, returning at about 16.00. If you want to go from Kazbegi to Gudauri you may be forced to pay the full fare to Tbilisi, although there are shuttles in ski season, taking half an hour (Kazbegi is very cold in winter, as low as −26°C, but accommodation is cheap). Marshrutkas take 2½–3 hours and charge GEL10; **shared taxis** (which might even stop for you to take a photo) charge GEL15. A taxi from Tbilisi airport will cost at least GEL200, as will a minivan (up to seven passengers) with driver from Tbilisi. There are local marshrutkas south from Stepantsminda as far as Khobi, but none goes northwards.

TOUR OPERATORS Various operators in Tbilisi (pages 59–60) offer multi-day trips to climb Mount Kazbek. Above the Khevi restaurant on the main square in Stepantsminda you'll find the **Mountain Travel Agency** (*Kazbegi 29;* m *555 649291, 599 269291;* e *dkhetaguri@gmail.com;* w *mtainfogeo.com*) who have guides available, as well as climbing gear, bikes, tents and horses (the name is a pun, as Mta means mountain). Alongside is **Mkinvari Rental** (*Kazbegi 26;* m *579 951771;* **f** *bikerentalmkinvari*), renting hiking and climbing gear and mountain bikes, and across the road is **Mountain Freaks** (m *593 583596;* w *mountainfreaks.ge*), a Polish company whose main office is just south of the square, which has guides and gear to rent too, and also operates the very useful shuttles to Juta and Truso (both GEL25 return, leaving at 09.00, returning at 17.00, perhaps more in summer), as well as up the Dariali Gorge to the north (GEL25; leaving at 12.30, returning at 15.30). Alternatively, a taxi to Truso or Juta should cost GEL80.

Rafting is available with **Rafting Camp Kazbegi** (m *595 983738;* **f**); it's also possible to rent horses, either through these agencies, by asking at your guesthouse, or by calling the number posted on notices in the centre of town.

WHERE TO STAY As well as the hotels, there are various homestays in Stepantsminda village and better ones across the river in Gergeti. Naturally, it is always worth looking at the rooms and checking out facilities like hot water before making a commitment. Prices are fairly standard: around GEL20 for a bed or GEL30–40 for half-board. There's also **Kuro Camping** (m *592 006363;* e *kurocamping@gmail.com;* **f**), a 10-minute walk north beyond the museum, where camping costs GEL13 per person, a bed in a hut GEL17, or a triple room GEL60; there's a 24-hour bar and free Wi-Fi.

Hotels

✳ 🏠 **Rooms Hotel Kazbegi** (156 rooms) Gorgasali 1; ☏ 32 271 0099, 32 240 0099; w roomshotels.com/kazbegi. Now one of Georgia's finest hotels, it's hard to believe that this was once a run-of-the-mill Intourist block. Up a cobbled street just north of the square (before Liberty Bank), a right & a left & a surprisingly bad road leads up to the hotel on the left, a 10–15min hike (or a taxi) above the town. Inside, the ground floor is a lovely flexible library-style space with roaring fires & views across the valley to Kazbek & the Gergeti Church. There's a bar with hipster staff, sofas & shared tables, & more of a real restaurant beyond the bar, though still informal. There's a casino too, but it's unobtrusive. The terrace, & below it, the swimming pool (& sauna) also have superb views to Kazbek. Bedrooms, also with views of Kazbek, are spacious & comfortable,

although missing details such as bedside lights. **$$$$$**

🏠 **Hotel-Restaurant Stepantsminda** (20 rooms) m 599 646880, 182296; e kazbegihotels@yahoo.com. This comfortable hotel on the square has large en-suite rooms, with a decent restaurant & stunning views. Mainly used by groups but it may have short-notice availability. English is spoken (ask for Nata). **$$$**

🏠 **Shorena's Hostel** ☏ 345 252607; m 598 398274, 599 074074; e shorenashoka@gmail. com; **f** ShorenasHotelBarRestaurrant [sic]. At the south end of the square, a friendly little place with a lively bar-restaurant. **$$$**

🏠 **Uptown Boutique Kazbegi** (9 rooms) Vazha-Pshavelas 14; m 551 901085; e uptownkazbegi@gmail.com; **f**. Just uphill of the central square, this is not all boutique but has pleasant rooms (all but 2 en suite) & a pleasantly hostel-like bar (with a wall for guests to leave messages on); excellent b/fast. **$$$**

🏠 **Hotel-Restaurant Easy** Kazbegi 15; m 597 433483, 592 901928; e info@hoteleasy. ge. Just north of the centre before the bridge, this is a decent new place (not huge) with plenty of parking space & a good view towards Kazbek; friendly English-speaking owner. **$$–$$$**

🏠 **Soul Kazbegi Hostel** (2 rooms, & dorms) Kazbegi 4; m 551 901085, 597 152991; w soulkazbegiguesthouse.com. A clean & sleek hostel, with 4-bed dorms & dbl & trpl, & shared kitchen. If no-one is around, ask at the Uptown Boutique Kazbegi hotel. **$**

Homestays

🏠 **Anano** Vazha-Pshavelas 7; m 595 099449, 593 344274, 598 589662; e ananoqushasvili@ yahoo.com. Actually up an alley opposite No 9, this guesthouse has rooms with private bathrooms & also offers tours; b/fast is an extra GEL10. **$$**

🏠 **Ketino Sujashvili** Kvemo Gergeti 22; m 571 032439; e ketinosujashvili@mail.ru; ⬛ ketino. sujashvili. On the 1st road left after the bridge (ie: below Khevisberi), this is a wonderfully welcoming guesthouse where you'll find great food & can learn to cook dishes such as khinkali as well. **$$**

🏠 **Nini's Guesthouse** Vazha-Pshavelas 56; m 599 191396, 599 975691; ⬛. A big place with 20 rooms, some with private bathroom, & a shared kitchen, balcony and garden. **$$**

🏠 **Nunu Maisuradze** Kazbegi Lane ✆ 345 252593; m 599 570915, 558 358535. This homestay is just off the main road leading up

from the main square, & has rooms with shared & private bathrooms & a shared kitchen (b/fast & dinner also available); there's also space for camping, and they have 4x4 vehicles for tours. **$–$$**

🏠 **Gogi Alibegashvili** Tabidze 44. An attractive big house on the 6th street up to the east (fantastic views) with Wi-Fi but no English spoken. **$**

🏠 **Guesthouse Gergeti** Khevisberi 3; ✆ 345 252480; m 598 382700, 599 265813; e ssujashvili@yahoo.co.uk; w hotelgergeti.com. Clearly signposted on the 2nd street to the left in Gergeti, this is a welcoming guesthouse, also known as Nazi Chkareuli's or Shorena Sujashvili's homestay. It's very popular with backpackers & somewhat crowded, with shared & private bathrooms. Meals available, or there's a shared kitchen plus a washing machine. **$**

🏠 **HQ of Nove Sujashvili** Khevisberi 27; ✆ 345 252418; m 595 177079, 593 392278. One of the best homestays (although oddly named), this is across the river in Gergeti, about a 15min walk from the square – head north across the bridge on the road to Russia, turn left & after crossing a stream either go diagonally left up a path between 2 walls & turn left, or keep going & take the road to the left. In either case, it's a decent 2-storey house just up to the right, opposite a cross & above No 25. They have 4- & 8-bed dorms & a private dbl, or you can camp in the garden, below a cliff with fine vertical strata. English is spoken, & Nana knows a lot about traditional cures & recipes. **$**

✖ **WHERE TO EAT AND DRINK** For food, meals at your hotel or guesthouse are the best bet, although there are one or two places on the main square.

✖ **Restaurant Khevi** Kazbegi 29 (on the square); m 551 171736, 598 259330; ⬛; ⊕ 09.00–22.00 daily. Slightly more modern & upmarket than Shorena's, this has zero atmosphere but does serve decent & authentic food. **$$**

✖ **Tsanareti** Arsha; ✆ 551 606112; ⊕ 09.00– 23.00 daily. On the Military Highway 4km south, this is the best restaurant in the area, a large & shabby establishment (divided into smaller rooms) that serves large portions of superb mountain food, notably khinkali, khachapuri cooked on a stick over an open fire, kuserbo (shredded fried potato with salty cheese) & chmerkuli (fried

chicken with a sauce of sour cream, garlic, & walnuts). **$$**

✖ **Cozy Corner** m 593 787745; ⊕ 10.00–22.00. Immediately across the bridge to the north on the Georgian Military Highway, this serves some of the best food in town (including fresh trout), but service can be poor. **$**

✖ **Shorena's** See opposite for contact details; ⊕ 08.00–23.00 daily. This friendly restaurant-bar at the hostel of the same name serves huge portions of the classic Georgian dishes; English spoken. **$**

OTHER PRACTICALITIES A few minimarket-type shops just north of the central square sell the usual range of goods; there's no obligation to patronise the one that calls itself 'Tourist Shop'. There are **exchange kiosks** on the square giving poor rates, but there is now also an **ATM** at Liberty Bank, just north. There's a **post office** (⊕ *09.00–17.00 Mon–Fri, 09.00–15.00 Sat*) further north just beyond the museum, and a hospital to the west at the south end of town, opposite the police station.

WHAT TO SEE AND DO At the far end of the square the Georgian Military Highway forks left, while the road to the right leads past the church and behind this what remains of the lower terminal of the former cable car to the **Stepantsminda Museum** (⊕ *10.00–17.00 exc Mon; GEL3*). The church is a very simple basilica, built in 1814, with a few nice external carvings and a separate gate-tower. The museum (currently closed for refurbishment) is in a large stone building at Kazbegi 2 with a veranda and attractive garden with Kazbegi's grave. Downstairs are manuscripts, photos of Kazbegi and his three brothers whose home this was, and stills from films of his stories, and upstairs is his furniture. The ethnographic section has material on the Mokheve people, the gates of the Betlemi Monastery and information on the 'Kazbegi Treasure', a hoard of gold and bronze. Beyond the museum the road splits, with the town hall ahead and the post office to the right.

Immediately to the south of the church is Rustaveli kucha, just south of which, one block above the square (*at Vazha-Pshavelas 24*) is the **Kazalikashvili Museum of Alpinism** (ie: mountaineering), which is small and run-down and may be left open and untended (or, equally, locked and untended), but gives a good insight into the allure of rock and ice.

For a short **local walk**, a good option is to head up to the graveyard that stands above Stepantsminda to the northeast. Simply make for the massive Rooms Hotel (page 186) and just beyond it you will come to a gate into the cemetery. There are superb morning views over the village, Gergeti and Mount Kazbek from here; the graves, some quite elaborate with etched faces copied from photographs of the deceased, are also interesting. A track continues up to the hilltop shrine of Elia, with views towards Mount Kazbek.

Kazbegi Nature Reserve

The Kazbegi Nature Reserve was established in 1976, covering an area of 8,707ha. It lies at the divide between the Central and Eastern Caucasian ranges, with average precipitation in Kazbegi town of 640mm/year and temperatures of –5.2°C in January and 14.4°C in August (an annual average of 4.9°C). At 3,652m (the Gergeti glacier weather station) it's far colder, with temperatures of –15°C in January, 3.4°C in August, and an annual average of –6.1°C.

There are 1,347 plant species in the reserve, of which 105 are trees. Around half the trees are birch, with pine, beech, and large areas of Rhododendron caucasicum, and smaller areas of barberry, buckthorn, aspen, willow, maple and juniper. There are many alpine flowers in the hay meadows, with campanulas and gentians above the treeline, and cushion alpines on the scree slopes. Mammals include the brown bear (*Ursus arctos*), Caucasian goat or tur (*Capra caucasica*), chamois (*Rupicapra rupicapra*), hare (*Lepus europaeus*), fox (*Vulpes vulpes*), marten (*Martes martes*), weasel (*Mustela nivalis*), wildcat (*Felis silvestris*), squirrel (*Sciurus* sp) and birch mouse (*Sicista kazbegica*).

Bird species include lots of raptors, such as the bearded vulture or lammergeyer (*Gypaetus barbatus*), Egyptian vulture (*Neophron percnopterus*), Eurasian black vulture (*Aegypius monachus*), Eurasian griffon vulture (*Gyps fulvus fulvus*), golden eagle (*Aquila chrysaetus fulva*), imperial eagle (*A. heliaca*), lesser spotted eagle (*A. pomarina*), white-tailed eagle (*Haliaetus albicilla*), pallid harrier (*Circus macrourus*), long-legged buzzard (*Buteo rufinus*), lesser kestrel (*Falco naumanni*), peregrine (*Falco peregrinus*); also the jay (*Garrulus glandarius krynicki*), black francolin (*Francolinus francolinus*), chukar (*Alectoris chukar*), Caucasian snowcock (*Tetraogallus caucasicus*), Caucasian black grouse (*Tetrao mlokosiewicz*), great rosefinch (*Carpodacus rubicilla*), black redstart (*Phoenicurus ochruros semirufus*), white-winged redstart (*Phoenicurus erythrogaster*), red-fronted serin (*Serinus pusillus*), water pipit (*Anthus spinoletta*), white-throated dipper (*Cinclus cinclus caucasicus*) and the occasional ring ouzel (*Turdus torquatus amicorum*).

The meadows are presently overgrazed and increasingly suffering from erosion; from Kazbegi southwards sheep flocks migrate along the verges of the Georgian Military Highway in spring and autumn as they move between their home villages and the high meadows, and the damage done can easily be seen. On the other hand, the provision of natural gas has reduced the damage done to forests by the cutting of fuel wood. The WWF (Worldwide Fund for Nature) is involved with projects here, including an ecotourism scheme. GCCW (the Georgian Centre for the Conservation of Wildlife) is also active, bringing groups of birders almost daily in May and June, and the economic impact has largely ended the poaching of Caucasian snowcock. June and July are also a good time to visit, with the rhododendron in bloom.

The Gergeti hike

The WWF started conservation work in Kazbegi, but has now been replaced by the US Agency for International Development (USAID); they did produce a map of hiking routes up the Truso Valley and to the Gergeti and Devdoraki glaciers but this is no longer available. The Gergeti route is an extension of the near-compulsory excursion to the Gergeti Trinity Church, which sits high on a ridge west of the town of Kazbegi, silhouetted against the massive bulk of Mount Kazbek. This was reached by a cable car built in 1988 and very soon abandoned; no-one here ever wanted it, seeing it as an imposition from outside and an assault on the religious identity of the Gergeti Church. The lower terminal behind the Kazbegi Church is now derelict, while the upper one beside the Gergeti Church has already virtually vanished.

North towards the church (*1hr 15mins; moderate*) The route starts by taking the Georgian Military Highway north from the square in Kazbegi and across the Tergi and turning left up the road to the attractive mountain village of Gergeti; this road is being paved as far as the village, but a totally new route is being built in the valley just to the north and up to the Sameba (Trinity) church, to cope with the huge numbers of 4x4 taxis that now bring tourists there. Following the road up the left/south side of the village, heading straight for the church, you'll come to a point where a ruined defensive tower can be seen in a small side valley to the left (with a sign to a car park and the Café-bar Gergeti); although it is possible to go up here on a steep path to the rear/west of the Trinity Church, it's far easier to turn right to cross on the level through the village and then swing up to the left, following green arrows with the Kazbegi Brewery logo. From here a track leads up to the village cemetery, about 30 minutes from Kazbegi. Sticking to the very rough jeep track, just above the village at 1,900m you'll pass the **Kazbegi Mountain Hut** (m 599 497764; w *kazbegi-hut.ge*; ⊕ *May–Oct*), funded by USAID, where you can ask for information and arrange a climbing guide (*US$100/day*) and rent gear; there's also accommodation (*GEL25 pp*).

At the cemetery, just above, the path crosses a jeep track and climbs past crooked birch (*Betula litwinowii*) then pine trees, with Caucasian chiffchaffs and green warblers, reaching the jeep track again in 20 minutes. From here the most direct route is to head left for 5 minutes and then take a steep path up through the forest for 5 more minutes (a minimum of 1hr from Kazbegi); this emerges from scrubby birch and on to the ridge, where you'll see the church to the left, less than 10 minutes away across the alpine grassland.

An easier route is to head to the right on the track, which loops up to the left to reach the ridge in 15–20 minutes (with short cuts possible).

The churchyard is entered through a gate-tower (with a chimney shaft) which opens directly on to a blind porch on the south side of the church; the main door is to the west. The Church of Tsminda Sameba or Holy Trinity was built in the 14th century, with the tower added a century later, and a big separate belfry; it's a remarkably large construction for such an isolated location, at 2,170m. In fact the ruins of another church were found in 1913 at 3,962m on the slopes of Mount Kazbek. Paganism is alive and well in these remote areas, with crosses made of rams' horns; when I was first here a freshly decapitated sheep's head sat on the parapet of the churchyard. Monks live all year round just below the church, and there are even reports of solar panels. The church's festival is held on 28 August, when sheep are sacrificed (attracting vultures for the next day or two). There are some decayed frescoes, and postcards for sale in the church, but the magnificent setting is the main attraction.

Above the church (*2hrs 45mins; moderate–hard*) Coming out of the church and turning left at a pile of stones, follow the gravel track which drops briefly then climbs up into the woods; turn left onto a path at the hairpin bend and then choose either the steadier climber's route or the more spectacular route along the Sabertse ridge, leading westwards just above the treeline (with a steep drop to the north but pastures and alpine flowers to the south). These paths meet at the Arsha pass (2,940m), where you get a view to the Gergeti glacier and back down to the church. Day-hikers can turn back here, or it's possible to camp on the meadows below the glacier at around 3,000m, 3 hours (10.5km) from the village of Gergeti; the new AltiHut 3014 should open here in the summer of 2018, at a height of, yes, 3014m. Near the snout of the glacier it's easy to see Caucasian snowcock, wallcreepers, snowfinch, twite, Guldenstadt's redstart and great rosefinch, as well as lammergeyer and griffon vulture soaring overhead. Only those experienced on ice, or with competent guides, should continue up the moraine on the right/south side of the glacier (about 7.3km long but retreating fast, and criss-crossed with crevasses) and then across it to reach the huge former meteorological station, which was the highest in the Soviet Union at 3,652m. Since 1998 it's been a basic climbers' hut, known as Mtis Qokhi Betlemi or the **Betlemi Hut** (m *599 497764;* f *BethlemiHut*); there are about 50 beds (book through MTA in Kazbegi), and it's also possible to sleep on a mattress on the floor; there's heat and light (to 23.00) and a kitchen of sorts, but no running water and no food available. A volunteer Polish mountain rescue team is usually based here. Camping is possible at the hut or below the Black Cross at 3,880m (where there are stone windbreak walls), but it can be very windy indeed.

Nearby, at 4,100m, is the **Betlemi (Bethlehem) Cave**, the setting of Ilia Chavchavadze's poem *The Hermit*, where a metal chapel has been deposited by helicopter.

Mount Kazbek, more properly known in Georgian as Mkinvartsveri ('Ice-Top'), is a long-extinct volcano 5,047m in altitude, and is by far the highest peak in this section of the Caucasus. It's laden with mythology, first of Amirani, the Georgian Prometheus, who was chained to the mountain as a punishment for his pride and whose shape can be made out in the rock from far away, and second of the tent of Abraham which was said to stand on the summit, protecting the Holy Manger, or the Tree of Life – or treasure. There are also legends of lost treasure connected with the Betlemi Cave.

Kazbek was first climbed in 1868 by Douglas Freshfield with colleagues from the Alpine Club of London and guides from Kazbegi; it's a UIAA (International Climbing and Mountaineering Federation) grade II climb (PD, with just 100m of ice climbing in the final couloir where there's usually a fixed rope) and is best tackled between June and early October (ski-touring is possible from March); the classic route on the icy south face is UIAA grade III+. Kazbek is far easier than peaks such as Uzhba in Svaneti, but around 50% of climbers fail to reach the summit. The climb takes four days as a rule – one day to the hut, one day training and acclimatising (perhaps going to the Betlemi Cave), one day to the summit and back to the hut, and half a day to return to town. It's a 1,855m climb from the town of Kazbegi to the Betlemi Hut – a good day's work if carrying food and climbing gear, although pack-horses are available as far as the hut – and 1,381m more to the summit. It's possible to climb from the hut to the summit and back in an 8–12-hour day, starting by 04.00. You'll need to rope up on the glacier and keep well left beneath the crumbling Khmaura Wall, which will be spewing rocks and dust onto you on the descent, then follow small cairns on the glacier, zigzagging through the crevasses, up to the Maili plateau (c4,580m; there can be Russian border guards here!); from here a narrow path climbs to the base of the summit and the final 40° ice couloir.

It's also possible to turn left at the top of the glacier to climb Ortsveri (4,258m), another UIAA grade II peak, which makes a useful warm-up.

The Arsha hike (*Full day; no experience needed*) This is actually a very pleasant and easy stroll (now signed as a mountain-bike trail) up the west side of the Tergi Valley to the south of Kazbegi. An obvious 4x4 track starts from the road bridge at the north end of Kazbegi; it's also possible to start from the homestays on Khevisberi in Gergeti, simply turning right and following the track southwards, to reach the floodplain after 5 minutes. From here a gravel track leads south but you'll soon take a path to the right to reach an obvious wellhead, surrounded by boggy patches and pools full of frogs and tadpoles, after 10 minutes; it's another 5 minutes to a modern pool (about 15m by 30m) beneath a scree slope, full of fresh-tasting mineral water, by an unfinished concrete building. It's a good place to relax and watch the vultures soaring above.

Continuing, you'll join a gravel track below a tiny, recently restored chapel and a defensive tower, passing the few houses of Pansheti village, and reaching a junction after 20 minutes; turning left you'll cross a new road bridge to reach the highway at km121/18, 3km south of Kazbegi and a few hundred metres north of the junction to Sno. Carrying on along the west side of the valley, you'll pass 1½ towers (and the starts of some good paths up into the mountains), go through a hamlet, and then briefly go up to the right above a marsh and past a cross, before following a gravel road straight to a bridge, 25 minutes from the junction. To the west there's a view directly up a valley with good waterfalls, which would be easy and fun to explore. Crossing the bridge, you'll reach the highway in a couple of minutes, opposite a pharmacy north of the centre of Arsha, just north of Sioni; from here you could hike on to Sno (page 184).

Alternatively, it may be easier to start by taking a taxi south from Stepantsminda and then walk back: from the bridge at km121 you can either turn right on to a gravel road after a couple of minutes or go on to some houses and turn right below a chapel, then after almost 1km take a path to the left to pass below scree and reach the mineral pool in 20 minutes. Go to the right around the boggy patch to the gravel track, then after a couple of minutes fork left to reach the first houses of Gergeti in 5 minutes more.

NORTH OF STEPANTSMINDA

The Georgian Military Highway continues north from Kazbegi on the left/west bank of the Tergi, passing through Tsdo (1,767m) and then, 7km from Kazbegi, Gveleti (1,850m), where griffon vultures nest on the cliff; just southwest of Gveleti a narrow path leads to two fine waterfalls. The road crosses to the right bank here, but immediately before the bridge a track turns left to continue along the left bank, then follows the Amali Valley as a good hiking trail through subalpine birch forest to reach the **Devdoraki Glacier**. This is the lowest of all those in the Caucasus, its tongue reaching an altitude of just 2,300m; the trail is 9km each way, taking a minimum of 4 hours return. The highway enters the wildest section of the **Daryal Gorge**, running for 12km on a narrow shelf below granite cliffs up to 1,500m high where lammergeyers nest. The gorge is also a migratory route for other raptors such as pallid harrier and imperial and steppe eagles. It takes its name from Dari-Alan or 'Gates of the Alans', named after the forefathers of the Ossetians, who arrived here in the 5th century AD. Before that it was known as the Sarmatian gates or the Iverian gates, the point at which Pompey's advance into Asia was halted in 65BC. At the southern entrance to the gorge, to the west of the road, are the ruins of the **Daryal Fortress**, popularly known as Queen Tamar's Castle, although it's far older than the 12th century. It was restored by the Russians and successfully held by General Gurko against Shamyl's forces in 1846. Tours go as far as a new monastery at the confluence with the Khdi River, just south of the frontier at the northern entrance to the gorge; it's possible to hike up the valley to the east here.

The frontier between Georgia and Russia at **Zemo Larsi** was closed by Russia in July 2006 and remained so until March 2010 when it was reopened for Armenian traffic, and to Georgians in 2013. The border facilities were modernised with USAID funding in 2009; there are still long queues. For those wishing to take a look, two or three people could take a taxi from Kazbegi to the tunnel that marks the actual border for about US$10. The old border crossing is at Chertov Most (Devil's Bridge), about 20km beyond Kazbegi, and the highway ends after 168km at Vladikavkaz ('Rule the Caucasus'), founded in 1783 to be the base for the subjugation of the Caucasus. It was renamed Ordjonikidze after the Georgian revolutionary Sergo Ordjonikidze, Stalin's hatchetman, whose brutality horrified Lenin and who was in the end killed off by Stalin himself. Although there are still traces of the fashionable 19th-century climatic resort and garrison town, it has been surrounded by soulless communist tower blocks and was then knocked about during the first Chechen war.

KHEVSURETI ხევსურეთი

Khevsureti is one of the most remote and least changed areas of Georgia, a country where adherence to ancient traditions is very highly prized. The Khevsurebi are known for their unique textiles, with beautifully embroidered stars and crosses, probably a simplification of the pagan sun motif. The men are popularly supposed to have worn Crusader-style chain mail until the 1930s, and at the time of the protests after the 9 April 1989 massacre they certainly appeared in Tbilisi wearing 'knee-length, richly patterned tunics with half-metre silver daggers strapped to their waists'. In the 1920s the population of Khevsureti was about 4,000, but nowadays many actually live in Tbilisi and only about 400 still live full-time in the mountains. You may still be able to buy socks made from the wool of their aboriginal strain of sheep, and dyed only with natural products. However, there are now relatively few sheep in Khevsureti, because their traditional grazing grounds on the Chechen side of the watershed are no longer available. The area is technically now the Pshav-Khevsureti National Park (758km²) but this only exists on paper. The Khevsurebi are known for their brevity and straightforwardness, and for their unique poetry; they may actually speak in verse on day-to-day matters.

Their religion is still very pagan, with shaman-like 'bearers of forbidden knowledge'; icons are forbidden, and there are no real churches, only tiny sanctuaries for strange sacrificial rituals which may involve the *dekanozi* or priest drinking blood and 'sacred beer'. Beer is brewed to an ancient recipe (utterly unlike the Germanic lager found elsewhere in the region); the Khevsur firewater is *zhipitauri*, like vodka but more lethal. On the altar you're likely to find deer antlers and ram's horns instead of a cross. They are surrounded by spirits or *vohi* such as Sakhlis Angelosi, guardian of the household; Mparveli Angelosi, guardian of wanderers; Goris Angelosi, guardian of the mountains; and Did Gori, the Father of the Great Mountain, responsible for storms and avalanches. Others are Otchopintre, a version of Pan, and Dali, the Georgian Artemis, while St George is identified as the god of war.

Despite the unrest in Chechnya, Khevsureti is quite safe as there are plenty of Georgian frontier troops (who will check your papers) and OSCE observers (unarmed foreign military officers) based here.

GETTING THERE AND AWAY Khevsureti is reached by the road up the Pshavis Aragvi Valley from an underpass at km26 on the Georgian Military Highway, south of the Zhinvali Dam; take the road at right angles which soon heads south down to a bridge, and then turns north through the village of Zhinvali (capital of Pshavi). It turns right up a side valley, crosses the stream and soon swings left to a junction about 3km from the highway. The Khevsureti road heads left here, while another turns right to Tianeti, in Kakheti.

A daily **bus** from Didube in Tbilisi (*at 09.00*) runs as far as Barisakho, the administrative centre of both Pshavi and Khevsureti; it stops at the bottom of the hill, from where you climb up to the village, busy with free-range pigs, dogs with clipped ears and a few bored soldiers. The bus continues to Shatili (*6hrs; GEL20*) on Wednesday and Saturday from mid-June to mid-October, returning at noon the next day.

 WHERE TO STAY, EAT AND DRINK There are guesthouses in Korsha, 2km further up the valley. Only about 40 families live here, but it's a good base, giving access to three valleys.

Batria Arabuli m 599 686510. Batria (Shota & Marina's son; see below) speaks Russian but not English. $
Guesthouse Korsha m 577 348435. Shota & Marina Arabuli are very talented artists & rent rooms for up to 5 or 6 people with shower

& washing machine, just before the museum in Korsha, which Shota runs. $
Shota Tsiklauri m 599 399379. At the top of the village, offering 4 rooms & good food; speaks Russian but not English. $

5

WHAT TO SEE AND DO In **Korsha**, there's a museum in the former church (there's an English sign; GEL1). The museum houses rare Khevsur chain mail, remarkable traditional costumes with patterns unique to each clan (like tartans), fearsome spiky knuckledusters and agricultural implements.

Beyond here there's not even a kiosk and you have to find your own transport. You may wait days for a lift, but it's great country for **walking** (including the crossings west to Juta and east to Khevsureti), and there's no shortage of water. You can walk north to the hamlet of Biso and then west on a steep jeep track to Roshka (2,050m), 10km from Korsha, where you can stay at the Guesthouse Roshka (m 599 399789) and a couple of homestays. There are two huge erratic boulders here, the smaller of which measures 19m by 5m by 7m. There's also a lovely **day hike** north to the Abudelauri lakes (2,600m), one green, one blue and one white; hikers can continue from here to Juta (page 184) over the Chaukhi (or Roshka) Pass, but it's poorly marked and much harder in this direction.

From Biso, a dirt road leads northeast up the Gudantistsqali Valley to Gudani (the last village in Pshavi) and Khakhmati; there are defensive towers in both villages, and Gudani and Khakhmati, and a guesthouse in Gudani.

From here a 4x4 track continues eastwards, climbing 1,000m or so with hairpin bends up to the Datvis-Jvaris (Bear Cross) Pass (*2,676m*; ☉ *from May/Jun–Oct/Nov only*), and then swings north into Khevsureti to follow the Argun down the northern slope of the Caucasus through Kistani to a bridge where trucks stop below **Shatili** (1,395m), the main village of Khevsureti (though it's cut off in winter). It's less than 100km from the Georgian Military Highway (under 50km from Barisakho), but it takes 4–5 hours to drive this distance. It's an almost unspoilt complex of more than 50 defensive towers and ancient houses with wickerwork balconies (some dating from the 6th century, though most are from the 10th–12th centuries) huddled together on a low cliff, facing another of Tamar's castles. They were largely abandoned in the 1950s then partially restored in the 1970s, when Shevardnadze also built a new village around the corner beyond a soccer pitch-cum-helipad; bizarrely, there's a row of villas with big balconies overlooking the Argun River. Now 15 towers have had urgent repairs, and one is to become a museum. The World Bank and UNESCO have a cultural heritage project here, with a new ecotourism hotel in two renovated towers, with a kitchen and real bathroom on the ground floor and a ten-bed room above (*GEL25 pp plus food*), run by Dato Jalabauri (m 599 533379; e *dato.jalabauri@gmail.com*; ◼ *Jalabauri*). Vazha Chincharauli (m 577 729362; e *vabula@posta.ge*) also provides accommodation, but speaks only Georgian and Russian. The lovely Nana Gogochuri (m 599 992025) also has a guesthouse, with spectacular views towards the defensive towers. The road continues north down the Argun Valley from Shatili through a border checkpoint and soon, below the plague huts and necropolis of Anatori, swings southeast up the Andaki Valley. It's about 8km (with shrines marking excellent mineral springs) up the Andaki to **Mutso** (1,590m), the only other real settlement in Khevsureti, perhaps the finest (though most ruinous) of Khevsur villages. Almost completely abandoned over a century ago, it had around 30 medieval tower dwellings on near-vertical terraces, but many have collapsed; it's now being restored in a reasonably restrained way. You'll climb up past massively built tombs (about 2m by 2m and 4m long), to a few towers on a narrow ridge, now being renovated.

The valley splits immediately south of Mutso, with Khone in a bowl to the southeast beyond Khonischala and two plague huts still containing human bones; it's just 2km further to Chechnya, but the border is (officially) open only to incoming refugees – there's a road just 3km beyond the border, north of Mount

Tebulos. Two hours of steep hiking south of Mutso is **Ardoti**, a few defensive towers with a church above, after which the valley splits again: to the southwest in the Chanchistsqali Valley is **Khakhabo**. The lower village is still inhabited, while Upper Khakhabo (2,150m) is a tiny cluster of ruined 11th-century towers. From the tiny hamlet of Andaki, to the southeast, hiking groups can make the tough crossing over the 3,431m Atsunta Pass into Tusheti, reaching Parsma (page 324) in about 12 hours.

The track north from Shatili across the border into Chechnya is of course closed, and even in quieter times you should not attempt to cross the border here. You'll see abandoned helicopters and armoured cars in the area, and maybe some traces of a quixotic 1980s railway project, and a half-built tunnel, used by Chechen fighters to store arms in the 1990s.

SAMTSKHE-JAVAKHETI

6

Samtskhe-Javakheti
სამცხე-ჯავახეთი

This chapter covers three historic provinces: first, the tiny and virtually forgotten **Tori**, around the spa of Borjomi; second, **Samtskhe** or Meskheti, the high volcanic tableland around Akhaltsikhe; and, then, **Javakheti**, on the border with Armenia. Although part of Georgia's historical heartland, with the cave-city of Vardzia at its centre, the present region of Samtskhe-Javakheti has a population that is 90% Armenian and is in many ways autonomous. In 1624, the Georgian ruler of Samtskhe converted to Islam for political reasons; many Georgians left the area, but many of those who remained also converted. These so-called Meskhetian Turks lived here until their deportation to Central Asia in 1944 and have not been allowed to return; their villages are now largely populated by people from Racha and Lechkhumi. When the Russians took control of the area in 1829, some Muslims emigrated to Turkey and Armenians came here from Turkey to take their land. Thanks to its bleak climate and poor transport links, it remains a poor and isolated region, although the roads have been improved in the last couple of decades.

NEDSVI

From the junction with the Tbilisi–Kutaisi highway at the west end of Khashuri, it's 32km southwest to Borjomi, following the Mtkvari into the Borjomi Gorge. Marshrutkas for Borjomi (*GEL2*) wait by a ticket kiosk a couple of hundred metres down the Borjomi road from the roundabout; Tbilisi–Akhaltsikhe marshrutkas also pass roughly hourly.

The road passes through the long thin village of Akhaldaba, from where you can hike up to the **Nedsvi Sanctuary**. At km12/85, at the north end of the village, there's a junction where a bridge crosses to the right bank (where there's a ruined tower); this road crosses the railway, continues to the right as Rustavelis kucha, and then swings right again to cross a stream and carry on up the valley as Kazbegis kucha. Just before km3 you should be able to find a path up to the ridge on your right/southwest side, to (yet another) **Tamar's Castle**, a small group of dramatically located ruins. It's another kilometre to the end of the road at km4 (measured from the start of Kazbegis); a very muddy forestry track continues up the valley, reaching some fields and houses after an hour's hiking.

Just beyond these the track crosses to the right bank, and after about another 15 minutes you'll reach some summer-only houses at the meeting of two valleys; after crossing a stream you'll find some graves and a ruined church in a grove of trees on your left, as well as a table and shelter. This is all that remains of the Monastery of Nedsvi and its three-naved basilica, built in the 9th century by Grigol Kandzdeli; forestry tracks continue up steep-sided conifer-lined valleys which offer very attractive hiking and camping. The monastery is in the Nedsvi Sanctuary, a 9,000ha enclave of the Borjomi-Kharagauli National Park (pages 201–6); it's unmanaged, but wildlife should be recovering. The road winds on up the wooded Mtkvari valley, with pedestrian suspension bridges across the river, and a couple of café-restaurants with mineral springs around km14.

BORJOMI ბორჯომი *Telephone code 367*

Just before km29/68 the main road up the left/west bank of the Mtkvari reaches the centre of the spa town of Borjomi, with shops, a market, and a bus station, just south of the centre. This has departures more or less hourly to Tbilisi and Akhaltsikhe, eight a day to Bakuriani, and to Gori (*07.45 & 10.45*), Batumi (*09.00*) and Vardzia (*Jun–Sep 08.45*). Buy tickets inside (but pay the driver if going to Bakuriani); heading for Akhaltsikhe, you're best off waiting across the road. The railway station, across the river, has closed but you can buy tickets on board the amazingly cheap but very slow trains to Gori (*GEL1*) and Tbilisi (*GEL2*), which leave at 07.00 and 16.45. Green local buses run south to Likani and north to Chvibisi.

At an altitude of 810–850m the spa offers both health-giving waters and a bracing mountain atmosphere; in August the average temperature is 20°C, but it freezes from late October until March or later, and in January the average temperature is –2°C.

It's a town of 16,000, with a large plant bottling the water which used to be shipped all over the Soviet Union. Baths were built here in the 1st century AD but the valley's 150 springs were forgotten from the 15th century until a Russian army, returning from fighting the Turks, rediscovered them in 1810; it was Grand Duke Mikhail Nikolayevich Romanov, brother of the Tsar and viceroy of the Transcaucasus, who renovated the spa in 1862 and built a summer residence in 1871 and then the Likani Palace in 1892–96. The railway opened in 1894 and Chekhov, Tchaikovsky, Mme Blavatsky, other members of the tsar's family and Stalin were among those who came to take the waters here. A bottling plant was built in 1896 and, from 1900, carbon dioxide was added to extend the water's life and allow exports. In 1995 a French–Dutch joint venture, the Georgian Glass & Mineral Water Company, bought it with the Borjomi brand name, only to find that others had also been given licences to use the name; this was sorted out, but the company then lost US$7 million when the Russian economy collapsed in 1998. It merged with two Ukrainian companies in 2004 and had 8% of the Russian market until it was banned from Russia for political reasons in 2006; determined marketing elsewhere has brought sales to 15% above their level before the ban.

WHERE TO STAY The homestays are mostly unmarked but the tourist information centre (see opposite) can advise on their whereabouts (the staff here claim there are more than 100 – probably an exaggeration).

Hotels

Golden Tulip (17 rooms) 9 April 48; 322 880202, 800 358 0846; w goldentulipborjomipalace.com. The fabulously restored house built in 1892 for the Iranian consul now houses this boutique hotel, with restaurant, gym, spa & sauna. $$$$$

Hotel Rixos (151 rooms) Meskheti 16; 322 292292; m 591 090944; e borjomi@rixos. com; w borjomi.rixos.com. A new 5-star place in the former Likani sanatorium that boasts of

being the most expensive hotel in Georgia. It has a particularly fine spa, with supposedly the best of Borjomi's mineral springs. $$$$$

Crowne Plaza Borjomi (101 rooms) Baratashvili 9; 322 221221; w crowneplaza.com/ borjomi. Opened in 2015 just outside the spa park (reached from 9 April, in fact), this 5-star place has a kitschy exterior but comfortable rooms and a good restaurant, wine bar, spa and pool. $$$$

Hotel Natali (19 rooms) Vepkhadze 20, Likani; m 551 581353, 591 819051;

e hotelnatali1@gmail.com; **w** hotelnatali.ge. On a track leading in to the national park, 3km south, this modern place is very peaceful & has large, comfortable rooms, all with balcony, fridge, kettle, hairdryer, toiletries & lots of power sockets. There's a meeting room for 60 on the 2nd floor & a more utilitarian restaurant below. **$$$$**

🏠 **Borjomis Khoeba** (65 rooms) Rustaveli 107A (at km 28/69); ☎367 223072; **m** 599 323247, 599 323249; **w** borjomiskheoba.com. The best place in town until the new 5-star hotels opened, this modern place just to the north of the town is also a medical centre & guests have access to the health centre, with its own natural & sulphur water. It has en-suite rooms with satellite TV & a restaurant, bar & swimming pool. **$$$–$$$$**

🏠 **Hotel Likani Palace** (5 rooms) Meskheti 27A, 1km south, immediately beyond the national park headquarters; ☎367 224249; **m** 599 939413, 599 255158; **e** likanipalace@mail.ru; **w** ecorest. ge. This hotel occupies the top 2 floors of a modern chalet, with its entry at the rear; there are 2 luxe rooms (with fireplace, kitchenette & a children's bedroom) & 3 others. Rates are FB, although there's a kitchen available, too, & there are discounts in winter. **$$$–$$$$**

🏠 **Hotel Meidan** (6 rooms) Kostava 2; ☎322 223908; **m** 599 152939. In the centre near some decent bars & restaurants, this small place is the best of the budget hotels. **$$–$$$**

Hostels & homestays

🏠 **Hostel Firuza** Baratashvili 3; ☎322 223935; **m** 599 151898; ⏰ May–Oct. Parallel to 9 April, rooms with balconies & shared bathrooms are available in this sanatorium which has very sensibly reinvented itself as a hostel. **$$**

🏠 **Marina Zulmatashvili's Homestay** (3 rooms) Ketevan Tsamebulis 2; **m** 598 184550; **e** marinasguesthouse@gmail.com; **w** marinasguesthouse1.wixsite.com/home; 🅵 MarinasGuesthouse. A good option; rooms have shared bathroom & English is spoken. Marina's can be reached by taking the rough stony track (Shroma) uphill to the right that leads off Kostava before it plunges downhill; turn left at the top of this to reach the house at the end. **$$**

🏠 **RiverSide Hostel** (3 rooms) Rustaveli 97; **m** 595 445585; **w** hotelborjomi@gmail.com; 🅵 riversideborjomi. Set in a big garden (with plenty of parking) off the main road about 1km northeast of the centre, this friendly place has dorm beds with lockers & a kitchen. **$$**

🏠 **Levan Jangiroshvili** (2 rooms; Leo's Homestay) Pirosmani 18; **m** 593 981595, 551 414422; **e** jango.geo@gmail.com; 🅵 YogainBorjomi. Just behind the museum, the owner speaks excellent English & is entertaining & full of information; unfortunately he's also a bit of a sharp operator & very pushy with travellers he finds on the street. Rooms for up to 8 people. **$**

✖ **WHERE TO EAT AND DRINK** There are several cafés along Robakidze, parallel to the south bank of the river west of the suspension bridge. All of these serve decent khachapuri, khinkhali and other Georgian staples, and have free Wi-Fi. There's also the Wine House (*Robakidze 2*).

✖ **Old Borjomi** Kostava 19; ☎367 223320; ⏰ 11.00–23.00 daily. This café-restaurant, facing the park, has decent Georgian food, is slightly more expensive than those on Robakidze but has a wider choice & better décor, plus Wi-Fi. **$$**

✖ **Pesvebi** Erekle II 3; ☎367 221702; ⏰ 11.00–23.00 daily. Simple but excellent Georgian restaurant, just beyond the station on a minor road by the railway. **$$**

✖ **Café-Restaurant My House** Kostava 31; **m** 591 212147; ⏰ 10.00–midnight. Facing the park, this is a generally peaceful (except when they're

doing karaoke) restaurant with good food & service plus Wi-Fi. **$**

✖ **Café Tourist Beer-Bar** At the rear of the Hotel Meidan on Dumbadze, the next street south. Georgian menu (including shashlik) & beer. **$**

✖ **Inka Café** 9 April 2; ☎367 222310, **m** 595 302077; **e** devidze18@rambler.ru; ⏰ 10.00–21.00 daily. In a nicely restored period building. Serves excellent cakes, pizza & khachapuri, & has good coffee. **$**

☕ **Aguna** Robakidze 2; ☎367 222340. Simple, rather Soviet, café with good basic Georgian food. **$**

OTHER PRACTICALITIES There's a **tourist information centre** (*TIC*; ☎367 221397; **m** 599 302513; **e** ticborjomi@gmail.com; **w** travelinborjomi.ge; ⏰ 09.00–18.00, *summer until 19.00*) on Rustaveli just north of the suspension road-bridge that crosses the river to Borjomi Park station. The helpful English-speaking staff provide maps and information on accommodation and travel, run tours to Vardzia plus rafting and horseriding, and can also supply permits for the Borjomi-Kharagauli National Park when the national park headquarters (page 204) is closed. The TIC is also the start of two hiking routes, one marked in green that loops northwest via Cross Mountain and Gogia Fortress, above the museum, and one marked in blue that goes southeast to the Ekaterina Park, the Tsar's Baths and Sadgeri, linking to the red (adventure) trail.

There are several **ATMs** and **pharmacies** along Rustaveli between the TIC and the bus station (most on the west side).

WHAT TO SEE AND DO The **Museum of Local Lore** (*Tsminda Nino 5;* ⊕ *Apr–Oct 10.00–17.00 exc Mon, Nov–Mar until 16.00; GEL3, GEL1/photo, GEL15 guide*) is signed to the west from the square north of the market; although dark, largely without captions, and with no English spoken, its exhibits do give interesting insights into the life of the Borjomi region. Starting at the top with tatty stuffed animals, there's then the Romanov porcelain collection on the floor below, and Bronze Age jewellery and agricultural implements, photographs of ancient churches and 19th-century spa life, and by the entrance, furniture made for the Romanovs from the antlers of deer they'd shot. You can also see a video made in 2002.

In the small park on Rustaveli below the museum stands a statue of Pyotr Ilyich Tchaikovsky, who used to holiday here, looking rather dandy.

Borjomi Spa At about km28.5 (just south of the TIC), a bridge crosses the river and the railway and enters the spa between the former post office (1900) to the south and the former Hotel Central (1890) to the north; this road, Kostava, passes an attractive park on the left, with a new church and the beautifully refurbished Borjomi Park station, now housing some rather touristy restaurants.

Kostava soon reaches the Borjomka stream and 9 April, lined by trees, stalls selling souvenirs and empty plastic bottles for mineral water, and late 19th-century villas, which leads up to the right with little seated pavilions jutting over the river, ending (after about 5 minutes) at the gates of the **Ekaterina Park** (⊕ *Jun–Sep 06.00–midnight, Oct–May 09.00–22.00; Jun–Sep GEL2, Nov–May free*). The last villa on the left (No 48, known as Firouze) is in the same style as the others but with glittery arabesque decoration in the ceiling of the balcony; it was built in 1892 for the Iranian consul, Mirza-Reza Khan, and has now been beautifully refurbished as a Golden Tulip hotel (page 198).

Inside the park a stately pile on the left (the original bottling plant) now houses a library, with historic photos in the entrance hall, and a covered pavilion on the right has taps spewing out the famous Borjomi water. Together with Narzan (from the northern Caucasus) this was the Soviet Union's favourite mineral water, with 300 million bottles a year being filled when times were good. It's flavoured with sodium carbonate, tasting something like Vichy water – slightly warm and salty, and a bit slimy.

A bridge crosses the stream to new toilets and a hall with a 3D panoramic model of Georgia (*GEL2*), while the main promenade leads on up the right side of the valley past cafés, bars and restaurants, a cinema and a play area, added when the park was refurbished in 2006. The paved path turns to gravel (near a swinging pirate ship!), and after 3km you reach an isolated but popular open-air pool that's recently been refurbished. They now charge GEL5, and a minibus shuttle is available (**m** *551*

644949). The path also gives access to the **Sadgeri Arboretum**, on the plateau immediately above the park, which covers 136ha and is laid out for invigorating walks for the spa patients in pine forests with splendid views. You'll also see the remains of a fortress, and the simple barn-like Church of St George, built in the 15th and 16th centuries on a cliff edge. Outside the park gate a stylish little terminal houses a **cable car** (⊕ *10.00–23.00 May–Sep; GEL4 each way*) to lift visitors the 100m to the arboretum and a Ferris wheel (⊕ *closed winter*) and café. Sadgeri can also be reached by a winding road which starts from 9 April and passes the 'Composers' House' where the next Tchaikovsky could seek inspiration on his summer holidays; it continues to Tsemi on the road to Bakuriani (pages 207–9).

Walking to Likani Ignoring the modern viaduct above the bus station and continuing up Meskhetis, the main road southwards, take the steps to the right at km29.2, and just after the first bend (to the right) you'll find yourself in a hillside cemetery with a big new nunnery and good views of Borjomi. Higher up, where the gravestones mingle with pines, there's a metal Soviet-period portal that leads left to a war cemetery. The ruined **Gogiatsikhe** (Castle of St George) on the ridge immediately behind the market is also visible from the cemetery; it's quite easy to scramble up to this. In medieval times this was the stronghold of the feudal lords of the Avalishvili family, looking across the valley to the 11th–12th-century **Petristsikhe** (Castle of St Peter).

The headquarters of the Borjomi-Kharagauli National Park is just north of km30/67, under 1km from the viaduct. You're already in Likani, and it's just another 500m to the gate of the former **sanatorium**, now the Rixos Hotel. Once reserved for the elite of the Soviet Communist Party, this was used for conferences and for Shevardnadze's meetings with Lyudvig Chibirov, then leader of South Ossetia. It was bought by Kazakh investors in 2006 and closed for renovation, although this was delayed because of the Georgia–Russia 2008 conflict, finally opening in 2015. With luck you should still be able to walk through the lovely park and to the quasi-Tuscan Romanov **mansion**, built in 1895 of grey-painted stone and pink-painted brick, at the south end of the park; still owned by the state, this is where Saakashvili stayed when skiing at Bakuriani. In a couple of years' time it should be restored and opened to tourists; Stalin's bed is still there, and even the nail he hung his hat on, and there's a table made by Peter the Great himself, without nails. There's a sharp bend where the road south leaves Likani at km31/66, where you can glimpse a Romanov folly/viewpoint to the left.

BORJOMI-KHARAGAULI NATIONAL PARK

For a distance of 60km the Mtkvari River runs northeast from the Meskheti Plateau down to the central valley of Inner Kartli; this is the Borjomi Gorge, marking the division between the humid Colchic habitats of western Georgia and the drier landscapes of the east. There's also influence from the arid Anatolian Plateaux to the south, so there's an intriguing mix of species here, as well as Tertiary relics and some endemic species (such as *Gladiolus dzavacheticus* and *Corydallis erdelii*). Rhododendrons bloom in April and May, and autumn colours are spectacular too. In 1880 Prince Mikhail Romanov established a royal hunting reserve, building rangers' huts and appointing a German chief forester; it became a nature reserve in 1935 and a national park in 1995, opening to the public only in 2001. What's more, this was the only protected area in Georgia to have a management plan, thanks to the help of the WWF and the German government. It now covers 85,000ha with

Shrosha

Ubisi ✝

E60 M27

Rikoti
Tunnel

under
construction

Surami Pass
949m

Kharagauli

Surami

Khashuri

Moliti

Marelisi

Nunisi

Kvishkheti

Mtkvari

Akhaldaba

Dedabera Pass
1780m

✝ Nedsvi

Kvazvinevi
2025m

Zanavi

Stepuri
Gorge

Lomis Mta
2198m

National Park

Borjomi

Khergianis
1885m

Green
Monastery ✝

A308

Sadgeri

Timotesubani ✝

Chitakhevi

Likani

Tsaghveri

Chobiskhevi

Kvabiskhevi

Dviri

Dabadzveli
Lakes

Bakuriani

Didi
Mitarbi

Andeziti

Mt Kokhta
2155m

Tsikhdvari

N

Bradt

Zachraskaro Pass
2454m

Mt Sakvelosmta

0 _____ 8km
0 _____ 5 miles

Shavi Klde
2850m

Lake
Tabatskuri

Aspindza, Vardzia

Akhalkalaki

a buffer zone of 450,000ha, now including Abastumani and Sametskhavario, the highest peak in the region at 2,642m.

Trips can be booked through tour agencies in Tbilisi or through the national park – its headquarters are 1km south of Borjomi in Likani (*Meskheti 23*; m *577 640480, 577 101895, 577 640444, 577 101857;* e *borjomkharagauli@gmail.com;* w *apa.gov.ge;* ⊕ *09.00–18.00 Mon–Fri, 09.00–15.00 Sat–Sun*). Staff speak very good English and can arrange guides, horses, accommodation and the rental of mountain bikes, snowshoes, and camping and hiking gear; they also sell a map (*GEL3*) and handicrafts, jam, honey, and hot drinks.

GEOLOGY AND NATURAL HISTORY The area is composed mostly of Tertiary sediments (clay, marl, sandstone) and Quaternary volcanic bedrock (andesite, basalt, dolerite), with plateaux of petrified lava flows. There are 30 mineral springs, of which Zvare, Mitarbi and Nunisi are supposed to have medicinal properties, in addition to Borjomi water. The climate is moderately humid, with cold snowy winters and long cool summers, lasting 3½ months below 1,100m and just two months above 1,500m, where snow lies for at least 150 days a year. Average precipitation is 687mm a year, although it's higher to the north with 1,842mm at the Rikoti Pass and 1,366mm at Kharagauli, and lower to the south with 576mm at Atskuri. Temperatures are also higher to the north, with an average in August of 23°C at Kharagauli, 19° at Borjomi and 16° at Bakuriani.

Forest covers 75% of the national park, mostly climax conifer forest; in fact it's the largest unpopulated forest in Europe. However, more than 60 species of Colchic trees and shrubs have been recorded here, including cherry-laurel, holly, chestnut, *Rhododendron ponticum*, yew and buckthorn. Forests dominated by oak (*Quercus iberica*), beech (*Fagus orientalis*) and hornbeam (*Carpinus caucasica*) can be found at up to altitudes of 1,800m, though mostly at lower levels, while spruce (*Picea orientalis*) and pine (*Pinus kochiana*) can be found from 1,000m to 1,800m, and Caucasian fir (*Abies nordmannia*) from 1,400m to 1,800m. From this altitude to 2,400m there's subalpine forest of crook-stem birch (*Betula litwinowii*), mountain ash (*Sorbus caucasigena*) and *Rhododendron caucasicum*, with alpine grasslands above 2,400m. To the south, the slopes of the Trialeti are dominated by the pine *Pinus sosnowskyi* with smaller species such as juniper, *Astragalus caucasicus*, meadow sweet, hawthorn, cornelian cherry and dog-rose. In addition the Nariani marshes, at 2,050m, are home to many wetland species. The Nedsvi and Ktsia-Tabatskuri reserves (9,000ha and 22,000ha respectively), described on pages 197–8 and 209–10, are detached from the main body of the national park, which lies to the west of the gorge.

The 55 species of mammal in the national park include red and roe deer, chamois, brown bear (*Ursus arctos*), wild cat, lynx, wolf, boar, badger, otter, pine marten, squirrel and some endemic species of bat (*Myotis emarginatus, Nyctalus lasiopterus, Barbastella barbastellus*). Nine bezoar goats (like small ibex) were reintroduced to the Atskuri section of the park in 2006.

Among the 95 species of bird are the golden and white-tailed eagle, black vulture, blackcock, crossbill and six types of woodpecker. There are also snakes, three endemic lizards, newts and Caucasian salamander.

HIKING IN THE NATIONAL PARK Meadows are found as high as 2,500m on the flanks of Mount Sametskhavario, and are still used for seasonal grazing. Problems of overgrazing, leading to erosion, have been reduced by the national park, and hunting and logging are also less of a problem than they were. There are nine four-man ranger stations around the edges of the park, notably (in a clockwise direction from Borjomi) at Kvabiskhevi, Atskuri, Abastumani, Marelisi, Nunisi, Kvishkheti and Zanavi. There should always be a ranger on duty, guarding against illegal logging more than poaching or anything else.

Atskuri lies at 950m on the road from Borjomi to Akhaltsikhe (page 210); Kvishkheti (600m), at the northeastern corner of the national park, is 1km west of the Khashuri–Borjomi road at km7/89; and Zanavi (850m) is 1km west of the same road at km19.5/77.5, south of Akhaldaba.

Specifically for tourists, there are guesthouses in Atskuri and Marelisi (pages 210 and 223) and a visitor centre at the park headquarters in Likani (page 201). There's a pleasant 3km **Nature Interpretive Trail** from the rear of the headquarters, with wooden sculptures by students of the Academy of Fine Art and labelled trees; it starts to the left of the building with poor switchbacks for a couple of minutes before taking a better path. This trail can be done self-guided or with a national park guide if preferred. There's a map at the start and nine educational boards, as well as a new barefoot section.

There are also twelve **hiking trails**, each marked with a different colour on maps and trail markings, and mostly open to horses too, with rangers' stations and tourist shelters (where you have to bring your own food and bedding). Detailed trail maps can be downloaded from the park website (w *apa.gov.ge*), and an excellent GPS-compatible map has been produced for the park by Geoland, with gradient profiles on the back.

At the eastern end of the park, the isolated Trail 4 has been washed-out and closed – it offered an easy day hike from Zanavi north to Nunisi (page 223). **Trail 1** (*Nikoloz Romanov Trail; 43km; about 14hrs; blue-&-white stripes*) from Likani to Marelisi leads north through the Likani Gorge (you can take a taxi to the ranger station, 1.5km north of the highway) to a campsite, where you can get water. It then climbs and swings west to reach (after 5–6 hours) the Lomis Mta tourist shelter where you can stay the night (GEL20; or you can camp; water is about 500m away). The next day you can either go over Lomis Mta (Lion Peak; 2,198m, with views all the way from Turkey to Russia) or loop around to the east, with a short detour to St George's Chapel. It is mainly downhill, reaching the Shavtwala Valley in 5–6 hours; to the left it's half an hour to the Sakhvlari tourist shelter, or you could go to the right and reach the park's Marelisi guesthouse (page 223) in another couple of hours.

From Marelisi or Sakhvlari you could return south on the longer, harder **Trail 2** (*St Andrew's Trail; 40km; about 15hrs; red-&-white stripes*) to Atskuri: this follows the Shavtwala through the Bjoliskhevi Gorge to Sakhvlari (950m) and the Megruki tourist shelter (1,018m) at the mouth of the Stepuri Gorge, an exciting side trip (especially if water levels are high after rain) of 5.5km each way. From here the trail climbs to the northwest, past the shepherds' summer settlements of Shertuli and Chishkara to a 1,920m pass west of Kvazvinevi (2,025m). It then follows a ridge past the Kvazvinevi ranger shelter (1,800m) to Rkinis Jvari (2,439m), the Iron Cross Peak on which St Andrew the First-Called placed a cross in the 1st century AD. It continues to the east side of Samteskhvario (2,642m), the highest peak in the park, and over Megruki (2,475m). After a steep descent it reaches the Amarati tourist shelter (1,910m, with views to the Turkish mountains), and then follows the Ochora Ridge and the Barghebis Ghele Valley to the Atskuri ranger station (*6hrs*). Alternatively, you can backtrack slightly from the Amarati shelter to follow **Trail 3** (*Panorama Trail; 16km; about 6 hrs; blue-&-white stripes*) south along the Ochivari Ridge to the Barghebis Ghele Valley and the Atskuri ranger station.

From south of Lomis Mta you can also descend south through a dramatic gorge to Kvabiskhevi on **Trail 6** (*Following Wildlife Traces Trail; 13km; 6hrs; yellow-&-*

white stripes), which also makes a good day hike from Likani. A *via ferrata* route should be available in the gorge by the end of 2018.

Since 2013, **horse tours** have been provided by a group of Polish-trained guides (w *horsetoursge.kaukaz.net; GEL25/hr, GEL60–100/day*) – the only English-speakers are Vazha Gelashvili (m *595 116343;* e *vajaborjomski555@rambler.ru*) and Jemal Ghonghadze (m *595 188461*), both in Borjomi. Otherwise if you can cope with Russian or Georgian you can call m 551 865019 or 593 120289 (Bakuriani); m 595 111005 or 558 231936 (Borjomi–Likani); or m 557 231722 or 592 946533 (Atskuri). There are also two **snowshoe trails**, from Atskuri and Likani ranger stations.

EAST OF BORJOMI While here you should also make a side trip up to **Bakuriani** (pages 207–9), once the Soviet Union's most popular ski resort but now only Georgia's second most popular (after Gudauri). Marshrutkas leave from Borjomi's bus station, with taxis waiting by the square just north. The road starts at about km26.3, 2km north of the centre of Borjomi; a bridge crosses the river to the Borjomi-Works station, where the railway from Tbilisi connects with a rather amazing **narrow-gauge railway** (known as the Kukuschka, or Cuckoo) on which tiny carriages are hauled by a large and ungainly electric locomotive at a very leisurely pace. Opened in 1902, the 920mm-gauge line was electrified (at 1.5kV dc) in 1972. The first 18km to Tsemi (where it crosses a 34m-high steel bridge designed by the Eiffel company) were upgraded in 2002 to allow the dizzy speed of 25km/hour, but the next 19km are limited to 15km/hour. Nevertheless, this is a popular excursion, and the coaches have recently been refurbished, with panoramic windows. There's also a narrow-gauge steam loco, dating from 1914, set on a plinth near the Borjomi station.

The road and railway pass the sprawling No. 1 water-bottling plant and then follow a valley to the southeast. At km9 they pass the minuscule hamlet of **Daba**, with the very simple basilica of St George, built in 1333, with some nice carvings, which can be seen from the railway, on the left/west side of the valley, or reached by road from km8.5. At km11 the road enters the village of Tsaghveri, from where a new 10km circular walk takes you along the railway to the Eiffel viaduct, down to Daba church and back. Above Daba more than 100ha of forest was burnt in 2017; this had already been burned by the Russians during the 2008 war, after which an NGO was restoring the forest, and 80% of the replanted trees were lost in the second fire.

A minor road (Toreli kucha) runs due east from Tsaghveri, through an impressive short gorge (with a ruined fort high above the left bank) and on to reach the village of **Timotesubani** (17km from Borjomi) in just over 3km; turning left at the junction in the centre, it's another 1km to the **Monastery of St Timothy**, just beyond the edge of the village at the end of the asphalt. Here the Church of the Virgin, built at the end of the 12th century, is famous for its frescoes, painted in 1205–15. This was one of the first churches in Georgia to be built in brick, but with a band and crosses of turquoise mosaic on the barrel dome. The gate-tower, older than the church, is also of red brick, and there's a 9th-century basilica next to the main church, with horrid new paintings. Entering through the south porch, built later in limestone, you'll see plenty of bare brickwork, but also plenty of fine surviving frescoes, including a Virgin and Child above the altar, a Crucifixion to the south of the iconostasis, and Paradise at the west end; there are also plenty of saints and a flute-player in the north transept. The frescoes have recently had emergency work to treat mould, caused by the heating installed by the monks when they returned here. Three buses (*GEL1.50*) a day leave from Borjomi at 10.30, 13.30 and 17.00 but only two return, at 12.30 and 15.20.

A rough road follows the main valley eastwards all the way to Citelisopeli, which was inhabited by Ossetians until the secession of South Ossetia. Hardy mountain bikers could turn left/north at Sinubani to cross the ridge to Tkemlovani and ultimately Kintsvisi (page 175), a church which is similar to that of Timotesubani. There's a signed mountain-bike route north over a ridge from Bakuriani to Timotesubani, allowing you to make a loop. There are a couple of guesthouses here, but there's more choice in Tsaghveri.

BAKURIANI ბაკურიანი *Telephone code 367*

From Tsaghveri the road swings right and climbs in hairpin bends out of the valley; the railway takes a far longer route, heading west to cross the Gujareti Gorge and winding slowly through dense pine forests. The road passes the quiet spa village of Tsemi and eventually reaches Bakuriani, 27km from the main road. Established in 1932 at 1,700m, Bakuriani is still largely a traditional village, subsisting on grazing and logging, with large hotels built in the last three or four decades set at a respectful distance across the subalpine meadows in a volcanic crater. There's snow from November to March, or even May, with the heaviest falls in December; in January the average temperature is –7.2°C, but in August it's a pleasant 15°C, making it ideal for walking. Bakuriani is lower than Gudauri, and the trees stop it from getting so cold, while the sun is not as fierce, so it's possible to ski in a T-shirt in March; Bakuriani is also more attractive in summer.

GETTING THERE AND AROUND Marshrutkas from Borjomi (*GEL3*) take 40–50 minutes while the trains take around 2½ hours to cover 37km. Marshrutkas leave at 1- to 2-hour intervals through the day, the last in each direction leaving at 17.00. The train journey is a fascinating and cheap (*GEL2*) alternative but *very* slow, perhaps stopping to load someone's firewood in the forest. Departures are at 07.15 and 10.15 from Borjomi, returning at 10.00 and 14.15, although there may be seasonal variations. Fares are collected on board and you are more or less guaranteed a seat; Direct marshrutkas from Tbilisi's Didube station (*GEL9*) take between 2½ and 3 hours. **Marshrutkas** usually turn right at the wood-faced police station and terminate 50m along Tamar Mepe opposite the Hotel Santa Claus, but some continue straight along the main road, Tavisuplebis and Davit Agmashenebelis, to pass near the slopes *en route* to the village of Andesiti, 5km west. Arriving at the railway station, you should turn left and go uphill past the waiting taxis to the bus station at the junction of Tamar Mepe, Rustaveli and Mta; from here head left/east to the main road and turn right towards the slopes. It's not far to the junction with Tsakadze, which leads east past the Villa Palace Hotel (not recommended), gear-hire shacks and the nursery slope, known as Otsdachutmetriani or the Twentyfive-metre-Field, where there's a 40m drag and lifts up to 420m long. It passes the turning to Kokhta I, the original lift and runs, and continues to make a 3km loop around a large meadow, lined with disused communist hotels, to finish just above km26 on the Borjomi road.

Alternatively, Davit Agmashenebelis continues southwards and then splits; the right fork continues (past the Hotel Melisi) towards Akhalkalaki, while the other, lined with modern hotels, leads to the Kokhta II lifts (to the left – also known as Tatra-Poma) and the new Didveli lift to the right.

In winter, in addition to taxis, there are **horse-drawn sleighs** which cost about GEL1/minute, if you negotiate well (*min GEL5*). You can also rent a Buran snowmobile, which will do 80km/h (*US$100/hr*), or slower ones for kids, plus quad bikes, toboggans and horses.

🏠 **WHERE TO STAY** There are a few simple places to stay right in the centre, and quite a few new apartment blocks, but the big modern hotels are all a kilometre or two to the south near the slopes. The main road southwards, Tavisuplebis, is lined with traditional wooden cottages, in which rooms are available in the ski season; however, there are only the simplest restaurants and cafés here, so you'll have to arrange meals too. On Tsereteli, the road parallel to Davit Agmashenebelis to the left, there are plenty of private houses, all of which rent rooms in winter; you'd be sure to find one in summer too, for about GEL15. In 2018 a mega-stylish Rooms Hotel (as in Tbilisi and Kazbegi) will open (with 100 rooms) at the foot of Kokhta Gora, where a Four Seasons Resort is also under construction.

🏠 **Hotel Crystal** (23 rooms) Nr the Didveli funicular; ☏ 267 40376/7; m 595 461461; w hotelcrystal.ge. Bakuriani's first 4-star hotel, this has a fine modern spa & an excellent restaurant. **$$$$**

✳ 🏠 **Hotel Apollon** (19 rooms, 2 suites) Davit Agmashenebelis 21; m 599 334499; w apollon. ge. South of the village centre (much further south than its street number suggests), this hotel is open all year & is rightly popular with expats in Tbilisi; it comprises 2 buildings (& 2 dining rooms), with a nice simple style & pine furniture, & en-suite rooms for 2–4 people plus families. There's Wi-Fi, TV in all rooms, plus video & an open fire in the common area, sauna, billiards & table tennis, as well as parking, a warm boot room & a garden/play area. They're very friendly & efficient & will do vegetarian food given notice, & Inga & her son speak good English. Price includes 3 meals a day. **$$$**

🏠 **Hotel Snow King** Lanebis Mimdebare 25; m 598 285020, 577 745020; e info.snowking@ gmail.com; w snowking.ge. A modern 4-storey ski hotel by the Otsdachutmetriani slopes with

comfortable rooms, restaurant & bar, & remarkably helpful staff. **$$$**

🏠 **Hotel Tbilisi** (70 rooms) Davit Agmashenebelis 23; m 551 067706, 551 953570; e hoteltbilisi73@mail.ru; f . A package-style hotel with small rooms with balconies, TV & fridge-freezer. They're very friendly, although there's no English spoken. GEL5 extra for a buffet b/fast. **$$$**

🏠 **Villa Fagus** (12 rooms) Tamar Mepis 3; m 593 715855, 595 244300. A chalet block, close to the bus & train stations; rates include 3 meals a day. **$$$**

🏠 **Villa Park** (20 rooms) Rustaveli 25; ☏ 24 0405; m 579 826862; e hotelvillapark@yahoo. com. Central (though 100m up a dirt track (Tsakadze) opposite JoyLand), but with facilities such as swimming pool, sauna & gym, & a buffet b/fast. **$$$**

🏠 **Hotel Tovlis Babua** (32 rooms; Santa Claus) Mtis 1; m 599 142783, 568 142783; e dima.mikaberidze@mail.ru. An older place right in the centre; no English is spoken. Rooms are en suite, with TVs. **$$**

✖ **WHERE TO EAT AND DRINK** By and large the best restaurants are in the hotels, but there are a few alternatives.

✖ **De Novo** Davit Agmashenebelis 23A; m 555 385393; f cafe.denovo; ⊕ 09.30–03.00 daily. In the courtyard of the Hillside Bakuriani apart-hotel (there's another branch at the west end of Tsakadze), this is a stylish, modern restaurant-café; the Baron restaurant, at the same site, is good & not too pricey, mainly serving Georgian food. **$$$**

✖ **Mgzavruli** Tsakadze 1; m 592 220520; ⊕ 10.00–23.00 daily. In the Mgzavrebi

Apartments building, this offers some of the best food in town, with a huge fireplace that's just what you need after a day on the slopes. **$$$**

✖ **Mimino** Tsakadze 3; m 571 332934, 568 660608; ⊕ 10.00–23.00 daily. Near the Otsdachutmetriani slopes, this is a lively place serving the classic Georgian dishes, but it can get pretty smokey. **$$**

OTHER PRACTICALITIES The best place for **tourist information** is the Community Centre at Davit Agmashenebelis 4 (☏ 367 240036/37; m 593 335058; e ticbakuriani@ gmail.com; ⊕ 10.00–18.00, summer until 19.00). There are **ATMs** at Davit

Agmashenebelis 26 and at the Hotel Villa Palace, Tsereteli 1. The biggest **food shop** is the Market, at the south end at the junction of Agmashenebelis and the Andesiti road.

WHAT TO SEE AND DO The Bakuriani ski resort (w *bakuriani.ski*) has 29km of runs in three main areas. A ski pass costs GEL25–40/day, GEL144–232/week (or GEL 122–190 for 5 days in a week), or GEL7 for a single gondola ride. Many of the hotels rent downhill skis, but you'll have to bring your own cross-country skis, snowboard or snowshoes.

The oldest ski area is on Kokhta Gora (Pretty Hill; 2,155m), with a 3.1km run (very difficult at the top) and also ski jumps; an old lift takes you to a restaurant and the radio masts on top. Behind, on the peak's southern side, is the Kokhta II or 'Tatra-Poma' lift, starting by the Trialeti Palace Hotel, which has a good restaurant (but not recommended as a hotel). The new Didveli area is 3km to the southwest (*GEL8 by taxi*) at the end of Davit Agmashenebelis (while ski facilities are being developed, the roads are not, with daily traffic jams, not enough parking, and cars without chains slipping and crashing on the steep Didveli road). It was created by oligarch Bidzina Ivanishvili, who provided free skiing for the first season (when the lift was not yet open to the top), and then donated to the state. An eight-person Leitner gondola takes you up to a quad Doppelmayr chairlift and then a funicular to the 2,682m summit from where there are seven interconnecting pistes, between 1,200 and 2,200m long (14km in total); there are coloured LED lights for night skiing. At the end of 2016 the disused Mitarbi area, 3km east, was revived when its Soviet-era lift was replaced and the slopes were widened; there are two Doppelmayr chairlifts, from 1,550m to 2,000m and then to 2,235m, plus a drag to 2,010m. The Mitarbi and Kokhta areas meet at the top of the Tatra lift, so it's possible to ski between all three areas.

There's snow-making, and there's also skating on a natural pond in January and February; there's one snowshoe trail, but Georgians aren't very interested. Otherwise, the big winter sports event here is the **Sukhia ski race** held in early March of even years (in odd years it's in Gudauri).

In summer there's good **walking**, of course, and mountain biking, although chairlifts don't start until 11.00. The best access to the peaks is by a jeep track to the left from Davit Aghmashenebelis by the Tatra-Poma lift; there's a pleasant hike to the right/south to the next two peaks. Unusually for a ski resort, Bakuriani also has a fine alpine **Botanical Garden** (*Borjomi St 57;* m *899 573830;* ⊙ *10.00–17.00 in theory*), founded in 1910 and reached through the green gates at km25.9 on the road to Borjomi. In an area of 17ha they have more than 800 subalpine species of flowering plants, including around 100 trees and shrubs. Incidentally, Bakuriani is known for a sort of 'chewing gum' made from pine resin, as well as a pine cone jam.

The **Cinema Didveli** is at Davit Agmashenebelis 5 (\ *0367 240300*). Joyland (\ *0367 240099;* m *595 240099;* f *Joyland.Bakuriani*) is a **tubing park** in the centre of the village (between Davit Agmashenebelis and Rustaveli) which is open daily from 11.00 to 20.00 for children and then in the evening for their parents with the EnJoy bar, restaurant and disco.

Beyond Bakuriani The village of **Tsikhdvari**, 9km west (signposted as a mountain-bike route), is lovely, with a mineral bath built by Mikhail Romanov. Turning right off Davit Agmashenebelis, an unsurfaced road continues southwards through the Trialeti range and eventually down, through a Greek-populated area, to Akhalkalaki; immediately beyond the 2,454m Zachraskaro Pass an even rougher road leads east to **Lake Tabatskuri**, at 1,990m (security personnel for the BTC pipeline may demand to see your passport here). The lake (14.2km² in area) and the headwaters of the Ktsia River, to its north, are an important stopover for waterbirds such as grey heron, velvet scoter, Eurasian crane, black and white stork, great white egret, red-beaked swan, and also griffon-vulture; they're protected in a detached part of the Borjomi-Kharagauli National Park. It takes about 2 hours by 4x4 (not in winter) to get from Bakuriani to the east side of the lake, where the birds are most numerous.

SOUTHWEST FROM BORJOMI

Beyond Likani, heading southwest on the main road to Akhaltsikhe, there are a few more things to see in the national park. From just before km37/60 it's a short drive north (in the Khitakhevi Gorge, but a couple of kilometres short of Khitakhevi village) to the lovely **Mtsvane (Green) Monastery**, a simple 9th-century basilica partly in a cave, with a deacon's nave to the south and porches to the south and west. At about km38.5/58.5 (10km south of Borjomi), a road is signed to **Chobiskhevi**, across the river 3km south; here, by the Gogichant stream, are the most important secular buildings in the national park, lantern-vaulted houses (a style associated primarily with the historic Tori province) built in the 8th–10th centuries. With horses, it's a lovely excursion to the southeast up the Chobiskhevi Gorge to Lake Tabatsveli, which was reached by a cable car in Soviet times but has been largely abandoned since then. Local marshrutkas from Borjomi go as far as Dviri, just across the river at km42/55.

The A308 continues to the small village of **Kvabiskhevi** (km46/51) from where, as mentioned on page 205, a trail leads to Lomis Mta, starting near the rangers' shelter and campsite, behind which you can climb up to the Mariamtsminda (Holy Virgin) Church, a three-naved basilica built in the 9th and 14th centuries. It takes 90 minutes to the Kvabiskhevi fortress (1,150m), from where you can continue to Lomis Mta. In Kvabiskhevi, Rusudan Khutsishvili has a guesthouse (m 555 726386; $$) with two double rooms.

As the road emerges from the wooded Borjomi Gorge, there's a clear change to the dry, bare landscape of the Anatolian highlands. At km51 the railway (now on the left bank) passes through a tunnel under a castle, and at km56/41 the road and railway reach **Atskuri** (950m), a small, dusty village under the remains of a 10th–13th-century fortress high on a crag. Atskuri was an important trade centre from the 6th century BC, with Greek pottery coming via Vani; St Andrew is said to have brought an icon of the Virgin Mary here, and a bishop's church was built later. The fortress was a Turkish stronghold until 1829, but then fell into ruin. Hiking routes lead north into the Borjomi-Kharagauli National Park from 2.5km east of the village, as described on page 205. Guesthouse Nick & George, at Atskuri 45 (3 rooms; m 555 259355, 551 916237; e maiaaitsuradze@gmx.com; w nickandgeorge. com; $$) works closely with the national park; horseriding is available with Nugzar Aitsuradze (m 555 259355, 551 916237).

AKHALTSIKHE The Mtkvari passes through the short Tsnisi Gorge and swings away to the southeast (along with a short cut to Vardzia and Armenia), while the road and railway briefly head west to the small city of Akhaltsikhe, 45km from Borjomi, 77km from Khashuri and 200km from Tbilisi. The capital of Meskheti (or Samtskhe), its name means 'New Castle', but in fact Lomsia was founded in the 9th century and destroyed in the 11th, and the fortifications on the easily defensible hilltops were built in the 12th century, long before Paskevich stormed the Turkish defences in 1828 and built a new fort. The town has a reputation for being multi-ethnic and tolerant, but it was an important centre for the Circassian slave trade in the 18th century. It's now a city of 20,000, about a third of whom are Armenian (Michael Aznavourian, father of French singer Charles Aznavour, was born here) – the Meskhetian Turks who were numerous in the region in the period following the Ottoman occupation have long gone, exiled to Central Asia by Stalin in the early 1940s. These days, Akhaltsikhe is somewhat down-at-heel, but it's hoped that the massive refurbishment (or Disneyfication) of the Rabati fortress will bring many more tourists; there are certainly some decent new hotels. In any case there is enough interest here for an overnight stay and it makes a good base for visits to Sapara Monastery and Vardzia cave-city.

Getting there and away

There's a fairly new road crossing to Turkey at Posof, and Mahmut Turizm **buses** from Tbilisi to Turkey can be caught at the Akhaltsikhe bus station at 13.00, costing US$15 to Trabzon or US$50 to Ankara. Alternatively, **marshrutkas** run hourly to Vale, 9km west and 7km before the border, from where you should be able to get a ride to the border (or a taxi from Akhaltsikhe costs about GEL20); however, there are unlikely to be taxis waiting on the Turkish side.

There's a ticket office in the bus station for marshrutkas to Batumi (*GEL18; 08.30, 11.30*), Gori (*GEL10; 08.15, 13.00*), Kutaisi (*GEL10; 11.45, 15,00 & 18.00*) and Tbilisi (*GEL10; at least 18 daily, between 06.20 & 18.00*), which all go via Borjomi, as well as 13 to Atskuri and at least nine as far as Khashuri (*GEL5*). There are others to Abastumani (*10.30, 12.30, 14.00, 15.30, 17.00*), Akhalkalaki (*GEL6; 08.15, 09.30, 11.00, 11.30, 15.00, 16.30*), Ninotsminda (*08.15, 15.00*), and Vardzia (*GEL5; 10.20, 12.20, 16.00, 17.30*), and you can also take a taxi to Vardzia for GEL50–60 return including waiting time; the drive takes about 90 minutes each way.

There are also buses to Yerevan (*GEL35; 07.00*) and Gyumri (*GEL15; 07.00*) in Armenia (or else go to Akhalkalaki, from where there are more frequent buses to Yerevan). Armenian buses to Gyumri have the old name Leninakan written in Cyrillic on their destination board.

Where to stay

There's a hotel upstairs in the bus station (m *599 108144*), charging GEL15 each for a very basic room and cold showers; the only television is the one always blaring by the entrance, but they're friendly and speak some German. You may also be offered a homestay at the bus station, otherwise there are quite a few cheap hotels opposite the bus station and on and near Rustaveli, the road to Vardzia and Akhalkalaki.

Lomsia (63 rooms) Kostava 10; \365 222001; m 577 327825; w lomsiahotel.ge. Easily the classiest place in this area, with a good bar & restaurant, although the b/fast is not as good as you might expect. **$$$$**

Hotel Rabath Gino Wellness (38 rooms) Kharischirashvili 1; m 599 880924; w gino.ge. This new fake-oriental palace, complete with purdah balconies, is just inside the Rabati fortress & you have to park outside & carry luggage in. It's grandiose, with a luxury spa, but service can be poor. **$$$–$$$$**

Hotel Grand Palace Tamarashvili 2; m 592 000533; w grandpalace.ge. In the former railway station, this is a big place that receives plenty of coach parties, but it's nicely done & not expensive. **$$$**

Hotel Rio (13 rooms) Akhalkalaki Highway 1; \32 319101; m 593 276169. A modern hotel 2km east of the centre towards Vardzia, this has bright, largish AC rooms with Wi-Fi; fitness club & swimming pool. Price inc b/fast. **$$$**

Hotel Tiflis (23 rooms) Aspindza 12; m 568 111188, 0790 909001; w hoteltiflis.ge. In a large historic building just off Rustaveli, this is a surprisingly decent new place with a restaurant & lounge-bar; rooms are AC & some have balconies. **$$$**

🏠 **Meskheti Palace** (24 rooms)
Natenadze 2; 📞 365 222210; 📱 577 244046;
✉ meskhetipalase@mail.ru; 📘. On the left as you
go up Kostava, this is a comfortable but somewhat
impersonal new hotel, with a PC available at
reception & English-speaking staff. **$$$**

🏠 **Hotel Prestige** (18 rooms) Rustaveli 76;
📞 365 220570 📱 579 997711; ✉ otelprestige@
gmail.com. A solid old building of pink stone, all
rooms have AC, cable TV & private bathroom &
some have balconies. Rates inc b/fast. **$$–$$$**

🏠 **Hotel Shin** (9 rooms) Sts Davit &
Konstantine 2A at Aspindza; 📞 365 221230; 📱 579
174174; ✉ qkurtanidze@gmail.com; 📘. Down
by the river north of Rustaveli (not far from the
Borjomi road, but about a 15min walk from the
centre), this solid building of pink tufa has good
plain rooms including a dorm, Wi-Fi & a beer
garden. **$$–$$$**

🏠 **Diana Kurtanidze's Village House**
(4 rooms) 📱 555 775434. In Kide, a couple of
kilometres north of the Borjomi road & 6km
from Akhaltsikhe, the dbl rooms have 2 shared
bathrooms. It's a charming place to sample village
life & enjoy organic food. **$$**

🏠 **Guesthouse Edelvais** (3 rooms) Aspindza
7; 📱 574 228820. A self-contained flat with 8 sgl
beds in all & a basic kitchenette & poor Wi-Fi. No
b/fast. **$$**

🏠 **Hotel Meskheti** Kostava 8; 📞 365 220420;
📱 570 100671. Formerly the Intourist, this Soviet-
era hotel in the centre has gloomy corridors but
fairly clean rooms with TV, shower & Wi-Fi. **$$**

🏠 **Hotel New Star** Tsikhisdjiri 21; 📱 599
937331. On the way up to the Rabati Castle from
the lower town, this has an old stone ground floor
with the entrance around the corner to the right;
simple AC rooms, super-friendly staff & excellent
b/fast. **$$**

🏠 **Hotel Old Rabati** Tsikhisdziri 6; 📱 551
945549. More like a hostel, with a café-bar, though
you'll probably get a nice room with AC & a huge
bathroom to yourself; some English spoken. **$$**

🏠 **Guesthouse Edemi** (9 rooms) Rustaveli
105A; 📞 365 220035; 📱 599 185159, 599 937338;
✉ 105edemi@gmail.com. About 1.5km east on the
Vardzia/Akhalkalaki road & up to the right near
the hospital, this has a big yard with some private
woodland; some rooms have shared facilities,
others en suite, inc 1 small chalet. **$–$$**

✖ Where to eat and drink

Other than in the better hotels, there are few places
to eat in Akhaltsikhe: just a handful of simple places on Kostava that serve
Georgian snacks and, if you're lucky, burgers and shwarma. There's a decent Smart
supermarket opposite the bus station. There are a couple of touristy restaurants
between the tourist office and the entry to the upper part of the citadel.

✖ **Café Iveria Tamar** Mepe 7; ⊕ 10.00–
midnight. Opposite the library & theatre (there's
also a pleasant café on the traffic-free theatre
plaza), this serves up inexpensive Georgian food
such as khachapuri & grilled meats; there's a nice
vine-shaded patio. **$**

✖ **Dubli** Tamarashvili 35; 📱 551 579071;
⊕ 10.00–midnight daily. On the main road a
little east of the bus station, this is a popular (but
smokey) place serving khachapuri, khinkali and
other Georgian dishes; service can be poor. **$**

✖ **Dzveli Sardaph** On the right near the top of
Kostava, serving a good range of Georgian classics
such as kharcho, ostri, mtsvadi, chikhirtma &, of
course, khinkali & khachapuri. **$**

✖ **Paemani** Kostava 41; 📱 365 223278. At the
top of Kostava, this has something of a cafeteria
ambience but serves decent enough food. **$**

✖ **Restaurant Old Pub** Orbeliani 2 (cnr of
Kostava); 📞 365 222929. Good cellar restaurant
with Wi-Fi. Traditional Georgian menu. **$**

🍷 **Natenadze Wine Cellar** Saakadze 20; 📱 571
000021; ✉ natenadzegio@gmail.com; 🌐 natenadze.
company; ⊕ 11.00–18.00 daily. Something special
– the only winemaker in Meskheti, where vineyards
were destroyed after the Turkish conquest of 1578.
Now ancient vines (up to 400 years old) grow
wild up trees, at an altitude of 1,000–1,650m in
Georgia's coldest & driest wine-making area. Giorgi
is discovering lost varieties & makes 1 blend a year, a
maximum of 1,200 bottles.

Other practicalities

The **tourist information** office (📱 *555 777241*; ✉ *ticakhaltsikhe@
gmail.com*; ⊕ *10.00–18.00 daily*) is just inside the entry to the Rabati Castle but is fairly

useless and has no maps and no accommodation list. There are clean, free toilets behind. There are a couple of **ATMs** here, on Kostava and in the Public Service Hall opposite the bus station at Tamarashvili 3 (where there's also open Wi-Fi).

What to see and do Turning right out of the bus station and then right under the railway, you can make your way up to the left through a rebuilt historic district characterised by narrow, roughly cobbled streets and darbazi houses that have the enclosed loggia-style balconies typical of the region. Tiskhisdzuri then Kazbegi lead to the hilltop **Rabati Castle**, controversially refurbished in 2011–12 in what was more like a total rebuilding and re-imagining – everything is very new and slick, in authentic Saakashvili style. The upper part of the 7ha site contains a gold-domed mosque, madrasah, church and a superb modern museum which makes a visit worthwhile whatever you think of the rest of the fortress.

Inside the main gate is the tourist information office (*where you should buy entry tickets for the upper citadel;* ☉ *10.00–18.00 Tue–Sun; GEL6*) and a clinically neat garden feature with a ladder of pools at the east end of the fortress beyond an open-air performance area; stairs lead up inside a rebuilt tower (with concrete floors) and onto the walls and on top of the gatehouse, with views across the city (the rebuilding did not extend to making the steps health and safety-compliant, so watch your children).

To the right, a bit of a maze leads past new hotels and restaurants to the gate to the upper citadel, where the keep and the mint (with a double gallery) just beyond the bare Ahmadiyya Mosque (built in 1752 on a church's foundations) are relatively authentic; the gardens and pavilions are not. Below the keep is the excellent **Museum of Samtskhe-Javakheti** (*same ticket/hrs as upper citadel*) with spot-lit displays that work very well as long as the bulbs are replaced as required. They start with clay idols with rather spooky obsidian eyes from the first half of the 3rd millennium BC and obsidian arrowheads, metal and pottery from the same period, followed by a priestess's ornaments and some clay vessels from the mid 2nd millennium BC. The end of the 2nd millennium BC saw the rise of the Daiaeni kingdom (part of the Hittite cultural sphere), with ritual axes of copper and antimony, and then the use of iron. From the 5th century BC the area came under Greek influence, with the kingdom of Arian Kartli developing as a rival to Mskheta, which came out ahead and created the proto-Georgian kingdom of Kartli. There are stone carvings from churches, founded in Javakh from the 10th century and in Samtskhe from the 13th century, and ended by the Turkish conquest in the late 16th century. Finally, there's Georgian weaponry from the 17th to 19th centuries and tiles, copper vessels and musical instruments.

There's a minaret outside the upper gate of the citadel (between the mosque and an equally bare 9th–10th-century church) – if you come out of the gate and take the road to the left from the car park you'll come directly to an **Ottoman hammam** that's now used as a wood store. It is interesting to note that this structure has been dutifully patched up with recycled chunks of church-style stonework – a true palimpsest of the first order. Carrying on, you could turn left to the St Marine church (old, but with modern paintings and windows), or turn right and cross the asphalted road (at Kazbegi 55) and fork right again you'll come to a very ruined little Catholic church with a separate belfry, from where you can go on down to Kazbegi by a basketball court. If you explore the backstreets on the far side of Kazbegi below the fortress you should also come across an austere **synagogue**, built in 1863.

Turning right from the bus station and then left at the same roundabout, you'll cross the river to the centre; keep to the right up Kostava from the statue of Tamar

6

(outside a new church), and at the top of the hill you'll pass the market to your right. If you go on and turn left and left again to return on Natenadze, on the other side of the pseudo-one-way system, you'll have seen all there is to see here – not a lot, although the neatly built houses of volcanic tuff are very Armenian in style.

Heading down Iadze (opposite the Hotel Meskheti) you'll reach the Armenians' large **Mardi church**, silhouetted on a small hilltop that's even more dramatic than the one occupied by the fort; built in 1868, its interior is bare and cold and not worth seeing, but the view is good. You can reach it by the rough steps up from the end of Iadze, or take a big loop left to reach it from the rear.

Tours usually include **Sapara** just east of town, where there's an ancient monastery similar to that at Zarzma; turn right/south off Rustaveli onto Saphara Street, fork left after 3km and continue up the valley for another 8km. It's possible to hike here from Akhaltsikhe in about 3 hours, or you can take a taxi (*GEL20 return*). There's been a monastery here since the 10th century, but the present Church of St Saba (the largest of ten) dates from the late 13th century, with fine early 14th-century frescoes in the Byzantine Paleologue style. Dramatically set on the edge of a gorge, with a fort above, it is a good example of the cruciform ground plan.

WEST FROM AKHALTSIKHE Heading west from Akhaltsikhe, a road soon forks left to **Vale** (where there's a 10th-century cruciform church, remodelled in the 14th century) and the Turkish border. The main road continues westwards and then divides, with the A307 heading north to Kutaisi; this passes Amara, west of which you'll see the Amaravepe castle ruins on a hill, and enters **Abastumani**, a tiny spa which is the site of Georgia's main astronomical observatory (previously a Romanov villa and a TB sanatorium). At km9 (to the east from a statue on a rock) is the *banya* or spa, and at about km10 the Observatory Hotel (m *577 230475*) is on the east side of the road opposite No 56. About another 1km to the north, opposite No 7, a track leads 100m west to a footbridge and a tiny cable car which runs up to the observatory every few hours (connecting in theory with marshrutkas from Akhaltsikhe). Alternatively you can take a path parallel to the cable car, 20 minutes downhill and probably double that uphill, or a taxi, costing GEL5 – a 3km road turns left to the north of the village. There are four or five telescopes and typically Soviet apartment blocks in usual post-Soviet disrepair, plus a nunnery and a few nice and fairly new guesthouses, all strewn along a thin ridge which offers great views of the forested hills just to the north, now part of the Borjomi-Kharagauli National Park. The Kapa guesthouse at Rustaveli 31 (m *599 518760*) has ten en-suite rooms, plus a summer cottage with three more rooms.

From a ranger shelter about 7km north of Abastumani a marked trail used to lead northwest and upwards, making a 10km loop on the south slopes of Mount Didimagala (2,588m) via the Didimagala tourist shelter, about 3km west of the road just south of the Zekari Pass. However, this has been closed due to a fire, but mountain bikes (not allowed in the main part of the park) are allowed to go on the jeep track to the shelter only.

Five minibuses a day run from Akhaltsikhe as far as Abastumani, but none continue northwards to the 2,182m **Zekari (Sun Gate) Pass** over the Lesser Caucasus; this is often closed by snow between October and June, but if you can get here a short hike to the east soon gives superb views. There's accommodation in the national park's Zekari tourist shelters (2,080m), about 50m above some shepherds' huts south of the pass; from here it takes 5 hours (return) to climb Mount Didimagala (2,588m), the highest in the region, to the west of the road. A summer-only road descends through Sairme (pages 239–40), known for its mineral waters, and Baghdati (page 239), to Kutaisi.

The Batumi road, the A306, continues westwards from the junction up the Kvabliani Valley below Okrostsikhe (Golden Fortress), the stronghold in early medieval times of the lords of Samtskhe-Javakheti province and an important obstacle to the Turkish invasions of the 15th and 16th centuries. Its huge towers and powerful walls are still visible. Crossing the river, you'll come to **Zarzma**, 29km from Akhaltsikhe, and see to the left the early 14th-century Church of the Transfiguration, with 16th-century frescoes, a fine large bell-tower and four smaller churches. Beyond here the road is very bad, and unsigned – in summer a marshrutka goes this way to Batumi, leaving Akhaltsikhe at 08.30 (the rest of the year it goes via Borjomi). It climbs southwest out of the valley, entering Adjara just before the 2,025m Goderji Pass (92km from Borjomi, 115km from Batumi), which is often blocked by snow between October and May.

EAST FROM AKHALTSIKHE TO VARDZIA To the east of Akhaltsikhe, the Akhalkalaki road (the A306) soon rejoins the Mtkvari Valley, crossing it at the first village, Mikadze (km5/107), and entering a dramatic gorge, bright with hornbeams in the autumn; on the north side of this you can see caves which prefigure those you're heading for at Vardzia.

Soon after emerging from the gorge, at km16/96, you'll see a statue of the national poet Shota Rustaveli, marking the entrance to the village of Rustavi, just to the left/ north of the road. Here, not the post-war industrial city of Rustavi southeast of Tbilisi, is where he was born. Although the river is still fairly sizeable (with a dam under construction at km19/93), the country becomes increasingly arid and unpopulated, although you'll see several ruined castles. The landscape is extraordinarily beautiful here in autumn when the hills turn a fiery red and yellow. Entering the sprawling village of **Aspindza** at km29/83, the castle ruins on a hilltop to the north are easily reached from just west of the centre; there's also the rough 9th-century Khvilisha basilica at the eastern exit from the village (km33/79). The Restaurant Leki (m *599 572916;* ☉ *09.00–22.00 daily;* $), just west of the village at km28, is a reliable source of classic Georgian food, followed by the Restaurant-Hotel-Laundry (ie: car-wash) Chiko (*km30/82;* m *593 906405;* e *salomenadiradze9@gmail.com;* w *chiko.ge;* $–$$; *restaurant* ☉ *08.00–23.00 daily;* $), a lovely modern place with a garden and terrace overlooking the valley. There are other guesthouses down towards the river, such as Bermukha (*Gogebashvili 16;* m *599 181763;* $) and the Guesthouse 1001 Nights (*Tamar Mepe 1;* m *599 957228,* e *aspindza.atasertigame@gmail.com;* $), with dormitory beds, and even a craft brewery, Amphora Beer (*Shoreti 21;* m *99 946500;* w *amphorabeer.com;* ☉ *always; free*). Continuing on the main road through the village you'll find ATMs, fuel and a couple of cafés including the Café-restaurant Europe (☏ *483 645379;* ☉ *10.00–22.00 daily*) and Café To Go (*km31/81*). About 1 hour from Akhaltsikhe, just before km44/68, traffic to Vardzia forks right off the A306 at **Khertvisi**, with the famous fortress (☉ *always; free*) directly ahead; it's immediately to the left after the bridge at the confluence of the Mtkvari and the Paravani, and can easily be reached by a road on its far side, where there are new signs and maps and a huge bus shelter. There were fortifications here by the 2nd century BC (reputedly destroyed by Alexander the Great), long before a church was built in AD985, when it was the administrative capital of the Meskheti region. The two main towers (one recently restored) were built by Tamar, and the present walls were added in 1354–56, according to the plaque over the entrance. Beyond it you'll see cave cells in the cliff above the houses to the left and 12th-century field terracing to the right, now being replanted with vines. Just below the castle is the Guesthouse Khertvisi (m *599 458883, 599 412095;* $), with shared bathrooms and a large garden, where you can taste local wine and mulberry vodka, as well as the Café Tourist. Now running south along the right/east bank of the Mtkvari, after about 8km the road (with newly added crash barriers) reaches a junction to the village of Nakalakevi then climbs steadily to Tmogvi village.

Just after the village is a dramatic defile known as Tamar's Gates, on the far side of which is the medieval castle of **Tmogvi**, wonderfully well placed to defend the approaches to Vardzia. It's best seen from a distance to the north, but from the road immediately opposite you'll see the curtain walls and the caves in the cliffs below, near the river. It's also possible to hike to the castle in an hour or so following a track along the left/west bank of the Mtkvari from the Jolda bridge just north of Nakalakevi, or from Vardzia. The castle was built in the 10th and 11th centuries and destroyed by the Persians in the 16th century; subsequent earthquakes have more or less completed the job of reducing it to rubble. The Tirebi Farmhouse Hostel (**m** *599 338871;* **$$**) is across the river from Tmogvi, a pleasant 30–40-minute hike from Tmogvi fortress; it's a peaceful spot, with friendly owners who serve delicious meals of their own organic produce. They have two en-suite rooms and two sharing a bathroom. In Tmogvi itself, there are some lovely guesthouses with gardens and pools with warm mineral water, including Tirebi (**m** *599 338871;* **e** *tirebi12@gmail. com;* **$$**), Aleksandre (**m** *591 901214;* **$$**) and Imedi (**m** *595 285750, 595 381898;* **$$**), and near the south end Tsiskari (**m** *598 968687, 790 606047;* **$$–$$$**).

From here the road drops to the turning (just north of km14/3) to the cave-nunnery of **Vanis-Kvabi** (or Kvabebi) to the left, a smaller equivalent of Vardzia itself, built, or excavated, between the 8th and 13th centuries. It's a very steep climb of about 400m on a concrete track to the base of the cliff, with no less than 16 levels of monks' cells and churches hidden in it. Founded in the 8th century, it was partially destroyed by an earthquake in 1089 and was reconstructed by Queen Tamar, becoming the court monastery by 1191. In addition to the 9th–11th-century church of St George, a hall church and belltower were built at the foot of the cliff in 1265, before it was all destroyed by the Persians in 1551 and the Ottomans in 1576; monks have now returned to live here. On the walls of the upper levels are the remains of inscriptions (of old Georgian poetry and prose), left by women hiding here in the 15th century.

VARDZIA ვარძია

It's another kilometre up the valley to Vardzia (16km from Khertvisi), one of Georgia's most impressive sights. It is the country's most famous cave-city and, largely because of its connections with Queen Tamar, a place of almost mystic importance for most Georgians. Having been in a closed border zone throughout the Soviet period, it's now receiving plenty of visitors, especially in summer. It's said that its name derives from 'Ak var, dzia' or 'Here I am, uncle' – Tamar's call when lost in the caves. First established by King George III in 1156 and consecrated in 1185, his daughter Tamar made it into a monastery, which became the chief seminary of southwestern Georgia (housing 2,000 monks) until an earthquake ruined it in 1283, slicing away a large portion of the rock face, weakened by tunnelling. Another quake in 1456 was followed by a Persian army in 1551, and it was abandoned after an attack by the Turks in 1578, so that now around 600 chambers survive of a total 3,000, which included stables, barracks, bakeries, wine presses and stores. Likewise, only half a dozen levels remain of the 13 which once penetrated 50m into the cliffs. The cave-city has been protected since 1938; there was some heavy-handed restoration with concrete in the 1970s, but more recent work has been more sensitive. Monks returned here in 1988, and some frescoes were damaged by candles, which are now only allowed outside. Heavy rain in 1998 caused a large section of cliff to collapse from 40–50m up; the Dutch government rapidly provided US$50,000 for emergency repairs, including to the stairs to the monastery bell-tower. Egyptian vultures are nesting in the caves, making their management yet more complex.

GETTING THERE AND AWAY Getting here is certainly much easier these days, with daily marshrutkas from Akhaltsikhe (*4 in summer, 2 in winter; GEL5*), taking about 1½ hours. Buy a ticket at the Akhaltsikhe bus station (the destination sign is in Latin script) or wait at the stops on Kostava and Rustaveli (although you may not get a seat for a while). They continue south past Valodia's Cottage and return at 08.30, 09.45 (to Tbilisi), 13.00 and 15.00. You can also take a taxi for GEL50–60 return including waiting time (or GEL130 from Borjomi) – this means you do not have to rush around the site in order to catch the last bus back at 15.00.

 WHERE TO STAY There's free camping next to the monastery, by the river or indeed anywhere along this lovely valley. Apart from the riverside Café Vardzia (m 555 739810), serving good Georgian food including fresh local trout, you'll need to eat at your hotel/guesthouse.

Vardzia Resort (27 rooms) 790 201515; m 591 321515; w vardziaresort.com. A fancier place, 2km north of the bridge, with a lovely garden, swimming pools & conference room. **$$$$$**

Valodia's Cottage (10 rooms) m 599 116207, 595 642346, Tbilisi 599 114506 (English & French spoken); e welcome@psity.ge, w accommodationvardzia.ge; f. This is the best place to stay, about 2km beyond Vardzia. It's a big, place with 2 low buildings with en-suite rooms & a lovely garden, where you can feast on their own trout & fresh vegetables; wine-tasting, rafting & bikes also available. **$$$**

Hotel Taoskari (7 rooms) m 599 543540, 599 228092; 577 749996; f. At the Vardzia bridge, with en-suite rooms & an open-air pool. **$$**

Guesthouse Vanya m 577 525226. Smallish new place about 1km south of the monastery (50m up the road to Upper Vardzia nunnery), the cheapest option, with filling meals. **$**

WHAT TO SEE AND DO Crossing the road bridge and turning right, it's a hundred metres to the car park for the cave-city of Vardzia, at about 1,400m altitude. There's a simple but relatively decent toilet block, as well as souvenir stalls. The site is officially open from 10.00 to 18.00, but they can be pretty tardy opening up out of season and can stay open until 19.00 in summer; nor are they likely to have change except in summer. Having paid your GEL7 (and GEL10 if you want an audio guide, or GEL25 for a guide), you have to walk up a road past two hairpin bends. This ends at the Ananauri sector of Vardzia, which, dating from the 10th century, is older than Vardzia proper, but was swallowed up by it; immediately above the end of the road is a cave used as stabling for horses (note the holes in the rock used to attach head ropes), while a small path (from the top bend in the path leading north) leads to a church. This is usually locked but you can peer in and see its smoke-blackened 16th-century frescoes.

The main path leads northwards below the cliffs to a bell-tower (built after the 1283 earthquake) and the refectory, and then (after a stretch where you're encouraged not to hang around, due to occasional rock falls) to the **Church of the Assumption** (1184–86), the pivotal point of the complex; in front of you is a famous fresco of Tamar (also 1184–86, one of just four painted in her lifetime) and her father George III, together with what seems to be an Annunciation but for the fact that the Virgin already has the child Jesus on her knee. You can head down a tunnel (with electric lights) outside, forking left to the pool known as 'Tamar's Tears', with beautifully cool and sweet water, or right to go much further to a refuge and ultimately to the upper level of the city (see below).

Returning outside, you can continue to the right to the top of a ropeway at the entry to some caves, now inhabited by monks, and then either head down the steep steps to the paved path below that leads back to the ticket office, or climb up to a much higher level with cliff face walkways. Either way you're pretty free to explore, although safety railings are beginning to appear; some of the chambers are interconnected, but thanks to the earthquakes most of them are now open to the outside world. There are a few frescoes, although most of the chambers are smoke-blackened; what are more interesting than the walls and ceilings are the floors, which are pitted with a surprising array of channels and receptacles for water and, of course, wine.

Vardzia is also becoming known for its natural attractions, notably wallcreepers, Egyptian vulture, golden eagle and lammergeyer, as well as rock martin, western rock nuthatch, blue and rufous-tailed rock thrush, rock sparrow, rock bunting, red-fronted serin, red-breasted flycatcher, olivaceous warbler, Caucasian chiff-chaff and red-backed shrike, as well as sun-bathing lizards and tortoises.

BEYOND VARDZIA About 1km south of the caves the road (much rougher here) reaches a hot spring where a steaming jet sprays water into a field. Turning right, you'll eventually reach **Zeda Vardzia** (Upper Vardzia, 3.5km from Vardzia proper), where the writer Peter Nasmyth reported finding an old church (built in the 11th century, with some interesting frescoes) surrounded by fields of marijuana; now nuns here make cheese and farm fish. A hiking and mountain bike trail continues west in the Erusheti mountains for about 3km to the abandoned village of Agara and another 3km to Lebisi, where there are *darnebi* or cave shelters where people hid from the Turkish invaders.

From half a kilometre back to the northeast from the Vardzia bridge (at km2/15), a road switchbacks its way up to the village of Apnia at the top of the cliff on the east side of the Mtkvari Valley. From here a very rough road leads northeast to **Kumurdo**, 12km southwest of Akhalkalaki, where there's a fairly large and complex cathedral built in AD964, with a large apse above the altar, two side apses at the east end and two more to the west; in the centre six pillars support the dome, which collapsed in the 16th century. At the west end an ambulatory was added in the second quarter of the 11th century.

The road on from Kumordo to Akhalkalaki is slightly better, but without a 4x4 you're best advised to travel from Vardzia to Akhalkalaki via Khertvisi. This is a delightful journey up the Paravani Valley, largely unpopulated, apart from a couple of trout farms (there's also a new hydro-electric station just south of Khertvisi, but it hasn't ruined the valley above). At km64.5, 3km short of Akhalkalaki, there's a footbridge created by placing an entire railway carriage across the river, although the floor has now rusted out.

AKHALKALAKI ('New Town'; 1,716m) Actually founded back in 1064, this is a small town of no importance now that Javakheti is governed from Akhaltsikhe, except as the site of a Russian military base, which closed in 2007, despite the protests of locals against the loss of jobs and the perceived loss of security from Turkey, in an area that is 90% Armenian (street signs are in three scripts, Georgian, Armenian and Cyrillic). It was also the terminus of a painfully slow railway from Tbilisi, a 160km-long branch completed only in 1986, but as part of the project to build a railway to Kars in Turkey a new Akhalkalaki International Station has been built midway between Akhalkalaki and Ninotsminda, and the spur into town has lost its services. In addition to the crossing to Armenia, 50km south beyond Ninotsminda, there's also a fairly new road crossing to Turkey at Çıldır, 34km to the southwest (and the road from Tbilisi has been improved), so the town may benefit a little.

Where to stay, eat and drink

Artsegi Hotel (9 rooms; aka Art-Seg) Mashtots 31; 362 22 3707; m 592 618575, 593 713033; e art-seg@mail.ru. This is a surprisingly good hotel, with a decent restaurant; turning off the main street by the Armenian church, it's across a small park next to the town hall. **$$$**

Guesthouse Anank (10 rooms) Darbinian 5; m 599 101835. With its entertaining owner & retro décor, plus a sauna, this is one of the nicest places to stay here. **$$–$$$**

Hotel Ararat (18 rooms) Kamo 13; m 592 618575, 593 618575. **$$**

Hotel Evrostar (8 rooms) Airport Turn; m 571 880900; 571 909456. Just outside the city on the Tbilisi road, this is a bit functional but comfortable enough. **$$**

Hotel Gold Javakishvili 11; m 579 150985. Just to the left as you leave town towards Ninotsminda, this also has a friendly café-bar. **$$**

Café Lux Charents 9; m 599 777212. By the school at the top of Tamar Mepe. **$**

Restaurant Kavkaz m 599 338011, 599 941733. Where the road to Turkey leaves town, opposite the ruins of the fort & matching petrol station. **$**

What to see and do Akhalkalaki is a drab town with lots of slots and betting shops, but there's a remarkably vibrant street market on Nalbandian. There are six marshrutkas a day from Akhaltsikhe (c70km), and others to Yerevan (Armenia) every hour or two. There are banks on the main road, Tavisupleba (Svoboda), with ATMs inside their lobbies rather than on the street. There's no tourist office, but there's a useful information board (in English) at the start of the Ninotsminda road.

Other than the remains of an **Ottoman fort** there's nothing much for tourists in the town itself; however, there's growing interest in the megalithic 'Cyclopean ruins' dotted across the Javakheti Plateau. These massive structures of basalt blocks 3m across remain enigmatic, their purpose and building techniques still largely unexplained. They date mostly from the 2nd millennium BC, although some are much more recent.

The easiest to visit is at **Abuli**, a dozen kilometres east of Akhalkalaki and easily reached by taxi on a rough road heading towards the twin peaks of Didi Abuli, the highest mountain in the area at 3,300m. There seem to be defensive and residential structures here, overlooking the Javakheti Plateau and Lake Paravani; it's not far as the crow flies from another important site at **Shaori**, at 2,760m on the slopes of Mount Patara Abuli, but this is reached from Poka and Aspara on the shores of Lake Paravani (page 221). On these extinct volcanoes are fearsome scree fields which the ancient builders used as additional defences – you'll need to be very careful to pick the right route up.

The third major site is at **Saro**, just north of Khertvisi (and 4km to the right/east on the Khizabavra road from km70.5/41.5), where there are also cave dwellings and food stores; nearby is a twin-nave church dating from the 7th–8th centuries. Here, as well as in Khizabavra and elsewhere, you'll also see *darnebi* or cave shelters, connected by tunnels, for protection from invaders. The villages of the Javakheti Plateau are also notable for their darbazi houses, with three sides buried in a hillside and a flat earth- and grass-covered roof; in the centre is a pyramidal chimney of stepped logs, and of course there are pits for storing wine and grain as well as cheese. There are also *menhirs* dotted across the bleak Javakheti Plateau, notably at Chikiani and Tezi (now Avranlo).

NINOTSMINDA AND BEYOND ნინოწმინდა

To the east, the railway and the A303 cross a high arid plateau dotted with a surprising number of lakes; the road was known for its terrible state but has been rebuilt thanks to the US$100 million Millennium Challenge fund, also providing bilingual education in this poor and largely Armenian area. It's 18km to **Ninotsminda** (or Bogdanovka) a town of 7,000 and, at 1,940m, one of the highest and remotest in Georgia. There are few direct marshrutkas from Tbilisi (*13.00 from Didube, 08.00 & 17.30 from Samgori; GEL3*) and it's usually easier to travel via Akhaltsikhe and Akhalkalaki, a GEL4–5 taxi ride away; the railway from Tbilisi to Turkey (opened at the end of 2017) passes the edge of town but the only stop is the Akhalkalaki International Station, midway between the two towns. There are two simple hotels, the Ninotsminda (*10 rooms; Tavisupleba 1B;* m *599 653111, 599 760004;* **$$$**) on the main highway, and the Ararat (*5 rooms; Teryan 2A;* m *555 777905, 571 999002;* e *ararathot@gmail.com;* **$$**), one block south. Just southeast of the central crossroads is the Boutique-Café-Ground Coffee (**$**), which may also have rooms.

Just 1km southwest of Ninotsminda (at 1,930m) is **Lake Khanchali**, which also has a sad and complicated history. Until 1961 it covered 1,310ha and was home to lake trout, Caucasian herring, barbel and migrating ducks and waders, but in that year it was drained to be adapted for fish farming. It remained dry until 1964, by which time the wildfowl had moved to Lake Çıldır, in Turkey, on their migrations. Fish farming was abandoned in 1968, and the lake gradually reverted to its natural state. In 1985 two-thirds was drained again to grow hay, while the southeastern third was used for fish farming until 1990; in 1997 the dam began to collapse and the whole lake was drained for a year while it was patched together. The Georgian Centre for the Conservation of Wildlife campaigned for the restoration of the lake, buying 900ha of lakebed to create the first private reserve in the Caucasus; it's now part of the **Javakheti Protected Areas**, a loose collection of lakes on the bleak plateau that is becoming known as a great location for viewing migrating birds. It's being transformed into the Javakheti National Park (m *577 640482;* e *tkarapetiani@apa. gov.ge*), linked to the new Lake Arpi National Park in Armenia, with birdwatching towers and an expensive new visitor centre on the edge of Akhalkalaki (*3km to the southwest on the Kartsakhi road;* m *577 640482*), where you can camp (*GEL5 pp*) and rent tents, bikes and e-bikes.

Amazingly, 24 bird species (of which four are threatened with extinction) still nest at the lake, including cranes, Dalmatian pelicans and white storks. Many waders stop to feed when the water is low in the lakes, including thousands of little stints and ruffs, as well as Armenian gulls, black-winged pratincoles, marsh, curlew and wood sandpipers and greenshank; occasionally one or two sociable lapwings are seen, and possibly Demoiselle crane and in late August Terek and broad-billed sandpipers. The steppe grasslands surrounding the lakes are home to overwintering bustards, as well as larks, pipits and wagtails (including a few citrine wagtails), and raptors such as pallid harrier, osprey, long-legged buzzard and steppe eagle.

Just west of the lake in **Sulda**, on the road from Akhalkalaki to the Turkish border, birdwatchers and international drivers can stop at a couple of guesthouses, Flora (*3 rooms;* m *595 211136;* **$–$$**) and Misha (*2 rooms;* m *599 492967;* **$–$$**), which both charge GEL40 for a double room including breakfast. Similarly, just short of the Armenian border on the A306, the Guesthouse Madatapa (m *551 550941, 599 172113;* $–$$) in Sameba at the south end of Lake Madatapa, is also ideal for birders. You can also rent horses in Sameba (m *551 085524; GEL5/hr, GEL50/day*).

From Ninotsminda the A306 leads southeast to the Armenian border, passing through **Gorelovka**, the goal of Philip Marsden's mid-1990s quest in *The Spirit Wrestlers*. Here in 1895, on what they called the Sacred Heights, the Dukhobors, a Tolstoyan Quaker-like sect of Russians, burnt their guns and refused to serve in the tsar's army, starting a long saga of persecution and eventual emigration to Canada (via Siberia, as a rule). Tolstoy campaigned vigorously for them, donating the profits from his final novel, *Resurrection*, to resettle more than 7,500 Doukhobors in Saskatchewan, and also funded a school in Gorelovka. Now some of their turf-roofed cabins remain, but few of the people. In 1990 nearly 7,000 Dukhobors still lived in eight villages in this region, but today their community has shrunk to only about 500 (140 of them in Gorelovka). A dozen or so still meet to pray in the Gorelovka orphanage on Sundays (there are no Doukhobor churches, as they believe God is in each person). When collective farms were broken up in 1997 the Dukhobors chose to stick with the principle of co-operative work and established the Dukhoborets collective farm. Unfortunately they left no land for the local Armenians, and in 2006 the local council removed almost 5,000ha, leaving the Dukhobors with only 600ha, between 6ha and 15ha per family. They're now moving back to Russia. Armenians call it Aragilneri Gyugh or Stork Village, and there are still plenty nesting on houses and power poles in summer.

The A303 and railway head northeast from Ninotsminda past Georgia's largest lake, **Lake Paravani** (2,047m), which is also threatened by a plan to farm non-native fish; at its southern end is Poka, known for the **convent of St Nino** (w *phokanunnery. ge*) whose nuns make excellent cheeses and jams that can be bought in Tbilisi or at their shop here, just to the west. This is also the access to the Shaori megalithic ruins (page 219). At the lake's northern end is the Dukhobor village of Tambovka. The villages on this cold and treeless plateau are notable for their savage speed-bumps, and for their grass-roofed houses. From km 46/100, after Lake Paravani, the road drops fast to Tsalka (page 346; 81km from Ninotsminda) and on to the outskirts of Manglisi, where the old road takes a rather hilly route passing near to Birtvisi and Betania (pages 345–6), before descending to Tbilisi, while the railway takes a loop to the south. A minor road from Manglisi to Koda, south of Tbilisi on the main road to Armenia, was rebuilt (and launched by Saakashvili with great fanfare as the new Silk Road) and is now the fastest route, used by the few marshrutkas that head up on to the plateau.

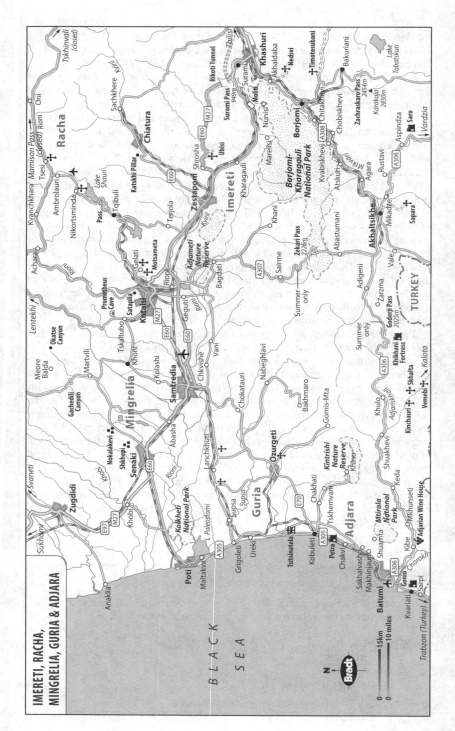

Imereti, Racha, Mingrelia and Guria

IMERETI იმერეთი

Imereti lies cradled between the High and Lesser Caucasus and the Surami range, inland from the coastal plains; it's a fertile, well-watered region that was one of the cradles of Georgian civilisation. The Imeretians are known as the most voluble and temperamental people in Georgia, and they also consider themselves the most hospitable. Its capital is Kutaisi, Georgia's second city until it was overtaken by Batumi, an attractive, friendly place which has a few creature comforts to offer the traveller.

The main road from Tbilisi crosses the Rikoti Pass from Khashuri and Surami (page 176) and descends steadily to Zestaponi, while the railway (and a back road) follows the next valley to the south. The main road has been improved, with lots of modern bridges cutting off sections of road that take a much longer route along the curves of the river (a process that will continue as the new East–West highway is inserted into this valley). Many of these still form village streets, and they can be used to make a far more enjoyable route for cycling; as most of these loops are to the north of the main road, cyclists should head westwards (ie: downhill). With a good, solid bike it would be possible to return by the Kharagauli road to the south, making a very pleasant loop. This is unsurfaced east of Kharagauli, but some repairs have been made.

HIKING TO THE NORTH OF BORJOMI-KHARAGAULI NATIONAL PARK The back road from Surami to Kharagauli passes through Moliti, where there's also a railway station; from here it's 6km southeast to **Nunisi** (400m), with an old church and thermal springs which are supposed to heal eczema, and the Samta Nunisi Park Hotel (*7 rooms;* m *599 225580;* ╲ *32 47 5202 (Tbilisi);* e *nunisi90@mail.ru;* w *nunisi. ge*), which was the starting point for the hike to Zanavi, currently closed due to wash-outs. Also on this route, the tiny village of **Marelisi** (450m) is becoming a centre for hiking into the Borjomi-Kharagauli National Park (pages 201–6); the park owns a guesthouse (m *599 951421, 577 101994;* e *welcome@borjomi-kharagauli-np.ge;* ⊕ *spring–autumn;* **$$**) 4km south of the station and 3km north of the park gate (a taxi is available and can also shuttle your baggage). It has four double rooms with food and hot water available, plus camping in the yard, and is becoming popular with Tbilisi expats at the weekends. Horses can be rented for easier forays into the park, and local people will provide meals and show visitors how they produce honey, bread and other local foodstuffs. The trails leads south up the Shavtwala Valley and then to either Lomis Mta and Likani, or Rkinis Jvari and Atskuri; see page 205 for details.

Kharagauli is the northern centre for the Borjomi-Kharagauli National Park, with special responsibility for the buffer zone. Rather more substantial than Nunisi and Marelisi, it consists of two main streets (across the river from the station and to the right) with some fine buildings of dressed stone built in 1933, one of which (*at Solomon Mepe 17*) is now a park office and visitor centre. Further west there's the large *Muza* sculpture by someone who'd obviously never seen a naked woman; the road heads into a gorge, passing a very odd sculpture, half-covered in ivy but seeming to represent grotesquified pagan myths.

Marelisi, Kharagauli and Moliti are served by marshrutkas from Didube (the last at 15.30) and trains, with the 09.00 and 21.45 departures from Tbilisi taking about 2 hours 30 minutes to Moliti, 2 hours 45 minutes to Marelisi and 3 hours to Kharagauli. From the west, trains leave Zestaponi at 02.00 and 13.25, taking 40 minutes to Kharagauli, 60 minutes to Marelisi and 75 minutes to Moliti. Chinese engineers are completing three new railway tunnels just west of Kharagauli to avoid the current 30km/h curves.

UBISI Emerging from the toll tunnel at km143.5 (or the old road over the pass), the main highway passes beehives and their keepers camping beside the road in summer and criss-crosses the Rikotula and the Dzirula streams many times, passing a new restaurant at about km149 and then attractive villages such as Khonevi (km155) and Boriti (km167) – all to be bypassed when the highway is extended west from the Rikoti tunnel.

Immediately after passing the piers for an unfinished concrete viaduct, to the left at km170/382, a road to Goresha turns left on a bend and drops to a bridge; it's well worth halting here to visit the charming little **church of Ubisi**, just before the bridge. Heading east, there's a good view of the church and the remains of fortifications above the unfinished viaduct. Built in AD826 by one Grigor Kansteli, it's a single-nave basilica, but with a double porch that more or less constitutes a southern aisle. The gate-tower, built of rounded river stones, has been doubled as well, and there are various other extensions tacked on to the main building. However, the bell-tower, a three-storey dwelling built by Demetre I in 1141 (when the church was also restored), with a ladder to reach the entrance, is separate. The 14th-century frescoes by Damiane, reaching almost to the floor, are lovely and rival the finest Byzantine paintings with a supple grace that seems very Western, especially the Last Supper above the altar and the Annunciation (with the Virgin turning in surprise) to the north. The excellent Restaurant Zgapari (m *551 047373;* f) sits between the main road and the river, specialising in locally foraged mushrooms.

TO ZESTAPONI In the long village of **Shrosha**, huge quantities of red ceramics are for sale, especially in a lay-by at km174 (km378 from the west), although the village itself is at km177; this is virtually the only place in western Georgia where qvevris are made for wine-making. The good Imereti Restaurant is just west of km180. The railway soon appears from the valley to the southeast (before the junction with the Kharagauli road at km183) and cuts across a bend in the river through a new tunnel; to the north the traces of the old single-track railway can still be seen and could also be used for a hiking or mountain-biking route from km184. At km189, a road bridge leads right into the village of **Shorapani**, while the highway (lined with stalls selling engine oil) loops to the left; to the right at km190 you'll see a ruined castle, then a rusty steam locomotive (a narrow-gauge 0-6-0 tank engine) on a plinth above the rail junction to Chiatura.

Another kilometre to the west, at km192, the road enters **Zestaponi**, a sprawling, grimy industrial town at the junction to Chiatura and Sachkhere, with a decent soccer team but not much else to recommend it. The transit route (lined with Western-style coffee shops) turns right over the first bridge crossing the Kviril

River, while westbound buses pick up and set down here, continue on the south bank to then take the second bridge and turn left to pass the railway station and a park (through a colonnade to the south). At the western end of town they head under the railway to the bus station at km195.5 (the end of the transit route and the road from Chiatura), then pass the metallurgical works (now Ukrainian- and American-owned) and finally leave the town at km199 (km353 from the west). At km204 the road passes the turning north to Tqibuli and Racha (page 245); the new Khareba winery is just another kilometre west. As for accommodation, the Hotel Parnavazi (*Farnavazi 5;* \ *492 252147;* m *579 535395;* f *hotelfarnavazi5;* **$$$**) is basically a grand casino and does not seem interested in passing trade; there is a restaurant like an airport control tower on top of the building, and a terrace and swimming pool. The Guesthouse Zedafoni, just south across the river (*Pushkin 43;* m *558 932746, 557 650645;* e *zedafoni@gmail.com;* **$$**) may be a better bet, and there's a motel at the Socar petrol station in the western outskirts.

From the railway bridge by the bus station a Wine Route sign points a couple of kilometres south to Kvaliti, where you can visit Archil Guniava's Wine Cellar (m *599 534295;* e *archilguniavawinecellar@gmail.com*) – winemakers in this area mostly use a blend of Tsitska and Tsolikouri, perhaps with some Krakhuna or Otskanuri Sapere, and remove the chacha (the skins, stalks and seeds) after just two months, producing beautiful yellow wines. About 20km west on the main road to Kutaisi (just after the start of the Imereti Bypass) there's also Nikoladzeebis Marani (m *551 944841;* e *georgianslowfood@yahoo.com;* f *qvevri.wine*), owned by Ramaz Nikoladze, head of the Slow Food movement in Georgia; he produces biodynamic Tsitska and Tsolikouri whites in qvevris with no chemicals or herbicides.

CHIATURA This small town, 40km north of Zestaponi (an hour by marshrutka; GEL4), sits amid one of the world's richest manganese deposits, perhaps 222 million tonnes; Bidzina Ivanishvili, who's worth almost US$5 billion, also comes from Chorvila, just east of Chiatura, so the town is not in the state of total post-communist decline you might expect. Many of the mines are on the cliffs around the town, reached by a network of cable cars which are becoming an offbeat tourist attraction (while the cliffs themselves were apparently once used for the Soviet Union's rock-climbing championships). The first manganese ropeways were built in the 1930s and the oldest cable car (No 25) dates from 1954, just after the mines were turned into a modern Stalinist industry; this was in part a reward for their having been the only Bolshevik stronghold in overwhelmingly Menshevik Georgia. Stalin himself hid here in his revolutionary days, holding up trains to steal the mines' pay chests. Now a couple of the cable cars are belatedly being modernised – to be replaced by new Swiss-made cars. The bankrupt state-owned Chiatura mines and the Zestaponi processing plant were bought by Stemcor, a British steel-trading company, then in 2006 sold to Ukrainian oligarchs in partnership with Miami-based Georgian-American Alloys (and the Vartsikhe dam which powers the mines and plant was added to the portfolio); profitable from 2012, the company was presented in 2016 with a US$90m tax bill then effectively seized by the state on environmental grounds after a court order. This is set to be a major test of the rule of law in Georgia.

Getting there and away Marshrutkas run roughly hourly (*GEL6;* ⏱ *09.45 until 18.00*) from the Okriba terminal at Didube in Tbilisi to the bus station at the first hairpin on the Zestaponi road (the turning to Zeda Rgani), taking about 3½ hours. They also run from Kutaisi every 40–60 minutes until about 15.00, taking an hour and a half but also charging GEL6, although some continue through town to Sacchere. There are two daily trains from Kutaisi I at 05.30 and 16.20, returning at 10.20 and 20.00, amazingly slow but cheap (*GEL1*).

🏠 **Where to stay, eat and drink** Tourist services are minimal: about a kilometre north of town, continuing on the main road (Maiakovski), there's the Nikoli hotel (*Mgvimevi 1;* m *598 432190, 599 759528;* **$$**), opposite the bridge to Perevisa, which has basic but adequate en-suite rooms and weak Wi-Fi, and the simpler Pirosmani (*Tabagrebi 7;* m *599 564708, 555 393052;* e *shori.gelashvili@mail.ru;* 🔲 **$$**), about 100m up the side-road to the left, which also has a hostel in a small newer single-storey building. The Newland Turkish supermarket (m *595 301025;* e *bormaniko@ yahoo.com*), by the City Hall on Ninoshvili, seems to have some rooms, as well as a café and children's play centre. The only place to eat is the tiny Café Sophie Comme Il Faut (**$**) on the main street, Ninoshvili, which doesn't offer much beyond beer, cakes and khachapuri.

What to see and do Just two **cable cars** are still in operation in the town centre. By the bridge just north of the main square (km40/68), one cable car rises southeast across the river while a tiny blue one climbs north to a clifftop mine from where you can hike down in a very long zigzag to the south. Just to the south, across a footbridge from the town centre, there's a triple terminal now being rebuilt, to link the cliffs to the east with a terminal just above the Zestaponi road.

Another unusual attraction is 15 minutes along the road to Zestaponi and Kutaisi at km29.5/78.5, just east of the point where it crosses the Kashura River: about 500m to the north you'll see the 40m-high **Katskhi Pillar**, a limestone monolith with a small church, wine cellar (obviously) and hermit cells on top. Marshrutkas will leave you by a brown sign with a monastery symbol, from where it's a 1km walk to the monastery (⊕ *10.30–18.00 daily; no access to the pillar itself*). A monk called Maxime has lived here alone for 24 years, hauling up food that's supplied by local followers. He's not a total recluse and does climb down a metal ladder (dubbed 'the stairway to heaven') twice a week. It seems that the hermitage was established in the 9th or 10th century and abandoned from the Ottoman invasions of the 15th century until 1944, when a way up was found again.

A couple of kilometres north of town (just beyond the hotels) and up to the left in the village of **Mghvimebi**, there's a cave monastery founded in the 10th or 11th century where Queen Tamar once hid, apparently; it's richly decorated inside and out, with some 13th-century frescoes. Look for a tiny shop selling candles and icons, from where you climb straight up. There are two more cable cars about 1km further up Maiakovski.

KUTAISI ქუთაისი *Telephone code 431*

Kutaisi dates from perhaps the 17th century BC and was established as the Greek colony of Aia (still the name of the city's football team) by the 7th century BC; it was the capital of Colchida (and thus the birthplace of Medea) from the second millennium BC, and from AD978 to 1122 capital of the united Georgia, Tbilisi being occupied by the Turks. It was again capital of Imereti from the late 15th century to 1810. Kutaisi was spared by the Mongols, but was burnt by the Turks in 1510, 1666 and in 1692; they were driven out in 1770 by Solomon I. Under communism it grew to be a city of 240,000, but its main employer, the Kamaz truck factory, soon closed and the city became the mafia capital of Georgia and perhaps the whole former Soviet Union. It has long since been cleaned up and may be revived by the National Parliament moving to Kutaisi, although little actually happens in the flashy new building other than voting; the real work is apparently still done in Tbilisi. Its population has now dropped to 150,000, a couple of thousand fewer than Batumi.

GETTING THERE AND AWAY

By air Kutaisi International Airport, 14km west on the highway at Kopitnari [map, page 222] (km255/297; 20 minutes), is Georgia's main arrival point for low-cost flights, with arrivals from an ever-increasing range of cities across Europe. There's an exchange desk and ATMs here, as well as a café and a duty-free shop. A new terminal, hotel and railway station are under construction.

Modern minibuses meet flights to take passengers to Kutaisi (w *georgianbus. com; GEL5*) as well as Batumi and Tbilisi. You shouldn't pay more than GEL30 for a taxi. In any case, the airport is on the south side of the main highway (ie: Kutaisi is to the right), with marshrutkas every 20 minutes between Kutaisi bus station (near the west end) and Samtredia (*GEL2; until 18.30*) as well as long-distance services. With the opening of the Imereti Bypass on the south side of the airport, traffic for Tbilisi now turns left/west from the airport then left again to join the highway at the Akhalsopeli/Bashi junction.

Cars can be rented at the airport through Sixt (m *571 549955;* e *reservation@ sixt.com.ge;* w *sixt.com.ge*) and RACE (*Rent a Car Enterprises;* m *514 577555, 514 896896;* w *race.com.ge*).

By bus At km223, after crossing a plateau covered with pine forest, buses from Tbilisi turn left on the former E60 to reach the Baghdati–Kutaisi road on the edge of town (km227.5) and turn right to cross the Rioni and directly reach the Okriba bus station [228 A4] of Kutaisi, 220km (137 miles) from Tbilisi, and 140km from Batumi. For a long time this was also the main route from Tbilisi to the west of Georgia, but in 2016 a bypass opened to the south of the city, cutting journey times to Samtredia and beyond by an hour. **Local buses** from Zestaponi (*15/day; GEL2*) carry straight on for 5km to enter the city to the north, via the Kutaisi I railway station [228 G4], which also serves buses to Tqibuli (*8/day; GEL2.50*) and Terjola (*6/day; GEL1.80*). Bus tickets are sold inside on the ground floor. The main Okriba **bus station** is at Chavchavadze Avenue 67, 3km southwest of the centre, close to Kutaisi II railway station [228 A4]. This is perhaps Georgia's most disorderly bus station, a scene of third-world chaos especially when it rains; it's also bad for food. There's a list of departures at w visitkutaisi.com/en/ travel-kit/transport/busmarshrutkas. Frequent buses for Tbilisi (*GEL10*) leave from several locations, long-distance marshrutkas westwards (roughly hourly to Batumi (*GEL10*), Poti, Ozurgeti and Zugdidi) leave from a concrete platform at the northwestern end, and those to more local destinations to the southeast, where there is a rusty ticket booth. Shared taxis to Tbilisi also wait just to the west by MetroMart and the railway bridge. Coming from Tbilisi, marshrutkas leave from the Didube terminal and also the rear of the railway station and the Akhmeteli metro station.

Marshrutkas for destinations to the north such as Oni in Racha province leave from Mkheidze, north of the river by the Chain Bridge [228 E1] beneath Bagrat Cathedral.

From the bus station, turn left then right up Gamsakhurdia and Rustaveli to reach the centre. Alternatively, bus 1 runs to the city centre and below the Kutaisi I

KUTAISI

Gelati & Motsameta monasteries

GELATI

Sataplia, Tskaltubo, Ambrolauri, Racha

Botanic Garden

Mtsvane Kvavila Monastery

Church of the Annunciation of the Virgin

Synagogue

Kutaisi Botanic Garden, Sataplia, Tskaltubo, Racha

Bagrat Cathedral

BAGRATI

Rioni

Bus stop

St George's Church

Marshruttkas to Gelati

Military Museum

Sports Museum

State Theatre

Kutaisi State Historical Museum (closed for refurbishment)

Davit Agmashenebelis Square

Kutaisi I railway station

University

Stairs

TBILISI

26 MAISI

KOSTAVA

GOGEBASHVILI

TAMAR MEPE

TSERETELI

Rioni

FLOW

D Giorgi's Homestay, Darejan

LERMONTOV

Market

Art Gallery

Biblusi

City Garden

RUSTAVELI

Opera

Stadium

Wonderland

PUSHKIN

Cinema

Kutaisi State Historical Museum (temporary site)

El Galeon

Veriko Anjaparidze Garden

Puppet Theatre

Tsulukidze Garden

TABIDZE

Besarion Gaboshvili (Besiki) Park

Cable car

Bus stop

Police station

GRISHASHVILI

D AGMASHENEBELIS

DAVIT AGMASHENEBELIS

DUMBADZE

Geguti, Tbilisi

Taibuli, Zestaponi

Bradt

N

0   300m
0   300yds

Inset

Bradt

N

0   500m
0   500yds

Javakishvili

Tskaltubo, Satsplia, Satsplia cave

Konstantines...

Parliament

Abashidze

Rustaveli

Bus stop

Bus stops

Davit Agmashenebelis

Hotel Aia, Tbilisi

Kutaisi II railway station

Bike Shop Kutaisi

Botumi, Zugdidi

Mtkvidze

Asatiani

Dumbadze

Rioni

Tabidze

see main map

Zurab Anjaparidze

Tsereteli

railway station every 5 minutes from 07.30 to 21.00 (*GEL0.40*); there are also slightly faster marshrutka minibuses (*GEL0.50*), but the regular buses have more space for baggage and are particularly cheap here.

By train Kutaisi has two railway stations: Kutaisi I [228 G4] facing east, and Kutaisi II [228 A4], by the main bus station, facing west. Trains to Tbilisi (*GEL7.50*) consist of a couple of carriages from Kutaisi I trundled down to the main line at Rioni station and attached there to a through train; the services at 09.00 from Tbilisi (arriving 14.30) and 12.15 from Kutaisi (arriving 17.15) are pleasant alternatives to a scary marshrutka ride, and the easiest way to get to Gori or Mtskheta. Going to or from western Georgia, you could use Rioni as a sort of parkway station; it's about 500m west of the road from Kutaisi to Baghdati, served by several marshrutkas every hour, and taxis meet trains here. A new Kutaisi Airport station should open in 2018, and will also serve as a handy interchange from the west. Kutaisi I also has two trains a day to Sachkhere. The Kutaisi II railway station is barely functional (buy tickets on the train) and only handles local trains to Tskaltubo (3/*day; GEL1*).

From Kutaisi I railway station, turn right to walk 1km into the centre.

WHERE TO STAY As well as the hotels listed, there are nice homestays on Ukimerioni Hill west of the Bagrat Cathedral, where large houses have attractive gardens, secure parking and balconies with great views of the city.

Hotels

Empire Hotel [228 E3] (25 rooms) Grishashvili 7; ✆0431 242328; w empirehotel.ge. Facing the Tsulukidze Garden, this excellent hotel has AC rooms (14 luxe), conference room & a classy bar-restaurant with terrace. **$$$$**

Argo [228 D4] Tabidze 51; 431 248171. This well-refurbished villa (built in 1913) is not exactly a boutique hotel as is claimed, but it has decent AC rooms, some with jacuzzi; b/fast is filling but basic. **$$$$**

Aeetes Palace [228 D3] (28 rooms) Tabidze 34; ✆0431 253533, 244407; m 590 314407; w aeetes-hotel.com. A modern, centrally located hotel close to the cable car station, with restaurant, bar & conference hall. **$$$**

Argo Palace [228 D2] (18 rooms) Debi Ishkhnelebi 16; m 599 779797, 599 376525; w argopalace.wordpress.com. A friendly, modern place with excellent homemade food, AC, parking & fast Wi-Fi. Rooms (& bathrooms) are smallish but each floor has a shared balcony overlooking the city. **$$$**

Best Western Kutaisi [228 D3] (40 rooms & 5 suites) Grishashvili 11; ✆32 219 7100; tf 1800 780 7234 (N America); w bwkutaisi.com. Excellent new hotel in the overlit 6-storey block by the White Bridge, with a rooftop bar/grill. Good deals on w bestwestern.com. **$$$**

Hotel Aia [228 B4] (7 rooms) Chavchavadze 8, just over 1km east of the bus station; ✆0431 223676; m 599 293676, 570 104149; e teonchi@ mail.ru. A comfortable, modern place that's handy for drivers in transit, but is linked to the city centre by bus 1 & various marshrutkas which run up Asatiani to the centre & back on Ninoshvili. There's good Georgian food a 5min walk west at the Baraka Delikatessen Restaurant (Chavchavadze 20). B/fast GEL10 extra. **$$$**

Hotel Gora [228 D2] (43 rooms) Debi Ishkhnelebi 22; ✆431 252170; m 599 574625; e hotelgora@gmail.com, 195706@mail.ru; w bigsale.ge/hotelgora. A grandiose new building, totally out of place in this area of low-rise family homes & guesthouses, but it gives good views towards the Bagrat Cathedral (but is an eyesore at night). Rooms are simple but do come with en-suite facilities. **$$$**

Hotel Old Town [228 E3] (9 rooms) Grishavili 3/4; ✆431 251451; m 595 300024, 599 516056; e dzvelikalaki@gmail.com; w oldtown.ge. New hotel primarily aimed at a business clientele, facing the Tsulukidze Garden. Rooms with AC, minibar & cable TV. Rates inc b/fast & Wi-Fi. **$$$**

Hostels

Hostel Kolga [228 D1] (6 rooms) Tsatskhvebi 12; m 579 531010, 555 000473; w hostelkolga.

com. Also on Ukimerioni Hill, this has pleasant private rooms & a 5-bed dorm with private bathroom, plus free transfers, kitchen, washing machine & iron. Swimming pool in summer. **$–$$**

🏠 **Hostel City Centre** [228 E2] Tsminda Nino 15; m 574 524040, 598 538738; e hostelcckutaisi@gmail.com. Certainly very central! Rooms with AC & balcony; b/fast inc. **$**

🏠 **Hostel Kutaisi by Kote** [228 D1] (14 rooms) Gorki 18; m 593 548507; e hostel.kutaisi@mail.com; w hostelkutaisien.wordpress.com, hostelkutaisi.com. On Ukimerioni Hill (reached by marshrutka 2), a small shop serves as reception for a good hostel owned by Poles working with the excellent local NGO ProMotion Georgia & spread over 3 separate houses; dorms with shared bathrooms, big sitting room & kitchen, washing machine & Wi-Fi. **$**

Homestays

🏠 **Hostel Paradise Road** [228 E3] Tsereteli 4th Lane 1; m 593 911900; 🅕. Owned by an English-speaking university professor, this lovely guesthouse is by the river but also close to the centre (just south of the temporary history museum); they've just added to the 6 original rooms, all en suite with balcony, AC & fridge. As they say, it's ideal for anyone interested in 'history, architecture & food' – & you'll probably taste their own wine! **$$–$$$**

🏠 **Darejan** [228 D1] (4 rooms) Chanchibadze 2nd Lane 4; m 551 125935, 595 720608; e darejan.khachapuridze@mail.ru. In a pleasant garden (with mandarins in autumn & a barbecue), this is a simple house 5mins from the Bagrat Cathedral. Car available for trips to Prometheus Cave & the canyons; Greek & Russian spoken. **$$**

🏠 **Guesthouse Bagrati** [228 E1] (4 rooms) Bagrati 25; ☎ 24 9278; m 599 510858, 577 936484; e bagratiguesthouse@gmail.com; w bagratiguesthouse.com. This friendly & comfortable place (in a historic house) could hardly be closer to the Bagrat Cathedral, with views from the terrace; some rooms also have balconies. **$$**

🏠 **Lali's Family Guesthouse** [228 D2] (12 rooms) Debi Ishkhnelebi 18; ☎ 431 248395; m 599 376525. Lali Jalaghiana has built a new wing here with nice big twin rooms with showers opposite (with solar water heating); only Georgian & Russian spoken. **$$**

🏠 **Giorgi's Homestay** [228 D1] (8 rooms) Chanchibadze 14; m 595 591511; e giorgihomestay14@yahoo.com. A hospitable & comfortable family home 5mins' (uphill) walk from the Bagrat Cathedral. Giorgi Giorgadze speaks good English & can show you how to play Georgian dominoes, as well as arranging tours & transfers. Price inc 2 good, filling meals. **$–$$**

✕ WHERE TO EAT AND DRINK

✕ **Sanapiro** [228 C4] Zurab Anjaparidzis 17; m 555 406240. This is the best restaurant in Kutaisi, &, as its name ('Riverside') implies, is indeed right by the Rioni just south of the centre. It serves classic Georgian dishes such as khinkali, khachapuri, shashlik & aubergine salads, with live music at w/ends. **$$$**

✕ **Baraqa** [228 F2] Tamar Mepe 5; m 597 225522. A popular place that specialises in khachapuri from around the country – imeruli, adjurali, etc – & in particular Svan kubdari. Service is excellent, & there's a choice of foreign beers & free Wi-Fi; it's even non-smoking. **$$**

✕ **Eto's** [228 E2] Davit Agmashenebelis 2; m 574 608600; ⏲ 10.00–23.45 daily. Facing the fountain on the main square, this is one of the best places for good Georgian food (notably lobio) & shish kebab, & b/fast, with good friendly English-speaking service. Alongside, Café El Paso is also (oddly enough) good for Georgian food. **$$**

✕ **Gora** [228 D2] Vazha-Pshavelas 1; ☎ 24 1735; m 590 498940; ⏲ 11.00–23.00 daily. In Besarion Gabashvili Park, by the Ferris wheel, this is a local favourite with its rustic style & semi-rustic location, as well as its authentic Imeretian food. **$$**

✕ **Palaty** [228 E3] Pushkin 2; ☎ 431 243380; 🅕 palatypalaty; ⏲ 09.00–23.30 daily. Popular & lively restaurant with friendly English-speaking staff; there's often live jazz or folk music upstairs. **$$**

✕ **Bagrati Brewery** [228 F3] Tamar Mepe 45. This is basically a standard Georgian restaurant, with decent food & service, that serves 1 fairly light & adequate own-brew beer. **$**

✕ **Crepamania** [228 F3] Tamar Mepe 21; m 557 565358; e crepomaniaa@gmail.com; 🅕 crepamaniakutaisi; ⏲ 11.00–22.00. A nice simple place serving crêpes & other snacks (to eat in or takeaway). **$**

🖵 **Our Garden** [228 E1] Bagrati 23; m 579 555445; 🅕 ourgardenkutaisi; ⏲ 11.00–03.00.

Opposite the Bagrat Cathedral, this café-bar has a garden with great views & is ideally placed for the guesthouses & hostels on Ukimerioni Hill. **$$**

💻 **Café Neta** [228 E3] Tamar Mepe 15; ☏431 243014; ⊕ 09.00–20.00 daily. Stylish little place for coffee & cakes. **$**

💻 **Coffee Bean** [228 E2] Tsminda Nino 11; 📱 574 270909; ⊕ 09.00–23.00. Near the puppet theatre, this serves excellent artisan coffee & is next to the attractive Our Café (Tsminda Nino 13; 📱 574 270909), Azzato Cake House & Sairme Bakery (Tsminda Nino 15) for cakes, salads, soups & desserts. **$**

💻 **Sanimesho** [228 E3] Tamar Mepe 16. Self-service bakery/café. **$**

💻 **Savane** [228 E2] In the City Garden; ⊕ 09.00–23.45 daily. This café is a pleasant place to take a break, especially at its outdoor tables. **$**

💻 **Tea House Foe-Foe** [228 E2] Rustaveli 5; 📱 592 132121; ⊕ 09.00–23.45 daily. In the foyer of the former Hotel Kutaisi, this has an arty junkshop vibe, with mismatching chairs & tables, lots of books, & large paintings including on the ceiling. They serve a long list of teas (*from GEL4*) & snacks, & have Wi-Fi. **$**

♀ **Sapere** [228 D3] Tabidze 18/2; 📱 577 560565; 🄵 SapereKutaisi; ⊕ 09.00–midnight. A stylish wine bar that also serves authentic Imeretian food; friendly English-speaking service. **$$**

♀ **#B12** [228 E3] Pushkin 10; 📱 597 104204; ⊕ 24hrs. New bar on the city's 'party street', with live bands most nights. **$**

♀ **Eldepo** [228 D3] Tabidze 30; ☏431 244273; ⊕ 24hrs. A lively (& smokey) pub that's good for beer, chacha & khinkali. **$**

✳ ♀ **Satsnakheli** [228 E3] Pushkin 8; ☏431 247696, 📱 595 286307; e satsnakheli16@gmail.com; 🄵; ⊕ 10.00–23.30 daily. Actually on an alley south from Pushkin, this is an excellent cellar wine bar (with a sheltered street-level patio), with a good range of Georgian wines shelved by region (inc Abkhazia), with organic/natural & sparkling wines, as well as chacha, teas, spices, juices, jams & honey; they do tastings (*GEL15*) & also store baggage (*GEL5*). You can also book tours with the ProMotion Georgia NGO, including a visit to a different winemaker every week (*GEL100*), Okatse Canyon (*GEL35*), Gachedili waterfall, etc. **$**

♀ **White Stones** [228 D3] Grishashvili 3; ☏431 244275; ⊕ noon–02.00 daily. Stylish & popular café/cocktail bar with a terrace overlooking the river & excellent live jazz; good real coffee & brownies etc, but not really a place to go for substantial meals (or dedicated service). Between 1915 & 1930 this was the meeting place of the Symbolist writers known as the Tsisperkantselebi (The Blue Horns – notably Grigol Robakidze, Paolo Iashvili, Titian Tabidze, Gogla Leonidze, Galaktion Tabidze, & painter Lado Gudiashvili). **$**

NIGHTLIFE AND ENTERTAINMENT Kutaisi has a strong theatrical tradition, with many famed actors and singers born here. The huge **State Theatre** [228 E2] (w *meskhishvilitheatre.ge*) dominates Davit Agmashenebelis Square, and the **opera house** [228 E2] (*Tsminda Nino 17;* ☏ *24 2432*) has a horrid modern exterior but puts on decent shows. The **Puppet Theatre** [228 E2] (*Tsminda Nino 11;* ☏ *45 205*) is always popular with children. **Kutaisoba**, the annual city festival, is on or around 2 May.

Pubs on Pushkin often have live bands playing; El Galeon [228 D2] (*Paliashvili 1;* 📱 *593 611605;* 🄵*;* ⊕ *18.00–04.00 daily*) is a lively rock club, with a terrace below the Red Bridge.

OTHER PRACTICALITIES **Tourist information** is available from an office by the Rustaveli bridge [228 D2] (*Rustaveli 9A;* ☏ *431 241103;* 📱 *595 807141;* e *tickutaisi@gmail.com;* ⊕ *09.00–18.00 daily, summer until 19.00*), and also at the airport [map, page 222] (📱 *595 088219;* e *tickutaisiair@gmail.com*).

The best places to **exchange money** are between Rustaveli and the bus station, on Tsereteli, or north of the market on Tsminda Nino. There are plenty of **ATMs** along Rustaveli, Paliashvili and Tsereteli and elsewhere in the centre.

The central **post office** is at Tsminda Nino 7 [228 E3] with other branches at Tamar Mepe 56 and Gamsakhurdia 32 (*all* ⊕ *09.00–17.00 Mon–Fri, 09.00–13.00*

Sat); **DHL** have an office at Davit Aghmashenebelis 3–5 (⏲ *09.30–18.30 Mon–Fri, 10.00–14.00 Sat*). For **internet** access, Ciber House is on Pushkin at Tamar Mepe [228 E3]; there's open Wi-Fi at McDonald's at the bus station [228 A4] and on the main square.

Flights and tours can be booked at the Wonderland Travel Agency [228 E3] (*Tsereteli 8;* \ *431 255656;* m *597 355656;* e *kutaisi@wonderland.ge;* w *wonderland. ge*) or at Kolkha Tour, upstairs in the cable car terminal at Veriko Anjaparidze Park [228 E2] (\ *431 251199;* m *597 577000;* w *kolkhatour.ge*). At the side of the cable car terminal you can buy tickets for a tour bus (*10.00, 11.00, noon Tue–Sun; GEL20/1 day, GEL30/2 days*) to the Gelati and Motsameta monasteries, Sataplia and Prometheus Caves and Martvili and Okatse Canyons.

Bikes can be rented at Davit Agmashenebelis 105 [228 B4] (m *568 767151;* ⏲ *10.00–20.00 daily; GEL30/day*); you can arrange to collect/return bikes at the airport. Bike Shop Kutaisi [228 A4] (m *598 102132*) is just over the railway bridge on the Samtredia road at the junction with Guganava. For books, the Biblusi shop [228 E2] (*Paliashvili 31;* \ *322 486844;* w *biblusi.ge*) has some foreign books and is next to a second-hand market where you can find antique Georgian books.

WHAT TO SEE AND DO

A tour of central Kutaisi Rustaveli forms the main axis of the city, leading from the Zugdidi road to the city centre; there are plenty of buses, but if you walk from the junction by the bus station it'll take about 30 minutes to a square where a brief one-way loop begins; almost at once you rejoin Rustaveli to cross the river by a stone bridge built in the 1860s, flanked by two steel bridges dating from 1866 (the first metal bridge in the Caucasus) and 1872. To the left, immediately before the river, is a monument to Galaction Tabidze (the young poet being sent on his way by his muse), and beneath the bridges are the limestone slabs from which the city derives its name – '*kwata*' means stony. Across the bridges to the left is the city's main marshrutka terminal (known as Tsitelikhidi or the Red Bridge), and beyond it you'll see an intriguing gable at the western end of the covered market passage that uses terracotta figures to detail the city's history and culture. To the right on the far bank of the river is the **Veriko Anjaparidze Garden** [228 D2], named after a famous actress, which was laid out as a royal garden in the mid 17th century and is now less attractive, even with some modern sculptures. It's separated from the nicer **Tsulukidze Garden** [228 E3] to the south by the Golden Marquee (a royal palace that's used for corporate events) and the terminal of a cable car [228 E2] (⏲ *noon–18.00 daily; GEL0.50*) which ascends to the **Besarion Gabashvili (or Besiki) Park** [228 D2], on the hilltop above the Tabidze monument, where there's a small funfair and zoo.

Continuing into the centre, the first building on the left on Rustaveli is the **David Kakabadze Fine Art Gallery** [228 D2] (*Rustaveli 8;* ⏲ *10.00–18.00 Mon-Fri; GEL1*). Temporary shows are held downstairs (and there's also sculpture in the courtyard), while the main collection is in one large room one flight up; this gives perhaps the best overview of Georgian art of any gallery outside Tbilisi. Opposite the door are two Pirosmanis, then paintings by local hero David Kakabadze including two called *Imereti* (1912 and 1934). There's a portrait by Ketevan Maralashvili of the poet Titsian Tabidze, looking like Oscar Wilde with his red carnation and cigarette. Then there's Lado Gudiashvili's *Autumn Festival*, with people in national dress celebrating the grape harvest, and a painting by Robert Sturua, father of the famous theatre director. The works on the facing wall are less famous but possibly more attractive, such as Valeri Margiani's *Kutaisi*, with the white rocks built up in impasto, and a portrait of Pirosmani by Samson Nadareishvili.

Just beyond the Art Museum on the right is the Classical Gymnasium (1902), the school attended by the poets Akaki Tsereteli (1840–1915) and Vladimir Mayakovsky (1893–1930), whose father, an impoverished Russian noble, worked as a forester in Baghdati, south of Kutaisi.

Just south of the Art Gallery, the former **Radium cinema** [228 E2] (Kutaisi's first; 1908) on the right at the top of Tsisperkantselebi, is worth a look; a little further south a courtyard marks the site of the Mon Plaisir cinema (Kutaisi's second cinema), with its lovely Art Nouveau proscenium arch now serving as a portal from Tsminda Nino (St Nino Street). Beyond this is a group of rather odd Soviet statues supposedly in praise of labour, although in fact one is also named *My Imereti*.

The centre of the city is the **City Garden** [228 E2] or Bulvari, a park full of trees where old men gather on benches and cafés serve the young. At its east end is **Davit Agmashenebelis Square** [228 E2], in the centre of which is the Colchis Fountain, based on gold jewellery found in the Vani archaeological site (page 240). In 2011, this replaced a statue of King David the Builder (who was crowned and started his campaign of unification here) by Elgudja Amashukeli, Georgia's best-known monumental sculptor, unveiled by Shevardnadze during the 1995 election campaign and moved by Saakashvili to a more dominant position in front of the Kutaisi I railway station [228 G4].

On the north side of the square is the huge, circular **Meskhishvili State Theatre** [228 E2] (⊕ *for performances only*), on the east side is the **Kutaisi State Historical Museum** [228 E2], one of the best outside Tbilisi. This is currently closed for long-term refurbishment and there's a 'temporary' display at Pushkin 12 (at Tsereteli) [228 E3] (⊕ *10.00–18.00 exc Mon, winter 11.00–16.00; GEL3*). On the ground floor is a cannon seized by Solomon I at the battle of Rukhi in 1799, a landau and music box and a huge wine press made from a hollowed linden tree trunk. In a beautiful hall upstairs, you'll see stone implements from the Palaeolithic and Neolithic periods, qvevri burial pitchers used in Colchis for burying women (men were wrapped in leather and hung on trees) and then jewellery and ceremonial axe heads from the 2nd and 1st millennia BC, and a fertility figure from Baghdati, with both breasts and phallus, produced sometime between the 8th and 6th centuries BC, which is the museum's most famous exhibit. From the Antique epoch (6th–3rd centuries BC) there are ceramics, beads and a *rhiton* or silver cup of fighting soldiers from Gomi. However, the museum's pride and joy is its early medieval collection, above all icons from the 10th century onwards, many from Svaneti and Racha. Note the fine icon of St George from the 12th century, the big 13th-century icon of an archangel from Gebi, and a large 16th-century cross from Barakoni. Also from the 16th century is the great triptych of the Virgin from Gelati, its Nativity scene showing Joseph clearly wondering what's going on. There are too many photos of ancient documents, plus 17th-century ecclesiastical vestments, 18th-century costumes, 18th- and 19th-century weaponry (including the sword of King Solomon II) and 19th-century musical instruments. In a side room, beyond some medieval ceramics and 12th-century frescoes on plaster from Vani, there are agricultural implements, a chacha still and drinking vessels, an 18th-century door from Martvili church, snowshoes, traps and guns, some 16th- to 19th-century deeds and 18th- to 19th-century coins. There's also a replica of an Imeretian peasants' house, with carpets on the wall and wooden vessels on the shelves. Finally, you'll see a priests' punishment belt and items of goldsmithery including decorations for horse harnesses.

It's also worth mentioning the **Kutaisi Sports Museum** [228 E2] (⊕ *office hours; free*), across the road to the west of the theatre, which has surprisingly eclectic coverage, with insight into social context as well as the usual cases of medals. A prize exhibit is George Best's shirt from a Northern Ireland–Soviet Union game, and there's also the bike of world champion cyclist Omar Kakadze, and a steel rod that a strongman wrapped around his arm. A couple of doors down there's also a **Military Museum** [228 E2] (☉ *10.00–17.00 Mon-Fri; free*), honouring the dead of World War II.

A kilometre north of the bus station along 9 April, or west on Abashidze from Rustaveli, the appallingly expensive **Parliament Building** at Abashidze Avenue 26 [228 A4] (by Spanish architect Alberto Domingo Cabo, inaugurated in 2012) is an astonishing sight, like a giant frog's eye rising out of the ground. This was the site of a 1980s war memorial by Merab Berdzenishvili which Putin suggested should be moved to Moscow if Georgia was spurning it. Saakashvili had it blown up in 2009 out of personal pique, but unfortunately flying concrete boulders killed two people in the courtyard of their home a considerable distance away. Guided tours are available on Wednesdays, Thursdays and Fridays in weeks when parliament is sitting, at noon, 15.00 and 17.00; booking is required (\ *32 228 1690/3; e toursparliament@gmail.com*).

The Bagrat Cathedral [228 E1] The city's great sight is the Bagrat Cathedral, which you'll see high on the Ukimerioni Hill across the river from the city centre. To reach it, head north on Tsminda Nino (Saint Nino Street) from the west end of the City Garden. This leads past the market and across the river on a mock-suspension bridge to Mkheidze kucha; the terminal for buses to Racha is just to the right here, and steps from behind here (or a road further to the right) lead up to Kazbegi kucha and the cathedral. There has been a fortress here since at least the 1st century AD; now there are remains from the 5th and 6th centuries, and late medieval fortifications, and the ruins of a 4th-century church. Occupied by the Turks, in 1769 it was bombarded from Mtsvane Kvavila by Solomon I and the Russian General Todleben. However, the fortifications are dwarfed by the Cathedral of the Assumption, commissioned by Bagrat III (who is buried here) in 1003 (as recorded by the oldest Arabic numerals in Georgia). It's a huge triconch cruciform church with a central dome on four free-standing pillars; later (although still in the first half of the 11th century), a portico was added to the west, with others to the north and south added in the 12th century. The cathedral was destroyed in 1691–92 by the Turks, leaving it roofless; it was disused, but immensely impressive, until 2008, when President Saakashvili launched a controversial plan to restore it as a working church. UNESCO, which had placed it on its World Heritage List in 1994, was very opposed to this (along with many other people and bodies) and in 2010 placed it on its list of World Heritage Sites in Danger. However, Saakashvili pressed on, owing to its importance as a symbol of national unification having been built by the first ruler of a united Georgia. The restoration is now complete, with a horrid green roof and a modern tower discreetly added on the north side, and UNESCO has now removed the cathedral from the World Heritage List. To the west on the same hill is **St George's Church** [228 E1], built in the 19th century, with a plain white interior.

Northern Kutaisi There are other interesting churches on the left bank of the Rioni, to the east of the centre. Behind the State Theatre, Varlamishvilis (named after a local painter) leads to the **Church of the Annunciation of the Virgin** [228 E1], built by French Roman Catholics in 1862; the ornate west porch was added in 1892. It's now a Georgian Orthodox church, with an interior that seems at odds with its Baroque exterior and Latin inscription (although the Orthodox church of

SS Peter and Paul, built in 1901 just south of Rustaveli, is not so different). In front is a virtual arboretum and the Kutaisi Sport Monument, with a list of Olympic champions (and, oddly, room for only one more). Just beyond, off Newport kucha, Jerusalem Street is the heart of what was the Jewish quarter, which had three synagogues in the 19th century. In 1926 a tenth of the city's population was Jewish, and 5% of Georgia's Jews still live here. The **synagogue** at the junction of Jerusalem and Gaponov, built in 1885, has been restored [228 F1] (🕑 *08.00–10.00 Mon–Fri, 09.00–noon, Sat; or ask at the nearby kosher food shop*); it now attracts reasonable congregations in summer after years of decline. A smaller synagogue, at Gaponov 49, built in 1835, is disused.

On the hill above is the **Mtsvane Kvavila (Green Flower) Monastery** [228 F1], with three churches including the 6th-century Church of the Archangels and a 17th-century church and bell-tower, as well as a pantheon that includes the grave of the composer Meliton Antonovich Balanchivadze (1862–1937), father of the choreographer George Balanchine. There's a good view back to the Bagrat Cathedral and northeast to the Gumat dam across the Rioni River; a newly published leaflet describes an 18km circular walk from the city along the river to cross the dam and return on the far side.

On the far (west) bank of the river, the **Kutaisi Botanic Garden** [228 F1] (📞 *31 245079;* ⓕ; 🕑 *10.00–18.00 Tue–Sun; GEL3*) is about 500m north from the chain bridge and the steps up to the Bagrat Cathedral. Founded in the mid-19th century, it became very run-down after the end of communism but has recently been refurbished. Even so, it's mainly about trees and shrubs, of which there are around 700 species; there are few non-woody plants here, apart from a small rose garden just to the left of the entrance. There are lots of fine Mediterranean cypress (*Cupressus sempervirens*) near the entrance, and further in various specimens of cedars (*Cedrus atlantica* and *C. libani*), Eastern red cedar (*Juniperus virginiana*), box elder (*Acer negundo*), Nepal camphor trees (*Cinnamomum glandiferum*), Caucasian zelkova (*Zelkova carpinifolia*) and Chusan palms (*Trachycarpus fortunei*), as well as a big Osage orange (*Maclura aurantica*) with huge green fruit, and a box hedge (*Buxus colchica*). At first it's tidy and well organised, with labels in Georgian and English, and lots of solid bamboo benches; towards the river it gets wilder.

Returning towards the city on Leselidze, after a few minutes you can turn right for a steep climb up Petre Iberi to reach Bagrati Street, at the rear of the Bagrat Cathedral.

AROUND KUTAISI

GELATI [map, page 222] Wonderfully set in the hills 10km to the north of Kutaisi, the monastery of Gelati is one of the most beautiful spots in Georgia. Marshrutkas (*20mins; GEL1*) leave from the rear of the State Theatre [228 E2] in Kutaisi daily at 08.00, 11.00, 14.00, 16.00 and 18.00, returning 25 minutes later. The Gelati-bound marshrutka has a little church symbol on its windscreen; it is best to arrive 20 minutes before if you want a seat. Buses from Kutaisi I to Tqibuli also pass the Motsameta and Gelati turn-offs, although you're unlikely to get a seat if you board here heading north. The turn-off is 3km from the edge of Kutaisi, from where it's a 2km uphill walk to the monastery. A taxi will charge about GEL5 for a combined trip to Gelati and Motsameta, including waiting time. You can stay in the very friendly Agro-guesthouse Korena halfway up the hill to Gelati (*signed to the left just before a small meat shop, between 2 sets of hairpins;* 📱 *558 587342, 593 314020;* ✉ *korena.office@gmail.com;* ⓕ *RuralGuesthouseKorena*), for GEL50 per head with all meals. The rooms are simple with a modern bathroom outside under the stairs;

there's a lovely garden and great views from the terrace to the monastery. Korena is a small local agro-tourism association and they offer tours to local sites.

Up a grassy slope from the road as you arrive at Gelati is a small church that's currently being restored. You may have to pay a nun a couple of coins to pass through the gateway. On the left as you enter is the Church of St George, built in the mid 13th century, burnt in 1510, and restored and painted in the 16th and 17th centuries. It tends to be shut except at weekends, when weddings are often held here.

The centrepiece is the great **Cathedral of the Virgin**, built by King David the Builder in 1106–25 (though in a style typical of the 11th century). The apses project to the east in a manner reminiscent of Abkhazian churches such as Bichvinta (Georgian churches usually have a flat east end). The narthex was added to the western end later in the 12th century, followed by chapels to the south in the 13th century and to the north in the late 13th or early 14th century. Burnt by the Turks in 1510, and again by the Lesghians (from the north Caucasus) in 1579, it was restored, then closed under communism, and reopened in 1988.

The interior is full of light, and painted, mostly in the second half of the 16th century, in fantastic colours (although a blue background is unusual in Georgian churches). The cupola, supported by the walls of the apse to the east and two columns to the west, bears a fresco of Christ Pantocrater, and on the spandrels the four evangelists were painted by Tevdore in the 17th century; the narthex was decorated with paintings of the first seven ecumenical councils (now in poor condition) in the first half of the 12th century. The north transept was painted in 1291–93 and in the 16th and 17th centuries, with portraits of King David the Builder (haloed and holding the church), Bagrat III and Giorgi II (both kings of western Georgia) and, across the corner from David, the Emperor Constantine and his mother Helena; above these is a fresco of Palm Sunday and above this, between the windows, the two saints Theodore. The south transept was painted in the 17th century – note in particular the Death of the Virgin, below saints George and Dmitri. Above the west door you'll see Pontius Pilate washing his hands, and Judas hanging himself.

However, the pride of the church (and one of Georgia's greatest works of art) is a remarkable mosaic (containing 2.5 million stones) in the apse of the Virgin and Child with the archangels Michael and Gabriel. Created c.1130 in a Byzantine style with specifically Georgian features, it was damaged by earthquakes later in the same century and subsequently. The lower half was restored by painting – although this is often denounced as communist vandalism, it seems that it was genuinely impossible to restore it as mosaic. The mosaics were then badly damaged by rain at the end of 2016 and the US embassy is apparently funding their restoration – now the metal roof has been replaced with turquoise-glazed ceramic barrel tiles. Gelati has been on UNESCO's World Heritage List since 1994, although the boundary has now been changed to exclude the Bagrat Cathedral (page 234).

Outside, the belfry stands to the southwest, built over a spring in the second half of the 13th century. Next to this, facing the west end of the cathedral, is the **Church of St Nicholas**, one of the oddest in design in Georgia. Also built in the 13th century, it's a two-storeyed construction that looks rather like an English market cross, with the church above an arcade in which you can see a section of tree trunk once intended for use as a coffin. Beyond this, to the west looking out over the valley (in good weather it's possible to see to the Black Sea), are the recently restored buildings erected in 1106 by King David to house the academy of Neo-Platonist metaphysical philosophy under Ioanne Petrisi; the portico, with four different types of column, was added in the 13th century. To the left is the south gate, built early in the 12th century; when King David died in 1125 he was buried as requested in the centre of the gateway, where churchgoers would walk over him and remember him for ever: an interesting way of combining self-abasement with a bit of egotism. The battered iron gate was made in 1063 in the Persian city of Ganja (now in Azerbaijan, on the main Tbilisi–Baku highway) and brought back by David's son Demetre I in 1129 from a campaign against the Persians.

From the gateway a track continues steeply into the trees; turning right near the top you can walk to a viewpoint overlooking Gelati and the valley beyond. In the hills to the south are two further small churches, St Saba and St Elijah, a pleasant 20-minute walk. The monastery car park has all manner of stalls selling souvenirs, religious knick-knacks, churchkhela and even hot dogs. There are a couple of restaurants in the village below, such as the Dzveli Gelati (m 595 412244, 599 562311; w gelati.ge; ⊕ noon–23.00 daily).

MOTSAMETA [map, page 222] Slightly closer to Kutaisi (a 2km walk to the right/east from the junction) is Motsameta Monastery. It's smaller and quieter than Gelati, although its cliff-edge setting is more spectacular by far. It commemorates the brothers David and Constantine Mkheidze, killed by Arabs in the AD720s for refusing to convert to Islam and then thrown into the gorge here. They are now saints, with their skulls in a casket behind the red velvet curtain, and your wish will be granted if you crawl three times under their tomb, set on two lions on the south side of the church, without touching it. The monastery was founded in the 8th century, but the present church and bell-tower were built by Bagrat III in the 11th century; the frescoes were destroyed by the Bolsheviks. It's busy but feels much less like a tourist site than Gelati. To the left of the gatehouse is a steep path down to the river, which makes this a very popular excursion in summer, when Kutaisi swelters.

Walking between Gelati and Motsameta This is a pleasant hike that takes an hour or two (c5km) and affords great views of both monasteries – it is best to start at Gelati. From the monastery gate, take the signed path to the right past a cemetery. The rough stone path descends and soon divides; take the right fork, which winds down through a village to reach the main road near the Gelati turn-off. Turn left to cross the river and walk along the road for about 600m before turning left into Motsameta village. You can then follow the railway track to the left (south) for about 500m until you reach the road to the car park and the path to Motsameta Monastery.

SATAPLIA, TSKALTUBO AND THE PROMETHEUS CAVE The most popular excursion from Kutaisi is to one or both of these spectacular karst caves just northwest of the city, both with striking stalactites, stone curtains and other formations. It's worth combining the two (GEL35–40 by taxi, waiting for 1½ hours at each) but remember that Prometheus is closed on Mondays and Sataplia on Tuesdays. The Prometheus Cave is bigger and has fancier lighting but there's not much else to it (other than a boat ride through part of the cave), whereas at Sataplia there are added attractions; it's best to go to Prometheus first as the electric boats' batteries run flat in the afternoons at busy times.

Sataplia [map, page 222] (⊕ 10.00–18.00 Wed–Mon; GEL6) Just 10km from Kutaisi is Mount Sataplia (Honey Mountain), a forested area in which a cave 300m in length (up to 10m high and 12m wide) and full of stalagmites was discovered in 1925 by Peter Chabukiani, a Kutaisi teacher. There are five karst caves here in all, although only the largest is open to visitors; in addition, about 200 footprints of dinosaurs have been preserved in Cretaceous limestone (120 million years old). This is said to be the only place where prints of both carnivorous and herbivorous dinosaurs are preserved together, although they are separated in time by several thousand years. Although Sataplia has been protected as a reserve since 1935, until recently it was mainly seen as an excursion for the people of Kutaisi, especially schoolchildren, and was not well preserved. New tourism infrastructure was completed in 2010 and visits are now properly controlled.

The reserve covers 354ha, on the slopes of Mount Sataplia (494m) and Mount Tsinara (520m), with a humid subtropical climate (with an annual average of 1,380mm precipitation). Nevertheless, the average temperature in January is as low as −5°C, and 24°C in August, with an annual average of 14.5°C (and 14°C in the cave). Colchic forest covers 95% of its area and 544 species of flora have been recorded (67 of them trees and bushes). These include hornbeam, alder, box (growing up to 15m high here), chestnut, beech, ilex, medlar, ivy, rhododendron, bilberry and blackberry. There are small mammals such as moles, squirrels, hedgehogs, hares, foxes, jackals and badgers, and birds such as larks, goldfinches, tits, jays, woodpeckers, hawks, sparrowhawks, cuckoos and hoopoes. The mountain bees that produced the plentiful honey that gave the mountain its name are now few in number.

To get there by public transport you'll have to take marshrutka 22, 31 or 35 (*every 10mins; GEL0.30*) along Rustaveli and Javakishvili to the first major intersection on the edge of town from where marshrutka 45 (50mins past the hour *Mon–Sat; GEL1.50*) may take you to the cave – or marshrutka 4 (*hourly; GEL1*) may leave you with a 2.5km uphill walk from the turning at the north end of Banoja village. At the entry there's a toilet and tiny shop; then the guided tour covers a total of 2km, starting with the hall over the dinosaur footprints (with sound effects) and then a cliffside walk, with views to Kutaisi, before heading to the cave where you'll see three halls carved out over 2,000 years, with an active stream still flowing in the second half. Outside again, there's a stylish café with a double terrace and an exhibition hall with good displays about the reserve; to the right the Colchic Forest Trail is a 300m loop, while to the left a trail leads 500m to a stunning modern viewing platform looking out over Kutaisi and Gelati.

Tskaltubo A dozen kilometres northwest of Kutaisi (or 5km from the Banoja junction near Sataplia, or 10km from km247/305 on the Kutaisi-Samtredia highway), Tskaltubo is a spa where mildly radioactive water at an average 35°C is used to treat arthritis, rheumatism, polio and fertility problems. In Soviet times, when this was the Ministry of Defence's main health resort, none of the hotels in Kutaisi was open to westerners, and they had to stay out here; when the hotels and sanatoria were taken over by refugees from Abkhazia, tourists had to stay in Kutaisi and come here for a day trip. The Soviet treatment centres in the central Mineral Water Park have been well refurbished; the biggest is Spa 6, right on top of the springs and offering a range of therapies from hot mud wraps to a 'slightly irradiated' bath, costing about US$15 each. Several of the huge Stalinist-Neoclassical sanatoriums ringing the park have now been refurbished, such as the Argo Spa Resort (*Rustaveli 8A;* m *595 509019;* e *hotargo@gmail.com;* w *hotelargo.ge;* **$$$**), the Hotel Imereti (*Tsereteli 8;* \ *436 22 1122;* m *597 918422;* e *imeretihotel@gmail.com;* w *hotelimereti.ge;* **$$$**) and above all the huge Tskaltubo Spa Resort (*Rustaveli 23;* \ *436 221417,* m *599 091610;* e *reception@tskaltubosparesort.ge;* w *sanatoriumi.ge*), the massive hydro-sanatorium where Stalin stayed, in the middle of the east side of the park. There are also a few new hotels to the north of the park, also huge and in the same heavy architectural style, such as the **Hotel Prometheus** (*88 rooms; Rustaveli 11;* \ *436*

220051, m *555 305491;* e *hotel.promete@mail.ru;* w *prometheus.ge;* **$$$**) and the **Tskaltubo Plaza** (*76 rooms; Rustaveli 15A;* \ *436 222393, 436 220808;* e *info@tph. ge;* w *tskaltuboplaza.ge;* **$$$–$$$$**), which both have excellent restaurants and spas.

Marshrutkas run from the junction of Chavchavadze and Rustaveli, near the bus station in Kutaisi (route 22), and from the market (route 30, every 20 minutes) (*both GEL2*) and after 15 minutes enter the spa, passing the station (served by three trains a day from Kutaisi II) and a large park dotted with pines. The town is spacious but run-down with little to see; the main attraction is the **Prometheus (or Kumistavi) Cave** [map, page 222] (*7km from Tskaltubo;* ☉ *10.00–16.00 Tue–Sun; GEL7*), found only in 1983 by a local caver and his dog. It's 145m deep, with 17 chambers up to 25m high, and a river (with waterfalls) runs through it; there are also 10–12 species of bat living here. Marshrutka 42 (to Kumistavi) comes here every 2 hours from the market in Tskaltubo (*20min; GEL2*); a guide will lead you on a 1,420m route on narrow cement walkways through six spectacular chambers, with the option of taking an electric boat (*GEL7*) for the last 380m.

GEGUTI AND VARTSIKHE

From Kutaisi's main bus station, marshrutkas (*GEL1*) leave regularly for **Geguti**, about 7km south (just beyond an interchange with the new highway) in the plains of the Rioni, known in classical times as the Phasis. This gave its scientific name, *Phasianus colchicus*, to the pheasant, which was discovered here, perhaps by Jason. Geguti is the site of the great ruined palace of the Georgian kings, one of the few secular buildings left in Georgia from medieval times. Now, it's a jumble of ruins covering 2,000m², set on a plinth 2.5m high housing heating conduits; you may be able to identify the large fireplace of the 8th-century hunting lodge, as well as one shattered arch of the 14m-wide dome of the 10th-century hall, and other ruins from the 12th and 13th centuries, including a church. The royal chambers are to the southwest, the treasury to the southeast, and the church and bathhouse to the northwest. In 1179 George III proclaimed his daughter Tamar his co-ruler here, and in 1360 David VII died here; later it fell into disuse and was destroyed in the 17th century. Arriving by bus, get off at the Restaurant Venezia (on the left) 1.5km from the village of Geguti, and walk up the paved road to the left for 5 minutes to the end where a series of unlocked gates on the right lead to the 'castle', which does look a bit like a tumble-down Tudor manor house.

Marshrutka 211 continues south to a dam across the Rioni, on the south side of which is **Vartsikhe**, once the Greek fortress of Rodopolis; from the lane leading to the Geguti 'castle', you can follow a farm track for 1.5km then turn left on the road about 3km short of the dam. From the dam it's another kilometre on to Vartsikhe, but the ruins are on the left immediately after the dam. There's not a lot to see, just 100m of ancient wall, some partially rebuilt, and another chunk of wall in a cemetery behind, by a small church. The fortress dates from the 4th–6th centuries, with a royal residence built here in the 9th–11th centuries. Vartsikhe is also known for its brandy. From the village it's 100m to the main road, where you can pick up buses between Kutaisi (to the left/east) and Vani. Also to the left, it's 2km to the road from Kutaisi to **Baghdati**, about 15km south (with hourly marshrutkas), birthplace of great Russian modernist poet Vladimir Mayakovsky (1893–1930), who went to school in Kutaisi until 1906 when the family moved to Moscow after the death of his father, who was a forester here. He grew up speaking Georgian and loved the country, returning four times. The museum in his family home (*Baghdati 51;* ☉ *10.00–17.00 daily; free*) has recently been revitalised and displays objects belonging to him and his parents, paintings, documents and copies of his works. The road continues south to the spa resort of **Sairme** (41km from Kutaisi, at 950m), just a cleft in the forested mountains with almost nothing but two well-refurbished hotels (*both* ☎ *32 240 4545;* w *sairme.com.ge*). The simpler Hotel Imereti (*106 rooms*) is open May–September only, while the plusher Hotel Sairme (*152 rooms*) functions all year; there is also the more basic Hostel Maia (m *579 244411*). Marshrutkas come here from Kutaisi at 10.50 and 17.50 daily (*GEL6*).

Beyond Sairme there's just a rough summer-only road over the beautiful Zekari Pass (2,226m) to Akhaltsikhe (pages 210–14). From a hairpin bend 6km south of Baghdati a track leads 10km left/east to **Khani**, where there are four dramatic waterfalls and some hot springs; it's a beautiful remote area for hiking with a couple of homestays – if you come with the daily marshrutka from Kutaisi you'll have to stay overnight.

VANI On the south side of the Rioni, Vani is reached by hourly marshrutkas (*GEL2*), the last leaving at 19.00 from Kutaisi and 17.00 from Vani. Beyond the Technical University the road follows the left bank of the Rioni, through beautiful oak forest, which forms part of the Adjameti Nature Reserve, and passes 500m east of the Rioni railway station. After 15km Vani buses turn right off the Baghdati road at a police post, passing Vartsikhe after 2km (30 minutes from Kutaisi); it's 7km to the road from Baghdati, and another 17km to Vani, where there's a big market opposite the bus station. There's a much better road on from Vani to the Kutaisi–Batumi road, 18km west (page 255), with hourly marshrutkas to Samtredia.

Cross the bridge over the River Sulori and the square beyond, and follow the sign (in English) to the 'Archeological Excavations'. You'll see the very obvious large **museum** (⊕ *10.00–17.00 exc Mon; GEL2*) on the hillside ahead, although it takes about 10 minutes to reach it, winding up Gorgasali; go under the footbridge and up the steps to the right to the entrance. Vani, known to the Greeks as Surium, was a major centre from the 8th to 1st century BC (at its peak from 600–400BC; it was destroyed by Mithridates VI Eupator in about 65BC), and many of the finest artefacts from ancient Colchis were found here. The best are all in the Treasury of the National Museum in Tbilisi (pages 149–50), but there are replicas here, as well as fine original pieces; what's more, captions are in English. By 1876 it was known that rain revealed gold objects on the hillsides here, and excavations began in the 1890s, with further work in the 1930s and from 1947 to 1963. Nowadays research is continuing, and the museum may also be closed for improvements, with a temporary display nearby; Vani was placed on the World Heritage List in 2007.

The ground-floor displays are mostly of weapons and tools, and the oldest and finest pieces are up in the gallery. In the 7th and 6th centuries BC, gold jewellery by superb craftsmen was buried with nobles, together with fine ceramics from the 6th to 4th centuries BC. From the 4th century BC on burials were in qvevri (clay vessels or *pithoi*), making it easier to conserve the contents, which now included Greek imports from Sinope. By 100BC foundries were casting bronze statues; on the gallery there's a fine torso of a youth, in front of a small treasury of beautiful gold ornaments and lots of tiny silver coins from the 3rd century BC. Across the footbridge is a small area of ruins, including city walls and sanctuaries; a few are covered, but visitors can clamber over the rest. There's a fine view north to Kutaisi and the High Caucasus, with attractive wooded hills to the south.

It's also possible to visit the **house-museum of Galaction Tabidze** (1892–1959), one of Georgia's finest and best-loved poets, near the Rioni in Chkvishe, about 4km north of Shuamta (where his cousin Titsian Tabidze, an equally fine poet, was born), on the main road about 3km west of Vani. It's a simple cottage with little on view (although the exhibits have been broadened to cover Titsian as well); what's more, the replica of Jason's ship, the *Argo*, which Tim Severin sailed here from Greece in 1984 and was on display, has been burnt! However, it's worth coming here on Galaction's birthday, 17 November, when there's always a celebration (followed on 23 November by Giorgoba – a good time to visit Georgia!).

RACHA რაჭა

Immediately to the north of Kutaisi is the small province of Racha (or Racha-Lekhumi), along the upper reaches of the Rioni River. Hemmed in by mountains up to 3,600m, it's a beautiful area which is mild enough in summer to produce both wine and tea, but so harsh in winter that most of the population move temporarily to the lowlands. It's also apparently the best source of seeds for Christmas trees (*Abies nordmanniana*), which unfortunately requires local men to climb 30–50m up without safety equipment. The people here are known for their strong traditional culture, with superb icons, honey and a unique genre of bagpipe music. Racha is also becoming known as a great venue for adventure tourism.

NORTH FROM KUTAISI The main road from Tbilisi branches off the Kutaisi highway about 5km west of Zestaponi and runs via Terjola, Tqibuli and Nikortsminda (page 245) to Ambrolauri, the chief town of Racha, and Oni, and then to Tskhinvali, capital of South Ossetia, although this road is now closed. From Oni the Ossetian Military Highway climbs to the summer-only Mamison Pass (2,820m), which you should not use to enter the Russian Federation. There are more marshrutkas from Kutaisi, but this road along the Rioni is very rough (although it's slowly being surfaced).

Marshrutkas from Kutaisi to Ambrolauri leave from the minor bus terminal on Mkheidze [228 E1], below the Bagrat Cathedral, at 10.00 and 14.00 daily, plus 09.00 on Tuesday to Sunday, returning at 13.00 and 17.00 (*GEL7*). The 09.00 continues to Oni (*GEL9*); there's another from the main bus station at 15.30 daily. Tickets can be bought from an office beneath a sign reading 'Windows' in English. A Tbilisi (Didube) to Oni marshrutka leaves at 08.00 daily in each direction (*GEL20–25*). It's also now possible to fly from Tbilisi (Natakhtari) to a new airport just south of Ambrolauri on the main road (w *vanillasky.ge; GEL50*).

Heading north along the right/west bank of the Rioni, you'll soon pass the Kutaisi Botanical Garden [228 F1] and the **Gumat Dam**, a typical Soviet hydro-electric scheme of the 1930s. About 25km from Kutaisi the road enters a fine limestone gorge, passing through the village of **Mekvena** (km36) where there's a guesthouse. The next village, **Tvishi**, 1km to the left/west at km41, is the first in Racha; known for its semi-sweet white wine, it lies below high cliffs on which you can see vertical lines caused by logged trees being slid down the slopes.

At Achara (*km54; 2hrs from Kutaisi*), a road turns left to Lajanauri (where there's a hydro-electric dam) and continues over a pass to Tsageri on the Tskaltubo–Lentekhi road. **Lentekhi**, at 820m, is nothing but a village, with the late-medieval ruins of a Dadiani palace, but it is the capital of Kvemo (Lower) Svaneti; this is far lower than Svaneti proper and has far less of interest to visitors, although guesthouses are appearing here. Guesthouse Leksura (*Tamar Mepe 34;* m *551 535067;* **$$**) is on the main street near Liberty Bank (with ATM), and the Riverside Hostel (m *591 812374;* **$**) is a little further east and across the river; on Chavchavadze (the road northwest to Bavari) are the Hotel Konstanta (m *579 591029;* **$$**), Hostel Nunu (m *595 284342, 595 558001;* **$–$$$**) and Mountain Inn (m *598 645630, 598 851049;* **$**). The only old churches are a couple dating from the 10th century just north of

Zachunderi, from where a very rough track continues over the 2,623m Zagar Pass (⊕ *Jun–Oct; 4x4 only*) into Upper Svaneti. Marshrutkas to Lentekhi leave three times a day from Kutaisi's main bus station, and take 4 hours. Continuing on the (gradually improving) main road up the Rioni Valley, the first village, across a bridge to the right, is **Zeda-Ghvardia**, known for its large caves. In fact the whole of Racha is a caver's paradise, and two 5km-long caves were discovered in 2001. This is the site of the Shareula tourist complex (page 245), a great base for rafting, riding, and hiking.

At km74 the road enters the district of **Kvanchkara**, known for its wine (page 84), which everyone will proudly tell you was Stalin's favourite; you can stay (and taste) at Guesthouse Kvanchkara (m *558 900962;* e *a81leco@yahoo.com;* f *alekosguesthouse;* **$$**). The valley opens up as you pass the 14th–15th-century hall church of Bugeuli on the far (south) bank, and after another 12km (at km82) you'll see the modern sprawl of **Ambrolauri** on the far side of the river, 14km from Kvanchkara (and 3 hours from Kutaisi). There's a modern tourist office at the junction into town (☏ *439 221618,* m *514 700055;* e *ticambrolauri@gmail.com;* ⊕ *10.00–18.00 daily*). It's still little more than a village, with a small daily market and fast food stalls opposite the bus station and few other services. If you head south up Kostava, the main road, from the roundabout with its much-photographed giant wine bottle, there are guesthouses (page 244) on the second street to the left (Kvanchkara) and the third (Rustaveli), opposite the Royal Khvanchkara wine cellar (*Kostava 13;* m *551 267722;* f ; ⊕ *10.00–16.00 Mon–Sat*). At the top of Kostava the post office faces the Bank of Georgia just before the main square, where you'll find a small and fairly simple hotel (page 244).

Continuing eastwards up the Rioni, the next village is **Tsesi**, where you'll see the Barakoni Church of the Virgin (km91/73), a large cruciform dome church built in 1753 (by Duke Rostom of Racha, a few years before he was tricked into being captured, overthrown and blinded by King Solomon I of Imereti), on the right, and then (after a bridge) the Mindatsikhe Castle, reached by a steep path up to the left.

Beyond this (at km112, 30 minutes from Ambrolauri) lies **Oni**, at the junction of the routes to North and South Ossetia. There are marshrutkas to Kutaisi (*09.00 and 15.00 daily; GEL9*) and Tbilisi (*08.00 daily; GEL25*), and taxis charge just GEL4 from Ambrolauri. Oni is famed as a stronghold of the mountain Jews, living in isolation here for 2,000 years or more. The community numbered around 3,000 in 1970 (when Oni was 55% Jewish) but has largely vanished to Israel, and now only five families remain. There is still a **synagogue** to the north of the centre on Baazovi that dates from 1895 and was restored in 2015. It was saved from demolition by the communists by a sit-in by women with babies (not just Jews), and now in order to pray women are needed to make up a minyan or prayer quorum, not usually allowed under Orthodox Jewish law. It can be visited by asking for the caretaker in the house with a rusty blue gate by the alley on the north side (on the Ossetian Military Highway). Further out on Baazovi is a cemetery with a mixture of Georgian and Jewish (and Soviet-era) grave markers. Northwest of the central square, there's a church with a wooden bell platform and a curiously large statue of Daniel and a lion outside. High on the hill across the river is a small, newish chapel that is worth walking up to for the view. The **museum** at Rustaveli 26 (⊕ *10.00–17.00 Mon–Fri (Jun–Sep daily); GEL2, tour GEL3*) has a very rich collection, starting in the entry hall with stone reliefs from 10th- and 11th-century church iconostases (and a stuffed bear, lynx and wolf). There's an art collection with ten paintings by Ucha Japaridze (1906–88), an important teacher who became rector of the Tbilisi State Academy of Arts, and others by Dimitri Nalbandyan (1906–93) and Elene Gugeshvili of the Famili Hotel Gallery; there's also a big painting on the stairs of Stalin at Gagra in 1952. The archaeological displays start with Mesolithic spearheads and a handmill, then Colchian and Celtic axes and Bronze Age metalwork (copper from Upper Racha was very important from the 8th to the 12th century BC), as well as 1st- to 3rd-century buckles with a unique (possibly Mesopotamian) astral design, and beads of the same period from Egypt and Syria. The Ethnographic store houses a jumble of 18th- to 20th-century chacha stills, copper jugs, wooden drinking cups, ceramic pots, a three-legged seat for the head of the family, musical instruments (and also accordions and a gramophone), grape-pressing troughs, qvevri, wineskins, scales, wooden bargeboards (balcony ornaments), one with a hammer and sickle, old religious books and more. On the balcony are more stone carvings including a superb Last Judgement from the first half of the 10th century (with old Georgian script) and a huge copper beer cauldron.

From Oni, a very lovely road, lined with mineral springs, leads northeast into the Caucasus for 25km past **Utsera** (1,042m) to **Glola**, site of another of Tamar's castles. **Shovi** (1,620m), a few kilometres east of Glola, was a popular spa in Soviet times, but now there are only a few fine villas and some moribund blocks set about a lovely meadow. The hotels listed on pages 244–5 offer basic rooms, but better accommodation should soon be available. It's well worth hiking on into the Mamison Gorge and to Udziro Lake, but you can't cross the Mamison Pass into North Ossetia, which is closed to foreigners. There's also a very bad road east from Oni to Tskhinvali in South Ossetia, which is also closed and unlikely to reopen in the foreseeable future. From 3km west of Glola a rough track leads northwest up the Rioni Valley to Chiora and **Ghebi** (1,350m), a large lively village surrounded by wildflower meadows and glaciers, which is also known for its traditional singing, especially of harvest songs and funeral laments. Ghebi has been populated since the Bronze Age, when a Colchic copper mine was established here. The Tbilisi–Oni marshrutka continues to Ghebi on Thursdays and Saturdays, returning the next day; there are also local marshrutkas from Oni to Ghebi at 16.30 and to Shovi at 16.00.

Ghebi is a great base for hiking and horseriding, with the Trails of Ghebi project seeing attractive hikes marked north and east from Ghebi; these go very close to the Russian border, so you'll need a permit from the border police in Oni (*Baazovi 169;* m *591 915692*) or Gona – don't forget your passport. The easiest option, marked with yellow stripes, follows the Cheveshuri valley east from Ghebi to the border police post at Gona (10km); then there's a river crossing (not possible when the water is high) and a path (8km) up to the meadows beneath Mt Dombistsveri (2,829m) and the Kirtisho Glacier, close to the Russian border. You'll have to return the same way. A longer route, marked with red stripes, follows the Rioni northwest from Ghebi (passing many mineral springs fenced to keep bears and other animals away) to cross the bridge at Brili and follow the river north to a camping site below Mt Uvali (3,191m); you can climb up to the Goribolo Pass (c2,930m) for views of the high peaks of the High Caucasus watershed.

A much tougher hike starts from the hamlet of Brili – keep left here up the Rioni valley (rather than crossing the bridge), pass a group of houses in the middle of a meadow and climb into the forest past a brick building (a Soviet Turbaza or mountain hut) with half its roof missing and up to a ridge (with views of the Edena glacier) and on to the turquoise Sasvano tarns, some of which are muddy but others are clean and fit to drink or swim in. It's possible to carry on to cross the Lechkhumi ridge, separating the deep and very long Rioni and Tskhenistskali valleys (and thus Racha and Lower Svaneti), but only about 50 hikers a year do so. The trail crosses the Vatsistsveri pass (2,910m) and Lapuri pass (2,600m) before dropping down to Zeshko, deep in the Tskhenistskali valley – but although it has been marked and will be designated as part of the Trans Caucasian Trail, the trail tends to get washed out and to be overgrown with 4m-high hogweed, comfrey and nettles, so be sure you know what you're doing and have a tent and supplies. The road down the valley from Zeshko is blocked by snow for about six months a year; about 3km down the valley from Zeshko it meets the 4x4 road from Lentekhi (page 241) to Ushguli in Upper Svaneti.

Where to stay, eat and drink

Ambrolauri

Hotels

🏠 **Hotel Metekhara** (16 rooms) Gamsakhurdia 2; ✆ 439 221221; m 596 221221; e hotelmetekhararacha@gmail.com. A boxy but comfortable modern place, with swimming pool & restaurant (**$$**). **$$$**

🏠 **Hotel Silovani** (20 rooms) Kostava 37; m 590 224243, 551 224322, 551 509515. A late (ie: not Stalinist) communist-era building with service standards still stuck in that era. **$$$**

Guesthouses

🏠 **Edena** Shishinashvili 21; m 577 522411. **$$**

🏠 **Elo** Kobakhidze 15; m 599 408567, 514 700055. **$$**

🏠 **Kidobana** Gogebashvili 23; m 598 258464. **$$**

🏠 **Racha Davit** Agmashenebelis 33; m 555 678010. **$$**

🏠 **Rachuli Oda** Shishinashvili 34; m 599 528007, 555 479963; e sosotomadze4@gmail.com. **$$**

🏠 **Saba** Rustaveli 27; m 593 982409; e bregadze.1955@mail.ru. **$$**

🏠 **Tanini** Kvanchkara 17; m 595 486121; **$$**

🏠 **Taripiri** Rustaveli 36; m 579 960960; e labaishvili78@gmail.com. **$$**

🏠 **Toma** Shishinashvili 41; m 555 8463261. **$$**

Glola

🏠 **Guesthouse Glola** (5 rooms) Shovi; m 577 305290

Ghebi

🏠 **Hostel Ghebi by Marika** m 593 548507; � hostelghebi. A very simple but very welcoming place; you can also rent horses (*GEL50, plus GEL50 for a guide*). **$**

🏠 **Into the Wild Hostel** (3 rooms) Patara Ghebi; m 599 567295. Activity-oriented hostel; shared bathroom & kitchen. **$**

Oni

🏠 **Hotel Sunset Shovi** (35 rooms) On the Ambrolauri road at km111; m 571 768855, 577 901901; w sunsetshovi.ge; ⏱ May–Oct. A comfortable but overpriced hotel set in its own nature reserve, with a good restaurant (**$$**). **$$$$**

🏠 **Hotel-Restaurant Orioni** (20 rooms) Davit Agmashenebelis Sq (junction of Kafianidze & Baazovi); m 591 255999, 599 343161. A big, modern place. **$$$**

✳ 🏠 **Famili Hotel Gallery** (8 rooms) Kafianidze (formerly Stalin) 18; m 599 231722, 593 660884; e nikagugeshashvili@gmail.com. Run by delightful artists Elene & Temur Gugeshvili (she's a painter and he is a wood-carver) who have a good collection of fossils, rock crystals, prehistoric metalwork & crampons, snowshoes & traps. Quite small but charmingly decorated rooms with shared bathroom. Also 3 larger but slightly cheaper en-suite rooms in a 200-year-old house at the end of the garden with 19th-century furniture. Great food; groups can press grapes (in season), distill chacha, make bread & churchkhela etc. 10 decent mountain bikes to rent. One of the best places to stay. **$$**

🏠 **Guesthouse M & B** (4 rooms) Baratashvili 7; m 599 157638, 558 385588. A nice place to stay, this has comfortable rooms, a hammock & good meals; some English & German spoken. **$$**

🏠 **Hostel #Onigram** Arno Oneli 31; m 592 922992; � onigram. A very hospitable place with great food, including Racha ham, and their own wine & teas of mountain herbs. **$$**

🏠 **Sunny Hostel** (14 rooms) Davit Agmashenebelis 54; w racha.ge; � travelinracha. Opening in the spring of 2019, this riverside hostel will be a cheery, modern & affordable base, with a range of excursions on offer. **$**

Shovi

There are 2 decently refurbished Soviet spa hotels here.

🏠 **Hotel Mamisoni** (28 rooms) m 599 514086. **$$**

🏠 **Hotel Racha** m 577 720808, 593 400880; e shovi.hotel.racha@gmail.com; w shovi-racha.com **$$**

Utsera
🏠 **Guesthouse in Utsera** (3 rooms) m 599 353464. Friendly place with good food & a shared bathroom; camping also possible. **$$**
🏠 **Klavdia's House** (3 rooms) m 599 353464, 591 299009; e utseraguesthouse@gmail.com. A comfortable guesthouse with a large garden, next to mineral springs. **$**

🏠 **Shorena Guesthouse** (8 rooms) m 593 548507; 🇫 shoreguesthouse. A traditional house with a glassed-in verandah, & friendly owners offering great food. **$**

Zeda-Ghvardia
🏠 **Shareula tourist complex** m 599 703939, 579 487788; w shareula.ge. Accommodation in chalets (ideal for groups), with restaurant & sports facilities. **$$**

NIKORTSMINDA By far the most important monument of Racha is 15km to the south of Ambrolauri, at Nikortsminda, where there's a beautifully decorated church set on a ridge on the edge of the village. Marshrutkas run several times a day from Ambrolauri, crossing the bridge south from the bus station and labouring up a modernised road (past the Khotevi Castle and Church of the Archangels at km9/63) to reach the village on a high limestone plateau. It's also possible to come directly from Kutaisi, taking a bus past Gelati to the logging town of Tqibuli and continuing by marshrutka on the Ambrolauri road up a winding road to a pass (a great spot for advanced paragliders) and past the artificial Lake Shauri (popular for fishing and picnicking) to Nikortsminda, 40km and 50 minutes from Tqibuli. From Ambrolauri, marshrutkas leave at 09.00 for Tbilisi and 09.30 to Kutaisi via Nikortsminda.

Just down a lane to the east of the bus stop, the **Church of St Nicholas** is built of mellow golden stone reminiscent of Somerset or the Cotswolds. It was built by Bagrat III in 1010–14 on a tight and tidy hexagonal internal ground plan; this was slightly spoiled in the mid-11th century by the addition of porches to the west and south, and a chapel to the south, which has a curved west end and Romanesque-style round arches. There was a porch to the north, but this has gone. None of this has interfered with the external carvings on all four façades. The finest is a figure of Christ on the north wall, above three perfectly proportioned blind arches. Inside, the hexagonal plan produces six apses radiating from the centre (instead of the usual four in the shape of a cross) which are all identical except that the eastern one (above the very simple blue-painted iconostasis) is marginally longer, and the western one leads into the porch. The dome is set on a splendid drum without squinches, pierced by 12 slim windows with finely carved architraves. The interior was fully painted in the 16th and 17th centuries, with the life of Christ (starting with the Nativity to the right of the entrance, together with a modern icon of the church's patron, St Nicholas) and portraits of local notables. The Annunciation is over the arch of the eastern apse, with Christ in Majesty beyond that; see also the wooden model church incorporated into the altar. The detached bell-tower, with its fireplace and spiral staircase, was added in the second half of the 19th century. Ask for the church key at the house with the two-storey glass front through the blue gate to the north of the church. The Nikortsmindoba festival is on 1 August. There are also great mountain views to the west and northeast.

MINGRELIA სამეგრელო

The subtropical region of Mingrelia (Samegrelo) produces tea, hazelnuts and citrus fruits, and its people are proud of their own distinct language (not a dialect of Georgian, they insist) and of their spicy cuisine, as well as dishes such as *elarji* (a shepherds' meal of *ghomi* or cornmeal polenta with cheese) and *kharcho* (a thick meat soup with walnuts added here). The highway westward leaves Kutaisi by the bridge over the railway next to the bus station and Kutaisi II railway station (with the new parliament and the High Caucasus visible to the right); it reaches the new Kutaisi airport (km255/297) after 20 minutes. From a roundabout at km256.5 there's a link to the Kutaisi bypass, and at km258 the Hotel Tsiskhkhavi is in a pleasantly rural setting by the Gubistskali River, at the start of the road north to Khoni and the Martvili and Okatse canyons (see opposite).

SAMTREDIA AND SENAKI The highway rejoins the Rioni at **Samtredia**, an industrial town and a major rail and road junction where the routes to Batumi swing south to cross the Rioni. Virtually all traffic into town uses the bridge at km264/288, about 500m east of the station, with vehicles heading west performing hazardous U-turns at the bottom; not an ideal spot to flag down marshrutkas but still feasible, and taxis do wait here. The bus station is a few hundred metres west of the railway station, but it's virtually abandoned and you'll usually have to cross the railway and head southwest to flag down a marshrutka at the junction of the roads to Poti (64km west; pages 251–4) and Batumi (104km southwest; pages 286–99). Buses from Zugdidi and Poti to Tbilisi also turn down the Batumi road to pick up the new highway just south of town, and there are ticket offices for buses to Turkey at the junction too.

The village of Kulashi, 6km north of Samtredia, was home to one of Georgia's largest Jewish communities; there are still three synagogues (the oldest dating from the 18th century), a cemetery, and the Museum of Georgian–Jewish Friendship (⊕ *10.00–18.00 Tue–Sun*).

Senaki is another industrial town (28km west of Samtredia) and the rail junction for Poti. Arriving from the east, the main road crosses the Tekhura River and the railway, then bypasses the town to the south; local marshrutkas turn off to cross back over the railway, then head down the old main road past the barracks where the 1998 mutiny began. In the centre they turn left to the rail and bus stations, then loop back over the railway by a level crossing, and stop again immediately across the tracks from the bus station; through buses and minibuses also stop here, in a yard 100m east of the footbridge (and about 200m west of km295/257). The road junction to Poti is at a level crossing just west of km301/251, 6km west of Senaki; from here it's 30km to Poti, 35km to Zugdidi or 121km to Sarpi.

🏠 **Where to stay, eat and drink** In Samtredia the modern Hotel Brend (*Javakishvili 7*; ☎ *411 220052*; m *568 674044*; e *nikoleishvili53mail.ru*; **$$**) is a block north from the railway station, although entry is at the rear on Chavchavadze. There is a simple restaurant to the left/west at the end of the pedestrianised street, and ATMs at the railway station and next to the hotel.

Senaki's hotels are aimed more at the wedding market than at travellers, so big glitzy buildings have cavernous restaurants and only a few rooms.

🏠 **Hotel EA Senaki** (24 rooms) Gvinjilia 5; ☎ 41 322 1717; m 595 002002/8/9; e georgian-hotel-ea@hotmail.com; w myhotels.ge/ea. On the main road just southeast of the centre, this has cottages around a court. **$$$**

🏠 **Hotel Oscar** (10 rooms) Mshvidoba 227B; m 598 565683, 568 936252; e restarantoscar@mail.com. This probably has the best restaurant

(**$$**), & is on the main road just southwest of the centre at km296/256. **$$$**

🏠 **Hotel Versailles** (35 rooms) Tsminda Nino 2/4; ☎ 413 275260; m 597 255111, 597 089592; e hotelversailles@myhotels.ge; w myhotels. ge/hotelversailles. In the centre, just west of the station. **$$**

MARTVILI AND THE CANYONS The road from Samtredia to Senaki is lined with long thin villages, each merging into the next, and each house has a garden full of citrus trees and a water tank on a tower (spot the polyhedral one painted like a football). From a junction 200m west of the rail and bus stations in Abasha (km280/272) a road leads 34km north to **Martvili** (hourly marshrutkas from Kutaisi; GEL4), where there's a very good Ethnographic Museum (*Tavisupleba 7;* ⊕ *10.00–18.00 Tue–Sun; GEL5*). Just south of the museum, a cable car rises to the monastery (the centre of Mingrelia's religious life in medieval times, when King David the Builder's mentor, St Giorgi Chkondideli, taught here – his festival is on 25 September), where there are two interesting 10th-century churches. In Salkhino, 15km from Martvili, you can stroll in the lovely park of the Salkhino Palace, built by Levan V Dadiani in the first half of the 19th century; it's known for its huge wine cellar, but the building is now closed.

In the foothills of the Caucasus to the north of Martvili, new tourist opportunities opened up in 2014, with roads and visitor facilities at some stunning canyons where you can swim, hike, camp and take boats through virtually untouched nature (**w** *martvilicanyon.ge*). The **Okatse (or Gordi) Canyon** is in Imereti, north of Khoni on the Satsiskvilo River near the village of Zeda Gordi. It's 2km long and no more than 5m wide at its narrowest points – too tight for boating, but you can swim, although the water is chilly all year. It's known for its dramatic waterfalls, up to 35m high (and 70m high in a side valley). There's also a quite stunning modern metal walkway (⊕ *10.00–18.00 Tue–Sun, closed in rainy weather; GEL5*) high above the water that, at times, is up to 15m away from the cliff. By public transport the only way to get here is the 10.00 marshrutka from Kutaisi bus station to Khoni (*hourly; GEL3*) and then another at 11.00 to the canyon, returning at 16.00.

About 6km north of Martvili, in Samegrelo (Mingrelia), the **Gachedili Canyon** is also superb, with the added attraction of dinosaur footprints and Colchic forest. You can take a boat (*GEL60 for up to 6 people*) on the Abasha River, or float in wetsuits and helmets, through the canyon, 2.4km long and 20–30m deep. Slightly further into the foothills, you can hike 4km from Meore Balda to the Toba waterfall, plunging vertically into a circle of cliffs, and on to the Oniore and Abasha falls; also near Meore Balde is the slightly less impressive **Balde Canyon**, also on the Abasha River, 1.5km long with cliffs up to 30m high.

It's possible to get to Martvili by marshrutka from Kutaisi (hourly; GEL4), but it's generally easier to take a tour or to hire a taxi for the day (*GEL60–70*).

🏠 **Where to stay**

🏠 **Guest House Martvilla** (8 rooms) Mshvidobis 7, Martvili; m 577 508090. Shared kitchen, & bikes to rent. **$$**

🏠 **Martvili Newhotel** (5 rooms) Mshvidobis 35, Martvili; m 597 400211. Owned by a very friendly doctor, this has simple rooms, a shared kitchen & great b/fasts. **$**

🏠 **Tamuna Guesthouse** (8 rooms) m 598 824982. The best accommodation at the Martvili Canyon, with a huge garden. Its very hospitable owners also run the restaurant next door. **$**

NOKALAKEVI About 18km northeast of Senaki (30 minutes by bus towards Martvili) are the ruins of **Nokalakevi**, capital of Egrisi (Lazica) from the 4th to 8th century AD, but there's evidence of settlement since the 8th century BC. In AD542–55 Shah Khusro I (and his famous general Mermeroes and his elephants) failed to capture the city; but in AD737 it was destroyed by the Arabs and remained in ruins until the first excavations in 1930 by the German Alfons Maria Schneider.

Large-scale archaeological work by the National Museum began in 1973, resuming from 2000 as an Anglo-Georgian expedition involving the National Museum and the universities of Cambridge and Winchester (w *nokalakevi.org*). Known to the Greeks as Archaeopolis (Old City), it's also been known as Tsikhegoji and Dzicha (Tsikhe and Dzicha meaning 'castle' in Georgian and Mingrelian respectively); Nokalakevi means 'ruins where once a town was'.

On a hill to the left a few kilometres north of Senaki (a pleasant jaunt), you'll see the ruins of **Shkhepi**, part of a chain of signal posts from the Black Sea. Continue through two villages to the gates of the ancient city (⊕ *Nov–Mar 10.00–17.00 Tue–Sun, Apr–Oct until 18.00; GEL5*) to the left immediately after the bridge over the Tekhuri River. In the museum (⊕ *10.00–16.00 Tue–Sun; GEL5*), the first room on the left upstairs displays relics from the 8th to 1st centuries BC, including ritual clay animals, silver and bronze bracelets (there were gold ones too, now in Tbilisi) and Greek ceramics, attesting to trade links across the Black Sea. To the right are *pithoi* (storage vessels) from the 4th to 1st century BC, and replica coins, agricultural implements, weapons (sling and catapult stones, and arrow- and spearheads), and pipes from a 'calorifer' (underfloor steam heating), as well as a few ceramic pieces from the 6th to 18th centuries AD.

The ruins are entered by a right-angled trap area and a gateway through a massive triple wall; the outer wall, of big blocks, was built in the 6th century AD, and the next two, of smaller stones, date from the 5th and 4th centuries. The walls enclose an area of 20ha, including a 4th–5th-century citadel and two churches on the mountain behind. There are a couple of modern houses, with beehives, inside the walls; you'll also see a gatehouse with external stairs and the Church of the 40 Martyrs of Cappadocia (with fragmentary remains of 17th-century frescoes, mostly hidden by a new iconostasis), both from the 6th century. Next to the church are the ruins of a tiny palace and the foundations of an older basilica, with those of a third church just to the west.

Beyond a house just outside the ruins, a tiny path leads up to a **fort** on a hill (as opposed to the citadel, higher up and reached by a jeep track to the north, a pleasant walk of an hour or so each way). At the far end of a very solid 19th-century girder bridge (for pedestrians and bikes only) across the river are the remains of a 5th-century bathhouse (with three rooms for three different temperatures, and red ceramic heating elements). As in most Georgian forts, there's a tunnel down to the river, to get water during a siege. On the far side of the river is a popular, if stony, beach, and a road leading up into a dramatic gorge with popular hot springs a kilometre or two along. The same team is now excavating at Khuntsi, just a few kilometres east of Martvili, which may turn out to be the site of the 6th-century fortress of Onoguris, where the Persians repelled a Byzantine siege in AD555 during the Lazic War.

ZUGDIDI (*Telephone code 415*) Heading northwest from Senaki, the Zugdidi road crosses the River Khobi at km311/241 and soon reaches the bus station of **Khobi**, opposite a massive sculpture of the sun, moon and stars, just east of a theatre with a matching sculpted frieze along its front and fly-tower. Marshrutkas from Batumi and Poti to Zugdidi join the main road here; a couple of kilometres north across the railway are the ruins of Khobi Monastery, founded in AD554, and a church which dates from the 12th and 13th centuries, as well as medieval walls and a bell-tower.

It's just over 100km from Kutaisi to Zugdidi (322km from Tbilisi), a city of 43,000 plus many of the 84,000 refugees from the neighbouring Gali district of Abkhazia now stuck in Mingrelia. Nevertheless, it's pleasant enough and there are a couple of things worth seeing if you decide to stay overnight. It's the capital of Mingrelia or Samegrelo, a province which has always gone its own way; it was ruled by the Dadiani family from 1046 at the latest until 1857 (paying tribute to the Turks from the 1460s until 1774, and nominally under Georgian rule at other times), and was the stronghold of the Zviadists (supporters of the ousted president Gamsakhurdia) and of the nationalists who wanted a military assault on Abkhazia.

Getting there and away The main bus terminal is 400m west of the main square at the railway station (reached by bus 1); tickets are sold in the hall opposite the railway ticket office. There are regular buses and minibuses to Kutaisi (*every 30mins 06.00–19.20; GEL7*), Poti (*11 daily; GEL6*) and Batumi (*8 daily; GEL10*), and every few hours to Tbilisi (*6hrs; GEL15*). There may be a bus or minibus for Mestia here but there's more likely to be something in the area by the Svan tower, where minibuses heading up to Svaneti wait for passengers. There are two trains a day to Tbilisi, but both now leave in the evening – the day train at 18.15 (arriving at 23.40) and the night train at 22.15 (arriving at 06.33). Just north of the Svan tower on Nikoladze, where marshrutkas to Mestia wait, there's a terminal for the comfortable Metro coaches to Tbilisi (m *599 201602; 3/day; GEL20*).

Where to stay

Hotel Grand Konstantine Gamsakhurdias 35; m 579 777701; f Grandhotelzugdidi. New in 2017, this is squeaky-clean & indeed quite grand, apart from the rather Soviet b/fast. **$$$**

Hotel Samegrelo (20 rooms) Kostava 54; ☏ 415 507445. Slightly newer & more expensive than the nearby Hotel Zugdidi but better value & with its own restaurant (**$$**). **$$–$$$**

Hotel Mars (14 rooms) Kostava 36; m 591 210055; f. A decent modern building with AC rooms, next to McDonalds at the south end of the main square. **$$–$$$**

Hotel Zugdidi (14 rooms, 1 suite) Kostava 5A; ☏ 415 254242. All rooms have clean, en-suite facilities with TV (not cable), hot water & towels, & there's a good little café-bar. Still, it's pretty over-priced. Rates inc b/fast. **$$–$$$**

Art Hostel (4 rooms) Rustaveli 29; m 568 535663; w arthostelgeorgia.simplesite.com; f. Another typical 2-storey house & yard, but with rather retro furnishings & a very warm welcome. **$$**

My Moon Hostel (4 rooms) Rustaveli 67; m 595 901590; e mymoonhostel@gmail.com; f. A 2-storey house with big paintings of Jim Morrison & Bob Marley but not very hostel-like otherwise; there's 1 ground-floor dorm with 6 bunks & private rooms upstairs, sharing a bathroom on the rear porch. There are shared kitchens & a nice garden shaded by a big fig tree. **$$**

Zugdidi Hostel (4 rooms) Rustaveli 8; m 558 102688, 591 654036; e zugdidihostel@gmail.com; f. Recently moved to the junction of Rustaveli & Kostava, this friendly place has dorms, 1 dbl, a small kitchen & a shared bathroom. **$**

Where to eat and drink As well as those listed, there are several decent cafés along Zviad Gamsakhurdias facing the park such as Kamea at no 13 (☏ *415 251185*) and the Tea House Café Alerti at no 6 (m *593 313538*).

Art House Rustaveli 87A; m 593 117030; ☺ noon–02.00 daily. Next to the tourist office, this bar has a charming big courtyard, good décor & music. A nice place for a drink, but the food is less good, & overpriced. **$$**

Diaroni Konstantine Gamsakhurdias 9; ☏ 415 251122; e diaroni2007@mail.ru; w diaroni.ge; ☺ 10.00–23.00 daily. 1 block east of the central park at its northern end, this restaurant is the best place for a full meal, with a grand dining hall & a terrace in front behind a cypress hedge. **$$**

El Barco Rustaveli 77 m 595 672929; ☺ 11.00–01.00 daily. This is an oddly named but cheery place serving a familiar range of Georgian & more local dishes. **$$**

✗ Mendzel Kostava 34; m 571 541515; **f** mendzel.ge; ⊕ 09.00–23.00 daily. This has been recommended for authentic Megrelian food, though it can be noisy & smokey. $$
✳ ✗ Hugo's Taverne Davit Agmashenebelis 19; m 599 461908. Just south of the centre on the main road, a simple place that serves great European (mainly German) food, with good friendly service. $$

✗ Dariali Kostava 58; m 593 248038. Good new 24hr khinkali joint, with a couple of decent cafés alongside. $
✗ Mego Bari Beria 2; m 599 550057; e youthforsamegrelo@gmail.com; ⊕ 11.00–03.00. A new social project with café-bar & co-working space, & live music & other events. $

Other practicalities There's a **tourist information centre** (m *591 445345, 598 469201;* ⊕ *10.00–13.00, 14.00–18.00 daily*) on Rustaveli just east of Zviad Gamsakhurdias Square. There are plenty of exchange offices and **ATMs**, including opposite the tourist information centre. The **post office** is on the south side of Rustaveli immediately west of Zviad Gamsakhurdias Square, and there's an **internet** café at the northern end of the square. The Atriumi cinema is at Zviad Gamsakhurdias 26 (m *599 380808*).

What to see and do The main square, Zviad Gamsakhurdias Gamziri, is quite attractive; long and thin, it has trees in the centre and a few cafés and bars. Buses go three-quarters of the way around the square to continue on Rustaveli, the main road westwards, past a market and so-called trade centre, bustling with people heading for the de facto border with Abkhazia, just a few kilometres north. A couple of hundred metres northwest of the bridge on Gulua you'll see a Svan defensive tower, built in the communist period to mark a Svan restaurant.

Heading northwards along the length of the main square, past the new esplanade behind the Public Service Hall to the right, you'll come in a couple of minutes to a park (with steps down towards a footbridge to the Svan Tower to the left) on the far side of which is the neo-Gothic palace of the Dadiani family, rulers of Mingrelia, until the Russians finally took over in 1857; it's now a **museum** (⊕ *10.00–18.00 Tue–Sun; GEL2*).

Alexander Chavchavadze's daughter Katarina (sister-in-law of the playwright Griboedov) married David Dadiani, the last prince of Mingrelia (although the poet Nikoloz Baratashvili was in love with her); their daughter Salome was the god-daughter of Catherine the Great and married Achille Murat, grandson of Marshal Murat and Napoleon's sister Caroline (it was Achille who introduced European-style winemaking to western Georgia). Thus, one of Napoleon's three death masks has ended up here, together with other bits and pieces of Bonapartiana. The palace was built in the 17th century and extended in 1873–78; it became a museum in 1921. Together with the relics of Napoleon and the Dadianis (such as paintings, textiles and weapons), it also houses a notable collection of Colchian gold and silver coins and 13th- and 14th-century manuscripts. To the side is the small Church of the Icon of the Mother of God (built in 1838), with a bare interior and unusual semi-circular sides to the porch so that its ground plan is a circle in a cross plan. The chasuble of the Mother of God, brought from Jerusalem to Khobi's Monastery of the Dormition, and now in the museum, is taken in procession to the church on 7 July.

On the right-hand side of the park is Nico Dadiani's **palace**, built in the 1880s and now being refurbished, and the **Botanical Gardens** established in 1840 by his mother Katarina Dadiani, complete with pond and picturesque ruin, which are free and make a nice spot for a stroll, especially in spring. In the village of **Rukhi**,

5km north on the main road towards Sukhumi, a new shopping mall is busy with shoppers carrying goods into Abkhazia; just beyond, a fortress dating from 1636 dominates the bridge over the Enguri at the de facto border crossing.

ANAKLIA This stands on the sandbanks at the mouth of the Enguri River where President Saakashvili decreed that a sparkling new pleasure resort should be built on the site of a Russian military base, as part of a barely thought-out scheme for a tourist zone stretching from the new Tetnuldi ski resort above Mestia to the Black Sea, as well as a new deep-water port and international airport. Alas, he ignored the man-eating mosquitoes and other problems, but a couple of oversized and overpriced hotels with casinos opened in 2012, and are used mainly for weddings; the port and its rail link are now under construction in 2018, due to be completed in 2021. It may be worth a jaunt from Zugdidi to enjoy the sense of space, and to cross the dramatic modernist cycle-bridge (540m long) across the mouth of the river to the **Aquapark** [map, page 222] (⊕ *11.00–19.00 daily; GEL15*), the largest waterpark anywhere on the Black Sea coast, with wave pools, slides and a bar.

In 2014 the beach in front of the Aquapark was the site of the Kazantip Republic Festival, something like Nevada's Burning Man, after it became impossible to stage it in Crimea. Since 2015 the GEM festival (*Georgian Electronic Music*; w *gemfestival. com*) has been staged here instead; initially nine days long, it briefly had state funding to expand to a month but will run for just four days in August 2018 (in 2017 one raver died and 20 fell ill from bad GHB drugs, and there were also financial irregularities). The Orthodox Church has been strongly opposed to the festivals, but local people welcome the economic boost.

Just inland, the marshland that Saakashvili hoped to build his airport on is a haven for migrating birds. About 15km south, the city of Lazika has a similar background, but consists of just one building, a very imaginative City and Public Service Hall on stilts above the marshland designed by Anglo-Georgian firm Architects of Invention. It's hard to believe that anything else will be built here.

Getting there and away From Zugdidi, 31km northeast, marshrutkas run six times daily (*between 10.00 and 17.00; GEL2*) from opposite the Svan tower on Gulua; if you get off where the road turns 90° left at the seafront, you'll see the walls of a fortress built in 1703 that effectively blocked the trade in slaves from the Caucasus to Constantinople.

Where to stay, eat and drink In addition to those places listed, a few houses offer rooms, and there's a café and a couple of food shops just inland from the fortress.

Golden Fleece Hotel (105 rooms) m 597 164164; w goldenfleecehotel.ge. Just south on the seafront boulevard, this is a rather grandiose 5-star establishment, with spa, pools & sauna. $$$$$
Hotel Anaklia (42 rooms) ✆ 32 260 9990/1; w hotelanaklia.com. Slightly Moorish-style luxury hotel with a large outdoor pool. $$$$

Hotel Palm Beach (52 rooms) m 596 007700; e p.beach242@gmail.com; w palmbeach. ge. This 4-star hotel (with organic restaurant; $$$) is on the seafront, & overshadows the fortress. $$$$

POTI ფოთი *Telephone code 493*

From the road junction 6km west of Senaki, it's 30km to Poti, founded by the Greeks (as Phasis) and re-established as a Turkish fort, which was the hub of the trade in Circassian slave-girls, the most highly prized in the Ottoman Empire. In a little-known episode, a group of Vikings once landed here; they had taken part in a Russian campaign against Constantinople in 1043 but were captured and ultimately released. In 1047 they were invited by Bagrat IV to join his army, fighting in the battle of Sasireti, after which they returned home, with Georgian coins which have since been found in Scandinavia. Development of the modern port began in 1858 and was boosted by the arrival of the Transcaucasian Railway in 1872. Nowadays it is Georgia's largest port, with a capacity of five to six million tonnes a year, largely containerised; a train-ferry terminal opened in 1999, to link Poti with Chornomorsk (formerly Ilyichevsk, Ukraine), Constanţa (Romania) and Varna (Bulgaria). Privatisation saw the shipbuilding yard sold to the Korean Hyundai Group and the Petrocas oil terminal to the Russian oil company Rosneft; the port itself (which was occupied by the Russian army in 2008) was sold to the sovereign wealth fund of Ras al-Khaimah (in the United Arab Emirates), and then in 2011 to the Danish APM Terminals. A Free Industrial Zone was opened in 2008, and, in 2017, 75% of its shares were sold to CEFC China Energy Company, as part of China's One Belt, One Road initiative to reinvent the Silk Road (see box, page 81). The Kulevi oil terminal, 15km north, is owned by the Azerbaijani state oil company; opened in 2008, it was built on 96ha of wetland, home to migratory waterbirds and supposedly protected by the Ramsar Convention.

It's a city of 50,000 people; unattractive and without much to see, but it does offer a couple of comfortable places to stay. It's also the base for the Kolkheti National Park (pages 254–5) whose headquarters and visitor centre are at Guria 222, south of town.

GETTING THERE AND AWAY There are comfortable day trains from Tbilisi (*5hrs; GEL12.50*) via Gori and Rioni. Marshrutkas leave more or less hourly for Tbilisi (*GEL15*), Batumi (*GEL6*), Kutaisi (*GEL5*) and Zugdidi (perhaps changing at Khobi; *GEL5*) from the yard of the closed bus station, west of the train station. Taxis and marshrutkas for Batumi also wait by the Tsotne Dadiani statue and pick up along Davit Agmashenebelis.

Ukrainian shipping company UkrFerry (e *poti@ukrferry.com*; w *ukrferry.com*) has ferries that ply weekly across the Black Sea to and from Constanţa (Romania) and Chornomorsk (Ukraine) (pages 65–6).

🏠 WHERE TO STAY

🏠 **Hotel Park Green** (45 rooms) Guria 181; ✆493 220808; e hotelparkgreen@gmail.com; ⓕ. A good modern holiday hotel across the main road from the Maltakva resort area; decent restaurant. **$$$$**

🏠 **Hotel Ankori** (24 rooms) Gegidze 22; ✆493 226000; e ankor.99@mail.ri. A good, modern hotel just to the right/east from the roundabout at the north end of Davit Agmashenebelis, with a nice restaurant & rooms with AC & cable TV with good Grundig sets. English is spoken at reception, & they'll exchange US dollars. **$$$**

🏠 **Hotel Poti** (10 rooms) Kostava 3/6; m 599 540815, 571 146855. A glass box over a shop facing the Tsotne Dadiani statue, opened at the end of 2014 but not as impressive as it sounds. **$$$**

🏠 **Golden Lake Hotel** In the centre of Maltakva (by the bridge); m 557 227587; ⓕ. South of Poti by the lake, this is run-down but cheap, & in a peaceful rural setting. **$$**

🏠 **Hotel Fasis** Rekvava 10; m 995 289979, 598 310104. Between the rail & bus stations, this is a decent budget option in a newish building; some English spoken. **$$**

🏠 **Hotel Paleostomi** ✆493 278202; m 555 159775; e bartianatia@rambler.ru. A further 1km to the south from Maltakva, a road leads 50m east to the hotel from the Restaurant Iasoni (Jason; km81/40), where marshrutka 20 terminates. An ideal location for birdwatchers, as the national park boat launch on Lake Paleostomi is immediately beyond the hotel. **$$**

🏠 **Hotel Prime** (9 rooms) Akaki 63 (not 53, despite the sign); ☎ 493 222235 m 592 929202; e primepoti@hotelsprime.ge; w hotelsprime.

ge/en/poti. In an older building just southeast of the centre (under 10min walk from the cathedral roundabout), this has adequate rooms with fast Wi-Fi & a bar & restaurant (reserve in advance for dinner; **$$**). **$$**

✕ WHERE TO EAT AND DRINK

✕ **Aragvi** Gegidze 18; ☎ 493 242727; ⊕ 08.00–midnight daily. Just 100m east of the Hotel Ankori, heading towards the station, this red-brick beer-restaurant has a double terrace with a view of the docks. **$$**

✕ **Nikoladze Art Café** Davit Agmashenebelis 7; m 595 909806, 577 345401; 🄵 artcafenikoladze; ⊕ 11.30–23.30 daily. Easily the most attractive place in town to eat & drink, with charming décor & lots of books, perhaps some live music, & a non-smoking area. **$$**

✕ **Restaurant Old Ship** Mshvidoba; m 790 936129; ⊕ 10.00–midnight daily. In a galleon just

west of the cathedral by the rowing club, this is not gourmet, serving the usual Georgian dishes plus some tapas, but it's a pleasant setting & there's Wi-Fi. **$$**

☕ **Café Room** Davit Agmashenebelis 30; m 591 307310; 🄵. A pleasant café that also serves decent Georgian food. **$**

🍺 **Beer House BH** Davit Agmashenebelis 37/1; m 570 108005; e office.armana@gmail.com; 🄵; ⊕ 10.00–midnight daily. At the north end near the dock gate, this pub serves a good mix of Georgian dishes such as khachapuri, khinkali, kebab & trout, etc. **$$**

OTHER PRACTICALITIES There are banks with **ATMs** on Davit Agmashenebelis, including at the south end Silk Road Bank at No 10 and Liberty Bank at No 12, Bank of Georgia at No 30, and at the north end, by the dock gates, TBC. South of the cathedral, Bank of Georgia, Tera Bank and TBC all have ATMs near the start of 26 May. The **post office** is at Tsminda Giorgi 16.

The city is clearly increasingly used to foreign visitors, with groceries for instance now signed in English and street names translated.

WHAT TO SEE AND DO Turning right from the bus station on Samegrelo you'll come to the beautifully restored railway station; turn right to cross the bridge to the big equestrian **statue of Tsotne Dadiani** (who led an uprising against the Mongols and was killed by being coated with honey and left to be eaten by insects), with the market (and exchange stalls) immediately on your right. Head west on Chanturia past the market, and you'll reach a huge roundabout and the circular **cathedral**. Built in 1906–07 and loosely based on Hagia Sophia in Istanbul, it was a theatre under communism and has now been restored for religious use.

Across the square to the north of the cathedral is the splendid new concert hall, while to the east 26 May leads to the **Museum of Colchian Culture** (*26 May 9*; ☎ 93 23502; ⊕ 10.00–18.00 *Tue–Sun*), with a world-class collection of artefacts from 3000BC to the 16th century, including fine iron axes and bronze carvings, ceramics and coins, as well as an exhibit on Jason and the Argonauts.

Heading north from the cathedral, you'll cross the Rioni Canal again on Davit Agmashenebelis, passing fine buildings built around the start of the 20th century, of which a surprising number are now being refurbished and repainted. A stadium is visible to the left, as well as the **lighthouse**, a cast-iron structure fabricated in London and erected here in 1864; refurbished in 2012, this is now open to visitors, with an exhibition at the base if you can't face the 153 steps. There is a theory that soccer was introduced to Georgia here, either from sailors or the English workers installing the light.

Eventually the road reaches a roundabout with a statue of Niko Nikoladze (mayor from 1894 to 1912) where it swings left to reach the port in around 200m; here, there's a big, modern grey ferry terminal, and a small chapel. Immediately north of the terminal is the yacht club, with electricity, water and fuel available for yachts, plus a shower, sauna and café terrace for their crews; it also organises races and other events. Turning right at the roundabout you'll eventually come to the bus and rail stations and then cross a bridge back to Tsotne Dadiani Square.

AROUND POTI
Maltakva To the south of the cathedral, Mshvidoba leads past a park with various statues, fountains, dodgems and an unserviceable Ferris wheel, to the sea. It's possible to walk south along the dirty grey beach for 3km to the Maltakva resort area, an impressively Modernist complex, built to hold water-skiing championships on the so-called Golden Lake. It's easier to follow the Batumi road, taking Akaki southeast from the cathedral and after about 1km turning right past a cemetery. Behind it is Lake Paleostomi, which is black with waterfowl in the migration seasons and in winter, although there's little to see at other times. From here, it's 2.5km south to the national park headquarters and another 1km to the Maltakva turning.

Marshrutka 20 from the market runs this way, mostly terminating 500m north of the Maltakva turning. You can walk through a turnstile to the right just south of this terminal, or take a road from just south of km80/39 (opposite a large ugly monument of Jason holding the Golden Fleece, and an English sign to Maltakva). This leads through a wood and then after 200m right to the complex; from the beach you should turn inland at a half-built hotel isolated by the sea and cross a long, modern rusty-coloured footbridge to the derelict spectator facilities. The campsite at the north end of the complex has closed, as has the Pioneer Railway in the park behind it, but you could camp wild.

Kolkheti National Park [map, page 222] Immediately east of Poti is the Kolkheti (Colchis) National Park, now recognised as globally important wetlands and listed as a Ramsar Site; the reserve is in four parts totalling 44,849ha (including 15,742ha of water). The coast both north and south of Poti and the wetlands inland, along rivers such as the Rioni, are very young, having formed only in the last 6,200 years. In other words, when Jason and the *Argo* came here from Greece in the 13th century BC, there was only open sea here. Then around 5000BC the connection from the Mediterranean to the Black Sea burst open, causing the biblical Great Flood, which in fact lasted for about 40 years and raised the sea level by about 100m. Now there is a coastal sandbank with peat bogs, up to 12m deep (ie: well below sea level) behind, with a system of lagoons. The largest is **Lake Paleostomi**, 18.2km² in area and up to 3.2m deep; it's a stopover for 21 threatened bird species, and there are 173 other bird species resident here. The best birdwatching is to the east of the lake, reachable only by boat. It was linked to the sea in 1934 by an artificial channel, the Kaparcha River, and the changes in salinity have wiped out many of the rare fish species; expansion of Poti port and the new Khulevi port to the north may cause further damage. Despite heavy human impact, there are still important communities of endemic and relict plant species in the wetlands. Among the most interesting is the wingnut tree, whose only relations are in China and Japan, as well as an endemic oak; it's also one of the only two remaining spawning grounds of the Atlantic sturgeon. You may also see three species of dolphin offshore. Many international and Georgian NGOs are now involved in the conservation of the Colchic wetlands, notably the WWF, the Poseidon Marine Association and the Georgian Centre for the Conservation of Wildlife. The park headquarters, with a modern visitor centre (✆ 577 101837; e zjibladze@apa.gov.ge; w apa.gov.ge; ⊕ 10.00–19.00 daily), is at Guria 222, 4km south of the centre of Poti, and a long way from Guria 212. The friendly staff can arrange boat trips and kayak rental (GEL10/1hr or GEL15/2hrs), with maps of paddling routes.

GURIA გურია

This is a small province, known both for its immensely complex polyphonic singing, and for its people who are both very political and very forthright, which many of us would see as a contradiction in terms; nevertheless, it was the home of Shevardnadze. The local tea industry has been revived since 2010 by the excellent Gurieli company (w gurieli.ge/en), and hazelnuts are an important crop, too.

The main road to Batumi passes through the leafy town of Lanchkhuti on its way from Samtredia to the coast, but the capital of Guria is Ozurgeti, 33km to the south

OZURGETI AND LANCHKHUTI It's drab and uninteresting, but Ozurgeti is the starting point for visits to some attractive old churches in the surrounding hills. The closest is the medieval monastery of Shemokmedi, 7km south. The others are to the north near Lanchkhuti; from Chkonagora, 9km east of Lanchkhuti, a road is signposted south to the nunnery of Sameba-Jikhetis – the road is steep and passable only in good weather, but the views over the Kolkheti National Park are great. It's best to take a guide with a 4x4 vehicle, and you may still have to walk the last bit; the Festival of the Virgin on 21 September is a good time to visit. The Maral monastery of Jumatis is to the south from Lesa (km37.5/19.5, 7km west of Lanchkhuti) off the Ozurgeti road. There is a small museum in Ozurgeti, just north of the central roundabout at Chanturia 1, displaying archaeological relics, old books and coins, and a sword that supposedly belonged to Napoleon. This used to be in the nearby Gurieli Palace (1873), now the Bishop's Palace.

Kvemo and Zemo Shukhuti, 4km east of Lanchkhuti on the main road, are known for their annual game of lelo, a mass-participation version of rugby in which hundreds of people spend the afternoon of Easter Day trying to move a 16kg ball across the stream between the upper and lower villages; it's pretty violent, and a man was killed in 2015.

Getting there and away Ozurgeti is reached by a railway from the coast, with day and night trains from Tbilisi (from GEL8.50), but it's a very roundabout route and you're best off taking a marshrutka (hourly; GEL3) from Samtredia or Batumi. Lanchkhuti is on the main road and railway between Samtredia and Batumi, and thus an easier stopping-off point.

Where to stay

🏠 **Hotel de Lux** Ninoshvili 60, Lanchkhuti; m 599 917933; e kesohotel@yahoo.com. By the main roundabout in the centre of town (km 31/26), this is simple but adequate; there are shops, cafés & fast food just to the west. **$$$**

🏠 **Guest House Achi** (7 rooms) Achi; m 597 990955. A village guesthouse in a dead-end valley 7km south of Ozurgeti. **$$**

🏠 **Guest House** Guriis Khibli (10 rooms) Dvabzu; m 555 530085, 599 787516. A friendly village guesthouse 5km from Ozurgeti. **$$**

🏠 **Hotel Brooks** (11 rooms) Guria 17, Ozurgeti; m 551 595000, 591 228200, 599 001252; e wasarela@mail.ru. **$$**

BAKHMARO There's a better road southeast from just south of Chokatauri, on the Samtredia–Ozurgeti road, via the Nabeghlavi mineral spring (famous for its sodium bicarbonate water, available in bottles all over Georgia) to Bakhmaro, in the mountains a mile above sea level just north of the Adjaran border. Once a Soviet children's health resort, in July and August it's full of Georgians who come to hike, watch the sunset, drink wine and chat by a bonfire. Rooms are cheap and you can buy some food, but you may want to bring extra food and camping gear because there are no amenities. Until recently it was only accessible from mid-June to mid-October, but there's now a small ski operation here (w *powderproject.ch*) using snowcat vehicles rather than lifts, and a new lodge. There's a great two-day hike (to be part of the Trans Caucasian Trail) from here to Gomis-Mta (2,100m), 17km southeast of Ozurgeti, camping overnight at a yayla or shepherds' summer encampment, and on into the Kintrishi Protected Area in Adjara (page 302).

ALONG THE COAST ROAD Heading south from Poti, immediately south of the checkpoint at km40 you'll cross a bridge over the Kaparcha River from Lake Paleostomi to the sea, and another 3km further south you'll finally leave Poti municipality and the province of Mingrelia, and enter Guria. The first village on the coast road is **Grigoleti**, settled by Old Believer religious dissidents exiled from Russia in 1912; some very comfortable new resort hotels have opened here (see opposite). Just south it meets the direct road (and, just south, the railway) from Tbilisi to Batumi, via Samtredia, Lanchkhuti and Supsa (at km48/69 on the coast road; km0/57 on the Samtredia road).

Just inland of the coast road, and southwest across the river from **Supsa** village, four big storage tanks mark the terminal of the refurbished oil pipeline from Baku, opened in 1999. This carries just 80,000 barrels a day or four million tonnes a year, which could be increased to 10 million or 12 million tonnes a year. When the land was privatised, the elite took the best farming land, and the rest got the marshy land across the Supsa River to the south, where the oil terminal was later built; however, the compensation offered was derisory, leading to a lawsuit and the detention of their lawyer on thoroughly dubious grounds.

There are fish restaurants by the coast road south to Kobuleti, notably opposite the station of **Ureki** (just south of km 53/66); this attractive little resort (also known as Magnetiti), on the coast, is famous for the healing properties of its iron-rich black sand. Soviet doctors sent patients for rest, relaxation and treatment at the resort's three sanatoria; then businessman Badri Patarkatshishvili started redevelopment aimed at creating a western-standard resort. Crossing the tracks or following the road from south of the station where there's a seasonal tourist office (e *ticureki@gmail.com*), it's about 20 minutes' walk to the small park (refurbished by Patarkatshishvili) with modern toilets and lots of benches, beyond which alleys lead down to the beach. The main road (Takaishvili) turns to follow the coast southwards only, where there are hotels (see opposite), but there are cheaper options available inland such as the Theodora (*Takaishvili Alley III;* m *557 248585;* **$$**), and even cheaper rooms above a shop inland from the square at Takaishvili 118 (**$$**). The small restaurants near the park are adequate, pleasantly rustic but a bit samey, all serving fish kefalia and kambula.

At km 59/60 there's a turning to Ozurgeti (20km east), just north of the new Black Sea Arena (and huge car park); the Kobuleti bypass starts at km62, and immediately south on the old coast road is the **Tsitsinatela amusement park** [map, page 222] (m *568 411741;* w *tsitsinatela.com;* ☉ *18.00–01.00 daily*), with a very obvious Ferris wheel, and the Miniature Park, an open-air exhibition of scale models of Georgia's architectural landmarks. At the mouth of the Natanebi river, there was a Russian fort here that was stormed by Turkish forces in 1853, at the start of the Crimean War, with nearly 1,000 Russians killed; the luxury Paragraph Resort & Spa (w *paragraphhotels.com*) has just been opened here by the Marriott chain and really does seem to be maintaining very high standards of comfort and service.

Where to stay, eat and drink

Grigoleti

Hotel Andamati (24 dbls, 6 half suites, 3 suites) 293 30035; m 599 446097, 593 555255. A classy place set in beautiful gardens with tennis court & seawater pool. Suites have DVD & jacuzzi. $$$–$$$$$

Hotel Spa Villa Reta 493 250555; m 571 250555; w villareta.com. This has all the creature comforts you might expect of such a place – AC rooms, Wi-Fi, swimming pool & health spa. $$$–$$$$

Hotel Central m 555 178201; e grigoleticentral@gmail.com; f. Down a track towards the sea at the highway junction, this is a cheaper option. $$

Ureki

Tbilisi (46 rooms) Takaishvili 200; m 590 222277, 599 364430; e marta-55@mail.ru, tsitso@ locks.ge; w urekitbilisi.ge. Ureki's only 4-star hotel. $$$$

Elegant Ureki Takaishvili 67; m 557 087788, 577 727377; e elegant.ureki@gmail.com; f ureki.elegant. A plain block not far from the beach, with a decent-sized pool; there's a café but no restaurant. $$$

George Takaishvili 107; m 597 806061, 592 806061; f hotelgeorgeureki. Overlooking the beach, this has a small pool. $$$

Kolkhida (76 dbls, 12 suites, 3 apts) Takaishvili 117; m 790 302203, 599 205445; e kolkhida.hotel@gmail.com; w kolkhida.ge. Just beyond the Edemi on the right, this was once the main sanatorium but is now a large & rather faded hotel complex, open all year, with 3 soccer pitches. $$$

Prime Takaishvili 129; m 592 929202; e manager@hotelsprime.ge; w hotelsprime.ge/ en/ureki; late May–late Oct. With a private beach & terrace bar, this is great for a family holiday. $$$

Edemi (16 rooms) Takaishvili 138; m 599 101393; e amiko1947@rambler.ru. This is a 4-storey block with friendly staff. $$–$$$

BeachCamp m 571 300125; w blackseacamping.com; summer only. In Kaprovani, 3km south of Ureki (the 1st right after crossing a bridge over the railway). Modern showerblock, electricity, Wi-Fi, café & mini-shop. €10 pp/night. $

ABKHAZIA აფხაზეთი

Abkhazia, the beautiful westernmost district of Georgia, has effectively seceded and, having once been the Soviet Union's most popular area for beach holidays, is starting to lure back Russian holidaymakers attracted by its relatively low prices, good beaches and sunshine. Western, non-Russian, visitors are rare, although bodies such as the United Nations and the Red Cross are working here. Part of the reason for this is – quite reasonably – the region's perceived instability, but there are also serious problems with visas, as Russia and Georgia disagree about Abkhazia's claimed independence. From the Russian perspective, Abkhazia has every right to be independent and is recognised as such; Georgia (and most of the world) sees Abkhazia as merely an autonomous republic within Georgian territory. Naturally, such a divergence of views has led to enormous problems since Abkhazia's de facto independence in 1994. The situation remains volatile and subject to change but at the time of writing it was possible for foreigners to enter Abkhazia from either Georgia or Russia and then return to that same country. In 2017 the slowly recovering tourism industry was hit by rising crime levels; even before that a sense of tension and paranoia was noticeable among local people, which is hardly surprising. The natural beauty of Abkhazia is delightful, but in between are abandoned concrete buildings and even ghost towns, the result of both post-Soviet collapse and the war of secession.

GETTING THERE AND AWAY Entry to Abkhazia from Russia and continuing on to Georgia is not possible (and ill-advised as individuals would be subject to arrest as illegal aliens) as Georgia does not consider the Russian–Abkhazian frontier an official entry point, nor the Georgian–Abkhazian border as a bona fide exit point. Boats no longer run from Trabzon in Turkey and so this is no longer a viable alternative.

However, short trips from Zugdidi are increasingly popular; you'll have to go to the Abkhaz Foreign Ministry's website at w *mfaapsny.org/en/council/visa.php*, and download the visa form, fill it in and email it to their Consular Service. A free permit is usually emailed back a week before travel, which you should print out and present at the Enguri checkpoint 10km northwest of Zugdidi; within three days you must go to SberBank of Abkhazia in Sukhumi to pay the US$20 fee, and take the receipt to the Consular Service to receive your **visa/exit permit**. There's no hassle at the Georgian checkpoint (which even has free Wi-Fi), but then you have to walk for almost a kilometre (there are horses and carts for cargo but no taxis) to the Abkhaz checkpoint (where you have to wait for half an hour while they call Sukhumi to confirm your permit) – but the true barrier is the third one, run by the Russian FSB, where you may be interrogated for half an hour ('Do you know any member of the Georgian government? of the Abkhaz government?'). Finally you can take a marshrutka to Gali and another to Sukhumi (the last leaves at about 17.00). 'Public transport' is even more random than in Georgia proper.

Returning to Georgia proper, the guards are obliged, in theory at least, to let you back in as, in official terms, you have not left Georgian territory. Coming from Russia, it is only possible to return to that country (you will need a double-entry visa), although as there should be no evidence of ever having visited Abkhazia from Russia in your passport, you will still be free to visit Georgia at a later date. The border situation might well change in the future – for better or worse – but for the time being a visit to Abkhazia is just about do-able for adventurous types. Sukhumi is more dangerous than Georgia proper, especially after dark, when women should definitely not go out alone. The lingua franca in Abkhazia is Russian and the currency used, Russian roubles – be sure to take some with you as Georgian lari are of no use whatsoever. US dollars and euro can be changed in Sukhumi but not necessarily elsewhere; Abkhazian ATMs do not work with foreign credit cards, and your SIM card probably won't work either. A useful website for more information is w *abkhazia.travel/en*.

On the food front, local specialities are *abhazura*, deep-fried spicy meatballs of pork and beef with pomegranate, and *ojakhuri*, grilled meat with fried potatoes, onion and garlic.

WHAT TO SEE AND DO   Should you decide to go (see box, opposite), here is a brief summary of the highlights.

South from Russia Entering in the far west from Sochi in Russia, you'll immediately reach **Leselidze**, site of a huge children's holiday camp and a training centre for the Soviet team before the Moscow Olympics, and then **Gantiadi**, where the Tsandripsh basilica, built in the 8th century, has perfect acoustics due to resonating hollows built into its walls. From here the road runs below cliffs (and the railway through a tunnel) to the town of **Gagra**, which claims to be the warmest place on the Black Sea, with bathing from February to November; you can see the ruins of a 5th-century castle, a 6th–7th-century basilica and a park stocked with subtropical plants. It is then 14km to the road south to **Bichvinta** (better known by its Russian name of Pitsunda), where a modern resort abuts the only forest of the relict long-needled Pitsunda pine *Pinus pithyusa*, stretching east for 7km along the beach. By the 14-storey hotels is the late 10th-century Church of the Mother of God, large and externally very rounded. Large numbers of Russian tourists are once again visiting this area and there are now plenty of beach hotels; the season runs from May to October and hotel rooms can be had for just 200 Russian roubles (*about US$4*), with better rooms in guesthouses costing from about US$10 in April, May or October to double that in August.

Once back on the main road, this swings inland to run parallel with the railway, and in 7km reaches Bzyb (or Bzipi), where there's an attractive 10th-century church and the junction to **Lake Ritsa**. This road follows a valley into the hills inland for 41km to the lake, in a stunning location at 950m, below the 3,256m peak of Mount Agapsta on the border to the northwest. Stalin used to come here to relax, and you can still see his dacha beside the lake. In normal circumstances there's a motel open here, as well as boat hire; in the Ritsa Nature Reserve you may see boar, roe and red deer, plus mountain goats and trout. Some of the world's deepest caves are in the Bzipi Ridge, including the Kruger Abyss, only found in 2005, and the Krubera or Voronya Cave, now explored to a depth of 2,197m, currently the world record.

The main road returns to the coast at Musera (site of Gorbachev's dacha) and continues to Gudauta, a resort which is also the site of the 10th–11th-century Abaata basilica and a Russian army base. About 5km north is Lykhny, site of the 14th-century palace of the Abkhazian kings and a 10th-century Byzantine church. It's another 20km along the coast to **Novy Afon** (known in Greek as Anakopia and in Georgian as Akhali Atoni), where the 9th–10th-century Church of St Simon the Canaanite (who came to this area with St Andrew in AD55 and is buried in Komani near Sukhumi) was the seat of the Bishop of Abkhazia. There's also a tower built in the 13th century by the Genoese. In 1875–86 the monastery of New Athos was built by monks from Athos in Greece; it's been described as 'a delirious fantasy of a building with silver domes bubbling up out of the mountainside, its walls painted in rich yellows and red, crowned by spires'. Under the Soviet regime it was converted into a holiday camp, and suffered badly from 'official' vandalism. Just inland is the Psyrtskha holiday camp, and beyond it the Anacopia Cave in the holy Mount Iveri, which was discovered in 1961 and opened to visitors (except on Sun and Mon) in 1975, with an electric-train tour of its beautiful rock formations. There are nine chambers over 100m in length and 40–60m in height, and the longest is 140m long.

Sukhumi The coast road soon crosses the Gumista River and enters Sukhumi, the capital of Abkhazia, which was founded in the 5th century BC as the Greek port of Dioscurias. It's known as Sukhumi or Sokhumi to Georgians but Sukhum to

Abkhazians; 'Sukhum/i' is often used as a compromise. The city has beautiful beaches and an elegant seaside boulevard, mixed surreally with Soviet concrete towers and abandoned buildings pocked with bullet holes. The ruins of Dioscurias have been underwater for over 2,000 years, and are still sinking slowly; the remains of the Roman fort of **Sebastopolis**, built in the 2nd century AD, survive by the quayside, and the 10th-century castle of King Bagrat stands on a 600m hill by the remains of an 11th–12th-century church. Also here is the 15th-century **Turkish fort of Sukhum-Kale** (Turkish for 'Water Sand'), rebuilt by the Russians in 1810. The **Botanical Gardens** were created in 1840, and the 32ha Forest Park, on a low hill to the northeast, was laid out in 1941–51. The Botanical Gardens were very fine before the war of secession but are now fairly run-down; in an area of 25ha they had 5,000 species and varieties of plants, including 1,300 trees and shrubs and 2,800 herbaceous plants, as well as 500 species in greenhouses and 20,000 specimens in the herbarium. Abkhazia is known for the great ages its inhabitants can live to, and Sukhumi's Centenarians' Choir (Nartaa) had members up to 130 years in age. Also here is the Abkhazian State Museum, with Greek statues and weapons and local history.

You will hear about the 'space monkey zoo' at the Institute of Experimental Pathology and Therapy in the hills above the city, but this is a truly horrible place, a concentration camp full of primates bred for experimentation in the Soviet space programme and now largely abandoned and traumatised.

From Sukhumi to Zugdidi
Continuing east along the coast, 6km from Sukhumi a rough road leads another 6km up the west/right bank of the Kelasuri River to **Kelasuri**, where you can see the Great Wall of Abkhazia, built by the 6th century AD as a defensive line along the river. You'll also pass the 11th–12th-century arched bridge of Besleti, 13km from Sukhumi. It's another 13km along the main road (passing Gulripshi, where there are dolmens dating from the 3rd and 2nd centuries BC) to **Dranda**, near Sukhumi's airport, where there's a 9th-century church by the River Kodori. About 30km further east a road leads inland to **Mokvi**, site of a cave-church built in the AD960s, with five aisles, and a cupola on four pillars. Beyond the town of Ochamchire (54km from Sukhumi, and heavily battered in the 1993 war) the road heads inland through rich subtropical farmland and hazel trees, soon passing the turning north to **Bedia**, where a 10th-century church was home of the Bedia Chalice, now in the Art Museum in Tbilisi (page 151). The church's frescoes include the only portrait of Bagrat III (AD975–1014), the first king of a unified Georgia, to be made during his lifetime; unfortunately it was damaged after the fall of Sukhumi. The overwhelmingly Megrelian (Georgian) populace of Gali region, towards the Georgian border, now lives under an apartheid regime, not allowed to vote, to use their language in schools or to join the public services, although this is Abkhazia's agricultural heartland, producing its only exports; as a result the people are alienated and crime levels are higher than elsewhere in Abkhazia.

Beyond the town of Gali the road reaches the border at the bridge over the Enguri, not far short of Zugdidi, with minibuses available on either side (but not between the checkpoints).

8

Svaneti სვანეთი

Svaneti, the land of the Svans or *Svanebi*, hidden in obscure recesses of the High Caucasus, is an area to which much mystery attaches itself. It's seen as more Georgian than Georgia proper, the repository of the country's soul, due to having been the last refuge from the Mongols – the holiest icons and richest treasures were carried up beyond the Enguri gorges for safe keeping in times of crisis, and artistic and religious traditions are felt to have been better preserved here than elsewhere. At the same time the Svans are seen as strong but unsophisticated, often disregarding the norms of law and order and speaking a language which split from Georgian by the 6th century and is largely incomprehensible to the people of Kartli and Kakheti. The Svans' fearsome reputation for brigandage is not wholly without foundation; indeed crime flared up during the Shevardnadze period, and during the civil war in Abkhazia, when refugees were fleeing from the Svan-populated upper reaches of the Kodori and Sakeni rivers, some were greeted by soup kitchens at the passes, but others were robbed by their fellow Svans. Until 2003 tourists were sometimes held up and robbed here but the situation changed dramatically thanks to investment and a clean-up campaign by President Saakashvili.

The typical Svan name 'Kurdiani' means 'thief', although the family has actually produced many well-known Tbilisi architects and artists. In fact, the Svans are very hospitable and friendly, and given the amazing beauty of the surrounding peaks, the clusters of defensive towers that dominate the villages, and the frescoes and icons of the churches, it is hardly surprising that these valleys are now enticing many visitors, just as in Soviet times.

More and more independent travellers are arriving and people can see the economic benefits of tourism: the total was still only 1,200 in 2005 but now an estimated 50,000 visit per year. The Saakashvili administration sought to develop tourism in Svaneti even further, turning the region into a 'Switzerland in the Caucasus', complete with ski slopes and modern hotels. One aspect of this was the enlargement of Mestia's airport to handle commercial flights. Another is the US$25 million spent in 2011 on rebuilding the rough, and occasionally frightening, 136km highway between Zugdidi and Mestia, built only in 1934; journey time was cut from 6 hours to just three. Such changes will undoubtedly boost the region's economy, although the harm they will do to an age-old and formerly isolated culture such as this remains to be seen. The Svan culture is probably strong enough to survive, but it's still sound advice to get there as soon as possible.

CULTURE AND HISTORY

The Svan culture shows clear ties with ancient Sumeria and Mesopotamia, though many Svans are blonde with green eyes. They've lived here since the 2nd (and maybe the 3rd) millennium BC, supplying high-grade copper, gold and other metals to

SVANETI

Bronze-Age Colchis, and the foundations of the oldest defensive towers can be dated to the 1st century BC. These towers are Svaneti's most distinctive feature, more elaborate than those in Khevsureti and elsewhere to the east, with fortified tops and roofs. There are now about 175 towers, dating from the 6th to 16th centuries (most being from the 9th to 13th centuries), and a couple of dozen have been restored. In Roman times, when the Svans ruled a vast tract from Sochi to Sachkhere, the Greek geographer Strabo called them 'a mighty people … foremost in strength and courage'; they were formally Christian by AD523 but even today their religion retains strong elements of paganism, such as sacrificing rams on religious festivals and placing their horns on the altar. The Svan sun god Lile may well be the same as the Sumerian Enlil, and the village of Lakhamu may be named after the Sumerian water god. Now, St Barbara (Barbol) is seen as an equivalent of the sun god, while St George (Dzgraeg or Jgöräg) is revered as an equivalent to the moon god; Däl, the goddess of hunting (and mother of Amiran) is equivalent to Diana/Artemis. Nominally under the control of Colchis, then Lazika (Egrisi), Svaneti became part of Abkhazia then of a unified Georgia from the early 11th century; it shared in Georgia's golden age under Queen Tamar (who ruled from 1184 to 1213), who visited Svaneti several times and is still revered there. The Svans were largely undisturbed by the Mongols (although Tamerlane's horde passed through in 1397), and came under a Russian 'protectorate' in 1833, local autonomy surviving until 1857 when Prince Constantin Dadeshkeliani stabbed to death the Russian governor and three of his staff, and was summarily tried and executed. The principality was abolished the following year and replaced by direct Russian rule; the last Tsarist governor was driven out in 1905, leaving Svaneti effectively independent again until 1924. The wheel and the aeroplane both appeared in Svaneti in 1935; given their eight-month winter and the poor state of the roads, many Svans are still happy to use heavy ox-sledges as a means of transporting goods. However, increasing numbers now live for most or all of the year in Tbilisi or other cities, as the disadvantages of the harsh mountain lifestyle become ever clearer. In Rustavi, built after World War II as a new industrial city, there are now Svan villages. In January 1987 terrible avalanches killed around 70 people, mostly children in a school in Ushguli, and around 4,000 residents of Zemo (Upper) Svaneti left. In all there are 45,000 Svans in Georgia, of whom 12,000 remain in Zemo Svaneti, about 2,500 of them in Mestia. Logging (probably about double the official level of 60,000m^3/annum) is leading to more avalanches and landslides, and 75–80 families are still leaving each year.

However, it has to be said that the bulk of the death toll is entirely self-inflicted, as young men keep on killing themselves in road accidents; when I was first in Mestia three families were mourning three young men killed in entirely separate incidents. The Mestia cemetery has a number of grave markers that have etchings of young men proudly standing in front of cars, the same vehicles that took them to their death. The road from Zugdidi to Mestia was until 2011 notorious as the most dangerous in Georgia, and was lined with shrines at accident sites. Under the shrine was a shelf laden with bottles and glasses, and friends would stop and drink a toast of chacha in memory of the deceased; the absurdity of drinking firewater in memory of someone who was probably drunk when he went off the road is lost on the Svans. There's a sense that this was linked to lack of hope during the brigand period, and more recent economic stability has reduced the collective death wish somewhat, but drink-driving remains a problem. It's also reckoned that between 1917 and 1925, 5% of the population (600 people) were killed in feuds, so now politeness is ingrained, and 'fool' is the strongest insult the Svans allow themselves.

A typical Svan village is actually composed of perhaps half a dozen separate clusters of around 30 households huddled around their defensive towers or korchi (singular

8

Death has always been nasty and premature for many Svans, even before the arrival of the motor car, so it's not surprising that many traditions have evolved to cope with it. Routinely 300 or 400 people come to a funeral, where there's lots of food, but no meat or dairy. Men don't shave for 40 days after a death, while women wear black; widows also often have a lapel badge bearing a photo of the deceased. Men also used to wear a black ribbon around the forehead at the funeral and go barefoot for a year after, but this has died out. In the home there is a shrine with more photos, and visitors will be given a drink, to pour a few drops on the floor, and toast the deceased with the rest. Forty days, three months and a year after the death, family and friends go to the cemetery; a table is set up on the grave with food and drink (and perhaps other household items such as a radio). The women wail and cry, then the men line up, hats off, to say prayers and, of course, toast the deceased with chacha (spilling a few drops on the ground first); then the table is removed from the grave, and the food is eaten.

As in every Orthodox church, tapers are lit by everyone who enters a church; those at the front left are for prayers for women, those at the front right are for prayers for men, and those at the back are for the dead.

The dead are commemorated on Mariamoba (St Mariam's Day, 28 August), and also in Khaishi on Jvedi Ham, the second Sunday in January, when the souls of dead relatives stay overnight with their families, and in Ushguli on Lipanali, the Monday after 19 January. Singing at funerals combines pre-Christian wailing traditions with Christian singing, by both men and women but not together.

'kor'). These are up to 28m tall (perhaps following a formula by which the height of the tower should equal the sum of the four sides), and unlike those of Ossetia and elsewhere they are crenellated and roofed. The standard tower also has three 'eye' windows in each of its four sides, for a total of 12. They were probably built by spiral scaffolding, with rocks hoisted up by oxen. In some villages the oldest and largest will be the 'war tower', standing separately on a hilltop. The traditional home or *machub* consists of one spacious room with living space in the centre separated by carved wooden partitions from the livestock stalls around the walls. Churches are generally tiny, just 5–6m², and they're single-nave basilicas, mostly built between the 8th and 14th centuries, with frescoes painted between the 10th and 12th centuries, both on the inside and the outside of the churches. They tend to be opened perhaps twice a year for festivals, but the key holder may let you in. Svan icons are remarkable for the standard of their chased metalwork, and the finest examples, made at the end of the 10th century and start of the 11th century, are kept safe in the homes of the leading families.

The national dish of Svaneti is kubdari, bread stuffed with beef, onions, herbs and spices; they also make particularly fine khachapuri, known as *teeshdvar* or *chvishtari*, made of corn flour mixed with cheese before baking. Svaneti is known for honey, potatoes and yoghurt (*martswen*). The local firewater (*arakh*) is an especially horrible form of chacha, made from bread due to the lack of grain, although a better apple spirit is also produced. It might be worth trying *khevi*, a sort of chewing gum made of fir-tree resin, which sells for GEL1 and takes a lot of work to get chewy.

Svaneti is known for its primeval and ethereal style of untempered three-part singing, with pentatonic harmonies (unlike the rest of Georgia), often accompanied by the changi, the Svan harp, which looks as if it's come straight off a Greek vase, or the lute-like chianuri.

A FEW WORDS OF SVANI

The Svan language (spoken by c40,000 people) has four local dialects and is not, Svans insist, a dialect of Georgian; however, the authorities are trying to force people to use Georgian in schools and for official business, and it is now on the UN's list of endangered languages. It has 18 vowels (eg: a, aa, ä, ää and u, uu, ü, üü) rather than five as in Georgian, and there's no 'i' at the end of almost every word (eg: in the place names Döz rather than Dizi and Ke rather than Khe).

yes	*ah-du*	hello, good day	*khocha-ladägh*
no	*desa, maama*	thank you	*ivasukhari*
good	*khocha*	how are you?	*imzhi khäri*

SVANETI FESTIVALS Until the 1950s there were 160 feast days a year in Upper Svaneti; around 50 festivals are still celebrated, not to mention the various inescapable ceremonies remembering the dead (see box, opposite).

Jvedi Ham	In Khaishi on the second Sunday of January, a 'Long Night' when the souls of the dead stay overnight with their families
Lipanali	In Ushguli from 18 January to the following Monday, commemorating dead family members
Lagami	In Latali and Lenjeri at the end of February, with a 'battle' of snow towers
Lamproba	In all the Svan villages ten weeks before Easter, commemorating St George and the spiritual unity of the village with candles (*lampari*) for each male in the family plus one for St George
Kashvetoba	In Lenjeri and Kala the third week after Easter, when women married in other villages return to their roots
Kaishoba	In Nakra, Pari and Becho eight weeks after Easter, the festival of the Archangels
Hulishoba	In Nakra, Becho and Ushguli ten weeks after Easter, the adoration of God the Father, with animal sacrifices and sports such as horse racing, arm wrestling and rock lifting
Giorgoba	In all the Svan villages on 6 May, the birthday of St George
Petre-Pavloba	In all the Svan villages on 12 July, the festival of Saints Peter and Paul
Kvirikoba	In Kala on 28 July, the main religious festival of Svaneti, commemorating Saints Kvirike (in fact the pre-Christian deity Kviria – see pages 266 and 278) and Ivlitta
Eliaoba	In Lenjeri and Tzvirmi on 2 August, the feast of the Prophet Elia
Livskhvari	In Ushguli on the first Sunday of August, marking the start of the hay-making season
Mariamoba	In all the Svan villages on 28 August, the festival of the Assumption of the Virgin Mary
Lalkhori	In Etseri on the first Sunday of October, a celebration of village solidarity
Giorgoba	In all the Svan villages on 23 November, commemorating St George's martyrdom

For **Kvirikoba**, on 28 July, almost everyone in Svaneti descends on the mountaintop site of Kala for a real 'gathering of the clans'. As you'd expect, there's a lot of alcohol-fuelled singing and some religious observance involving the sacrifice of bulls or goats. Dating from Roman times or before, it's linked to the pagan deity Kviria, protector of the fertility of soil, man and animals. In addition you can buy hand-carved wooden drinking vessels, traditional Svan felt hats and other craftwork direct from the artisan, as well as traditional Svan food. Outsiders are welcome.

The Svanetoba festival was established in 2016, taking place in Mestia the day after Kvirikoba; however, in 2017, it was held in Chuberi and Nakra earlier in July. Every village or group of villages had a display of their unique foods, drinks and handicrafts, and local choirs and dance groups performed. See w wearesvaneti.org for future dates.

GETTING THERE AND AWAY

Now that Mestia Airport has been expanded, there are regular **flights** to Mestia from Tbilisi, though only in good weather (*09.00 Mon, Wed, Fri from the Natakhtari aerodrome near Mskheta*), with a free transfer from Rustaveli metro (*07.30, returning from Mestia at 11.00; GEL65*); this is operated by Vanilla Sky (*Vazha-Pshavelas 5, Tbilisi;* m *599 659099;* w *vanillasky.ge;* ⊕ *10.00–18.00 Mon–Fri, 10.00–14.00 Sat*). The plane then goes to Kutaisi and back, a very short but very scenic hop across the mountains (GEL40), before returning to Tbilisi. Otherwise, the only other way in is by road via Zugdidi. There's a **marshrutka** from Tbilisi's main railway station at 06.30 daily and others at 07.00 and 08.00 from the Samgori metro station (*8hrs; GEL30*), but it's far more comfortable to take the overnight **train** (or a Metro bus) to Zugdidi, and make your way to the Svan tower near the river from where marshrutkas leave for the drive up the Enguri Valley to Mestia (*3–4hrs; GEL20*). Although there are no official departure times – it could be any time between 07.00 and 11.30 – it is best to arrive as early as possible; buy your ticket from the kiosk with the 'Mestia' sign. If you miss the marshrutkas you'll probably be able to get a ride in a jeep until mid afternoon (page 249). On the return journey, the day train to Tbilisi actually leaves at 18.15, followed by the night train at 22.15; there are also Metro buses at 01.30, noon and 19.00 (page 249). Most marshrutkas returning to Zugdidi leave Mestia early in the morning, from around 06.00; if you ask nicely they may drop you off at the railway station where the Kutaisi marshrutkas leave from, otherwise it is a 10-minute walk. There are a couple of marshrutkas from outside the Hotel Mestia to Tbilisi at 07.00 and 08.00 and to Kutaisi at 08.00; it's best to book ahead, at shops opposite the Hotel Svaneti (*Tamar Mepe 14*) or (less reliable) immediately east of the Hotel Mestia (m *551 131222*).

FROM ZUGDIDI TO MESTIA By road, Svaneti is best reached from Zugdidi, although there is also a very poor road (4x4 only) from the less interesting region of Kvemo (Lower) Svaneti. Leaving Zugdidi, Mestia traffic turns right off the road to Abkhazia after a railway bridge (at a typically Megrelian cemetery; km0/198), then heads north across the plains straight towards Elbruz (across the border in Russia, and the highest peak in Europe at 5,642m), between two near-continuous rows of houses, then climbs up a side valley before cutting across to the west to reach the Enguri Valley at Georgia's largest hydro-electric station. Many vehicles will go the 100-odd metres to the left to a viewpoint over the dam at km33 (half an hour from Zugdidi); they also tend to make a café-stop at km53 (Barjashi), km63 or km99 (the Restaurant Mariami). The road, often strewn with rock falls, follows the side of the valley high above the reservoir, passing through half a dozen tunnels. Above the head of the reservoir (km61; where you can see how quickly it's filling with silt) the road relatively soon reaches **Khaishi**, the first of the Svan villages (comprising 20 separate little settlements), about 80 minutes from Zugdidi (at km71/127; c590m). Khaishi is known for its honey, but may be submerged by a proposed dam. The road crosses to the right/north bank after a couple of minutes at km73, where a road leads north to Chuberi and the Lakhami and Nenskra valleys, as the gorge closes in; tiny **Dizi** (km90/108) is the site of the quarry which produced much of the marble for the Moscow metro's fabulous stations. At km93 a road turns north up the Nakra Valley towards the Nenskra Pass. The valley opens out and becomes more heavily populated as the road turns east into the upper Enguri Valley, with fantastic views of Elbruz, Ushba, Tetnuldi and Shkhara, and passes above **Lakhamula** (km101; centre of a group of 11 hamlets), then below the village of **Pari**, once inhabited by notorious robbers who were eventually driven out by Cossacks.

The road climbs through a couple of hairpins to the crossroads of **Etseri** (km112/86; 1,450m; a group of hamlets including Iskari, Pkheutreri, Barsi and Kurashi) where there's a patched-up Soviet bus stop, a map (with various routes missing) and signs in English and Georgian north to Mazeri via the Bakhi Pass; an unpaved side-road climbs fairly steeply north for 10 minutes to the Etseri school where more bilingual signs point to the Archangels' Church of Pkhutreri (600m left) and St George's Church of Kurashi (1.3km ahead). Continuing northwards up the road to Iskari hamlet, the second house on the right is **Hanmer House** ❋ (m *599 629789, 595 791419;* e *a.hanmer@gmail.com;* f *hanmer.house.svaneti*), a welcoming guesthouse at about 1,550m altitude that's an ideal jumping-off point for the lovely hike over the Bakhi Pass to Becho (page 268) and also for visiting the two churches and the highest Svan tower. The Anglo-Canadian-Zimbabwean and Georgian owners offer accommodation in six sizeable rooms with three shared bathrooms, plus one en suite, for GEL20 per person (*GEL60 FB*) as well as camping; there's a shop, shared kitchen and kettles with tea and coffee in the rooms. They make several kinds of cheese and offer photography lessons, tours and horse rental.

The lovely Archangels' Church is at the end of a ridge at the far end of the hamlet of Pkheutreri, with an open porch around three sides. Continuing up the hill from Hanmer House into the hamlet of **Barshi**, you'll see the Dadeshkeliani tower, the highest in Svaneti at 28m and well restored; not far behind it are a small private family church and a fortified house. Turning right at the top of Barshi, near the northern end of Etseri village, a track leads across to **Kurashi**, basically an extended family farm, where St George's Church is an odd double structure with an open porch all around. There's also homestay accommodation in Barshi with Beka Gurchiani (m *599 917623*) and in Kurashi with Vakhtang Khorguani (m *599 744663*).

Etseri lies on the Trans Caucasian Trail from Mestia (see box, page 275), which continues west into a far less touristed area with abandoned villages and few guesthouses. Initially it's not far north of the Zugdidi road, reaching around 1,500m, then from Pari it follows a dirt road up to Gheshderi and then a rebuilt trail via Paledi over a pass to Kichkhuldashi (1,600m; with a tiny church dating from the 12th or possibly the 4th century). There's another low pass above Lashkrashi to Nakra (1,182m), then a forestry road leads towards the much more challenging (but spectacular) Utveri Pass (2,720m); there's quite a long descent to Zemo Marghi (1,240m), just above Kvemo Marghi (840m) in the Nenskra valley. Accommodation is thin on the ground here, but there are two guesthouses (*Babi* m *599 244162;* $; & *Nenskra* m *551 761919, 595 186677, 599 315153;* e *tsindeliani85@mail.ru;* $) in Kvemo Marghi (part of Chuberi village), and a hotel up the valley at Tita (but unfortunately a huge new dam is being built a few kilometres further up the valley). It's about 6km down the valley road to the junction just east of Khaishi, on the Mestia–Zugdidi road, from where a pretty wild crossing of the Svaneti range is possible to Mukhuri in Mingrelia, and ultimately to Bakhmaro and down to the Black Sea.

Heading eastwards from Etseri, one of the best day hikes in Georgia (with great views of Ushba to the north and the Svaneti ridge to the south) is the crossing of the Bakhi Pass (2,416m) to Tvebishi, one of the 11 hamlets of **Becho**. This is also part of the Trans Caucasian Trail and has been hugely improved, with new switchbacks on the descent to Tvebishi; it's 10km from the Etseri crossroads, taking 6–7 hours, and horses are also available. The total climb from the crossroads to the pass is almost 1,000m, with a descent of 800m; there's a clear trail to the pass, then you should follow the ridge southeast for about 600m before dropping through trees to the Meziri Church of the Archangels and then a great viewpoint. Across the Dolra River from Tvebishi is Mazeri (or Mazeer; the northernmost part of Becho, 7km from the main road), where there are quite a few good new guesthouses, including Becho Guesthouse Svaneti (m *599 139072;* **$$**) in Ushkhvanari, halfway between Mazeri and the main highway, run by Jenari and Lela Kvitziani, a cosy place with particularly good food; and Peak Mazeri Guesthouse (w *hotel-svaneti-mestia.com;* **$$**, *camping €4 pp*) right at the top of Mazeri village, where they have horses to rent and camping is also possible. Beyond this, in a remote meadow at about 1,620m, the Grand Hotel Ushba (🕾 *371 2923 7524;* m *790 119192;* w *grandhotelushba.com/EN;* **$$$$**) is grand only in the ambition of its name and in its warmth and hospitality; run by an energetic Norwegian (pages 274 and 353) in co-operation with a local family, it's a great base for hiking west to Etseri and Chuberi, east to Mestia over the Guli Pass, or north up to the Ushba Glacier (page 281). Local guides are available (*from GEL25 pp*) for hiking (and other activities, and the upper valley is also popular for ski-touring and other winter activities).

Until 2011, a bulldozer was always waiting to repair the Etseri–Becho stretch of the Zugdidi–Mestia highway, but it's fairly normal now, with a guesthouse with camping at Lankhvri and then the excellent new Becho House (m *514 033303, 599 311850;* w *bechohouse.ge;* **$$$**), a fairly upmarket guesthouse with a spacious garden; they speak good English here. This is just before the junction to Becho at km119/78; the road north up the Dolra valley is rough at first but the top half is now paved; there are also a couple of good guesthouses halfway up the valley in Ushkhvaneri. There are no marshrutkas on this road, but guesthouses will pick you up from the main road or you can hitch a ride. There's also a great hike (pages 275–6) from here to Mestia.

The Mestia road continues through a bit of a gorge and then drops to **Ienashi**, a biggish settlement with defensive towers; this is the central part of the village of **Latali** (km127–130) which means 'guard' and is the first of the truly Svan villages, having always been free from the feudal system. Latali, spread across the tongue between the Mulkhura and Enguri rivers, is perhaps the loveliest part of Upper Svaneti, and there are signs for new hiking routes. The traditional religious centre of Upper Svaneti, there were once 68 churches here for barely more than 1,000 people. The Matskhvari Church of the Saviour, a small one-nave basilica built in 1140 on the hilltop above the settlement of Matskhvarishi (at the west end of Latali), has fine 12th-century frescoes, including one of the coronation of Demetre I by the Svan painter Mikhail Maglakeli (1142), the only medieval painting on a secular theme in Svaneti. There's also the church of Jonah in Ienashi itself, also with ancient frescoes. Places to stay include Guesthouse Latali (m *577 518211;* **$$**) and Family Hotel Laleta (*5 rooms;* m *599 134011;* w *laletahotel.com;* **$$**), with excellent, largely vegetarian meals – they also have the Kakuchela hostel (*same details; $*), with bunks in dorms and a shared kitchen. About 3km further on, the road passes above **Lenjeri**, the first of the 'villages of Mestia' (and itself the centre of six hamlets) with half a dozen towers; just south of the road the Lashtkhveri Church of Taringzel (the Archangels) has a famous fresco of Amirani (the Georgian Prometheus) killing the devil Devi, painted on the northern façade in the 14th and 15th centuries, and a contemporary fresco of St George killing the pagan Roman emperor Diocletian (in place of the dragon) inside. At the eastern end of Lenjeri, the Matskhvari Church of Nesgun has 9th–10th-century frescoes by a master called Giorgi. Good places to stay include Lenjeri Guesthouse (*Mukran Shukvani 56;* m *559 336009, 595 223550;* f *lenjeri.guesthouse; $$*) and Udesiani Family Guesthouse (m *591 810286,* f *udesianisGusethouse [sic]; $$*).

MESTIA მესტია

It's another 2km to the town of Mestia itself, at 1,470m, where the old town sits above the modern Seti Square on the right bank; at its west end, by the road from Zugdidi (once Stalin Street, now Pharjiani Street), are the striking police station and Public Service Hall, both built in 2012 by the German architect Jürgen Mayer H. At the square's east end, beyond a hideous statue of Queen Tamar, is a commercial block in vaguely Alpine style, built in 2012 where Saakashvili demolished some older buildings and unoccupied since then. The new museum and airport (also by Jürgen Mayer H) are on the far left bank, along with some apartment blocks. The old town's backstreets are pure Svan, with steep stony alleys, hairy free-range pigs, rough stone houses and defensive towers – in 1887 the climber Douglas Freshfield counted 80 towers in Mestia alone, but now there are 66 at most, with just 175 in all Svaneti.

WHERE TO STAY Marshrutkas will drop you in the square, where in summer you're likely to be met with offers of accommodation. There are now plenty of adequate homestays and guesthouses here and in the surrounding villages, and a few hotels.

Hotels

Hotel Tetnuldi [270 E4] (36 rooms) Margiani 9; m 599 732525, 599 370055; w tetnuldi.ge. Reached by the unpaved Avtandil Khergiani St & opened in 2010, this is a ski-lodge-type chalet that is squeaky clean but not perfectly maintained. All rooms have satellite TVs, Wi-Fi access & balconies with great views. Local tours can be arranged & there's also a restaurant & bar. **$$$$**

Hotel Mestia [270 D3] (14 rooms) Seti 27; m 577 721252, 599 949419. Immediately east of the square, this is newly renovated & has bike rental & internet facilities. The hotel may function in winter only, but the restaurant is usually open. **$$$**

Hotel Svaneti [270 D3] (12 rooms) Tamar Mepe 5; m 599 648822, 599 549142, 599 132163. An odd-looking but perfectly comfortable structure just east of Seti Square; poor service, but there's a decent bar-restaurant. **$$$**

Hotel SvanSeti [270 D3] (10 rooms) Seti Square 21; m 557 945604; f. Central but quiet, with good-sized rooms & excellent service. **$$$**

Homestays

Guesthouse Ushba [270 D3] (11 rooms) Tamar Mepe 7; m 599 555217; e ushbahouse@ yahoo.com. A recommended place to stay on the main street, along with their Café Ushba (page 271). **$$$**

Davit Zhorzholiani [270 D3] (5 rooms) Seti III 1, right next to St George's Church; m 599 344948, 591 926723; e setiguesthouse@gmail. com. Rooms for up to 4 are available including all food & hot showers; they have a car available & can organise treks & trips, & make their own chacha! **$$**

Guesthouse Koka [270 A3] (6 rooms) Betlemi Alley 4; m 599 910831, 598 127617; e kokachartolani@gmail.com; w mestiahotel.

MESTIA

Kergiani Museum

Airport

DAVIT AGMASHENEBELIS

Margiani Museum of Architecture

BEQNU KHERGIANI

Liberty $

Hike to Cross Mountain, Koruldi Lakes

KHAKIANI

MULKHRA

Mulkhra

TAMAR MEPE

Church of St George

LOSELIANI

MARGIANI

Seti Square

Police

Seti

GAB LIANI

SELLA

Hike to Cross Mountain, Koruldi Lakes

PHARJIANI

Hospital

Filling stations, Zugdidi

Ushguli

Svaneti Museum of History & Ethnography

Bradt

N

0 — 200m
0 — 200yds

For listings, see pages 269–72

Where to stay

1 Davit Zhorzholiani.........D3
2 Guesthouse Koka.........A3
3 Guesthouse Ushba.........D3
4 Hotel Mestia.........D3
5 Hotel Svaneti.........D3
6 Hotel SvanSeti.........D3
7 Hotel Tetnuldi.........E4
8 Irma Jatchvliani.........B4

9 Keti Margiani.........E1
10 Manoni's
    Guesthouse.........G3
11 Natia's Guesthouse.........G3
12 Nino Ratiani.........A4
13 Roza Shuqvani.........B2
14 SvanLand.........G1
15 Tsiuri Gabliani.........B4

Where to eat and drink

16 Café Laila.........C3
17 Café Lanchvali.........F1
18 Café Old House.........E1
   Café Ushba.........(see 3)
19 Erti Kava.........D3
20 Panorama Café.........D4
21 Rea Dessert Café.........E2
22 Sunseti.........D3
23 Woodstock.........F2

com. Newly extended, with a big entry hall & rooms with 1 power socket & a rather cramped bathroom; there's good food & drink with free tea & coffee, & camping is possible. Tours & transfers as far as Batumi can be arranged; you'll need a torch to walk outside after dark. **$$**

🏠 **Irma Jatchvliani** [270 B4] (6 rooms) Gabliani 9; m 599 855545; ❱ hotel.in.mestia; w hotel-mestia.ge. Another comfortable homestay in the centre with basic & better rooms, & a barbecue in the garden; 4x4 vehicle available for tours. **$$**

🏠 **Keti Margiani** [270 E1] (7 rooms) Lanchkhuti 7; m 598 759767, 591 810025; e ketimargiani@gmail.com. Alongside the museum in the family tower (page 273), Keti runs an excellent guesthouse with perhaps the best views in Mestia & fantastic b/fasts; only 1 shared bathroom, however. **$$**

🏠 **Manoni's Guesthouse** [270 G3] Boris Kakhiani 25; m 599 568417, 551 664821, 590 602040; e manonisvaneti@yahoo.com. To the right just beyond the bridge on the airport road, this is a very hospitable guesthouse, recently extended. **$$**

🏠 **Natia's Guesthouse** [270 G3] (6 rooms) Khakiarni 14. On the airport road, this is a fairly cheap & simple place with 6 bedrooms sharing just 1 bathroom. **$$**

🏠 **Nino Ratiani** [270 A4] (10 rooms) Jondo Khaftani 19 (at km138/60); 📞41 042 1182; m 599 183555, 590 527818; e ninoratiani@gmail.com; ❱ NinoRatianisguesthouse. Nino is very well connected, & speaks some English, while her daughter Tamuna is fluent; they're just 2mins from the square back along

the Zugdidi road, with clean, white, light, airy rooms, modern bathroom & large quantities of delicious Svan food. Nino's is understandably popular, so it is best to book in advance. **$$**

✴ 🏠 **Roza Shuqvani** [270 B2] (6 rooms) V Sella 17, Lekhtagi; m 599 641455, 598 309919; e rozashukvani@gmail.com; w roza-mestia. blogspot.ca; ❱. Mestia's best & friendliest guesthouse, with clean, simple rooms for up to 6 (with big old beds & 1 power socket) plus shared modern bathrooms. Access is by a steep lane that's a bit muddy but vaguely lit. They've also just opened a 3-storey hotel (same prices) a couple of minutes to the west (Parjiani 1st Alley 9) with 17 rooms, mostly en suite, a sauna & a restaurant with an attractive glassed-in balcony. **$$**

🏠 **Tsiuri Gabliani** [270 B4] (4 rooms) Gabliani 20; m 599 569358. Tsiuri is an English teacher who also speaks German, with a good library. The street is named after her father, a fine mountaineer; it's next to the 'hospital', 2mins from the square, down the lane by the Public Service Hall. **$$**

Camping

🏕 **SvanLand** [270 G1] Davit Agmashenebelis 17; m 599 912573, 591 699629; e merabson@yahoo. com, campinglegabi@yahoo.com. About 1km upriver from central Mestia (but before Lakhrami), this is Svaneti's only dedicated campsite (although various guesthouses allow camping on their lawns, eg: at Nos 12 & 23). There's a good washblock (with hot showers) & Wi-Fi, & the helpful owners are fluent in English, French & Russian & can organise horses, 4x4 vehicles & hiking guides. *GEL 10/tent.* **$**

✕ **WHERE TO EAT AND DRINK** All guesthouses and homestays provide large quantities of food, and independent restaurants are beginning to open up in the town as tourist numbers grow.

✕ **Café Laila** [270 C3] Seti Sq; m 577 577677; e swanuka@yahoo.de; ❱ CafeBar.Laila; ⏱ 09.00–03.00 daily. The most modern & tourist-friendly place in town, with Wi-Fi plus live music most evenings in summer, but there's a limited menu & service can be sulky, while the local drinkers can also be annoying. **$$**

✕ **Café Lanchvali** [270 F1] Lanchvali 8; m 591 711181; ❱; ⏱ 10.00–08.00 daily. A modern place with a wooden deck, below the Margiani tower (& owned by the same family); good Svan food & more European drinks. **$$**

✕ **Café Ushba** [270 D3] See Guesthouse Ushba (page 269). Just beyond the Hotel Svaneti, this is a fair restaurant with a terrace above the street. **$$**

✕ **Panorama Café** [270 D4] Japaridze 12A; m 577 788388; ❱ Panorama.Mestia; ⏱ 09.00–02.00 daily. Excellent new place set back from the main strip (behind the Svanseti), with great views from the rooftop terrace; good b/fasts & authentic Svan dishes. **$$**

✕ **Rea Dessert Café** [270 E2] Tamar Mepe 32; m 593 991761; ⏱ from 10.00 daily. A friendly smoke-free café serving a vegetarian-friendly mix of Georgian & international dishes, & of course desserts; b/fast from 10.00, live music from 20.00. $$

✕ Sunseti [270 D3] Tamar Mepe. Just east of Seti Square, with a quiet terrace at the rear on the lane leading to St George's Church, this bar-restaurant is one of the nicest places to eat in town, with good kubdari & salads; mostly competent service. $$

✕ Woodstock [270 F2] Davit Agmashenebelis; m 599 075729; f woodstockmestia; ⊕ 11.00–

01.00 daily. Behind Liberty Bank at the start of the road to Lakhrami, this cosy café serves good coffee & some of the best food in town. $$

✕ Café Old House [270 E1] Lanchvali 1 (at Beqnu Khergiani St); m 551 809090. One of the few options for a break away from Seti Sq; excellent Svan food. Wi-Fi. $

✕ Erti Kava [270 D3] Seti Sq 25; m 599 134011; f ertikava; ⊕ 08.00–20.00 daily. The best coffee in town, & also hot chocolate, mulled wine & snacks. $

OTHER PRACTICALITIES The **tourist information centre** [270 C3] (*7 Seti Sq*; m *790 357375*) is pretty useless and usually has no local maps (except in Georgian script), although they do speak good English; there's no Wi-Fi here but you can pick it up at the Public Service Hall, to the west of the square. You will find maps of the town at either end of Seti Square (although the one at the east end doesn't show the new road to the museum and Ushguli, and the one at the west end has *You Are Here* marked at the museum, while the one at the museum has it marked at Seti Square…). There are two 24-hour **filling stations** in Mestia (on the Zugdidi road) and two **ATMs** at the Seti pharmacy [270 C3] just west of the police station, and another at Liberty Bank [270 F2] to the east just before the bridge, and an **exchange office** [270 C3] (⊕ *09.30–17.00 daily*) immediately east of Seti Square. The **hospital** [270 B4] is a few hundred metres west along Gabliani from the Public Service Hall; it's behind the rather grander Pharmadepot – there's a small 'Emergency' sign (in English) on the left at the end of the road.

WHAT TO SEE AND DO One of the greatest pleasures here is to roam the town's backstreets, which, away from the sterile central square, show all the characteristics of any typical Svan settlement – defensive towers, wandering pigs and dung-rich farmyards. There is a handful of specific sights too, however.

Church of St George [270 D3] East of the main square down Seti III Alley is the Church of St George, built in the 19th century to replace an 11th-century ruin; this is where the museum's icons were housed until the church reclaimed its building. Now it has a plain interior and a minimalist iconostasis; there's a good metal icon of St George killing Diocletian and painted icons of Christ and the Virgin and Child from the 12th century. Outside, the grandest memorial is a boulder commemorating the climber Mikhail Khergiani (1932–69), who died in the Italian Dolomites when he got bored with climbing on a rope; there's now a museum in his home (see opposite).

Svaneti Museum of History and Ethnography [270 D4] (*Ioseliani 7*; ⊕ *10.00–18.00 exc Mon; GEL7; GEL10 for an optional English-speaking guide*) Now part of the Georgian National Museum, this has a smallish but exquisite collection that's beautifully displayed (and you're free to take photographs, without flash). Its impressive new home, opened in 2013, is under 1km up the new road to Ushguli; it can also be reached by following Ioseliani south from between Seti Square and St George's Church and crossing two bridges.

The six exhibition halls begin with archaeological displays, including a stone hammer swung on a rope for quarrying and 'stones of sin', rocks with holes in them to be hung around the neck to atone for crimes and found only in Svaneti. There are also bronze Colchian axes, Hellenistic glass and cornelian beads, medieval signal-arrow heads with a hole to make sound, and two-pronged ones for hunting game. Coins, found mostly in church treasures, include a 5th-century BC Colchian silver hemi-drachma and a gold stater of Alexander the Great from the 4th century BC, as well as British, Russian and French coins and, bizarrely, Malaysian coins from 1948. The highlight is the collection of icons from the 10th century onwards, all showing a remarkable quality of metalworking – most are from the 11th to early 13th centuries, the so-called Georgian Renaissance or Golden Age. One of the finest, though not made in Svaneti, is of the Forty Martyrs of Sebaste, from the 11th or early 12th century. Note also the 13th-century icon of the Archangel Gabriel from Latali (at the entrance to the gallery), an 11th-century Christ from Mestia, and 11th- and 13th-century icons from Ipari of St George spearing the Emperor Diocletian.

There are also some astounding Gospels from the 9th–13th centuries – perhaps only the Labskaldi one quite matches the *Book of Kells* for artistic richness, but to have half a dozen ancient books of such grace and finesse in one place is amazing. Among them are the famous Adishi Gospels, the oldest surviving illuminated manuscript of the Gospels in Georgian, produced in Tao-Klarjeti (now in Turkey) in AD897, supposedly brought by Queen Tamar and later removed for safety to Adishi in Svaneti – until the Soviets seized them in 1937. Also here are 14th–15th-century documents on wood from Kala, and psalms printed on Solomon II's press in Tbilisi in the early 18th century. Finally, the ethno-cultural exhibits, from the 17th to 20th centuries, include armour, daggers, saddles, hunting arrows, snowshoes, musical instruments, costumes, jewellery and powder horns, and a ritual copper cauldron that would hold two sacrificed oxen. There are also fascinating photos of Mestia in 1890, showing very little sign of change since. You'll exit to a lounge and café, with sofas, good toilets (under the stairs) and great views of Mestia's towers to the northeast.

Margiani Museum of Architecture [270 F1] (*Lanchvali 7;* m *595 974138;* f *margianismuseum;* ⊕ *09.00–17.00 Tue–Sun; GEL4*) This museum (aka Margianis Machubi), where you can visit both a defensive tower and a machubi house, is at the top northeastern corner of central Mestia, just beyond a cemetery chapel and the defensive tower, which is left open, with fixed external steps then five flights leading up to the roof. The machubi house, which dates from the 12th century, has a central fireplace (with a chimney of fireproof *mukhra* wood, and a metal plate for cooking bread, by a wooden basin for mixing dough). The fire would have been virtually the only source of light, although there is now a sole electric bulb. Around the room, clockwise from the chest between the windows in which dishes are kept, there's a store for food and chacha, then stalls for sheep along one wall, and larger stalls for cows along two walls. Between 12 and 20 people would have lived in this room, sleeping above the animal stalls for warmth; yet there's only one chair, reserved for the oldest man of the family. Carved on the wooden stalls is a repeated sun or eternity motif, like an orange or apple flan seen from above, which also appears on Georgian coins.

Khergiani Museum [270 G1] (*Khergiani 13;* m *599 912573;* ⊕ *10.00–17.00 Tue–Sun; GEL2*) Not far below the Margiani Museum, Khergiani Street leads from the main part of Mestia eastwards to a cluster of nine towers, the hamlet of Lakhrami (or Laghami). Here you can visit the Khergiani Museum, beyond the 13th-century Matshovris Church, which has a fresco of Adam and Eve barely visible

on the façade (and others inside), and just before the two-storey Church of the Transfiguration, dating from the 10th century. The museum is both a memorial to Mikhail Khergiani, one of the world's leading climbers when he died (page 272), and a traditional Svan house; however, opening hours are erratic. You can return by the main road, Davit Agmashenebelis, on the valley floor, passing the high school, where you can pop over a stile to a *narzan* (mineral water) spring in the yard.

Skiing The old Zuruldi ski resort, immediately south of Mestia, fell into disuse around 1993, but was re-invented as **Hatsvali**, as part of President Saakashvili's plans for transforming Svaneti. A Doppelmayr lift from just above the museum in Mestia to the base station opened at the end of 2017, and a Leitner quad-lift (⊕ *10.00–16.00 all year, weather permitting, with a break in Nov; GEL5/ride, GEL40/day, GEL232/ week*) runs from the base at 1,800m to a restaurant at 2,345m atop Mount Zuruldi. There's one small hotel and one ski rental shop at the base, also reached by a road turning right off the Ushguli road at the edge of Mestia. Open from late December to the end of April, there's a red run (2,600m), a blue run (2,565m) and a learner's slope, with more easy slopes opening in late 2018. The new **Tetnuldi** resort is being built above Mulakhi, with a first phase opened in 2015. There's a free shuttle from Seti Square in Mestia to the base (15km), where there are ticket and gear rental kiosks and a snack van; Poma lifts (⊕ *10.30–16.00 daily; GEL40/day*) go to 3,165m, also reached by a 4x4 road in summer. There are ambitious plans for the resort, which will have the biggest vertical drop in the Southern Caucasus (1,500m), and the longest runs, up to 9.5km. There are currently nine pistes totalling 30km, with new runs and lifts opening every year, and there's a huge northeast-facing area which is a paradise for skiers with skins or snowshoes. There are also plans for short lifts in villages such as Mazeri, Etseri, Ushkhvanari, Lentekhi and Ushguli; Svaneti is also ideal for ski touring, which is being developed by the Norwegians of the Grand Hotel Ushba and Svaneti Backcountry (w *svanetibackcountry.com*).

Hikes around Mestia

Chalaadi Glacier (*10km; 3–4hrs each way*) The easiest and most popular hike from Mestia follows the Mestiachala Valley beyond the airport before crossing the rushing river by a shaky Soviet-era pedestrian suspension bridge and continuing for 2km up to the Chalaadi Glacier. Walk or get a ride along Davit Agmashenebelis, past Lakhrami to the road bridge just beyond the airport, then follow the jeep track along the left/east bank (past Lavladashi village and the new Mestiachala hydro-electric power station) to the footbridge and café (at 1,627m). Soon after crossing this, you'll pass a border guards' post and then climb up the side valley to the glacier, now somewhere above 1,800m altitude; return the same way (or via the airport). You can climb on to the ice, covered with rocks and gravel, with the fully fledged river flowing from beneath the glacier.

From the bridge it's also possible to make a multi-day trip following the Mestiachala and Tyuibri valleys to the northeast towards the Lekzyr Glacier and ultimately the Mestia Pass (3,757m), which would be open from June to October if one could freely cross the border, but this is not currently possible.

Koruldi Lakes (*16km; 8hrs return*) A cross was erected on a hill high above Mestia in around 1994, and it's an excellent, if exhausting, walk up, taking about 2 hours to climb 800m over 4km. Having got this far, it makes sense to continue along the ridge to the lovely Koruldi Lakes, giving a total of 16km (which can also be done by horse or mountain bike; farmers use a 4x4 road to the east).

The Trans Caucasian Trail (*TCT;* w *transcaucasiantrail.org/en*) is the ambitious project to create a 1,500km hiking route from the Black Sea through Georgia and Armenia to the Iranian border – it'll be the region's first route designed for multi-day unsupported backpacking, along the lines of the Appalachian or John Muir Trails, rather than the day-hikes that are more usual here. Not surprisingly, therefore, it's been conceived and created by expats from the USA and Britain. In the summer of 2016 they scouted the route, identifying as many existing trails as possible (plus lots of access points on 4x4 tracks, for construction and rescue, and side-trails to cultural sites and stopovers), mapped on the OpenStreetMap website, and in 2016 and 2017 teams of volunteers began construction in Upper Svaneti, mainly replacing long-washed-out bridges and rescuing some badly degraded sections of trail. The hike from Mestia to Ushguli has become suddenly very popular in the last few years, so they chose to work on the other side of Mestia, on a 60km section of the route towards Becho and Chuberi; also in the last few years, places like Mestia have become crowded with tourists and risk losing the simple charm that attracted the tourists in the first place – so the TCT (like this book) aims to spread the load by bringing tourist traffic to small, remote villages where the first family homestays are just opening. By late 2018, the trail onwards from Ushguli to Lower Svaneti and into Racha, now hiked by about 50 tough hikers a year (mainly Poles and Czechs), will be improved too, permitting a continuous 14-day hike (including the Mestia–Ushguli trail, with new variants).

Further east, South Ossetia will have to remain as a gap in the TCT, which will start again from the Georgian Military Highway, using the routes described on pages 195 and 325 east from Juta to Khevsureti and Tusheti, although they want ultimately to move off the dirt roads onto parallel trails.

The team uses experience of working in US national parks to build trails to a high standard to cope with high numbers of heavily laden hikers, and the markings follow European standards; the Svaneti Trekking Association has also been active in marking trails. Official bodies took a long time to get on board, but the team has always worked well with local communities, consulting and offering economic opportunities. Ultimately there'll be a second, north–south, route linking the Greater and Lesser Caucasus ranges too.

There are two possible routes out of town, the better probably being to take Lanchvali Street past the Margiani Museum of Architecture, then bearing away to the right before crossing a stream and returning to the left to the cross and viewpoint at Tskhakvazagari, popularly known as **Mount Mestia** or Cross Mount (2,200m). At the top you have a bird's-eye view of Mestia, an astounding panorama of the High Caucasus and the Enguri Gorge, and lush alpine meadows full of cows and brightly coloured plants, as well as a surprising number of cowherds' huts. The path (now marked with red-and-white stripes) continues via the Lamaaja signpost (2,400m) to the small lakes in a grassy basin just beyond a 2,700m ridge. Returning to the Tskhakvazagari cross, you can descend more directly to Vittorio Sella Street (in Lekhtagi) and Seti Square. It's also possible to continue to Mazeri in the Becho valley – before the lakes a trail drops left into a valley then a less clear path climbs steeply to the Guli Pass (2,954m) and winds down to the abandoned village of Guli (where there's still a church that women are not allowed to enter, although it's open only on the three Tuesdays following Easter), from where it's a short walk on a track to Bagvdanari (17km from Mestia, a hard hike taking c10 hours), just below Mazeri.

Mount Zuruldi (*8km; 8hrs return*) From Seti Square signs lead south along Ioseliani and across the main road beyond the museum, up the hill south of Mestia. Crossing the Ushguli road again, this swings sharply left/east, passing the Hatsvali resort at the foot of Mestia's ski runs and continuing to climb steadily to Mount Zuruldi (2,340m), on the ridge between the Mulakhi and Enguri valleys. You can also return by following the ridge via the top station of the Hatsvali chairlift to Heshkildi (where there are summer huts and accommodation for hikers), from where a track soon joins the Hatsvali road at a hairpin bend. Continuing from Heshkildi, a trail continues below the ridge for 6km via the hamlets of Ieli (1,700m; with towers, two old churches and Zeynab Kipian's guesthouse) and Tsvirmi to the Ughvir Pass (1,923m) and down to Bogreshi (1,500m) and Adishi, making a less busy start to the Mestia–Ushguli hike.

Chkhuti ridge (*Up to 8km each way; 6–8hrs*) This is perhaps the best day-hike from Mestia, and also the first stage of the four-day hiking route from Mestia to Ushguli (see below). Cross the bridge from the central square and instead of heading uphill right to the museum, fork left on Revaz Margiani St past a new church with a graveyard containing an unusual pyramidal grave marker. Pass the Hotel Tetnuldi, named after the 4,974m-high pyramid-shaped peak at the head of the valley, and fork right (the road to the left is a link from the airport road) to climb gently past some new chalets (supposedly built for Saakashvili, and now a hotel), keeping Tetnuldi peak in the gun-sight of the road. As this jeep track climbs higher, you'll notice the twin peaks of Ushba surfacing above the Mestia ridge like a terrier's perky ears. About 3km from the hotel you'll arrive at an abandoned Soviet-era alpine lodge complete with rotting three-tier accommodation, the remains of a swimming pool and a curious semi-circular restaurant, all close to collapse and unlikely to survive many more years. Skirt to the right around the lodge on a steep track that climbs up to alpine meadows (at c1,900m) and then swings right to Zardlashi in Mulakhi; taking a path into the forest to the left, you'll climb through a meadow where Tetnuldi appears again and can then follow the narrow Chkhuti ridge as far as you like – it's about an hour to a good viewpoint at 2,750m and another 45 minutes to three cairns at 3,100m, from where you can either return the same way or follow a ridge southeast then south (crossing a 2,100m pass by a small church) to Zhamushi in Mulakhi, although this is much harder than the standard route below.

From Mestia to Ushguli (*60km; 4 days*) This increasingly popular trek, now marked with red-and-white painted stripes, can be done with overnight stops in homestays in remote villages, or by camping. The full trip starts by hiking from Mestia to Mulakhi, as above, but many people choose to take a jeep or marshrutka to Zhabeshi, the top hamlet of Mulakhi, and start a three-day trek there.

From Seti Square (1,400m) it takes around 7½ hours for the 14km to Zhabeshi, going past the Hotel Tetnuldi and the Soviet alpine lodge then climbing to the right over a ridge just above 1,900m to the Mulakhi Valley. The marked hiking route stays high to the left when a dirt track drops to the hamlet of Zardlashi then through Murshkeli, Zhamushi (the centre of Mulakhi), Cholashi, Majdeveri and **Chvabiani** (1,640m), where there are 15 towers (there were once 60) and a Makhtsovari

Church, the oldest in Svaneti, dating back to the 4th century. It's a simple basilica with a three-sided apse, although it once had aisles to the south and north, and a porch to the south. Now it has a modern metal roof, to protect the frescoes and icons inside; ask for the key at the last house in the village. There's also a tower, built in the 10th century, and you may notice the tiny St George's Church, isolated in the fields to the left as you enter Chvabiani.

Continuing from Chvabiani or staying high on the scenic hiking route, you'll arrive at **Zhabeshi**, at about 1,600m at the head of the valley. Here, there's accommodation with Mariana Ioseliani (m *595 323508;* **$**), Temur Gujejiani (m *599 255997, 591 228572;* **$**), Sopho Chartolani (m *598 919236;* **$**), Mamuka Naverani (m *595 563155;* **$**), Avghan Naveriani (m *598 465846;* **$$**), Lola Kakhiani (m *591 352477;* e *irmanaveriani@gmail.com;* **$**), Givi Kakhiani (m *599 519089;* **$$**), Mevlud Kakhiani (m *591 952487;* **$$**) and Zurab Kakhiani (m *591 816772;* **$$**). There are other homestays in Cholashi and Chvabiani, and in Lakhiri, just above Zhamushi, where there are still 14 towers.

From here the trail leads southeast, climbing steadily through birch forest for 8km to a plateau at about 2,700m (the top of the new Tetnuldi ski area, with great views of Mt Tetnuldi, only about 5km to the southeast, and many other Caucasian peaks), before dropping slightly to the south for 4km to the very remote village of **Adishi** (or Hädish; 1,900m), 9km from the nearest road and cut off by snow for six months of the year. Only two families were left here, but sustainable tourism is yielding benefits here in summer and there are now 12 families in residence and the village's maze of alleys, towers and wooden balconies is finally seeing some conservation work. Although tiny, it has four churches (notably the Saviour and St George churches) and eight towers, in which treasures from all over western Georgia used to be brought to be kept safe from invasion. There's accommodation in summer with Gia Avaliani (m *598 126469;* **$**), Mukhran Avaliani (m *599 186793;* **$$**), Mamuka Kaldani (m *595 305953;* **$**), Omar Kaldani (m *599 309055;* **$**), Elisabed Kaldani (m *599 931418;* **$$**), Tarzan and Nino Kaldani (m *790 870794;* **$$**) and Zhora Kaldani (m *599 187359;* **$**).

Next the trail leads southeast, climbing up the north/right side of the Adishchala Valley for 5km before crossing the river (not far below the spectacular Adishi glacier) and climbing steeply south for 2km to the Chkhutnieri Pass (2,720m). Guesthouses in Adishi can arrange for someone with a horse to help you cross the river for GEL50 if the water is high. From the pass the trail drops steeply to the Khaldeshala Valley (not far below the Khalde glacier) and follows a rough track downstream (southwest) through **Khalde**, a village burnt down by the Russians in 1876 for refusing to pay new property taxes, where the Lalhor Church of St George is worth a visit (and there's just one small summer-only café and homestay), to **Iprari** (Ipräl; 1,890m), 15km from Adishi. There's accommodation here at the Hotel Ucha (*19 rooms;* m *595 557470, 599 250578;* e *uchaiprali@yahoo.com;* **$$**), and with Jokola Pirveli (m *599 197207;* **$**) and Erekle Pirveli (m *599 328505;* **$**). There's another church (less than 5m long) painted by Tevdor, supposedly the court painter of King David the Builder (although there's no real evidence), close to the Hotel Ucha, where you can ask for the key.

The final stage, of only 10km, climbs gently up the Enguri Valley, parallel to the road, reaching Ushguli (at almost 2,200m) after a couple of hours. A much harder option (but potentially saving a day) is to cross straight over the Khaldeshala River and climb steeply to the Kareta Pass (3,077m) and drop to reach a dirt road about 3km northeast of Ushguli.

BY ROAD TO USHGULI Seti Square in Mestia is the place to look for a jeep (in fact a Mitsubishi Delica, as a rule) to Ushguli. A return trip should cost around GEL200 – not bad if this is shared between four (be at the square by about 09.00). Your guesthouse will probably be able to hook you up with a group, or ask at the Café Laila (page 271), which arranges day trips in summer, leaving at 09.00 and returning at 18.00 (*GEL30*). The 46km road has been improved so that even a day trip gives time for a bit of a hike, but it's better to stay overnight. A public marshrutka also runs at least once a week from Tbilisi and Mestia to Ushguli – call one of the Ushguli guesthouses for information.

A new road starts to the west of Seti Square and crosses the narrow gorge of the Mulkhura River before joining the old road from the left by the modern museum. The road is newly paved with concrete past the junctions to the Hatsvali ski resort (6km to the right from km3.5) and the new Tetnuldi slopes at the top of Mulakhi (also being developed for skiing), and up to the Ughveri Pass (1,923m). There's a *narzan* (mineral spring) to the right 500m along the Ushguli road (marked by red stains on the rocks), by a washed-out bridge. Following the south/left bank of the Mulkhura River, you'll pass the various hamlets of **Mulakhi** village, all with small groups of defensive towers, on the right bank – first Ghvebra, then Zardiashi, Artskheli and Zhamushi (also hit in January 1987 by a lethal avalanche which killed 26 and led to many families abandoning the village). The road crosses briefly to the right bank then back before Cholashi, as the towers of Chvabiani come into sight ahead, in front of the giant peaks of Tetnuldi (4,974m) and, to the right, Shkhara (5,068m, the highest peak in Georgia). At the junction to Chvabiani (with two ancient churches; pages 276–7) and Zhabeshi, the Ushguli road hairpins sharply right and climbs to the pass (☉ *Apr–Dec only*), with good views of Ushba. The road switchbacks down into the Enguri Valley at Bogreshi (27km from Mestia, at the start of the track to Adishi; page 277) where the concrete ends, opposite **Nakipari**, where there are seven towers and the Jgrag (St George) Church, decorated with frescoes in 1130 by the court painter Tevdor; these have survived untouched since then, and there are also some fine icons including a silver one of St George.

The road follows a power line by the Enguri River, passing the isolated **Kukdiani 'Tower of Love'** after 5 minutes; legend has it that a girl shut herself up here after her lover (who was married to another) drowned in the river while hunting. It's worth a visit (*GEL1*) if you haven't climbed up one of the towers in Mestia. It's another 30 minutes up the wooded valley to Khe (39km from Mestia), the first part of the village of **Kala**, where the 9th-century St Barbara's Church houses a 6th-century icon and 12th-century frescoes; there's also a café just to the north. Up a steep track to the south is the hilltop Lagurka Church of SS Kvirike and Ivlita (opened once a month, not in winter) which hosts Svaneti's most important pilgrimage and festival, Kvirikoba, on 28 July, marking the martyrdom of the three-year-old St Quiricus and his mother St Julietta (page 265). Built in 1112, with splendid frescoes painted then by Tevdor, it houses the fabulous gold Shalkiani icon of the Crucifixion, dating from perhaps the 6th century; outside, there are great views of Ushba.

The next hamlet, as the road follows the increasingly precipitous Enguri Valley, is Lalkhori, where a bridge crosses to the right bank and the Taringzeli (Archangels) Church of Iprari, 1km up the Khalde road; this also has frescoes painted by Tevdor in 1096, as well as ancient icons. From Davberi, a little further up the Ushguli road, it's possible to hike southwards to the 2,848m Latpari Pass and down a summer-only 4x4 road to Chvelpi (1,121m), on the Ushguli–Lentekhi road in Lower Svaneti.

From here it's just 4km to Ushguli, the road switchbacking up a cliff face to reach a high pasture, close to 2 hours' drive from Mestia. The road passes above Murkmeli (meaning 'Towertown'), the first part of Ushguli (almost uninhabited, with ten towers, one close to collapse), before crossing the Enguri by a bridge between Chazhashi ('Horsetown'; to the right) and Chvibiani ('Downtown') and Zhibiani ('Uptown'), the main parts of Ushguli (to the left).

USHGULI უშგული

Finally, 46km and at least 2 hours from Mestia, the road reaches Ushguli, claimed to be Europe's highest permanently inhabited settlement at an altitude of almost 2,200m; although there was a contender for the title on the other side of the Caucasus in Daghestan, they have both been overtaken by Bochorma (2,345m) in Tusheti (page 325). It's also a stunningly beautiful spot, with small clusters of towers huddled together amidst alpine pastures and beneath the highest peak in the country; fittingly, it's a UNESCO World Heritage Site (although it's odd that this is the only protected area of any kind in Svaneti). It is divided into three main settlements, with a total of seven churches built and painted between the 9th and 12th centuries. Ushguli has more towers per capita than elsewhere in Svaneti (about 33 for around 50 families or 220 inhabitants), and they show far more variation than elsewhere; one in Chazhashi, possibly the oldest in Svaneti, has 18 'eyes', as do the joined 'Twin Towers' of the Ratiani family in Zhibiani.

To the right of the bridge, Chazhashi was terribly damaged by the avalanche of 1987 but still has many medieval buildings, including the 'war tower' dominating from a hillock. The much-needed restoration of Ushguli's historic buildings began in 2014 with the tower of the ethnographic museum (*GEL10*), which houses some beautiful gold and silver icons and crosses, many from the 11th and 12th centuries, some from the 6th century and some even older. On the ridge above are some isolated towers that are supposed to have been Queen Tamar's summer home; her burial place is unknown, but the Svans naturally hope that it's here. When television arrived in Svaneti in 1975, the communists took great pleasure in installing the relay (now long gone) on Tamar's Towers. Across the bridge to the left is Chvibiani, and beyond it Zhibiani, the last and most spectacular part of Ushguli, where domestic artefacts, icons and a magnificent 11th-century carved door are displayed in another barn-like ethnographic museum (*GEL10*). On the far side of the village is the Jgrag Church of St George, and isolated on the ridge to the east is the Lamaria Church of the Assumption of the Virgin, set against the backdrop of Shkhara in the finest setting of any Svan church. It's a small basilica built in the 9th century, with a defensive tower and 10th–12th-century frescoes, somewhat deteriorated, including a portrait of Queen Tamar, plus scenes from the Amirani legend on the exterior. Pridon or Vladimir Nizharadze and Nanuli Chelidze are the people to ask for to open the museum and church.

If you visit Ushguli in wet or snowy weather be sure to have good footwear as the village streets, such as they are, tend to be permanently covered with a thick layer of cow manure; some have a stream flowing along them; some have both. Locals recommend wellington boots but slurry-proof hiking boots are probably the best option.

The road (4x4 only) passes to the south of Zhibiani and continues to the Zagar Pass (2,623m; 9km from Ushguli) and Lower Svaneti. There are great views here of the Svaneti ridge to the right and the main Caucasus range to the left, dominated by the peaks of Ailama and Tsurungali as it swings to the southeast. After passing through abandoned villages such as Koruldashi (where the river is poisoned by an abandoned Soviet arsenic mine), this reaches the asphalt a few kilometres before Lentekhi (the main town of Lower Svaneti; page 241) and takes a recently modernised road down to Tskaltubo and Kutaisi.

🏠 **WHERE TO STAY, EAT AND DRINK** As well as those below, others that have been recommended are Guesthouse Ailama (m *598 760630*), Giorgi Ratiani (m *599 971194*) and Malkhaz Khachvani (m *598 153538, 599 111425*; e *shorenadevdariani@ gmail.com*) in Zhibiani; and Gogi Charkviani (m *598 939359*) and Otar Nizharadze (*Guesthouse Caucasus-Ushguli;* m *599 317086, 596 119132;* e *solomonmdivnishvili@ gmail.com*) in Chvibiani (*all* **$$**).

✴🏠 **Guesthouse Ushguli** (6 rooms) m 599 974873, 599 773094, 595 710164; e teagigani47@ gmail.com. Laert Charkviani knows a huge amount about Svan culture & runs the best guesthouse in Chvibiani, with easy road access & a café. **$$**

🏠 **Villa Lileo** (4 rooms) m 599 912256; e ratiani.dn@gmail.com, likuna-788@mail.ru. A welcoming homestay, near the top of Zhibiani, with excellent food & a cosy atmosphere. Dato Ratiani is quite a character but it is his hard-working mother

who is the real dynamo driving this place, while his wife Nanuli runs the museum. **$$**

🏠 **Guest & Art House Gamarjoba** (4 rooms) m 599 209719 (Russian), 595 229814 (English); w gamarjoba-ushguli.com. A relative of Nana in Mestia, Temraz Nijaradze offers rooms in his house just below the small church of St George of Zhibiani, with hot water & lots of excellent food, as well as a display of rather surreal art by his brother Fridon. **$–$$**

HIKES AROUND USHGULI The most popular hike is to the **Shkhara Glacier** (*16km; 6hrs return*), source of the Enguri River. From the Lamaria Church a track drops to a bridge to the right/north bank of the Enguri and then follows it northeast through grassy meadows to where the freezing-cold river gushes from beneath the ice. You can climb on to the glacier and explore an ice-cave, with the bulk of Shkhara (5,068m), just a few kilometres away, looming overhead (you're at about 2,600m here). Climbers can camp here at 2,280m to enjoy the many challenging routes on the Shkhara wall.

It's possible to hike to **Iprari** either directly down the valley (*14km; 5hrs one-way*) or by a full day's hike along the ridge to the southwest via the peak of Latpari (2,830m) and the Lagurka Church. Well-equipped hikers can follow a trail south from Chazharshi and southwest along the Svaneti ridge to reach the Davberi-Chvelpi 4x4 road (page 278) and descend either to the north back towards Mestia or south towards Lentekhi. Hiking towards Racha, follow the road over the Zagar pass, as on page 279, and down through Koruldashi to a junction 2km beyond Tsana (1,700m; where there's accommodation in summer). Here an old road leads northeast up the Zeshko valley to Zeshko (1,812m) and just beyond it, an abandoned Soviet climbers' training camp. There are three permanent residents in Zeshko (more in summer), offering beds to hikers. From here a stunning but very difficult trail crosses a pass into the completely overgrown Tskhenistskhali valley, where hogweed grows to 4m and stinging nettles to 2m (and there are bears and far more dangerous horseflies), and over another pass into Racha (as described on pages 243–4). The trail has supposedly been remarked and repaired, as part of the Trans Caucasian Trail, but this area is so wet that it's always at risk from landslides and all-devouring vegetation.

BACKPACKING AND CLIMBING IN SVANETI This is the prime area for backpacking and climbing in Georgia, and the possibilities are described in a couple of guidebooks. Those published before independence assumed that hikers could freely cross the watershed into the Russian Federation, so these hikes have to be adapted as there-

and-back trips. Peter Nasmyth's *Walking in the Caucasus*, the booklet *Mountaineering Routes of Georgia*, produced by Geoland for the Georgian National Tourism Administration in 2014 and Richard Bærug and Shako Margian's *Europe's Unknown Fairytale Land* all have more current coverage. The Svaneti Trekking website (w *svanetitrekking.ge/eng/index.htm*) is a useful online resource. Nevertheless, routes are still hard to follow and the terrain is extremely rough in places.

From west to east, the easiest crossing of the Caucasus is by the **Nakra Pass** (3,203m, practicable from July to October), starting from Lakhani on the Zugdidi road – but of course you can't cross into Russia. Finishing at Terskol, in the valley immediately south of Elbruz, this gives fantastic views of Europe's highest peak (5,642m). This route was taken by British climber Douglas Freshfield in 1868, and was the scene of fierce fighting in 1942, when the Germans tried to break through from the north to seize the oil fields of Baku (turning back after the defeat at Stalingrad). It's also possible to hike from the Nakra Valley east to the Dolra Valley via the Ledesht Valley, glacier and pass.

It was Freshfield who explored this area and made the first ascents of most of the peaks, in wool and tweed and with alpine guides from Chamonix, as was the norm. In 1868 he climbed Kazbek and the east peak of Elbruz, then in 1887 Tetnuldi, Gulba, Shoda, and a reconnaissance of Shkhara, and in 1889 Laila, while searching for fellow climbers Donkin and Fox, lost on Koshtantau. In 1888 John Cockin made the first ascent of Shkhara, while Albert Mummery climbed Dykhtau, then the highest unclimbed peak in the Caucasus at 5,180m.

The **Dolra Valley**, above Becho and Mazeri, gives superb views under the distinctive twin peaks of Ushba (4,710m), a beautiful mountain with the reputation of being a 'killer queen' and the most technically difficult peak in Europe, only climbed in 1903 by a Swiss–German-Austrian expedition (the lower north peak (4,694m) was climbed in 1888 by Cockin). Now, the south summit (the higher and easier one) is rated as French TD, UIAA grade IV–V, and can be climbed in a trip of four days. Starting from Mazeri, the first camp is at 2,367m, above the 200m-high Becho waterfalls, and the second is on the Ushba Glacier at 4,000m (the main difficulty is the crossing of a suspended glacier between 3,000 and 3,800m); then the route follows the northwest ridge for 600m before some hard ice-climbing for 400m to the final ridge and snow dome. Shkhelda (4,370m), just to the north of Ushba, is rather easier (UIAA II–IV); between these two peaks is the Ushba Pass (4,100m), a very hard and high route. The glaciers in this area are retreating and the upper part of the Ushba Glacier is now dangerous.

Easier routes from Mazeri involve hiking to the foot of the Ushba Glacier (2,500m) and the waterfalls, or to the Guli Glacier (2,900m); it's possible to swing east to the Guli Pass (3,100m), south of Ushba, and then down to Mestia. In summer, border guards are posted 7km north of Mazeri; you'll probably only need to carry your passport but it's possible you'll need a permit from their office down the Becho valley in Uskhvanari – check locally. From Mazeri the route follows the left/east bank of the Dolra and passes through a gorge to the confluence of the Dolra with the Becho, from the north, a couple of hours from Mazeri. From here routes lead west to the Nakra Valley, north to the Becho Pass (3,367m; ☉ *Jun–Sep*) and the Baksan Valley, northeast to the Akhsu Pass (3,830m; crossed by Freshfield in 1889), and east to Ushba and Mestia. It's another 2 or 3 hours to the Guli Glacier and bivouac, start of the climbing routes on the south side of Ushba; it's not much further to the Guli Pass, from where it's about 4 hours down to Lenjeri or Mestia.

There are **two possibilities from Chvabiani** to the Semi Pass and the Upper Tsanner Pass, at the top of Mulakhi, both starting by following the right/north bank of the Tviber through a gorge known as the Gates of Georgia, where the trail follows a metre-wide shelf for about 50m, to the confluence of the Tviber with the Kitlod at 2,400m, 5 or 6 hours from Chvabiani. You should cross the Tviber using the ruins of a bridge, unless there's a snow bridge upstream, then continue up the left/east bank of the Tviber, reaching the Tviber Glacier in about 6 hours (permit required from the border post in Zhabeshi). Again, it would be possible to continue to the pass (3,580m) and down to Chegem if politics permitted. It's an easy pass, with safe glaciers and no need for anything more than a rope.

Having made the crossing of the Tviber, a path follows the right/north bank of the Kitlod to the Kitlod Glacier; with a short climb on snow, it takes about 6 hours to reach the Semi Pass (3,850m). From here there's a stunning view of the sheer white Bezengi Wall, 12km long, and the lovely pyramids of Tetnuldi (4,974m) and Gestola (4,860m), as well as Elbruz and Ushba to the west. It's possible to continue northeast and then east along the watershed for 4 or 5 hours to the Upper Tsanner Pass (3,990m), from where there's a view of the other side of the Bezengi Wall and the 5,204m peak of Dykhtau to the north. This is the most spectacular of the hikes currently possible in this region.

Tetnuldi (4,974m) is approached from Adishi, starting up grassy slopes to the north, then bypassing moraines to the left after 3–4 hours and reaching the first camp at 3,013m after another hour or two. Alternatively, it's possible to drive a jeep from the Ughveri Pass to a hut at 2,786m (or to hike from the pass in 5–6 hours) then take a horse track to the camp.

9

Adjara აჭარა

In the far southwest of the country [map, page 222], Adjara (or Achara) is the warmest and wettest of Georgia's provinces, with 2.4m to 2.8m of rain per year. Average temperatures on the coast range between 4°C and 6°C in January and 20°C and 23°C in July, and it's horribly humid in summer. It's cloudier than Abkhazia, which claims 100 more sunny days per year.

Christianity arrived here in the 1st century AD, but the region has been under Turkish domination for much of its history and now many of the population, especially in the mountains, are Sunni Muslim in faith although ethnically and linguistically Georgian. People are fairly religious in the mountains, but less so in Batumi, where there's only one mosque. The Adjaran men's traditional costume (as seen in dance troupes) is particularly camp with its tight trousers. Russia took over in 1878, and after the convulsions of the war and revolution (including a brief British Protectorate), created an autonomous republic within Georgia in 1921 as a condition of peace with Turkey. Nevertheless 340,000km² of historically Georgian territory still lie within Turkey, including many of the finest Georgian churches (see the ITM/ERKA map of Georgia), and the Georgian population of Turkey has not always been well treated.

After the break-up of the Soviet Union Adjara was ruled as the personal fiefdom of Aslan Abashidze, whose family had been in charge here since the 15th century, and never tolerated much opposition (Tbilisi streets are named not after Aslan but other Abashidzes who were fine poets). Abashidze was appointed chair of the Adjaran Soviet by Gamsakhurdia in 1991, and always had strong support from the generals commanding the Russian (nominally CIS) base outside Batumi. He ruled firmly, keeping the Mkhedrioni out of Adjara, and handed over very little tax to Tbilisi; nor did he go to Tbilisi himself – although elected as a deputy, he never attended parliament and should technically have been dismissed. Meanwhile the Adjaran opposition lived in Tbilisi, due to threats against them in Batumi. It was unclear why Shevardnadze didn't stand up to him, given all Abashidze's insults and his talk of challenging for the presidency; as he had plenty of funds due to his take of the trade passing through Batumi from Turkey, he easily persuaded opposition parties outside Adjara to throw in their lot with him. Abashidze claimed to have been the target of frequent assassination attempts, which he blamed on the Shevardnadze government. No-one outside Adjara took this very seriously, but the streets of Batumi were full of young toughs in plain black clothes wielding Kalashnikovs.

All this changed after the Rose Revolution – in May 2004 Abashidze staged a confrontation with Saakashvili and had three bridges linking Adjara to the rest of Georgia destroyed. Saakashvili gave him ten days to disarm and return to constitutional rule, sending the army to conduct a major exercise just across the border, while activists were smuggled in to lead protests and seduce Abashidze's guard away from him. Fortunately he was also persuaded to go peacefully and was flown to Russia, and Adjara returned to being a normal part of Georgia.

On the coastal road from Poti or Samtredia, the new Kobuleti bypass takes off to the left at km62/59, just before you enter Adjara [map, page 222] at the bridge over the Choloki River at km65. This is also the terminal of the minibuses that run the length of Kobuleti from the station. The dunes just south cover the Pichvnari archaeological site (page 298), while a thin strip of bog inland from the road forms the 770ha Kobuleti Nature Reserve. This protects the Ispani Marshes, ecologically valuable wetlands similar to those near Poti (pages 254–5); there's access at km50.5/68.5, while the shiny new Kobuleti and Kintrishi Protected Areas Visitor Centre (*opposite Davit Agmashenebelis 316, km47.5/71.5;* m *577 101897;* e *tamar7gogitidze@gmail. com*) opened in mid 2017. The road enters the long, thin coastal sprawl of Kobuleti 2km from the bridge. A settlement has existed here since the 5th century BC; now it's chiefly a beach resort, although there is also a small port. With the closure of Abkhazia, this is now one of Georgia's chief Black Sea resorts, although the beach is black sand and everyone is aware of the polluted state of the Black Sea. It looks like one long thin tourist strip, but in fact there are normal shops in the residential area along Rustaveli, just inland. The residents insist on cladding their buildings, even blocks of flats, with corrugated galvanised iron, which is perhaps not to all tastes.

GETTING THERE AND AWAY There are plenty of marshrutkas up and down the coast road; services to Tbilisi (*Didube; GEL20*) leave every hour from the railway station (km44; served by trains between Tbilisi and Batumi). Marshrutka 123 (*GEL0.50*) runs from near the Batumi cable car station (at the top of Gogebashvili) and the Roman Catholic church to central Kobuleti (north of km71/48); local routes 1 and 2 run from Kobuleti station the whole length of the strip to the north end of the resort. There's a cycle track stretching for about 10km from north to south alongside the main road (nominally limited to 40km/h), and cycling is also allowed along the beachfront promenade.

WHERE TO STAY The main road along the coast, Davit Agmashenebelis (formerly Lenina), is lined with hotels and guesthouses – there are plenty to choose from, though they close by the end of September. There are also quite a few signs advertising '*komnaty*' and '*sdaetsya*' (Russian for 'rooms') on the stretch of road north of km73/142. Camping Zekari (m *571 392424; GEL15 pp;* $) is just north of km66/53, just beyond the built-up strip.

Georgia Palace Hotel & Spa (156 rooms) Davit Agmashenebelis 275; ℰ 32 224 2400; w gph. ge. Just south of km71/48, this former sanatorium has been refurbished & reopened as a 5-star luxury hotel. It still functions as a health spa with all manner of treatments available (including the Kerala Ayurvedic Centre). Guests have included Katie Melua as well as the Polish & Ukrainian presidents. All rooms with AC, Wi-Fi & cable internet, minibar & satellite TV. $$$$$

Kobuleti Beach Club (9 suites) Davit Agmashenebelis 373A; m 599 569677; e kbchotel@gol.ge; w kbchotel.ge. Near km66.5 & the last of a number of other isolated hotels to

the north, this British-owned place has excellent staff, a Moroccan restaurant & a swimming pool. $$$$$

Hotel Condori (32 rooms) Davit Agmashenebelis 280; ℰ 32 226 6444; m 599 150300; e hotel-condori@mail.ru. A decent, mid-range hotel built in 2006 that has rooms & suites with cable TV, minibar & internet connection. $$$–$$$$

Hotel Chveni Ezo (9 rooms) Davit Agmashenebelis 492; m 599 791907; e chveniezo@mail.ru; ☐ chveniezo. Simple, clean en-suite rooms with generous balconies; there's beach access directly opposite (at km70/49). $$$

Hotel Palermo (35 rooms) Davit Agmashenebelis 448; m 558 800005, 577 223108; f . A big comfortable place, in gardens set well back from the road; Georgian & Lebanese food. **$$$**

Hotel-Restaurant Chero (22 rooms) Davit Agmashenebelis 454; m 599 616168, 571 024545; f restaurantchero. A mini-hotel that's of note mainly for its excellent restaurant (see below). **$$$**

Solidarity (51 rooms) Davit Agmashenebelis 269; \ 32 231 1244; m 599 145168; e rusiko_m@mail.ru, hotel.solidarity@ profkurort.ge; f . A modern façade hides fairly standard rooms with balconies, as well as a conference hall; it's right on the beach. **$$$**

Hotel Omega 177 Davit Agmashenebelis 288; m 568 775549. A modern hotel with smallish rooms that come with microwave, fridge, kettle & balconies. **$$–$$$**

Caffe Princessa (20 rooms) Davit Agmashenebelis 390; \ 426 266656; m 557 332337; e taraghana1722@gmail.com. Simple, clean & comfortable rooms, some with 3 or 4 beds making it ideal for families or groups; also a popular café-restaurant. **$$**

Savane (25 rooms) Davit Agmashenebelis 362; \ 426 266538; m 5555 020101; w savane. ge. Comfortable but noisy rooms in two buildings & a luxuriant garden with small outdoor pool (at km71/48). **$$**

✕ WHERE TO EAT AND DRINK

✕ **Hotel-Restaurant Chero** (See above) Davit Agmashenebelis 454. This hotel has an excellent restaurant, serving fantastic khinkali, shashlik (with sulguni), khachapuri, BBQ chicken & grilled fish. **$$**

✕ **Bora-Bora** Davit Agmashenebelis 466; m 593 766978; ⏲ 24hrs in season. A bit fast-foody in style, but with live music in summer; it's next door to the lively Lounge Bar Monroe. **$**

✕ **Green Café** Davit Agmashenebelis 134 (just south of km73/46); m 595 018757; ⏲ 10.00– midnight. Affordable snacks such as khachapuri, served indoors & on 2 terraces (1 very green). **$**

✕ **Retro** Davit Agmashenebelis 486 (km70/49); m 577 511722; w retro.ge; ⏲ 10.00–23.00 daily. Gia Agirba's famous Adjaran khachapuri, also in Batumi & Tbilisi. **$**

OTHER PRACTICALITIES There are several **ATMs** north and south of the museum, and to the north at Davit Agmashenebelis 468, 488 and 492. The town centre lies just north of km74/45, 500m north of the modern railway station, but this is a fairly dull area. There is a helpful **tourist information** kiosk here, facing the main square (with cinema and supermarket) at Davit Agmashenebelis 121–139 (*km74/45;* \ *422 29 4414;* m *593 937991;* e *tic@welcomebatumi.com;* (⏲ *09.00–19.00 daily*). Just south is the **Kobuleti Museum** (⏲ *10.00–14.00 & 15.00–18.00 Tue–Sun; GEL2*), a surprisingly grand building housing good archaeological and ethnographic displays.

TOWARDS BATUMI The railway south from Kobuleti hugs the coast, while the road begins after 4km to climb away from the coast into the fringes of the Lesser Caucasus in a steep series of hairpins. Owing to the influence of the mountains, it's cooler in summer and warmer in winter than in Batumi; there's thick subtropical vegetation, with groves of bamboo as well as plantations of tea and citrus fruits. The road climbs past the ruins of the 6th-century Byzantine fort of **Petra** (*or Tsikhisjiri;* ⏲ *always; free*) at km80/39, then drops from km82/37 to **Chakvi**, a small coastal resort with a station at km86/33 and the Hotel Oasis (*155 rooms; Batumi 16;* \ *32 247 2233;* m *592 296060, 592 847272;* w *hoteloasis.ge;* **$$$–$$$$**) to the west from the main bus stop at km87.5/31.5, 1.5km south of the railway station. This is now part of the upmarket Dreamland development (\ *32 247 2233;* m *555 380034;* w *dreamland.ge*).

In 2005, a 657m-long road tunnel was opened through the ridge south of Chakvi; a second bore was added in 2010, and a new link to the Kobuleti bypass should open in 2018. To reach the Batumi Botanic Gardens (page 299) you can turn left north of km89/30; the old road climbs then begins to drop towards the gate of the Agricultural Institute of the Academy of Science and of the Botanic Gardens; this road rejoins the main road through the tunnels before km93/26. The road is reunited with the railway at **Makhinjauri**, a pleasant small resort of 15,000 residents; just south of the station (km94/25), the most striking building is a restaurant built in 1917 by a Japanese architect, with a wrap-around veranda and nicely carved wooden lattices. Behind this is the Hulus Castle Hotel (*Tamar Mepe 20;* m *557 589811;* e *huluscastle@mail.ru;* $$$$), a retro-styled place with swimming pool. Finally, after passing the former Chess Palace, the very kitschy Batumi Art Center and the new (but misnamed) Batumi Central railway station [289 G1], the road and railway swing west along the shore of a bay to Batumi (km102/19), one of the most attractive and relaxed cities in Georgia. Most people will arrive by the route described here, but it's also possible to arrive from the Turkish border crossing at Sarpi, 19km south, and served by plentiful taxis and minibuses, or by the rough highway from Akhaltsikhe, to the southwest of Borjomi, untouched by public transport except in summer (page 215).

BATUMI ბათუმი *Telephone code 422*

Batumi, with its sheltered natural harbour, existed as a Greek trading colony by the start of the 2nd century BC at the latest; its name is probably derived from the Greek words *bathys limen* (deep harbour). Later it was a Genoese trading colony, and then became known as a multi-ethnic city, home to Georgians, Russians, Armenians, Jews and Muslims. Under Turkish rule from the 16th century it was just a tiny fishing village, but once the Russians arrived in 1878 it began a very rapid development. It was a free port from 1878 to 1886 and became the terminal of the railway from Baku in 1883 and of the oil pipeline in 1906. In 1902, Stalin organised a strike after the sacking of 400 workers from the Rothschild refinery; 15 lives were lost, and Stalin was sent to Siberia for three years. A week after the Armistice of November 1918, 15,000 British troops landed in Batumi to protect Georgia and the Caspian oilfields from Germany and Bolshevik Russia; the last troops left on 9 July 1920, leaving the way open for the Bolshevik invasion and the takeover of Georgia. The democratic prime minister Noe Zhordania and his government fled from Batumi early in 1921. Now, it's a city of around 150,000 people, the second-largest and perhaps the liveliest in Georgia, and handles a great deal of trade with Turkey, both by land and sea.

From 2009, the Saakashvili government used an array of incentives to trigger a building boom aimed at turning Batumi into the Las Vegas of the Black Sea. The new architecture is glitzy, verging on kitsch, particularly around Evropus Moedani (Europe Square) and especially all along the seafront, from the towers in Miracle Park to the New Boulevard well south of the city. The Sheraton and Radisson hotels, built in 2010 and 2011, are now dwarfed by the Porta and Technical University towers, although plans for Donald Trump to co-finance, with the Silk Road Group, a Georgian 'Trump Tower' development have so far come to nothing. The city is a popular destination for Turks, Arabs and Iranians, and their languages, and Russian, are more obvious here than English – whereas Tbilisi seems to be oriented towards Europe, Batumi is closer to Beirut or Dubai.

In 1990 the city covered 18km^2, but it now sprawls over 65km^2, with very high levels of car use and just 0.3% of the population cycling, and unsurprisingly congestion and pollution have become serious problems; a Sustainable Urban Mobility Plan is being developed, and cycle lanes are appearing across the city.

GETTING THERE AND AWAY

By bus and train Until 2015, passenger trains to and from Batumi actually ran only as far as Makhinjauri, 5km north of the city centre, but then a new rail and bus terminal called **Batumi Central** [289 G1] opened; about 2km north of the city, it's not at all central but is named after the attached shopping mall, immediately south of the Batumi Art Center (see opposite). It's squeaky clean but fairly simple, with tickets, café and a tourist information centre on the lower level, and WCs and a bus station to the north, with services to Tbilisi, Kutaisi, Moscow and Istanbul, plus shared taxis to Tbilisi, Zugdidi, Mestia, Kutaisi and Yerevan. In addition to the day trains to Tbilisi (*at 07.30 & 17.10; GEL42 (US$18) 1st class, GEL19 (US$9) 2nd class; 4hr 55min*) there's a sleeper train to Tbilisi at 00.30, which from July to October runs all the way to Yerevan. You'll need to book several days ahead for this. Buses 10, 13, 15 and 17 (*GEL0.80*) and marshrutkas 20, 21 and 31 (*GEL1*) run between the station and the city centre; taxis cost about GEL15.

The **bus station** [289 G2] (422 230162/3) lies just off Tsereteli, not far east of the centre next to the railway lines; the ticket hall is closed so you have to buy tickets from kiosks at the relevant bay. Look out for the Soviet-era hammer and sickle on a plinth in the yard, marking the site of a factory where Stalin worked before the Revolution. Marshrutkas leave for Tbilisi, Kutaisi, Poti and Zugdidi almost hourly until 18.30, with some later overnight departures to Tbilisi (*GEL18*); marshrutkas to Akhaltsikhe run via Kutaisi and Borjomi, leaving at 08.30 and 10.30 (*6hrs; GEL18*). Marshrutkas run up the Adjariskhali Valley as far as Khulo. Other marshrutkas for Kutaisi and Tbilisi leave when they're full from the junction of Gogebashvili and Chavchavadze (by the cable car) [289 F2], and shared taxis wait at the rear of the old railway station [288 D5] (Zubelashvili/Vazha-Pshavelas) and the ferry terminal [288 D1]. The Georgian Bus service to Kutaisi airport (*2hrs; GEL15*) leaves from Ninoshvili 1 [288 B2], behind the Radisson Blu hotel (book in advance); Eurobus (032 2305939; m 595 990000) also has services from the bus station to Tbilisi via Kutaisi Airport. There are also comfortable Turkish buses to Trabzon (*3hrs; GEL25*) that leave fairly regularly throughout the day to Trabzon (*3hrs; GEL25*) and less frequently to Ankara, Istanbul and elsewhere. From Trabzon airport, just to the right outside the terminal, Havas (w *havas.net*) operates frequent shuttle buses directly to Hopa, from where you can take a taxi to the border.

Metro Georgia (422 242244; m 514 242244; w *geometro.ge*) operates buses to Tbilisi (Ortachala) at 01.00, 09.00, noon, 15.00 and midnight, with Wi-Fi, air conditioning and reserved seats; these leave from the new BTM terminal much further east on Mayakovsky at Gogol 1 [289 G1] (422 242612; m 577 159400), reached by marshrutkas 39 and 42. They take longer than the marshrutkas, but are far more comfortable and restful; fares are GEL25 by bus or GEL18 by marshrutka. Metro and other companies also have buses from the Gogoli terminal to Turkey (*Trabzon 5hrs; GEL30, Istanbul 22hrs; GEL70*); they also pick up on the way out of town at Abuseridze 67. Tickets can be reserved through Adjara Tour [289 E6] (*Chavchavadze 48, cnr Melikishvili;* 422 228778; m 577 788888; 09.30–19.00 *Mon–Fri, 09.30–18.00 Sat–Sun*).

By air The recently refurbished **airport**, 6km south at Khelachauri [map, page 222] (*buses 9 & 10;* 422 235100; w *batumiairport.com*) at present has flights from Ukraine with Ukraine International Airlines and Georgian Airways, Minsk with Belavia, Tbilisi with Georgian Airways [288 D7] (*Abuseridze 1;* 422 235116, m 593 180404; e *bus@georgian-airways.com*), Istanbul with Pegasus and Turkish Airlines, which has a sales office at Baratashvili 27 [288 D3] (422 223222; e *batummd@thy.com;*

BATUMI

A **B** **C** **D**

1

Ali & Nino
Ferris wheel
Miracle Park
Alphabetic Tower
Chacha Tower
Ferry terminal
☆ Gate

Promenade

2

BLACK SEA

31

Radisson Blu 27
State Theatre
BK Books
Turkey 26
RACE
29
Wine Room
39
KUTAISI
45
G A M S
Z
19
Air Arabia
St Nikoloz
Buses to Kutaisi airport

33

KOSTAVA
ZHORDANIA
MELASHVILI

3

Seaside Park

Promenade

Summer Theatre
10

28
Evropas Moedani
Medea
Vinomania Batumi
Mimino

Cinema Apollo

K GAMSAKHURDIA

GENERAL MAZNIASHVILI
Wine Store Batumi

Khareba Winery
1
36
37
Armenian church
KTW
K GAMSAKHURDIA

34
7
Circus
15
Turkish Airways
5

BARATASHVILI

4

2

Take Five
40
☆

RUSTAVELI
NINOSHVILI

Naniko
+

24
25
TAVDEDEBULI
44
Nugeshi
43
City Hall
Azerbaijan
ASATIANI
Puppet & Youth Theatre
Art Museum

MEHMET ABASHIDZE
GORGILADZE
$
$
PARNAVAZ MEPE
GORGASALI
Polyclinic

5

20
Biblusi
32 41
26 MAY

☆ Sector 26

University

Esenin House
$
35

VAZHA-PSHAVELAS

Synagogue
11

State Museum of Adjara
Iran
Taxis

MELIKISVHILI

26 MAY

DHL

6

6 May Park

21
Ukraine

30

TNT

Zoo

PARNAVAZ MEPE
GORGASALI
KHIMSHIASHVILI

7

Dolphinarium

Aquarium

46

4
Post office, Georgian Airways, Black Sea Mall, airport, Sarpi, Turkey

TAKAISHVILI
LERMONTOV

CHAVCHAVADZE
A305

↓ San Remo, Hotel 19, Marina, Aquapark
A **B** Batumi Mall ↓ **C** 6
8
D ↓

For listings, see pages 291–4

Where to stay
1 Batumi Surf Hostel...........C3
2 Batumi Tennis Club........B4
3 Boni.....................................H1
4 Chillout Hostel.................C7
5 David...................................D4
6 ERA Palace.........................C7
7 G Bakuri.............................D3
8 Gulnasi's Guesthouse.....D7
9 Iliko....................................E3
10 Intourist Palace...............B3
11 Irise.....................................D5
12 Lavro...................................F3
13 Luna....................................E2
14 Mercury..............................E3
15 Metropoli...........................D3
16 Oscar...................................E2
17 Peria....................................F3
18 Premier Hotel Batumi.....H1
19 Ritsa....................................D2
20 Sheraton.............................B5
21 Tsereteli.............................C6

Off map
Camping Robi...................G1
Hotel 19.............................A7
Marina................................A7
Sputnik..............................H2

Where to eat and drink
22 Arhavi.................................E2
Batumi Pizza................(see 34)
23 Bereg Café.........................E2
24 Café Batumi.......................C4
25 Café Saamo.......................C4
26 Chacha Time.....................C2
27 Clouds................................C2
28 Coffeetopia.......................C3
29 Conte..................................C2
30 Culinarium........................C6
31 Dzveli Gemi.......................B2
32 Fanfan................................B5
33 Heart of Batumi...............D2
34 Kafé Bar
      Maspindzelo.................C3
35 Kaltenberg.........................C5
36 Literaturuli........................D3
37 Luca Polare........................D3
Mamapapuri................(see 34)
38 Mevlana.............................E2
39 Munich...............................D2
40 Neocca...............................B4
41 Old Boulevard...................B5
42 Porto Franco......................E3
43 Prague Pub........................C4
44 Princess Café.....................C4
45 Radio Café-Bar..................D2
46 Retro...................................C7
47 Sofra Lokantası.................E2
48 Temelas Dukani................E4
Veronica........................(see 20)
Winter Garden Café...(see 10)

Off map
San Remo............................A7

⊕ *09.30–17.30 Mon–Fri*) and Sharjah with Air Arabia [288 D2] (*Zhordania 24;* ✆ *422 254025;* w *airarabia.com*).

By sea It's also possible to arrive by sea, at the stylish **ferry terminal** [288 D1] at the north end of Zhordania – see pages 65–6 for details of services (or ask at the 'Inquiring Office' in the terminal). Some cruises call here, too. There's a weekly car ferry from Chornomorsk in Ukraine (*U&G Agency, Kutaisi 34;* ✆ *422 274119;* e *ugagencybatumi@gmail.com; foot passenger US$110, 34hrs*). The Kometa Express hydrofoil in theory leaves Batumi on Thursdays at 10.30 for Sochi in Russia, returning on Fridays at 10.30 (m *593 333966; Sochi +7 918 4091296; GEL260*).

GETTING AROUND There's no shortage of **taxis**, but for more comfortable and reliable vehicles try Taxi 2 (✆ *577 419797*), Taxi 555 (✆ *422 273718*), Taxi 777 (✆ *422 231070;* m *577 511070*), or Taxi 929 (m *599 929929*).

The Batumi Velo **bike-sharing** system has automated stations around town and all along the Boulevard. You have to register at the tourist information centre at Ninoshvili 2 (with your passport), and pay GEL10 for ten days, which gives you 3 free hours plus top-ups at GEL2/hour, or GEL20/year with 5 free hours. It may be easier to just rent bikes the old-fashioned way, with various types of bikes and tandems for rent opposite the tourist information centre and at various places along the boulevard. There are cycle tracks south along the Boulevard and north from just beyond the cable car terminal to the Batumi Art Center; for bike shops see page 295.

City transport is provided by both buses and marshrutkas; the latter race around more or less everywhere while buses stop only at designated stops (which now have real-time displays in Georgian and English) meaning they are slower (but cheaper). Marshrutkas cost GEL0.50 (pay the driver as you leave) while bus tickets cost GEL0.80 for two rides – in the central area (including the airport) you validate just one whereas to go out to Makhinjauri or Sarpi you validate both. You can pay the conductor when you board a bus, but tickets are cheaper from supermarkets with a Bat-Bus logo or tourist information centres. Routes 1/1A and 7/7A are circular, providing a handy city tour.

Car rental is available through the usual international firms at the airport and also:

🚗 **Mimino Rentacar** [288 C3] Rustaveli 13; m 579 012801; w miminorentcar.com
🚗 **RACE** [288 D2] (Rent a Car Enterprises) Melashvili 11; m 514 577555, 514 896896, airport 514 577555; w race.com.ge

🚗 **Rentacar Naniko** [288 B4] Leselidze 49; ✆ 214 7675; m 574 288855; w naniko.ge

TOURIST INFORMATION The tourist information office is at Ninoshvili 2 [288 B3] (✆ *422 294412;* m *577 909091;* e *tic@gobatumi.com;* w *gobatumi.com;* ⊕ *09.00–20.00 daily*), at the entrance to the seaside park; the helpful staff speak English and can provide excellent maps and leaflets. There's also a kiosk at the airport (✆ *422 294414;*

NOTE ON STREET NAMES

Note that in its wisdom the city has named two streets Gamsakhurdia (Konstantin and Zviad), two for Abashidze (Mehmet and Haidar) and two for Khimshiashvili (Selim and Sherif).

m 593 937991; ⊕ *09.00–18.00 daily*) and others by the cable car on Gogebashvili [289 F2] (✆ *422 294410; m 577 909093; e tic@gobatumi.com*) and at the Sarpi border post (*m 577 909093; e tic@gobatumi.com*), both open 24 hours.

WHERE TO STAY Batumi has a good choice of hotels, owing to the flow of businessmen across the border from Turkey and to serious promotion of its casinos in Turkey, Azerbaijan, Iran and Russia, where gambling is banned. Some of the flashier ones not only offer prostitutes, but are said to take serious offence if guests fail to avail themselves of their services. Currently, there is serious multi-million-dollar investment from Armenian, Kazakh and Tbilisi business concerns in southern Batumi and all along the coast south to the border, and even future US president Donald Trump expressed an interest in building here (page 286). Refugees from Abkhazia were paid US$7,000 per family to move out of communist blocks such as the Hotel Medea, which have been gutted or demolished and rebuilt. An offshoot of the fantastic Rooms Hotels in Tbilis and Kazbegi is expected to open early in 2018 on Gogebashvili at Parnavaz Mepe.

Camping is possible at Camping Robi by the main road in Chakvi [map, page 222] and at the Botanical Garden.

Hotels
Hotels are listed from north to south.

Boni [289 H1] (34 rooms) Mayakovsky 4; ✆ 422 271939, 422 274820; m 577 125206. Surprisingly good for its location near the bus station, this is a modern block with a sauna (with cold pool), café-bar-restaurant & billiards, & English is spoken. **$$–$$$**

Premier Hotel Batumi [289 H1] (28 rooms) Mayakovsky 15; ✆ 422 292202; m 579 092202; w hotelpremier.ge. Formerly known as Batumi 2000, the only reason to stay here is to be close to the bus station, but it's actually clean and efficient, though pricier than the Boni. **$$–$$$**

Oscar [289 E2] (9 rooms) Gorgasali 6; m 557 537842, 599 388500. A small place; rooms with shower & TV, & some with AC. Everything's basic but clean. **$$**

Ritsa [288 D2] (14 rooms) Z Gamsakhurdia 16; ✆ 422 273292; m 593 414293; e hotelritsa@ hotmail.com. A stylish, city-centre hotel with luxe rooms (with nice wrought-iron balconies), as well as standard. **$$$–$$$$**

Mercury [289 E3] (32 rooms) Chavchavadze 10/12; ✆ 422 277501–3, m 558 606000. A good and fairly new city centre hotel that satisfies both business folk & Peace Corps Volunteers, this has a bar, bistro, sauna (GEL12/hr), roof-top swimming pool & PCs with internet access. In addition to standard rooms & suites it has sgl & twin 'student' rooms. **$$–$$$$**

G Bakuri [288 D3] (28 rooms) Baratashvili 23; ✆ 422 274788; m 577 125209; e bakuriltd@ yahoo.com. A decent modern block up the alley by the Circus, with a bar but no other facilities; rooms are with shower, TV, & phone. **$$–$$$**

Metropoli [288 D3] (15 rooms) Nodar Imnadze 5 at Baratashvili; ✆ 422 276353; m 599 161815; e metropol_hotel_batumi@hotmail. com. A good, modern building with twin rooms; also a huge AC apt with a remarkably small TV & 3 balconies. Snacks are available in the top-floor bar; limited English is spoken. **$$–$$$$**

Iliko [289 E3] (7 rooms) K Gamsakhurdia 42; ✆ 422 273892; m 557 240042; e hoteliliko@mail. ru. A small, slightly grubby place shoehorned into a courtyard opposite Biblusi Books, with cramped twin rooms with bathroom, Wi-Fi & TV. **$$**

David [288 D4] (12 rooms) Baratashvili 33; ✆ 422 271718; m 592 091010; e hoteldavid_11@ mail.ru. The best in town until the Intourist Palace and Sheraton opened, with big stylish rooms & a good restaurant, sauna, & tennis facilities; a café is being built next door. Good English is spoken, & there's internet & cable in all rooms. With standard twin rooms (good Sony TVs, full bath, minibar, hairdryer), & deluxe rooms (with jacuzzi), inc b/fast (no credit cards). **$$$–$$$$$**

Peria [289 F3] Zurab Beridze Seshakhveri (formerly Pereulok Kalieva) 13; ✆ 422 251576; m 599 262870. A modern building with restaurant-bar & Wi-Fi, pretty decent but limited English spoken. Rather post-Soviet sgl rooms. **$$–$$$**

Adjara BATUMI

9

Lavro [289 F3] (8 rooms) Pushkin 29; m 558 551453; ▪. In the market area, this has basic but cheap rooms for 2 or 3 people. $–$$

Luna [289 E2] (4 rooms) Zubelashvili 4; ☎422 277277. A small pension in a pink-painted house on a square near the mosque. There are 2 bathrooms, a living room & kitchen, with fans but no AC. $$

Intourist Palace [288 B3] (146 rooms) Ninoshvili 11; ☎422 275525; m 577 612020; w intouristpalace.com. A Stalinist block of 1939 (on the site of the Alexander Nevsky Cathedral) which John Steinbeck thought 'the finest and most luxurious in the Soviet Union'; it was totally remodelled & reopened in 2006 as a Turkish-run 5-star hotel, with gym, hammam & 4 swimming pools (2 indoor, 1 outdoor & 1 for children). It's come a long way from the days when staff refused even to tell me the phone number for reservations. Rooms all inc b/fast, tax, plasma-screen TV & power showers. $$$$–$$$$$

Batumi Tennis Club [288 B4] (14 apts) ☎422 222662; m 571 331774, 593 241085; e dimitri.bliadze@yahoo.com. Set in the park off Ninoshvili, these are lovely motel-style apts (but without car access), each with a terrace, small garden & pavilion. There are 8 artificial grass courts, costing US$10/hr, & a bar above reception in the centre of the courts. Prices inc b/fast & 1hr of tennis daily. $$$–$$$$

Irise [288 D5] (15 rooms) Vazha-Pshavelas 39, at Gorgasali; ☎422 221301; m 599 552991, 558 850303; e infoirise@mail.ru; ▪. A small, newish hotel over a café-bar, with only Georgian & Russian spoken. Basic twin rooms with shower & TV, inc b/fast, or larger rooms are available. $$–$$$

Sputnik [289 H2] (152 rooms) Shervashidze Rise 28; ☎422 276066; m 577 226487, 577 650808; w hotel-sputnik.com. It's great to see this Soviet classic restored to life, on a hilltop 2km south of the bus station with great views; comfortable rooms, 3 restaurants & a swimming pool in beautiful subtropical gardens.

Sheraton [288 B5] (202 rooms) Rustaveli 28; ☎422 229000; w sheratonbatumi.com. An unmistakable & tasteless building that can be seen from all over town, especially at night when it is illuminated. This state-of-the-art 5-star hotel has everything you might expect: conference facilities, 2 restaurants, 3 bars, health centre, business

centre, spa & outdoor & indoor swimming pools. Rooms have hypoallergenic pillows, minibar, satellite TV & complimentary high-speed internet. Prices inc taxes & b/fast. $$$$

Tsereteli [288 C6] (12 rooms) Gorgiladze 33; ☎422 276684; m 557 247575, 571 751001. A small place with budget rooms in a period building & better ones in a modern wing. All rooms have AC, with satellite TV, minibar & balcony. There's a restaurant & bar, & parking & laundry are available. Prices inc simple b/fast. $$$–$$$$

ERA Palace [288 C7] (57 rooms) Gorgiladze 77; ☎422 220000; m 577 504506; e erapalace@gmail.com; w erapalace.ge. A stylish modern, 8-storey, 4-star hotel of modernist design with a good range of rooms – suites, semi-suites & standards, all with AC, satellite TV, minibar & bath; they've recently expanded into the building next door, too. Rates inc b/fast. $$$$–$$$$$

Hotel 19 [288 A7] Khimshiashvili 15B; m 593 051919, 593 131919; w hotel19.ge. On the19th floor of the SeaTowers building on the New Boulevard, each room has a balcony looking over the Black Sea. It's more like an aparthotel, with limited service & no restaurant, but the location is special. $$$

Marina [288 A7] (33 rooms) Selim Khimshiashvili 10; ☎422 244400; m 599 136565; e hotelmarina@marigroup.ge; w marigroup.ge. South of the city centre on the New Boulevard (hidden behind a Bank of Georgia branch) but close to the beach, this is part of a complex (built in 2006) that also includes a Mexican restaurant, cafés, tennis courts, fitness club & swimming pool. All rooms come with cable TV, internet, AC & balcony. $$$

Hostels

Batumi Surf Hostel [288 C3] (2 dorms & 3 dbls) Melashvili 33/35; m 599 104094; e batumisurf@gmail.com; ▪ batumisurf. This welcoming ground-floor hostel opening onto a courtyard (rather than the adapted apts that often pass themselves off as hostels) has rooms for 5, 7 or 8, plus two 4-bed rooms that can serve as private dbls, 5 bathrooms, kitchen, washing machine & a chilled common room; excellent English. $$

Chillout Hostel [288 C7] Parnavaz Mepe 133, at Takaishvili; m 555 526762; e chilloutbatumi@gmail.com;

�È chillouthostelbatumi. In an attractive residential area just south of 6 May Park, with characterful bars & restaurants, this friendly efficient hostel is open in the summer only. **$**
✴ ⌂ **Gulnasi's Guesthouse** [288 D7] (20 rooms) Lermontov 24A; **m** 557 065859, 599 797224; **e** homestay@mail.ru. Through the gate

under a 2-storey house, it's the house on the right of the yard at the back. The best budget option, with en-suite rooms for up to 6 plus garden with camping space & use of 2 kitchens, with free tea, coffee & wine/chacha to taste; English spoken. Tours, transfers & meals can be arranged. **$**

✗ WHERE TO EAT AND DRINK There are relatively few really good restaurants in Batumi, although you'll see signs with pictures of khachapuri outside cafés serving the cholesterol-laden Adjaran version of this snack. Other local snacks include *borano* (a fried cheese), *sinori* (a dough coil filled with curd and garlic), and honey-soaked *baklava* as a dessert. For a special occasion or a splurge, the **Veronica Restaurant** (**$$$$**) at the Sheraton Hotel [288 D5] is worth considering, as are **Clouds** (**$$$$**) on the 19th floor of the Radisson [288 B2] and the **Winter Garden Café** (**$$$$**) at the Intourist Palace [288 B3]. More humbly, there are several cheap and characterful **Turkish lokantas** along Khulo and Kutaisi, near the mosque – most of these serve the standard Turkish cheese-and-olives breakfast, *pide* (the Turkish version of pizza), tea (*çay*) and strong coffee (*kahve*) made the Turkish way in a bed of hot sand (no alcohol, as a rule).

Restaurants
✗ **Culinarium** [288 C6] Haidar Abashidze 5; **m** 555 155799; ⏱ 18.00–01.00 daily. The Lyon-trained patron produces a limited choice of excellent Franco-Georgian dishes (there's no written menu); wines & service are also good. **$$$**
✗ **Munich** [288 D2] Kutaisi 8; ☏ 422 227284; ◈ munichinbatumi; ⏱ 10.00–01.00 daily. Occupying a whole red-brick block (between Zhordania & Kostava), this is a lively place serving German-style sausages, pork, schnitzel & beer, & also fish. Service varies, & it's not particularly cheap. **$$$**
✗ **Old Boulevard** [288 B5] Ninoshvili 23A; **m** 577 242006; ⏱ 09.00–midnight daily. To the south side of the Sheraton, this is an excellent upmarket place with live music from 20.00. Good modern Georgian food, including a buffet. **$$$**
✗ **San Remo** [288 A7] Rustaveli 34; **m** 593 37466, 555 5188857; ◈ sanremo1234; ⏱ 11.00–02.00 daily. On a glass-floored pier south of the centre, at the start of the New Boulevard, this is great for evening drinks; it's also a slightly pricey fish restaurant. **$$$**
✗ **Porto Franco** [289 E3] K Gamsakhurdia 40; ☏ 422 276222; ◈ RestaurantPortoFranco; ⏱ 09.00–22.00 daily. Excellent restaurant serving Georgian food such as (Adjaran) khachapuri & khinkali in a grand setting with an open kitchen. **$$–$$$**

✗ **Bereg Café** [289 E2] Gogebashvili 9; ☏ 422 222570; **m** 595 610707; ⏱ 08.00–02.00 daily. Pavilion-style café with terraces overlooking the entrance to the harbour & the Sanapiro fish restaurant; very popular for drinks but the food & service are less enticing. **$$**
✗ **Dzveli Gemi** [288 B2] (Old Ship) Seaside Park; **m** 599 417758, 558 883884; **e** img333@mail.ru; ⏱ noon–midnight daily. In a (new) wooden galleon on the Boulevard, this is the most interesting of the touristy places in the seaside park, serving Georgian food. **$$**
✗ **Heart of Batumi** [288 D2] Mazniashvili 11; **m** 568 940515, 599 067970; ◈ batumisguli; ⏱ 11.00–23.00 daily. An 'art-café' with good friendly service & excellent food, including various aubergine dishes, as well as pork & other meat dishes. **$$**
✗ **Kafé Bar Maspindzelo** [288 C3] Melashvili 35; **m** 593 789235, 599 556778; ⏱ 09.00–02.00 daily. Named after a dish of ground fried meat with sour cream, they also serve good fish; like Mamapapuri (**m** 598 092906; **$$**) immediately north & Batumi Pizza (**m** 599 502386; **$$**) immediately south it's next to the Batumi Surf Hostel & accustomed to foreigners. **$$**
✗ **Radio Café-Bar** [288 D2] Zhordania 9; **m** 555 974977; ⏱ 08.00–midnight daily. A small café with a small menu of perfectly cooked dishes, such as pasta, salads, steak, fish & desserts, as well as coffees, wine & excellent cocktails. **$$**

✖ **Kaltenberg** [288 C5] 26 Maisi 17; m 577 416565, 595 330183. A big pubby place that's fine for an evening of beer & Georgian fast food. $

✖ **Princess Café** [288 C4] m Abashidze 45; ☎ 422 273733. A fairly basic place selling standard Georgian fare including Adjarian khachapuri. $

✖ **Retro** [288 C7] Takaishvili 10; ☎ 422 276116; m 579 511722; w retro.ge; ⏱ 09.00–23.00 Mon– Wed, 09.00–03.00 Thu–Sun. Gia Agirba's famous Adjaran khachapuri, also in Kobuleti & Tbilisi. $

Turkish lokantas

✖ **Arhavi** [289 E2] Kutaisi 36; m 577 585385; ⏱ 10.00–01.00 daily. A very clean & efficient cafeteria-style place, with menu & prices displayed above the counter. Wi-Fi. $

✖ **Mevlana** [289 E2] Khulo 3; m 577 535369; ⏱ until late daily. Spick & span cafeteria-style place, immediately north of Antalya Fast Food. $

✖ **Sofra Lokantası** [289 E2] Kutaisi 27; m 557 726363; ⏱ until late daily. One of the better lokantas on this street. $

Cafés

🍴 **Fanfan** [288 B5] Ninoshvili 27; m 591 150051; ⏱ 09.00–02.00 Mon–Sat, 09.00– midnight Sun, May–Sep. A unique arty café in a fin de siècle building built in 1905, with an attractive outside terrace; there's often live jazz. The food, from the short but slightly pricey menu, is excellent. $$

🍴 **Literaturuli** [288 D3] K Gamsakhurdia 18; ☎ 422 272013; ⏱ 10.00–23.00 daily. For American- or Italian-style coffee, cakes & savouries in a bookish setting (some English titles for sale), this is expensive but good. $$

🍴 **Café Batumi** [288 C4] M Abashidze 39; ☎ 422 277766; ⏱ 10.00–00.30 daily. Also known as Privet iz Batuma, a good, relatively pricey café with nice historic photos of the city. $

🍴 **Café Saamo** [288 C4] M Abashidze 37; m 577 479526. Opposite the Batumi, brightly lit & less interesting, but with decent coffee, beer & snacks. $

🍴 **Coffeetopia** [288 C3] K Gamsakhurdia 6; m 514 030505, 555 495112; w coffeetopia.ge; ⏱ 08.00–01.00 daily. Facing the State Theatre, this rivals London's hipster coffee bars for its range of new-wave coffees, from Aeropress to Japanese syphon & a cold brew, as well as the strong Turkish brew. $

🍴 **Conte** [288 C2] Zviad Gamsakhurdia 1/5; w casbatumi.ge. Part of the Contemporary Art Space gallery, this is a relatively unpretentious little place with live music some evenings, films or talks on Sat nights, & children's drawing sessions in the afternoons. $

🍴 **Luca Polare** [288 D3] Irakli Abashidze 3; ☎ 422 380802; w lucapolare.com; ⏱ 08.00–02.00 daily. The best ice cream in town, as well as sandwiches, salads & cakes. $

🍴 **Neocca** [288 B4] Vazha Pshavela 1; m 557 778888; w neocca.com; ⏱ 09.30–01.00 daily. Founded in 2012 as a specialist in coffees imported from 15 different countries, there's no point coming here for interesting wines & beers, but there's decent pizza, pasta & Turkish dishes; there's live Turkish music from 20.30 Tue–Sun, & service is excellent. $

Bars

🍷 **Chacha Time** [288 C2] Mazniashvili 5; m 597 561198; w chacha-time.com; ⏱ 15.00–01.00 daily. An attractive hipster bar that's quite serious about its 20 varieties of chacha, offering a varied flight of 5 for GEL15 plus interesting cocktails. $

🍷 **Prague Pub** [288 C4] Marjanishvili 8; ☎ 422 274415; m 558 286060; ❚ PubPragueBatumi; ⏱ 11.00–late daily. At the rear of the Art Museum, a cheery place with outside seating, Wi-Fi, & football on TV or karaoke on Fri & Sat nights. $

🍷 **Temelas Dukani** [289 E4] Baratashvili 43; m 599 640027, 577 433398; ❚ temelasduqani; ⏱ 10.00–02.00 daily. Wine is produced in Adjara, but in this pleasant wine cellar you'll mainly be drinking Kakheti's finest; decent Georgian food too. $

ENTERTAINMENT AND NIGHTLIFE Occasionally there's something worthwhile on at the **State Theatre** [288 C2] (*Rustaveli 1;* ☎ *422 270613/4;* m *555 366399;* w *batumitheatre.ge*) or the **Summer Theatre** [288 B3] (☎ *422 294524*) on the boulevard west from Tavdedebuli; the **Puppet and Youth Theatre** [288 C4] (*Mehmet Abashidze 49;* ☎ *422 270593;* w *puppet-show.org*) has recently been refurbished. There's just one cinema, the lovely **Cinema Apollo** [288 C3] (*M Abashidze 17;* ☎ *422 227227*), although the Batumi International Art House Film Festival (w *biaff.org*) in mid-September also uses the huge Batumi Art Center, 2km north.

The annual **Batumoba** festival takes place the first weekend of September, with an opening parade, various performances and exhibitions, and a closing gala concert on Europe Square. Also the first week of September, the **Batumi Music Festival** (w *batumifest.ge*) takes place in the Batumi Art Center. In July, the **Black Sea Jazz Festival** is held at the Batumi Tennis Club [288 B4].

There are plenty of tacky discos and casinos in town, but Take Five [288 B4] (m *595 797935*) and Sector 26 [288 A5] (m *557 189292*), both on the Old Boulevard, and the Gate dance club [288 C1] (*Barbius 6;* \ *422 222112;* w *thegateclub.com*), in Miracle Park just east of the Alphabetic Tower, seem better than average.

Brewery Shumeruli [289 F4] (*Pushkin 35;* m *579 942277*) is a big 24-hour pub that puts on live bands.

SHOPPING There's a good **food market** to the east along Tsereteli and beyond the bus station. Goodwill (w *goodwill.ge*) is a large 24-hour **supermarket** at Chavchavadze 3 [289 F2] and in the Batumi Mall at Gorgiladze 88 [288 C7]; Nugeshi is a smaller 24-hour supermarket on the north side of Tbilisi Moedani [289 E3] and the north end of Marjanishvili (actually on Tavdedebuli) [288 C4], and there's a big Carrefour in the Black Sea Mall, to the south on Chavchavadze [288 D7] (⊕ *10.00– 22.00 daily*). There are also some decent **wine shops**: Daniela's House of Wine [289 E2] (*Zviad Gamsakhurdia 43*), Wine Room [288 D2] (*Zviad Gamsakhurdia 11*), Wine Store Batumi [288 D3] (*Mazniashvili 18*), Vinomania [288 C3] (*Bakhtrionis 29*), KTW [288 D3] (*Konstantin Gamsakhurdia 28*) and Khareba Winery [288 D3] (*Konstantin Gamsakhurdia 14*). There are some pretty classy **fashion shops** on the northernmost block of M Abashidze: Diana Kvariani, Sopho Bakuridze, Flabour Georgian Designers, Club Georgian Designers and New Store Georgian Designers. Probably the only place for **English-language books** is Biblusi [288 C5] (*Mehmet Abashidze 62, at Vazha-Pshavelas, diagonally opposite the city library;* w *biblusi.ge;* ⊕ *09.30–19.00 daily*); also at Chavchavadze 60 [289 E6] and K. Gamsakhurdia 44 [289 E3]. BK Books is also worth a look [288 C2] (*Mehmet Abashidze 9;* \ *0422 212444;* ⊕ *10.00–22.00 daily*). There are **bike sales/repair shops** on the block of Pushkin between 26 May and Vazha-Pshavelas [289 E6], including decent rental bikes at Pushkin 114 [289 E6].

OTHER PRACTICALITIES It's easy to exchange money in Batumi; there are **exchange counters** everywhere, even folding tables on the pavement around the market and Tbilisis Moedani, at the top of Chavchavadze, and near the cathedral, and also at the bus station and the Hopa Bazaar. In addition to the standard dollars, euros, roubles and Turkish lira, some of them will also exchange pounds sterling, though at an awful rate. There are **ATMs** across the town, with many on Konstantin Gamsakhurdia and Chavchavadze.

There are a few **internet** places on Zviad and Konstantin Gamsakhurdia [288 D2] and Chavchavadze, at Melikishvili 23 [288 B5] and in the Circus foyer at Baratashvili 23 [288 D3].

Post office
✉ [288 D7] Chavchavadze 90, at Lermontov; ⊕ 09.00–17.00 Mon–Fri, 09.00–14.00 Sat

Couriers
DHL [288 D5] 26 Maisi 44; \ 422 274608; ⊕ 09.30–18.30 Mon–Fri, 10.00–14.00 Sat

TNT [288 C6] Gorgiladze 40; \ 422 223275; ⊕ 10.00–19.00 Mon–Fri, 10.00–13.00 Sat
UPS [289 E5] Tavdedebuli 36; \ 422 277358; ⊕ 10.00–18.00 Mon–Fri, 10.00–14.00 Sat

A TOUR OF BATUMI If you leave the bus station and cross Tsereteli and the railway, you'll reach Gogebashvili, the main road along the harbour front. To the right is the modernist **church of Sts Peter and Paul** [289 G2] (*Javakishvili 55*), opened in 2000 and easily the most active Roman Catholic church in Georgia, with Sunday Mass at 10.00 in English, 11.30 in Georgian, 14.00 in Armenian and 17.00 in Latin, and also services at 09.00 in Georgian (except Sunday). Confusingly, you head due north from the bus station to the sea, and the town lies to the west on a headland projecting into the Black Sea. Turning to the left/west, opposite the north end of Chavchavadze you'll find the terminal of the modern Doppelmayr **gondola** [289 E2] (⊕ *11.00–23.00; GEL15 return*), which takes 10 minutes to climb to a 257m hilltop southeast of the city, where there's a café-bar (serving good pastries, cakes and real coffee in the morning, then shashlik, pizza and other meals); there's nothing else to do but enjoy the view from the terrace (with telescopes).

Continuing along the coast, you'll pass the port headquarters on your left and the ferry terminal on the right, always crowded with anglers. This is the start of the seafront promenade to the west and then south. Just to the south is the **Orta Jame mosque** [289 E2] (*Chkalov 6; also entered from Kutaisi*); built in 1866, it's not particularly ancient and much like any small-town Turkish mosque, but it's more unusual in Georgia. The new **Miracle Park** [288 C1] occupies the headland at the entry to the harbour, dotted with various exotic mismatched towers, all elaborately illuminated at night; you'll pass first the **Chacha Tower** [288 D1] on your left, a 25m-high Moorish clock tower that was meant to spout chacha from its fountains for 10 minutes every evening, but it never worked. Next is the **Ferris wheel** [288 C1] (⊕ *10.00–20.00 daily; GEL3*), 55m high and taking 10 minutes for each revolution; going for a spin is an enjoyable and convenient way to get an overview of the city. To the right by the water is the **Ali and Nino statue** [288 C1], named after the romantic novel by Kurban Said (page 352), comprising two human forms that move together and become one. Beyond the 21m-high lighthouse, built in 1882, is the **Alphabetic Tower** [288 B1], a 130m-high double helix bearing the Georgian alphabet (ie: the nation's DNA) with a globe and viewing platform reached by a lift at the top. To the south of the park are the Radisson Blu hotel (and the future Kempinski) and another tower with, bizarrely, another Ferris wheel set into its side; this was built to house a Technical University but is to be sold and converted to a hotel.

Running south from here along the shore is one of the city's finest features, the Boulevard or **Seaside Park**; originally 150m long and laid out in 1881 by German and French gardeners (plus a Georgian who'd worked at Kew), it's now 7km long and dotted with funfairs, cafés and restaurants, as well as toilets and bike rental stations; the beach, unfortunately, is stony, but still popular. Looking south along the boulevard the skyline is dominated by the rocket-like, rather Stalinist-looking tower of the Sheraton Hotel, with the twin towers of the Hilton beyond and then the apartment blocks of the New Boulevard.

Running east to the tourist information kiosk on Ninoshvili is a series of dancing fountains; continuing inland just north of the Intourist, on Konstantin Gamsakhurdia (formerly Lenina), you'll cross Rustaveli to the square behind the theatre (with a copy of Giambologna's bronze statue of Neptune (1567) in Bologna, gaudily gilded in true Saakashvili style). and then the plaza of Evropas Moedani (Europe Square) on the right, lined with pastiche buildings and an astronomic clock in the northeastern corner. It's named after the Association of European Regions, the only international body to treat Abashidze's Adjara as a real entity, earning his eternal gratitude. At the centre of Evropas Moedani stands an enormously tall plinth with a **statue of Medea** [288 C3] holding a glistening Golden Fleece, a controversially expensive monument by Davit Khmaladze that was unveiled by Mikheil Saakashvili in 2007. There are three casinos around the square, notably in the Wyndham Hotel, rising ludicrously high from behind the façade of the city's former post office. Continuing inland, the tree-lined Konstantin Gamsakhurdia also hosts some of the city's more expensive shops, and the **Armenian church** [288 D3] at No 25, built in 1887–98 by the Austrian Robert Marfeld; it continues through the Old Town to Tbilisis Moedani, the square which serves as the terminal for most of the city's marshrutkas. Beyond this is the central **market** [289 E3], heaving with people and more like a Turkish bazaar than anything Soviet.

If you head north on Parnavaz Mepe from Konstantin Gamsakhurdia you'll enter the (relatively) Old Town, a tightly packed area of Neoclassical houses, with balconies, columns and pediments, built about a century ago, and pass the newly restored **Church of St Nikoloz** [288 D2], built in 1865. Opposite this is the **Piazza** [288 D2], the only really outrageously kitsch development to be shoehorned into the Old Town (the others are safely out of the way on the New Boulevard); modelled on Venice's Piazza San Marco, it's ringed by expensive shops and restaurants and an Irish pub, and the campanile houses a luxury hotel.

To the south of Tbilisis Moedani is the former **Roman Catholic church** [289 E4]. Built in a sort of Baltic-Gothic style, with Arts and Crafts-like murals and stained glass and consecrated in 1902, it's now the busy Orthodox cathedral, although it remains largely unchanged. The church is brightly lit at night. Just beyond it is the former railway station, now the **TBC Bank and Gallery** [289 E5], with very occasional exhibitions. Turning right/west here you'll come in three short blocks to the **synagogue** [288 D5] at Vazha-Pshavelas 33, opened in 1904 and reopened in 1998 after a thorough refurbishment; on the right-hand side of the street opposite, Khariton Akhvlediani, at No 4, is the **State Museum of Adjara** [288 C5] (✎ 422 271175; ⊕ 10.00–18.00 daily; GEL3). There's an excellent archaeological collection here, as well as Arab metalwork, miscellaneous tools and weapons, a display on the tea industry (including relics of the Chinese merchant Lan Chun-Chao who established the first plantations in Adjara), and photographs of Batumi's development in the 19th and 20th centuries. In the yard, there's a whale's skeleton and a few medical monstrosities, as well as the toilet. Staff here used to hold the key to the two-room Stalin Museum, in the little white wooden house at Pushkin 19 where he stayed for a couple of months in 1901–02, but this is currently closed; it took a reverential viewpoint now out of fashion in the rest of the world, with paintings and photos depicting him as the idealistic, youthful union organiser, rather than the paranoid dictator he later became.

Immediately to the west, Vazha-Pshavelas crosses Gorgiladze (formerly Gorki, then ERA kucha or Association of European Regions Street); across it to the right is the **Art Museum** [288 C4] at Gorgiladze 8 (✎ 27 3894; ⊕ 11.00–18.00 exc Mon; GEL2), which opened only in 1998, in a lovely building built in the 1930s to house a Museum of Communism. The upstairs gallery displays the older paintings, including pieces by Akhvlediani, Gudiashvili, Kakabadze and Pirosmani (a cow being milked, instantly recognisable), as well as local prodigy Rusudan Petviashvili; downstairs are pieces by more contemporary painters. Diagonally opposite it, facing Roses Square, is the **City Hall** [288 D4], built around the start of the 20th century.

Gorgiladze continues south to Khimshiashvili and the new promenade, but a block to the right, by a statue of a female aviator flying a toy plane with a child, is the main entrance to **6 May Park** [288 B5] (w *parkbatumi.ge*), surrounding a large lake; the oligarch Bidzina Ivanishvili paid for its refurbishment, with very funky low-level lighting, and also for a high-tech rebuild of the dolphinarium at its far end (see below). There's a small Zoo Corner (⏀ *closed Mon; free;* w *parkbatumi.ge*) on the inland side, with primates, birds, marsupials and hoofed animals. The Russian poet Sergei Esenin lived at Melikishvili 11 (formerly Engelska), on the northern side of the park, in 1924–25 between his fourth and fifth marriages (not to speak of his homosexual affairs); born in 1895, he was one of the most radical of the young poets at the time of the Revolution and an ardent supporter of the Bolsheviks, although he was refused party membership as he considered himself too much of an individualist. In 1922 he married the American dancer Isadora Duncan and set off to travel in Europe and America, but he suffered a nervous breakdown and declined into alcoholism, with hallucinations. He then married Galina Benislavskaya, travelled to Batumi and Baku, then in 1925 married Sofia Tolstoya, Leo Tolstoy's granddaughter, and on 28 December 1925, hanged himself in Leningrad, leaving a suicide poem written in his own blood. In Nice, in September 1927, Isadora was strangled instantly when her scarf caught in the wheel of her sports car. There's a pleasant residential area inland from the park, with good bars, cafés and restaurants.

In the southwestern corner of the park, the modern **dolphinarium** [288 B7] (w *dolphinarium.ge; box office* ⏀ *10.00–14.00 & 15.00–18.00 Tue–Sun*) puts on a show (*17.00 Tue–Sun (16.00 out of season), 14.00 Sat–Sun & in high season; GEL15*), and you can also swim with dolphins for 15 minutes (*ages 3–16 GEL100, 17+ GEL150*). Immediately south at Rustaveli 51, the **aquarium** [288 B7] (⏀ *11.00– 18.00 Tue–Sun; GEL2*) stands on the campus of the State Maritime Academy (1929) and the Marine Ecology and Fisheries Research Institute; it's worth a visit, although many of the fish are in fact from the tropics. Buses 1/1A and 7/7A and marshrutkas 116, 120 and 155 come this way. At a roundabout just south of the Maritime Academy the main road turns 90° left and then right, at the start of a new seaside boulevard, Sherif Khimshiashvili (not to be confused with Selim Khimshiashvili, running east from 26 May Park); this is the start of a strip of **surreal architectural statements**, starting with the horseshoe-shaped Alliance tower, then the Public Service Hall and Sky Tower by Ardagari Lake and the fabulous 'Splashdance' animated fountain and lightshow, installed at great expense by a French company to be the centrepiece of the new tourist zone. There are cafés, discos, bowling, tennis courts, a casino and so on, although the Chinese pagoda, the Dutch windmill and the Parthenon now house humdrum tourist eateries rather than the original themed restaurants. Continuing south you'll pass the Upside Down restaurant (yes, upside down) and the Colosseum Marina hotel (yes, based on the Roman original), and the boulevard ends at the castellated Europark Palace Hotel and the tatty **Aquapark** (*Khimshiashvili 12;* ☏ *422 210101;* m *577 774455;* ⏀ *09.00–21.00 summer only; GEL30*), with pools and water slides.

Returning to the centre, the **Archaeological Museum**, behind Soviet arches at Chavchavadze 77 [289 E6] (at Melikishvili; ☏ *422 276564;* w *bam.ge;* ⏀ *10.00–18.00 Tue–Sun; GEL3*) displays finds from Pichvnari, on the coast between Kobuleti and the Choloki River, where a joint Oxford University/Georgian team has been working since 1988. Meaning 'Place of the Pine Trees' in Georgian, Pichvnari is the site of a Greek trading settlement from the mid-5th century BC, on the site of an earlier Colchian settlement; there are late Bronze Age, early Iron Age, Classical and Hellenistic levels over an area of 100ha. Visitors would be made welcome at the site but there's not a lot to see, as the digs are in sandy soil and quickly filled in. The museum has photos of the dig, Stone Age pottery, Greek- and Roman-era articles including drinking bowls and medieval Arabic coins, and finds from graves at Gonio (pages 299–300); upstairs a large gallery is used for temporary shows.

One of Batumi's most interesting attractions is in fact 9km to the north: the **Botanic Gardens** at Green Cape (Mtsvane Kontskhi), reached by bus 15 (*GEL0.80*) or minibus 31 (*GEL2*) from Parnavaz Mepe, which turn off along the old road before the tunnel. Get off at the hairpin at km28/93, go through the main gate and then right (the green gate to the left leads to the Agricultural Institute, which has beautifully labelled plants but they're mainly standard herbs and palms, bamboos and so on). Fork left to the gate and *kassa* (ticket office) (✆ *422 270033*; **w** *bbg.ge*; ⊕ *10.00–17.30 daily; GEL8*), and go on to the administration building halfway down the hill. From here the main part of the garden is ahead to the north, with a rose garden, Australian, New Zealand, Himalayan, Mediterranean, East Asian, Mexican and North American sections, and at the far end a park. If you return and gradually go down to the south, through some big mature eucalyptus trees, as well as citrus plantations, you'll cross above the railway tunnel to the Green Cape, with attractive viewpoints. You can leave by the Mtsvane Kontskhi gate from where marshrutka 101 (*GEL0.70*) leaves frequently, reaching the old road in 500m, just before its junction with the new highway from the tunnel. Guides are available, and there's an electric shuttle which will carry you from end to end of the garden for GEL6.

Founded in 1912, the gardens cover 113ha with more than 5,000 species of plants (and 1,200 varieties of rose) from around the world, as well as 40,000 specimens in a herbarium. In addition to Caucasian flora, there are species from moist subtropical climes around the world, including Japan and the Himalayas (and there's good birdwatching too, with sightings of Krueper's nuthatch, green warbler, Caucasian chiffchaff and five species of woodpecker all possible). It's a great spot for a picnic in wonderfully lush surroundings, and the presence of the sea just below the trees always adds an extra frisson.

TO GONIO AND THE TURKISH BORDER

GONIO Turkish trucks and businessmen in black SUVs race up and down the main road south from Batumi to the Turkish border; this starts by turning right off the road east to Akhaltsikhe just north of km105, at the entry to the village of Angisa. At km106.5 there's a turning to Batumi's airport, 200m to the southwest, before the road crosses the Chorokh River at km109; there's good birding here, with dirt roads alongside the river and an old bridge just west of the modern road bridge. Just north of km113/6 you'll find the gate to the **fortress of Gonio** [map, page 222] on the left, with a mini-fort aptly placed in a playground across the road. Founded in the 3rd century BC as Apsaros (after the son of King Aeetes killed by Jason), a Roman fort built in the 1st century AD was home to five cohorts, or 1,200–1,500 men, until it was abandoned in the 4th century. What is seen now is the outer wall of the Byzantine (from the AD540s) and Ottoman (after 1548) fort of Asparunt; it's a square of about 200m, with oranges, plums, strawberries and palms being grown inside, and mature eucalyptus trees outside, against a backdrop that's reminiscent of the gentler parts of the Nepalese foothills, with luxuriant vegetation.

There's a ticket kiosk (⊕ *10.00–18.00 Tue–Sun; GEL3, audio guide GEL5*) and toilets inside the gate, from where a paved path leads to the centre, where there's a museum (with poor English captions) and souvenir shop. The earliest finds are from the 8th century BC, and you'll also see sling/catapult stones, amphorae and coins, and photos of the wonderful 2nd-century AD Colchian goldsmithery of the Gonio Treasury, found in 1974 and now in the Archaeological Museum in Batumi (see opposite). Nearby are the remains of Roman baths (with mosaic floors) and barracks (with underfloor heating) and perhaps a temple; in the southwest corner are the remains of Roman handmills and a kiln. Excavations by the south gate have revealed lots of Roman, Byzantine and Ottoman pipework. Outside the south wall a 5th-century burial site has been found, as well as a theatre and hippodrome from the 1st–3rd centuries. The grave of St Matthew the Apostle (Matthew Levi) is said to be by the cross to the left of the museum; he was one of 70 Minor Apostles who replaced Judas, and came to Georgia with St Andrew the First-Called and Simon the Zealot. It's possible to climb up onto the 5m-high walls behind the ticket office and walk around the square, with 18 of the original 22 towers surviving.

There's a beach at Gonio but it's not that attractive – a bit of pebbly wasteland with wrecked Soviet-period bunkers, grazing cows and frogs splashing about in ponds – and it's known for its Uzbek prostitutes. You're better off continuing south to Kvariati if you're after sun and sand. Shops and exchange offices are 1km south of the fortress.

Getting there and away Marshrutkas charge GEL1 to Gonio or to the Turkish border at Sarpi, 19km south of Batumi, and buses 16 and 17 cost GEL0.80. A **taxi** to the border shouldn't charge more than GEL10, and you may be able to share. It's a very busy route, and you'll be accosted by drivers yelling 'Sarpi, Sarpi, Sarpi' as you arrive at Batumi's bus or train station. Minibus 88 (often with 'Sarpi' on a sign in Latin script) runs from Tbilisis Moedani, in the centre of town, and along Chavchavadze; you should be across the border in Hopa within a couple of hours, and in Trabzon in another 3 hours.

Where to stay, eat and drink

Gonio Inn (20 rooms) Pirveltsodebuli Hwy 5th dead end; \ 422 212002; m 555 657766; w gonioinn.ge. Down a lane by the beach with a sea view, this is a decent modern place with an adequate restaurant ($$). **$$$**

Guesthouse Gonio (7 rooms) m 577 242855. 1.5km south of the fortress & 5mins from the beach, with a swimming pool & summer café. **$$$**

Hotel Eva (16 rooms) \ 422 524040; m 593 353727. A modern hotel with a restaurant & bar, 1km from the sea at the south end of Gonio. All rooms come with TV, minibar & AC. **$$$**

Hotel Magnolia (19 rooms & suites) Pirveltsodebuli Hwy 31; m 599 366076, 574 482181; f hotelmagnoliagonio. On the east side of the main road, not far south of the fortress, this new place has simple rooms with satellite TV, minibar & bath; AC in the suites. **$$$**

Reggae Hostel (4 dorms) Pirveltsodebuli Hwy 52; m 568 783703; f reggaehostelgonio. This cosy Polish-owned hostel has 4 dorms (GEL15/bed) with 2 shared bathrooms, a kitchen & a big garden with hammocks. **$**

KVARIATI To the south of Gonio (14km from Batumi at km116/3) is Kvariati, also being developed for tourism, with some spacious new beachfront hotels. At the moment it's still a very pleasant resort for those looking for rest and contact with nature, and it's better for swimming than Batumi; in addition to the buses to Sarpi, marshrutka 33 comes here.

Where to stay, eat and drink

Egrisi (21 rooms) m 598 657545; w hotelegrisi.com. A large, new 4-storey place with excellent service, & a couple of independent restaurants nearby. **$$$$**

ERA Palace \ 422 212424; m 557 590021; e era.kvariati@gmail.com; w erapalace.ge/kvariat. A modern 14-floor tower (with just 1 lift) with restaurant ($$$) & swimming pool. **$$$$**

Hotel Martini (12 rooms) m 599 556464; w martini.ge. At the south end of the village, this has 4 sgls & 6 dbls, & a cottage with 2 trpl bedrooms. All rooms are en suite with satellite TV, fridge & balcony. Large swimming pool, billiards, restaurant ($$) & bar. **$$$**

SARPI The road finally runs below a cliff (with a sculpture of St Andrew by a waterfall) to reach the Turkish border at Sarpi (km119/0), crammed into a tiny space below hills before the Customs Terminal, a funky jigsaw tower built in 2011 by Jürgen Mayer H, the German architect responsible for the new look of Mestia in Svaneti. There is a stony **beach**, where the water is cleaner than in Batumi. Right behind the gate of the customs area is a **tourist information kiosk** (m *577 909093*), with helpful English-speaking staff who can book beds in Sarpi, Kvariati or Gonio, as well as Batumi. You can exchange money, get a free SIM card or gamble in a slot club, all 24 hours a day. Buy tickets on board bus 16 or 17 to Batumi, or just grab a marshrutka or taxi. Sarpi holds the **Kolkhoba Festival** on 20 August (in theory – check the date), a Laz festival based on the legend of the Golden Fleece which was revived in 1978.

🏠 **Where to stay, eat and drink** A bed in a private house in Sarpi will cost US$10–15 in August or US$5–10 at other times; most of the houses on the road up to the right from the border crossing have rooms to rent.

🏠 **Sarpi Resort Hotel** ☏ 412 222500; m 577 430003, 577 233240. Just north of the border beyond the church, this has comfortable 2-storey bungalows with AC, as well as a gym & the decent Laimi restaurant ($$) with friendly helpful service. $$$

MOUNTAINOUS ADJARA

The humid mountains immediately east of Batumi protect tertiary relict forests with some of the highest levels of endemicity in Georgia. Rare species include lynx, golden eagle, black vulture, falcon, Caspian snowcock, Krueper's nuthatch, great rosefinch and Caucasian salamander, and relict plant species. In addition, the mountain villages inland from Batumi are home to the bulk of Adjara's Muslims, living a pretty traditional lifestyle – child marriage and bride kidnapping (only sometimes by agreement) are only now being abandoned, and there's still a huge stigma against divorce or leaving a forced marriage. **Mount Mtirala** ('Weeping'; 1,336m) is the rainiest place in Europe, with 4.1m of precipitation a year. The mountains of the Lesser Caucasus, with its ravines and thick forests, block the passage of clouds from the sea and make this the greenest corner of Georgia. It would be worth protecting as a national park anyway, but there's the added interest of the autumn migration of up to 280,000 raptors a day at a bottleneck on the coastal flyway. This is dominated by European honey buzzards and steppe buzzards (over half a million each), but you may also see black kite, Montagu's harrier and various eagles, as well as black storks.

In September and October the **Batumi Raptor Count** (w *batumiraptorcount. org*) is becoming a well-known attraction, countering the local tendency to shoot birds, coupled with the Batumi Bird Festival in the last week of September. Organised by Bird Conservation Georgia (*Sabuko, Melashvili 5, 6010 Batumi;* ☏ *422 241777;* m *557 900909;* w *sabuko.org*), their main counting posts are in the villages of Sakhalvasho and Shuamta, where they have set up guesthouses (m *599 216 580;* e *visit@batumiraptorcount.org;* f *guesthousessakhalvasho; 5 nights all-inclusive* €*140; $$*). To reach Sakhalvasho, take the main road north from Batumi and turn right on the first road after the tunnel, then take the gravel road to the right below the school to a house marked with the BRC logo (or ask for Ruslan Dilaverov's house, 'Ruslanis sachli'). The nearest hotel is the Oasis in Chakvi (page 285); you can buy snacks and drinks in the village. In Shuamta (7km inland), the Adjaran Department of Tourism has constructed a viewing platform with stunning 360° views; it's a steep walk from the car park, but there's a shelter and toilet.

MTIRALA NATIONAL PARK AND KINTRISHI NATURE RESERVE [map, page 222]

Access to the 15,806ha **Mtirala National Park** is to the east from Chakvi; the park headquarters are just east from km 87/32 (*Chavchavadze 13*; m *577 101889*; e *mtiralapa@yahoo.com, teogvianidze@gmail.com*; w *apa.gov.ge*). The park has a visitor centre in Chakvistavi, 15km inland from Chakvi; there's also a small hostel, campsite and a family-run restaurant (m *593 967495*). Marshrutkas from Batumi (every 30 minutes) run only as far as Khala.

Enthusiastic local rangers can lead you on a 3-hour loop trail (also a 2-hour hike to a 12m-high waterfall), and there's a longer circuit (15km) to the Tsivtskaro shelter, that can be tackled with mountain bikes; this is also the start of the Trans Caucasian Trail (see box, page 275), via Mt Khino to Gomis-Mta in Guria (page 256). Zip-lining and canyoning are also available at the entry to the park.

To the north is the **Kintrishi Nature Reserve** (18,893ha), reached by a long drive inland from its headquarters in Kobuleti (page 284). The visitor centre is at Tskhemvani, 24km east (marshrutkas run only as far as Chakhati), and the road continues through the Kintrishi River Gorge, with a dozen wonderful old bridges attributed (as always) to Queen Tamar, to Khino, where there's a ruined cathedral. It also lies on a new east–west horseback itinerary through the mountains.

 Where to stay, eat and drink Guesthouses in Chakvistavi include Gela Kontselidze (m *557 651764*; **$$**), Guram Kontselidze (m *558 466828*; **$$**), Eteri (m *558 719006*; **$$**) and Mary (m *577 469944*; **$$**).

La Belle Verte Just north of Korolistavi; m 568 999917; e labelleverte.mtirala@gmail. com; w batumicamp.com. On the southern edge of Mtirala National Park (take marshrutka 141 or follow the road for 9km up the south side of the Korolistskali River from the Batumi Art Center) is this delightful ecolodge and yoga centre run by a Russian-Armenian couple. Camping is also available, as well as plentiful organic food. **$$$**

ADJARISKHALI RIVER VALLEY [map, page 222]

To the south of Mtirala the road from Batumi to Akhaltsikhe follows the Adjariskhali River inland to the Goderji Pass (2,025m), which can be closed by snow any time between October and May, forcing a lengthy detour via Kutaisi. This is a luxuriantly fertile region, with a profusion of vines, tangerines and watermelons, as well as magnolia, oleander, eucalyptus and cypress trees, with yellow azalea (*Rhododendron luteum*) on the higher slopes. Along the Adjariskhali there are also ten well-preserved Turkish bridges, built in the 10th–12th centuries, spanning side-streams with surprisingly slender stone spans.

South of Batumi airport, the road heads inland up the valley of the Chorokh River (flowing out of Turkey) then forks left/east at Adjariskhali (km15); to the south on the border is the **Machakhela National Park**, with little infrastructure as yet, other than guesthouses in Chkhutuneti, about 13km southeast. At km16, the **Adjarian Wine House** [map, page 222] (m *577 214002*; w *awh.ge*) is an attractive new winery with a small vineyard of local grape varieties such as Chkhaveri; they also make chacha and serve food. Continuing up the lovely wooded valley, at km24/135 the little Restaurant Chadrebi serves traditional Adjaran dishes. In **Mkhunseti** (km28) a sign in English leads left up a bad track to a museum in a modern barn to the right and then left to a dramatic waterfall (behind a café-restaurant with a tank to keep the trout fresh). Across the main road and down some steps is **Tamar's Bridge**, a simple 19.5m span of volcanic stone without parapets. Rafting trips start here, organised by Active Tours (m *555 701201*), GeTur (m *555 701999*; w *en.getur.ru*) and Rafting.ge (m *557 305490, 574 773030*; f *Rafting.ge*), all in Batumi.

At **Keda**, about 42km from Batumi (reached by marshrutka 77), there's a seasonal tourist office and various ruined fortresses in the hills around; the area is known for its pink tomatoes and wines from Tsolikauri and Chkhaveri grapes. About 5km on up the valley is **Vaio**, known for its knitting and wicker baskets, as well as wine and chacha; there are guesthouses here and 5km off the highway at Gobroneti (see below). There are also **mineral springs** (good for intestinal conditions) in this area at Kokotauri and Gundauri.

At Dandalo, there's another famous bridge and just above to the north is the 11–12th-century **Takidzeebi (or Otolta) Fortress**, with ruined walls (18m by 52m) and a tower; from here a dead-end road leads north up the Chvanistskali Valley. It's not far up the main valley to **Shuakhevi**, a small spa where there's another seasonal tourist information centre; there are guesthouses nearby in Nigazeuli, 6km north of the road and 78km from Batumi (see below). Just beyond, at Zamleti, a minor road leads southeast up the Skhalta Valley to the **ancient churches** of Kinchauri, Skhalta, Vernebi and Kalota. It's not much further to **Khulo** (943m), centre of an area known for its 19th-century wooden mosques, *chiponi* bagpipes and plaited cheese; there's a small museum and a seasonal tourist information centre. A tiny ancient cable car (*GEL5 return*) crosses a gorge to Tago, at 1,700m on the hill to the south, while 3km east of Khulo a dirt road leads north into the hills to the start of a jeep/horse trail to Bakhmaro (page 256).

Khulo is as far as marshrutkas come, apart from a daily summer-only service over the Goderji Pass to Akhaltsikhe. Near the pass at 2,635m is **Khikhani Fortress**, with the ruins of 11th-century walls, towers and a church. Traces of fossilised trees can be found near the pass, where the Batumi Botanic Garden is creating a subalpine garden; **Goderji** (*2,025m;* w *goderdzi.ski*) is also the newest of Georgia's ski resorts, with the country's longest ski trail and six hotels (with 435 beds) now under construction. There are now two runs and two lifts, but potentially it could cover three times the area of Gudauri or Bakuriani. Currently there's one small hotel and some cottages here, and a dozen guesthouses in Danisparauli, 3km west. It's about 110km (3 hours' drive) from Batumi, but from the east it's usually reached by a snowcat shuttle (*GEL150–250*) over the last 18km from Adigeni, on the main road west of Akhaltsikhe.

From the pass a jeep track leads 6km south to the lovely **Green Lake** (Mtsvane Tba; 2,058m), also reached by hiking from the village of Beshumi, just east of the pass. The hills are dotted with the yaylas or huts of the Adjaran herdsmen who spend the summer camping up here.

🏠 Where to stay, eat and drink
Rooms in the guesthouses below start at GEL20–30 per person without meals, or GEL35–50 including three meals.

Goderji
🏠 **Hotel Meteo** m 598 095016. A chalet-style former weather station has been converted into a decent little hotel. **$$**

Gobroneti
🏠 **Guesthouse Tskarostvali** m 599 944662. Owned by Amiran Bolkvadze. **$**
🏠 **Guesthouse Zebo** m 593 933403. Owned by Zebur Bolkvadze. **$**

Khulo
🏠 **Taliko Shantadze** m 577 103940. **$**

Nigazeuli
🏠 **Avto** m 593 628378. **$**
🏠 **Giorgi** m 593 464845. **$**
🏠 **Imedi** m 555 128195, 595 368032. **$**
🏠 **Kvemourebi** m 577 290848. **$**
🏠 **Mtsvane Sakhli (Green House)** m 558 793307, 591 981722. **$**

Vaio
🏠 **Lado Shavishvili** m 599 783659. **$**

10

Kakheti კახეთი

The easy-going, wine-growing province of Kakheti, to the east of Tbilisi, is justifiably popular for easy excursions of a couple of days (or even day trips from the capital), but it also gives access to Davit-Gareja and Tusheti, much harder trips along very rugged roads, but well worthwhile if you have the time. The *rtveli* or grape harvest in September and October is a fine excuse for a visit.

GETTING THERE AND AWAY

A new **minibus** service offers day-trips from Tbilisi to Telavi, Gremi, Kvareli and Sighnaghi for GEL85, on Tuesdays and Thursdays from mid-March to mid-October and on Saturdays from November to March. Contact Donkey Express (m *568 809168;* e *donkeyexpressgeo@gmail.com;* w *donkeyexpress.online;* f *donkeyexpressgeo*). Being Georgia, departure is only at 10.00 (from Fabrika, Ninoshvili 8) with three 40–60-minute stops and 2–3 hours for lunch in Sighnaghi.

EASTWARDS FROM TBILISI

The main road from Tbilisi runs to the south side of the Gombori Mountains, around their eastern end and then back to the northwest to reach Telavi, the capital of Kakheti; almost all marshrutkas and tour buses take this route, but it is also possible to cut directly across the 1,650m Gombori Pass by a quiet, winding road that has seen considerable improvement in recent years. This is a glorious route with expansive views towards Tbilisi that you are only likely to experience if you drive yourself or charter a taxi. However, some shared taxis between Telavi and Tbilisi also go this way in preference to the longer route via Gurjaani.

In either case, you'll head out of Tbilisi on the airport road, past the Isani and Samgori metro stations (terminals for marshrutkas to Kakheti; page 98) with the white tower blocks of Varketili along the ridge to the left. There's some striking Saakashvili-era modern architecture along this road: first the green-glass Interior Ministry (security police) headquarters (by the Italian architect Michele de Lucchi) to the left/north, then the offices of Saakashvili's party, the UNM, to the right, and the treasury of the National Bank of Georgia to the left. After the flyover junction to the airport, with its needle-like monument, the six-lane dual-carriageway becomes a four-lane highway, passing the huge Lilos Bazroba or open-air flea market to the left (page 133), and the Castel brewery to the right, before leaving the city at about km21/139, by the intersection with the city's eastern bypass; from here it's single carriageway, with overtaking lanes up some hills. From km23/136, it's 22km north to Martkopi, 5km northwest of which, on Mount Ialno, is the **Monastery of St Anthony**, founder of Georgian monasticism, who spent his last 15 years as a hermit on a rock pillar that still stands to the east; the church, founded in the 6th

10

century, was rebuilt at the end of the 17th century (the belfry was built in 1629). At the top of a hill at km27 on the main A302, the direct route to Telavi via the Gombori Pass turns left/north, passing through **Ujarma**, on the Iori River 45km from Tbilisi, where you can see an old stone church, the remains of a two-storey palace and fortifications with nine square towers (at km47.5). This was the residence of King Vakhtang Gorgasali, who died here in AD502; destroyed in the 10th century by the Arabs, the fortifications were restored in the 12th century. The road to Shuamta and Telavi turns right in Otaraani, but if you continue up the left/east bank of the Iori to km56 it's possible to hike in about 30 minutes up to the 10th-century castle of **Bochorma**, around a six-apse domed church built in the 7th century.

NINOTSMINDA AND TSINANDALI
ნინოწმინდა, წინანდალი

The main road soon descends from the Samgori steppe to cross the Iori and enter Kakheti at km35/125; you'll see the ruins of the 6th–7th-century fort of **Khashmi** to the north from a viaduct, and a few oil wells, and pass south of the village of **Patardzeuli**, with the modern KTW (Kakhetian Traditional Wines) winery's tasting rooms, shop and café at km39/121, before, at km45/115, the old road turns left to run through Ninotsminda and Sagarejo. Buses to Telavi use the bypass to the south, stopping for passengers only at the roundabout at its far end; if you want to visit Ninotsminda you should take one of the local marshrutkas to Sagarejo, leaving from immediately outside the Samgori station.

There are no house numbers or street signs, so look out for small signs with a monastery symbol leading up to the solid tower of Ninotsminda (St Nino, one of many), to the left of the old road around 2km from the junction, and 3km west of the centre of Sagarejo. The site of **Ninotsminda Church** has been used for Christian worship since the 5th century, and the present cathedral was built in AD575. It was largely ruined by earthquakes in 1824 and 1848, but is nevertheless profoundly impressive, the earliest large cruciform church to survive (anticipating the Jvari Church of Mtskheta). It has a tetraconch ground plan with corner niches, and because the church is half ruined this is a good place to study the detailed arrangements. In the eastern apse are the remains of a 16th-century fresco of the Virgin and Child, and the western end of the church has recently been converted into a chapel. The bell tower was built in the mid 16th century by Levan I; it shows strong Safavid-Persian influence, although it seems oddly primitive and almost African in feel. Around these are well-preserved defensive walls built in the 16th and 17th centuries.

Continuing across the Tvaltkhevi Bridge into Sagarejo, a roundabout marks the town centre, with a market just north; walking east along the main road, you'll fork right after 5 minutes and go downhill for almost 20 minutes to reach the roundabout at the end of the bypass (km50/110), where you can catch a bus onwards towards Telavi (marshrutkas for Tbilisi via Ninotsminda wait here too, as well as taxis). Halfway down the hill you'll pass a small and very attractive old basilica.

EASTWARDS FROM SAGAREJO Continuing eastwards, a left-turn at km51.5 gives access to the **Mariamjvris Nature Reserve**, one of the country's older reserves, protecting endemic pines in 1,040ha of the Gombori Mountains, and to the 10th–11th-century **Manavi Fortress**, once the summer residence of the kings of Kakheti (known as 'Come and See Castle', as enemies always failed to take it). This is visible from km58 on the main road, high on a hill to the left/north, with the Church of

Giorgi-tsminda (Saint George) below it. At km64.5 you can go up to the restored 16th-century **Chailuri Fort** just to the right; the walls are in good shape but there's nothing to see inside. The Hotel Ambasadori Kachreti is a luxury hotel and golf resort in the middle of nowhere at km84 (**** *32 243 9494, 32 272 9417/9;* **m** *591 225004;* **w** *ambassadori.com/kachreti*), popular mainly with Muslims coming for golf and discreet drinking. In the same area a 'farm' offshoot of Tbilisi's Rooms hotel is due to open in 2019.

Eventually the main road climbs out of the Iori Valley, and then from km94/66 drops steeply through woods into the Alazani Valley, past the junction to Sighnaghi (pages 331–5) at Chalaubani (km 94.5), the Nakeduli Restaurant (km99.5), and Vardiskheli (Cool Water) at km101.5, where there's a fountain and stalls, before reaching a roundabout at Bakurtsikhe (km103/57, 1½ hours from Tbilisi). The name implies that there is a castle here, but it is in fact known for its *kurgan* or burial mound from the 3rd millienniun BC. In theory, the main road is the one to the right, towards Azerbaijan, but most traffic turns left towards Telavi, 45km northwest.

GURJAANI This road passes through Bakurtsikhe and after km6/67 a road leads up to the west; turning right after 1.5km you'll come to the Church of the Virgin of **Kvelatsminda**, the only ancient double-domed church in Georgia and perhaps Gurjaani's main claim to fame. Built in the 8th century, it's a three-aisled stone basilica rather than a cruciform church, with two octagonal brick domes over the nave which are too small to dominate it. The church also has external galleries and lateral chapels, one of which projects to the northeast. Just beyond at km6.5, there's a turning (signed in English) up to the west to the early 19th-century house-museum (⊕ *10.00–18.00 Tue–Sun; GEL2*) of the great actress Nato Vachnadze (1904–53), opened in 1989 due to the efforts of her sons, film directors Eldar and Giorgi Shengelaia. Just after km9/65 and the turning to Lagodekhi (pages 329–30), you'll reach two roundabouts in **Gurjaani**, known as a spa and a centre of winemaking; at the larger, second roundabout is a taxi and bus stand with a fine mosaic frieze of wine- and churchkhela-making. Tamar Mepe leads northeast from here to the centre, passing the Akhtala *kurort* or **health resort**, with mini-volcanoes belching forth healing mud in a public park (with new WCs). You can have treatment here for an hour, or have daily treatments for up to two weeks, except on Sundays; the mud is at its best in the mornings. At the bottom of Tamar Mepe, Guramishvili leads to the right to the former railway station and the Lagodekhi road; there's not a lot to see here, but it's a pleasant place with lots of trees lining the streets.

Heading back towards Tbilisi, Agmashenebelis leads west from the smaller roundabout to a park with great views of the Caucasus and a military museum with five Svan-style towers for the five years of World War II; it's usually closed but there are some interesting paintings to be glimpsed through the windows. Continuing towards Telavi, a tiny old **chapel** stands on the right at km12/61 in Chumlaki; there's no lock on the door, and inside it's very dark, totally blackened by smoke. There are no specific features of interest, but the place has an intriguingly pagan feel to it. After km17/56 there's a turning to Zegaani monastery, 1.8km to the left; there are two churches here, built in the 5th and 6th/7th centuries, with 16th-century frescoes in the tiny older one, as well as a lovely garden.

At km18/55 a road turns right to Kvareli (pages 327–9), 17km to the northeast; to the right of the junction is **Velistsikhe**, an old Silk Road village which is developing as a centre of wine tourism. At Lomtadze's Marani (**m** *599 154781, 597 070222;* **f**) you can see the family's winepress and marani (with 24 qvevri installed in 1900–05) and taste their dry red, white and orange wines; Velistsikhe Veranda (**** *322*

237700/22; m 595 997517; e *mepurishvili500@mail.ru;* w *ktw.ge*) has a shop, tasting area and an ethnographic corner. It's also worth finding the Qvevri Wine Cellar (m *599 937909;* e *nareklishvili76@yahoo.com, i.nareklishvili@icloud.com*) and Wine Cellar Numisi (m *599 561031, 571 165519*), with a 16th-century cellar-museum 1km from the main road. Artisan cheese-making is also starting here (with Swiss aid), with MM Cheese (m *571 334353*) making excellent sulguni.

Beyond a railway crossing the Telavi road enters Mukuzani, known for its dark, velvety and full-bodied Saperavi wine – look for the Maranuli Winery (m *577 401111;* w *maranuli.com*). There's a simple basilica to the left of the road. About 5km further (km24/49) is Shashiani, where Tamari's Wine Cellar (m *595 336103;* e *tamari. wines@gmail.com*), on the main road, produces a gutsy Saperavi and also uses Kisi and French grapes such as chardonnay and cabernet. And in the historic village of Vachnadziani (km27/46), with various ancient churches, the Vachnadziani Winery (\ *322 988391, 591 442181;* e *ana.tavtetrishvili@gmail.com;* f *vachnadzianivalley;* ⊕ *09.00–18.00 Mon–Fri*) produces Saperavi and Rkatsiteli wines in qvevris.

🏠 Where to stay, eat and drink

🏠 **Gurjaani Wine House** (4 rooms) Rustaveli 28; m 790 512244, 599 512244; w whg.ge. There's a pleasant B&B in this family house, & behind it a summer garden & sizeable tasting room with qvevri & an 1864 winepress; visitors can take wine from qvevri & bottle it & watch chacha-, bread- & churchkhela-making, & there's good food with their own wines. **$$$**

🏠 **Hotel Rebi Gurjaani** (17 rooms) Akhtala 12; \ 353 222102; m 551 898932; e rebigurjaani1@gmail.com; f hotel. rebigurjaani. A fairly basic hotel with no English spoken. **$$$**

🏠 **The Rolé House & Café** (3 rooms) Davit Agmashenebelis 5; m 555 350874; f rolehouse. A small but very neat & friendly guesthouse/café in the town centre. **$$$**

🏠 **Juisher Mikeladze's Guesthouse** (4 rooms) Gonashvili 32; \ 353 223376; m 595 154780; e datomelkidzee@gmail.com. **$$**

🖵 **Coco Café** Vazha-Pshavela; m 599 514068; e cafecoco097@gmail.com. A nice modern café opposite the new cathedral (across the main road from the town centre), with a rooftop terrace; tasty pastries & strudels to eat in or take away. **$**

TSINANDALI From km31/42 there's a string of villages, with vineyards behind them, until km37/36, at the far end of Tsinandali, where you reach the entrance to the **Alexander Chavchavadze house-museum** (w *tsinandali.com;* ⊕ *10.00– 17.00 daily, to 19.00 in summer; park GEL2, park & museum GEL5*). You'll cross a typically communist irrigation channel, huge and out of place, before following a cypress-lined avenue to a handsome pair of wrought-iron gates and the ticket office. The house is set in an ornamental garden of 12ha with many fine, mature examples of rare trees, including umbrella pines, cedars, magnolia and lime trees, as well as bamboos and palms. This was praised as a wilder version of Kew; Alexandre Dumas simply called it the 'Garden of Eden'. To the right as you enter, the garden is relatively formal, leading to a big villa which was a government guesthouse and is now the Hotel Tsinandali (*18 rooms;* \ *322 253581–3;* m *570 701212;* w *hoteltsinandali.ge;* **$$$$**). To the left the garden is slightly less formal, with a box maze; however, it's too densely planted with trees to be an 'English park', as claimed.

Behind the house to the northeast are industrial buildings which house the famous **Tsinandali winery**, founded in the 1830s by Alexander Chavchavadze. It can be visited by tour groups, who can taste the dry white wine (85% Rkatsiteli grapes and 15% Mtsvane Kakhuri or Green Kakhetian), although not the 1814 vintage, the oldest in the collection. The house, garden and winery are now run by the Silk Road Group. A Radisson Blu hotel is to open here by the end of 2018, and from 2019 there'll be an open-air classical music festival featuring orchestras of the calibre of the Israel Philharmonic. There's more affordable accommodation in Tsinandali village, at Tsinandalis Edemi (\ *350 235200*; m *599 260215*; **$$**), where they make good wine; and Mangaliti (m *577 113743, 599 502250*; **$**).

The house itself is a relatively small and unpretentious two-storey manor house of local sandstone, built in 1818 by the poet Alexander Chavchavadze, leading spirit of the Romantic Movement in Georgia. Born in St Petersburg (where his father was Georgian ambassador) in 1786, he joined the Russian army and served against Napoleon and the Turks before settling in Georgia, marrying Salome Orbeliani, a member of one of Georgia's grandest families. This was a summer house, and his main residence was in Tbilisi; although he wrote poetry, Chavchavadze's main importance was as translator of Voltaire and the French Romantic poets and as chief animator of the circle of writers and critics who created Georgian Romanticism. Many of the leading Russian Romantic writers also came to Tbilisi, usually with the army or government; these included Alexander Griboedov (1795–1829), who married Chavchavadze's daughter Nina when she was just 16. He was a notorious philanderer and is generally supposed to have seduced her (although the museum staff might disagree) and then been forced to marry her; almost at once he was sent on a diplomatic mission to Tehran which went tragically wrong when a mob stormed the Russian legation and killed all the Russians, brutally hacking Griboedov's head off. The teenage widow became a symbol of grief, and is portrayed as such on their shared tomb in Tbilisi's pantheon.

Chavchavadze himself died in 1846 in a bizarre accident in Tbilisi, when his cloak caught in the wheel of his carriage and he was thrown out, hitting his head on the ground. In 1854 the house was burnt by Chechen rebels, who kidnapped the Chavchavadze princesses and their children and servants and rode off into the Caucasus with them lashed across their saddles. Their leader Shamyl demanded the return of his son Djemmal-Eddin (or Jamal Al-Din), who had been handed over to the Russians as a hostage 15 years before, at the age of eight, and given a Russian education and then a commission in the army. Negotiations took nine months, but eventually the hostages were exchanged (together with 14,000 silver roubles for the rebels); alas, the last thing Djemmal-Eddin wanted or was suited to was a life in a rebel village in the Caucasus, and deprived of the glittering social life of the court he faded away and died within six months. Just one of the Chavchavadze children avoided capture by hiding in a hollow tree, which can still be seen beyond the maze. You'll be given a guided tour of the house, still with original furniture and lots of pianos, including the French one (with a folding keyboard) given as a wedding gift by Griboedov to Nina, supposedly the first grand piano in Georgia. There's also a reproduction of the Winterhalter portrait of Chavchavadze's wife Salome, and embroidery by their daughters. The former drawing room is now an exhibition hall (also used for concerts), after which you'll emerge into a summer gallery over the wine cellar and toilets. There's a café (⊕ *until 18.00*) with a terrace on the side of the house near the ice-house.

KISISKHEVI Crossing the bridge (at km38/35) from Tsinandali, you'll have the Shumi winery (see box, page 315) on your left and the Marani winery to the right. Beyond them to the left is Kisiskhevi, home to a church with a circular tower built of river stones.

🏠 Where to stay

🏠 **Schuchmann Château** (20 rooms) m 790 557045, 577 508005; e i.datunashvili@yahoo. com; w schuchmann-wines.com. Attractive to the upmarket wine enthusiast – guests can have a free 15–20min tour of the winery (page 314) followed by a tasting (with bread, cheese & olives). They also offer classes in baking & making churchkhela & chacha, & in Sep you can try barefoot grape-pressing. You can stay the night in attractive wood & stone rooms (with no need for AC); there's a good restaurant (⊕ 10.00–22.00 daily; $$$), wine spa & swimming pool. $$$$

🏠 **Villa Alazani** m 577 414842; w villaalazani.com. A simpler option, this is owned by a group of former foreign correspondents (& therefore well stocked with interesting English books, as well as old rugs draped over the gallery); they also make wine, but only about 1,000 litres a year, & don't bottle any. You'll rent the whole house (from US$100 for 2 people to US$200 for 8), with b/fast provided. $$$$

TELAVI   თელავი   *Telephone code 350*

From Tsinandali it's 5.5km to the city limits of Telavi (at km43), and 3km more to the centre. The city sits at 568m on a hilltop above the Alazani Valley. In the 2nd century, it was mentioned by the Greek geographer Ptolemy as 'Telada', and was the capital of Kakheti in the 11th century and again from 1615 (when Gremi was destroyed by the Persians) to 1762 (when Tbilisi took over); with a population of just 28,000 it's still the largest town in Kakheti.

GETTING THERE AND AWAY There are three **bus** yards on either side of Alazani Avenue immediately below the market; to the left is the 'New Bus Station' [311 D2] (📞 *350 272983*), packed with buses to regional destinations including Lagodekhi, Pshaveli and Tbilisi (there's a *kassa* and toilets at the bottom end), while a little further down you can cut through the market to the right to the 'Old Bus Station' [311 E1] (📞 *350 271619*), a large yard used for the frequent local departures to Akhmeta, Alvani, Alaverdi, Gremi, Gurjaani, Tsinandali and Kvareli. Just north beyond Agmashenebelis is the Roki bus station [311 D1] (📞 *350 274390*), for buses to Tbilisi (*every 40min 06.00–18.00; GEL7*). **Shared taxis** to Tbilisi via the Gombori Pass (*GEL12, 1½hrs*) wait at the crossroads by the market at Alvani and Chavchavadze [311 D2].

🏠 **WHERE TO STAY** As well as the hotels, there are also some good homestays (although not all of them speak English), especially on the streets above the Public Service Hall (turn right off Erekle II Square past the theatre). A 100-room Golden Tulip is expected to open in 2018 in the former Intourist Hotel, overlooking the citadel.

Hotels

🏠 **Château Mere** [311 B1] (24 rooms) Vardisubani 15; m 595 990399, 595 990390; w mere.ge. The best place to stay in the area is this fake castle at the start of the road to the Gombori Pass; it has large rooms with an eclectic bohemian style, a fairly grand restaurant ($$$$) & its own winery & cellar. $$$$

🏠 **Erekle II** [311 F3] (7 rooms) Lionidze 1; m 596 377377; w hotelerekle.ge. A new & genuinely boutique art-hotel in what was the home of King Erekle's 24 children, just outside the citadel walls; there's a lovely blend of old & new, with ancient walls & contemporary art. There's a good restaurant (serving local natural wines) & 24hr bar; excellent English spoken. $$$$

🏠 **Old Telavi** [311 D3] (37 rooms) Cholokashvili 1; 📞 350 270707, 350 279009; m 596 440707, 596 450707; e oldtelavi@gmail.com; w oldtelavi.ge. In 2 blocks (one 19th-century, one modern) on either side of the road, with well-equipped comfortable rooms; the modern block has a rooftop café, now with lift access. $$$–$$$$

🏠 **Teliani Valley** [311 G3] (5 rooms & 2 suites) Tbilisi Highway km3; m 599 363600, 577 500257; e nana-teliani@mgroup.com; w telianivalley.com. One of the more modern & dynamic Georgian wine companies, Teliani Valley has a modern guesthouse at its winery on the eastern edge of town. Prices inc b/fast & winery tour with a tasting. $$$–$$$$

For listings, see pages 310–13

① Where to stay

1	Alaznis Veli................E1
2	Erekle II................F3
3	Eto Jajanidze................E4
4	Guesthouse
	Kavkasionis 33.........D1
5	Guesthouse Marinella....C2
6	Guesthouse Tin-Tina......D2
7	Kakheti................D4
8	Lali Khosroshvili's
	Guesthouse................D4
9	Marleta's B&B................E2
10	Old Telavi................D3
11	Rcheuli Marani................B2
12	Svetlana Tushishvili......E4
13	Sweet Home................D4
	Off map
	Asmat Sekhniadize.....E4
	Château Mere................B1
	Guesthouse Erma.......D4
	Merab Milorava........E4
	Teliani Valley................G3
	Zuzumbo................D4

⊗ Where to eat and drink

14	Bravo................E4
15	Dzveli Galavani................D3
16	Kaploni................E4
	Mala's Garden........(see 16)
17	Pirosmani................E2
18	Rosato................E4
	Starz Café &
	Restaurant................(see 15)
	Off map
	Nikala................B1

TELAVI

🏠 **Alaznis Veli** [311 E1] (Alazani Valley; 30 rooms) Alazani 75; 📞350 274144; m 595 500155; w alaznisveli.com.ge. This plain, white building, just north of the bus station, has rooms with satellite TV, minibar, AC & bath; conference hall & sauna. The same company owns the homelier Kakhuri Ezo (Kakhetian Yard) just off the Tbilisi highway at Davitashvili 7 (📞350 274144; m 599 007704; $$$), with 4 dbls & a wine cellar. $$$

🏠 **Rcheuli Marani** [311 B2] (24 rooms) Chavchavadze 154; 📞350 273030; m 592 758899; e rcheulimarani@rcheuli.ge. The oldest of this small chain (with sister hotels in Batumi, Tbilisi & Sighnaghi) is just west of the centre in an attractive red-brick building with traditional balconies. It has spacious rooms but seems tired & neglected. $$$

🏠 **Zuzumbo** [311 D4] (20 rooms) Kartuli Universiteti 5; m 591 110106; e hotelzuzumbo@gmail.com; w hotelzuzumbo.com. A new but characterful place with a cheery restaurant, up on the hill by the university where it catches a cooling breeze in summer. $$$

🏠 **Kakheti** [311 D2] (20 rooms) Vardoshvili 1; 📞27 0151; m 599 135511; e hotel.kakheti@gmail.com; w hotelkakheti.ge. Across the road to the west of the market, this is a fairly functional 3-star, with decent rooms with Wi-Fi, & a restaurant (🕒 from 09.00). $$–$$$

Homestays

🏠 **Guesthouse Erma** [311 D4] (12 rooms) Kartuli Universiteti 25; 📞350 270183; m 558 141447, 557 323205; w erma.ge. At the top of 26 May, this is a modern 3-storey block with functional rooms & a simple bar-restaurant. $$$

🏠 **Eto Jajanidze** [311 E4] (4 rooms) Akhvlediani 27; 📞350 277070; m 598 782050; e familyhoteleto@yahoo.com. Just uphill from Nadikvari, the very hospitable Eto speaks English & has a comfortable traditional house. Good meals, internet access & a nice shady garden. $$

🏠 **Marleta's B&B** [311 E2] (4 rooms) Bagrationi 13; m 577 722771. To the east of the market off Chavchavadze, this is a fine guesthouse, & there's good food (including cheeses) from their farm. $$

🏠 **Guesthouse Marinella** [311 C2] (6 rooms) Chavchavadze 131; 📞350 273946; m 577 516001; e maria.marinella@mail.ru, ekaterine222@gmail.com; w marinella.ge. A solid grey house on the main road west, with good food & views over the Alazani River. $$

🏠 **Svetlana Tushishvili** [311 E4] (5 rooms) Nadikvari 15; 📞350 271909; m 577 756625; e sspiridon@rambler.ru; w globalsalsa.com/telavi. Rooms in a lovely AC apt with shared bathroom & swimming pool. English spoken. Transfers & ½- to 2-day trips to wineries, Davit-Gareja & Kakheti can be arranged for cGEL10/hr. Excellent b/fast (inc pancakes) & very good sociable dinners (GEL20 inc wine). $$

🏠 **Sweet Home** [311 D4] (16 rooms) 26 May 35; 📞350 235570; m 551 811500; info@shome.com.ge. Solid 3-storey brick building with simple rooms & balconies, pleasant courtyard & restaurant. $$

🏠 **Asmat Sekhniadize** [311 E4] (6 rooms) 9 April 83; m 599 565074; e barabintimur@mail.ru. $–$$

🏠 **Lali Khosroshvili's Guesthouse** [311 D4] (7 rooms) 26 May 2nd lane 4, which runs uphill from Kostava east of the theatre; 📞350 271824; m 593 981862; e ingabel2020@yahoo.com. 5 older rooms with 3 bathrooms, plus new en-suite rooms. Great food, & a wine marani. $–$$

🏠 **Merab Milorava** [311 E4] (4 rooms) Akhvlediani 67; 📞350 271257; m 599 737371. Just uphill from Nadikvari. Merab offers rooms in a cottage in a lovely garden for 4 or 5 people, with safe parking, or a car is available. $–$$

🏠 **Guesthouse Kavkasionis 33** [311 D1] (10 rooms) Kavkasionis 33; 📞350 274028; m 551 159915; e gela.gelashvili555@gmail.com. North of the centre near the bus stations, this is a modern place with garden & barbecue; friendly service, bikes available. $

🏠 **Guesthouse Tin-Tina** [311 D4] (4 rooms) Bakhtrioni 22; m 593 123201; e tintinaguesthouse@gmail.com. Run by a friendly young couple, this is a delightful place with shared bathrooms, living room & kitchen. $

✕ WHERE TO EAT AND DRINK

✕ **Kapiloni** [311 E4] Barnov 10; 📞350 278767; m 599 985115; 🕒 09.00–midnight daily. Perhaps the best in town at the moment, opposite the Erekle II statue; good meat & veggie dishes, also German beers & a 'beer menu' including olives & Mexican potatoes. $$$

✗ Mala's Garden [311 E4] Rustaveli 4; m 599 543593; ☷; ⊕ noon–23.00 daily. Lively & popular new place with plenty of outdoor seating (of course) & excellent Georgian food, especially grilled meats. $$$
✗ Bravo [311 E4] Nadikvari 11; ☎350 278127; m 593 152713; ⊕ 10.00–midnight daily. Lively new café-restaurant (with terrace) serving decent Italian food, with good service. $$
✗ Dzveli Galavani [311 D3] Cholokashvili 6; m 350 230363; ⊕ 09.30–22.00 daily. A friendly place serving simple but good Georgian food such as khinkali, & beer. $$
✗ Nikala [311 B1] Vardisubani; m 551 449941, 599 198834; e kobiashvililasha@yahoo.com. Very authentic Kakhetian food at this rural restaurant

just west of the Château Mere on the Gombori Pass road; rooms available ($$). $$
✗ Rosato [311 E4] Tavisupleba Sq; ☎350 236860; m 577 272763; ⊕ 09.00–midnight daily. Formerly Shua Kalaki, a nice terrace-café in the park opposite the citadel; decent affordable food & drinks. $$
✗ Pirosmani [311 E2] Chavchavadze 52; m 574 878777, 579 020757; ⊕ 10.00–23.00 daily. Out to the west, this is a cheery & reliable place serving standard Georgian dishes. $
✗ Starz Café & Restaurant [311 D3] Cholokashvili 4; m 571 600608, 599 001221; ⊕ 08.00–02.00 daily. Good pizza & shawarma, a salad bar, plus good coffee & cakes; a better option than Blitz at No 2. $

OTHER PRACTICALITIES There's a helpful **tourist information centre** [311 E4] (☎ 350 275317; e tictelavi1@gmail.com; ⊕ 10.00–18.00 daily, summer to 19.00) at Erekle II 9, clearly signed, upstairs in a traditional house on the main square; they're accommodating and have free Wi-Fi and city maps. **ATMs** are along Erekle II [311 D3] and Ketevan Tsamebulis 11 [311 D3]. The **post office** [311 D3] (⊕ 09.00–17.00 Mon–Fri, 09.00–14.00 Sat) is by the town hall at Erekle II 12. The **market** [311 D2], on Alazani Avenue near the New Bus Station, is fantastic, and has stalls selling good hot snacks, but the best food is often outside, where the local foragers offer their mushrooms and herbs. Sopho Gorgadze makes great cheeses at her farm just outside Telavi; you can buy it at Marleta's B&B [311 E2] (*Bagrationi 13; m 577 722771*).

The city's **festivals** are Telavkalakoba at the end of October and Erekleoba on 7 November; there's also a wine festival on the first Saturday of October and the Telavi International Music Festival the second week of October.

WHAT TO SEE AND DO It's now hard to find the quaint old streets lined with elms (*tela*) and wooden-balconied houses which used to characterise Telavi, but some have been restored along Cholokashvili, and you should also see the zigzag patterns of river stones that are still typical of the region. The city is unusual on account of the four separate citadels here, most obviously the 17th-century Batonistsikhe ('the Lord's Castle'; see below) but also the 9th/10th-century Dzveli Galavani ('Old Walls'), the 16th-century Korchibashishvilebis Tsikhe and the 18th-century Vakhvakhishvilebis Tsikhe, all pretty ruinous. It's much cheaper and less touristy than Sighnaghi (pages 331–5), and a good base for visiting the surrounding villages and wineries. Heading up the hill from the market is a broad boulevard (Ketevan Tsamebuli) with a stream and trees in the middle; at the first crossroads you can turn right/west into a residential quarter nicely refurbished with cobbles and single and double balconies (although there's still too much traffic); the 16th-century church of the Holy Virgin [311 D3] is large and plain, with a high cupola. Turning left takes you along Erekle II, the city's main street, lined with relatively tasteful post-war blocks, housing the post office and so on, which leads to the large **Freedom Square** [311 E4], with the Public Service Hall [311 E4] ahead and **Batonistsikhe citadel** [311 E3] to the left. Closed for refurbishment until sometime in 2018, this contains various churches and palaces, now housing a school and museum. Entering on the far (east) side, you'll find the

Interest is growing fast in the wines of Kakheti, increasingly famed as the home of natural qvevri wines; new hotels are opening, both in towns and in the vineyards themselves. The wines are widely available, so it's strange that tours of the wineries are so awkward and expensive; the only wineries to offer free visits are Shumi and Vaziani (see opposite and below). The Kakheti Wine Guild runs a Wine Tourism Center [311 F4] (*Rustaveli 1, Telavi;* \ *350 279090;* m *551 468283;* w *kwg.ge;* ⏰ *10.00–19.00 daily*), which organises winery visits with a driver. Alternatively, Dato (David) Luashvili (m *551 300620, 593 761216;* e *davi.luashvili@gmail.com;* w *kakhetidavidtours.weebly. com*) is an excellent guide in Telavi who speaks good English, drives carefully and doesn't smoke when with clients; he charges GEL90/day for four people and can also take you to Davit-Gareja (*GEL150*) and elsewhere. Other drivers (*from GEL10/ hr*) include Vakhtang Butskhridze (m *597 141914, 577 658877*), Davit Tsatiashvili (m *599 909194*), Spartaki Simona (m *551 740760*), Nukri Bragvadze (m *551 150044*), and Mamuka Jangulashvili (m *555 156715*). In Sighnaghi, Goga Shabalaidze (m *598 722872;* e *goga_shabalaidze@mail.ru*) is also a good guide.

On the edge of Telavi are big industrial wineries that produce export-quality wine but aren't very interested in independent tourists; to the east, there are some small, more welcoming, places. Alternatively, some family winemakers also welcome visitors (but probably won't speak English). The only free tastings are at Shumi and Vaziani; otherwise you'll pay from GEL10–15 per person, depending on the snacks provided and the number of wines you try.

OUTSKIRTS OF TELAVI

GWS Achinebuli village; \350 276051; e l. aladashvili@gws.com.ge; w gws.ge. GEL30 for a tour of the production area & cellar & a tasting.
Kakhuri Tbilisi Hwy 1; \350 270200/10; w kakhuri.com; ⏰ 10.00–18.00 daily. GEL15 pp (5 wines), GEL10pp for 10 or more wines.
Kote Makhatelashvili Davitashvili 15; \350 230303; m 599 571857; w elgitour.ge. Kote makes wine at the Kakhuri Ezo hotel; tastings cost GEL5 for 2 wines with cheese, bread & walnuts.
Marani Milorauli Wine Cellar Akhvlediani 67; m 551 774444; e smilorava@yahoo. com. Decent small-scale qvevri wines (accommodation also available); GEL15 pp inc cheese, bread & churchkhela.
Shalauri Cellars Shalauri village; m 577 727270, 577 474616; e shalauricellar1@gmail. com; ⨐ shalauriwinecellar. On the eastern edge of Telavi, this new qvevri winery charges GEL20 to taste 3 wines or GEL30 for 5 wines.
Telavi Wine Cellar Kurdghelauri village; \350 273707; w marani.co; ⏰ 10.00–16.00 Mon–Fri. €11 for a 1hr tour & tasting of 4 wines.
Teliani Valley Tbilisi Hwy 3; \350 234848; w telianivalley.com. This is the only winery

you need to book for (1 day in advance); GEL20–40.
Vaziani Mshvidoba 42; \322 904774; m 599 885258; w vaziani.ge; ⏰ 10.00–17.30 daily. Free, & well done, but it's a tasting only, without a tour.

EAST OF TELAVI

Nicolashvili's Wine Cellar Zardiashvili 55, Gurjaani; \353 223419, 555 680693; w winecellar.ge; ⏰ from 09.00 Mon–Fri, from 10.00 Sat–Sun. You can taste & buy in their century-old cellar; they also do a day's tour of local wineries, & offer accommodation.
Schuchmann Château m 577 252213; w schuchmann-wines.com; ⏰ daily. Charges GEL15–35 for a very professional tasting of 3–5 wines with bread, cheese, walnuts & olives. You'll see the 50 stainless-steel fermentation tanks, some 3,000-litre qvevri & a huge cellar (inc a riddling rack for sparkling wines). This German-owned winery-hotel, founded in 2009, aims for 'quality not quantity', although they do now produce 2 million bottles/year, & more than 20 wines from 10 grape varieties. Just 30% of their production, labelled Vinoterra,

is in qvevri, including a splendid deep amber Rkatsiteli. They also produce sparkling wine (a Chardonnay Blanc de Blanc & a better Merlot/ Malbec Rosé Brut). Also offers accommodation (pages 309–10).

Shumi ✆ 322 381137; m 599 289982; e vazioni@shumi.ge; w shumi.ge. Across the river from Tsinandali at km38, they offer free tastings, & have a museum housing a good collection of items, starting with ceramics dating from the 4th to 2nd millennia BC & silver sleeves from the 3rd millennium BC for grafting, & qvevri from the 12th century; in front is a collection of 294 indigenous varieties of vine (& 92 European ones), all used to make their Zigu wine, fortified with chacha. They're only just beginning to make qvevri wines, & don't always have an English-speaking guide available.

Tsinandali winery At the museum café (pages 308–9); w tsinandali.com; ⊕ 10.00– 18.00 daily. Charges GEL7 for entry to the museum & a sip of their white wine, or GEL25 for a proper tasting of Saperavi red, a qvevri-made Rkatsiteli white & a chacha.

NORTH OF TELAVI

Alaverdi Monastery m 595 101166; e maranisince1011@gmail.com; w since1011. com; ⊕ 11.00–18.00 Mon–Fri, 11.00–16.00 Sat, 13.30–18.00 Sun. Wine-making has a special significance here, as one of the places that kept knowledge of traditional techniques alive for the long Soviet period when anything but industrial production was banned (& only 4 varietals were used). In partnership since 2006 with the Badagoni wine company, the monks have opened up an 11th-century cellar with 40 qvevri & are making their wines more widely available (some red wines are even aged in oak nowadays). Tours cost GEL65 pp (minimum of 7) & visit the demonstration vineyard (with 104 varieties), the old cellar & other historic buildings, with tasting of 3 wines (perhaps the lovely amber Khikhvi & a deep red Saperavi) & a chacha, with bread, walnuts & churchkhela. Not to be confused with Alaverdi Alcohol Drinks Company (w alaverdi.ge), a new winery built in 2001 in Chumlaki near Gurjaani, which produces

more modern industrial wines.

Avtandil Abuladze Old Wine Cellar, Eniseli; m 599 398733

Babaneuris Marani Babaneuri; m 551 433551, 555 776551; w babaneuri.com. Just northeast of Kvemo Alvani, this is a lovely place (with 5 en-suite rooms available, $$$$; & a good restaurant; $$$$) making limited quantities of unfiltered natural wines in qvevris.

Danieli Winery m 599 624411; w danieliwinery.com. This boutique winery in Argoichki, just north of Kvemo Alvani, uses technology rather than tradition to produce consistent export-friendly wines, notably a dry white Kisi. Horseriding also available. No set hours or prices – be sure to call ahead.

Graneli Khareba, near Kvareli m 577 987791; e meghvineobagraneli@mail.ru; w graneliwine.ge; shop ⊕ 09.00–22.00 daily. A large winery with a good line in brandies; tastings should cost GEL10, but may be free.

Khareba Kvareli m 790 120001, 593 303636; w winery-khareba.com. Very popular with tour groups, more for their famous tunnel cellar (*GEL5*) rather than their tastings (*GEL12*). They make European-style, qvevri & sparkling wines, & have a decent restaurant ($$).

Kindzmareuli Corporation Chavchavadze 55, Kvareli; ✆ 790 100061; m 595 330433; w kindzmaraulicorporation.ge; ⊕ 09.00–18.00 daily. A large modern winery with a well-organised tourist offering: tastings GEL2 per wine.

Kindzmarauli Marani ✆ 322 361850; w kmwine.ge. A modern winery using both stainless steel tanks & some qvevri, a demonstration plot of 423 indigenous grape varieties, & a tasting room in a tower. GEL20 for a minimum of 5 wines.

Petriaant Marani Zemo Khodasheni; m 593 444229; e petriaantmarani@gmail. com; w petriaantmarani.ge; ⊕ 09.00–20.00 daily. Near Akhmeta, this small family winery produces only white wine, & offers a tasting with bread, cheese, walnuts & dried meat (*GEL20*), dinner (*GEL35*) or dinner & tasting (*GEL50*).

continued overleaf

palace of **King Erekle II** [311 E3], a relatively small and low two-storey building built in the 1750s in the Persian style, one of the least expected buildings in Georgia (*GEL6 foreigners, GEL1 Georgians*). It's a lovely building, and also houses a small museum of history and ethnography. Beyond the palace are two **churches**: a tiny and very simple basilica, built of stone in the 17th and 18th centuries, which is always open although there's little to see, and a larger brick church, built by Erekle in 1758, which may still be closed. There's also a pantheon, bringing together the graves of sundry Kakhetian notables, and the ruins of the 11th-century royal baths. Beyond these (near the school, and accessible through the west gate) is a new semi-underground **art museum** [311 E3] with a façade of clay pots that should open in 2018 (another Saakashvili project that was put on the back-burner after he left the presidency). The collection of the former art museum included works by local painters (there are lots of views of Gremi and Alaverdi) and five paintings by Elena Akhvlediani (born in Telavi in 1901), many 17th- to 19th-century German and French paintings, a few Dutch ones, and Russian landscapes.

Going back through the east gate, you emerge by the large **equestrian statue** of King Erekle II, by Merab Merabishvili. There's a fine view to the east from here, and about 100m below is a small park with a famous 900-year-old plane tree, below the shell of the Hotel Telavi. On the far side of the hotel, Nadikvari runs through a pleasant residential area that has a number of homestays and past another citadel wall to **Nadikvari Park** [311 F4], nicely done up with a funfair, open-air theatre and viewpoints over the Alazani Valley, and the terrace of a modernist white café-bar (which has step-free access all the way from the road).

WEST OF TELAVI

SHUAMTA Heading west from Telavi, it's about 2km to the city limits, and another 1km to the junction (at about km7) of the road to Tbilisi via Gombori (30km west). Taking this road for about 8km to km57 and turning left and left again, you'll soon reach the **nunnery of Akhali (New) Shuamta**, where you can see a large cruciform brick church built in the second quarter of the 16th century and decorated with frescoes of the founders King Levan of Kakheti, Queen Tinatin and their son Alexander. Tinatin became a nun and was buried here; her tomb was found in 1899, and she is remembered on 3 September. Alexander Chavchavadze is also buried here, by the north wall. However, the nuns who have returned here are somewhat fierce and unwelcoming.

The real attraction is another 3km up the road, the **nunnery of Dzveli (Old) Shuamta**, beautifully set on an isolated hilltop amid hornbeam forest. There are three churches here; the southernmost is a triple-church basilica dating from the 5th–6th century, with a barrel vault and its original alabaster iconostasis. Immediately to its north is a tetraconch cruciform church with an octagonal dome, dating from the early 7th century (and modelled on the Jvari Church), and to the east is a smaller version of the same, also 7th century. There is supposedly a tunnel from here to Ikalto.

Families from Telavi often come to the lovely **Tetris Khlebi Waterfall** above Shuamta on the side of Mount Tsivgombori; it's a good spot for a picnic and a stroll, or even taking a ride on one of the horses for hire.

IKALTO Marshrutkas head west from Telavi every 15 minutes or so to Akhmeta and Alaverdi, all passing through the village of Ikalto, famed as the site of the academy at which the national poet Shota Rustaveli studied in the 12th century; students kept a jug of wine under their desks, to renew their inspiration as required. At km54/19 (8km west of Telavi) there's a signpost to the academy, 1.8km south up a good road along a valley. Halfway up you'll see the tiny chapel of St Stefane on the far left bank which, although open, is of no real interest. At the end of the asphalt you'll find the three churches and the ruins of the academy crammed together in a relatively small compound, beautifully set among cypress trees.

Ikalto was founded in the third quarter of the 6th century by St Zenon, one of the Assyrian Fathers who established Christianity in Georgia, but the main church is the 8th–9th-century **Church of the Transfiguration** (Gvtaeba), which is the oldest in Kakheti to have a central dome supported by four free-standing pillars. The belfry over the porch at the west end was added in the 19th century; its interior was whitewashed by the Russians, also in the 19th century, so there's little to see, although Zenon is buried to the right of the altar. To the east is the original 6th-century **Church of the Trinity** (Sameba), a small basilica with an odd interior plan, with apses off the side of the sanctuary, and steps to a chamber over the porch. In the northeastern corner of the complex is the 8th-century wine-press, with qvevris on the ground. Just to the south of the main church is the 7th-century **Kvelatsminda Church**, another bare, undecorated basilica, and behind it the ruins of the academy's **refectory**, built at the start of the 12th century and destroyed by Shah Abbas in 1616. The stone walls and window arches remain; Georgians find the ruins very moving because of the association with Rustaveli, but although they are doubtlessly 'romantic in the extreme', foreigners may find them of less interest.Immediately west of Ikalto (before the Alaverdi junction) is Atskuri, with the 10th–13th-century church of St George on a hill 2km south. The Khatoba Festival held here on 14 August retains pagan elements such as the sacrifice of sheep.

🏠 Where to stay, eat and drink

Turning south/left at km53.5 (right at km19.5 if heading towards Telavi), an asphalt road leads about 1km to an attractive, modern hotel owned by the Villa Ikalto winery (w *savaneti.com*) and two associated guesthouses. There's a couple of nice new restaurants along this stretch of road, too.

🏠 **Castle Tamarioni** m 790 102000. Similar to the Savineti, also with a good restaurant, a wine cellar & chacha distillery. **$$$$**

🏠 **Hotel Savineti** (36 rooms) m 790 102040. Just to the right of the Bazieri, 800m south of the Akhmeta road. Small but nicely presented rooms (but with huge leather sofas on the landing), with plenty of lights & power points; the bar-restaurant offers good food & wine (of course) & there's a swimming pool. **$$$$**

THE PANKISI VALLEY From the junction to Alaverdi (9km north) at km57/16, the main road continues for 16km (past Zemo Khodasheni and the modern Badagoni winery) to **Akhmeta** (28km from Telavi), a winemaking town of no particular importance (except as the birthplace of theatre director Sandro Akhmetili) near the point where the Alazani River emerges from the hills. There are two ATMs at a roundabout (km73/0) where taxis wait, just south of the bus station; a few hundred metres west on Kazbegi there's a tiny rectangular basilica on the right that dates from the 6th century.

Kvetera, a ruined town-fortress, lies hidden in the hills to the west of Akhmeta; 9km along the road to Tianeti, you should fork left on to the upper road, and left again after 2km. In another kilometre you'll find the fortress and its tiny jewel of an 11th-century church. Built of white tuff, with blue tiles, it has a most unusual semi-diamond-shaped ground plan, with four equal transepts and four smaller niches between them. Tianeti itself, on the upper Iori River, is a tranquil village set in the foothills of the Caucasus; it's surprisingly close to Tbilisi, which can be reached by a poor road to Gldani, in the northwestern suburbs; or you can continue to Zhinvali, on the Georgian Military Highway.

A road follows the Alazani north into the **Pankisi Valley**, home to Georgia's Kists, ethnic Chechens who settled here from the late 17th century to the early 19th century. The Kists are Muslim and are frequently accused, especially by Russia, of kidnapping and terrorism. There are Saudi-funded Wahabi mosques in the villages, and some local men, most notoriously Murad Margoshvili (aka Muslim al-Shishani) and Tarkhan Batirashvili (aka Umar al-Shishani), have joined the Chechen fighters in Syria; but the people are predominantly peaceful Sufis, and a new Sufi mosque is being built in Birkiani, and in fact this is really a very interesting and welcoming place to visit. It's much like the rest of Georgia but with ducks, turkeys and geese instead of pigs, and many women wearing headscarves; you need to take your shoes off before entering buildings. It's a great base for exploring into the mountains to the north, and it's even possible to hike to Tusheti.

From Akhmeta, marshrutkas and shared taxis (*both GEL2*) run via Duisi and Jokolo to Birkiani; from Ortachala in Tbilisi there are marshrutkas to Duisi at 07.30 and 14.20 (*returning 06.00 & 11.40; 3hrs; GEL10*), and others to Akhmeta at 10.00, 14.00, 17.00 and 19.00 (*GEL8*), while shared taxis from Tbilisi cost GEL12 to Akhmeta or Duisi. The valley's main festival is Pankisoba, usually in late July, although it took place in September of 2017.

The first villages in Pankisi are inhabited by Pshav people (who inhabited the whole valley until the Kists arrived), notably Matani, where there's an interesting disused cemetery and the Cholokashvili fortress (birthplace of Kakutsa Cholokashvili, who led anti-Soviet guerrillas until 1924). Pankisi's main village is **Duisi**, where there's a community centre with an ATM at the southern end and a small museum (300m south of km15/7; you'll need to get someone to call the curator). It's well worth timing a visit to be here for the female Sufi ceremony at the mosque on Fridays (from 11.00 to noon, as a rule) when they move in a circle, praying but not dancing. In **Jokolo**, 3km north, you can visit the mosque and church, as well as a felt-making school and some tiny waterwheels. The asphalt ends just north at km22/0 in Birkiani, and it's another 3km, through increasingly wild scenery, to the **Batsara Reserve**, a unique forest of yew trees, up to 25m high, 1.2m in diameter and 2,000 years old. Trails lead up to the lovely Batana Lake and on in to Tusheti, while a jeep track continues past a rarely open hotel near the Chinese-built Khadori hydro-electric station to a waterfall at the intake to the power station.

 Where to stay For accommodation in other villages, see w pankisi.org.

Guesthouse Melissa Duisi; m 591 012516; nataborcha@yahoo.com. 2 dbl rooms & a shared bathroom, & another lovely garden. **$$$**

Leila's Guesthouse Jokolo; m 551 232266. On the other side (to the west) of the shops & the Restaurant Pankisi (which opens only for booked events), this has rooms for 2, 3 & 5 & a lovely garden. English & Russian spoken. $$$

Nazy's Guesthouse Jokolo; e nazy@nazysguesthouse.com; w nazysguesthouse.com To the right past the church (1888) from the shops,

this is the best base in this area. Nazy speaks excellent English & is keen to give as much help & information as you might require. Laundry & bikes are available, as well as guides & horses for hiking & horseback expeditions into Tusheti. $$$

ALAVERDI Turning right at the junction 2.5km west of Ikalto, it's 9km north through the vineyards to the great **Cathedral of St George** (⊕ 08.00–18.00 daily) at Alaverdi, 20km from Telavi. From Akhmeta, it's 15km east from a junction off the Pankisi road to Kvemo Alvani, and then 3km south to Alaverdi. Founded by St Joseph, another of the Assyrian Fathers, the present church was raised in the early 11th century, one of the largest medieval churches built in Georgia. Built of *shirmi*, the tuff (or travertine) stone ubiquitous in Kakheti and Armenia, it was damaged by the Mongols (with repairs in brick in the late 15th century), by Shah Abbas in 1616, and again by an earthquake in 1742, after which it was restored by Erekle II. It was surrounded with defensive walls in the early 18th century, with the gate-tower added in the following century. From the destruction of the Bagrat Cathedral in Kutaisi in 1691–2 until the construction of Tbilisi's Sameba Cathedral in 1995–2004, this was the highest church in Georgia, its dome rising 50m from the ground. It's a triconch church, but with an ambulatory to the west as well, the north and south apses being incorporated into a rectangular plan.

The interior is pretty worn; frescoes from the 11th to 13th centuries and the 15th century were whitewashed by the Russians in the 19th century, and gradually uncovered and restored from 1967. They include St George over the outside of the west door, the Virgin and Child over the altar, and others in the south transept. There's supposedly a hand carved in relief on a flagstone to the left inside the entrance; the story goes that a local prince was captured by the Turks, and before being killed cut off his hand, so that it could be taken home and buried in holy ground. This is also the burial place of Queen Ketevan the Martyr, who was tortured to death by Shah Abbas in 1624. To the northwest of the church are the ruins of the Persian governor's summer palace, built in 1615, including a two-storey octagonal brick pavilion.

The Alaverdoba pilgrimage and folk festival lasts for two weeks from 14 September, the feast of the Exaltation of the Life-Giving Cross (relics of which were given by the Patriarch of Jerusalem to King Levan in the 16th century), and climaxes on 28 September, the feast of St Joseph of Alaverdi. Like several other Kakheti churches, Alaverdi was thoroughly renovated in 2010, with future plans to adapt the sacristy as a treasury to display the church's treasure of icons, vestments and manuscripts. It's also known for its very traditional **winery** (active since 1011; page 315), with a display plot of over 100 grape varieties right in front of the church. Across the road is a strictly non-smoking car park and the Matsoni House restaurant, specialising in natural local products such as matsoni, cheese and honey, and a toilet block to the north. Marshrutkas continue north to the village of Alaverdi and Kvemo Alvani, and return after half an hour, making this an easy excursion from Telavi (their signs mostly read 'Alaverdi' in Latin script). In the village you can stay at the Guesthouse Alaverdi (m 593 161635, 577 540541).

TUSHETI თუშეთი

The region of Tusheti was effectively autonomous as a tribal democracy until the end of the 17th century, and a road was not built here until 1978–82. Until the 1940s people here had a totally self-reliant life, growing enough wheat, hops and potatoes to keep them through the winter; they then tried to declare independence from the

Soviet Union but were crushed by the Red Army, the men being sent to the army or the gulag and the women and children deported to Alvani, since when they have lived a seasonally migratory life. The scenery is almost as spectacular as in Svaneti, with peaks up to 4,500m, deep gorges and high waterfalls, and well-preserved pine forests of *Pinus kochiana*. It's similar in many ways to Svaneti, with traditions of hospitality coupled with building spectacular defensive towers or *koshkebi*; but, unlike Svaneti, there were never any reports of robberies here. There's also plentiful evidence of the survival of animist religion here, with the horns of sacrificed goats or sheep placed on stone shrines or *khatebi* close to most villages – women are not permitted to approach these shrines (although photography from a distance is fine). Tusheti delicacies include *kotori*, a bread with a cheese and potato filling, the hard, dry *kalti* cheese, the smoked cottage cheese-style *dambal kacho* and very salty *gudiskweli* or *chogi* cheese, made of sheep's milk in a bag (*guda*) of sheepskin, with the wool on the inside. In 2017 the top prize at Slow Food's International Cheese Festival in Italy was won by a guda (not Gouda) cheese from Tusheti. Pork is forbidden in Tusheti – in fact local people won't eat it the day before they travel to Tusheti as it will still be in their gut.

The **Atingenoba Festival** is held in Tusheti 100 days after Easter, with bareback horse races and human pyramids; men brew *aludi* beer (dark, malty and not very strong) in sacred places where no mature women are allowed; in 2017 a brewery began to make beer all summer long, not just for festivals.

KVEMO ALVANI Just 3km beyond Alaverdi, on the far bank of the Alazani, is Kvemo (Lower) Alvani, a village which in summer is very quiet but in winter acts as home to the bulk of the population of Tusheti, with only about 20 people remaining there on the far side of the Caucasus watershed; the transhumance in late September or early October, when they drive their livestock over the pass and down to Kvemo Alvani and then to Shiraki and Vashlovani, is a fascinating sight. There's a couple of guesthouses in decent modern houses, Alvanis Veli (m *558 001070*; 🅕 *alvanisveli*) just south of the centre on the Alaverdi road, and Guesthouse Alvani (*Antsukhelidze 94*; m *599 708047*) just north of the centre. It's also the administrative centre for the Tusheti National Park [map, page 321] (w *tusheti.ge*), which comprises a total of 16,297ha in the Tushetis, Batcharis and Babaneuris reserves. The Babaneuris Reserve, just northeast of Kvemo Alvani (to the left at km47/82), has yews about 1,000 years old, from 950m to 1,350m altitude. The Tushetis Reserve (also to the north) protects possibly unique virgin forests of pine (2,000–2,200m) and birch (2,300–2,600m).

Although the national park is still relatively new, it has managed to support a number of guesthouses (*see* w *tusheti.ge*), and these are already doing fantastically well, with perhaps 10,000 visitors in 2017. Tours are available from Tbilisi for around US$100/ day, as well as hiking and horse-trekking trips of various durations. Local specialists include Caucasus Trekking Company (m *595 629927 (Apr–Oct)*, *599 728162; France* ☎ *+331 6947 2397 (all year)*, *+336 3378 0441 (Nov–Mar);* e *caucasustrek@msn.com;* w *caucasus-trek.com*), Tushetiland (m *557 488911;* w *tushetiland.ge*) and Tusheti Tour (m *593 744090, 568 647945;* e *sualak2013@gmail.com;* w *sualak2013.wordpress. com*). Devi Asmadiredja, based in Birkiani in Pankisi (e *deyazoye@googlemail.com;* w *deviadventure.wordpress.com*), is an inspiring Indonesian-German guide who specialises in custom and off-the-beaten-track adventures, including photography and horseriding trips, and in interaction with local communities, including working with local artisans, cooking and music lessons.

One particularly interesting project is the development of **ski-touring and snow-shoeing**, as Tusheti is virtually abandoned in winter (m *577 907272;* w *caucasus-trek*); you'll have to rent snowshoes in Tbilisi (or Gudauri).

OMALO A poor road, only passable from June to mid-October, and even then for 4x4s only, runs over the 2,927m Koja (or Abanos, meaning hot baths) Pass and down into Tusheti. At the roundabout in the centre of Kvemo Alvani, you'll find an ATM and local taxis, and 4x4 vehicles waiting for passengers to Omalo (*GEL200/vehicle, with up to 7 sharing*); there's no waiting place for vehicles returning from Omalo so you (or your guesthouse) will have to call around. Hotels in Telavi can also arrange transport to Omalo. In fact, Georgian hiking trips may use horses for almost the entire journey from Alvani, taking two days to reach Omalo, with a decent wild campsite halfway. There's talk of a 5km road tunnel from Pankisi to Tusheti, which would be a social and environmental disaster. A government-funded helicopter flies in to Omalo once a month in winter, serving the border guards and the very few elderly people who stay here in winter, but there's talk of flying every Tuesday from 2018/2019 and carrying tourists too.

The route turns off the road to Gremi and Lagodekhi in Pshaveli (km52/77), where drivers stock up on fresh bread at the junction; just a village, it is nevertheless the main settlement in Pshavi or land of the Pshavs, relatives of the Tushetians and Khevsurs living on the south side of the Caucasus watershed. The poet Vazha Pshavela ('son of Pshaveti') was born here and returned in the 1880s to live as a peasant. It takes 3–5 hours to cover the 70km from Pshaveli to Lower Omalo in a jeep, winding up from the mossy forest across bare eroded slopes to reach the pass, where there is supposedly a free Wi-Fi hotspot, after 2 hours; there's an easier descent to a ranger station at km52/20 and a bridge at km58/14, where there's the base of an old defensive tower and side tracks up to the hamlets of Khiso (to the right/east) and Shtrolta, Chiglaurta and Khakhabo (to the left). The track follows the Khisos Alazani River through the Chanchakhovani gorge to the turning to

Kumelaurta (to the right at km 64/8) and then switchbacks up to km67/5 and the left turn to the National Park Visitor Centre (named after US journalist and Clinton aide Brooke Shearer), where you can buy hiking maps (*GEL2*). It's not far to the new village of Kvemo (Lower) Omalo (1,890m), where the airstrip, boarding school and clinic sit on a plateau just above the Pirikiti Alazani; Zemo (Upper) Omalo, a cluster of fortified tower-houses at 2,070m, is high on the slope just to the north, near the 12th–13th-century citadel of Keselo, where you can visit a small ethnographic museum, and the Shalva Alkhanaidze photographic collection, thousands of images taken in Tusheti between 1927 and 1978, lost until 2005 and put on show here in 2017. It's not really a citadel, just six high towers (almost too well restored) with just a bit of low wall between them. Omalo is also the base of the OSCE (Organization for Security and Co-operation in Europe) monitors, ensuring that no Chechen fighters cross the border; Georgian frontier troops may check your passports.

Where to stay, eat and drink
As well as those listed, there's a free campsite near the National Park Visitor Centre. There are lots of new homestays and guesthouses, all much the same, but all full in July and August – be sure to book, or bring a tent. Late June and September are the best times to visit, as high summer now gets very hot.

Kvemo Omalo

Guesthouse Nazo (4 rooms; Natia Khvedaguridze) m 577 538582, 577 585929; e nkhvedaguridze@gmail.com; f. **$$$**

Elisabeth's Guesthouse (3 rooms; Elisabed Ichirauli) m 555 020171; e ichirauli@mail.ru. Horses & guide available for overnight trips. **$$**

Guesthouse Bukhurta (Eka Brarvaidze) m 593 579508; e nkindolauri@mail.ru. **$$**

Guesthouse Javakhe (9 rooms; Paata Arshaulidze) m 558 797222; e paataarshaulidze@gmail.com; f javakhe.tusheti. A big new 'hotel', friendly, some rooms en-suite (hot water only in evening). **$$**

Guesthouse Kamsuri (7 dbls; Gela Bakhturidze) m 595 54411, 558 758478; e tushiase@yahoo.com, gelabakhturidze@gmail.com. In the centre of Lower Omalo; 1 shared bathroom, dining room & sitting room with cable TV. **$$**

Guesthouse Keselo (6 dbls; Nani Arshaulidze) m 558 209901, 598 941270, 577 472111; e arshaulidze@gmail.com, nani_arshaulidze@yahoo.com. At the top of Lower Omalo, with lots of open space with a campfire; 2 shared bathrooms. **$$**

Guesthouse Old Omalo (8 rooms; Kakha Tatrulaidze) m 557 719777, 555 910077; e kaxa.tatrulaidze@gmail.com. Jeep & horse tours available. **$$**

Guesthouse Tevdore (6 rooms; Leila Kindolauri) m 593 531796. At the top of Lower Omalo, this also has a kiosk & sells tea, coffee & khachapuri. **$$**

Guesthouse Tusheti (6 dbls, 2 trpls; Vaja Shabalaidze); m 599 790092, 599 231132; e hoteltusheti@yahoo.com. Isolated (at km67/5 on the road from the Abanos Pass) & relatively flashy; no English spoken. **$$**

Guesthouse Tsasne (14 rooms; Muradi Ichirauli) m 557 127722. **$$**

Lali's Guesthouse (Lali Ichirauli) m 593 324841. **$$**

Hostel Tizhe (Eteri Markhvaidze) m 599 905337; e inga_chvritidze@mail.ru. This claims to be cheapest in Omalo. **$**

Mamuka Kindolauri (3 dbls, 1 trpl) m 593 323586, 599 313913, 593 531796. **$**

Green House Welcome Break (Levan Sulakauri) m 593 744090; e mr.sulakauri@mail.ru. At the south end of Lower Omalo, this has a camping area. **$**

Zurab Mouravidze (1 dbl, 2 trpls) m 598 540545, 598 252123; e mouravidze@gmail.com. **$**

Sakhavitse Meaning 'a place where khavitsi is made', this new café is dedicated to the Tushetian curd fondu (also known as datkhuri), made from milk from their own small herd of cows. They also sell aludi beer, traditionally only brewed for festivals but now available all summer. **$**

Zemo Omalo

For eating, Arbuzi, a rather boho bar (serving vegetarian food), the café at Guesthouse Shina, & a bakery next to the Guesthouse Lasharai are the only choices here.

🏠 **Guesthouse Lasharai** (7 dbls, 2 trpls; Vefkhia Rainauli) m 591 012621, 555 645254; e guesthouselasharai@yahoo.com; w guesthouselasharai.com. Comfortable new place at the top of the village square. **$$$**

🏠 **Guesthouse Shina** (6 dbls, 2 trpls; Sergo Meltsaidze) m 595 262046, 597 170707; e hotelshina@gmail.com; w shina.ge. Nice new guesthouse at the top of the village square; also a café serving pizza, khachapuri, & sandwiches. **$$$**

🏠 **Guesthouse Omalo 2005** (6 rooms; Micheil Othiuridze) m 599 672243, 599 293756. At the top of Upper Omalo, close to the citadel. **$$**

🏠 **Guesthouse Sargiri** (6 rooms; Vazha Kardlidze) m 599 775543, 555 300221; e fatimishidze2016@yahoo.com. **$$**

🏠 **Tushuri Koshki** ('Tusheti Tower'; 8 rooms; Nugzar Idoidze) m 599 110879, 593 769135, 599 067999; e nidoidze@yahoo.com. In a 5-storey 18th-century tower. **$$**

Elsewhere

🏠 **Hotel Loeli** (4 rooms) Shtrolta; m 555 715709, 599 218139; e hotelloeli@yahoo.com. A possible hiking destination,1.4km from the road to the Abanos Pass. **$$**

🏠 **Kekhi Guesthouse** (4 rooms) Khakhabo; m 557 143907; e gio.bakuridze@gmail.com. A bit further from the main road (& a shorter hike from Omalo). **$$**

HIKING IN TUSHETI Having got to Omalo, you can't drive much further (although the horse trails are gradually being converted to jeep tracks). Hiking, biking and horseriding (going as high as 2,900m) are necessary to see Tusheti's amazing scenery and very isolated settlements. Tusheti is defined by the gorges of the three branches of the Alazani River (the Khisos Alazani in the Chanchakhovani gorge, from the Abanos Pass; the Tushetis Alazani in the Tsovata and Gometsari gorges to the west; and the Pirikitis Alazani to Dartlo and Girevi, which meet below Omalo to form the Chaghma Gorge, below Shenako and Diklo, before flowing into Daghestan and ultimately the Caspian Sea. Trails follow the rivers in their higher courses, but nearer Omalo the trails are mostly high on the mountain ridges. Hiking signs have recently been installed by the Czech Development Agency, which has also fitted solar panels and thermal batteries in many villages.

An easy day walk leads east to Shenako and Diklo – a path marked with red stripes leads past the barn-like church of Upper Omalo and down to Lower Omalo (1.5km; 20 minutes down/30 minutes up), from where a jeep track continues across the plateau and drops down to the left into the Pirikitis Alazanis gorge from a sign describing the Tushetian dog rose (*Rosa tuschetica*) and other local endemics. It takes 30 minutes (following yellow stripe markings) down to a bridge and 20 minutes up to a sign at Tatikboseltana (1,740m), 4.5km from Lower Omalo. From here the yellow stripes continue on the jeep track to Shenako (2.5km) and red stripes mark a narrow path along a steep slope to the abandoned village of Ageurta (2km; 30 minutes) and on by a disused quarry road (1.5km; 20 minutes) to **Shenako** at 1,920m. This small village is slightly more picturesque than Lower Omalo and seems slightly Nepali, with its enclosed balconies; it's known for its 16th-century church, the only old one in Tusheti, sitting on the hilltop at the top of the village (women are not allowed on the direct path to the church). It has a dome and an apse but no real nave, and two open aisles on the exterior. From here the track drops and climbs steeply across a valley; at the top the yellow stripes continue along the track to Diklo (4km; 1 hour from Shenako) while the red stripes mark a path to the right, also to Diklo (6km; 1 hour 50 minutes). Staying on the track, this climbs slightly to reach a sign (at Chatekhiltana, 2,120m) after 20 minutes, the junction of a path west to Chigho (8km; 3 hours 30 minutes) and Dartlo (16km; 6 hours; see below) – it crosses the Diklo or Sonekhi Pass (2,560m) and drops down to 1,750m and up to Chigho (2,400m). It's just a bit too long (32km) and difficult (hugging the edge of a vertiginous cliff, at times only 50cm wide) to make a day hike back to Omalo by this route, alas. It's another 10 minutes to **Diklo** (2,150m), visible on the col ahead, from where a path continues for 3km to Dzveli (Old) Diklo, a ruined fortress on a spectacular cliff above the Tushetis Alazani River, and on into Dagshestan (closed, of course). Diklo was attacked by the Daghestani leader Shamil in 1838 and abandoned for the next 13 years. The WWF is funding an ecotourism project, providing alternative energy sources to boost tourism, and other sustainable sources of income, such as making honey and carpets using natural dyes and the wool of the aboriginal Tusheti mountain sheep. There are festivals here on 20 July and 10 August.

To loop back on the path marked with red stripes, swing left past the animist shrines to a simple cemetery with picnic tables and information signs, then climb over a low ridge and follow the path along the slope (high above the river) to a clearing with a ruined hut and over another low ridge, dropping and continuing along the slope to reach a water tank after an hour; from here there's a short steep climb until you see Shenako and keep right to rejoin the track above a boggy patch. From Shenako it's 7km back to Lower Omalo, if you stick to the jeep track.

Other fairly easy hikes from Lower Omalo head west to Khakhabo (4km, marked with red stripes), Chiglaurta and Shtrolta, perched above the road to the Abanos Pass (page 321), and south to the lovely Oreti Lake at just over 3,000m (you'll need a guide for this one); the two can be linked in a three-day hike via Khiso.

The much longer multi-day hikes to the northwest leave from Upper Omalo, to the right of the Keselo citadel – it takes 5 minutes to a col, then the jeep track curves to the right while red stripe markings show a short-cut path down to a clearing called Kue (1,980m; 20 minutes from the col), where the track splits. To the right one branch (marked with red stripes) crosses the valley and heads for the Ghele pass (3km; 1 hour), from where you can drop steeply down to the Pirikitis Alazani valley (1,750m) and back up to **Chigho** (2,400m), known for its pagan festival of Lasharoba, 100 days after easter, when a ram is sacrificed 100 days after Easter, honouring the spirit of war. Halfway up to Chigho you'll meet the narrow path to Diklo and Shenako (pages 323–4). Alternatively, a jeep track continues from Ghele up the Pirikitis Alazani for 10km to **Dartlo** (1,990m; 11km, 3½ hours from Upper Omalo), the second most-important village of Tusheti, but it's nicer to take the path on the left/north bank from Chigho. The World Bank has funded a project here to restore (perhaps excessively) Dartlo's 30-odd towers and houses with typical wooden balconies; other villages have been neglected but should soon be fixed up, and perhaps more sensitively. There are also accommodation options (see opposite); and jeep tours are run by Levan Pataraia (**m** 599 681661).

The main hazard in the Diklo–Chigho–Dartlo area is the fierce sheepdogs guarding the flocks – shepherds will call them off, but the key rules are not to walk through the flocks, not to seem afraid and to pick up stones (or even pretend to), and to sit down if pressed; at the National Park visitor centre outside Omalo you can buy a map showing the potential locations of sheepdogs.

Above Dartlo is **Kvavlo**, with a beautiful tower with a tetrahedral roof. There are more towers, and shrines to those drowned in the river, as the trail continues west up the Pirikiti Alazani past Chesho and further into the mountains. Just up a side-valley to the north is **Parsma** (1,960m, with fine medieval towers, also with pyramidal tops, and houses linked as a virtual fort); continue up the valley to reach the village of Girevi, just 11km south of the Chechen border, where there's a border police checkpoint.

Most hikers will return to Omalo, but it is possible to continue from Girevi by a long, tough trail to Khevsureti – allow five days for the 70km from Omalo to Shatili. This follows the upper Pirikiti Alazani and then the Kvakhidistqali through Chontio and virtually abandoned settlements such as Baso and Hegho, before the tough climb on scree to the **Atsunta Pass** (the highest in Georgia at 3,431m; closed early October–March), between Tebulos (4,493m, the highest peak of Tusheti) to the north and Amugo (3,839m) to the south. This is an unpopulated region, but as you camp in alpine meadows you may come across the occasional shepherd. Descending into the Andaki Gorge and heading northwest through Ardoti, you'll eventually reach **Mutso**, the first Khevsur village, from where a rough track leads virtually to the border and then south to **Shatili** (page 194). The route is well enough marked now, so there's no need for a guide, but don't forget your passport. There's a jeep track to Girevi (a driver will probabaly charge cGEL100); in summer there's quite a bit of traffic as far as Dartlo, but it's peaceful enough from there to Girevi.

The other option from Kue (marked with yellow stripes) stays on the north side of the Gometsari valley, reaching Mirgvela (*3km; 45mins*), where there's a guesthouse, and **Bochorma** (2,345m), 4km further, which is officially the highest populated village in Europe because one 76-year-old man lives there year-round; he's the local doctor and makes his house-calls on horseback. There's accommodation in the next village, Dochu, from where you can drop down to the river and loop back to the south to return to Omalo via a 2,570m pass; alternatively, from Mirgvela there's a lower track to Lower Omalo. Beyond here the Gometsari and Tsovata valleys are the least populated part of Tusheti, with little formal accommodation and no phone signal; there are also 18th-century tombs in which plague victims are said to have voluntarily shut themselves up. A jeep track now extends as far as Verkhovani (23km from Omalo), from where you can hike across the Nakaicho Pass (2,903m, with great views to the north) north into the Pirikiti Alazani valley east of Girevi. With a guide you could follow the unpopulated Tushetis Alazani valley southwest and then make the three-day crossing to Pankisi; or returning to Omalo, you could take a lovely forested path (marked with red stripes) on the south side of the valley through the hamlets of Iliurta, Bukhurta and Gogrulta.

Finally, from Kue, there's also a 10-minute walk east to a good new viewpoint over the Pirikitis Alazani gorge towards Shenako, where you might supposedly see some of the 100 last bezoar goats in Tusheti (although the population is recovering). From here an unmarked path climbs back up to the jeep track at km0/72 (the official start of the Abanos Pass road); you can bypass Upper Omalo and follow the road past a clifftop viewpoint to return directly to Lower Omalo.

Where to stay, eat and drink

Dartlo

Guesthouse Samtsikhe (11 rooms; Beso Elanidze) m 599 118993, 599 785302; e bes.el@ posta.ge. 8 dbls & 3 trpls with shared bathrooms, & extra beds in neighbouring houses; also café & craft sales. **$$**

Hotel Dartlo (13 rooms; Mariam Otiuridze) m 598 174966, 598 246405; w dartlo.ge. At the top of the village. **$$$**

Diklo

Gia & Nino m 599 775372, 551 133593. **$$**

Dochu

Guesthouse Kruiskari (6 rooms; Usupi Torgvaidze) m 599 285647; e hotelkruiskari@ yahoo.com. 1 dbl with en suite, 2 trpls with shared bathroom. **$$**

Girevi
🏠 **Guesthouse Nakudurta** m 599 334465. **$$**

Mirgvela
🏠 **Guesthouse Mirgvela** (8 rooms;
Vaja Itiuridze) m 599 636103, 597 066000;
e mirgvela@yahoo.com. **$$**

Shenako
🏠 **Nino Sekhniashvili** (6 rooms) m 558
639722, 593 173708. **$$$**
🏠 **Guesthouse Old Tusheti** (Eldar Bukvaidze)
m 558 272006; e gocha_tel@yahoo.com. **$$**

🏠 **Guesthouse Shenaqo-Veranda** m 599
400159. Guesthouse & fast food, in the pines off
the Omalo road. **$$**
🏠 **Guesthouse Your Home** m 599 102944.
At the top of the village by the church. **$$**
🏠 **Irodi Bukvaidze** (3 dbls, 1 trpl, 1 sgl)
m 558 639722, 577 101876; e hotelshenaqo@
yahoo.com. **$$**
🏠 **Nino & Zao Jijuridze** m 599 001915.
Excellent food, especially their cheese. **$$**
🏠 **Shenako Guesthouse** (3 rooms) m Elene
Gagoidze 599 481812, Erekle Bukvaidze 599
481812; e hotelshenako@yahoo.com. **$$**

EAST OF TELAVI: FROM GREMI TO KVARELI AND LAGODEKHI

NAPAREULI, GREMI AND NEKRESI Alvani lies on the road along the left/north bank of the Alazani, from Akhmeta to the Azerbaijani border. Heading east, it passes through **Napareuli** (km59/70), a village known for the Twins Wine Cellar (❨ *322 728141;* m *551 747474, 557 148282;* w *cellar.ge*), the first modern qvevri winery, founded in 1994; they also have a hotel-restaurant and a wine museum (see box, page 316).

After a junction from Telavi (11km south) the road reaches **Gremi**. It's now little more than a pleasant village (known for its brandy), but there was a city here by the 6th century AD, and it was the capital of Kakheti from 1466 until 1616, when it was utterly destroyed by Shah Abbas. High on a rocky ledge at the west end of the village (with good steps leading up from the main road), a few crumbling ruins remain of the fort, built in 1565, and the palace and three-storey tower, built of red brick on stone blocks. The dome church is in great condition; it was built in 1565, with paintings completed in 1577, and reconsecrated in 1989. Along with the tower at Ninotsminda, the **citadel of Gremi** is the best example of Georgian adaptation of Persian styles of architecture, such as patterned brickwork (ie: arches in relief). There's a poor museum (⊕ *10.00–18.00 Tue–Sun; GEL3*) by the church displaying ceramics, spear- and arrowheads and various implements; it's worth paying for if only as a way to get the church opened and go up the tower, which gives great views to the Caucasus. They also have a shop and they'll lay on a tour to Nekresi for US$3. The real museum (⊕ *10.00–18.00 Tue–Sun; GEL3*) is below the church to the west, by the main road (through an underpass from the car park/toilets), and displays ceramics from the 4th and 3rd millennia BC to the 14th century AD, bronze daggers from the 12th to 7th centuries BC, and has useful information in English on the area that was covered by the capital. Nearby are two small churches (just on the west side of the hill) and the foundations of a caravanserai and covered market, all built in the 15th and 16th centuries and being restored; there is also a replica of a two-domed bathhouse that was across the road. Beyond a café (and Monastic Hotel) is an Armenian church of mixed brick and stone, with a typical raised altar.

Marshrutkas from Telavi (towards Kvareli and Lagodekhi) run via Eniseli, immediately beyond Gremi, where the Château Eniseli-Bagrationi winery (w *eniselibagrationi.ge*), founded in 1887, includes a six-room hotel (see opposite). Also in Gremi is a winery at a social enterprise for socially vulnerable people, Temi Community (m *591 633633;* w *temi-community.org;* ⊕ *07.00–21.00 daily*); call them ahead to visit the marani and taste their organic Saperavi, Rkatsiteli and chacha, or to rent bikes.

At km85.5, 9km east of Gremi, a rough road (you can take a shuttle bus for GEL3) leads 3km up into the hills to the left/north to **Nekresi**, site of one of the oldest churches in Georgia, a little basilica dating from the third quarter of the 4th century, when palace ruins were also converted to a marani. Inscriptions found here are claimed to date from the 1st to the 3rd centuries AD, making them the earliest examples of the Georgian alphabet. In the 6th century this monastery was the base of the Assyrian Father Abibos, who was martyred by the Persians after pouring water on a Zoroastrian sacred fire; in the next century a three-church basilica, perhaps the finest example of the genre, was added (and painted in the 16th century), followed in the 8th and 9th centuries by a bishop's palace (with a tower added in the 16th century), and a cruciform church, by the present entrance. Frequently raided by the Lesghians, it was finally destroyed in the 18th century. This is the only place in Georgia where pigs are still sacrificed, because a Persian army was driven away by rolling pigs' heads down the hill at them.

🏠 Where to stay, eat and drink

🏠 **Hotel Château Eniseli-Bagrationi** (6 rooms) Eniseli; w eniselibagrationi.ge; m 577 624648; 🆕 chateau.eniseli. A very comfortable base for oenophiles (a tour of the vineyard & winery is included), with a terrace, garden & restaurant. **$$$**

🏠 **Lake Lopota Resort** Just north of Napareuli from about km62; 📞 322 400400; m 591 700777; w lopota.ge. Lake Lopota started the trend of luxury resorts in the Kakhetian foothills & has tennis & mini golf facilities, bikes, pedalos, a spa, 3 swimming pools & of course fancy bars & restaurants. **$$$$**

🏠 **Guesthouse Gremi** Gremi; m 579 948895. **$$**

🏠 **Guesthouse Nona** Shilda, just east of Gremi at km80; m 599 979838, 599 060059. English-speaking. **$$**

KVARELI (*Telephone code 352*) Continuing eastwards from Gremi for half an hour, you'll come to Kvareli, a small town (home of the Kindzmarauli and Khareba wineries), which has become an upmarket tourist spot since President Saakashvili bought a house on one of the lakes here (he was probably also responsible for the cycle tracks that no-one uses). Marshrutkas from Ortachala in Tbilisi come to Kvareli via Gurjaani every 30 minutes (*08.00–18.00; GEL8*); from Telavi marshrutkas run every 40 minutes (*09.30–17.30; GEL3*). From the highway junction (km92) the tree-lined Chavchavadze Avenue leads north for 2km, through the town to the marshrutka terminal on Gogebashvili; returning south for about 200m you'll see the Church of St John the Baptist to the right, with the helpful **tourist office** (*Rustaveli 8;* 📞 *352 221340/50;* e *tickvareli@gmail.com;* 🕐 *10.00–18.00, summer until 19.00*) hidden behind it. There's an ATM on the main square and another at Bank Republic opposite the Koté Marjanishvili museum.

🏠 Where to stay, eat and drink
In addition to the places listed, there are also guesthouses in town, such as Iva Kuprashvili (*Rustaveli 12;* m *592 122438;* **$$**), Liana Baidashvili (*Leist 33A;* 📞 *352 220955;* m *593 758458;* **$$**) and Salome Varamishvili (*Marjanishvili 53;* 📞 *352 220989;* m *593 173425;* **$$**). There are few places to eat in town other than the hotels: the Yard of Wine (m *599 458955;* e *yardofwine@gmail.com;* **$$**), up against the fort walls behind the Château Kvareli, is an entertaining option.

In town
🏠 **Château Kvareli** (26 rooms) Kudigora 1; m 790 924090, 599 466595; w chateaukvareli. ge. The best hotel in town, on the south side of the square near the fort. Above its huge lobby are comfortable rooms & there's a good restaurant (**$$$**). Free winery tours are offered to guests, at Kindzmareuli Corporation (see box, page 315). **$$$$**

Villa Guesthouse Davit Agmashenebelis 27; m 558 373206, 514 150404. The first of a group of guesthouses on the road east to Kvareli Lake; bikes can be rented here. $$$

Guesthouse Kora Chavchavadze, 3rd lane; m 577 227715, 595 395844. $$

Hostel Qvareli Inn Kudigora 1A; m 599 466595; **f** Kvarelilnn. At the rear of the Château Kvareli is a hostel with dorms (some en suite) with triple-decker bunks, deep new mattresses & a kitchen with hot plates but no pans or cutlery. $$

Hotel-Restoran Shua Kalakshi Tsereteli 7; ✆352 221446; m 557 406633, 514 043838; e eka. elo@mail.ru. New, smallish but grandiose. $$

Kavkasioni Chavchavadze 32; ✆352 221751; m 598 383412; e todadze.e@mail.ru. A long way south, a newish but drab place. $$

Outside Kvareli

Kvareli Lake Resort (19 rooms) 7km east along Davit Agmashenebelis from the centre; ✆322 303030; w kvarelilakeresort.ge. Rooms

here have panoramic views. Food not as good as at other hotels. $$$$$

Royal Batoni Hotel (31 rooms) m 595 996611, 595 996600; w batoni.ge. Part of the Ilia Lake complex, built in 2011 in the Duruji Gorge (known for its healthy populations of raptors), across the river just west of Kvareli but 7km by road (turning off the main road west at km87). This castle-like hotel is kitschy but comfortable, with a terrace & infinity pool overlooking the lake. Rooms have wonderful mountain views & stylish bathrooms with transparent walls (& curtains, thankfully). $$$$$

Kvareli Eden Hotel & Wine Spa Davit Agmashenebelis 78A; ✆322 97 0165; m 577 600303; w kvarelieden.ge. Nearer town (but still set in vineyards) this is a striking Mediterranean-style building with a luxurious (& very expensive) spa, where you can soak in a copper tub filled with wine, in addition to the usual steam rooms, massages & aromatherapy; there's also a bowling alley. $$$$

What to see and do Hidden under the tourist office is the National Bank's **Money Museum** (⊕ 09.00–13.00 & 14.00–18.00 Mon–Fri; free). This exhibits Georgian coins dating as far back as the 6th century BC (from Vani), a stater issued by Alexander the Great in the 4th century BC, Roman denarii, Parthian coins, 8th-century Arabian coins minted in Tbilisi, 11th-century Bagratid coins from Georgia, irregularly shaped copper coins issued by Tamar, then more from 13th- to 18th-century Georgia, 16th-century Venetian gold ducats, and Austrian and Polish thalers. It ends with roubles issued by the Transcaucasian Federation and the USSR, coupons issued in 1993–94, and finally a colourful display of modern notes, from Europe, Iraq (Saddam), Iran (Khomeini), Israel, the Central Asian 'stans', Asia, the Antipodes, the USA and (very nice) Madagascar.

Just to the right, at Rustaveli 13, is the **house-museum of theatre director Koté Marjanishvili** (1872–1933), which opens slightly erratically (⊕ in theory 10.00–18.00 Tue–Sun; GEL3); actually two nicely restored houses, it displays his personal effects, photos and theatre posters and has a fine garden with sculptures.

Opposite the tourist office and church is a white building like a Corbusier chapel; built in 1978, this is the **house-museum of Ilia Chavchavadze** (1837–1907) (⊕ 10.00–17.00 exc Mon; GEL0.50), the editor of popular newspaper *Iveria*, founder of critical realism in Georgian literature, and creator of Georgian theatre, translating Molière and Gogol and introducing the plays of Shakespeare. He also reformed the alphabet, and became a deputy in the Russian duma or parliament. As leader of the moderate reformist and nationalist tendency, he was officially declared a secular saint after his murder by either tsarist or Bolshevik agents – just who is disputed, and both seem to have had an interest in removing him. The Iliaoba Festival is held on 8 November on Ilias Gora, a hill (on the northeastern edge of town) with the country's largest statue of him, which is a popular picnic spot. In the garden behind the museum is the defensive tower in which he was born in 1837 while the family hid from an attack by Lesghian tribesmen – this is seen as deeply symbolic, as he spent his life defending Georgian culture. Beyond the tower is the 17th-century house in which he lived until the age of 11; most striking is the huge marani wine cellar with 40 qvevris, and two limewood wine presses, one for Saperavi grapes and one for Rkatsiteli.

About 500m to the south of the tourist office and church on Chavchavadze, the remains of an 18th-century **fort** rise to the right beyond the Public Service Hall, which looks like a small glass tower with a couple of gigantic white bras draped over it; the square of walls, with seven towers, is intact, but inside there's only a football pitch, visible through a gate on the north side.

The **Kindzmarauli Wine House** (*signed in English; Chavchavadze 55;* m *790 100061; 595 330433;* e *office@kindzmarauli.ge;* w *kindzmaraulicorporation.ge;* ⊕ *09.00–18.00 daily*) is about 200m south of the main square. Tastings cost GEL2/ glass, and you can buy wine from GEL10; its history dates back to the establishment of a royal castle and wine cellar here in 1533.

The **Khareba Winery** (w *winery-khareba.com*), across the river to the east (go back to the main road, turn left to cross the bridge, left on to the Lagodekhi road and at once left again) is famous for its 8km ex-military tunnels (at a constant 14°C), 3km of which is now in use for wine storage. They do good tours (*GEL5*) and tastings in fluent English (*from GEL12*) and you can eat at the Restaurant Saperavi ($$$), with good views, very cheap wine but not so good service.

LAGODEKHI (*Telephone code 335*) From Kvareli you have the choice of returning by a direct road (17km) to Mukuzani, or continuing through vineyards for 41km to Lagodekhi, set on a plateau between forested hills on the border with Azerbaijan; the junction is at km93/36, a few hundred metres to the east of the Kvareli junction (beyond the bridge). Coming from Tbilisi or Sighnaghi, the road crosses the Alazani Wetlands, mainly marshy, seasonally flooded woods with good birdwatching; the road from Kvareli joins this road at km129/0, a few kilometres west of Lagodekhi. There are marshrutkas from Kvareli (*hourly; GEL4*); from Telavi (*5/day; GEL7; or change at Kvareli*); and from Isani metro station in Tbilisi via Tsnori (*at least hourly 08.00–18.15, last to Tbilisi at 17.30; GEL8*); shared taxis from Isani cost just GEL10. These arrive at the bus station at the corner of St Nino and the main road, Zakatala.

⌂ **Where to stay, eat and drink** A few places to eat can be found along the main road (*Zakatala*), where there is also a small market and a couple of ATMs. There's camping space at several guesthouses and at the Protected Areas administration (page 330).

Hotels

⌂ **Chateau Bruale** (7 rooms) Tkhilistskaro; m 592 951370; w chateaubruale.net. Midway between Kvareli & Lagodekhi, this is a charming new hotel & winery (also producing hazelnuts!) with a beautiful garden. $$$

⌂ **Waldhotel** (6 rooms) Vashlovani 197; m 593 839983; e waldhotellagodekhi@gmail. com; f waldhotellagodekh. To the left inside the gate to the Protected Areas administration, this is the nicest hotel here, open all year, with 1 room with disabled facilities plus camping space

nearby. The Enpard Terrace (named after the EU's agricultural co-op scheme) is a nice cafeteria-pizzeria ($$). $$$

⌂ **Hotel Hereti** (14 rooms) Kostava 15; m 591 111211, 593 280502. Head uphill on St Nino & take the 1st left for 1 block to the main square to find this basic hotel, which looks pretty dysfunctional from the outside but has tolerable rooms. $$

⌂ **Hotel-Restaurant Lagodekhi** (13 rooms) m 555 543802. Opposite the Hereti, this is more a restaurant than a hotel. $$

Homestays

⌂ **Kiwi House** (6 rooms) Vashlovani 35; m 557 427819, 551 245072, 557 499489; e thekiwihouse.lagodekhi@gmail.com. Known in Georgian as Kivis Sakhli, there's nothing Antipodean here (despite the name); they just grow kiwi fruit where other Georgians have a grape vine. Miriam and her son speak some English & are very hospitable. Has dbl & trpl rooms, some with mini-kitchen, & a garden with barbecue pit & camping space; they're adding more rooms with a bar & terrace on top. **$$$**

⌂ **Gardenia** Vashlovani 127; m 551 550500, 599 457500. An old family house with a few renovated rooms, a huge balcony & qvevri in the marani. Great food; camping space & hammocks in the garden. **$$**

⌂ **Guesthouse Vashlovani** (6 rooms) Vashlovani 92; m 599 856657. Solid modern building with garden & good food. **$$**

⌂ **Hotel Bio-Yard** (10 rooms) Vashlovani 167; m 595 293945, 595 767799. Organic food,

camping space & swimming pool; also home to Blues Village, with mini-festivals every w/end in summer. **$$**

⌂ **La Deka** Janelidze 6, 577 384384, 551 501967. Nice new place with great food & friendly hosts, a block west of Vashlovani; garden with hammocks, rooms with private bathrooms. **$$**

⌂ **Lago** (5 rooms) Zakatala 63; m 899 349932; e hotel_lago@yahoo.com. 4 blocks from St Nino on the main road, just east of the centre; an unassuming bare-brick house with swimming pool, barbecue, table tennis & marani. **$$**

⌂ **Lile** (11 rooms) Davit Agmashenebelis 93; ☎254 25988; m 599 580963. Friendly homestay. 1 block east of Vashlovani – head north from the bus station, go past the sports ground, keeping it on your left, & you will see it on the left after a 20min gentle uphill walk (there's a side gate to the park at the top of the road). Rates inc meals. **$$**

⌂ **Robinson Crusoe** Davit Agmashenebelis 107; m 599 398832. Recently renovated, with lavish food & homemade wine. **$$**

What to see and do The local museum at Vashlovani 30 (*above No 35, oddly;* ⏱ *10.00–18.00 Tue–Sun; GEL1*) has reopened after EU-funded refurbishment; there's a simply awful display of religious embroidery, then a decent archaeological collection including eneolithic (Copper Age) stone blades and an early Bronze Age clay bowl from the 4th millennium BC, a stone handmill, an antler ploughshare, some unlabelled jewellery, and Hellenistic pots from the 1st and 2nd centuries BC. The ethnographic collection includes metal pots and trays, guns and daggers, local costumes, snowshoes and farming equipment.

Bikes can be rented at Zakatala 12, just west of the centre.

AROUND LAGODEKHI Very strong tobacco is grown in the Lagodekhi area (as well as kiwi fruit and peanuts), but immediately to the north the mountains rise very steeply to the Caucasus watershed, and it's just a few kilometres to the wild and largely untouched **Lagodekhi National Park** (w *apa.gov.ge*). The first national park in the Caucasus, it was founded in 1912 by a Polish general in the Tsarist army, on the basis of Prince Demidov's hunting reserve, with forests of chestnut and hornbeam, plus red and roe deer, wolves, bear, lynx, chamois and tur. Red deer numbers dropped from 750 in the 1980s to 150 in 2003 due to poaching, but are over 300 again. Bearded vultures (lammergeier) live here all year, and griffon and cinereous vultures are here from May to September, plus Egyptian vultures passing through on migration. It covers 17,932ha (from 400m to 3,500m), but borders the Zakatala Nature Reserve (in Azerbaijan) and the Tliarata Federal Sanctuary (in Daghestan), so the total protected area is considerable; entry is allowed only to the lowest part, but even a short walk from town soon takes you into fantastically unspoilt forest. It's 1.5km up from the main road to the Protected Area headquarters at the edge of the forest (*Vashlovani 197;* m *577 101845;* e *gsulamanidze@apa.gov.ge*), which can provide detailed maps and rent tents (*GEL10/day*) and horses (*GEL50/day*), as well as taking bookings for overnight shelters (*GEL15*). You can register here if staying overnight in the park, but you'll need to take your passport in any case. There are plenty of information boards and waymarked trails, including the short nature interpretation loop for families with 12 information boards. The Black Grouse Waterfall Trail (*9.5km; 4–5hrs; marked with yellow and black stripes*) leads up the Shromoskhevi Valley and back the same way, with 12 interpretative stations. The flagship route is to Shavi Kldeebis Tba (Black Rock Lake), straddling the border with Daghestan (48km, 3 days, late May–early Oct); you spend the first day largely in forest climbing from 567m at the visitor centre to 1,936m at the Meteo shelter (11.5km), where there's a spring; there's room for 16 inside, and camping outside. The trail is marked with red stripes, and is open to horses too. From here you're hiking in stunning alpine terrain, past the border police checkpoint (2,650m) to the lovely lake (2,780m, 12.5km from the Meteo shelter). A new overnight shelter was constructed in 2016 so instead of returning the same way it;'s now possible to loop back to the west, via the peak of Kaputsikh (2,176m) and down to the visitor centre.

The Ninoskhevi or Great Waterfall trail starts from the village of Gurgeniani, about 7km northwest of Lagodekhi, and is a beautiful day hike (*8.5km; 4–6hrs*) to the lovely 40m-high waterfall. There's also a trail between Matsimi (3km east of Lagodekhi) and Machis Tsikhe (Machi Castle) on the Azerbaijan border, which runs through hornbeam forest for about an hour to a border police post (don't forget your passport; Azerbaijan starts at the river to the right), and on to the ruins of the 5th-/6th-century castle, destroyed in the 17th century. Return the same way; it's 5km each way, taking 4–5 hours.

SIGHNAGHI AND BEYOND *Telephone code 355*

From the Lagodekhi border, the A302 heads south across the Alazani to the junction with the Telavi road 103km from Tbilisi, and 50km from Lagodekhi. The main attraction along this road is the walled city of **Sighnaghi**. High on a ridge, with stunning views across the Alazani Valley to the Caucasus, Sighnaghi was ringed by a 4.5km wall and 28 towers in 1772 by Erekle II (who settled Armenians and Imeretians here to make this a trading centre on the Silk Road). They surround a remarkably large area with a small town at its centre. With its cypress trees and fine 18th- and 19th-century buildings, it's reminiscent of an Italian hill town, featuring a cascade of piazzas: Solomon Dedashvili Square at the top; Davit Agmashenebelis in the middle by the town hall; and Erekle II at the bottom. This was more or less the first town to be identified by the Saakashvili government as a future tourism hotspot and underwent extensive renovation in 2007. Sighnaghi became just a bit too pristine for its own good and, somehow, just a bit soulless, but it has weathered and mellowed a little since then; it is particularly attractive at night when the town's balconies are beautifully illuminated. Branded as 'The City of Love', its wedding palace was to be open 24 hours a day to attract Georgian wedding parties as much as foreigners; this may not have worked, but some excellent hotels and restaurants are attracting plenty of visitors and the town has become a compulsory stop on most itineraries.

GETTING THERE AND AWAY From Lagodekhi, the junction to Sighnaghi is on a hairpin bend at the south end of Anaga, at km110.5 (49.5km from the border). It's 6km of hairpins (despite the 4km sign) up to the town, with a lovely new surface; however, there's little traffic so if you're in a hurry it's better to get off the marshrutka in Tsnori (km117.5/42.5, where the famous gold lion, made in 2300–2000BC and

SIGHNAGHI

↗ *Anaga*

City wall

Knowledge Café, Tsnori →

Bodbe Nunnery, Lost Ridge Inn,
↓ Living Roots Ranch, Tbilisi

N

Bradt

0 ————— 200m
0 ————— 200yds

For listings, see pages 333–4

Where to stay

1	Abramichi Guest House	5	Hotel Crown	9	Hotel Signagi
2	Brigitte	6	Hotel Kabadoni	10	Nana Kokiashvili
3	Galvanis Kari	7	Hotel Old Sighnaghi	11	Nato & Lado's Guesthouse
4	Guest House Central	8	Hotel Pirosmani	12	Zandarashvili Guesthouse

Where to eat and drink

13	Art Café Qedeli	16	Okro's Wines	***Off map***
14	Natakhtari	17	Pheasant's Tears	Knowledge Café
15	Nikala		Shio's (see 5)	

now in the National Museum, was found in a kurgan or burial mound) and change to a marshrutka, taxi (*GEL10, or GEL3 shared*) or a shared taxi, waiting at the junction about 300m west.

Sighnaghi is more commonly reached from the Tbilisi direction, turning off at Chalaubani km94.5, by a petrol station and police checkpoint. The road passes a weird monument at km9/12, and beyond Nukriani, after which you soon have a view of Bodbe Church.

Marshrutkas (*GEL6*) leave six times a day from Tbilisi's Samgori metro station (also calling at Isani) and take 90 minutes, so a day trip from the capital is possible.

Taxis wait at the top and bottom of the piazzas, while marshrutkas leave from a large yard (with a ticket kiosk and toilets) behind the police station, across the road from the tourist information centre. Departures are at 07.00, 09.00, 11.00, 13.00, 16.00 and 18.00 to Tbilisi, at 09.00 to Telavi (returning at 15.00) and every 30 minutes from 09.45 to 16.45 and at 17.30 to Tsnori. The Bodbe services (6/day) go to the village, not the nunnery.

↑ WHERE TO STAY *Map, opposite*

In addition to those below, there are a dozen or so more guesthouses in town.

Hotels

Hotel Kabadoni (21 rooms) Tamar Mepe 1; 322 240400; w kabadoni.ge. Excellent by any standards, from the friendly welcome in perfect English to the huge suites, restaurant, wine-bar, 2 terraces & the spa with saunas, gym & swimming pool. **$$$$$**

Hotel Signagi (14 rooms) Chavchavadze 1; 355 231002; m 595 960770; e hotelsignagi@yahoo.com. Formerly the Hotel Nugo, this has been renovated but still seems a bit functional. Fantastic location with views on 3 sides, comfortable rooms with TV & bath. **$$$$**

Hotel Crown (12 rooms) Davit Agmashenebelis 10; 355 231393; m 555 559190, 599 477634; e shotanikvashvili@mail.com. A fairly grand neoclassical block; all rooms have AC, bath, TV & minibar. There's also a bar & decent restaurant (page 334). **$$$–$$$$**

Hotel Pirosmani (18 rooms) Davit Agmashenebelis 6; 322 243030; m 599 164104, 555 559190; e hotel_pirosmani@mail.ru. Another of the Rcheuli Group hotels, the spacious rooms here have bath, TV, AC & minibar. There's Wi-Fi, tours are available & there's a restaurant too. **$$$–$$$$**

Galvanis Kari (13 rooms) Mosashvili 38; 355 231046; m 595 765538; w galavniskari.ge. About 600m out along Chavchavadze by a gate in the city walls (hence its name, Fortress Gate); a decent modern building with a pleasant garden (& beehives) & comfortable rooms (those with balconies cost a bit more); friendly but no English spoken. **$$$**

Hotel Old Sighnaghi (8 rooms) Dadiani 19; m 574 279797; e old.sighnaghi@gmail.com; old.sighnaghi. Great central location and comfortable rooms; lights & Wi-Fi are weak but the heating is not. B/fast in the independent restaurant downstairs is not inc. **$$$**

Brigitte (13 rooms) Tamar Mepe 13; 355 238080; m 551 188080, 579 939898; w brigitte.ge. A friendly & cosy hotel with great views, swimming pool, restaurant & wine cellar. **$$**

Homestays

Abramichi Guest House (4 rooms) Gorgasali 29; m 595 611655; abramichi.guesthouse. A welcoming place with wine & fruit on arrival, great b/fasts, en-suite rooms & a terrace. Good tours offered. **$$$**

Guest House Central (5 rooms) 9 April 30; 355 230056; m 592 404031, 599 281393; e sighnaghi@live.com; . On Erekle II Sq, this has AC rooms with private bathrooms, shared kitchen & a garden looking towards Bodbe; English & Russian spoken. **$$**

Nana Kokiashvili (4 rooms) Sarajishvili 2; 355 231829; m 599 795093. Entered through the gift shop on the corner with Dadiani; spacious, potentially chilly, rooms with balconies, good b/fasts (GEL10 extra); English spoken. **$$**

Nato & Lado's Guesthouse (7 rooms) Pirosmani 5; m 599 212988, 595 338351;

e natolado@gmail.com. Behind the green gate is this welcoming backpackers' guesthouse, run by Nato who speaks good English (but very quickly). You can sample their own wine & folk singing, & take tours to Davit-Gareja or to Nato's home village to make wine & chacha (Nov–Feb); good roof terrace, all rooms will soon be en suite. **$$**

🏠 **Zandarashvili Guesthouse** (8 rooms) Tsminda Giorgi 11; ☎ 355 231029; **m** 555 383837; **w** zandarashvili-guesthouse.com. Great food & wine; also offering tours. **$$**

Hostels

🏠 **Guest House Central** (2 dorms) Below the guesthouse (page 333) is a small hostel with its balcony facing Bodbe. **$**

🏠 **Hotel Old Sighnaghi** (8 rooms) Dadiani 19; **m** 574 279797; **e** old.sighnaghi@gmail.com. Just uphill from the hotel there's a hostel in a former carpet workshop – a big space, possibly chilly & without curtains, but attractive, with old loom frames, old carpets hanging & futon beds, & a kitchen & bathroom. **$**

✖ WHERE TO EAT AND DRINK Map, page 332

There are plenty of other places to eat in addition to the options available at the hotels and guesthouses.

✳ ✖ **Pheasant's Tears** Baratashvili 18; ☎ 355 231556; **m** 599 534484; **w** pheasantstears.com; **f**; ⏰ 10.00–22.00 daily. The best place to eat in town, this wine bar has wonderfully authentic, natural qvevri wines matched with great organic & foraged food. **$$$**

✖ **Art Café Qedeli** Baratashvili 15; ☎ 23 1048; **m** 557 644355; **e** signagi@heim.ge; **f** QedeliCommunity. Supports a home for the disabled in Bodbe, where they produce the baked goods. **$$**

✳ ✖ **Okro's Wines** Chavchavadze 7A; **m** 599 542014, 551 622228; **w** okroswines.com; ⏰ noon–22.00 daily. Punning (Okro means 'gold') on the name of owner & winemaker John Okruashvili, who offers knowledgeable & generous tastings (from GEL20 for 4 wines & a chacha with snacks); food is also excellent & the terrace offers fabulous views. All his wines are natural, including petnaz or sparkling. **$$**

✖ **Shio's Restaurant** Davit Agmashenebelis 10; **m** 551 355818; ⏰ 10.00–23.00 daily. In the brick cellar of the Hotel Crown, this can be smokey but the food is authentic & the atmosphere cheery. **$$**

✖ **Natakhtari** Kostava 1; ☎ 31 449; ⏰ 10.00–22.00 daily. Traditional Georgian fare in a touristy setting. **$**

✖ **Nikala** Loloshvili 4; ☎ 18 9256; ⏰ 09.00–22.00 daily. Serves all the Georgian favourites with the usual erratic service. **$**

🖥 **Knowledge Café** Tsnori; **m** 595 964656; **f** tsodniscafe; **w** codnebi.ge; ⏰ 10.00–20.00 daily. A social enterprise in Tsnori, down in the valley below Sighnaghi where you may find yourself changing buses, this is a lovely café, bookshop & library that also puts on films, reading sessions for kids & activities for older people. **$**

OTHER PRACTICALITIES There's a **tourist information centre** at Kostava 10 (☎ 355 232414; **e** ticsignagi@gmail.com; ⏰ 10.00–18.00 daily, summer until 19.00) through the second door from the left of the wedding palace (an attractive 19th-century building), on the east side of Davit Agmashenebelis Square, at the bottom of town. They have good maps of the town (not always available in English) and can book you a bed from about GEL20 without food, GEL25 with half-board. The **Zedashe Cultural Center** (**e** zedashemusic@gmail.com; **w** zedashe.com) is not a building but an organisation running a fine choir and putting on concerts. A wine harvest festival is held in early October.

There are various **ATMs** in the centre of town; the **post office** (*Davit Agmashenebelis 9;* ⏰ *Mon–Fri 10.00–15.00*) is opposite the Hotel Pirosmani, and there's internet access at Kostava 13.

WHAT TO SEE AND DO To the right/east (facing the Hotel Solomoni) is the **Sighnaghi Museum** (**w** museum.ge; ⏰ 10.00–18.00 Tue–Sun, Nov–May until 17.00; GEL3), which was renovated in 2007. In addition to archaeological and ethnographic displays that include Stone Age artefacts, bits of mastodons, chain mail, musical instruments and so on, there is also a permanent exhibition of paintings by Niko Pirosmanashvili, Georgia's most famous painter, who was born not so far away in the village of Mirzaani. At the top of the piazza you can fork right and head down the Tsnori road to the small **basilica of St George**, built in the 17th–18th centuries, with a bare interior and a separate, 12-sided, brick bell-tower set on the base of a defensive tower. There are three **house-museums** in Sighnaghi, commemorating obscure musicians. There's not a lot else to see, but it's a nice place in which to stroll through the backstreets; the most photogenic balconies are on Sarajishvili and Dadiani to the west of Bebrebis Baghi (the Old People's Garden, the triangular plaza southwest of the upper one). The best views of the Caucasus are from the very end of Tamar Mepis, to the northeast, and along Chavchavadze.

Guesthouses and hotels can all arrange tours of wineries and Davit Gareja, but to really connect with the area's food and wine culture, contact the excellent **Living Roots** (m *599 534484, 599 480086, 599 581175;* w *travellivingroots.com*), who can arrange tours of the Pheasant's Tears organic vineyard and cellars in Tibaani, a cooking course, or a visit to Lamara who knows all about foraging and medicinal herbs and makes silk. Guided **horseriding** (*GEL35/1hr to GEL85/3hrs*) is available at the Living Roots Ranch – take the Tbilisi road and follow the Bodbiskhevi/Zemo Machkhaani road, ie: go straight on where the main road takes a hairpin to the right. In conjunction with Pheasant's Tears, Living Roots can arrange meals at the new Crazy Pomegranate restaurant down in the vineyard (the food is similar to that at the wine bar in town but slightly more complex (and less fast), using fermented/pickled foods, for instance). They will also be opening the Lost Ridge Inn (m *555 588831;* w *lostridgeinn.com*) in 2018 near the ranch, along with a garden restaurant specialising in grilling and other uses of naked flames, plus an organic brewery, artisan bakery and a cider and charcuterie counter.

AROUND SIGHNAGHI Immediately north of Anaga, to the north of Sighnaghi, is **Kardanakhi**, where there are various ancient churches (the Sabatsminda monastery, the 13th-century cross-domed church of St Barbara and the 4th-century basilica of St Nicholas) and some good wineries such as Khvtisia (m *577 220525;* e *z.khvtisiashvili@gmail.com*), and Nikala's Marani (m *599 963317;* e *nikalasmarani@gmail.com*), as well as the larger-scale Shalvino (◖ *322 367226;* e *info@shalvino.ge;* w *shalvino.ge*).

It's just 3km from Sighnaghi to the nunnery of **Bodbe** (also known as Ninotsminda), where St Nino, who converted Georgia to Christianity, is buried. Heading south beyond the bottom square and up Baratashvili, you'll soon fork left on the Tbilisi road, and again after about 1km (about 200m after a petrol station and km8/14); a taxi will charge about GEL5 return including a wait. You can take a marshrutka towards Tbilisi, but you'll be getting off after about 5 minutes, just beyond the petrol station, where an asphalt road leads down to the left. It's about 1km more through oak and pine woods to a junction on a bend; the nunnery is 300m to the right in a grove of cypress trees. Across the car park are the pretty decent Pilgrim Refectory (known for its pies) and an outdoor café.

The rather tatty 19th-century buildings were used as a hospital in the communist period and have only fairly recently reopened as a nunnery. Below it stand the older three-storey bell-tower and St George's church, largely red brick in the western European style with a nave, aisles and chancel, though its core probably dates from the 8th–11th centuries. A church was first built in the 4th century, over the grave of St Nino, the illuminator of Georgia. Most of the kings of Kakheti were crowned here; it has attractive, slightly naïve frescoes, including Adam and Eve on the ceiling of the nave and a Last Judgement at the west end, plus a Baroque golden iconostasis. There's also a big, new church in classic medieval Georgian style just below. Following signs past the gift shop and the nuns' tranquil cemetery, you can take steps a long way down the hill (allow 15 minutes to come back up) to a tiny chapel where you may witness locals queueing up to collect water from the holy spring that is said to have burst into life after Nino prayed at the spot.

If you turn left at the bend and then right, a good unmade track will take you down the escarpment to Tsnori, about an hour's pleasant walk through pomegranate orchards (less pleasant uphill). Turning right onto the Sighnaghi–Tsnori road, you'll reach the main highway at km117/43, 500m west of the centre of Tsnori; alternatively you can make your way through some residential lanes to reach the main highway further west in Sakobo (about km116/44). There's a supermarket facing the taxi rank and Tbilisi marshrutkas, and a busy market uphill from the highway at about km117.5, while the bus yard is below, in front of the former railway station.

By road, it's 8km from Sighnaghi down to Tsnori; turning right towards Lagodekhi and turning right immediately after the bridge under the railway, it's 13km to **Khirsa**, where St Stefan Kirseli, one of the 13 Assyrian Fathers, founded a monastery in the 6th century. It's a fairly large church, untouched except for the addition of two wings and a modern iconostasis; the saint's tomb is to the left of the altar. This should not be confused with the Khirsa Ozaani of the Ascension, 12km south of Tsnori (just south of Tibaani village, in a beautiful forest); a domed church built in the 10th century, it has frescoes from the same time.

From Tsnori a rough road continues southeast into the desert (dominated by wormwood, *Artemisia fragrans*), to the small town of **Dedoplis-Tskaro** (terminal of a freight-only rail branch). This passes through **Mirzaani**, the home village of painter Pirosmani (1862–1918) where you can visit the house-museum (⊕ *Tue–Sun 10.00–17.00; GEL3*) in his home. Pirosmani Memorial Day is on the third Saturday of October, when celebrations include a concert of Georgian folk music and dance, and a recreation of Pirosmani's painting of a supra, at the round table in the centre of the museum. Marshrutkas run hourly (*until 18.00; GEL7*) from Ortachala in Tbilisi to Rustaveli 37 in Dedoplis-Tskaro. You can find accommodation at the Guesthouse Megzuri (*Megobroba 97;* m *599 19633;* **$$**), and at the Vashlovani National Park headquarters (*Baratashvili 5;* m *577 101849;* **$**), where you can also camp. There are two restaurants, at Rustaveli 18 and 139.

An even rougher track continues from Dedoplis-Tskaro a long way eastwards to the **Vashlovani National Park**, the driest part of Georgia (with just 300–500mm of rain per year) and where temperatures may exceed 40°C in summer. There's very dry steppe and savannah flora (*Tulipa eichleri* is endemic to the banks of the Iori), with light forests of pistachio trees and *Paliurus* thorns, and three species of juniper, including the rare black juniper *Juniperus foetidissima*, and the endemic pear tree *Pirus sakhokiana*, with grassland dominated by *Bothriochloa ischaenum*. Cinereous vultures nest in low junipers, and Egyptian and griffon vultures and great imperial and steppe eagles are also seen here. Animals include wolves, bears, boars, lizards, tortoises, and the very rare goitred gazelles (reintroduced from Azerbaijan in 2009) and striped hyenas; there are too many snakes for it to be safe in summer, although they concentrate on hunting hamsters; there are also many endemic invertebrates, and fossils. The track from Dedoplis-Tskaro ends at a birdwatching spot in the Pantichara Gorge, where bee-eaters, rollers, swallows and bearded and griffon vultures can be seen. This is near the Mjniskhura visitors' village, where you can camp or sleep in a bungalow (*GEL40 for 2*) or dorm (*GEL25 pp*); a permit is needed and guides are available for GEL50/day. To the south of Dedoplis-Tskaro, a rough track leads a long way south to the **Dalis-Mta Reservoir**, where there's good fishing and 134 species of birds; it's another 8km southwest to the Kila-Kupra and Takhti–Tefa mud volcanoes, up to 4m in diameter (you may have to hike the last few kilometres in). Northwards from Dedopolis-Tskaro, a yet rougher track leads past the Artsivi (Eagle) Canyon (beautiful but spoiled by littering) to **Khornabuji**, a limestone pinnacle above the Alazani Valley, topped by the ruins of a fortress rebuilt by Queen Tamar and then by Erekle II, and abandoned in the 17th century; it's not an easy climb up (c45 minutes). The winter transhumance from Tusheti brings sheep and cows here, and fierce sheepdogs are a hazard at that season; but horseriding is a great way to see Vashlovani – contact an operator such as Expert Guides Georgia (page 60).

DAVIT-GAREJA დავითგარეჯის

Also in Kakheti, though usually visited separately as a day trip from Tbilisi, is the Davit-Gareja complex of monasteries. In what is now virtual desert on the Azerbaijani border at 400–878m is a group of **cave monasteries** founded in the mid 6th century by St David (one of the 13 Holy Assyrian Fathers), and his disciple Lukian, after his stay on Tbilisi's Holy Mountain. Over two dozen monasteries have been identified, but only a few are widely known or visited and just three are in use; the roads are still bad, and although cars can get here, it's best to have a 4x4. There's no way to get here other than by mountain bike, car or a trip organised by a tourist agency; it's about 70km, or under 2 hours, each way from Tbilisi. A day trip costs around GEL150 for two people, or about half that if you have your own car; if not you'll usually be accompanied by both a driver and a pretty knowledgeable guide. From mid-April to early November a minibus operated by Gareji Line (m *551 951447*; f *gareji.line*) leaves daily at 11.00 from the Pushkin statue near the northeastern corner of Freedom Square in Tbilisi, stopping for lunch at the Oasis Club (run by the same Polish owners; page 338), then visiting the monasteries for about 3 hours and returning after 19.00. If you're thinking of moving from Tbilisi to a hotel in Sighnaghi or Telavi, ask about a transfer including the detour to Davit-Gareja, which makes a very cost-effective combination. A cheaper but fussier way to reach the monastery complex from Tbilisi is first to take a marshrutka to Gardabani or Sagarejo, then hire a taxi for the round trip from there. This does involve far more hanging around at bus stations, however. Don't be tempted by the daily bus to Udabno village, it's tiny and you won't find a taxi to get to the actual monasteries. There's no government involvement at all, with lots of graffiti, bad paths and no safety warnings; it's not at all easy for the elderly or less able to reach Udabno Monastery or enter the caves. Two hours is enough time to see the Lavra and Udabno monasteries.

HISTORY The area has been populated for at least four millennia, as shown by Bronze Age tombs and pottery; it was then a forested area, but iron smelting eventually led to deforestation in the first half of the 1st millennium BC, and thus climate change and desertification. When the monks arrived in the 6th century they had to construct channels and reservoirs for water, and their 9th-century frescoes show their close relationship with nature, notably an image of wild deer being milked, referring to the deer that gave the first monks sustenance (but not on Fridays). The monasteries were constructed from natural sandstone caves which were expanded by heating the rock with fire then pouring on water to split it; all have a church with a main nave and a lesser deacon's nave to the north, as well as cells, stores and other chambers. Above, a dozen of the monasteries built towers to send signals between them. The high point of the monastic community was from the 10th century to the coming of the Mongols in the 13th century, although most survived until the early 17th century, when Shah Abbas massacred 6,000 monks (all subsequently canonised) during the Easter Night procession. The monasteries were re-established, but declined and were abandoned in the 19th century, although three have now been re-established.

Their greatest crisis has come in the last 50 years, during which the Soviet army used the area as an artillery range, often aiming directly at the monasteries. From the late 1980s nationalists demanded an end to military training in the area, and it was finally halted in 1991. The military were keen to train here because of its resemblance to Afghanistan, but once that war had finished in 1989 they lost interest. In 1994 the first cultural and biological survey of the area was undertaken, and some water channels were reopened. Another monastery, abandoned in the 12th century, was rediscovered in 1995, with domes of a type otherwise unknown in Eastern Christendom, as were 10–12th-century frescoes and graffiti, which have given interesting information on the development of the Georgian alphabet. In mid 1995 the Georgian army resumed training in the area, and in 1996 artillery firing; this was suspended in 1997 after protests and legal action, which was seen as proof of the development of 'civil society' in Georgia. The army appealed to the Supreme Court, but the Church finally joined the battle against it, and the cultural (and touristic) value of the area was eventually preserved.

It's pretty much a lunar landscape in many places, but it's transformed from April to early June when the steppe flowers bloom; the dominant species is the bearded grass *Botriochloa ischaenum*, with other grasses such as *Festuca sulcata*, *Stipa capillata*, *S. lessingiana* and *S. pulcherrima*. There's a healthy population of snakes, lizards and rabbits, and a remarkable range of raptors, such as eagles, vultures, buzzards and owls, that prey on them. In addition there are wolves, bats in many of the caves, and there were goitred gazelles until relatively recently. May and June are also the best time for birds, notably nesting vultures and displaying chukar, as well as huge tadpoles.

TOWARDS DAVIT-GAREJA The best way in is via the A302 (the Tbilisi–Telavi/Sighnaghi road), turning off at km51, just east of the roundabout at the east end of Sagarejo. Taxis wait here, where the Tbilisi–Sagarejo marshrutkas terminate; they should charge about GEL60 return, including an hour at Davit-Gareja. From here it takes a little over an hour to the main monastery at Davitis Lavra, crossing the railway and turning right (on asphalt, briefly) before km2, and crossing the Iori River at km8. Following signs to **Udabno**, the road climbs to a low col after 20 minutes, passing between two salty lakes (with poor grazing), and turns sharp right after another 10 minutes to skirt around Udabno village to the left. This is one of several villages in the area built for Svans moving from the mountains (there was a fresh influx in 1988 after a terrible avalanche in Ushguli); the Oasis Club hotel and restaurant (m *574 805563;* e *oasisclubudabno@gmail.com;* f *oasisclubudabno;* **$$$**) has accommodation in pod-like cabins of reclaimed building materials and provides an excellent (but pricey) lunch. They also rent bikes and horses and provide tours of the monasteries with knowledgeable guides, and also stage Monday Movie Nights and other events.

The road on from Udabno is much rougher; you'll soon turn 90° left on to the unpaved road from Rustavi and Gardabani (with huge motorway-scale signs), from where it's 5km to Davitis Lavra, passing dramatically eroded hills and the tower of Chichkhituri Monastery (founded in the 12th century) and then a seismological station (which records around 100 tremors each year), reaching the Lavra about 25 minutes from Udabno. You can also turn right towards Rustavi to visit the Monastery of St John the Baptist (see opposite), about 7km from the junction.

It's also possible to come from the west via **Rustavi**, although the road is much worse. Established on virgin land immediately after World War II, this was Soviet Georgia's leading industrial centre, and its metallurgical plant was the republic's largest employer, closely followed by chemical and pharmaceutical works; these are mostly closed, with Georgia's first 'European-standard' prison (with closed cells) built instead. The country's largest used car market (7 days a week) has also evolved here. People moved here from all over the country, especially from mountain areas such as Svaneti, and its population is now in the region of 150,000, but the work conditions were so bad that workers retired at 45 or 50. It's worth noting that the town has no connection with the poet Rustaveli, who came from Meskheti (page 215).

There are a couple of adequate places to stay in Rustavi: the Hotel Rustavi (*60 rooms; Megobroba 32;* \ *341 22 2212;* m *599 192599;* w *hotelrustavi.ge;* **$$**), a communist block in the centre; and the Grand Vejini (*57 rooms;* m *568 154949, 595 555172;* e *grandvejini@gmail.com;* f *GrandVejini;* **$$$**), a modern business hotel to the north at the start of the bypass, which offers much better food.

It's also possible to take a marshrutka (*GEL2*) from Didube to Gardabani, the last town before the Azerbaijani border, just beyond Rustavi, from where a taxi will charge GEL50–60 to the monasteries and back. The road to Davit-Gareja starts by turning left in front of the immense administration block of the Rustavi metallurgical plant (far grander than the city hall, to show exactly where the true power used to lie), crossing the railway and turning right to pass through a post-industrial wasteland for a considerable distance. Turn left (on an unsigned asphalt road) just after a barrier gate when the biggish white village of Jandara comes into view ahead, and then turn right at the top of the rise (with the white wall of a collective farm on the left), onto a very rough track (also unsigned), which climbs past wrecked armoured personnel carriers onto the very scrubby dry steppe. The Monastery of John the Baptist is visible to the left once on the plateau, where the road becomes slightly smoother; to reach it fork left and soon left again to go down a valley, forking right (with an abandoned collective farm to the left) to park just below the monastery. Returning to the top of the valley and continuing over a ridge, keep to the right where the Sagarejo road joins from the left.

THE MAIN MONASTERIES Set into a cliff face, the **Monastery of John the Baptist** (Natlismcemli), 12km from the main Lavra, was founded in the 6th century, but the main church was completed and painted only in the 13th century (there's a portrait of Queen Tamar in the rear right-hand corner). The refectory, with its Persian-style vaulting, was added in the 17th century, and there's a 19th-century tomb. Above is a tower decorated with blue tiles; it clearly used to be taller, as the foot of a tile cross survives.

Arriving at the main **Lavra Monastery** (Davitis Lavra), park at the houses (there's a fairly horrid toilet in the field), and walk up past the Church Shop (selling icons and candles but no water or snacks). It was founded by St David in the 6th century and is now occupied by notoriously fundamentalist monks who take great exception to noise and especially to inappropriate clothing. Tourists are not allowed in the inner court or, of course, the monks' cells. Inside, go around to the right and down steps in the rock to the lower court: David and Lukian are buried here in the Church of the Transfiguration (Peristvaleba) or Rock Church (plain and with modern icons), near a spring known as the Tears of David. The diagonal lines of the rocks above the outer court and the cells are striking, and very photogenic; channels also lead water off the bare rocks outside the main doorway.

A bad path starts immediately above the Church Shop, reaching a viewpoint over the Lavra in a couple of minutes. This is the path to the **Udabno Monastery** (literally 'Desert'), constructed between the 8th and 10th centuries, on the far side of the ridge; this is in both religious and artistic terms the most important of the monasteries. The trail climbs to the left (alongside a railing) for about 10 minutes and then from a hairpin to the right for another 10 minutes to reach the ridge, with vast views of the desert in all directions. Heading down to the left you'll pass cave-churches with trees growing in their entrances; after No 37 (each has a crudely painted number) you should go up to the left to the refectory. The monks knelt at the stone table down the middle, with their food hidden from each other in hollows; the frescoes of Bible scenes were painted in the 13th and 14th centuries. Just a bit further on, the main church has superb frescoes from the late 10th and early 11th centuries, including the life of St David on the north wall (with a deer feeding on milk), the Virgin and Child in the apse, a Last Judgement on the east wall, and a Deesis in the east apse. The path then continues for 5 minutes along the cliff edge, pocked with cave chambers, before climbing back to a new chapel on the ridge just before a triangulation point, from which you can return to the left past the ruins of a 6th-century chapel, reaching the hairpin bend on the path in about 15 minutes. From the ridge you have superb views across the desert, deep into Azerbaijan, and there are amazing sunsets here.

The monastery with the best frescoes (painted 1212–13, including portraits of Tamar and her son Giorgi IV Lash) is **Bertubani**, which has been 2km inside Azerbaijan since the dying Soviet Union moved the border in 1991 to run across the Udabno ridge (813m; known in Azerbaijan as Keshishdag). Georgia is offering a land swap to regain control of Bertubani and Chichkhituri, but Azerbaijan is being bolshy.

From Lavra it's also possible to hike 11km to **Dodos Rq'a** (meaning 'the range of Dodo', one of David's disciples), towards the Sagarejo road. Also one of the original 6th-century monasteries, this has 8th–9th-century frescoes with the oldest surviving traces of Georgian inscriptions; monks have recently returned here, and are not very friendly to tourists.

11

Kvemo (Lower) Kartli
ქვემო ქართლი

Kvemo Kartli, or Lower Kartli, is the area to the southwest of Tbilisi, far smaller and less important than Shida (Inner) Kartli, but attractive and convenient for short trips from the capital. Its population is largely Azeri, while there are also traces of German colonists, who settled in the area of Bolnisi in the 18th century and were deported to Central Asia at the start of World War II, after which they went to Germany; wine in this area is more Germanic in taste than the Georgian norm. The Azeris are hardworking farmers, and you'll see women in typically Islamic leggings selling apples, onions, pomegranates, persimmons and sweetcorn by the roadside.

MARNEULI AND BOLNISI მარნეული, ბოლნისი

You're most likely to see this area on your way to or from Armenia; the traditional route to Yerevan was that built by Russian military engineers in 1834–75, but as this passes through Azerbaijan the main route is now via Sadakhlo. It's also possible to take the A304 via Bolnisi and Gyumri; it's well worth stopping to see a group of churches south of Bolnisi, which are among the loveliest in the country. Marshrutkas run from Samgori, picking up near Isani and Ortachala; there are also some to Marneuli (with signs in Cyrillic and Georgian scripts) at Station Square and the Dinamo Stadium. The A304 turns off the Rustavi/Baku highway in the outskirts of Tbilisi and climbs on to the steppe, and at km9/88 signs for 'Kvemo Teleti Wine Route' and 'Teleti St George's Friary' show the way to Shavnabada monastery, high on a hill to the right looking as if it should be in Tuscany – it's becoming known as a winery (m 599 455765) with excellent Saperavi qvevri wines. From km11/86 the road drops steeply to the village of Kumisi (where a Canadian firm is drilling for natural gas) and climbs again to Koda, start of the new road (km18.5) to Tsalka (page 346). These villages are both notable for their solid houses of grey tuff, far more typical of Armenia than of Georgia. At km26/71 you'll see the huge Algeti statue on a hill to the left/east; it's a war memorial, depicting a mother handing a sword to her two small sons. From here the road drops to **Marneuli**, not a tourist destination in any sense, but rather a thoroughly drab industrial town, although there is an ATM at Cholokashvili 3. Known as Borchali until 1947, the town was famous for its carpets, and the reWoven project (w *rewoven.net*) is working to revive the weaving tradition in the surrounding villages, whose Azeri names are known worldwide as the names of classic rug designs. Email e info@rewoven.net to view and perhaps buy rugs.

Passing the modern bus station and turning left at the central roundabout by the Public Service Hall, the A310 passes the Marneuli military airbase (formerly Soviet, brought up to NATO standards by Turkey and then bombed by the Russians in 2008) and continues through Azeri-populated villages with gaudy mosques. After

KVEMO (LOWER) KARTLI

N

Bradt

0 ——— 10km
0 ——— 10 miles

Mgebriani
Tedzami
Rkoni
Ertatsminda ✝
Chardakhi
Ksani ✝ Shiom-
Mtkvari ghvime
Saguramo
Zedazeni
Mtskheta
✝ Jvari
Tbilisi National Park
St Anthony ✝

Armazi ✝
Digomi
M27

TBILISI

Tbilisi Sea

Telavi

Algetis National Park
Manglisi
Betania ✝

Beshtaneshi
A303
Birtvisi
Orbeti
A303
Kojori
Kumisi
Shavnabada monastery ✝

Lake Tsalka
Tsalka
Akhalkalaki
Trialeti
Tbisi
Tetri-Tskaro
Algeti
Koda
Rustavi

Pitareti ✝
Khram
Kveshi
Bolnisi
Marneuli
Baku
M27

Darbazi
A304 Bolnisi
Kvemo
Bolnisi
Bolnisi Sioni ✝
Zugrugasheni ✝
Sakdrisi
Kazreti
Poladauri
Debet
A310

Dmanisi
Dmanisi archaeological site
Patara Dmanisi
Mashavera
Sadakhlo

Guguti

Tashir, Gyumri, Yerevan
A R M E N I A
Alaverdi, Yerevan

29km it reaches the village of Sadakhlo and 4km further on the modern **border post**, with 24-hour duty-free shops and toilets. In addition to international services to Armenia, there are local buses from Marneuli to Sadakhlo; taxis wait at the border, and charge GEL 45–50 to Tbilisi.

Going straight across the Marneuli roundabout, the A304 heads southwest across a fertile valley, and at km49/48 (about 1¼ hours from Tbilisi) it reaches **Bolnisi**, a marginally more attractive town that stretches for 6km along the road. Bolnisi was founded in 1818 by colonists from Württemberg in Germany who called it Katharinenfeld; from 1921 to 1944 it was named Luxemburg after the German revolutionary Rosa Luxemburg, and since then it has been Bolnisi. There's a tourist office (*Sulkhan-Saba 115;* \ *358 222319;* e *ticbolnisi@gmail.com;* ⏱ *10.00–18.00 daily, summer until 19.00*) at the junction to the Sioni church. Most of the surviving German houses are on three streets (originally Katharinenstrasse, Nikolaistrasse and Gartenstrasse) east of the mill and south of the main road, most obviously the Rathaus or town hall (c1845) at Parnavaz Mepe 41, opposite the Lutheran church (1854). The Walkerhaus, a former German school, was restored for the bicentenary of the Germans' arrival in Georgia in 2017, along with the church of Asureti (Elisabethtal), on the road from Koda to Manglisi. In Asureti you can ask for the rather grumpy Manfred Tikhonov, who makes good red wine and has restored a typical Swabian half-timbered house. The Lutheran church (1866) of Trialeti (Alexandershilf), south of Tsalka, is also being restored.

WHERE TO STAY, EAT AND DRINK The population of **Marneuli** is 85% Azeri, so you should make a point of stopping at the Mugham Azeri restaurant (*26 May;* m *591 600157, 514 399797;* e *mehriban.muradova@gmail.com;* $$).

In **Bolnisi** the obvious place to stay (or eat) is the German-owned Hotel Deutsche Mühle (*Sioni 4;* ✆ *322 61 4750;* e *service@muehle-bolnisi.com;* w *muehle-bolnisi.com;* $$$$). This beautifully restored watermill now offers both German and Georgian food, indoors or on the terrace. They can also organise local tours and give information on the area's German heritage.

BOLNISI SIONI AND ZUGRUGASHENI CHURCHES The church of **Bolnisi Sioni**, 9km south of the town of Bolnisi, is an outstanding example of the earliest Georgian church architecture, and the only surviving example of the original type of three-aisled basilica (without transepts). It's striking for its simplicity and calm (set in a tranquil rose-planted churchyard), and for the lovely green tuff of its western façade (added in the 17th century). The turning to Sioni is at the tourist office at the west end of the town centre. From here it's 7km to Sioni, an easy road to walk, although there are also marshrutkas, mainly at peak hours.

Walking down to the bridge you'll see a few typically German houses, solidly built of stone, and a former watermill (now a hotel; see above) by the river. Ten minutes from the main road you'll pass the railway station and start to climb steadily to a pass 5km from Bolnisi; it's another 1km to the large village of Kvemo Bolnisi that sprawls (in a most un-Germanic way) across a fertile valley; its new mosque is one of the largest in Georgia. You need to fork right at the entrance to the village to bypass it; the church visible ahead on a hilltop is not Sioni but Zugrugasheni. With the village to your left, you'll pass a couple of small abandoned chapels of striking green tuff, below the bare limestone outcrops to the right. It takes 25 minutes on foot to reach the end of Kvemo Bolnisi, and then just ten more to reach the village of Sioni, where you'll find the wonderful Bolnisi Sioni church to the left.

Entering by the west door, you descend a flight of steps into the dark church; the only natural light comes from the door and from a few narrow lancet windows. It's a remarkably long church by Georgian standards, with a six-bay nave. The only frescoes are in the apse, and have faded with time; likewise the carved capitals in the nave have been damaged. The lintel over the north door (now replaced with a copy) gives the church's construction dates as AD478–93; this is the oldest inscription in the Georgian language found within Georgia itself (slightly older ones were found in Palestine). To the northeast a chapel added in the 8th century projects beyond the main apse; there's another, shorter, chapel on the church's southeastern corner. There are also the remains of ambulatories or external aisles along both sides of the church. The separate bell-tower, its steps swathed in vines, dates from 1678–88.

To reach the **church of Zugrugasheni**, 2km away on the far side of the valley (and very visible south of Bolnisi on its hilltop), you can go back to Kvemo Bolnisi, or turn left from the Sioni church into the village and go left twice more to follow a track due east towards the church; it takes 15 minutes to reach the bridge and another ten to wind up to the church, strikingly set high on a hill with a high thin barrel dome to add to the effect. The nearest houses are at a farm further up the valley, so it's a nice spot to camp. Built in 1212–22, it's still a very impressive building. It has a two-bay nave and aisles, plus a separate deacon's nave to the north, and lateral chapels on either side of the apse. To the south a porch has been demolished. Externally there are fine carvings and high niches marking the position of the apses inside the east end. The barrel dome, with its ornamental platform bands, is typical of the 18th century in style.

11

A **mountain-bike route** designed by Czech consultants and named the Griffon Way (f *griffonway*) comes here from Tbilisi, via Kojori, Kiketi, Ardisubani, Jorjashvili, Dagheti and Bolnisi; it continues (with extra loops and detours to fortresses and churches) to Samtsevrisi, Opreti and Shulaveri, on the main road south of Marneuli.

FROM BOLNISI TO DMANISI AND THE ARMENIAN BORDER
Continuing along the main A304 towards Armenia, at Kveshi there's a turning west to Pitareti and Darbazi. It is about 8km from the junction to Tandzia and the River Khram and a taxi could be taken to reach this (they wait by the roadside at the junction), although it needs to be a 4x4 in order to cope with the rough track. The bridge across the Khram has been washed away but you can cross on metal cables; on the far side is the ruined fortress of Khuluti, beyond which you'll cross some fields and follow a jeep track up a gorge to the isolated **church of Pitareti**. Built by Tamar's son Giorgi IV in 1213–22, it has a cruciform, almost square, plan, with three virtually equal apses, a single-bay aisle, and a tall central drum, and only a porch to the south to spoil its regularity; there are excellent carvings on the eastern façade. The church was surrounded in medieval times by a double wall, with a two-storey gate-tower added in 1696. At Darbazi, reached by turning left before Tandzia, are the remains of a 12th–13th-century royal palace. Pitareti can also be reached by 4x4 or mountain bike from Tetri-Tskaro to the north, 59km from Tbilisi (reached by two marshrutkas per hour from Samgori metro); this was the centre of a Greek community, most of which has now emigrated. In Samshvilde, also on the Khram 4km south of Tetri-Tskaro, there's a cupola church built in AD759–77.

Just west of the junction on the main road, the fortress and church of Kveshi sit on a rocky crag just north of km61.5. At km68/29 a side road heads southeast for 3km to Kazreti, whose apartment blocks are soon very obvious; this is the terminus of the Soviet railway from Marneuli and the commercial centre for the upper Mashavera Valley. Just west is **Sakdrisi**, where traces of gold mining almost 5,000 years ago were excavated in 2006; at the end of 2014 the government controversially gave RMG Gold permission to mine there, destroying the remains. At km75/22 marshrutkas to Dmanisi turn right at a roundabout, while the very quiet road to Guguti and the Armenian border heads south and enters a limestone valley rather like a Derbyshire dale; at km79/18 it reaches Patara Dmanisi (2¼ hours from Tbilisi), known for its cheese factory, sweetbriar jelly, walnuts, hazelnuts, and its mineral springs. Patara means 'Little', and Didi ('Big') Dmanisi is on the hill above the roundabout at the start of the road to the town of Dmanisi, 11km west towards Tsalka.

A rough track to the right as you reach Patara Dmanisi leads to the **Dmanisi archaeological site**; turning left at a bend you'll come to the remains of a medieval fortified town, covering 13ha, with 13th- and 14th-century fortifications and the ruins of a palace and baths, and to the right a 7th-century basilica with a three-bay nave and apse, and a narthex or separate porch added by Giorgi IV in 1213–22. There are no frescoes inside, but good external stone-carvings. Finding an unsigned path straight ahead from the bend in the road brings you to the far more important hominid site, where a skull of *Homo erectus* about 1.7 million years old and remains of *Homo sapiens* about 200,000 years old have been found (pages 14 and 149), as well as Palaeolithic artefacts and the remains of extinct species of rhino, elephant, giraffe, ostrich, bear, sabre-toothed tiger, deer and cow. The site is managed by the Georgian National Museum, and there is a new visitor centre (✆ 322 998022; ⊕ May–Oct 10.00–18.00 Tue–Sun; GEL3); homestays are also to be provided.

Other less ancient archaeological sites in the area include Gadachrili Gora near Imiri, south of Marneuli on the main road to Armenia, where evidence of winemaking dating back to 6000BC has been found, as well as traces of wheat and legumes, agricultural implements and pottery; rice, honey and fruit were fermented in China c7000BC, but this is the first evidence of grapes being used. In 2014 a site at Nadikhuri, near Bolnisi, revealed agricultural tools and unusual channels.

The road climbs through open beech forest, and then out on to the high plateau that characterises Armenia; the first **border post** is at km97 (3 hours from Tbilisi), just south of the tiny village of Guguti.

🏠 **Where to stay** There are a couple of homestays in Tetri-Tskaro, with Haykush Kyrakosyan (*Tavdadebuli 29;* m *599 398720;* $$) and Gia Vaniani (*Vazha-Pshavelas 6;* m *599 198620;* $) – both have shared bathrooms and nice gardens.

BETANIA AND MANGLISI ბეთანია, მანგლისი

It's odd that in both Britain and Georgia it's the A303 that goes west from the capital to the country's finest ancient monument, from London to Stonehenge and from Tbilisi to Vardzia. The Georgian A303 starts as Chavchavadze Avenue, passing Vake Park and the 'mountain resort suburb' of Tskhneti, before reaching the junction with the minor road from Freedom Square that winds up between Mtatsminda and Narikala as the Kojoris Gzatketsili or Kojori highway. This passes through **Kojori**, 16km from Tbilisi, which, at 1,280m, was a summer resort for the Georgian nobility; it was also the birthplace of composer Aram Khachaturian, and in February 1921 the site of a last stand by Georgian troops, including the heroic pupils of the Cadet School, against the invading Red Army. You can hike through the village and up to a ruined 17th-century castle just to the southwest, and 1.5km to the northeast on a wooded spur of Mount Udzo is the Kabeni Church, much visited by barren women. This is a dome church built in the 9th century and altered in both the 12th and 18th centuries. Marshrutkas 10 and 106 run to Kojori once or twice an hour from Orbeliani Square in Tbilisi, making this a popular outing for picnicking and strolling.

In **Kiketi**, just south of the road 4km west of Kojori, the Gotsa Family Winery (*Tabidze 3;* m *599 509033;* e *bgotsa@gmail.com;* w *gotsawines.com*) welcomes visitors to taste its organic wines and has two comfortable rooms ($$$).

A rough road turns right 22km from Tbilisi to the **monastery of Betania**, in the wooded Vere Valley, 10km north; its church is a masterpiece of Georgian architecture and is also famous for supposedly housing part of the Virgin Mary's robe. Set on a ridge, it's surrounded on three sides by trees, with only its high barrel dome reaching above. The monastery was founded in the 11th century, and the cruciform church was built in the 12th and 13th centuries; the frescoes were painted in 1207, and include one of just four portraits of Queen Tamar painted in her lifetime. Tourists have been robbed here, so don't go alone. Just to its west is the Darbazuli Church of St George the Triumphant (1196).

Continuing along the A303, at Orbeti there's a turning south to **Birtvisi**, site of a medieval fortress. This is just north of a minor road from Koda, on the main road to Armenia, to Manglisi, which was rebuilt (and launched by Saakashvili with great fanfare as the new Silk Road) and is now used by most of the relatively few marshrutkas that come this way, and by trucks to Akhalkalaki and Turkey.

The Birtvisi Canyon is described as a 'rock labyrinth' by the Sustainable Tourism Centre, who offer trips of one or two days' easy trekking and simple climbing, for US$50–100 each, depending on numbers (best from September to November). They also run mountain-biking trips across the Trialeti range, starting from Manglisi, the next major village along the main road; there's a lovely 11th-century church set in the trees here. From Manglisi, at 1,200m, the trail climbs north to 1,800m in the 6,822ha **Algetis National Park** (founded in 1965), and descends to Rkoni (page 165), 25km and 5–6 hours away; from here a rough 4x4 track runs north to Ertatsminda and Kaspi. It's also possible to hike to Rkoni from Choliani, north of Lake Tsalka, via the Sabolia Gorge and the Kldecari (Rocky Gate) Pass. The reserve was founded in 1965 to protect the forests of spruce (*Picea orientalis*) and Caucasian silver fir (*Abies nordmanniana*) which cover 80% of its area, as well as more than 1,000 plant species and over 80 bird species. There's no visitor centre but national park staff in Manglisi (*Kurorti 4;* m *577 101801, 577 907272;* e *gkavtaradze@apa. gov.ge*) are happy to help. Manglisi is reached by regular marshrutkas from Tbilisi, leaving Station Square hourly between 11.00 and 18.00 (*exc noon; GEL4*).

Further to the southwest the road reaches the Trialeti Plateau, passing to the southwest of several lakes. From the first large lake, Tsalka, a three-day trekking route leads north to the Tedzami Canyon and Rkoni. **Lake Tsalka** is the centre of Georgia's Greek population, still speaking Pontian Ancient Greek. This area was unpopulated as it was laid waste by every army invading from the south, but it is very fertile and ideal for raising cattle and growing potatoes; nevertheless, about a third of the population has emigrated in recent years, although Svans have come in to replace them. At Beshtasheni, 5km north of the highway at the east end of Lake Tsalka, there are Cyclopean fortified settlements dating from the 3rd and 2nd centuries BC, with massive stone walls 6m high. The Trialeti area is also known for ancient petroglyphs portraying horses, deer and birds and the sun, crosses and grids, which could be up to 2.5 million years old. On the southern shore of the lake, the town of **Tsalka** was known for Swiss-style cheese before World War I; just 2km southeast, the Dashbashi canyon was carved through a volcanic plateau by the River Khram and has a very moist microclimate, as well as frozen waterfalls in winter.

The A303 used to be a very bad road, and although it's been improved most traffic from Tbilisi to Akhalkalaki and Vardzia still goes via Borjomi rather than the direct route over the bleak plateau with its fearsome speed-bumps (page 221).

WHERE TO STAY In Manglisi, there are two guesthouses, run by Givi Chokheli (*Stalin 38;* m *599 428444;* **$$**) and Akaki Gogichadze (*aka Hotel Manglisi; Gantiadi 1;* m *599 010111;* **$$–$$$**). There are several guesthouses in Tsalka: the Trialeti Hotel above a supermarket at Aristotle 3 (m *551 143423, 599 535919;* **$$**), Davit Giorgadze (*Aristotle 18;* m *599 221001;* **$$$**), with gym and billiards table, Nanuli Bolkvadze (*Aristotle 15;* m *599 483384;* **$$**), Levan Tserediani (*Chavchavadze 21;* m *595 073114, 599 985497;* **$$**), on the road south, and Melsida Mezirova (*Griboedov 2, off Chavchavadze;* m *599 856982;* **$$**).

FOLLOW BRADT

For the latest news, special offers and competitions, subscribe to the Bradt newsletter via the website www.bradtguides.com and follow Bradt on:

 BradtTravelGuides
 @BradtGuides
 @bradtguides
 bradtguides
 bradtguides

Appendix 1

LANGUAGE

If you have any knowledge of Russian already, you might as well concentrate on that; most older people speak Russian, and there's no prejudice against it, and many younger people now speak English. You can study Georgian at summer schools organised by the Centre for Kartvelian (Georgian) Studies at Tbilisi State University (*Chavchavadze 1, 380028 Tbilisi;* ℡ *32 229 0833*), or at the International Centre for the Georgian Language (*Gogebashvili 18;* ℡ *32 298 3285;* e *rusiko@causcasus.net*). Web-based introductory courses in Georgian can be found at w 101languages.net/georgian and udemy.com/conversational-georgian-language, as well as the Peace Corps' course at w livelingua.com/course/peace-corps/Georgian_Language_Lessons.

There are various useful phrase books; my favourite is the *Curzon Dictionary and Phrasebook*, by Nicholas Awde and Thea Khitarishvili (Curzon, London, 1997), which uses a transliterated version of Georgian, easy for us but unintelligible to most Georgians. *Speak Georgian/kartuli ena* by Khatuna Gelashvili (Sulakauri Publishing; w georgianlanguage.ge, 2006) is small and handy, and there's also a *Speak Georgian* app (2016). *Everyday Georgian (Biliki I & II)* by Nana Shavtvaladze (Tbilisi, 2009) is more a conversation primer than a phrase book. The *Hippocrene Concise Dictionary* by John J Torikashvili (Hippocrene, New York, 1992) uses Georgian and Latin script; the same publishers also have *Beginner's Georgian* (2012) by Dodona Kiziria. *Georgian – A Learner's Grammar* by George Hewitt (Routledge, London, 1996) is for students rather than travellers, and *Georgian: A Reading Grammar* by Howard Aronson (Slavica Publishers, Indiana University, Bloomington, corrected edition 1990) and *Text Book of Georgian Language* by Meri Nikolaishvili (Tbilisi, 2000) are even more academic.

GEORGIAN ALPHABET This is only a rough guide, as there are many variants, especially in handwriting. Georgian is entirely phonetic – anyone familiar with Welsh knows what that leads to, but every letter is pronounced, and always the same way. Note that *p* and *f*, and *b* and *v*, are fairly interchangeable, and there are no capital letters.

a	ა	k'	კ	t'	ტ	dż	ძ	d
b	ბ	l	ლ	u	უ	ts	წ	
g	გ	m	მ	ph	ფ	ch'	ჭ	
d	დ	n	ნ	k	ქ	x	ხ	
e	ე	o	ო	y/gh	ღ	j	ჯ	
v	ვ	p'	პ	q'	ყ	h	ჰ	
z	ზ	zh	ჟ	sh	შ			
t	თ	r	რ	ch	ჩ			
i	ი	s	ს	ts	ც			

ESSENTIAL VOCABULARY These words and phrases have been transliterated for English-speakers. You can also find transliterations for German-speakers, which can occasionally catch you out. The names of many dishes and drinks are on pages 76–86.

airport	*aeroporti*	I don't know	*ar vici*
avenue	*gamziri*	I don't understand	*ar mesmis*
beautiful	*lamazi*	included	*shedis*
bed	*sats'oli*	inner	*shida*
beer	*ludi*	lake	*tba*
big	*didi*	let's go	*tsa-vayd-et*
bread	*puri*	lower	*kvemo*
breakfast	*sauzme*	map	*r'uka*
bridge	*khidi*	mother	*deda*
bus station	*avtobusebis sadguri*	mountain	*mta*
car	*mankana*	museum	*muzeumi*
castle	*tsikhe*	my name is …	*me mkvia …*
cheap	*ee-api*	new	*akhali*
cheers!	*gaumarjos!*	no	*ara*
	(response: *gagimarjos*)	old	*ds-weli*
cheese	*qu-weli*	open	*ghia*
church	*eklesia*	please	*inebet, tu sheidzleba*
closed	*dak'et'ilia*	river	*mdinare*
cold	*tsiva*	room	*otakhi*
come here	*modi ak*	small	*patara*
expensive	*ds-weeri*	sorry!	*bodishi! map'at'iet!*
father	*mama*	spring	*tskaro*
fine	*kargad*	square	*moedani*
food	*satch'meli*	station	*sadguri* (also *voksal*)
fruit	*khili*	stop! (bus)	*gacheret!*
go	*tsadi*	street	*kucha*
good	*kargia*	thank you	*madloba*
goodbye	*nakhvamdis*	town	*kalaki*
good morning	*dila mush-wido-bisa*	train	*mat'arebeli*
gorge	*khevi*	upper	*zemo*
grandfather	*papa*	vegetables	*bost'neuli*
grandmother	*bebia*	very	*dsarlian*
hello	*gamarjoba*	warm	*tbili*
help!	*mishvelet!*	water	*ts'kali*
home	*sakhli*	welcome	*mober-zandit*
hot	*tskhela*	what is your name?	*ra gkvia?*
hotel	*sastumro*	when?	*rodis?*
how are you?	*rogora khar?*	where is?	*sad aris?*
how many?	*ramdeni?*	who, what, which?	*romeli?*
how much?	*ra ghirs?*	yes	*diakh, ki, ho*
I am …	*me var …*	you're welcome	*arapris*

NUMBERS

0	*nuli*	16	*tekvs-met'i*
1	*erti*	17	*chwid-met'i*
2	*ori*	18	*tvra-met'i*
3	*sami*	19	*tskhra-met'i*
4	*otkhi*	20	*otsi*
5	*khuti*	21	*ots-da-erti*
6	*ekvsi*	30	*ots-de-ati*
7	*shwidi*	40	*ormotsi*
8	*rva*	50	*ormots-da-ori*
9	*tskhra*	60	*samotsi*
10	*ati*	70	*samots-da-ti*
11	*tert-met'i*	80	*otkhmotsi*
12	*tor-met'i*	90	*okhmots-da-ati*
13	*tsa-met'i*	100	*asi*
14	*totkh-met'i*	101	*as-erti*
15	*tkhit-met'i*	200	*or-asi*

1,000	*at-asi*	second	*meore*
10,000	*ati at-asi*	third	*mesame*
100,000	*asi at-asi*	fourth	*meotkhe*
one million	*milioni*	fifth	*mekhute*
once	*ertkhel*	sixth	*meekvse*
twice	*or-jer*	tenth	*meate*
first	*p'irveli*	twentieth	*meotse*

DAYS AND TIME

Monday	*orshabati*	yesterday	*gushin*
Tuesday	*samshabati*	What time is it?	*romeli saati a?*
Wednesday	*otkhshabati*	It is … o'clock	*… saati a*
Thursday	*khutshabati*	now	*akhla*
Friday	*p'arask'evi*	hour	*saati*
Saturday	*shabati*	minute	*ts'uti*
Sunday	*k'wira*	in the morning	*dilit*
		in the afternoon	*nashuadghevs*
today	*dghes*	in the evening	*saghamos*
tomorrow	*khwal*		
the day after			
tomorrow	*zeg*		

Appendix 2

FURTHER INFORMATION

BOOKS

Travellers' tales Herodotus and Strabo both wrote about Georgia in classical times.

Anderson, Tony *Bread and Ashes: A Journey through the Mountains of Georgia* Vintage, 2004. A rather episodic but very atmospheric and informative account of hiking through much of the Georgian Caucasus.

Bitov, Andrei *A Captive of the Caucasus* Weidenfeld & Nicholson/Harvill, 1993. Full of associative anecdotes, more a journey through the literary culture of Russia than through Georgia and Armenia.

Bullough, Oliver *Let Our Fame Be Great: Journeys among the Defiant People of the Caucasus* Allen Lane, 2010.

Dumas, Alexandre the elder *Adventures in the Caucasus* (1859) Owen/Chiltern Books, 1962.

Farson, Daniel *A Dry Ship to the Mountains* Michael Joseph, 1994/Penguin, 1995. Following his father's footsteps (see following entry).

Farson, Negley *Caucasian Journey* Evans, 1951/Penguin, 1988.

Griffin, Nicholas *Caucasus: In the Wake of Warriors* Review, 2001. Published in the USA as *Caucasus, A Journey to the Land between Christianity and Islam*, taking us through Georgia, Armenia and Azerbaijan on the trail of Shamil.

Keun, Odette *In the Land of the Golden Fleece* London, 1924.

Maclean, Fitzroy *Eastern Approaches* Cape, 1949/Penguin, 2004.

Maclean, Fitzroy *To Caucasus* Cape, 1976.

Marsden, Philip *The Spirit Wrestlers* HarperCollins, 1998. A beautifully written quest to find the surviving Doukhobors, a dissident Russian Orthodox sect, ending up in Javakheti.

Nansen, Fridthof *Through the Caucasus to the Volga* George Allen & Unwin, 1931.

Nasmyth, Peter *Georgia, in the Mountains of Poetry* RoutledgeCurzon, 2006. An updated version of *Georgia: A Rebel in the Caucasus* (1992), this is a beautifully evocative account of travels in post-Soviet Georgia.

Pereira, Michael *Across the Caucasus* Geoffrey Bles, 1973.

Russell, Mary *Please Don't Call It Soviet Georgia* Serpent's Tail, 1991.

Severin, Tim *The Jason Voyage* Arrow, 1990.

Shaw, Peter *Hole: Kidnapped in Georgia* Accent Press, 2006. A gripping account of Shaw's 2000 kidnapping ordeal, which also offers insights into the social and political background.

Steavenson, Wendell *Stories I Stole* Atlantic Books/Grove Press, 2003. An evocative view of 1990s Georgia through the eyes of a young foreign correspondent.

Steinbeck, John *A Russian Journal* Viking, 1948/Penguin, 1999. Including 44 pages on Georgia, with photos by Robert Capa.

Thubron, Colin *Where Nights Are Longest* Atlantic Monthly Press, 1984.

History and politics

Allen, W E D *History of the Georgian People* Barnes & Noble, 1971.

Almond, Mark *Post-Communist Georgia: A Short History* CreateSpace Independent Publishing Platform, 2012. A pretty negative view of the first 20 years of Georgia's post-Soviet history.

Asmus, Ronald D *A Little War That Shook the World: Georgia, Russia, and the Future of the West* Palgrave Macmillan, 2009. An account of the five-day war of 2008 by an American diplomat who was involved at the time.

Aves, Jonathan *Paths to National Independence in Georgia 1987–90* School of Slavonic and East European Studies, 1991.

Aves, Jonathan *Post-Soviet Transcaucasia* Royal Institute of International Affairs Post-Soviet Business Forum, 1993.

Aves, Jonathan *Georgia: From Chaos to Stability* Royal Institute of International Affairs, Former Soviet South Project, 1996.

Awde, N (ed) *Ancient Peoples of the Caucasus: A Handbook* Curzon, 1999.

Baddeley, J F *The Russian Conquest of the Caucasus* Nabu Press, 2010 (paperback reprint of a 1908 classic, also free online).

Braund, David *Georgia in Antiquity* Clarendon, 1994.

Chervonnaya, Svetlana *Conflict in the Caucasus – Georgia, Abkhazia and the Russian Shadow* Gothic Image Publications, Glastonbury, 1995.

Coppieters, Bruno and Legvold, Robert (eds) *Statehood and Security: Georgia after the Rose Revolution* American Academy Studies in Global Security, MIT Press, 2005.

Cornell, S E and Frederick Starr, S (eds) *The Guns of August 2008: Russia's War in Georgia* M E Sharpe, 2009. An edited collection of essays by Russian, Georgian, European and American experts on the Caucasus.

Curtis, Glenn E (ed) *Armenia, Azerbaijan and Georgia* Bernan Lanham, Maryland, 1995.

de Waal, Thomas *The Caucasus: An Introduction* OUP USA, 2010. Written after the 2008 war, an interesting look at the American and Russian roles in the Rose Revolution and Saakashvili government.

Djilas, Milovan *Conversations with Stalin* Penguin, 2014. Based on three visits to Moscow in the 1940s, this shows the Yugoslav vice president shifting from awe to disillusion.

Gahrton, Per *Georgia: Pawn in the New Great Game* Pluto Press, 2010.

Goldenberg, S *A Pride of Small Nations: The Caucasus and Post-Soviet Disorder* Zed Books, London, 1994.

Goltz, Thomas *Georgia Diary: A Chronicle of War and Political Chaos in the Post-Soviet Caucasus* M E Sharpe, 2006. An entertaining and perceptive account of journalistic travels across the Caucasus.

Jones, Stephen F 'Georgia: A Failed Democratic Transition', in *Nations & Politics in the Soviet Successor States* (ed) I Bremmer, Cambridge UP, 1993.

King, Charles *The Ghost of Freedom, A Modern History of the Caucasus* Oxford UP, 2009. Starting with the arrival of Russian imperialists at the end of the 18th century, this deftly picks through the complex strands leading to the modern nations of the Caucasus.

Kleveman, Lutz *The New Great Game* Atlantic Books, 2003. A compelling account of the politicking and arm-twisting involved in extracting oil and gas from Central Asia and the Caspian, and building pipelines across the Caucasus.

Kotkin, Stephen *Stalin Vol 1: Paradoxes of Power, 1878–1928* Penguin, 2014. The latest biography of Stalin, using new archive material to understand his formative years in the Caucasus.

Lang, D M *Last Years of the Georgian Monarchy 1658–1832* Columbia UP, 1957.

Lang, D M *Modern History of Soviet Georgia* Grove Press, 1962.

Lang, D M *The Georgians* Thames & Hudson, 1966.

Lee, Eric *The Experiment – Georgia's Forgotten Revolution 1918–21* ZED Books, 2017. An excellent account of Georgia's experiment with democratic socialism which might have led to a less oppressive alternative to the Bolshevik nightmare (W ericlee.info/theexperiment).

Rayfield, Donald *Edge of Empires, A History of Georgia* Reaktion/Chicago UP, 2012. A wide-ranging examination of Georgia from the earliest civilisations to the Saakashvili era.

Sebag-Montefiore, Simon *Young Stalin* Weidenfeld & Nicholson, 2007. The prequel to the successful Stalin: Court of the Red Tsar. The story of his childhood in Georgia and the revolutionary exploits across the Caucasus that made him what he later became.

Shevardnadze, Eduard *The Future Belongs to Freedom* Sinclair Stevenson, 1991.

Skinner, Peter *Georgia – The Land Below the Caucasus* Mta Publications/Central Books, UK, 2014. A new history of Georgia from Hellenic times to the Soviet takeover of 1921 with 20 detailed maps and well-chosen photos.

Suny, Ronald *The Making of the Georgian Nation* IB Tauris, London 1989; 2nd edition Indiana UP, 1994.

van der Leeuw, Charles *Storm over the Caucasus* Curzon, 1998.

Waters, Chris (ed) *The State of Law in the South Caucasus* Euro-Asian Studies, Palgrave Macmillan 2005. Not just the law, but the way in which judicial, governmental, commercial and criminal interests are bound together in the Caucasus.

Wheatley, Jonathan *Georgia from National Awakening to Rose Revolution: Delayed Transition in the Former Soviet Union* Ashgate Publishing, 2005. A very academic approach to recent Georgian history.

Wright, J F R et al (eds) *Transcaucasian Boundaries* UCL Press, 1996.

Literature Some excellent new Georgian writing has been published in English by the Dalkey Archive (w *dalkeyarchive.com/product-tag/georgian-literature-series*).

Cobham, Leah *Nino's Song* TWH Publishing, 2016. An insightful women's-eye view of Georgia, presented in prose, poetry and diary excerpts.

Coffin, Lyn & Jokhadze, Gia *Georgian Poetry: Rustaveli to Galaktion* Slavica Publishers/ Indiana UP, 2013. An anthology of nine poets (some in both English and Georgian) from the 12th to the 20th century.

Heighway, Elizabeth (ed & trans) *Contemporary Georgian Fiction* Dalkey Archive, 2012. A good collection of short stories, written by 20 authors over a span of 50 years.

Karumidze, Zurab *Dagny, or a Love Feast* Dalkey Archive Press, 2014. A complicated and ambitious phantasmagoria of mysticism and eroticism via Stalin, Bach's Art of Fugue and much else, this tells the story of Edvard Munch's muse who died in a Tbilisi hotel in 1901.

Khantadze, Archil (trans) *12 Short Stories – A Key to the Georgian Mentality* Shemetsneba, 2009. Folk tales, really, that offer humorous insights into the Georgian mind.

Khantadze, Jumber *The Amorous Detective and Other Stories* Shemetsneba, 2012. Stories of Georgian life under communism that read a bit like oral history.

Lermontov, Mikhail *A Hero of Our Time* Penguin, 1977. Look out also for the Nabokov translation (1958).

Morgan Jones, Chris *The Searcher* Pan Macmillan 2016. A fast-moving thriller with a reluctant hero thrown into the chaos of Georgia's conflict with Russia.

Nicholson, Anthea *The Banner of the Passing Clouds* Granta, 2013. Odd insights into Georgian life under communism (from the 1950s) and during the civil war.

Pasternak, Boris *Letters to Georgian Friends* Penguin, 1971. Letters written by the author of Dr Zhivago in 1931–59, notably to the poets Titsian Tabidze and Paolo Iashvili, both to be killed in Stalin's purges.

Pushkin, Alexander *Journey to Arzrum (ie: Erzurum)* Ardis, 1974. Also included in *Tales of Belkin and Other Prose Writings* Penguin, 1998.

Rustaveli, Shota, translated by Lynn Coffin, *The Knight in the Panther Skin* Poezia Press, 2017. An excellent new verse translation of the national epic; also available are earlier translations by R H Stevenson (SUNY Press, 1977) and Venera Urushadze (Sabchota Sakartvelo, 1986/Nova Science, 1999).

Said, Kurban *Ali and Nino* Vintage, 2000. Set in Baku, an Azeri-Georgian Romeo and Juliet by a mystery author; full of romantic colour and period detail.

Tabidze, Galaktion, translated by Merabishvili, Innes *Discover Galaktion: Galaktion Tabidze: A Selection of His Poems in a New Parallel Translation* Critical, Cultural and Communications Press, 2017

Wildlife guides

Flint, Vladimir Field *Guide to the Birds of Russia and the Adjacent Territories* Princeton UP, 1984. English, Russian and scientific names.

Gavashelishvili, Lexo et al *A Birdwatching Guide to Georgia* Buneba, 2005. Available through w nhbs.com in Europe or Buteo Books in the Americas, an excellent guide to birding sites which covers flora and other wildlife.

Knystautas, A *Birds of Russia* Collins, 1993. Good photos, English and scientific (not Russian or Georgian) names.

Food and wine

Capalbo, Carla *Tasting Georgia – A Food and Wine Journey in the Caucasus* Pallas Athene, 2017. A superb guide to Georgian cuisine, with 70 recipes, fabulous photos and a lot of information on food and wine culture.

Goldstein, Darra *The Georgian Feast* University of California Press, 1993.

Feiring, Alice *For the Love of Wine* University of Nebraska Press, 2016. Everything you need to know about natural qvevri wines.

Hercules, Olia *Kaukasis* Octopus/Mitchell Beazley, 2017. Less definitive than Capalbo's book but perhaps more useful for home cooking.

Hudin, Miquel and Kholodilina, Daria *Georgia: A Guide to the Cradle of Wine* Vinologue, 2017. The definitive guide to Georgia's wines, region by region, with winery profiles and hundreds of tasting notes.

Saldadze, Anna and Gigauri, David *Be My Guest – The Georgian Recipe for Cooking Success* Sulakauri Publishing, 2013.

Tuskadze, Tiko *Supra – A Feast of Georgian Cooking* Anova Pavilion, 2017. Authentic family recipes.

Miscellaneous

Baerug, Richard *Europe's Unknown Fairytale Land* Sulakauri (Georgia)/Forlagshuset i Vestfold (Norway), 2016. An account of the first hiking and skiing circuits of the whole of Svaneti, with excellent photos by Shako Margian (Georgia), full of cultural background, as well as practical guidance.

Bender, Friedrich *Classic Climbs in the Caucasus* Diadem, London/Menasha Ridge, Birmingham, Alabama, 1992.

Gachechildze, Revaz *The New Georgia: Space, Society, Politics* UCL Press, 1995. A geography text.

Häberli, Katharina and Harker, Andrew *Under Eagles' Wings: Hikes, Bikes, Horseback and Skitours in Georgia* H & H Travelogue, 2005.

Kolomiets, Yury and Solovyev, Aleksey *Trekking in the Caucasus* Cicerone, 1994.

Nasmyth, Peter *Walking in the Caucasus: Georgia* MTA Publications/IB Tauris, 2005.

Rayfield, Donald *The Literature of Georgia: A History* Clarendon, 1994 (revised 2010).

Salkeld, Audrey and Bermudez, Jose *On the Edge of Europe: Mountaineering in the Caucasus* The Mountaineers, 1994.

Salkeld, Audrey and Bermudez, Jose *The Forgotten Range of Europe: An Anthology of Exploration in the Caucasus* Teach Yourself, 1993.

Soltes, O *National Treasures of Georgia* Philip Wilson, 2001.

Wheeler, Angela *Architecture Guide to Tbilisi* DOM Publishers, 2018.

Other Europe/Asia guides
For a full list of Bradt's Europe and Asia guides, visit w bradtguides.com/shop.

Brummell, Paul *Kazakhstan* (3rd edition) Bradt Travel Guides, 2018

Darke, Diana *Eastern Turkey* (2nd edition) Bradt Travel Guides, 2014

Holding, Deirdre *Armenia: with Nagorno Karabagh* (4th edition) Bradt Travel Guides, 2014

Ibbotson, Sophie *Tajikistan* (2nd edition) Bradt Travel Guides, 2017

Ibbotson, Sophie and Lovell-Hoare, Max *Uzbekistan* (2nd edition) Bradt Travel Guides, 2016

Mitchell, Laurence *Kyrgyzstan* (3rd edition) Bradt Travel Guides, 2015

Roberts, Nigel *Belarus* (3rd edition) Bradt Travel Guides, 2015

Taylor, Neil *Estonia* (7th edition) Bradt Travel Guides, 2014

WEBSITES

w **agenda.ge** Online news.

w **amcham.ge**, **yell.ge** For business contacts.

w **biodiversity-georgia.net** Every single species (provisionally).

w **bu.edu/iscip** Academic material.

w **cenn.org** The Caucasus Environmental NGO Network (CENN) website; for a round-up of environmental and NGO activities.

w **cia.gov/library/publications/the-world-factbook/geos/gg.html** The CIA Factbook.

w **civil.ge** Detailed news from Georgia, especially relating to civil society and NGOs.

w **depts.washington.edu/dtcg** The University of Washington's Georgian Digital Test Collective.

w **georgia.travel** The Georgian government's useful tourism website.

w **georgia.usembassy.gov** US government information (US embassy in Tbilisi).

w **georgiatoday.ge** The website of *Georgia Today*.

w **jam-news.net** Online news.

w **messenger.com.ge** The website of *The Messenger*.

w **rferl.org/p/55440.html** Radio Free Europe's weekly online newsletter with background analysis (*see also* w *rferl.org/section/Georgia/155*).

w **sarke.com** The website of the *Daily News* and *Weekly Economic Review*.

w **svanetitrekking.ge/eng/index.htm** Guide to trekking in Svaneti.

w **tabula.ge/en** Online news

w **tbilisiguide.ge** A useful online resource about Tbilisi.

w **usa.mfa.gov.ge** The Georgian embassy in Washington.

Index

Page numbers in **bold** indicate major entries; those in *italic* indicate maps.

INDEX OF ADVERTISERS